A Companion to the Vietnam War

A COMPANION TO THE VIETNAM WAR

Edited by

Marilyn B. Young and Robert Buzzanco

Blackwell
Publishing

BLACKWELL PUBLISHING
350 Main Street, Malden, MA 02148-5020, USA
9600 Garsington Road, Oxford OX4 2DQ, UK
550 Swanston Street, Carlton, Victoria 3053, Australia

First published 2002 by Blackwell Publishers Ltd
First published in paperback 2006 by Blackwell Publishing Ltd

1   2006

Library of Congress Cataloging-in-Publication Data

A companion to the Vietnam War / edited by Marilyn B. Young and Robert Buzzanco.
     p. cm. – (Blackwell companions to American history; 7)
   Includes bibliographical references and index.
   ISBN 0-631-21013-X (hb)
     1. Vietnamese Conflict, 1961–1975—United States. 2. United States—History—1961–1975. 3. United States—History—1969–. I. Young, Marilyn Blatt. II. Buzzanco, Robert. III. Series.

DS558 .C66 2002
959.704'3373—dc21

                                                                                    2002022763

ISBN-13: 978-0-631-21013-9 (hb)
ISBN-13: 978-1-4051-4983-9 (pb)
ISBN-10: 1-4051-4983-3 (pb)

A catalogue record for this title is available from the British Library.

Set in 10/12 pt Galliard
by Kolam Information Services Pvt Ltd, Pondicherry, India
Printed and bound in the United Kingdom
by TJ International Ltd, Padstow, Cornwall

For further information on
Blackwell Publishing, visit our website:
www.blackwellpublishing.com

Contents

About the Contributors

Amy E. Blackwell received her M.A. in history in 1997 from the University of Houston. As a researcher, writer and editor, she contributed to several works on US military history ranging from the Revolutionary era to the Persian Gulf War.

Mark Bradley is Associate Professor of History at the Northwestern University. He is the author of *Imagining Vietnam and America: The Making of Postcolonial Vietnam, 1919–1950* (2000).

Robert K. Brigham is Associate Professor of History at Vassar College. He is the author of numerous books and essays on the Vietnam War, including *Guerrilla Diplomacy: The NLF's Foreign Relations and the Vietnam War* (1999) and *ARVN: A History of America's Ally in Vietnam* (2001).

Robert Buzzanco is Associate Professor of History at the University of Houston. He is the author of *Masters of War: Military Dissent and Politics in the Vietnam Era* (1996), which received the Stuart L. Bernath Prize for best book in diplomatic history in 1996, and *Vietnam and the Transformation of American Life* (Blackwell, 1998). In 1998 he was named as outstanding young scholar in his field by the Society for Historians of American Foreign Relations.

Kenton Clymer is Professor of History at the University of Texas at El Paso. He is the author of *John Hay: The Gentleman as Diplomat* (1975), *Protestant Missionaries in the Philippines: An Inquiry into the American Colonial Mentality* (1986), and *Quest for Freedom: The United States and India's Independence* (1995).

Robert Dean is an Assistant Professor of History at Eastern Washington University.

William Duiker is Professor Emeritus at Pennsylvania State University. He is the author of *Sacred War: Nationalism and Revolution in a Divided Vietnam* (1994), *Twentieth-Century World History* (1998), and *Ho Chi Minh: A Life* (2000).

Carolyn Eisenberg is Professor of History at Hofstra University. She is the author of the prize-winning book, *Drawing the Line: The American Decision to Divide Germany, 1944–1949* (1996). She is presently working on a new book on Nixon and Kissinger's Foreign Policy.

Michael S. Foley is Assistant Professor of History at the College of Staten Island, City University of New York, and Executive Secretary-Treasurer of the Peace History Society. He is author of *Confronting the War Machine: Draft Resistance During the Vietnam War* (forthcoming).

Anne Foster teaches history at St. Anselm College. She writes about the history of US relations with Southeast Asia during the first half of the twentieth century.

H. Bruce Franklin is the John Cotton Dana Professor of English and American Studies at Rutgers University in Newark. He is the author or editor of eighteen books, including *War Stars: The Superweapon and The American Imagination* (1990), *M.I.A. or Mythmaking in America* (1993), and *Vietnam and Other American Fantasies* (2001). A former Air Force navigator and intelligence officer, he resigned his commission in protest against the Vietnam War and became a prominent antiwar activist.

Lloyd Gardner is Charles and Mary Beard Professor of History at Rutgers University, where he has taught since 1963. He is the author of two books on the Vietnam War, *Approaching Vietnam: From World War II to Dienbienphu* (1989), and *Pay Any Price: Lyndon Johnson and the Wars for Vietnam* (1997).

Christopher E. Goscha is a Ph.D. candidate at the Sorbonne University and assistant professor at the Université de Lyon. He is currently completing his thesis on "The Asian Context of the Franco-Vietnamese War: Networks, Relations and Economy (1945–1954)".

David Hunt is Associate Director of the Honors Program and Professor of History at the University of Massachusetts Boston. He is co-editor of *The American War in Vietnam* (v. 13, 1993).

Michael E. Latham is an Associate Professor of History at Fordham University. He is the author of *Modernization as Ideology: American Social Science and "Nation Building" in the Kennedy Era* (2000) and a co-editor of *Staging Growth: Modernization Development, and the Global Cold War* (2003).

Shaun Kingsley Malarney is an associate professor of cultural anthropology at International Christian University in Tokyo. He has been conducting anthropological research in northern Vietnam for over a decade. He recently published a book *Culture, Ritual and Revolution in Vietnam* with Curzon Press that examines cultural change in revolutionary and post-revolutionary northern Vietnam.

George Mariscal is Associate Professor of Spanish and Chicano Literature at the University of California, San Diego. He was drafted into the US Army and served in Vietnam in 1969. He is a board member of Project YANO, a counter-recruitment and anti-militarism organization based in San Diego. His anthology *Aztlán & Viet Nam: Chicano and Chicana Experiences of the War* (1999) was the first collection of Mexican American writings about the war.

Alfred W. McCoy teaches Southeast Asian History at the University of Wisconsin-Madison. His first book, *The Politics of Heroin in Southeast Asia* (New York, 1972), sparked controversy at the time of its publication, but is now regarded as authoritative and has been translated into eight languages. Three of his books on Philippine history have won that country's National Book Award. In March 2001, the Association for Asian Studies awarded him the Grant Goodman Prize for his career contributions to the historical study of the Philippines.

Edwin E. Moise is a Professor of History at Clemson University. His most recent book was *Tonkin Gulf and the Escalation of the Vietnam War* (1996).

Chester J. Pach Jr. is Associate Professor of History at Ohio State University. He is the author of *Arming the Free World: The Origins of the United States Military Assistance Program, 1945–1950* and *The Presidency of Dwight D. Eisenhower* (both 1991).

John Prados is a senior fellow of the National Security Archive in Washington DC. He is the author of several books, including *The Presidents' Secret Wars: CIA and Pentagon Covert Operations Since World War II* (1986), *Keepers of the Keys: A History of the National Security Council from Truman to Bush* (1991), *Combined Fleet Decoded: The Secret History of American Intelligence and the Japanese Navy in World War II* (1995), *The Hidden History of the Vietnam War*

(1995), and *The Blood Road: The Ho Chi Minh Trail and the Vietnam War* (1998).

Barbara L. Tischler teaches history at the Horace Mann School in the Bronx, New York, where she is also a Dean of Students. She is the author of *An American Music: The Search for an American Musical Identity* (1986) and the editor of *Sights on the Sixties* (1992).

Stein Tønnesson was trained as a historian and is now Professor of Human Development Studies at the Centre for Development and the Environment, University of Oslo, Norway. He is the author of *1946: Déclenchement de la guerre d'Indochine* (1987) and *The Vietnamese Revolution of 1945* (1991). At present he leads a research project on Energy and Security in the South China Sea.

Karen G. Turner is Professor of History at Holy Cross College and Senior Research Fellow in East Asian Legal Studies at Harvard Law School. She has published articles and books on Chinese law and is the author of *Even the Women Must Fight: Memories of War in North Vietnam* (1998).

James Westheider is Assistant Professor of History at University of Cincinnati's Clermont College. He is the author of *Fighting On Two Fronts: African Americans and the Vietnam War* (1997).

Introduction

The Vietnam War stands as America's longest and most divisive foreign conflict. In the aftermath of World War II, beginning with the decision to support French efforts to reimpose its colonial rule in Indochina, the United States gradually increased its commitment in Vietnam, from aid to the French to eventually replacing them altogether. From first to last, the American goal was to suppress the Communist-led Nationalist insurgency, initially throughout Vietnam, and after the establishment of the Republic of Vietnam, in the south. By the 1970s, this massive intervention had failed and scholars have spent the quarter-century since then examining the causes, impacts, and consequences of the war.

The Vietnam War continues to haunt us to this day, resurfacing predictably on anniversaries of the end of the war or more unpredictably when a contemporary foreign policy issue seems to echo the experiences of the 1960s, such as Colombia, or with new revelations of old atrocities, as in the case of former Senator Bob Kerrey. The war revealed the limits of postwar US global power, tore apart the liberal consensus that had defined American politics up to the 1960s, prompted mass protest in the streets, and intersected with social movements for civil rights, women's liberation, and participatory democracy, among others.

The purpose of this volume, then, is to examine the war in its many contexts. Wars transform whole societies and individual lives and Vietnam was clearly no exception to this historical process. We have structured this collection to look at the various societies affected by the war – the Vietnamese especially but also the Americans. We have incorporated both scholarship on established figures and episodes as well as new writing that offers insight into issues such as class, race, and gender. Our authors represent many of the best-known scholars writing about Vietnam as well as a new generation, whose knowledge of Vietnamese language and history adds a dimension to the history of the war absent from earlier accounts.

The essays in this collection add up to a vital contribution to any study of Vietnam. Whether read by itself, used as a companion to texts or monographs on the war, or utilized as a teaching tool, we hope that this volume will present its readers with a fundamental understanding of Vietnam and offer intelligent and creative new ways to look at that war.

CHAPTER ONE

Hanoi's Long Century

STEIN TØNNESSON

The Vietnam War was "the quintessential conflict in the long history of warfare in our century," says Gabriel Kolko, who thinks it was "virtually preordained" that the USA would try to attain a vital military success to compensate for its failures in Korea and Cuba. He concedes, though, that "it was mainly chance that designated Vietnam as the primary arena of trial" (Kolko, 1994, pp. 419, 436–7). Eric Hobsbawm, the great British narrator of modern history, thinks differently. He finds it "almost impossible to understand" why the USA came to embroil itself in "a doomed war" (Hobsbawm, 1994, p. 244). Although the two of them differ, they also have something in common: the notion of a short and tragic century. Hobsbawm has even subtitled his book "The short twentieth century, 1914–1991." Kolko and Hobsbawm's century was full of suffering and lacked a meaningful direction, starting as it did when lights went out in Europe, and ending in bewilderment. "Darkness" is Hobsbawm's last word, and Kolko's final sentence reads: ". . . a dark night of despair will overcome our world" (Kolko, 1997, p. 168).

From an Asian perspective the twentieth century was long and progressive. The Chinese started their century in 1842, with the Opium War and the loss of Hong Kong, and approached the year 2000 as an almost unified nation enjoying rapid economic growth. The long Vietnamese century began sadly with the French seizure of Saigon in 1859, followed by the "loss of country" in the years up to 1884. After colonization, however, a new generation developed nationalist ideas, formed strong movements in the 1910s–30s, and utilized a favorable opportunity for national liberation in 1945. Yet

This essay is based on a Norwegian-language article, "Utsikt over det 20. århundre – fra Hanoi," *Samtiden*, No. 2–3, 1997, pp. 92–110. I'm grateful to the editor of *Samtiden* for permission to reuse the material. I would like to thank Philippe Papin for help concerning pre-colonial Hanoi, and express my gratitude to Luu Doan Huynh and David G. Marr for their helpful comments to an earlier draft. On most points I've followed their advice, but not always. Responsibility for mistakes and errors of judgment thus remains entirely with me.

thirty years of sacrifice and struggle were needed before the nation could be unified in 1975. "Mistakes" were later made (in the official, Vietnamese parlance), but reforms from 1986 opened a new progressive stage, this time marked by an attempt to catch up economically. Growth is expected to continue.

This essay is an attempt to see the twentieth century from Hanoi's angle, with a "long-century approach." It is a mixture of travelogue and historical introduction, not chronological, but looking at how some main global trends have manifested themselves in Hanoi and Vietnam.

Global Trends

Which are the century's main trends? The long century was marked by population growth, urbanization and advances in science, production and communication. It saw the dissolution of empires and the construction of nation-states to serve as building blocks for a new global order. There were revolutions, and there were wars, and they were linked to a fundamental struggle over the nature of the world order.

Until 1989, the order was contested between proponents of liberal capitalism and state-directed socialism. Both used nation-states as building blocks, but while the former emphasized free markets, individual freedoms, limits to state authority, and electoral democracy, the latter aimed for social justice through rational economic planning, collective ownership and trade based on reciprocity or solidarity. Towards the end of the century, the liberal order triumphed. Many countries abandoned socialism and integrated themselves in the capitalist world. Thus the prevailing order was one of increasingly free markets both nationally and internationally, and of nation-states with elected governments.

The history of these global trends is marked by four economic and political turning points: 1930, 1945, 1950, and 1978–9.

Turning Points

The long twentieth century had two halves, one imperial and one multi-national. In the first half, many countries were colonized by Europeans and Japanese, who expected the century to be imperial. However, their empires were challenged by nationalist movements, and also by two federations: the United States of America (USA) and the Union of Soviet Socialist Republics (USSR). Both were increasingly powerful; both aimed for a world of nation-states. The imperial system suffered a first blow in 1930, the first turning point, when the great depression caused immense poverty, leading to revolts, not the least in Vietnam.

The second turning point was in 1945, when a Soviet–British–US alliance laid the foundation for a multi-national world by winning the first world war – often called "the Second World War" – and founding a number of new institutions with a global reach, notably the United Nations. The war's immediate losers were Nazi Germany and militarist Japan, but in a longer perspective the main loser was the imperial system. Japan was immediately relieved of its colonies, and the Europeans gradually gave up theirs. The USA and USSR took over as global leaders.

This global watershed is reflected in the history of Vietnam. The August Revolution of 1945 brought the Indochinese Communist Party – founded in 1930 – to power. The Nguyen dynasty's last Emperor – a French puppet – abdicated, and a Democratic Republic was formed. Despite this promising beginning it took 32 years before Vietnam gained UN membership, and 50 before it got normal diplomatic relations with the USA. By the mid-90s, the Vietnamese leaders had familiarized themselves with the main institutions of the capitalist order, such as the International Monetary Fund and the World Bank. Still, as late as 1999, neither Vietnam nor China had gained membership in the World Trade Organization, the main multi-national embodiment of liberal capitalism.

Why did it take so long for Asia's two main socialist states to join the global system? The answer lies in the third turning point: 1950. The Chinese communists had just won their civil war and proclaimed the People's Republic. It signed a treaty of alliance with the USSR, and sought to inspire revolutions in other Asian countries. However, counter-revolutionary regimes had been formed in South Korea, Vietnam, and Taiwan. Thus the cold war, which had developed between the Soviet Union and the USA, spread to Asia and divided the continent. In Indochina, the French had returned by late 1945, and after a period of truce with the Democratic Republic, war broke out and, a little later, a new French client state was installed under the former emperor. France hoped to defeat the army of the Democratic Republic, and construct a new nation-state, friendly to France and acceptable to the USA. 1950 was thus a watershed also in Vietnam, where the two camps in the cold war recognized two separate regimes – for the same nation. The two fought each other until 1975, when Vietnam was finally unified, on communist terms.

Vietnam's national unification happened just as the communist movement reached its global apogee. Never before and never after did so many states and political parties base themselves on communist doctrines as in the second half of the 1970s. The tide turned in 1978–9, the long century's fourth turning point, when internal conflicts between communist states provoked open warfare both in Indochina and Afghanistan. International communism had started its decline.

The essay will now make four big sweeps, each looking at one of four significant contradictions: town–country, empire–nation, revolution–reaction, war–peace.

First Contradiction: Town–Country

Between 1900 and 2000 the world's population went from 1.6 to 6 billion. This was an unprecedented growth, and most of it happened in Asia. The shift from west to east is reflected in the balance between France and Indochina. At the time of colonization, there were at least three times more Frenchmen than Indochinese. In the colonial period, the French population stagnated, while the Indochinese doubled. During the two first Indochina Wars, 1946–54 and 1959–75, France baby-boomed, but Indochina boomed more. By 1975, Indochina had surpassed France, and in 1997, when

Table 1.1   Total population in millions (Indochina and France), 1875–1997

	1875/80	1913	1926	1936	1950	1960	1975	1982	1997
France	39	41.5	40.9	41.9	41.8	45.7	52.8	54.4	58.6
Indochina	12	16.4	21.1	23.0	31.4	39.4	58.5	66.3	91.9
Vietnam*	10.5	14.2	17.7	19.0	25.3	31.7	48.1	56.0	76.4
Cambodia	1.1	1.6	2.5	3.0	4.2	5.4	7.2	6.9	10.5
Laos	–	0.6	0.9	1.0	1.9	2.3	3.2	3.4	5.0

Sources: Maddison, 1995, pp. 104–5; Brocheux and Hémery, 1995: 248; 2001: 249; US Bureau of the Census (http://www.census.gov/cgi-bin/ipc/idbagg); UNDP 1999.
*The figures for "Vietnam" 1875–1948 are totals for Tonkin, Annam and Cochinchina. 1960 combines South and North Vietnam (NVN had two million more inhabitants than SVN).

Hanoi hosted a summit of Francophone countries, Vietnam alone had far more inhabitants than France.

The Vietnamese today are young. Some 35 percent are under 15. Thus the vast majority have no personal memory of the wars against France or America, not even the Chinese invasion in 1979, but many remember that troops were away in Cambodia during the Third Indochina War, 1978–89. The three Indochina wars may have cost up to six million lives, and they drove other millions away as refugees. So much suffering. So many dead. Yet in the statistics their numbers drown in childbirth. Nativity was always much higher than mortality. The only exception was 1945, when a famine in the north took an estimated one million lives (Marr, 1995, p. 104). Population growth continued in Vietnam through all three Indochina Wars, and only slowed down when they were over. The annual population growth, which as late as 1960 was almost 4 percent and in 1970 remained over 3, in 1997 went down to 1.8. The fertility rate (number of children for each woman) declined from 5.8 in 1975 to 2.6 in 1997 (UNDP, 1999). Thus Vietnam follows the East Asian trend.

Rural families usually have more children than urban ones. Thus urbanization is caused primarily by migration, not by urban fertility. In the 1990s, for the first time in world history, more people lived in urban than in rural areas. Back in 1900 there were less than twenty cities in the world with more than one million inhabitants, and only three Asian ones: Tokyo, Beijing and Calcutta. By mid-century the number of cities with more than a million people had risen to 50. Indochina's biggest city, Saigon, had passed its first million by then. French-occupied Hanoi had only some 200,000 inhabitants, but in 1971, the year before the US "Christmas bombing," it reached its first million, if we include the suburbs. In the years 1950–85, the cities in the world with more than a million inhabitants quintupled to 250.

Throughout the century, Europe remained the most urbanized continent, with Latin America closely behind. However, the most rapid urbanization happened in Africa and Asia. And here it will continue well beyond 2000, since two thirds of the population still live in the countryside. Vietnam remains a nation of village-based peasants, with only one fifth of the population in urban areas. The main explanation for its late urbanization is poverty, but the exodus from southern cities after 1975 also played a role, and the socialist government gave priority for many years to the countryside, keeping migration to the cities to a minimum. Hanoi long remained a small town in a densely populated delta.

Is Hanoi now on its way to becoming a mega-city? Probably, but not necessarily. The Red River Delta could be "urbanized" without a massive displacement. Through careful planning and investments in infrastructure, one could transform the network of villages into an inter-connected urban system, interspersed with rice-fields. Then people could stay in their villages while being urbanized. This may be desirable, but is unlikely to happen. More and more people are now moving into Hanoi, Haiphong, Da Nang and, above all Ho Chi Minh City – the new name for Saigon. By the late 1990s, it had 4.5 million inhabitants. In 1989, greater Hanoi officially passed 3 million.

In Tonkin – the French name for northern Vietnam – the only form of human habitation is the village, wrote the French geographer Pierre Gourou in 1931. One of his assistants in surveying village society in Tonkin was the young historian Vo Nguyen Giap. Later, as the first commander of the People's Army of Vietnam and the strategist behind the victory against the French at Dien Bien Phu in 1954, he made an effort to integrate Vietnamese villages in the larger framework of a struggling nation. Young teachers and poor peasants replaced conservative, elderly landowners as village leaders, so they could mobilize the village communities in active warfare against the city- and garrison-based colonial army. The wars in Vietnam were decided in the villages. It was said in pre-colonial Vietnam that the power of the emperor stopped at the village gate. Each village was ruled by a self-nominated council of village elders, who negotiated the tax level (money, soldiers and labor) with the emperor's *mandarins* (public officials). The power of the Emperor rested on his army, perhaps also on the need for someone to organize irrigation systems above the village level.

Hanoi was the administrative center for the northern region of an empire which from 1838 was mainly called *Dai Nam*, but also carried other names, like *Viet Nam*. The Chinese and Europeans called it *An Nam*. Present day *Ha Noi* already existed as a city with a fortress in the period when the Red River Delta was a part of China, and was capital for the independent Viet dynasties from the eleventh century onwards, under the name *Thang Long* (Soaring Dragon). The Nguyen dynasty, who ruled 1802–1945 from the southern city of Hue, chose the name Ha Noi for the former capital. Many of its edifices were torn down and the stones used for mausoleums in Hue.

The words *ha noi* mean "inside the river." The city lies between three rivers, the *To Lich, Kim Nguu* and the big Red River *(Song Hong)*. Much of Hanoi is under the water level and is protected by a long dyke. One of the most outrageous plans to be discussed by the Pentagon in the 1960s was to bomb the dykes of the Red River Delta. One of the worst corruption scandals of the globalizing 1990s involved the construction of private houses on top of the dyke, hence endangering it. From the dyke one sees a substantial part of the city, but to get a better view one can mount the tower of the Citadel, constructed in 1812. The Vietnamese flag with its yellow star on a red background has been flying from that tower since the French left in 1954.

Eighty years earlier, the colonizers had started the construction of a French concession under Hanoi's dyke. This happened after French forces had conquered the Citadel and declared free trade on the Red River. The French were compelled to withdraw after their commander was killed, and only kept the concession. This backlash led to acrimonious debates in the French National Assembly, paving the way for the assertive political climate that ensured French aggressiveness in Africa and Indochina during the 1880s.

Pre-colonial Hanoi had three separate parts: in the middle a Citadel with a long wall around it, in the south a Temple of Literature *(Van Mieu)* and "university" *(Quoc tu Giam)*, and in the east, along the Red River, an agglomeration of commercial villages. The Citadel housed the mandarins with their horses and soldiers. Regular examinations to select mandarins were held on a big square where the National Library is now. In the Temple of Literature, which was dedicated to Confucius, those who successfully passed their exams got their names engraved on a stael mounted on the back of a turtle – a symbol of longevity. Three commercial villages or guilds *(phô phuong)* were inhabited by Chinese merchants, the rest by Viet artisans. Each *phô phuong* had its own specialty, be it silk, silver, hats or furniture, and each was separated from the next by a bamboo fence. Each had its village temple. Regular markets were held in front of the Citadel's five gates. The Tô Lich River was Hanoi's artery, with busy traffic of river boats.

The mandarins did not themselves trade, but the Viceroy depended on the river for communication with the provinces and the imperial court in Hue. The proximity to three rivers gave the Citadel an ideal, strategic position, but also made it vulnerable to attacks from ships mounting the Red River. The French captured the Citadel in 1873, and again in 1884. In 1883–5, the French defeated Dai Nam as well as China in war, and the court in Hue was forced to accept two separate French protectorates for the two remaining parts of the imperial realm, Tonkin and Annam. The southern region, Cochinchina, had been colonized 1863–7, and the King of Cambodia had accepted a French protectorate in 1863. These four entities – Tonkin, Annam, Cochinchina, and Cambodia – were made parts of the French Indochinese Union, founded in 1887. In 1893 a French protectorate was also established for the Lao principalities on the eastern fringe of the Siamese empire. They were merged into a new state, Laos, which became the fifth part of Indochina.

The French thus merged five lands into a Union, a number of principalities into Laos, and in Hanoi they fused the Citadel, the *phô phuong* and the French concession into an integrated city under a French mayor. Most of the Citadel was torn down and new French quarters constructed, with a big cathedral, broad avenues, and spacious villas. The walls between the *phô phuong* were torn down, and ditches were transformed into streets so Hanoi got its "native quarter," close to the *Ho Hoan Kiem* (Lake of the Returned Sword).

Hanoi was conceived as a Eurasian amalgam, in a century believed to be imperial. The French laid streets and a tramway, built a long bridge over the river, a row of piers, installed telephones and, eventually, an airport. The city-planner Ernest Hébrard fashioned out a new "Indochinese architecture" from a mixture of Chinese, Japanese, Indian, Southeast Asian and European styles. Many immigrants settled down, not only Viets, but Chinese, Indian Muslims and European Christians. Yet Hanoi preserved much of its village atmosphere. In 1943 it had only 120,000 inhabitants, of whom 5,000 were Europeans and 5,000 Chinese. The statistics from 1943 do not include the Japanese garrison, which was modest most of the time. The Japanese Army was present, but the French continued to rule.

Construction work continued until 1945, but then there was decay. A brief Japanese–French war in March, Revolution in August, the First Indochina War 1946–54, mobilization of North Vietnamese resources for sustaining insurgency in South Vietnam 1959–75, US bombing 1966–8 and 1972, and a lack of priority for urban development until the late 1980s, were factors contributing to Hanoi's dilapidation. Buildings were damaged in street fights and bombing. Frenchmen, Indians, and many Viet Catholics left the city when the communists took over in 1954. The Chinese disappeared in 1978, when some 200,000 Chinese were chased out of northern Vietnam in connection with the Sino-Vietnamese conflict. Both in 1955 and 1978, new families moved into the deserted or confiscated houses. In big villas, each family was allotted only one or two rooms. One house could thus provide shelter to many families, sharing a kitchen and a rest room. The buildings were poorly maintained. Few new buildings were built after 1954, except for some apartment blocks on the city's southern outskirts. During the 1960s and early 1970s the Vietnamese leaders saw no reason to invest in Hanoi since it might well be bombed to pieces. Plans were made for a modern, socialist capital in a more suitable adjoining area once Hébrard's colonial city had been leveled by US bombs. But central Hanoi was not destroyed. The Americans mainly bombed industries on the outskirts of the city, and even left the vital bridge intact.

During the war, the population of Hanoi grew almost as rapidly as in the countryside, so the multi-generation houses were crowded. In 1954 each person in central Hanoi had an average of 5.1 square meters living space. By 1982 this had gone down to 2.3, in 1991 to 1.2. This does much to explain the private building boom in the 1990s. In the last decade, many peasants have moved into the city. Some live in guest houses where each room can accommodate 10–30 people, sleeping at intervals.

After the Chinese left in the 1970s, Hanoi became almost purely Viet. Only small groups of East European and Swedish advisors, who mostly lived in seclusion, disturbed the picture of national conformity. Trade and crafts were concentrated in state-owned stores and workshops. Loudspeakers woke people up at 5 a.m. to healthy exercise and news. The buildings remained the same, but the atmosphere had changed. It was gentle, but uniform and thoroughly unfree. The streets smelled from mould and garbage. Noisy East European trucks spewed black exhaust. Old, sinewy and dead-eyed women drew garbage carts through the narrow streets. But crowds of children were laughing, and waves of smiling cyclists gave the impression of a city on the move. People in white shirts, conic hats and green helmets learned how to live closely together and keep their virtue. By 1987–8 Hanoi started to free itself from the chains of the surveillance state. Amidst the decay the Hanoians were able to revive a street life which could not but seduce a visitor. Hanoians who had grown up earlier would later feel nostalgia for the conviviality of the frugal 1960s, 70s and 80s.

War, revolution and socialism saved Hanoi from the capitalist destruction of Asia's other colonial towns. Little has survived of Singapore's Chinatown, although there is a model on the museum island Sentosa. Colonial Hanoi survived. US bombing and communist rule were less destructive, from an architectonic point of view, than transitions to capitalist modernity. There was decay, but not destruction. Even the French streetcars ran in 1989, although they moved so slowly that one could almost walk as fast. In the 1990s the tramway was scrapped. The destruction of the imperial legacy began.

Second Contradiction: Empire–Nation

World history in the long century was a history of rise and fall of empires. Europeans tried to tie up their colonies in relationships of mutual dependence, but failed. In the 1950s–60s, most colonies gained independence. Europeans turned inwards, concentrating on their own modernization and building the European Union. When France left Vietnam in 1954–5, Western Europe ceased to play a role in the country, but some of the French role was taken over, in the north by China and Russia, in the south by the USA.

Was there anything left of the colonial project, apart from the buildings? Yes, such obvious features as frontiers, infrastructure and administrative culture. Just as in Africa the European empires had outlined the modern state system. They mapped territories, initiated wars and negotiated treaties to define borders, and they linked up cities through modern infrastructure. Or to be precise, the Europeans decided, planned and administered; the work was done by Asians, sometimes forcefully recruited.

The two foremost state builders in Indochina were Governors General Paul Doumer (1897–1902) and Albert Sarraut (1911–14, 1916–19). Government revenue derived from state monopolies on opium, salt and alcohol, and was used to build a system of "colonial roads," a north–south railway, and two railways to China. Roads were also built to Laos and Cambodia, and the French encouraged Viet migration to these countries, where the Viets functioned as merchants, artisans, fishermen and officials. In 1900 Hanoi became the capital of all of Indochina. A number of monumental buildings were constructed: The Governor General's Palace, the Palace of the Superior Resident for Tonkin, a theater modeled after the Paris opera, a main post office, new military headquarters within the Citadel, a hospital, and a Pasteur Institute to fight malaria. Albert Sarraut founded the Hanoi University.

Why was Hanoi selected as the capital? The Nguyen dynasty, who continued to rule Annam and Tonkin in name, had its court in Hue. Saigon, which was Indochina's capital in the period 1887–1900, was by far the largest city, including many European settlers (colons). Those factors were used as arguments for choosing Hanoi. An impartial administration was needed, at safe distance from the reactionary court in Hue and the self-interested colons in Saigon. A more important reason was Hanoi's proximity to China. The French purpose in colonizing Tonkin was to cultivate markets in southern China. This was why the railroads to China were built. They never returned the French investments, but proved useful for the transportation of arms to North Vietnam during the Vietnam War. Because of the Sino-Vietnamese conflict, the railways were closed in 1978, but reopened in 1996.

It should be noticed that the French did not make Hanoi the capital of a country matching the territory of today's Vietnam. Hanoi was given a double function. First, it was capital of Tonkin. This put it on the same level as the capitals of the four other Indochinese countries (Hue, Phnom Penh, Vientiane, Saigon). Second, Hanoi became capital of French Indochina, including Laos and Cambodia.

Like the other colonial powers, the French encouraged a double set of native identities, thus causing ambivalence among local nationalists. On the one hand France based its rule on the pre-existing states. Thus the monarchs in Luang Prabang, Phnom Penh and Hue were left on their thrones, stimulating separate Lao, Khmer and Viet identities. On the other hand the French shaped an overarching Indochinese identity. The expectation was that the Union, from 1945 called Federation, would be gradually democratized. The populations would elect representative councils, operating under French leadership. Plans were discussed, and councils were formed, but the Vietnamese Revolution and the ensuing war forced the French to give up their plans of federation. This is a paradox, since the Indochinese Communist Party actually shared the federal ambition. In the war between the French colonialists (who wanted a French-led federation with five parts) and the Viet communists (who preferred a Viet-led federation with three parts), both felt a need to appeal to local national sentiment. Thus they gave up their federal ambitions and endorsed separate nationhoods for Laos, Cambodia and Vietnam. The Indochinese Communist Party became the *Vietnamese* Workers Party in 1951, and independent parties were formed for Cambodia and Laos. (In 1976 the Vietnamese *Workers* Party changed its name to Vietnamese *Communist* Party.)

The term Indochina survived only as a geographical notion, an integrated military theater and, eventually, a set of so-called "special relationships" between the independent nation-states of Vietnam, Laos and Cambodia.

Third Contradiction: Revolution–Reaction

World politics in the twentieth century was shaped by communist revolutions. They provoked repression and containment, and led to ill-fated experiments in centrally planned economies. Can they still, today, form part of a meaningful historic trajectory? Perhaps, if they are integrated in a tale of national liberation and unification. This, of course, is easier for historians of China and Vietnam than for those who write about Russia.

The two main revolutions were the Russian and the Chinese, the former a city-based coup, the second a country-based People's War. Vietnam's August Revolution in 1945 resembled the Russian more than the Chinese, although many rural villages had joined the Viet Minh before the revolution. The August Revolution was a swift sequence of revolts in a number of towns and cities, ending with the proclamation of the Democratic Republic of Vietnam on September 2 1945. Just as in Russia, the revolution led to war. The leaders of the Democratic Republic were forced to leave Hanoi in December 1946, and spent eight years away from the capital. Only after winning the battle of Dien Bien Phu in 1954 could they return.

Revolutions are conceived by intellectuals, carried out by fanatics, and taken advantage of by scoundrels, claimed a bitter veteran in a letter to the party leadership in 1996 (La Van Lam, 1996). The intellectual phase in Vietnam lasted until 1945.

Thirty years of fanatic warfare followed. Le Duan, who was secretary general of the party from 1960–86, was not perhaps a scoundrel, but he wet-blanketed all economic, cultural, and intellectual life while letting cliques and opportunism grow. When he died, the party loosened its grip. This helped unleash economic growth and cultural creativity, while at the same time making it easier for scoundrels to trade influence for black dollars. In the late 1990s, the Communist Party was torn by factional struggles between market-oriented reformers, disappointed veterans, and worried military officers with security and budgetary concerns.

Back in the intellectual phase, the would-be national leaders had been subjected to severe French repression. The clandestine parties and the French security police indulged themselves in a drawn out, cynical power struggle, learning from each other, recruiting agents within each others' ranks. Le Duan was one of the victims in the 1920s–30s. The young historian Vo Nguyen Giap was also arrested, but the French interrogators were so impressed by his intellect that they set him free, perhaps in a vain hope that he would moderate his views.

At that time the Vietnamese debated intensely how to achieve their liberation, and there were many rival parties, with varying degrees of support in different regions. The revolutionary struggle also transcended colonial borders, using modern communicative networks in a wider region (Goscha, 1999). Inside Indochina, Saigon was the main center of revolutionary politics, but the communists were solidly entrenched in some rural regions of south and central Vietnam. The Red River Delta was the main area of recruitment for a Chinese-inspired nationalist party which attempted a revolt in 1930 that was crushed by the French. Abroad, the main leader was a veteran by name of Nguyen Ai Quoc, who later changed his name to Ho Chi Minh. He took part when the French Communist Party was founded in 1920, presided over the foundation of the Indochinese Communist Party in Hong Kong 1930, and also played a leading role in creating the communist parties of Thailand and Malaya. In 1931 he was imprisoned in Hong Kong, and given a prison sentence. After he had served his term, the British did not expel him to Indochina where a death sentence was waiting, but sent him, in January 1933, to China. Not long after, he arrived in the Soviet Union where he barely survived Stalin's purges. Meanwhile, in Indochina, the French Popular Front Government instituted political freedoms so the local communists could emerge from clandestinity. It was then that Giap examined the conditions in the villages, as assistant to Pierre Gourou. By 1938–9, the French had reverted to harsh repression.

In 1940, when Indochina was under threat from Japan, the communist leaders in Saigon attempted a revolt, but their comrades in the north refused to take part. The French drenched the revolt in blood, thus virtually destroying the south-based communist party. A sectarian Buddhist movement, the Hoa Hao, took over formerly communist strongholds. From 1941 to March 1945 the Communist Party survived mainly in the colony's jails – and in exile. Ho Chi Minh left the Soviet Union in 1938, and traveled through China to Yunnan, near the Indochinese border. Some activists, including Giap, came across the border from Hanoi. Together they formed a national liberation front: Viet Nam Doc Lap Dong Minh, *Viet Minh* for short, and at the same time, a new communist leadership was established in the north. A guerrilla army was also formed, under Giap's command, to join the Allied struggle against Japan and the French Vichy regime. Despite French attempts to wipe it out, the Viet Minh survived with secret headquarters among the minority peoples in the border region.

In March 1945, well after the fall of Vichy and the formation of de Gaulle's French government, the Japanese removed the French regime in Indochina. Since Japan was not really able to take over the administrative and repressive functions of the French, an opportunity arose for the Viet Minh and other nationalist movements to expand their influence. A new nationalist government was installed in Hue, and political prisoners were set free. Amidst the terrible famine of 1945, the Viet Minh became a mass movement in north and central Vietnam. In the south another movement was formed, the Vanguard Youth, also under communist control.

The two weeks from August 15 to September 2 1945 mark the proudest moment in communist Hanoi's long century (Sidel, 1998, p. 307). Under the leadership of cadre coming in from the nearest villages, Hanoi rose up first. Shortly after, Ho Chi Minh arrived to lead a provisional government. Revolts followed in all the other Vietnamese towns, including Hue where the emperor abdicated, but there was little response in Laos and Cambodia, where the kings remained on their thrones, and non-communist governments were formed. They felt no urge to join the Viet Minh. Thus Ho Chi Minh's government gained authority only in the three Viet lands, not the whole of Indochina.

A mass rally was held on Hanoi's Ba Dinh square, in front of the Palace of the Governor General, on September 2 1945. Ho Chi Minh quoted from the French declaration of the rights of the citizen and from the American declaration of independence, and proclaimed the Democratic Republic of Vietnam. President Ho, who was standing on a stage, in simple cloths, but under a royal parasol, gazed at the masses and asked softly over the microphone if they could hear him. "We hear," the masses replied. Thus the bond was made between leader and people. With the meeting on Ba Dinh Square the capital of French Indochina was transformed into the capital of Vietnam. The revolutionary leaders in Saigon recognized the authority of Hanoi, but never forgot their frustration at being surpassed by the northern comrades. The meeting on Ba Dinh is represented by a painting on the end wall of Hanoi's Historical Museum. The simultaneous rally in Saigon ended in an ugly incident, and is rarely referred to.

The August Revolution became a national icon. When the war against France was over, the Ba Dinh square was redesigned to look more like the Red Square in Moscow and Tian An Men in Beijing. On the southern side, in 1945, lay the Palace and Residence of the Governor General, a park, and two pagodas – including the famous one-pillar pagoda. Hébrard's Eurasian buildings were in the north. When Ho came back in 1954, he refused to live in the Governor General's Residence. Instead a tiny house was built from precious wood, in the park outside, with a conference table downstairs, a sleeping chamber and a study upstairs. It was made in the style of one of the ethnic minorities whom Ho had got to know as a guerrilla leader. A conspicuous office for the Communist Party was set up north of the square, and later a National Assembly. In the last decade of the century a Ho Chi Minh museum and a war memorial were added to the buildings surrounding the national *lieu de mémoire*.

However, the main new building was to be a mausoleum. Ho Chi Minh died on September 2 1969, exactly 24 years after his proclamation of independence, and the year after the Tet offensive had failed to fulfill his hope of national unification. The unmarried President, often just called "the Uncle," had written one of the century's loveliest political testaments. All peasants were to be exempted from tax for a full year as soon as the war was over. Ho wanted his body to be cremated, and the ashes should be divided in three, one pile for each of the regions. Suitable hills should be selected, where trees could be planted around the grave, and a small shelter be built so visitors could have a place to rest.

The party ignored Ho's wishes, removed all of the above from the testament before its publication, and had the body embalmed by Soviet experts. Then they replaced the Governor General's Residence with a small-scale copy of the Lenin mausoleum. Thus they did their best to distort the peculiar myth that Ho had constructed around himself. He had known Lenin, Stalin and Mao, but wanted his own kind of legacy. Ho's shortsighted lieutenants had other plans. By having the mausoleum ready for the victory parade in 1975, they wanted to demonstrate Hanoi's precedence as capital, as well as its alignment with Moscow. The mausoleum is still in place, so the will of Ho Chi Minh remains to be fulfilled (Boudarel and Nguyen, 2002, pp. 142–4).

Fourth Contradiction: War–Peace

Like many other centuries, the twentieth was a century of war: international wars, wars of national liberation, civil wars. One often hears that there was more suffering in the twentieth century than in any other century. This is true in a numerical sense. Since there were so many people in the world, there were also more who suffered. But the number of people living long and peaceful lives also grew tremendously, not the least in Vietnam. The widespread western view that the twentieth century was particularly tragic, and also without a meaning, does not seem right from an Asian perspective.

The Vietnam War was tragic. Did it still have meaning? Some say that even though America lost in Vietnam, it did prevent the further spread of communism. Thus the war was meaningful from an anticommunist perspective. This is hardly convincing. Vietnam was one of the countries in the world where the communists had the strongest popular following, the best leaders, the most effective organization, and the least effective adversaries. To much of the world, Vietnam became a symbol of national resistance, an example of how a poor people could withstand the onslaught of the world's mightiest power. Such a place was a poor choice for America to take a stand. No polls or votes were taken to measure public opinion, but it seems likely that a clear majority of the Vietnamese, although they did not share the communist vision, identified themselves with their leaders in the struggle for national independence and unification. For the communist leaders, the war was full of meaning, and the victory was worth all the suffering. But could they have reached their goals with less sacrifice?

In 1995 and again in 1997, the former defense ministers Vo Nguyen Giap and Robert McNamara met in Hanoi to discuss the war they had waged. In the 1960s, McNamara had loaded the Pentagon's computers with figures showing that the adversary was taking unsustainable losses. This, he thought, would force Hanoi to the conference table. His calculations were proven wrong. McNamara lost faith, and was relieved of his duties by President Johnson, but the war continued. McNamara came to Hanoi in 1995 with three purposes in mind: confess to his mistakes, find the truth about the other side's calculations, and ask Giap to admit his mistakes. To McNamara the behavior of the Vietnamese had been irrational. When you take unsustainable losses, it is rational to seek a way out. Instead the Vietnamese had just continued to fight. There must have been misunderstandings. If they had been avoided, millions of lives could have been spared.

Neither Giap nor any other Vietnamese leader would confess to any mistakes, or share the US responsibility for the suffering inflicted on their people. "We did not attack your country," they exclaimed. "You came to our country. We had to resist." For the Vietnamese communist leaders, national unification was worth almost any sacrifice. They had a nation to unify, a revolution to defend, a history of national subjugation to avenge, and they were thinking of themselves as in the vanguard of a global wave of national liberation.

Fifty years earlier, Giap had been asked McNamara's question by Abbot Low Moffat, head of the Southeast Asia Division of the US State Department. He visited Hanoi in December 1946, just before the outbreak of the First Indochina War. Moffat ventured a question about the loss of civilian life which would inevitably follow if general warfare broke out. Giap's reply, according to Moffat, was that there "must be sacrifice, sacrifice." The local US Consul then suggested that sacrifice should be for a definite end, but what end could it serve? Giap only repeated the need for sacrifice, and added that the Vietnamese might not win, but that in any event the French would not win either (US Senate, 1972, p. 40). This was the kind of attitude that led Vietnam to its victories. The Vietnamese did not "win" in a strictly military sense. Neither did they expect to do so, but they wore their enemies out by sacrificing lives. Giap planned it. He said it. And he did it. Giap was the main brain behind the construction of an army and a state so thoroughly organized that the population could be motivated, or compelled, for thirty years, to endure the unendurable. And the population continued to grow. Children born during the First Indochina War sacrificed their lives in the Second. A heroic, patriotic tragedy. Again, was it meaningful?

The question should be related to the wider history of Hanoi's and Vietnam's experience with war and nation-building. When the European War broke out in 1914 (and Europe's "short century" began), the Vietnamese were a colonized people. Perhaps a hundred thousand young men were sent to Europe, to serve the French war effort. Many never returned, while others gained precious knowledge about war and modernity. Revolts in the 1920s–30s were futile, but in 1942, the Japanese demonstrated the fundamental weakness of the European empires, and in March 1945, they demonstrated it locally by conquering the French-held Hanoi Citadel within just 24 hours. For more than a year after the August Revolution, revolutionary Hanoi gained a respite, so it could prepare itself for the long resistance struggle. A French expeditionary corps, after having seized control of south Vietnam, landed in Haiphong and marched into Hanoi in March 1946, but only after having signed

an agreement with Ho Chi Minh. However, Franco-Vietnamese relations soon
deteriorated, and the First Indochina War broke out in Hanoi on December 19
1946, only days after Moffat had left. By then the government had already evacuated
a significant part of the population. During the subsequent fighting, Hanoi
was almost emptied. The government urged people to stay away from the city and
take part in the resistance struggle. Patriots and leftists followed up, but the majority
of Hanoi's citizens returned. After some time there was an influx of newcomers,
people who found it difficult to live in villages controlled by the communists.
Thus Hanoi became a spawning garrison and merchant town with relatively few
Viet Minh supporters. The enthusiasm in Hanoi when Giap's Army came back in
October 1954 was not overwhelming. Business people, officials and Catholics left the
north for the south, where they would form the main foundation for the South
Vietnamese regime. In Hanoi, party leaders and public institutions took over the best
French villas, and streets were named after communist martyrs.

The French had made Hanoi an integrated city with a mayor and modern administrative services. The Democratic Republic was more ambitious and instituted a system
of districts, subdistricts, wards, blocks and cells. This made surveillance easy. Instructions went down and reports came back up. The system stood its test when the US
bombing began in 1966 (Logan, 2002, p.149). It generated a natural sense of
solidarity, thus reinforcing social discipline. The main impact of the bombing was
probably to facilitate the government's efforts to motivate the citizens for further
sacrifice, but the bombs also destroyed the industries which had been built with
Chinese and Soviet help. Relatively speaking, US bombs did not kill many people in
the Red River Delta. The worst aspect of the war for the northern families was to send
their sons south, and never see them again. There was enormous relief in 1975, when
the war was over, and the surviving sons could return.

In his book about the conquest of Saigon in April 1975, General Van Tien Dung
tells how he, on victory day in Saigon, received a phone call from "the heart of the
Fatherland": "Hanoi, the capital of the whole country, heroic Hanoi, home of Uncle
Ho and our party, had accomplished this victory, along with the entire country.
Forests of people, seas of people, flooded the streets singing" (Van Tien Dung,
1977, p. 246). Thus spoke the general who had commanded so much sacrifice. To
him, the war had been full of meaning.

The tone was different when, many years later, one of the surviving conscripts, Bao
Ninh, published the novel *The Sorrow of War*. It tells about the soldier Kien who came
back to Hanoi, after taking part in Saigon's conquest. He and his friends had not
called themselves Hanoians, but "Thang Long soldiers," thus proudly reviving their
home town's long lost dragon name. (The idea that the Vietnamese had a long
tradition of fighting foreign [Chinese] domination was a strong motivating force
during their wars). Now, in the autumn of 1975, most of Kien's friends were dead,
and the Hanoi that greeted him, was not as he had expected: "The streets revealed an
unbroken, monotonous sorrow and suffering. There were joys, but those images
blinked on and off, like cheap flashing lights in a shop window. There was a shared
loneliness in poverty, and in his everyday walks he felt this mood in the stream of
people he walked with" (Bao Ninh, 1994, p. 138).

This was what Bao Ninh's figure felt in post-war Hanoi: A grayish sadness, and under the sadness the longing and sorrow that the war had left behind. While Kien was working on his traumas, a new generation of boys went out to fight, in Cambodia and at the Chinese border, where white-painted grave markers with dates from January 1979 form endless rows. The Sino-Vietnamese war was brief and dramatic. The war in Cambodia was a protracted counter-insurgency, with the Vietnamese Army in the unfamiliar role of repressing guerrillas and propping up a client state. The Third Indochina War was harder and harder to make meaningful.

In the 1980s, Hanoians privately realized how much their country had lost through all its wars. The party had thought that the stamina with which the long wars had been won could be channeled into fulfilling Ho Chi Minh's hope of "building the country a hundred times more beautiful." But industries and infrastructure had been shattered. War veterans were rewarded with positions for which they were not competent, and resources were diverted to imposing the central planning system on the south. Peasants reacted to the collectivization of land by working more slowly. They only started to work hard again around 1990, when the land was given back to the households. While socialist Vietnam slowed down, the neighboring capitalist tigers enjoyed a period of fabulous growth. China also joined the tigers in 1979. Hanoi noticed that the world was changing, and that something had gone badly wrong. A sense of crisis had emerged when Le Duan died in 1986. A reform policy was proclaimed under the slogan *Doi Moi*, and radical market-oriented reforms were carried out in subsequent years. Re-education camps were closed, and the surveillance system relaxed. Singapore's elderly capitalist statesman Lee Kuan Yew, one of those who thought the Vietnam War was meaningful because it stopped communist expansion, became advisor to the Vietnamese government. Relations with the USA were normalized in 1995, when Vietnam also joined the Association of Southeast Asian Nations (ASEAN). In the 1990s, Vietnam turned out to be a weak nation, still proudly independent, but without any allies. The country got through the Asian crisis 1997–9 without major scars, but continued to lag behind its neighbors economically. Some party veterans were disappointed by the disappearance of socialist values and institutions, and some western leftists saw corruption and growing inequality as evidence that the Vietnamese people, after winning their war through so much suffering, had lost their peace to the forces of global capitalism (Kolko, 1997; Logan, 2002, p. 224). Most commentators, however, agreed with the younger generation that Vietnam should open up, and compete in the global market. They saw no other way to get out of poverty.

In the process of transition to a market economy the wars became less meaningful, at least to the young, who could not care less about history. Still, if forced to take a longer perspective, even they may see their future way to prosperity as a prolongation of a tragic, yet meaningful long century.

REFERENCES

Bao Ninh 1991: *Than Phan Cua Tinh Yeu* (Hanoi). Trans. Phan Thanh Hao and Palmos, F., 1994 *The Sorrow of War*. London: Minerva.

Boudavel, G. and Nguyen Van Ky 2002: *Hanoi, City of the Rising Dragon*. New York: Rowman and Littlefield.

Brocheux, P. and D. Hémery 1995, 2001: *Indochine: la colonisation ambiguë*. Paris: La découverte.

Goscha, C. 1999: *Thailand and the Southeast Asian Networks of the Vietnamese Revolution, 1885–1954*. Richmond: Curzon.

Gourou, P. 1931: *Le Tonkin*. Paris.

Hobsbawm, E. 1994: *Age of Extremes: The Short Twentieth Century, 1914–1991*. London: Michael Joseph.

Ho Chi Minh 1989: *President Ho Chi Minh's Testament*. Hanoi: Vietnamese Communist Party.

Kolko, G. 1985: *Anatomy of a War*. New York: Pantheon.

Kolko, G. 1994: *Century of War: Politics, Conflicts, and Society Since 1914*. New York: The New Press.

Kolko, G. 1997: *Anatomy of a Peace*. New York: Routledge.

La Van Lam 1996: Open letter to Dao Duy Tung (Politburo member), January 6 1996 (downloaded from vinsight@netcom.com, news dated February 21 1996).

Li Tana 1996: "Peasants on the Move: Rural–Urban Migration in the Hanoi Region." Singapore: Institute of Southeast Asian Studies Occasional Paper, No. 91.

Logan, W. S. 2000: *Hanoi, Biography of a City*. Seattle: University of Washington Press.

Maddison, A. 1995: *Monitoring the World Economy 1820–1992*. Paris: OECD.

Marr, D. G. 1995: *Vietnam 1945: the Quest for Power*. Berkeley CA: University of California Press.

Masson, A. 1929: *Hanoi pendant la période héroïque,1873–1888* [Hanoi During the Heroic Period]. Paris: Paul Genthner.

Sidel, M. 1998: *Old Hanoi*. Kuala Lumpur: Oxford University Press.

Thrift, N. and Forbes, D. 1986: *The Price of War: Urbanization in Vietnam 1954–85*. London: Allen and Unwin.

Turley, W. 1975: "Urbanization in War: Hanoi, 1946–1973," *Pacific Affairs*, 3 (1975), 370–97.

Tyler Maclaren, F. 1995: "The French Colonial Quarter in Hanoi, Vietnam: a Preservation Approach." Calgary, Alberta: MA Thesis, University of Calgary.

United Nations Development Program (UNDP) 1999: *Human Development Report*. Oxford: Oxford University Press. For Vietnamese statistics, see: http://www.undp.org.vn/efault.htm.

US Senate 1972: *The United States and Vietnam: 1944–1947. A Staff Study Based on the Pentagon Papers*. Study No. 2, April 3. Washington DC: US Government Printing Office.

Van Tien Dung 1977: *Dai thang mua xuan*. Hanoi. Trans. J. Spragens, Jr., *Our Great Spring Victory*. New York: Monthly Review Press.

Wright, G. 1991: *The Politics of Design in French Colonial Urbanism*. Chicago: University of Chicago Press.

PART I

The Vietnamese in Context

CHAPTER TWO

In Search of Ho Chi Minh

WILLIAM DUIKER

A quarter of a century after his death, the Vietnamese revolutionary Ho Chi Minh remains one of the most controversial figures of the twentieth century. Although his name is instantly recognizable to millions of people throughout the world, there are still major differences in the interpretation of his character and his legacy to future generations of Vietnamese people. In death as in life, Ho Chi Minh remains one of the great enigmas of our century.

One explanation for this phenomenon can be traced to the frustrating lack of verifiable sources of information about his life. As a revolutionary in opposition to the French colonial regime in Indochina, Ho Chi Minh spent many years in exile and others living a clandestine existence inside his own country. During much of that period he lived and traveled incognito under a variety of pseudonyms. It has been estimated that during his lifetime Ho adopted over fifty assumed names. Many of his writings were penned under such names, while countless others have been lost or were destroyed in the course of a generation of conflict.

Ho Chi Minh contributed to the problem by maintaining an air of mystery about his life. For years he denied that the shadowy public figure that emerged immediately after World War II as President Ho Chi Minh was in actuality the same person as Nguyen Ai Quoc, the founder of the Indochinese Communist Party (ICP) and a prominent agent of the Comintern (the organization created by Vladimir Lenin in 1919 to promote revolution throughout the world) of the prewar period. Even after his true identity was revealed, Ho remained extraordinarily secretive about key events in his life, and his two brief ventures into the field of autobiography, which were written shortly after World War II and later published in the Democratic Republic of Vietnam (DRV) were written under an assumed name. Only in recent years have researchers in Hanoi been able to confirm that they were written by Ho Chi Minh himself.

These problems have been compounded by the inaccessibility of existing sources. Until recently, few archival materials held in Hanoi were available to Vietnamese researchers, much less to foreign scholars. Information relating to his activities in China and the USSR was also off limits, and rarely divulged by either the Chinese or the Soviet governments. Virtually the only interval of his life that had been exposed to careful exploration was the brief period that he spent in France after World War I. The opening of French colonial archives during the early 1970s placed that area for the first time under scholarly scrutiny.

There is more to the mystery of Ho Chi Minh, however, than the mere absence of verifiable facts about his life and revolutionary activities. Questions of interpretation bedevil the efforts of the rash biographer seeking to present a balanced picture of his life and his role in the Vietnamese revolution and the international communist movement. A few of these questions have entered the arena of public debate. While few knowledgeable observers would dispute the fact that Ho Chi Minh was a leading figure in the Vietnamese struggle for independence against the French, for example, many would question his patriotic motives by alluding to his record as a Comintern agent and his lifelong commitment to the Marxist–Leninist principle of proletarian internationalism. The patriotic image so assiduously cultivated by Ho and his colleagues in the communist movement, some allege, was simply a ruse to win support for the revolutionary cause from the Vietnamese people.

Compounding the problem of determining the nature of his ideological persuasion are disagreements about his personal character. In Hanoi today, Ho is presented as a symbol of revolutionary humanitarianism, an avuncular figure devoted to the welfare of his compatriots and to the liberation of all the oppressed and exploited peoples of the world. To many who met him, Vietnamese and foreigners alike, Ho was a "sweet guy" who, despite his prominence as a major world figure, was actually a selfless patriot with a lifelong commitment to the cause of bettering the lives of his fellow Vietnamese. Critics, however, point to the revolutionary excesses committed in his name, and accuse him of being a chameleon personality, a wolf in sheep's clothing.

Yet another question about Ho Chi Minh lies in the nature of his leadership. While Ho Chi Minh was the founder of the ICP and a leading figure in the international communist movement, an "event-making man," in Sidney Hook's classic phrase, he did not possess a dominant personality in the manner of many other modern revolutionary leaders such as Lenin, Stalin, or Mao Zedong, and appeared to lead by persuasion and consensus rather than by imposing his will through the sheer force of his personality. This was especially the case during the later years of his life, when Ho Chi Minh may have lost effective control over the leadership of his party to younger colleagues, whose own policy decisions contradicted some of the fundamental principles that he had espoused during a political career extending nearly half a century.

To these familiar questions, the prospective biographer must add others of his own. What motivated Ho Chi Minh to join the international communist movement rather than to follow the Western liberal democratic tradition, as was apparently his initial inclination? Was there something in the Confucian world view that predisposed Vietnamese intellectuals such as Ho Chi Minh to the Marxist version of the classless utopia, or was he drawn to Marxism–Leninism by the practical aspects of Leninist revolutionary strategy? What was the secret of his extraordinary appeal to his compatriots? Finally, what will be his ultimate legacy to the Vietnamese revolution, a question that is now being played out in Vietnam?

Today, as the passions of the Vietnam War begin to subside and additional source materials become available in a variety of languages, there are grounds for modest optimism that a more definitive understanding of Ho Chi Minh's life and activities will become possible in the coming years. The main channel of information is issuing from Vietnam itself, where the field of Ho Chi Minh studies has become a veritable growth industry as the Hanoi regime has attempted to utilize his many achievements as a means of mobilizing popular support for its current policies. A Ho Chi Minh Museum, designed by Soviet and Czech architects, has been erected behind the forbidding Lenin-style mausoleum in Ba Dinh Square in Hanoi. The museum represents an ambitious effort to place Ho Chi Minh in the context of his times, and museum officials are assiduously attempting to collect new materials relating to his life for display or placement in the archives. Smaller museums have been opened in his home province of Nghe Tinh and in Ho Chi Minh City (previously known as Saigon). In the meantime, his collected works have been published, and a number of research organizations, including the influential Marxist–Leninist Institute in Hanoi, have created special branches to study his life and thought.

Unfortunately, research on Ho Chi Minh in Vietnam is still severely hampered by political constraints, as well as by the prevailing belief in Hanoi that biography is more a collection of facts than of analysis. A few bold researchers have gone beyond official interpretations, notably in exploring his activities as a Comintern agent and in portraying new aspects of his personal life, but in general those Vietnamese who transgress the bounds of official sanction risk censure, or worse. At the same time, key aspects of Ho's political career, such as his relationship with senior colleagues within the party and government leadership and his role within the international communist movement, remain largely unexplored.

Fortunately, additional sources of information on Ho's life are gradually becoming available in other countries as well. The process began in Paris, where a gradual declassification of archival materials relating to the colonial era in Indochina has been underway in France since the early 1970s. More recently, new information on Ho's life has appeared in Moscow, where the archives of the Comintern were briefly opened up to researchers after the collapse of the Soviet Union. Ho Chi Minh lived and worked in Moscow on several occasions prior to World War II, and a number of documents relating to his activities as a Comintern agent are now stored in the Ho Chi Minh Museum in Hanoi.

Somewhat less has been accomplished toward opening up the field of Ho Chi Minh studies in China. Ho spent several years of his life in China, and worked closely with such leading members of the Chinese Communist Party (CCP) as Liu Shaoqi, Zhou Enlai, and Ye Jianying. Throughout the Vietnam War, China was probably the most important supporter and supplier of the Hanoi regime. Up until now, however, relatively little has been released in China about the nature of that relationship, except for official accounts that have been slanted to meet the political needs of the moment. Recently published official documents and memoirs by veteran CCP party members offer occasional insights into various aspects of China's role in the Vietnamese revolution, and on Ho Chi Minh's relations with Chinese leaders. But the Chinese archives on the subject remain tightly closed, and scholars are apparently offered little encouragement to pursue the subject. Until Sino-Vietnamese relations improve, or a more liberal attitude toward scholarly research on the history of the party reigns in Beijing, it is doubtful that crucial aspects of Ho Chi Minh's relationship with China will be brought to the light of day.

In summary, there are clear signs of progress in lifting the veil of obscurity on the life and activities of one of the most significant individuals of the twentieth century, but key questions have yet to be answered. The remainder of this article will attempt to provide an overview of Ho Chi Minh's life as one of the major figures of the twentieth century, based on the information at hand.

Early Life

The questions about Ho Chi Minh begin with his childhood. Born in 1890, the son of a Confucian official who served in the imperial bureaucracy during the early years of the colonial era, the young Ho Chi Minh, like so many anti-colonialist leaders of his era, was by birth and upbringing a member of the traditional elite. He received tutelage in the Confucian classics by his father and other scholars in his home village, and then was given the rudiments of a Western education at the prestigious Imperial Academy (*Quoc Hoc*) in the imperial capital of Huê. But in 1910 his father was dismissed from his post under controversial circumstances. French sources raise questions about the competence of his performance as an official, but there may have been doubts about his loyalty as well. A close acquaintance of several leading Vietnamese critics of the colonial regime such as Phan Boi Chau and Phan Chu Trinh, he was reputed to hold strongly anti-French convictions. Reduced to a humble existence as an itinerant scholar, he died penniless two decades later.

The impact of these events on the young Ho Chi Minh must be deduced from fairly fragmentary evidence, much of which has been unearthed by Vietnamese researchers through interviews with surviving members of the local community who were knowledgeable about events connected with Ho's childhood. It seems clear that as an adolescent the young Ho absorbed some of his father's animus against the French. In 1905, he was invited to join Phan Boi Chau's anti-colonialist organization, which then had its headquarters in Japan, but he rejected the offer for reasons that have not yet been fully explained. Three years later, Ho took an active part in peasant anti-tax demonstrations that had broken out throughout Central Vietnam, and was censured by school authorities for that reason. He left school shortly after, and after teaching briefly at a school run by progressive intellectuals in the port city of Phan Thiet, he decided to seek employment on a French passenger steamship as a means of finding passage to Europe. By that time, he had already decided to devote his life to the liberation of his country from colonial domination, but was uncertain as to whether the objective could best be achieved by reformist measures or by violent action.

First Travels Abroad

After a brief stay in France, where he submitted an application to attend the Ecole Coloniale (an institution established to train candidates to serve as administrators in French colonial territories) in Paris, he returned to the sea and traveled to Africa and the countries of the Western hemisphere. According to his own account, the experience served to introduce him to the fact that the exploitative practices of Western imperialism were not limited to French Indochina alone, but were common to colonial territories throughout the entire world. Ho Chi Minh then left maritime service and spent several months in the United States where, under the name Paul Thanh (his family name was Nguyen Tat Thanh), he worked briefly in New York City and Boston and allegedly undertook a short visit to the South. It is unclear what effect this experience had on his intellectual development, for there is no evidence that he was involved in any overt political activities. But he appears to have been exposed to the seamy underside of American society, which became the source for countless articles written in later years which criticized racial discrimination against Blacks in the South as well as the inequities of the capitalist system as it was practiced in the major cities along the eastern seaboard.

Sometime in 1913, Ho Chi Minh left the United States and went to Great Britain, where he worked as a manual laborer and then as a cook's helper at the Carlton Hotel in London. Little else is known about his activities during this period, but there is some fragmentary evidence that he may have joined a British labor union and made his first acquaintance with the writings of Karl Marx. If so, it may have marked the first tentative step toward his future career as a professional revolutionary.

Apprentice Revolutionary

A few months before the end of World War I, Ho Chi Minh left Great Britain and returned to France. By the summer of 1919 he had become a member of the French Socialist Party (FSP) and joined with other Vietnamese emigrés living in Paris to draft a public appeal to the leaders of the victorious powers attending the peace conference at Versailles; the appeal, signed by Nguyen Ai Quoc (Nguyen the Patriot, the name by which he would be known for the next two decades), demanded national independence for the Vietnamese people on the basis of the famous "fourteen points" that had recently been presented by US President Woodrow Wilson to the conference. Ho Chi Minh's identification with that petition thrust him into the public eye for the first time and launched him onto a revolutionary career that would span five decades. For the next three years, his activities were carefully monitored by the French security services. During that period he made the transition from a reformist patriot to a committed Leninist revolutionary.

The process was a fairly rapid one. During the final months of 1919 he was still consorting with Phan Chu Trinh (then living in exile in Paris) and other Vietnamese reformist intellectuals. But the following summer he became acquainted with Lenin's famous "Theses on the National and Colonial Questions," a document just presented to the Second Congress of the Comintern in Moscow, which convinced him that the liberation of the colonial countries could best be achieved by an anti-imperialist global revolution. Later that year he became a founding member of the French Communist Party (FCP) and soon emerged as one of its most prominent spokesmen for the cause of revolution in the colonial world. Ho was also the driving force behind the Intercolonial Union, an organization for colonial subjects living in France.

Why Ho Chi Minh had decided to abandon the path of moderate reform and embrace Lenin's strategy of violent revolution is not well documented, but evidence from French police files, as well as his own writings during the period, suggest that he, like many of his contemporaries throughout colonial Asia in the early twentieth century, had lost faith in the sincerity of colonial officials who had promised to carry out a "civilizing mission" (in French, "mission civilisatrice") throughout the possessions under their jurisdiction. What makes the case of Ho Chi Minh somewhat distinctive is the fact that to the end of his life, he expressed his admiration for the French revolutionary ideals of "liberty, equality, and fraternity," and the ideals of the American Declaration of Independence.

In July 1923, Ho Chi Minh traveled secretly to Moscow, where he worked at Comintern headquarters and received training in carrying out revolutionary operations. For years, little was known about this interval of his life, except for the occasional reminiscence by an acquaintance or a scattering of speeches that he presented as a delegate to the Fifth Comintern Congress, held in the summer of 1924. But the opening of Comintern archives in recent years has shed new light on his activities during this period, and how they affected his future growth as a revolutionary. Two points stand out. Firstly, it seems clear that his experience in Moscow did little to diminish his initial belief in the validity of Marx's concept of the communist utopia. In speeches and articles that he wrote for publication in various journals, he praised the Soviet experiment with a fervency that was sufficiently intense to draw the attention of friends and colleagues.

Secondly, it was in this first visit to Moscow that Ho Chi Minh began to exhibit the independent approach toward strategy and tactics that would characterize his later career as a revolutionary in Asia. Letters that he wrote to colleagues, as well as speeches presented to meetings of the Peasant International (the Krestintern, an organization established in 1923 to promote revolutionary activities in rural areas), emphasized the importance of the colonial question and the vital role of the peasantry in the Asian revolutionary process.

Such ideas were still within the general framework of the revolutionary strategy that had been adopted for preindustrial societies at the Second Comintern Congress in 1920. Lenin had called for a two-stage approach, beginning with a broad-based united front of the urban and rural masses to destroy the power of imperialist authority, to be followed by a second stage led by the working class that would begin the transformation to socialism. After Lenin's death in 1924, however, few European Communists gave more than lip service to such concepts, and reverted to the Marxist view that most peasants were acquisitive by instinct and thus unreliable allies for the proletariat in the revolutionary struggle. Conscious that his ideas were now out of the mainstream, Ho Chi Minh frequently expressed his frustration at the lack of attention given to colonial affairs in European communist parties, and in one sardonic remark to a colleague described himself as "a voice in the wilderness."

Forming a Communist Movement in Indochina

In the late fall of 1924, Ho Chi Minh was given permission to travel to Canton, where he took employment as an interpreter for the Comintern mission to Sun Yat-sen's revolutionary government there. A few months previously, the Comintern agent Maring had persuaded Sun to enter an alliance with the newly-formed CCP. In return, Moscow agreed to dispatch a mission to Canton to help Sun to reorganize his own Guomindang (Nationalist Party) along Leninist lines. Ho immediately began to gather anticolonialist emigrés living in South China into a new organization called the Vietnamese Revolutionary Youth League. His growing talents as a revolutionary organizer were quick to bear fruit, and by the late 1920s the League had enrolled over 1,000 members inside French Indochina. French officials soon recognized the League as the most serious threat to the colonial regime in Indochina. One factor in the League's success was undoubtedly the nature of its program, which reflected Ho's adaptation of the Leninist theory of the two-stage revolution to the Vietnamese environment. The program stressed both patriotic and revolutionary themes and was aimed at a target audience consisting not only of workers and poor peasants, but also of patriotic members of the middle class and the landed gentry as well.

In accordance with Leninist tactics, Ho and his colleagues in Canton sought to establish cooperation with other anticolonial parties operating in Indochina, while at the same time attempting to recruit members of such organizations into the League. Such activities were quite successful in promoting the recruitment of talented individuals into Ho's organization (most of the leading members of the League had originally been members of non-Communist organizations operating in the area), but they also aroused an attitude of mutual suspicion between the League and its nationalist rivals that would last long after the former had been replaced by a formal communist party.

In other respects as well, Ho Chi Minh's balanced approach combining patriotism and social revolution was not an easy one to maintain in the conditions of the time. In the spring of 1927, Sun Yat-sen's successor Chiang Kai-shek denounced Sun's alliance with the CCP and cracked down on Communist activities in South China. Targeted for arrest in a police crackdown, Ho was forced to flee from Canton and took refuge in Moscow. The headquarters of the League was shifted to Hong Kong.

The end of the Nationalist–Communist alliance was a devastating blow to Ho Chi Minh, not only in terms of his personal situation but also for its impact on the strategy that he had devised for promoting revolution in China. In the summer of 1928, the Comintern formally abandoned the broad-based Leninist united front strategy and adopted a more sectarian approach for Asian communist parties, focusing on class struggle and proletarian hegemony over the movement. Contact by Communist parties with bourgeois and peasant organizations was now discouraged.

By then, Ho Chi Minh had already left the USSR. Hoping to return to Asia as soon as possible, he spent several months in Western Europe awaiting funds from Moscow, and then in the summer of 1928 traveled by ship to Bangkok, where he spent over a year organizing Vietnamese emigrés in the northeast plateau of Thailand, while seeking an opportunity to restore contact with his colleagues in the League.

In Ho Chi Minh's absence, the League had suffered severely from the consequences of Chiang Kai-shek's coup in China and the policy shift in Moscow. By the summer of 1929 it had split into two factions, each claiming to represent the true spirit and line of Marxism–Leninism. Just before the end of the year, desperate colleagues invited Ho to come to Hong Kong to resolve the dispute. Arriving at the beginning of February, he convened a meeting of representatives of the two factions and successfully reunited them into a single Vietnamese Communist Party (VCP).

Whether Ho was fully aware of the full implications of the change of line in Moscow is unclear, although there is little doubt that it ran counter to his own instincts. In any event, the party program that was drafted in February under his direction essentially ignored the new Comintern strategy and reflected the broad Leninist model that he had adopted several years earlier in forming the Revolutionary Youth League. At the first meeting of the party's new central committee held in October, however, that decision was reversed. Under Comintern instructions, the party adopted a narrower "class struggle" approach in accordance with the current line in Moscow. At the same time, party leaders dropped Ho's emphasis on nationalist independence by adopting a new name that did not evoke the memories of the Vietnamese past: the Indochinese Communist Party (ICP).

For many years, historical writings published in Vietnam and elsewhere were virtually silent on the significance of these events and how they affected Ho Chi Minh personally. Recent evidence, however, suggests that Ho had indeed begun to come under suspicion in Moscow for his unorthodox views, and was replaced by the Comintern as the leader of the Vietnamese revolutionary movement by Tran Phu, an ambitious young revolutionary who had been trained in Moscow; he was appointed as director of a newly-formed Comintern office located in Hong Kong. During the next few years, Ho was occasionally criticized for his "nationalist" leanings by Tran Phu or other colleagues trained in Moscow.

It was one of the guiding assumptions of Soviet leaders at the time that a new high tide of revolution in Asia was on the horizon, and that communist parties throughout the region should prepare to ride it when it appeared. In the spring of 1930, widespread unrest broke out in towns and villages scattered throughout Indochina, thus appearing to vindicate Moscow's prediction. At the heart of the unrest were peasant anti-tax demonstrations in the coastal provinces of Nghe An and Ha Tinh. Party leaders were taken somewhat by surprise by the rapid course of events taking place inside the country, but attempted to provide guidance to the movement in accordance with Comintern instructions. Ho Chi Minh was skeptical of the movement's prospects for success, but agreed with his colleagues that the ICP must align itself with the oppressed masses of Indochina, whatever the cost. In the ensuing crackdown by the French colonial authorities, most of the leading members of the new party were arrested, while Ho Chi Minh himself was picked up in a police raid in Hong Kong. For the next two years, he languished in a British jail.

Years in the Wilderness

In 1933, Ho was released from jail in Hong Kong with the aid of a British lawyer. He then returned to Moscow, where he remained out of the public view for the next five years. Ho's second extended period of residence in the USSR came at a time when the Soviet experiment was under considerably more stress than had been the case during the previous decade. The decision to collectivize the countryside provoked bitter resistance from peasants and led to massive loss of life in rural areas, while Stalin's purge trials led to the imprisonment and execution of thousands of old Bolsheviks who had assisted Lenin in bringing the Communists to power in Russia.

Ho Chi Minh's own reaction to these events has never been recorded. Sources in Hanoi have passed over the period virtually without comment, while foreign observers merely note the possibility of illness, or speculate that he was still under suspicion by Stalin for his unorthodox beliefs. In recent years, however, sufficient evidence has appeared to corroborate the fact that Ho was indeed under suspicion by Stalin, and may even have been placed on trial for his failure to adapt rapidly enough to the shifting Comintern line. That Ho survived at all during the bloody era of the purge trials is probably an indication that he had friends in high places who were able to shelter him. Otherwise, it was a time of almost total inactivity for one of the Comintern's most experienced agents, and one that must have sorely tested his loyalty to the movement. But Ho had learned how to be circumspect in the face of strong ideological winds emanating from the Kremlin.

The Founding of the Vietminh Front

Sometime in the fall of 1938, Ho wrote a request for reassignment to an unnamed acquaintance at Comintern headquarters. "Send me somewhere," he asked plaintively, "where I can be useful." Shortly after, his request was granted, and he was permitted to leave the Soviet Union and return to China. Although the details of his new assignment are not available, it seems likely that he was directed to report back to Moscow on conditions in China and perhaps to pass Soviet advice on future strategy to leading members of the CCP. Fortunately for Ho Chi Minh, the ideological storms of the mid-1930s had now begun to subside, while the new Comintern line announced at the Seventh Congress in the summer of 1935 was closer to the one that he had espoused for the past decade. Communist parties were now authorized to seek alliances with other organizations and governments in resistance to the rising danger of world fascism.

Ho proceeded first to Yan'an, then the wartime headquarters of the CCP North China. After remaining there for about two weeks, he traveled south to Guilin, where he was employed at an officers' club and wrote articles describing conditions in wartorn China. It was at this time that he made his first attempt to restore contact with the ICP leadership inside Vietnam, calling on his colleagues to adopt a broad united front approach that would win over the widest possible spectrum of the population in Indochina to the Comintern's new antifascist line against Germany and Japan.

In the summer of 1940, Ho Chi Minh was finally able to restore personal contact with leading members of the ICP. With Japanese military forces advancing rapidly in China, Tokyo demanded and received from French authorities the right to station its troops in Indochina in preparation for a future takeover of Southeast Asia. Ho now resumed leadership over the ICP and took charge of planning for the creation of a new united front that would seek to unite all patriotic elements to seek independence from France and newly-arrived Japanese occupation forces. In May 1941, at a meeting of the central committee held just inside the Vietnamese border, he presided over the formation of the League for the Independence of Vietnam, popularly known as the Vietminh Front. It was a defining moment in the history of the Vietnamese revolution.

Ho Chi Minh's activities during this period are relatively well documented in the historical literature as a result of numerous memoirs by participants in the movement. Curiously, however, almost nothing is known about Ho's brief stay in Yan'an, a time when he presumably met with Chinese leaders to discuss the future course of revolution in the two countries. By now, the CCP had come under the firm leadership of Mao Zedong, whose strategy of "people's war" would be applied with ultimate success against Japanese occupation forces, as well as against the government of Chiang Kai-shek after the close of the Pacific War. Mao's writings on revolutionary strategy are reminiscent in many respects of Ho Chi Minh's own ideas on the subject, and it has sometimes been declared that the ICP borrowed liberally from the Maoist model in waging their own revolution. In fact, Ho Chi Minh had reached his own conclusions about the course of the Vietnamese revolution independently, although he apparently made use of his period of residence in China to study Mao's military ideas and to translate Chinese tracts on guerrilla warfare into the Vietnamese language.

During the next four years, Ho Chi Minh honed the Vietminh Front into an effective weapon to use against Japanese forces and the French colonial regime. With many of his rivals, such as Tran Phu, having died in French prisons during the 1930s, Ho was now the recognized leader of the ICP. His efforts were rewarded in August 1945, when Vietminh units seized Hanoi from surrendering Japanese military authorities and announced the formation of the independent Democratic Republic of Vietnam (DRV). The August Revolution, which consisted of a political uprising by patriotic forces throughout the country supplemented by the fledgling military units of the Vietminh Front, has become enshrined in party histories as the uniquely Vietnamese approach to the annals of modern revolution, with the patriotic masses operating under the firm and correct guidance of the ICP. More recently, a number of foreign scholars have taken issue with this portrayal, emphasizing the spontaneous and disorganized character of the August revolution. Be that as it may, it is safe to say that without the leadership of the party and the prudent guidance of its chief strategist Ho Chi Minh, the August Revolution would not have succeeded in consolidating power in North Vietnam under the suspicious eyes of Nationalist Chinese occupation forces who had been ordered to northern Indochina by the victorious allies.

Prelude to Conflict

Immediately following the surrender of Japan to allied forces in the Pacific in mid-August 1945, Vietminh units occupied Hanoi and other major cities and rural areas throughout the northern half of the country. On September 2, Ho Chi Minh, identifying himself only as "a patriotic figure long active in the service of his country," declared the independence of Vietnam from foreign rule and announced the formation of a new provisional republican government with himself as president. It was now that Ho Chi Minh (who publicly denied his previous identity as the Comintern agent Nguyen Ai Quoc) emerged in the eyes of the world as the leading force in the Vietnamese revolution. He spent much of the next year in negotiations with French authorities, who now occupied the southern half of the country and sought to restore their political and economic presence throughout Indochina; Ho simultaneously appealed for diplomatic recognition of his new government by major world powers like the USSR, Great Britain, and the United States.

In his appeal for international recognition of the DRV as the legitimate representative of Vietnamese national aspirations, Ho Chi Minh was disappointed, as none of the leading world powers responded to his request. He did have some initial success in dealing with the French, however. A preliminary agreement, recognizing Vietnam as a "free state" in the French Union, was reached with the French official Jean Sainteny in March 1946. But further peace talks at Fontainebleau, outside of Paris, broke down that summer, when the French refused to include the southern provinces of Vietnam in the new "free state." To prevent a deadlock, Ho signed a *modus vivendi* to resume discussions early the following year. Two months after his return to Vietnam in October, war broke out.

This brief period prior to the outbreak of the Franco-Vietminh conflict is one of the most thoroughly explored eras in the history of modern Vietnam. Memoirs by key foreign officials such as Jean Sainteny and Archimedes Patti, a US intelligence officer who had helped to recruit Ho as an agent for the OSS, monographs by foreign scholars and journalists, as well as a number of studies of the era by researchers in Hanoi, have thrown considerable light on the events following the August Revolution from various perspectives. All sources attest to Ho's diplomatic prowess and his extraordinary qualities as a political leader. Still, this period remains one of the most controversial in Ho's life, for it was now that the debate over the "real Ho Chi Minh" began. The controversy has its roots in his negotiating style. In his talks with French, Chinese, and US officials, he frequently claimed that he was surrounded by militant elements and pleaded for help in bringing about a compromise settlement of the dispute with the French. Similarly, in carrying out his domestic program, he consciously adopted a conciliatory pose with members of rival parties, while cajoling his followers to make compromises in order to secure eventual triumph.

Was his pose genuine? Was it true that there were factional splits in the party between radicals and moderates? Or, as skeptics charged, was Ho only posing as a moderate as a means of realizing his goal of winning international recognition of the DRV, at which time he and his colleagues would set out to create a socialist society on the Stalinist model? The debate came to a head in late 1946, when tensions in relations with France were leading inexorably toward a military conflict. Ho pleaded with French acquaintances to accept a compromise in order to arm him against radical forces in his government. At the same time he ordered preparations for a surprise attack on French military forces that had been returned to Hanoi after the March agreement. Did militant elements within Vietnam force a decision to resort to war in December, just as a new government in Paris appeared willing to pursue a compromise settlement, or was the decision reached with his full knowledge and agreement? Although the answer remains in dispute, recent evidence suggests that Ho Chi Minh was convinced of the inevitability of war and used all his diplomatic skills to postpone it until his forces were prepared. Although there were undoubtedly divisions within the party leadership over strategy and tactics, Ho effectively used the threat of a takeover by the militants as an instrument in achieving his negotiating objectives.

The issue is especially poignant for US observers because of the lingering debate over Washington's failure to respond to Ho Chi Minh's appeal for support against the French. Some have argued that had the Truman administration granted diplomatic recognition to the DRV, the later Vietnam tragedy could have been avoided. Ho actively encouraged such views, declaring his admiration of American society in meetings with US visitors and even hinting a willingness to accept a US military and economic presence in a future independent Vietnam. To his colleagues, however, he presented a different message, underlining the importance of playing off one capitalist state against another as a means of dividing his potential adversaries. Never were Ho's diplomatic skills more in evidence than in his desperate struggle for national survival in the months following the end of the Pacific War.

The Franco-Vietminh War

With the outbreak of conflict with the French in December 1946, the DRV returned to its original base in the mountains north of the Red River Delta. Until the opening of negotiations at Geneva nearly eight years later, Vietminh leaders did not re-emerge to public view. Rumors even circulated that Ho Chi Minh had died of illness in the Vietminh redoubt in the Viet Bac. Only in November 1953, when he astounded the world by holding an interview with a reporter of the Swedish journal *Expressen*, did he return to public view. Formal peace negotiations began at Geneva the following May, and resulted in a cease-fire agreement two months later. Ho was not a member of the DRV delegation at Geneva, but he became actively involved in the search for a settlement, holding conversations with Indian prime minister Jawaharlal Nehru and Zhou Enlai, Beijing's chief delegate at the conference, to sound out their views on conditions for an agreement.

Because of the clandestine character of the Vietminh struggle and the paucity of documentation available from either the Vietnamese or the French side, relatively little has been known about Vietminh policy and wartime conditions in Vietminh-held areas. Even less has been available about Ho Chi Minh's own role in the making of strategy. For years, it has been General Vo Nguyen Giap, the DRV Minister of National Defense, who has been identified by most foreign observers as the primary architect of victory over the French. Recent evidence, however, suggests that Vietminh strategy was usually hammered out by senior party leaders in consultation with advisers from the CCP, with Ho Chi Minh playing the key role as consensus-maker. Ho also played a major part behind the scenes during the negotiations, prevailing upon his colleagues to accept a compromise settlement that assigned the northern half of the country to the DRV, with the promise of national elections to bring about reunification in 1956.

A more murky issue surrounds Ho Chi Minh's role as chairman of the ICP (renamed at the second national congress in February 1951 as the Vietnam Workers' Party, or VWP) and chief arbiter of its ideological principles. Although Ho still retained enormous prestige within the party leadership, he had begun to assign questions relating to ideology and domestic affairs to VWP General Secretary Truong Chinh and other senior colleagues. With the strengthening of Chinese influence over the Vietminh movement after the establishment of the People's Republic of China in 1949, the VWP began to adopt some of the more radical elements of the Maoist model that had been recently put into practice in China. To what degree Ho sought to intervene on behalf of his own ideas on such issues remains unclear. There seems little doubt that by now, his influence on issues related to foreign policy was greater than on those in the domestic arena.

The Construction of Socialism in North Vietnam

The five years immediately following the end of the Geneva Conference in 1954 represent a relatively brief interlude of peace in the tortured history of modern Vietnam. During this period, Ho Chi Minh and his colleagues had their first real opportunity to create the kind of society that they had envisioned since the formation of the ICP over two decades previously. After the establishment of the DRV in the fall of 1945, the new government had adopted a moderate approach based on the establishment of a multiparty parliamentary system and a mixed economy. But that experiment had aborted with the outbreak of war in December 1946. On their return to Hanoi in the fall of 1954, party leaders signaled that they would initially follow the same line, adopting a gradualist economic strategy reminiscent of that previously followed in Soviet Russia under the New Economic Policy (NEP) and in China immediately following the end of the Civil War in 1949. Not until 1958 did the era of socialist transformation get underway in North Vietnam with a push to collectivize the countryside and nationalize the small industrial and commercial sector.

From the beginning, however, the regime's domestic policies were marked by tension and controversy. A land reform program aimed at equalizing landholdings and eliminating the power of the rural landed gentry class quickly got out of hand and resulted in revolutionary excesses. At a stormy meeting of the Central Committee in the fall of 1956, Ho Chi Minh felt compelled to accept public responsibility for the errors committed during the campaign, although it was General Secretary Truong Chinh who lost his position after the affair. In the meantime, a movement promoted by intellectuals to achieve greater freedom of expression in the DRV was repressed by the government under the weight of ideological orthodoxy. The violent character of the land reform program and the squelching of intellectual dissent were quickly seized upon by critics as an indication of the Stalinist character of the regime and the totalitarian instincts of Ho Chi Minh himself. Ho's defenders were forced to respond that Ho had not been directly involved in the implementation of such policies, and was shocked at the results.

At present, the evidence is insufficient to either confirm or refute such allegations, but it suggests that while Ho Chi Minh lamented the abuses of the land reform program, he strongly supported its ultimate goal of eliminating the landlord class and distributing excess land to poor and landless peasants. On a few occasions he intervened in an effort to protect veterans of the Franco-Vietminh conflict from persecution or punishment on the part of local cadres, but he took no decisive action until the issue had reached crisis proportions. He was similarly ineffective in moderating the effects of the government's crackdown on dissident elements. At present, too little is known about Ho's influence on domestic policies to do more than speculate on his views on such issues.

The War Against the United States

At the Third Congress of the VWP held in September 1960, party leaders attempted to maintain the momentum of socialist transformation begun two years earlier when they called for the inauguration of the nation's first five-year plan. In fact, however, the demands of a new conflict in South Vietnam were already beginning to undermine the regime's domestic agenda. In January 1959, Hanoi decided to return to a policy of revolutionary war in the South, and at the Third Congress, the party placed equal emphasis on the dual goals of reunification with the South and nation-building in the North. Within months, the conflict in South Vietnam had begun to take precedence, and for the next decade the entire country was embroiled in a bitter fratricidal war with the new US-supported non-Communist regime in Saigon. The five-year plan was quietly abandoned.

Ho Chi Minh, who passed his seventieth birthday in May 1960, had now become the living symbol of Hanoi's struggle to unify the entire country under party rule. It was widely assumed in world capitals that up to the last months of his life at the end of the decade he was directly involved in strategical decisions relating to the conduct of the struggle in South Vietnam. The reality is by no means so clearcut. While it is clear that Ho took part in meetings of senior leaders relating to foreign policy issues up through the early 1960s – making several visits to Beijing and Moscow to seek support from Hanoi's fraternal allies in the process – there are several indications that by mid-decade encroaching age and illness had begun to take their toll, rendering him increasingly incapable of playing an active role in the day-to-day conduct of the war.

A final judgment of his role in the Vietnam War, then, remains to be written. It seems clear that during the early stages of the conflict, when party strategists were debating how to combine political and military forms of struggle in the most effective way to bring about the collapse of the Saigon regime, Ho Chi Minh urged caution, warning that an overly aggressive posture could provoke the United States into a direct role in the South. At the same time, he consistently urged his colleagues to avoid damaging their close relations with either Moscow or Beijing. Ho had been increasingly depressed by the intensification of the Sino-Soviet dispute, not only because it complicated Hanoi's efforts to achieve its goal of national reunification, but also because it weakened the socialist countries in their global competition with their capitalist adversaries. By now, his sense of solidarity with the socialist camp in the struggle against global imperialism had become sharply defined.

During the early to mid-1960s, Ho Chi Minh made several trips to the USSR and China to reduce the bitterness of the Sino-Soviet dispute and maintain good relations with both allies. The results were mixed. By 1963, anger at the reluctance of Soviet leader Nikita Khrushchev to give firm support for DRV strategy in South Vietnam led party leaders in Hanoi to abandon Ho's policy of maintaining amicable relations with both Communist powers and lean instead toward China. Two years later, the situation was reversed. New leaders in Moscow showed greater willingness to provide assistance to Hanoi, while relations with the PRC had soured over Beijing's insistence that the DRV renounce its relationship with the USSR. The DRV now inclined toward the Soviet Union.

The involvement of Vietnam in the quagmire of the Sino-Soviet dispute must have distressed Ho Chi Minh, but by now he was virtually powerless to affect policy. As a recently-published account by his private secretary Vu Ky makes clear, during his final years he did not regularly attend meetings of the Politburo, although he was kept abreast of the situation in South Vietnam by his colleagues. After the United States intervened directly in the conflict in 1965, Ho vocally expressed the view that Hanoi must not back down under US pressure. At the same time, while agreeing that revolutionary forces must directly confront American troops on the battlefield, he urged his colleagues to leave open the door to a negotiated settlement that would enable Washington to withdraw from South Vietnam without loss of face. To the end, Ho Chi Minh's instincts on issues related to foreign affairs earned the close attention of his colleagues.

It is somehow fitting that even at the moment of his death, Ho Chi Minh inspired a sense of mystery. In 1965 he had begun to draft a testament for publication after his death. Revised periodically, it dealt primarily with the period after the achievement of final victory in the South, when the regime would begin to turn its eyes to the problems of nation-building and national reconciliation. Ho urged his colleagues to prepare for the challenge. The party, he stressed, must be purified to enable it to serve the people more effectively. Elements in South Vietnam that were hostile to the revolution should be given an opportunity, through legal or educational means, to serve the new order. The rural masses, who had provided the footsoldiers of the revolution during a generation of conflict, should be rewarded by a one-year remission of the agricultural tax. He appealed for comrades throughout the world to seek the restoration of the unity of the socialist community. Finally, Ho specified that he should be cremated and given a simple funeral service, with his ashes scattered throughout the three regions of Vietnam – North, Center, and South.

After his death in September 1969, party leaders carried out his cherished dream of unifying the country under party rule. But they ignored a number of his requests and published an altered version of his testament. Agricultural taxes were not reduced, nor was Ho's body cremated. Rather, it was embalmed and placed, Lenin style, in a massive mausoleum erected in Ba Dinh Square, where he had declared Vietnamese independence three decades previously. When rumors leaked out twenty years later that portions of Ho's testament had been tampered with and eventually ignored, the regime finally published the true version, while explaining that conditions in Vietnam had compelled them to ignore certain provisions in his testament.

Problems of Interpretation

The appearance of new source materials in locations scattered around the world has begun to take some if not all the mystery out of the life of Ho Chi Minh. But the mere amassing of facts about this extraordinary public figure will not end the debate over the significance of his career, because the controversies surrounding him are not simply a matter of what happened and when, but deal with his inner motivations, the driving force of his ideas, and the underlying character of the man as well. Inside Vietnam and abroad, the real Ho Chi Minh lies in the eyes of the beholder.

The most prominent public debate has taken the form of a sometimes bitter dispute over whether he was primarily a nationalist or a communist. Those who assert the former argue that his commitment to Leninism was essentially tactical, to be employed as a tool to bring about the liberation of his country from imperialist domination, and that he had little interest in the Marxist vision of a classless utopia. But others point to Ho's record as a Comintern agent and his half century of service to international communism, as well as the performance of the Hanoi regime after 1954, as evidence that Ho's protestations of patriotism and political moderation were essentially a smokescreen to seduce observers and assist the party in realizing its totalitarian objectives.

Ultimately, this is a sterile argument. Whatever the original motivation of Karl Marx and other radical thinkers of his generation, most Communists in the twentieth century, and certainly those born and raised in colonial societies, have had strong nationalist leanings, whatever their commitment to the Marxist vision. Pledges of support for the international communist movement and the success of the future world revolution notwithstanding, communist regimes in the last half of this century have acted primarily out of concern for national security or the realization of primordial goals of national destiny. Nothing more effectively demonstrates this fact than the bitter fratricidal conflicts that broke out among the revolutionary regimes in China, Vietnam, and Kampuchea after the end of the Vietnam War in 1975.

Such was quintessentially the case with Ho Chi Minh. Accounts of his childhood leave no doubt as to his early exposure to widespread concern in Vietnam over the survival of the nation and the race. As he himself conceded in an article written in 1961, his original interest in Marxism–Leninism stemmed from the potential use of Leninist strategy as a vehicle for the liberation of colonial peoples. Whatever else can be said about Ho Chi Minh, he was certainly a convinced Leninist. Throughout his long and active life as a revolutionary, his primary immediate concern was always the liberation of his country from imperialist domination. In several volumes of his writings and collected speeches, there are remarkably few references to Karl Marx and the ideal of a communist society. Ho clearly had little interest in ideological questions.

On the other hand, there is ample evidence of Ho Chi Minh's conviction that socialism was the most appropriate developmental model for preindustrial societies in Asia and Africa. Ho's oft-expressed admiration for the principles of the French and American revolutions should not disguise the reality that he was a lifetime critic of the capitalist system, a system that in his view had brutally exploited the peoples of Africa and Asia, and the working masses in Europe and the Americas as well. Whether he viewed the Soviet or the Maoist model as appropriate for application in Vietnam is a more difficult question. The most that can be said is that he apparently preferred a consensus-building gradualistic approach to the "heaven-storming" strategies adopted in China and the Soviet Union, and ultimately by his own colleagues. Comments that he made periodically to foreigners that Vietnam was not ready for communism can best be interpreted as a tacit recognition on his part that the road to a fully developed socialist society would be long and tortuous, not as an indication that he was a closet capitalist.

A third source of disagreement concerns the issue of his basic character. The official interpretation in Hanoi has portrayed him as Uncle Ho, a self-effacing father figure for all Vietnamese and the staunch defender of oppressed peoples around the globe. In the eyes of some observers, this portrait of simplicity and Confucian humanheartedness sits in sharp contrast with his role as a Comintern agent and with the oppressive character of the DRV regime. In recent years, it has been further undermined by the determination of his successors to create a personality cult of President Ho as a means of carrying out the political objectives of the regime.

Ho Chi Minh consistently objected to the launching of a personality cult in his name. Yet there is no doubt that he actively encouraged the popularization of the familiar image of the kindly Uncle Ho, an image that first materialized in early September 1945 when, as president of the newly-established provisional government of Vietnam, he spoke to a throng of thousands at Ba Dinh Square in Hanoi while dressed in rubber sandals and a faded khaki suit. Ho cultivated that image sedulously for the remainder of his life and undoubtedly shared in the efforts of his colleagues to cash in on that reputation to mobilize the Vietnamese people to rally in the service of the state.

This is not the place for a detailed examination of Ho Chi Minh's essential character. Suffice it to say that the real Ho Chi Minh was undoubtedly a much more fascinating, subtle, and complex individual than either the saintly figure portrayed by the Hanoi regime, or the shifty-eyed totalitarian presented by his adversaries. Although his public image was undoubtedly calculated for its effect and reflected an individual of considerable ego, his image of simplicity and incorruptibility is probably genuine. While he was clearly not a ruthless leader in the manner of a Stalin or a Mao Zedong and viewed terrorism as a blind alley, he was ever prepared to use whatever means were necessary in pursuit of his cause. While he was a convinced idealist in pursuing his ends, he was a wily opportunist in selecting his means.

One of the most interesting subjects of recent speculation deals with the possibility that Ho Chi Minh may have had amorous relationships with a number of women, and may even have been briefly married, thus raising doubts about the official portrayal of Ho as a lifelong celibate dedicated selflessly to the cause of the Vietnamese nation. So far, evidence of his numerous affairs has been strenuously denied by official sources in Hanoi. If true, such evidence clearly adds a new dimension to our limited understanding of Ho's personal life.

The Legacy of Ho Chi Minh

For most Asian specialists and other Vietnam watchers abroad, the study of Ho Chi Minh's life is now one of primarily academic importance. For the Vietnamese people, however, it has become a matter of more crucial significance, since it defines one of the central issues in the Vietnamese revolution – the relationship between human freedom and economic equality in the new Vietnam. Since the end of the Vietnam War, Ho's successors, who are still in power in Hanoi today, have tirelessly referred to his memory to sanctify the Marxist–Leninist model of national development. A few dissenting voices, however, have argued that the central message of Ho Chi Minh's career was the determination to soften the iron law of Marxist class struggle with the French revolutionary trinity of liberty, equality, and fraternity.

In the end, of course, Ho Chi Minh's importance as a posthumous factor in determining policy in Hanoi will decline, and the decision on the future course of the revolution will be made by the Vietnamese people themselves. Ho will become simply another historical figure in Vietnam's rich pantheon of national heroes. There are signs that this transition is already taking place, as a generation of young Vietnamese, most of them born and raised well after his death and the end of the war, know him only in the mythical terms employed by the propagandists of the regime. For the time being, however, Ho remains a powerful force in postwar Vietnam, revered by millions and undoubtedly detested by countless others. For good or ill, Ho Chi Minh managed to reflect in his person two of the central forces in modern Vietnam – the desire for national independence and the quest for social and economic justice.

SELECT BIBLIOGRAPHY

Brocheux, Pierre 2000: *Ho Chi Minh*. Paris: Press des Sciences Po.
Duiker, William J. 2000: *Ho Chi Minh: A Life*. New York: Hyperion.
Fall, Bernard B. 1967: *Ho Chi Minh on Revolution, 1920–1966*. New York, Praeger.
Fenn, Charles 1973: *Ho Chi Minh: An Historical Introduction*. New York: Scribners.
Gaspard, Thu Trang 1992: *Ho Chi Minh a Paris* [Ho Chi Minh in Paris]. Paris: l'Harmattan.
Hemery, Daniel 1990: *Ho Chi Minh: de l'Indochine au Vietnam* [Ho Chi Minh: From Indochina to Vietnam]. Paris: Gallimard.
Ho Chi Minh 1977: *Selected Writings*. Hanoi: Foreign Languages Press.
Huynh Kim Khanh 1982: *Vietnamese Communism, 1925–1945*. Ithaca: Cornell University Press.
Kobelev, Evgenyi 1983: *Ho Chi Minh*. Moscow: Progress Publishers.
Lacouture, Jean 1968: *Ho Chi Minh: A Political Biography*. Trans Peter Wiles. New York: Vintage.
Patti, Archimedes 1980: *Why Vietnam: Prelude to America's Albatross*. Berkeley: University of California Press.

CHAPTER THREE

Belated Asian Allies: The Technical and Military Contributions of Japanese Deserters, (1945–50)

CHRISTOPHER E. GOSCHA[1]

The military service of foreigners takes on great importance in terms of the numbers of men involved and [it] offers a considerable variety of cases. One sometimes associates it with the pejorative idea of mercenaries, which is often unjustified. The military use of foreigners is brought about by the inadequacy of the [armed forces as a] vocation or the military means of the population in relation to the military needs of the State.

André Corvisier, *Dictionnaire d'art et d'histoire militaires*

Introduction

It may seem strange to some to speak of the Japanese in connection with the "first Indochinese war" (1945–54). This is especially disconcerting for those who have grown accustomed to seeing only the two principal actors involved in the conflict: France and the Democratic Republic of Vietnam (DRV). In both Western and Vietnamese historiographies concerning this war, most studies of the Japanese focus on the events leading up to the coup of March 9, 1945, when the Japanese overthrew the French in Indochina. This, coupled with the Japanese capitulation a few months later and a famine-driven groundswell of popular Vietnamese discontent, brought the Viet Minh to power during the "August Revolution" of 1945.

And yet, as paradoxical as it may seem, the Japanese presence in Indochina did not completely disappear with Tokyo's surrender to the Allies in that same month. Why? Because several thousand Japanese soldiers refused to give themselves up at the end of the Pacific War. They deserted. In fact, they deserted throughout the territories the Japanese had occupied during the war – in Burma, Indonesia, Thailand, and Indochina. Even in China, many joined the ranks of Mao Zedong and his adversary, Chiang Kai-shek.[2] Others simply disappeared, like the famous deserter Shoichi Yokoi, who hid in the jungles of Guam for 27 years. He did not return to Japan until 1972, where he would pass away in September 1997.[3]

If the tiny island of Guam allegedly harbored around one thousand deserters in the wake of WWII, it was estimated that as many as 5,000 Japanese deserted in Indochina. Several hundred of them joined the Viet Minh's ranks and played important roles in officers' training schools, elite combat units, as well as in mining and pharmaceutical posts. Many of them brought valuable expertise as advisors, not only in matters of military science, but also in monetary and scientific techniques.

There is nothing strange about the Vietnamese use of these "Asian foreigners." The phenomena is well known to historians studying Southeast Asia and Europe. For the West, one has only to think of the well-known "Swiss Guard" or the "Deserters' Battalion" (*Freibataillonen französischen Deserteuren*), which Frederick II incorporated into the Prussian army in the eighteenth century. It consisted of soldiers from the defeated Saxon army and French prisoners taken from 1756–7. One can even cite the example of the famous French "Foreign Legion" (*Légion étrangère*), created in France in 1831 in order to provide useful employment for the all too numerous political and military refugees of that epoch.[4] It numbered around 35,000 men in 1952, precisely when its troops were heavily engaged in the war against the Viet Minh. While it would be an exaggeration to speak of these Japanese as an "Asian Foreign Legion," these examples should nevertheless remind us that the use of foreign troops by local Asian states at war is part of a larger historical process in both time and space.

However, for historians studying the first Vietnam war, this subject remains taboo. During the war, French propaganda used the presence of Japanese deserters in the Viet Minh's ranks in order to discredit the Vietnamese resistance in the eyes of a potentially sympathetic world.[5] On the other side, Vietnamese leaders denied it and nationalist historians have since then played down the contributions of "foreigners" in their resistance in favor of writing the "glorious Vietnamese victory" over "foreign invaders." Lastly, historiographies in Vietnam, France and the US rarely conceptualize this war beyond their own narrow nationalist and ideological purviews.

In taking up this delicate subject, my aim in this essay is to shift our study of these Japanese deserters working for the DRV away from nationalist and political orientations towards a more concrete discussion of their military, technical and economic contributions. Picking up on Corvisier's citation above, this article argues that there is nothing particularly shocking or deplorable about finding Japanese soldiers in the service of the DRV during the war against the French. Given the fragile state of the Vietnamese army in the early days of the war, the DRV used these foreigners in a bid to make up for that dangerous gap between the weakness of the revolutionary State's own military possibilities *at the outset of the war* and the need to fight a war against a technically and militarily superior adversary. Moreover, these Japanese deserters offer us a unique chance to explore the grayer areas of the wars for Vietnam and to think about how Asian actors fit into a conflict involving more than the French, the Americans and even the Vietnamese themselves.

We begin our study with a rapid summary of the coming to power of the Viet Minh in August 1945 and the different political and strategic conditions which developed in northern and southern Vietnam. This allows us to understand better the very different geo-political situations our "belated allies" would encounter when they crossed over to the DRV. In the second part of this study, I try to give a more precise estimate of the actual number of deserters who joined the Vietnamese, where they settled, and what their motives were for deserting. Working from this base, I examine in the two remaining sections the contributions of these Japanese deserters to the Viet Minh. As for the period under study, the focus is on the first years of the Indochinese war from the birth of the DRV in mid-1945 to the outset of the Cold War in Southeast Asia in 1950, symbolized by the recognition of the DRV by the communist world and the arrival of another group of Asian counselors who would have a much greater impact on the Vietnamese army (and society) than these wandering Japanese.[6]

The Birth of the Democratic Republic of Vietnam

The coming to power of the Viet Minh in southern and northern Vietnam

On August 19, 1945, the Viet Minh came to power in Hanoi. In the following days, this nationalist front led by the Indochinese Communist Party (ICP) took control of most of the provincial cities in central and northern Vietnam, setting up numerous "people's committees" (*uy ban nhan dan*) as it made its way toward the south. Determined to keep power at all cost, the ICP consolidated its internal control in the north by banning or eliminating opposing nationalist parties, by creating a powerful police force, and by forming "self-defense forces" (*tu ve*). On September 2, 1945, Ho Chi Minh officially declared the birth of the Democratic Republic of Vietnam.

In the south, the revolutionary situation was more complicated. For one, the ICP had fewer leaders there due to the effective repression of the French police a few years earlier. Even when southern radicals were reunited in Saigon in 1945, they remained remarkably divided among themselves. The ICP did not have one, but several voices in the south. More importantly, the communists were far from being the only nationalist group to seek power. There were also many non-communist nationalist and religious groups, like the Hoa Hao and the Cao Dai. These religious sects had been organized and armed by the Japanese towards the end of the war. Despite this competition, on August 23 one of the best known communist leaders of the south, Tran Van Giau, managed to obtain a fragile national union and to take power in Saigon in the name of a "People's Resistance Committee" (*Uy Ban Khang Chien Nhan Dan*), which was subordinated to the ICP in Hanoi with the arrival of northern communists by September.

The Allied decision in Potsdam in July 1945 – giving the disarmament of the Japanese north of the 16th parallel to Chiang Kai-shek's troops and the southern part to the British – not only influenced the different regional situations in Indochina, but it also affected the subsequent dispersion of Japanese deserters. In late September, Chinese nationalist divisions moved into northern Vietnam. More concerned with their own economic and strategic interests, Chinese military leaders on the scene were largely opposed to the immediate return of French troops to northern Indochina. It was only following the diplomatic accords of February and March 1946 that the Chinese began to leave Indochina (though their departure would not be complete until September). Chinese occupation was not necessarily bad for the Viet Minh. Whatever the historical differences between the two, the Chinese presence in North Vietnam allowed the DRV to "breathe" – to consolidate its revolutionary hold, to strengthen and improve its army, and to try to win allies in both Asia and the West. From August 1945 to the outbreak of the war in Hanoi in December 1946, the government of the DRV in Vietnam north of the 16th parallel could recruit among the Japanese without fear of direct French interference.

This was not the case in the south, where the Allied occupation played itself out in a very different way. Unlike the Chinese, once in place, the British facilitated the return of the French to southern Vietnam to the 16th parallel.[7] On September 23, an armed coup removed the Viet Minh from power in Saigon, pushing the communists, the Hoa Hao, and the Cao Dai towards the south and the southwest as the French Expeditionary Corps re-took the main cities and roads. Faced with a veritable war in the South, Vo Nguyen Giap and Ho Chi Minh replaced Tran Van Giau by Nguyen Binh, a nationalist militant forged in the prison of Poulo Condor. Working heavily from Zone VII (eastern Nam Bo), Binh quickly took over the military leadership of all of Nam Bo and was named Major General in 1948. Less concerned than Giau with the theoretical applications of Marxism–Leninism, Binh turned to creating an army to fight the Expeditionary Corps throughout the southern country-side. None of this was easy. And southern leaders immediately recognized the need for trained military instructors, essential for forming officers and NCOs in the basics of war. They would be key to the creation, deployment, and leadership of the DRV's first combat units and operations planning. Like Vo Nguyen Giap in the north (see below), Nguyen Binh and others did not hesitate to recruit their first instructors from among the Japanese officers who had stayed on in Indochina. Indeed, Japanese officers worked in Nguyen Binh's General Staff and even as his bodyguards.[8]

The DRV's military position at the outset of the Franco-Vietnamese war

The Vietnamese army began to take shape in the early 1940s, when the Viet Minh established its first guerilla units in the mountains straddling the Sino-Vietnamese border and Nguyen Binh began organizing a semi-independent force in the north-eastern delta. The Viet Minh force was further strengthened with weapons para-chuted in by the Americans operating in southern China against the Japanese. The Office of Strategic Services even helped the Viet Minh form their first military academy, called the "Politico-Military School of Resistance Against the Japanese" (*Truong Quan-Chinh khang Nhat*), which trained 200 "military cadres" in mid-1945.[9] However, this resistance against the Japanese was very limited in scope, and the time needed for forming sufficient officers for an army was even shorter. Once transferred to Hanoi, this school was renamed the "Politico-Military Academy of Vietnam" (*Truong Quan-Chinh Viet Nam*), while the "Vietnamese Liberation Army" (*Viet-Nam Giai Phong Quan*) became the "National Defense Army" (*Ve Quoc Doan*). In September 1945, there were roughly 278 students enrolled in the DRV's nascent national military academy.[10]

Acquiring weapons was a problem from the start to the finish of the wars for Vietnam. Vo Nguyen Giap equipped his first troops with weapons taken from the former Indochinese Guard and from stocks of French arms which had been given to the Viet Minh by the Japanese in August–September 1945. The Viet Minh also bought weapons from Japanese and Chinese soldiers. Others were obtained via the black market, from the overseas Chinese in Haiphong and Cholon as well as from all over Asia, where the badly organized disarmament of the Japanese contributed to a flourishing regional contraband market.[11]

From 1945, the National Defense Army developed under the authority of the Ministry of Defense, led by Giap and eventually by his General Staff. In January 1947, French intelligence services estimated that the Vietnamese army had at their disposal some 2,000 guerillas trained in China in the early 1940s, about 4,000 Vietnamese colonial troops trained by the Japanese, and former *tirailleurs* from the Indochinese Guard. They also had some soldiers repatriated from France in 1945–6, and still more recruited among the Vietnamese communities living in northeast Thailand. In all, there were about 28,000 men in the Vietnamese army at the end of 1946. One year later, this number increased to 40–45,000 troops. A recent history of the Vietnamese General Staff puts the army's numbers in October 1946 at 85,000 men.[12] In addition, there were numerous militia groups, especially the *tu ve* and various "Suicide Squads" (*doi cam tu*), especially under Nguyen Binh's orders in the south. In the north as in the south, these militias were poorly armed and badly disciplined, but they were ferociously patriotic and/or indoctrinated. They constituted an important para-military force for the Viet Minh in 1945–6, until the DRV could establish a regular army in the classical sense of the term.[13]

And yet, in spite of the heroic efforts made by the Vietnamese to develop their army, in 1945–6 they were still far from prepared to fight the divisions and tanks of Generals Leclerc and Valluy. This fact has been openly admitted for over two decades by members of the Vietnamese military elite, who were directly involved in the events of the time.[14] Their nascent army was extremely heterogeneous, weapons lacked spare parts, the officers had little real combat experience, and the troops were still poorly led and experienced.[15] It would be a serious mistake to confuse 1945 with 1954 (let alone 1975!). Although it is difficult to sum up in a few paragraphs the extremely complex geo-political and military situation of the time, it was in this context that Japanese deserters would cross over to the Viet Minh.

As for the Vietnamese opposed to the return of the French, they saw in these Asian deserters very experienced soldiers and technicians versed in the most modern military and economic techniques of the day. Whatever the contradictions inherent in Japan's anti-Western propaganda and the violence of their own imperialist ambitions during the first half of the twentieth century, their pro-Asian propaganda and the technical might of their army, not to mention the legendary fanaticism of their troops, won over the admiration of many Vietnamese.[16] When Nguyen Binh went to meet Ho Chi Minh for the first time in Hanoi in late August or September 1945, he showed up with Japanese boots, a Japanese sword, and a Japanese pistol.[17] An important military leader in the south defended the recruitment of Japanese deserters by comparing the Vietnamese policy with that of the Indonesians in their fight against the Dutch: "We must base our actions on the example of Sjajhir and Sukarno in the Dutch Indies[,] who used Japanese fighters to spread panic in the ranks of the Anglo-Indian army."[18] They were not alone in resorting to such action. Chiang Kai-shek and Mao Zedong recruited Japanese deserters to serve as technicians and officers in their respective armies.[19] It is in this context, not an ideological one, that the DRV urged Japanese to serve their state militarily and technically, even if belatedly.[20] Let us turn now to these deserters to determine their numbers, their motives, and the nature of their distribution in the North and South.

Japanese Deserters in the Viet Minh

Defectors in North Indochina

Desertion was easier for the Japanese stationed north of the 16th parallel than in the southern part of Indochina. Not only had the Chinese maintained a less stringent surveillance of northern Indochina, but they also wanted to recruit Japanese for their own army. Although these disarmed Japanese were theoretically confined to very precise areas, in practice they could move around quite freely, leaving their detention camps in the morning to return at night. The Chinese had interned roughly 20,000 Japanese in areas of Quang Yen/Yen Lap, 5,000 in Tourane (Da Nang), 3,000 near Nam Dinh, 3,500 in Hanoi, and undoubtedly many more in Thai Nguyen province.[21] As noted, the Chinese nationalist presence and refusal to overthrow the DRV allowed the Viet Minh to recruit among the Japanese population without fear of direct French intervention. And they did. This would not begin to change until after the March 6th Franco-Vietnamese Accords, when the French began to return partially to the North. Yet this agreement limited France's military presence above the 16th parallel to about 15,000 soldiers; the DRV continued to operate as a "Free State."

At the time of the Japanese surrender, it was estimated that there were around 97,000 Japanese soldiers and civilians stationed in Indochina.[22] According to Japanese and American sources, in September–October 1945 there were around 48,000 soldiers and 2,000 civilians in Vietnam north of the 16th parallel.[23] Approximately 30,500 Japanese were repatriated to Japan through the port of Haiphong on April 29, 1946; 1,500 civilians were evacuated shortly thereafter; and another 3,000 escaped to Hainan island in the South China Sea. Around 15,000 Japanese remained in an "indeterminate" position (but not necessarily "deserters") in northern Indochina in late December 1946.[24] Most of the others would be repatriated in the following months. These statistics are, of course, estimates, as the French Diplomatic Advisor to the High-Commissioner of Indochina in 1948 rightly pointed out in 1948.[25]

It is thus difficult to establish the exact number of desertions. A French report based on captured Viet Minh documents and the declarations of returned Japanese deserters estimated that there were roughly 4,000 of them in Tonkin and Annam north of the 16th parallel in December 1946.[26] Given our examination of many of these documents, 4,000 must be considered as an absolute maximum, and 1,000 to 2,000 as the more likely minimum.[27] What is certain is that the number of deserters would decrease continually as they returned to their units, disappeared, or died in battles of decolonization, or due to illness and, more rarely, suicides. Demoralized by the conditions of life in Viet Minh camps and often exhausted by rough treatment and living conditions, many Japanese would abandon the Viet Minh. Others left because they were disappointed by the low quality of their Vietnamese troops.[28] Moreover, between April and September 1946, having re-established a military footing in the north, the French initiated their "Mission Tokyo" aimed at recovering the large number of Japanese deserters in northern Indochina before running the risk of retaking the north by force. The returnees, however, were few. The DRV maintained very strict police surveillance over them. Even later, when the famous Japanese Colonel Saito arrived to locate the Japanese deserters – something he had done in the South with considerable success (see below) – he ran into very efficient Vietnamese police monitoring.[29] Lastly, the Viet Minh would hide or, in rarer cases, execute Japanese (and European) deserters who had come under suspicion or who simply knew too much to risk letting them talk to foreign intelligence services.[30]

The problem for the historian, however, resides in the difficulty of determining just how many of these deserters actually crossed over to the Viet Minh. Of the possible maximum of 4,000 deserters in northern Vietnam, not all of them joined the Viet Minh. It seems reasonable to suggest that a maximum of 1,000 to 2,000 Japanese were effectively in the service of the DRV army and state between 1945 and 1950. It must be emphasized, again, that this number diminished inexorably and rapidly during these five years.

Deserters in Southern Indochina

At the time of the Japanese surrender, there were around 68,000 Japanese troops (including 3,000 civilians) south of the 16th parallel in Indochina.[31] Around 20,000 Japanese were repatriated via the town of Cap St. Jacques (Nha Trang) in April 1946, and most of the others in the months that followed. Most of the desertions in the south occurred just after the Japanese surrender, as the British and French took control of the south. Worried about their fate under the imminent Allied occupation, many Japanese disappeared without waiting to find out what the British would do. This was especially the case for the war criminals. In early 1946, the Japanese High Command provided the "official" figure of 620 deserters in southern Indochina. A well-informed French intelligence officer considered this "well below the reality."[32] A French study in late 1946 estimated that there were probably 1,000 Japanese who had deserted following the Japanese capitulation. This study calculated that about 560 of the 1,000 deserters were scattered throughout the provinces of Tay Ninh, Thu Dau Mot, My Tho, Saigon-Cholon, Bien Hoa, and Rach Gia.[33] Another estimate, based partly on British archives, put the number of deserters at "roughly" 1,000 in March 1946.[34] Indeed, according to the military intelligence section of the Supreme Allied Commander, as of March 30, 1946, there were among the "dead, deserted or missing" in southern Indochina 731 soldiers and 76 civilians from the Japanese army, and 59 sailors and 61 civilians from the Imperial Navy, making for a total of 927 men.[35] Again, not all of them were deserters working for the DRV.

This figure would diminish rapidly in southern Indochina, where the French could attack the Japanese problem much earlier than in the north. In early November 1945 and late April 1946, 250,000 pamphlets written in Japanese were air-dropped over Viet Minh-controlled zones, while another 180,000 were distributed on the ground by Japanese units. Until April 22, 1946, the location of the deserters was left to Japanese authorities. They succeeded in recovering 168 deserters. From April 22, a more methodical search program began under the auspices of the "Control Mission for the Japanese Army" (*Mission de Contrôle de l'Armée japonaise*) in Saigon. Under French control, it dispatched 200 officers and troops to locate the deserters, but only recovered ten.[36] Following this failure, from mid July, a new "Control Mission for Japanese Deserters" (*Mission de Contrôle des Déserteurs japonais*) was run by a French officer fluent in Japanese. Following his death, Japanese Colonel Hiroo Saito took over this highly secret operation.[37] Saito had been trained in the most prestigious intelligence schools of the Japanese army. During the war, he had served as an officer on the General Staff of the 55th Division in Burma. By 1948, he would succeed in returning some 350 Japanese deserters. Due to this success, he was later sent to the North to mount a similar mission, but with much less success (see above).[38]

Taking into account all this evidence, it would seem reasonable to assert that there were 500–600 deserters in the South at the end of 1946. If one includes Saito's successes in 1948, there could not have been more than 300 deserters in Nam Bo after 1948. Indeed, in March 1948, an agent of Colonel Saito learned from discussion with the heads of the General Staffs of the 8th and 9th Zones that there were 200 Japanese attached to the 8th zone, 100 in the 9[th,] and "a sizeable number" in the 7th. In short, there were not many more than 300 Japanese working for the Viet Minh from 1948 in the south.[39]

The Beginnings of Japanese-Viet Minh post-1945 Collaboration

The North

In Bac Bo, the first contacts between the Japanese and the Viet Minh were both diplomatic and military in nature. The diplomatic cooperation, if it can really be called that, was extremely limited. It was most notably associated with a handful of Japanese intellectuals *de gauche*, who had been educated in France in the 1920s and 1930s and attached to the diplomatic and military services in Indochina during the war. Some remained in Vietnam after the war. Two in particular were surprisingly active in northern Vietnam up to the March 6 Accords. The most remarkable was a Westernized scholar named Kiyoshi Komatsu.[40] Born in Kobe on June 13, 1900, Komatsu had traveled to France in 1921, where he quickly took to learning French and would later become one of Japan's most famous writers on French literature. Later, he would pride himself on having befriended André Malraux and even Georges Bidault, President of the French Council. But even more important, Komatsu had already met Ho Chi Minh in Paris in 1921.[41] They thus knew each other in 1945. During the Japanese occupation, Komatsu had worked closely with various Vietnamese groups demanding national independence, especially in the South.

After the Viet Minh took power in August 1945, Komatsu went to Hanoi, where he allegedly created the "International Committee for the Aid and Support of the

Government of the DRV." He directed the committee in collaboration with a Frenchman of Russian origin named Solovieff, who had been doing business in the Far East since the 1930s. But the most important collaborator for Komatsu was his compatriot, Komaki Oomiya. Also educated in France in the 1920s, Komaki had worked in Indochina since the 1930s as a specialist in mining, banking, and juridical questions. Like Komatsu, during the war he worked in secret with Vietnamese nationalists opposed to the French. Although this organization seems to have received a green light from the Chinese and the Americans in Hanoi in 1945, it is still not clear whether it was an individual initiative or received support from somewhere else. In any case, the main idea was to help Vietnam on the diplomatic front, since the young Republic had not yet been recognized by any foreign nation. After his release from an internment camp by a "Soviet agent," Komaki began working as an intermediary between the Vietnamese, the French, and Chinese and Soviet delegates, especially during the negotiations of March 6.[42]

While the French put an immediate stop to this organization following the March Accords, another organization, known as the "Organization for Collaboration and Mutual Aid for the Independence of Vietnam," picked up where Komatsu and Oomiya had left off. According to one Japanese participant, this "Organization of Collaboration" was active in the north after the March Accords, operating under the direction of Lt. Colonel Muraiyama and his adjunct, Major Oshima. These officers tried to help Vietnam obtain independence in any way they could, to naturalize Japanese deserters as "new Vietnamese" (*Viet Nam Moi*), and to lay the ground for a new relationship between Japan and Vietnam in the future. They obviously refused to obey the imperial edict to give themselves up to Allied troops. For strategic and economic reasons, they anchored their *jusqu'au boutiste* (last stand) movement in the regions of Thai Nguyen, Phu Tho, and Tuyen Quang. According this source, their numbers were around 1,500 soldiers, employed in the rudimentary munitions workshops and in the military ranks of the DRV. We know that some Japanese were allegedly running an arms factory in Thai Nguyen in 1946, and French intelligence figures confirm a very high number of Japanese deserters in this very province.[43] Of the 799 Japanese deserters identified by the French in northern Vietnam in November 1946, 595 were located in the province of Thai Nguyen, or 75 percent of the total on this list. Around 280 of them were employed in the Viet Minh arsenals there. In my opinion, this military support – rather than a diplomatic one – most attracted the Vietnamese in late 1945.

The South

Similar overtures occurred at the same time in the South. On October 12, a meeting of Vietnamese leaders took place at Bien Hoa to discuss the utilization of the Japanese against the French. Among those present were a special governmental delegate sent to the South by Ho Chi Minh, Vu Duc (Hoang Dinh Giong), Huynh Van Nghe (a ranking ICP member who had worked in secret organizations in Bangkok in the early 1940s), and the veteran communist leader, Ha Huy Giap. During this meeting, Vu Duc evaluated the position of the Japanese deserters with regard to the Viet Minh. He learned that the deserters had mixed feelings towards the Vietnamese, depending on the regions. Some Japanese had shown themselves sympathetic to the Viet Minh's cause. After a long discussion, Vu Duc divided the Japanese deserters in Nam Bo into three main groups: the "neutrals," the "nationalist socialist elements," and those who wanted to "help them tacitly." Vu Duc called this third group the "revolutionary elements," worthy of recruitment by the Viet Minh: "As we are the revolutionary army, we can use these Japanese revolutionaries to help us." Duc asked that an "official committee" be created to enter into contact with them.[44] Undoubtedly aware of these directives, Huynh Kim Truong, a Viet Minh commander in the South, gave his complete approval of the recruitment of Japanese *already* underway by his subordinates: "We have learned that you have sent an emissary to recruit Japanese [soldiers], you have our complete approval on this subject and we wish you brilliant results."[45] Military memoirs recently published in Vietnam confirm the early presence of Japanese deserters in the ranks of the Viet Minh in the South at the end of 1945.[46]

Motives behind the Japanese desertions

It would be a serious mistake to think that all these Japanese soldiers crossed over to the Viet Minh on "pro-Asian" or "anti-Western" grounds. This counted, as we shall see, but very often they left simply for fear of being arrested by the Allies, condemned as war criminals, and executed. This was especially the case in the South, where the rapid reoccupation by British troops, followed by the troops of General Leclerc, did not leave much time for reflection. Reading through pages of the detailed interrogations of numerous returning deserters, one gets the impression that following the unexpected Japanese defeat in August 1945, hundreds of Japanese soldiers and officers suddenly found themselves caught up in the middle of a nationalist uprising and anti-colonial war, neither of which they really understood. Devastated by their own debacle, many drifted into the Viet Minh less because of ideological or pan-Asian sentiments than the fact that their world had come crashing down around them. They suddenly found themselves lost, directionless, playing the part of "leaderless samurais," *ronin*, in Indochina in particular and Asia in general.

Indeed, the reasons for most of these desertions were, in the end, very human. Many of the common soldiers and civilians preferred to remain in Indochina, where the economic possibilities were considerably better than in Japan, which had been economically and militarily devastated by the war. One such deserter, Yoshikawa Tomizo, cited the "miserable situation in Japan after the war" as one of the main reasons for his decision to desert. Others, with similar ideas in mind, traded in their weapons and changed their names in order to open small shops, transport services, and import–export businesses in both DRV zones and the French-controlled towns of Saigon, Haiphong and Hanoi. Some even chose to return to their prewar farming jobs as cultivators in Vietnam. Many of these deserters were married to Vietnamese women. Among the officers of the Kempeitai and military intelligence services, many spoke Vietnamese and/or Chinese well, and had extensive cultural or economic knowledge of the country. They used these advantages for money-making ends.[47]

Given that the repatriation of the Japanese in Southeast Asia was originally intended to take five years, many Japanese decided to try their luck in Indochina rather than wait in an internment camp for the ship to Japan. Others, truly destitute, were seduced by the promises of preferential treatment in the DRV's army – which was often the case, at least in the early days. There was also the collective choice, a psychological situation in which an officer could get his men to follow him thanks to bonds of friendship and loyalty forged in combat. Of the 400 Japanese names missing from the repatriation ships leaving Haiphong in March–April 1946, 98 belonged to the 82nd Infantry Regiment, or about 25 percent of the total; 70 belonged to the 34th General Infantry Brigade, or 17.5 percent of the total; and 40 belonged to the 83rd Infantry Regiment, or 10 percent.[48] It is hard to believe that these ordinary soldiers all left on idealistic, pro-Viet Minh grounds. It is more likely that they decided collectively to check out permanently. They were undoubtedly scared and fearful of being arrested and condemned by the Allies to prison or worse.

It is worth noting that some of these deserters were incorporated into the ranks of the Viet Minh against their will. They were simply captured and forced to work as technicians and advisors for the Viet Minh. Given the critical state of the DRV economy and army from December 1946, Vietnamese leaders were in many ways following an old Southeast Asian practice (more Thai, in fact, than Vietnamese) which involved taking technically valuable "hostages" or "slaves." The leaders of the DRV knew perfectly well that once pushed out of the cities, they would need highly educated engineers, technicians, and administrators in order to operate their war state. As they left Hanoi in December 1946, the DRV took as hostage doctors and educated men like Pham Le Bong and Nguyen Tien Lang. The latter, secretary of the French Résident Supérieur in the 1930s (and the son-in-law of the famous intellectual Pham Quynh), became the personal secretary to General Nguyen Son, chief of military forces in Trung Bo in 1946. Several dozen Japanese, if not more, were "recruited" in this way, especially to serve in the Viet Minh barracks and arsenals in Thai Nguyen in 1946.[49]

Not all the deserters necessarily joined the Viet Minh. This was especially the case in the south, where the Japanese army and intelligence services had for many years collaborated with the religious sects, the Cao Dai and Hoa Hao in particular. Several deserters were to be found in the General Staff of the Cao Dai General Trinh Minh The. Besides helping Nguyen Giac Ngo, Captain Kanetoshi worked for Trinh Minh The as a military instructor and advisor. In the course of a conversation with Colonel Saito, the Cao Dai "Pope," Pham Cong Tac, said of Kanetoshi: "He is our master." There were also a dozen Japanese who worked for the famous Binh Xuyen para-military, brigand forces led by Le Van Vien ("Bay Vien").[50] Although it is impossible to establish exactly how many Japanese dissidents participated in these two groups, it is doubtful that there were more than a few hundred. In the north, as in China, several dozen Japanese decided to join the non-communist Vietnamese nationalists of the "Vietnamese Nationalist Party" (VNQDD) and the "Dai Viet" parties. These groups were as opposed to the return of the French as they were to Vietnamese communist efforts to take power. However, the Japanese presence in the ranks of the VNQDD did not last long, especially following the latter's annihilation by the Viet Minh in northern Vietnam in mid-1946.[51]

Other reasons for deserting were more moving. For example, there was a notable increase in departures for the Viet Minh after the Japanese Emperor's repudiation in early 1946 of the myth of the divinity of the imperial dynasty.[52] This announcement triggered an already deep malaise in the minds of ranking officers, most of whom had been intensely indoctrinated and shaped by the cult of the divine Emperor. It disturbed them profoundly and led them to isolate themselves in the maquis, where the Viet Minh welcomed them with enough to eat and the chance to carry on the "cause" in the Vietnamese army.[53]

Some Japanese officers deserted in order to continue the struggle against "the White Man" and in favor of the "Asians." Again, several of the deserting officers had been trained in top-secret, ultra-nationalist, and pan-Asian military and intelligence academies. This may have been the case of the officers trained in the Nakano Academy, such as Ishii Takuo and Muraiyama. According to one military study, the Japanese who went through this elite program "were influenced by a pan-Asian mystique and were initiated into the grandest and most secret projects of Japan's politics of expansion, and received special technical training for the geo-political zone in which they would take command." The Allies believed that these men may have received special protection on the part of the General Staff of Marshal Terauchi at the end of the Pacific War, allowing them to elude capture by the Allies.[54] Moreover, although Japanese officers had been put to the test in combat in Burma and the Philippines, the Japanese Expeditionary Corps had never been entirely defeated by the Allies in continental Southeast Asia or in Indonesia. Some of these officers must have only bitterly accepted the idea of surrendering to Westerners without a fight. Disgusted by their unexpected defeat, several of them simply disappeared, never to return to a country that no longer wanted to hear of them. Others truly saw themselves fulfilling their Asian mission by helping the Vietnamese.[55]

Shame, of course, was also part of it. Many deserting officers simply could not bear the thought of returning to their homeland and family vanquished. They would have at least preferred to have died for the cause. Surviving their fallen comrades was worse. The battle-hardened Kanetoshi of the 55th division later told his interrogators that he had deserted because he had been "tormented by Japan's defeat," something which had been "unthinkable" for him. Not only was it "shame," but he could never bear the idea of returning to Japan when so many of his fallen comrades would never be able to do so. For Kanetoshi, aiding the Vietnamese independence movement was a way of carrying on the war, a way of life – the only one he knew. Fate also had its place in such psychologically disconcerting circumstances. When an envoy sent to recuperate Japanese deserters in the forests of Nam Bo asked colonel Ishii Takuo "why" he did not "want to return" to his Japanese homeland, the latter responded laconically that "one could not take back the seeds which had already been sown."[56]

Japanese Contributions to the Viet Minh, 1945–50

The contributions of these Japanese deserters to the Viet Minh can be divided into two major categories: 1) military and 2) technological and scientific ones. The former was by far the most important, but the second should not be underestimated.

Military contributions

As noted, the training of officers and military cadres was top priority for the DRV from 1945. Besides a handful of very important officers trained in Chinese military academies, the Viet Minh had virtually no other superior officers to command in battle. The fact that the colonial system had trained but very few Vietnamese ranking officers before the war only aggravated an already critical deficiency. This was especially the case in the south, where war broke out almost immediately. It is therefore not surprising that the Viet Minh recruited Japanese soldiers and especially the experienced officers who remained in Vietnam. The reports made by returning Japanese officers to their French and Japanese interrogators leave no doubt as to their early contributions to the southern Viet Minh.[57] Japanese officers who stayed on directly advised such key Vietnamese military leaders as Nguyen Binh, Nguyen Thanh Son, Nam Lua, Nguyen Giac Ngo and Vo Van Duc in the rapid, if superficial, training of hundreds of young Vietnamese recruits in late 1945 and 1946; in the first efforts to stop the return of French armed forces to Nam Bo; and in early operational and strategic planning. Ranking Japanese officers, such as Ishii Takuo, Toshihide Kanetoshi, and Nishikawa[58] were directly involved in early Viet Minh military operations against the French between 1945 and 1947. Kanetoshi was for a while "Chief of Staff" of Nguyen Giac Ngo's troops in the 9th zone. Assisting him, Shida Shigeo (Ly Dang Hai), helped train three classes of young Vietnamese soldiers, in all 550 men.[59] In the north, Ngo Van Chieu, a young Vietnamese combatant, received an officer's training in one of the first officers' academies established in Hanoi in 1945–6. In his memoirs, he reveals that a "former Lieutenant-Colonel in the General Staff of the 38th Japanese Army" worked as a "technical advisor" for the Vietnamese instructor of this school.[60]

The role of Japanese officers in military academies: The Quang Ngai example

Japanese deserters played a particularly important role in the running of the "Infantry Academy of Quang Ngai" (Truong luc quan trung hoc Quang Ngai) from 1946 to 1949.[61] Created by Nguyen Son, this officers' school employed at least six Japanese officers as military instructors. They were known by their Vietnamese names: Dong Hung, Tam, Ngoc, Thong, Quang, and Tong.[62] Another document mentions "Nguyen Van Thong" (Ishii Takuo), "Phan Lai" (Igari Kazumasa), "Nguyen Thinh Tam" (Saitoh), "Minh Ngoc" (Nakahara Mitsunobu), "Long" (Konishi?), and "Hai" (Nabeyasi). All were military instructors.[63] Of the 46 Japanese officers present in the Viet Minh ranks in the southern part of Trung Bo in 1948, 36 worked as military instructors, or 78 percent of the total number.[64]

The memoirs of Vietnamese and Japanese present in the Quang Ngai academy at the time corroborate these French sources. The Japanese–Vietnamese Association reveals that Dong Hung (Kikuo Tanimoto) led the 1st company in Quang Ngai, Minh Ngoc (Mitsunobu Nakahara) the second, Phan Lai (Kazumasa Igari) the third, and Phan Hue (Tokuji Kamo) the fourth company.[65] Nguyen Viet Hong, a former Vietnamese military cadet trained by the Japanese at Quang Ngai, confirms that in

1946 General Nguyen Son confided the direction of these first four companies to Minh Ngoc (Mitsunobu Nakahara), Dong Hung (Kikuo Tanitmoto), Phan Lai (Kazumasa Igari) and Phan Hue (Tokuji Kamo). That same year he recruited four more Japanese officers, including Shoichi Igawa of the General Staff of the 34th Mixed Infantry Brigade in the region of Hue-Da Nang. Igawa became a close advisor to Nguyen Son, according to Vietnamese sources.[66]

In recollections recently published in Vietnam, Nakahara Mitsunobu (Minh Ngoc) confirms his role in the Quang Ngai Academy and his military collaboration with General Nguyen Son. It was Nguyen Son himself who convinced him and another officer named "Ikawa", almost certainly Major Shoichi Igawa,[67] to work for the Vietnamese cause by giving military training in the new Quang Ngai Academy. In early 1946, these two Japanese went to Tuy Hoa to help the Viet Minh fight against the French Expeditionary Corps, which was then attacking southern Trung Bo. Nakahara provided crucial advice to Son concerning command operations before going to north as a special advisor to the DRV's general staff preparing for all-out war against the French. Indeed, he fought in the battle of Nam Dinh when war broke out in all of Vietnam in December 1946. In 1948, Nakahara once again saw Nguyen Son in Inter-Zone IV (upper central Vietnam), where the Japanese deserter was busy training more military cadres.[68]

What did these Japanese teach precisely? Documents found on the body of one of the Japanese instructors from the Quang Ngai Academy, Chief-Sergeant Oshikiri, give us a better idea. Oshikiri's personal notebooks contain an intensive course on "Tokkohan" ("Special Assault Forces"). Oshikiri taught his young Vietnamese students how to sabotage, to organize smash-and-grab-attacks, to plan effective ambushes, in short, how to fight against a militarily superior foe.[69] Japanese instructors also provided the basics of officer training and military science. They organized and directed company and battalion exercises, all the while drilling in assault, attack, and night combat. They gave instruction in commanding, tactics, navigation, orientation, battle communications and movements, etc. In 1945–6, Japanese instructors in the south formed hundreds of Vietnamese officers in these matters. Japanese soldiers accompanied Viet Minh troops into battle and commanded troops against the French. They also helped in developing radio communications and military intelligence gathering.[70] Recent Vietnamese publications concede this point today. And it was not limited to Quang Ngai, as we shall see.[71]

The role of Japanese officers in positions of command
Japanese military techniques were introduced by a number of ranking Japanese officers in positions of command in the Viet Minh. The case of Major Ishii Takuo is particularly revealing. He crossed over to the Viet Minh in the South and became, in my view, one of the most important Japanese deserters ever to serve in the Vietnamese army. At the time of the Japanese capitulation, Ishii was only 27 years old. As a major, he was allegedly the youngest officer in the Japanese army at the time. Colonel Saito had been his superior in the General Staff of the 55th Division in Burma.[72] He was not your normal Japanese officer. Ishii had first been trained at the Nakano Academy, an elite and ultra secret superior officers' training school.[73] He was

well versed in the most modern Japanese methods of war, as well as the finer methods of clandestine warfare. Moreover, he had already commanded within the General Staff of the 55th Division in Burma, and had taken part in the difficult battle of Rangoon. For military reasons above all, Colonel Saito believed this taciturn, bearded and chain-smoking man to be extremely dangerous in the hands of the Viet Minh.[74] He was.

Ishii deserted his unit on December 17 1945 in Banam in Cambodia. He brought with him other "veterans" of Nakano and from the 55th Division, including Kanetoshi. Once rallied to the Viet Minh, he traded in his passable English to learn Vietnamese. In exchange for his military collaboration, the Viet Minh named him "colonel" (*dai ta*) in their army. Thus began his career as military instructor for the DRV. In May 1946, he left Baria for Quang Ngai in the company of Pham Van Bach, president of the Resistance Committee of Nam Bo. Under the leadership of Nguyen Son and Pham Van Dong, southern Trung Bo served as the principal relay for the transfer of men and arms from the north to the south.[75] According to a French source, in June 1946 Ishii assembled the Vietnamese "regiment" (more likely a company) commanders between Hue and Phan Thiet for intensive military training as full-scale war with the French loomed. In July, he provisionally headed the Military Academy of Quang Ngai.[76] He placed other Japanese officers whom he had known before in this school, such as his friend the instructor Saitoh, who was also named colonel by the DRV (see above). In late 1946, the latter took over at the Quang Ngai Academy,[77] while Ishii allegedly became "Chief Advisor" of Viet Minh troops in the South.[78] According to French and Japanese intelligence, in July 1946 he went to Pleiku to help lead combat operations. But his real value was officer and combat training. In August 1946, Nguyen Son sent him to Tuy Hoa to found another military school. In 1947, this graduate of Nakano offered elite training to 130 Viet Minh candidates and in late June 1948 he provided military training to cadres of the 7th, 8th, and 9th zones further south.[79]

Similar cases existed in the north. Mawayoshi Hiro joined the Viet Minh and led Vietnamese troops against the French paratrooper landings in Bac Kan in 1947.[80] In December 1948, "Bao," the Vietnamese name of a Japanese "colonel" who had served in Burma, trained Vietnamese cadets and personally led a Vietnamese company into battle against the French at Phu Thong.[81]

This "technical transfer" to the Vietnamese was all the easier since several of these instructors knew Vietnam well. Four of the seven officers identified at the Quang Ngai Academy in 1946 had worked for the Kempeitai in Hue and Phan Thiet. Men such as Minh Ngoc had considerable geographic, linguistic, and cultural knowledge due to their experiences during the war. Thirteen of the forty-six deserters identified by the French in southern Trung Bo in 1948 could speak Vietnamese either "perfectly" or "very well," and nine could speak "well." Nine of them were married to Vietnamese women.[82] Over fifty years later, Nakahara Mitsunobu wrote the account of his time with Nguyen Son in Vietnamese.[83]

One of the results of the Japanese presence in the Viet Minh army was an increase in French losses at the beginning of the war.[84] During the first battles in the north, for example, the Vietnamese used Japanese soldiers in the front lines. Several Japanese bodies were discovered outside Ho Chi Minh's former residence when the French re-took Hanoi in late 1946.[85] During the battle of Hue in early 1947, the French estimated that they had engaged a Japanese assault unit consisting of around 150 soldiers. Because of their superior training and experience, these Japanese were responsible for a dozen deaths and many wounded in Expeditionary Corps. In 1947, in collaboration with Nguyen Son, Ishii laid an ambush which resulted in 70–80 deaths on the French side.[86] The casualties among these Japanese troops must also have been very high, as French sources reveal.

These Japanese officers working in Vietnamese military academies of the Viet Minh, and especially the officers from Nakano like Ishii and Muraiyama, were assets for the DRV at the outset of the war, when the military needs of the Vietnamese State were greatest and when Vietnamese possibilities were weakest. On that note, it would be interesting to compare the military contributions of these Japanese deserters with those of the Europeans who worked for the Viet Minh at the same time.[87]

The transfer of modern military science in Asian ways

In many ways, the defeat of the Japanese and the desertion of these soldiers and officers after WWII provided the DRV with a precious Asian source for learning modern military science at a time when they needed it most but had the least access to it.[88] The technical contributions of Toshio Komaya (Nguyen Quang Thuc) and Koshiro Iwai are particularly instructive. Between 1947 and 1949, the former worked as an advisor to the 59th Regiment. Located in northern Vietnam, Toshio worked as a military advisor to the Chinese-trained Vietnamese officer, Nam Long. He accompanied Le Quang Ba into southern China in mid-1949 in a bid to help the CCP defeat the GMD. As the Chinese communist victory approached, Toshio was transferred to the operations section of the general staff of the newly formed Viet Bac inter-zone. He played a particularly important role in helping to organize and plan a new level of modern military operations against the French, thanks to the massive aid now being provided by the Chinese to the DRV. Indeed, he participated in organizing the frontier battles designed to open the border to China via Cao Bang in mid-1950. However, surviving Vietnamese officers who worked with him are most thankful for his training of cadres and officers, the development of Viet Bac's military intelligence, and his crucial operational work in the planning and mapping of major northern battles.[89]

Koshiro Iwai, called Sau Nhat at the time, made similar technical contributions. Since 1947, he had led Vietnamese units into battle against the French in Lang Son and conducted special operations behind enemy lines. By 1949 he had been named a battalion deputy commander. He was most appreciated, however, for the technical training he provided in general staff work, battle preparation, and military intelligence. The Vietnamese army no longer hides the very important advisory and intelligence role Koshiro Iwai played during the frontier battles against the French in 1950 as a member of the famous 174th regiment. He also solved problems that allowed the Vietnamese to employ their newly acquired Chinese artillery more effectively against French positions. His contributions and fidelity were so precious that he was admitted into the Vietnamese Workers Party in 1952.[90] In exchange for all these services, the DRV allocated a higher salary to these allies than to their own troops, at least at the beginning of the conflict.[91]

However, the military knowledge imparted by these Japanese officers was not always well adapted to the needs of the Vietnamese army, still badly armed and supervised at this time. Division General Vuong Thua Vu reveals in his memoirs, published in 1979, that a high-ranking Japanese officer named "Ai Viet" ("he who loves Vietnam") served in his General Staff in December 1946 as a "military delegate" (*phai vien quan su*). Revealingly, an acerbic debate broke out on the eve of full-scale war with the French between this Japanese officer, who advocated a classical defense of Hanoi against the Expeditionary Corps, and Vuong Thua Vu's General Staff, which stressed the strategic importance of the *tu ve* and guerilla tactics (*du kich*). Given the superior firepower of the French, General Vu (rightly) considered Ai Viet's defense plan to be suicidal, "not at all in harmony with the technical and tactical level of the [very weak Vietnamese] forces of the time."[92] To put it another way, modern operational and tactical military science could only be applied efficiently to the DRV's army in the North from 1950, once Chinese military aid allowed Vo Nguyen Giap's northern army to take on the French Expeditionary Corps in modern battles and not simply hit-and-run guerilla actions.

Technological and economic contributions

Japanese technical advice also made itself felt in the economic realm. Although the sources are sparse, the presence of Japanese engineers and monetary advisors among the Viet Minh in the North is confirmed by a highly-placed actor at the time: the former Minister of the Economy, Le Van Hien. In his diary, recently published in Vietnam, Hien is remarkably frank about the presence of a handful of Japanese technical advisors attached to the Ministry of the Economy into the early 1950s. They often worked at his side, advising him on the planning, organization, and management of the economy and of the resources of the DRV in the north.[93] Hien mentions five principal Japanese deserters by their Vietnamese names: Thuan, Thanh, Lam, Hien, and Duong. Some of these engineers had worked in the mines in Tonkin (those of Minh Khai in particular) during the Japanese occupation.[94] It was this mining expertise and familiarity with Tonkin's natural resources that made them so precious to the Viet Minh. "Thuan" is a good example. An engineer by profession, he worked as an economics advisor to Le Van Hien in "the study of the planning and construction" of the DRV economy and in a lead foundry feeding northern Vietnamese weapons factories. Impressed by his technical abilities, Hien writes in his memoirs that he considered him to be one of his most skilled advisors.[95] Another example comes from two Japanese engineers stationed near Lao Cai who applied scientific methods to exploit minerals for the Viet Minh.[96] It appears that some of these Japanese were, indeed, highly-skilled. On July 24 1950, Le Van Hien wrote as follows concerning one of his Japanese mining specialists named Lam Dong Luong:

> I discussed at length with Luong the development of Vietnam's mines. Luong had a profound knowledge of the mining situation. During the Japanese occupation, [he] had

exploited many areas. [He] knew much about uranium mines. By his own hands, he had located this mineral and was present when a Japanese delegation came to consider the possibilities of exploiting this uranium. According to Luong, following these investigations, the Japanese began to exploit [the uranium mines in Tonkin] and he thought that they were going to have the nuclear bomb thanks to the primary resources of Vietnam.[97]

Some Japanese financial experts also worked for the DRV as advisors in the management of the government's banking and monetary policies, one of the Viet Minh's most pressing problems during the entire war against the French. If their numbers were limited, their influence was perhaps not. Once again, Le Van Hien reveals that a Japanese named "Tung" (Hoang Dinh Tung) was one of his most important monetary advisors. This should not be surprising, since this "Tung" was none other than the former director (*giam doc*) of the local branch of the Bank of Yokohama in Hanoi. After the Japanese defeat in 1945, he rallied to the DRV and served as an advisor to the "National Bank of Vietnam" (*Quoc Gia Ngan Hang Viet Nam*). According to Hien, Tung played an influential role in the making of Vietnam's early "banking policy" (*chinh sach ngan hang*).[98] Another deserter, Shinsuke Yamamoto, deserves mention. He had graduated from the Tokyo Imperial University, one of the most prestigious educational centers in all of Japan. He worked for a steel company for several years, before joining the Navy. He arrived in Saigon in February 1943 and worked as the Director of the Hanoi branch office of the Navy's accounts office until August 1945. Unsurprisingly, the DRV used him to work for them in their accounting departments and especially in monetary matters related to issuing money. He would also provide military training in his time off.[99]

A Japanese source provides similar information on a certain Mr. Fujita. The latter was a former employee of the "Yokohama Specie Bank" in Hanoi, and was transferred to the Bank of Indochina on March 9, 1945. He continued to work there during the Chinese occupation. In late 1945, he was recruited by agents of the Viet Minh who had infiltrated the bank. Fujita crossed over to the Viet Minh at this time and helped the DRV "in organizing a new banking system and stabilizing a new currency system," largely confirming Le Van Hien's description of Tung.[100] As the former minister wrote of Tung's contribution during a meeting of a sub-commission of the National Bank in September 1949: "Since Hoang Dinh Tung previously worked for the Bank of Yokohama, he has concrete experience and can thus provide us with many suggestions regarding the organization [of monetary policy]."[101] This is not surprising, given the monetary war the French were waging on the DRV's currency at this very time. This Japanese economics advisor was most probably Isamu Fujita, who worked at the Yokohama Shokin Guinko branch in Hanoi.[102]

A final area where Japanese deserters versed in modern Western techniques made a significant contribution was in the medical field. One of the most important figures was the Doctor Phuong, that is, Tamiya Takazawa. Although we know little about him, this Japanese deserter figures often in the memoirs of Le Van Hien. From December 1949, the DRV authorized him to create a laboratory to manufacture medicines (*phong bao che thuoc*), which the Vietnamese army desperately needed to treat their wounded and sick. This "pharmaceutical industry" was also intended to lessen the Viet Minh's dependence on costly imports. According to Hien, the Japanese in his entourage played an important role in the construction of this medical laboratory. Dr. Phuong became its director in December 1949.[103] To encourage their support of the resistance, a "correct and generous policy" (*chinh sach dung dan, rong rai*) was applied.[104] French documents speak of eleven nurses and two doctors identified among the 81 deserters working for the Viet Minh in northern Vietnam around 1951.[105]

Conclusion

It is difficult at this stage of our research to know exactly how many of these Japanese deserters remained in the Viet Minh's ranks after the arrival in force of Mao Zedong's troops on the Vietnamese border around 1950. There were probably no more than a few hundred Japanese residing in the north and even less in the south. And of these, only a few dozen were truly valuable for the DRV by the early 1950s, such as Toshio Komaya and Koshiro Iwai. The others, much less important, undoubtedly lived in small groups which were carefully monitored by the Viet Minh. As the ICP/DRV aligned itself officially and ideologically with the communist world from 1950, Vietnamese and Chinese communist leaders must have been more suspicious of these Japanese "allies," due as much to their problematic political history as to the threat that they represented as potential spies. In any case, there were certainly not thousands of Japanese deserters working for the Viet Minh in 1950. However, there were indeed Japanese working in the General Staff of the Vietnamese army, in positions of military command and as trusted technical advisors. In 1951, according to a recent military history published in Hanoi, the Vietnamese General Staff decided formally to return the Japanese (and European) advisors serving in its bureaus. They returned them via China and Eastern Europe, the "internationalist road".[106]

Meanwhile, military authorities in Japan were still worried about the fate of their errant soldiers and their possible manipulation by the Chinese. In early 1949, T. V. Soong, the famous diplomat and businessman from nationalist China, asked Louis Rondon, a French friend and associate who had long been active in Asia, if he could use his contacts in Tonkin and southern China to organize the repatriation of the Japanese deserters remaining in Tonkin. Soong was acting on behalf of a Japanese General.[107] Indeed, in December 1949 the Japanese General Yuichi Tsuchihashi arrived in Hanoi to try to repatriate these deserters before Mao Zedong's troops could consolidate their presence on the Indochinese border.[108] He appealed to these men over the radio and even made a direct appeal to Ho Chi Minh himself.[109] Though we do not know the results of these efforts, Japanese sources reveal that after the Geneva Accords of 1954, 71 Japanese left the Viet Minh and returned to Japan. A few more gradually returned over the years.[110] A handful would remain in Vietnam well into the 1970s. This was the case of Shinsuke Yamamoto, who was discharged from the DRV army in 1950. In 1957, the Vietnamese government informed his family that he had become a farmer in Rach Gia.[111] Others would never return...[112]

In this article, I have tried to suggest the importance of factoring "Asian foreigners" into my analysis of the Franco-Vietnamese war. While I do not deny the nationalist origins of the Vietnamese army, nor the importance of the French or

American military engagements, it is time to think about how other, Asian actors fit into a more complex geo-historical "picture" of the wars for Vietnam.[113] I have also tried to suggest how "modern" military science could enter Vietnam via a little-known Asian intermediary and not just a "French" or "Western" one. While one should not exaggerate this Japanese technical transfer, it may have been more important than we may have suspected for the early years of the war, when the military needs of the Vietnamese revolution were *greatest*, but when its own military possibilities were *weakest*. Japanese contributions in officer training schools, in basic military science, in battle formation and command operations, as well as economic and mining advisors were probably very important in the first two or three years of the war against the French. It is also likely that they played important roles as commandos in the heavy fighting against the French between 1945 and 1948. It is in this early technical and scientific gap that one might place the contributions of these belated Japanese allies to the Viet Minh. Japanese involvement was most important in the first two or three years of the war, when Vo Nguyen Giap, Nguyen Son, Vuong Thua Vu, and Nguyen Binh had to create an army out of nothing – and very quickly – which could stand up to the troops of the Expeditionary Corps.

By 1948, and especially by 1950, their presence and importance would decrease markedly due to high mortality rates, desertions from the Viet Minh, and as the DRV made every effort to nationalize its ranks and its General Staffs in particular. "Staying on" became increasingly more difficult as the people's nationalist army took form. But a handful of extremely important Japanese advisors would remain to work in military intelligence and the operational work of the DRV General Staff. And these Asian foreigners would not be the only ones. Just as the Vietnamese General Staff was sending many of its Japanese volunteers home via China in 1950, it began welcoming, in true internationalist style, another group of Asian, foreign counselors. Indeed, during the second half of the Franco-Vietnamese war and well into the American one, hundreds of Chinese advisors would have an even greater impact on the Vietnamese army (and society) than their Japanese predecessors. The French and the Americans were clearly not the only foreign powers "involved" in Vietnam. And the Vietnamese were not always alone in fighting Vietnam's enemies.

NOTES

1   I wish to thank Colonel Bodinier, General Bach and the French Ministries of Defense and Culture and Communications for formal authorization to consult the classified documents used in this essay.
2   For more on the Japanese who remained in China, see: Donald G. Gillin with Charles Etter, "Staying On: Japanese Soldiers and Civilians in China, 1945–1949," *Journal of Asian Studies*, vol. XLII, no. 3 (May 1983), pp. 497–518 and "Report no. 5425, China," August 3, 1948, "Military/Japanese Serving with the Chinese Communist Forces in Manchuria, May 1948," WO208/4782, Public Records Office [hereafter, PRO], Great Britain.
3   "Shoichi Yokoi, Holdout Japanese Soldier, Dies," *International Herald Tribune* (September 27–28, 1997), p. 4.

4   André Corvisier, *Dictionnaire d'art et d'histoire militaires*, (Paris: Presse Universitaire Française, 1988), p. 296.

5   "Constitution d'un dossier relatif à la collusion nippo-Viet Minh," Saigon, February 5 1947, pp. 1–2, Conseiller Politique [hereafter, CP], carton 247 [hereafter, c.], Centre des Archives d'Outre-Mer [hereafter, CAOM]. The DRV's propaganda announced to the world that the French gave refuge to European fascists and Nazis in the Foreign Legion. In private, some in the French High Commissioner's office recognized the limits of attacking Japanese-Viet Minh collaboration, since "we would have to respond to the same accusation concerning the former troops of Rommel" fighting in the Foreign Legion for the French in Indochina. Ibid., p. 2.

6   It would be interesting to compare the contributions of Chinese and Japanese military advisors to the Viet Minh. Qiang Zhai's study of Chinese military advisors to the DRV has provided a very important corrective to our study of the Franco-Vietnamese war, by showing just how important the Chinese were to training, equipping and even commanding the Vietnamese army from 1950. Qiang Zhai, *China & the Vietnam wars, 1950–1975*, Chapel Hill, North Carolina University Press, 2000.

7   "Nam Bo" was the DRV's word for Cochinchina or southern Vietnam; "Trung Bo" was the word for Annam or Central Vietnam; whereas "Bac Bo" referred to Tonkin or northern Vietnam.

8   Nguyen Hung, *Nguyen Binh: Huyen thoai va Su That* [Nguyen Binh: Myth and Reality], (Hanoi: Nha Xuat Ban [hereafter, NXB] Van Hoc, 1995), p. 191; interrogations of Japanese returnees, discussed in Christopher E. Goscha, *Le contexte asiatique: Réseaux, relations et économie*, (Thesis, Paris, Ecole Pratique des Hautes Etudes, 2000), section japonaise; and Tran Kim Truc, *Toi Giet Nguyen Binh* [I Killed Nguyen Binh], (Saigon: Dong Nai, 1972), pp. 69–72.

9   Vo Nguyen Giap, *Chien dau trong vong vay. Hoi uc* [Fighting in a Situation of Encirclement: Memoirs], (Hanoi: NXB Quan Doi Nhan Dan, 1995), p. 357 and *Chien khu*, special edition (November 25 1945), including photos of the American officers in this military academy.

10 Vo Nguyen Giap, *Chien dau trong vong vay*, pp. 358–9; *Chien Thang*, no. 612, (October 21, 1945), p. 1; and "Truong Quan-Chinh Viet-Nam bat dau khai-giang," *Cuu Quoc*, no. 43, (September 14, 1945), p. 1.

11 Goscha, *Le contexte asiatique*, Southeast Asian and Japanese sections.

12 Bo Tong Tham Muu, *Lich Su Bo Tong Tham Muu trong Khang Chien Chong Phap (1945–1954)* [History of the General Staff during the Resistance against the French (1945–1954)], (Hanoi: NXB Quan Doi Nhan Dan, 1991), p. 97. This source put 27 regiments in Bac Bo and 25 companies in Nam Bo.

13 On the eve of the outbreak of the war in North Vietnam in 1946, it is estimated that there were 8,000 men enrolled in the *tu ve* in Hanoi. Vuong Thua Vu, *Truong Thanh trong Chien Dau: Hoi Ky* [Matured in Battle: Memoirs], (Hanoi: NXB Quan Doi Nhan Dan, 1979), p. 93.

14 Vuong Thua Vu, *Truong Thanh*, pp. 85–6.

15 It is worth noting that top command positions in the Vietnamese army in 1945–6 went to Vietnamese officers who had been trained in Chinese military academies in China and who had seen battle there. I am thinking of Generals Vuong Thua Vu, Nguyen Son, Le Thiet Hung, Hoang Sam, Nam Long and Le Quang Ba. I examine this question in "Entremêlements sino-vietnamiens: Réflexions sur le Sud de la Chine et la révolution vietnamienne entre les-deux-guerres," *Approches Asie*, no. 16, (1999), pp. 81–108.

16 Ever since the Japanese victory over the Russians in 1905, the Japanese and their military science had drawn the attention of a number of Vietnamese (and Asian) nationalists. The famous anti-colonialist Phan Boi Chau began the *Dong Du* (Voyage to the Orient) movement in order to send hundreds of students to Japan to undergo mainly *military training* in Japanese *military academies*.

17 Nguyen Hung, *Nguyen Binh*, pp. 87–8.

18 French captured and translated document: Garde Nationale, VIIe Zone Militaire, Chi Doi 4, "Huynh Van Tri à Nguyen Binh," no. 402–T.M, PC du Chi Doi IV, dated December 11, 1946, c. 10H3827, Service Historique de l'Armée de Terre [hereafter, SHAT].

19 Gillin and Etter, "Staying On," pp. 505–15.

20 See the Vietnamese tract addressed to Japanese deserters entitled, "Hoi Binh Si Nhut Chanh Phu Viet Nam Cong Hoa Dan Chu," in CTFEO, BCR, "Les services spéciaux japonais et le problème japonais en Indochine," no. 7804/1000/B.2, December 30, 1946, a study by Battalion Chief Barada, pp. 179–80, dossier [hereafter, d.] 118, c. 57, Haut Commissaire en Indochine [hereafter, HCI], CAOM.

21 CSTFEO, EM/2B, no. 1530/2, "Note sur les Japonais au Tonkin," Saigon, February 21, 1946, p. 1, c. 10H4309, SHAT and "Activité Viet Minh," January 1946, c. 10H600, SHAT.

22 Présidence du Conseil, Etat-Major de la Défense Nationale, 2nd Section, no. 958/DN/2, "Note de renseignements: Les Japonais en Indochine," Paris, February 27, 1947, p. 1, d. 6, c. 4Q43, SHAT.

23 "Le problème japonais en Indochine," p. 138.

24 "Le problème japonais en Indochine," pp. 138–9 and "Hanoi to Secretary of State," April 18, 1946, 851G.00/4–1846, US National Archives (hereafter, USNA). In Tonkin, they were concentrated in Cat Ba, Van Ly, Thai Nguyen, Phuc Yen, Hoa Binh, Dong Trieu, and Hanoi.

25 HCFIC, AP, no. 865/CP/Sat, "Eléments japonais demeurés en Indochine," June 11, 1948, d. 375, c. 121, HCI, CAOM.

26 "Fiche no. 7," in CSTFEO, EM/2B, no. 2818/2, "Le général de corps d'armée Valluy, Commandant Supérieur des TFEO, à M. le Conseiller de la République, Haut Commissariat de France en Indochine," July 10 1947, Saigon, signed Valluy, d. 3, c. 10H602, SHAT.

27 4,000 is most certainly a wild exaggeration. Japanese sources put the total number of deserters at around 800. See: Vietnamese Association in Japan, *Vietnam*, 50 – no. 4, (1976). A document from the 38th Army claims that the number of deserters in northern Indochina only amounted to 348 (though this number only referred to military personnel). See: Headquarters of the 38th Army, *Jokyo Hokoku (Hokubu Futsuin)* [Report on the Situation in Northern Indochina], dated April 30 1946, (Library of the National Institute of Defense Studies) (in Japanese). My thanks to Kyoichi Tachikawa who kindly shared this information with me.

28 A travel diary written by a Japanese instructor in the bataillon "Pham Hong Thai" leaves no doubt. Speaking of his Vietnamese colleagues, he writes dryly: "They're a bunch of idiots. Their discipline is even worse." SDJ, no. 53, DJ. No. 95, July 26, 1946, "Objet: Traduction de journal écrit par un déserteur japonais," d. Renseignements, c. 10H4363, SHAT.

29 Uy Ban Khang Chien Hanh Chinh Nam Bo, So Cong An Nam bo, "Hoat dong cua gian diep [Saito] cua nguoi Nhut o Viet Nam" [Activities of the Japanese Spy Saito in Vietnam], no. 135–A-2, February 5, 1950, d. 4–D-IV, c. 10H4356, SHAT et CTFIN,

EM/2B, "Note au sujet de Saito, Mission J," no. 4732/2, October 19, 1948, d. Japonais, 1946–1954, c. 10H2959, SHAT.

30   See excerpts of the DRV circular published in *Chien Dau*, June 19, 1948, in d. D414, c. 90, Collection Etats-Associés, Archives du Ministère des Affaires Etrangères; SDJ, no. 75, DJ no. 29, January 25, 1948, "Objet: 8e rapport de l'opération C", d. renseignements, c. 10H4363, SHAT; and the order of Nguyen Binh regarding the repatriation of the Japanese, in d. 1249, c. 138–139, Nouveau Fonds, CAOM.

31   Mission de Contrôle de l'Armée Japonaise, no. 4279/SDJ, "Le problème des déserteurs japonais en Indochine du sud", August 7, 1946, p. 2, d. Mission de récupération, c. 10H4363, SHAT.

32   CSTFEO, EM/2B, no. 1895/2, Saigon, March 22, 1946, "Activités japonaises", February 1946, c. 10H600, SHAT.

33   "Le problème des déserteurs japonais en Indochine du Sud," Saigon, August 7, 1946, p. 2 and "Le problème japonais en Indochine," p. 136.

34   CSTFEO, EM/2B, no. 1895/2, "Activités japonaises," Saigon, March 22, 1946, d. February 1946, c. 10H600, SHAT.

35   Intelligence Division, Headquarters, Supreme Allied Commander, South East Asia, "Japanese Demobilisation Report no. 7," March 30, 1946, p. 5, WO203/4940, PRO. For Thailand, it is estimated that there were about 220 "dead, deserted or missing," 148 in Burma, 521 in Malaysia, 527 in Sumatra, 636 in Java, 25 in Bali, 1,663 in British Borneo, etc. For the total in Southeast Asia, there were about 10,275 "dead, deserted or missing." See *Idem*. A Japanese officer stationed in Indonesia during the war wrote in his memoirs that there were roughly 1,700 Japanese deserters in Indonesia after the Japanese surrender. Takao Fusayama, *A Japanese Memoir of Sumatra 1945–46: Love and Hatred in the Liberation War*, (Ithaca: Cornell Modern Indonesia Project, 1993), p. 102. This number appears to be exaggerated, too.

36   "Le problème japonais en Indochine," pp. 142–4.

37   Ibid.

38   CFTFIC, EM/2B, no. 4732/2, "Note au sujet de Saito, Mission J," Hanoi, 19 October 1948, p. 1, d. Japonais 1946–1954, c. 10H4363, SHAT.

39   SDJ, no. 187, DJ no. 54, le 26 mars 1948, d. Renseignements, c. 10H4363, SHAT.

40   See Vinh Sinh's excellent article, "Komatsu and French Indochina," forthcoming in the Japanese journal, *Sekai*. I would like to thank Professor Vinh Sinh for sharing a copy of this article (in English) with me.

41   "Lettre de Komatsu adressée à Nguyen Ai Quoc," November 19 1921, d. 1920, Notes de la Sûreté, c. 364, Service de Protection du Corps Expéditionnaire, CAOM and "Le problème japonais," p. 160.

42   On Solovieff and Oomiya, see: Kiyoko Kurusu Nitz, "Independence without Nationalists? The Japanese and Vietnamese Nationalism during the Japanese period, 1940–45," in *Journal of Southeast Asian Studies*, vol. XV, no. 1 (March 1984), pp. 117–24, 131–2; "Le problème japonais," pp. 162–6; and Archimedes L. A. Patti, *Why Viet Nam?* (Berkeley: University of California Press, 1980), pp. 176–81, 304–6, 553, 563.

43   "Le problème japonais," pp. 166–70 and Présidence du Conseil, EM/DN, 2nd Section, no. 958/DN/2, "Les Japonais en Indochine," February 27, 1947, pp. 1–3, d. 6, c. 4Q43, SHAT. According to a British military report at the time, Muraiyama was a member of *Nakano* and *Akira Kikan*, another top secret Japanese intelligence service active in Asia during the Pacific War. Kyoichi Tachikawa informs me that Japanese officers involved in repatriating soldiers from northern Indochina do not recognize this person.

44 Translation of the captured document: "Procès-verbal: Une réunion extraordinaire du Comité de Résistance de l'Est Nam Bo Viet Nam," October 12, 1945, signed by Pham Van Nhan and Huynh Van Nghe, in CSFF, EM/2B, no. 660/2, 9 December 1945, c. 10H528.

45 Regiment I, no. 35/BTM, "Lettre de Huynh Kim Truong à Nguyen Van Ngo [Quy]," Thu Dau Mot, January 16, 1946, translated into French in d. Affaires avec [les] Japonais, c. 10H4363, SHAT. Vu Duc forgot to mention that other Japanese troops had been recruited by the French and were being used at this very time to crush the Viet Minh and retake Vietnam for the French.

46 Bo Quoc Phong, *Phong trao Nam Tien (1945–1946)* [The Movement towards the South (1945–1946)], (Hanoi: NXB Quan Doi Nhan Dan, 1997), p. 130.

47 I have found information regarding these Japanese in the archives of the DRV. See, among others, the naturalization request of Tomisawa in Phong Hanh Chinh, "Uy ban Hanh chinh Bac bo kinh gui ong Bo truong bo Tu Phap, Hanoi," no. 87/HC, August 13, 1946, d. Xin nhap quoc tich Viet Nam, c. 9, Gouvernement de fait, CAOM.

48 "Liste des déserteurs japonais absents à l'embarquement à Haiphong en mars, avril 1946, établis d'après des documents américains," c. 10H2959, SHAT, confirmed in part by Japanese sources, cited in Furuta Môtô and Oka Kazuaki, "Tu binh linh quan doi thien hoang den chien si Viet Minh" [From a soldier in the imperial army to an officer in the Viet Minh], in Van Tao, ed., *Cach mang thang tam: Mot so van de lich su* [The August Revolution: Some Historical Questions], (Hanoi: NXB Khoa Hoc Xa Hoi, 1995), pp. 315–16.

49 For more on this, see: *Le contexte asiatique*, Japanese section.

50 CSFFEO, EM, Mission de Contrôle de l'Armée Japonaise, "Capitaine Kanetoshi," no. 685 [?] [sic]/SDG, Saigon, October 9, 1946, c. 10H4363, SHAT. Saito extracted another Japanese officer, Mr. Matsumoto, from Colonel Trinh Minh The. SDJ, no. 640Z, DJ no. 139, "Projet de récupération générale des DJs en Cochinchine et en Annam du sud," September 12 1948, d. Mission de récupération, c. 10H4363, SHAT.

51 Bui Diem, with David Chanoff, *In the Jaws of History*, (Bloomington: Indiana University Press, 1999, 2nd edition), p. 41; Hoang Ton Van, "Viet Nam mau lua," *Dai Viet*, no. 9, [1994], pp. 64–70; and CTFIN, EM/BRN, "Liste des Japonais dont la présence a été repérée en Indochine du Nord depuis le 21 avril 1946," c. 10H2959, SHAT. My thanks to François Guillemot for the Dai Viet article.

52 "Le problème japonais en Indochine," p. 4.

53 This comes through powerfully in Japanese and French interrogations of returned Japanese concerning the reasons leading them to desert in the first place.

54 "Le problème japonais en Indochine," p. 37. According to documents seized by the latter at the end of the war, it seems that some Japanese officers went over to the Viet Minh on the direct order of the Japanese High Command in mid-August. This remains to be verified from Japanese sources.

55 *Le contexte asiatique*, Japanese section. This seems to have been the case for the deserting officers of the 55th Division in particular.

56 Ishii to an emissary of Hiroo Saito, in Mission des Déserteurs Japonais, no. 3523, Japs/ 2B, "A M. le Chef de bataillon Bixella du colonel Saito: Compte-rendu," pp. 9–10, undated but around 1947, c. 10H4363, SHAT. On those who returned and how they have been perceived, see the excellent work of Beatrice Trefalt, "Tarzans and living spirits of the war dead: Japanese stragglers in New Guinea," paper delivered for the conference *Remembering the War in New Guinea*, (19–21 October 2000) at the Australian National University, Canberra.

57   These interrogations are discussed in the *Le contexte asiatique*, Japanese section.

58   Nguyen Hung, *Nguyen Binh*, pp. 175, 191–2; Vuong Thua Vu, *Truong Thanh*, pp. 79, 92–3; and Thai-Lan, *Ai Giet Nguyen Binh?* (Saigon: Dong Nai [?], 1959), p. 70. British military intelligence identified Captain Ishikawa, a member of the Japanese intelligence service Hikari Kikan, as an advisor to Nguyen Binh in early 1947. See Appendix A in "Activities of the Japanese Special Services since the Armistice," FO959/14, PRO.

59   *Le contexte asiatique*, Japanese section.

60   Ngo Van Chieu, *Journal d'un combattant viet-minh*, (Paris: Editions du Seuil, 1955), p. 94.

61   The Vietnamese recognize this publicly. See: *50 nam truong luc quan trung hoc Quang Ngai, 1.6.1946–1.6.1996* [50 Years of the Infantry Academy of Quang Ngai], (Quang Ngai[?], Ban lien lac Bac-Trung-Nam, 1994), pp. 31–2, 45, 52–3. For more on this school, see: *Tu Dien Bach Khoa Quan su Viet Nam* [Encyclopedic Military Dictionary of Vietnam] (Hanoi: NXB Quan Doi Nhan Dan, 1996), p. 888.

62   CSTFEO, EM/2B, no. 3787/2, "Rapport sur la collusion nippo-viet minh," August 9, 1946, p. 6, d. Mission Française au Indes, c. 10H600, SHAT. Japanese sources confirm this. See: *The Association of Viet Nam in Japan*, 96, no. 1, (1996). Excerpts kindly translated from Japanese by Kyoichi Tachikawa.

63   "Bulletin de renseignements du 9 octobre 1946," c. 10H3826, SHAT. These names were verified by a careful comparison with SDJ no. 603/SDJ, DJ no. 106, "Objet: renseignements sur les D.J.," Saigon, August 29, 1948, c. 10H4363, SHAT.

64   CSTFEO, EM/2B, no. 3741/2, "Note de renseignements sur le 6ème secteur du Vietnam," p. 10, d. August 1946, c. 10H600, SHAT. The French estimated that there were approximately 200 Japanese deserters in Quang Ngai province. During the interrogation of a former captain in the Vietnamese People's Army, an American intelligence officer learned that Japanese instructors had first trained him in Quang Ngai around 1948. Interrogation of January 8, 1973, private source.

65   Vietnamese Association in Japan, *Vietnam*, 96, no. 1, (1996) (in Japanese).

66   *Tuong Nguyen Son* [General Nguyen Son], (Hanoi, NXB Lao Dong, 2nd edition, 1995), pp. 74–5 and also *50 nam truong luc quan trung hoc Quang Ngai*, p. 50.

67   My thanks to Kyoichi Tachikawa for this information, based on his interview with ex-Major Sakakibara of the General Staff of the 38th Army and in charge of repatriations after WWII from northern Indochina.

68   Minh Ngoc-Nakahara, "Nho tuong Nguyen Son" [Remembering General Nguyen Son], *Xua va Nay*, no. 38, (April 1997), pp. 9–10 and "Gap Nakahara Mitsuboni," in Mac Van Trong, ed., *Cam on cac ban* [Thank You, Friends], (Hanoi: NXB Lao Dong, 2000), pp. 81–5.

69   "Projet d'instruction à diffusion réduite," in "Le problème japonais," pp. 153–4 and SDJ, "Jugement du chef de la SDJ d'après le carnet d'un D.J. saisi sur son cadavre," April 9 1947, c. 10H3826, SHAT.

70   This is based on the testimonies of a dozen ranking Japanese officers on their military activities in southern Vietnam between 1945 and 1947, including that of Kanetoshi, in *Le contexte asiatique*, Japanese section.

71   "Nhung Nguoi Nhat tai Quang Tri" [The Japanese in Quang Tri], in *Cam on cac Ban*, pp. 161–4.

72   SDJ, no. 640Z, DJ no. 139, "Projet de récupération générale des DJs en Cochinchine et en Annam du sud," September 12, 1948, d. Mission de récupération, c. 10H4363, SHAT and *The Association of Viet Nam in Japan*, 50, no. 4, (1976) (in Japanese). This Japanese source reveals that Takuo Ishii was born on May 20 1919.

73 See: *Le contexte asiatique*, Japanese section.

74 In January 1946, Marshal Terauchi, the Supreme Commander of the Japanese Expeditionary Corps in the Southern Region, told General Gracey that the remains of the 55th Division were in Baria, numbering 5,816 troops. The Division Commander was Lt. General Sakuma Ryozo and his Chief of Staff was Lt. Colonel Saito Hiroo. In this General Staff there was a certain "Major" Ishii Takuo. "Message no. 452, 5 January 1946, from Field Marshal Count Terauchi, Supreme Commander, Japanese Expeditionary Forces in the Southern Region to Major General D. Gracey, Commander, HQ, SACSEA," WO208/671, PRO.

75 Even after the outbreak of the war in the north, vast areas of central Vietnam remained in the hands of the Viet Minh, which may explain the continued presence of Japanese officers and officers' training schools in this key region situated between the northern and southern deltas.

76 *50 nam truong luc quan trung hoc Quang Ngai*, p. 32.

77 SDJ, no. 603//SDJ, DJ. No. 106, August 29, 1948, d. Renseignements, c. 10H4363, SHAT.

78 SDJ, no. 640Z, DJ no. 139, "Projet de récupération générale des DJs en Cochinchine et en Annam du sud," September 12, 1948, d. Mission de récupération, c. 10H4363, SHAT.

79 No. 603/SDJ, DJ no. 106, "Renseignements sur les D.J.," Saigon, August 29, 1948, c. 10H4363, SHAT. A southern Vietnamese source claims that a certain Nguyen Thong was a former Japanese officer in the General Staff of a "Japanese division," who served the Vietnamese as an advisor in zone VII in 1946. Thai-Lan, *Ai Giet Nguyen Binh?*, p. 70.

80 "Doi Vo Chong Nhat-Viet" [A Japanese-Vietnamese Couple], *Cam on cac ban*, pp. 90–1.

81 Le Van Hien, *Nhat ky cua mot bo truong* [Diary of a Minister], Da Nang, Nha Xuat Ban Da Nang, 1995, vol. I, pp. 467–8.

82 "Renseignements sur les D.J."

83 Concerning the Japanese officers serving in Quang Ngai, see: *The Association of Viet Nam in Japan*, 50, no. 4, (1976).

84 This was also the case in Indonesia, according to Takao Fusayama, *A Japanese Memoir of Sumatra*, pp. 98–102.

85 Présidence du Conseil, EM/DN, 2nd Section, no. 958/DN/2, "Les Japonais en Indochine," February 27, 1947, pp. 5–6, d. 6, c. 4Q43, SHAT. Christophe Dutrône has kindly shown me the photos recovered from the bodies of Japanese soldiers who died in the battle of Hanoi in late 1946–early 1947.

86 SDJ, no. 628/Z, DJ, no. 108, "Objet: renseignements sur le commandant Ishii," September 1948, d. Renseignements, c. 10H4363, SHAT.

87 The Vietnamese army has recently admitted the presence in its ranks of a Ukranian named Skrzhinskii Aleksandrovich from 1947 to 1955 and a German, Erwin Borchers ([Ho] *Chien Si*) between 1947 and 1954. See: *Tu Dien Bach Khoa*, pp. 574 and 306. Judy Stowe met the family of Skrzhinskii and kindly provided me with information on his work in Vietnam. Borchers was a communist and very trusted by Truong Chinh since 1944. In fact, Truong Chinh introduced him into the ICP in 1945. General Giap mentions in his memoirs the presence of a certain unit of Germanic deserters of the French Foreign Legion, who were active in Tonkin and led by a German known by his Vietnamese name "Ho Si Thang." The latter was killed in combat in 1948. Vo Nguyen Giap, *Chien dau trong vong vay*, pp. 273, 276. According to other sources, Borchers (*Ho Chien Si*), Kubiak (*Ho Chi Thuan*), and Schroeder (*Le Duc Nhan*) worked for the General

Staff of the Vietnamese army, in charge of important guerilla units. However, in 1948 they were transferred to the Political Education Department for tending to prisoners of the Expeditionary Corps. See Jacques Doyon, *Les soldats blancs de Ho Chi Minh* (Paris: Fayard, 1973), pp. 29–71 and Pierre Sergent, *Un étrange Monsieur Frey* (Paris: Fayard, 1982). I will examine European deserters to the Viet Minh in a forthcoming study. On European deserters, see my "Crossing Over: Foreigner Volunteers in the Viet Minh and the Difficulty of Remembering French Decolonisation in the 20th Century," paper for the conference *Decolonisations, Loyalties and Nations: A History of Diminishing Choices*, Amsterdam, The Netherlands, (30 November–1 December 2001), forthcoming.

88 Neither the USSR nor the Chinese communists were in a position to help the DRV's army between 1945 and 1950. And the French were obviously not going to provide military training to their enemies.

89 Do Van Tuan, "Chien Si Viet Nam Moi: Toshio Komaya-Nguyen Quang Thuc" [The New Vietnamese Fighters: Toshio Komaya-Nguyen Quang Thuc], *Su Kien va Nhan Chung*, no. 70, (October 1999), p. 27.

90 "Anh Koshiro Iwai-Dong Chi Sau Nhat cua Trung Doan 174" [Koshiro Iwai-Comrade Japanese no. 6 of the 174th Regiment], *Cam on cac ban*, pp. 260–4 and Dang Van Viet, *La R.C. 4: Campagne des frontières (1947–1950)*, (Hanoi: Editions en Langues Etrangères, 1990), pp. 66–7, 73.

91 "Etat des soldes des 'Annamites Nouveaux' (Japonais)," Annexe II, dans c. 10H4258, SHAT; SEHAN, no. 1417, "Bulletin de renseignements," August 26, 1946, c. 10H4309, SHAT; and Doyon, *Les soldats blancs*, p. 60.

92 Vuong Thua Vu, *Truong Thanh*, pp. 79, 92–3.

93 Le Van Hien, *Nhat ky*, vol. I, p. 72.

94 Le Van Hien, *Nhat ky*, vol. I, pp. 153, 174–5, 378. On January 28, 1946, the Japanese mining engineer, Tosiuori Sugimoto, asked the DRV to make him a Vietnamese citizen. See his file in d. Viec nhap quoc tich Viet Nam, c. 9, Gouvernement de fait, CAOM. This was also the case with another Japanese engineer named Katada Hirochi.

95 Le Van Hien, *Nhat ky*, vol. I, pp. 378, 457.

96 Le Van Hien, *Nhat ky*, vol. II, p. 347.

97 Le Van Hien, *Nhat ky*, vol. II, p. 263, entry for July 24, 1950. On French investigations into such rare mineral deposits in northern Indochina, see: Bureau Technique et Commercial, Haiphong, "Lettre à M. le colonel [x]," Haiphong, April 1 1947 and Laboratoire métallurgique et industriel, "Echantillon," Haiphong, September 4 1933.

98 Le Van Hien, *Nhat ky*, vol. II, p. 85, 89.

99 Yamamoto Maseko, *Betonamu ni Kieta ani* [My Brother who Disappeared in Vietnam], (Tokyo: Nishida Shoten, 1999) (in Japanese). My thanks to Professor Sinh Vinh for providing me with a copy of this book and Kyoichi Tachikawa for the translation of certain excerpts.

100 Kiyoko Kurusu Nitz, "Independence without Nationalists?," p. 131. However, a list compiled by the French in early 1950 of the remaining Japanese deserters in Tonkin mentions a certain Fujita, who was said to have been a former director of the Yokohama Bank's office at Vinh. After the Japanese defeat, the Viet Minh sent him to Son Tay as a military instructor. He was then transferred to Thai Nguyen as a financial advisor. CCFAEO, EM/2B, no. 564/FAEO/2S, "Liste nominative des déserteurs japonais au Tonkin," 15 February 1950, d. 50, c. 10H544, SHAT.

101 Le Van Hien, *Nhat ky*, vol. II, p. 110.

102   My thanks to Kyoichi Tachikawa for this information, based on his interview with ex-major Sakakibara who was on the General Staff of the 38th Army and was responsible for repatriating Japanese from northern Indochina.

103   Le Van Hien, *Nhat ky*, vol. II, pp. 161, 165, 214.

104   Le Van Hien, *Nhat ky*, vol. II, p. 214.

105   List in d. Japonais, 1945–1954, c. 10H2959, SHAT.

106   *Lich Su Bo Tong Tham Muu*, p. 406. Other "deserters" also came out via China. See the list in Russian and French in "The Ambassador of the Czech Republic at Moscow to the Ministry of Foreign Affairs, Soviet Department," Prague, no. 24/TAJ. 52–DJ/k, "The Repatriation of Czechoslovakian Citizens from Vietnam," dated November 20 1948, d. 24, c. 3, Archives of the Ministry of Foreign Affairs of the Czech Republic, Prague.

107   "Hanoi to Secretary of State," March 1949, 851G.01/3–549, Department of State, US National Archives.

108   Yuichi Tsuchihashi, *Gunpuku seikatsu no omoide*, (Tokyo: Keiso Shuppan Service Center, 1985), (in Japanese), pp. 583, 591, 595, 602–3, confirms this in his memoirs. The results were limited: four couples, their four children and four soldiers returned. Tsuchihashi returned to Japan in May 1950. My thanks again to Kyoichi Tachikawa for bringing this to my attention.

109   "Consulate Hanoi, to State Department," November 12, 1949, 851G.00/11–1249.

110   Kiyoko Kurusu Nitz, "Independence Without Nationalists?," p. 131 and Furuta Môtô et Oka Kazuaki, "Tu binh linh quan doi thien hoang den chien si Viet Minh," p. 317, citing official sources. I do not know if all the Japanese were returned at this time or not.

111   Yamamoto Maseko, *Betonamu ni Kieta ani*.

112   Takuo Ishii was killed in battle in Vietnam on May 20 1950. Vietnamese Association in Japan, *Vietnam*, 50, no. 4, (1976).

113   From a military history point of view, it would be very useful to know more about these deserters, their numbers and contributions elsewhere in Asia, especially in Indonesia, Thailand and China. It seems that we may have a real regional phenomenon, not without historical parallels in Europe.

CHAPTER FOUR

The Realities and Consequences of War in a Northern Vietnamese Commune

SHAUN MALARNEY

If one spends time in contemporary northern Vietnam and talks with people about their experiences during the American war years, one quickly recognizes that people's recollections generally fall into one of two categories. One prominent tendency is to nostalgically describe those times as among the best ever for the people of North Vietnam. Similar to recollections of many older Americans who lived through the Second World War, these accounts emphasize the unity and fortitude the North Vietnamese showed and the sheer wonder of having defeated such a powerful enemy. A second recollection style emphasizes how difficult that period was. In an expression that one frequently hears, the war years were "terribly hard" (*kho qua*) as people experienced poverty, food shortages, and the ever present specter of the death or maiming of one's self or loved ones. Both of these narratives capture part of the North Vietnamese experience, but they fail to bring out some of the smaller though significant occurrences that colored people's experiences during the period, and also some of the profound but narratively unelaborated consequences that still inform social life. This article's purpose is to bring out some of these details as they were manifest in Thinh Liet commune, a community of three villages (named Giap Nhat, Giap Nhi, and Giap Tu; population approximately 5,000 *circa* 1965) located some ten miles south of Hanoi. Although Thinh Liet's experiences were unique and cannot be construed as representative of all communities in northern Vietnam, an examination of the realities and consequences of soldiers leaving for the front, the air war against North Vietnam, and the death of soldiers on the battlefield, help to give us a sense of how the war has affected and continues to affect those North Vietnamese who did not travel to the front lines.

War Begins

When the North Vietnamese government decided in 1959 to provide military support for the insurgency in southern Vietnam, the residents of Thinh Liet commune were only five years removed from their last war. Dozens of local men and women had participated in the resistance war against the French and a number of residents had also been present for the decisive victory over the French at Dien Bien Phu. The realities of the coming war became clear in the commune in the early 1960s when local men slowly began heading off to serve in the army. Some who left were young men called up to serve, others were older men who had remained in the military after the French War. One of the first indications of the situation's seriousness came when Thinh Liet lost its first son, a Giap Tu resident, in 1962. As hostilities intensified, the number of men heading off increased and a small number of young men and women also went off to serve with the "Youth Volunteers" (*Thanh Nien Xung Phong*) near the front lines.

The growing military struggle gradually transformed local social and cultural life. Given that the government had a strong desire to maintain morale for the war effort, local cultural and ideological organs stepped up the dissemination of official propaganda for the war and against the United States and the South Vietnamese regime. From as early as the 1950s, the North Vietnamese had applied the tag of "American imperialists" (*de quoc My*) to the American government, largely due to the US government's extensive support of the French military in its war with the Viet Minh. After the failure to hold an election to reunify Viet Nam in 1956, official propaganda intensified its references to the "American-Diem clique" (*bon My-Diem*) and other reactionaries dedicated to dividing Vietnam and destroying the revolution. With posters, films, plays, radio broadcasts, and the extremely important meetings with local residents, local officials and traveling artistic troupes outlined the necessity of struggle as well as its glory. Indeed, while the previous war had been described as "The Resistance War Against the French" (*khang chien chong Phap*), the new war was referred to as "The War of National Salvation Against the Americans" (*Chien Tranh Chong My Cuu Nuoc*). Warfare and the necessity of it began to pervade all areas of life. Officials argued that everything, from family habits to production activities to the proper organization of wedding ceremonies, were to be devoted to this cause. Although many residents recall the intensity of the propaganda at this time, some now assert that it was not needed as much as perhaps the government then thought. One elderly Thinh Liet resident felt that what motivated them was the desire to protect their own territory. Just as the residents of one Thinh Liet village had fought a brief though somewhat bloody skirmish in the 1940s with another village over a perceived encroachment on their land, so were some local residents ready to fight when the US brought the war into their own locality.

While the necessity of struggle and warfare took on a heightened meaning in local cultural life, Thinh Liet social organization also began to change. One of the most important social innovations of the French War period was the creation of the category of "policy family" (*gia dinh chinh sach*). This category included those families that either had family members serving in the military or had lost a family member while in military service. Ho Chi Minh and the North Vietnamese government had recognized that the maintenance of support for the war effort necessitated the active support by the government of those who served in the military and their families. When the American War broke out, they realized this policy by providing extra food rations to policy families and a number of other perquisites such as easier access to good medical care, education, and party membership. At the administrative level, the government also created the position of "Social Policy Officer" (*Pho Ban Chinh Sach Xa*). When the North Vietnamese government established the structures for administration of rural communities in the 1940s, one position on the communal administration's executive committee was a "social affairs" officer. In the period after the French War these men had responsibility for local policy families, but as the American War intensified, the Social Policy Officer position was created in order to have an official who tended exclusively to the needs of the policy families. Through this position, the government hoped to maintain a positive relationship with those families as their numbers swelled during the war.

The departure of Thinh Liet men for the military brought with it the necessity for local women to take up a number of roles previously occupied by men. Although this did not translate into the assumption of such positions of power and authority in the commune as President of the Communal People's Committee or Secretary of the Commune's Communist Party cell, it did entail expanded roles for them in production in the agricultural cooperatives. Official rhetoric exhorted women to follow the "three responsibilities" (*dam dang*) – responsibility for the household, for production, and fighting – and Thinh Liet women certainly made good on the first two. The fact that they participated more on these projects, however, did not result in an increase in productivity during the period. Accurate figures are impossible to obtain, but residents agree that productivity dropped off noticeably during the war and recall that they frequently had very little to eat. Reasons for the drop in productivity included the departure of some of the best young laborers for the front, disruptions in production caused by air strikes, and a decrease in the number of available laborers. At times local farmers were even forced to work their fields after the sun went down. Reasons for hunger were partly linked to the drop in productivity, but were also related to the general shortages of foodstuffs and the structure of the North Vietnamese economy. Under the cooperative system, the government decided both the type and quantity of foodstuffs that residents received. In terms of meat, for example, residents usually could only buy one pound of meat per month, though they were free to consume whatever fruits and vegetables they could grow on small family plots. To make matters worse, Thinh Liet cooperatives were also required to send off large amounts of their rice harvest to feed the military. In the place of rice the government gave residents wheat flour supplied by the Chinese and Russian governments. Given that wheat was not a regular part of the local diet, residents had neither the knowledge nor the means to make anything tasty with it. People usually made an unleavened pan cake that they fried up with lard. Anyone who regularly ate these cakes is quick to comment that they were among the most unpleasant things they have ever eaten.

One final aspect of social change during the war period was the almost complete mobilization of local society for the war effort. While some young men and women headed off to serve with the military or the Volunteers, most of the remainder of the population helped out in whatever way they could. Many of the young served in the local "militia" (*dan quan*). This unit, which was directed by the army, consisted of one platoon (*trung doi*) responsible for shooting at American aircraft, a second platoon responsible for apprehending any shot down pilots, and five other platoons that rescued and gave medical aid to those injured during air raids. All told, over 425 people joined the militia and most of the members were actually women. Beyond this number, almost all residents contributed their labor when repairs were needed to local roads, bridges, dikes, fields, or houses after an air raid. Like other localities across North Vietnam, Thinh Liet residents, often in the face of extreme hardship, banded together on several occasions and contributed enormous amounts of labor to make sure that the local infrastructure stayed in good repair so the war effort could go on. These moments of communal effort retain an important prominence for those inclined to some of the more nostalgic recollections of the period. It should be noted that although public support for the war ran high, there were still young men who did not want to serve and avoided induction, and people did become war weary after many years. Desertion, however, was difficult as the standard punishment was a reduction in the food rations for the deserter's family.

The Air Raids

Given that American soldiers never invaded the Red River delta during the American War, the main contact that most residents had with direct combat was through the air war against North Vietnam. The United States began bombing the north in February 1965 with the commencement of Operation Rolling Thunder. Direct bombing of the Hanoi region did not begin until June 1966, though American aircraft were a regular part of the skies from 1965 to January 1973. Throughout these years, the main activity of American planes over the region was the collection of intelligence through reconnaissance photographs, some taken from high altitude, some taken by aircraft coming down low over the terrain. One of the main purposes of these photographs was to ascertain and track the movement of supplies to the front. The North Vietnamese received a large portion of their war material from the Chinese and Soviets through the port of Hai Phong. The most common method for transporting this material was to send it west via truck or train from Hai Phong to Hanoi. To reach Hanoi it had to cross the Red River on the eastern side of the city, after which it could be rerouted on Highway One where it would travel to redistribution points further south. Thinh Liet was intimately involved in this process as Highway One and the Giap Bat rail yard, the major rail hub located south of Hanoi, both sit on the commune's western boundary (Giap Bat was a former Thinh Liet village and the government had appropriated the land for the rail yard in the early 1960s). During the war, the government also constructed a narrow gauge rail line that ran from the Red River to Highway One and crossed directly through the commune's southern rice fields. With its proximity to such militarily important infrastructure, Thinh Liet had a steady flow of aircraft throughout the war.

When American aircraft passed into North Vietnamese territory on a course toward Hanoi, an extensive warning system went into motion. One obvious component of this system were air raid sirens located throughout the commune, but an equally important component were loud speakers in public places as well as small speakers placed in every home. Originally these latter speakers had been intended for use by the agricultural cooperatives so that cooperative leaders could inform individuals of their daily work assignments. In war time, they provided an excellent device for propagandizing about the war effort and warning residents of approaching aircraft. Thinh Liet residents were warned via an announcement given by officials in the commune's People's Committee, who received their information from authorities in Hanoi. The standard message delivered over the loud speakers informed the community of the direction from which the planes were coming and how many minutes remained, and then instructed all but essential personnel to take cover immediately. Authorities indicated the direction of the aircraft by sometimes stating which province the planes were then over, but the more important instructions came through the use of a system of numbers, one through four, that indicated the compass direction. This was critical for the local anti aircraft emplacements to train their guns. Generally speaking, residents did not have very long to prepare. When planes reached the coast near Nam Dinh or Thanh Hoa provinces, or when they passed over the mountains to the southwest via Laos (the majority of planes to the region came this route after taking off from bases in Thailand), they usually reached the Hanoi area in only fifteen to twenty minutes.

The sounding of the sirens sent everyone in motion and their pace picked up as the authorities announced every few minutes how much time remained. Local officials were extremely strict about people fulfilling their assigned responsibilities during an air raid. For most residents, their primary responsibility was to take cover in a shelter as soon as possible. During the war, an extraordinary number of shelters were constructed throughout the commune. Local records indicate that there were 1,918 shelters (*ham*) and 560 meters of trenches. Some shelters sat near homes, others out among the rice fields. Some accommodated only one person, others as many as seven or eight. The most popular form of shelter was called an "A Letter Shelter" (*ham chu A*). The design of these shelters displayed the remarkable ingenuity that the North Vietnamese showed throughout the war. The basic plan for the A-Letter Shelter involved digging out a rectangular area of ground, usually to a depth of one meter. A bamboo frame was then put in place in which several supporting poles were placed down the middle of the length of the hole, and then a single bamboo beam was placed on top of these posts. Further bamboo poles were then laid from the ground to the top post, giving the structure an A shape similar to a pup tent. The true ingeniousness of the shelter lay in the fact that the sides were covered with thick rolls of rice straw that were bound together and then covered with dirt. Unlike a shelter made of metal, wood, or concrete, in which bullets or shrapnel could ricochet or cause the shelter to collapse, the dirt and rice straw slowed down or stopped virtually all projectiles. The bamboo frame was also so flexible that it almost never collapsed, but if it did, it was usually not heavy enough to hurt or crush the occupants. Most residents felt that the only way to be severely injured in an A-Letter shelter was if it sustained a direct hit from a bomb, but then virtually no shelter could withstand such an occurrence.

When the sirens sounded, all of the very young and old took cover in the shelters. Only a few dozen people were allowed to stay above ground during an air raid, and they were only allowed to do so in order to man the anti-aircraft weapons placed around the commune or handle the communications regarding the raid with the central authorities. The militia's anti-aircraft defenses in the commune consisted of two main components. All members of the militia received rifles or AK-47s which they used to shoot at low-flying aircraft, and then the local unit also received three large caliber anti-aircraft weapons of Soviet manufacture. Generally speaking, Thinh Liet militia members shot only at planes flying at low or middle altitudes. Thinh Liet did not have anti-aircraft missiles. The closest weapons of this variety were deployed near Ngoc Hoi to the south of Thinh Liet, and these were manned only by active military personnel. The three anti-aircraft guns of the Thinh Liet militia were deployed on the southwest side of the commune in an area that served as a cemetery for the village of Giap Nhi, and also to the northeast out among the rice fields. Occasionally dummy emplacements made of bamboo were erected in order to deceive the American military. Those who remained above ground remember countless incidents in which they shot off numerous rounds at American aircraft, but they never succeeded in downing one. A number of people did participate in the pursuit and capture of American pilots, but again, a plane never crashed nor was a pilot ever captured on Thinh Liet soil.

The majority of planes that Thinh Liet residents saw during the war were reconnaissance planes. Local authorities still demanded that residents take cover in the shelters, but if there had been no bombing for a long time, people sometimes lingered outside of their shelters to watch the action above, particularly if a dog fight was visible. Many residents felt that they had been through so many such experiences that the presence of an incoming aircraft did not scare them as they knew whether it was really heading toward them and when they should take cover if it was. To some, the war had become so routinized, such a normal part of life, that they just went about their business when the planes were coming or stood around and watched as if it were a film or a game.

Although some residents tell stories of their nonchalance when enemy planes approached, such stories only relate to the years between the cessation of American bombing in March 1968 and the beginning of the Christmas Bombings in December 1972. In the period between December 1966 and October 1967, and at the time of the Christmas bombings, Thinh Liet was bombed ten times. The reasons why Thinh Liet was bombed were easy to ascertain. Not only was there the railroad track for supplies to the south of the commune, there was also the Giap Bat rail yard on its western edge and a number of factories in an adjacent area. These facilities were apparently the targets when American planes came in on their raids, but on numerous occasions, the bombs or rockets missed their targets and landed within the commune's residential areas. Officials reckon that perhaps as many as one hundred homes in the commune were destroyed and even more damaged during the raids. Significantly, 54 people died in the raids and 44 were seriously injured. The first raid against Thinh Liet occurred in December of 1966 and injured only one person. Over the next eleven months, four more raids were conducted. There was a certain irony in the consequences of these raids. At this early point in the war, the North Vietnamese government emphatically sought to instill a "spirit of hatred" (*cam thu*) against the Americans. If there were any who by this point had yet to come over to this position, the 1967 bombings likely provided the convincing they needed. The reason for the rising sentiment against the Americans related to the random destructiveness of the bombings. On May 20 1967, several bombs fell among Thinh Liet homes and tore part of the roof off the Giap Nhi communal house. The communal house, a building that had formerly served as the center for worship of the village guardian spirit but at that point, following official secularization campaigns, served as a warehouse, was still considered sacred by many residents. Several months later another bomb that landed in the Giap Nhi cemetery destroyed numerous graves, scattered pieces of caskets throughout the area, and made it impossible for many residents to find their ancestors' graves. The destruction of these two sacred sites infuriated residents. The death of innocent people did so even more. During the May 20 1967 raid three people, including a young mother and her child, died when a bomb hit their shelter. Later in the year four people were killed in a similar incident. One of the saddest stories of 1967 was that of a Giap Nhi man who lost his wife in an air strike at the beginning of the year, married again several months later, and then not long after lost that wife when their home sustained a direct hit. She had taken shelter in a bunker under the home. Residents describe 1967 as among the most "savage" (*ac liet*) years of the war and a large percentage of the local population left the commune to take refuge in communities not threatened by American aircraft. Those who remained proudly note that despite such hardships as the May 20 1967 raid, they still went out to work in the fields the next day, and even have the photographs to prove it. As one elderly man said, they "turned their hatred into activity" and would not sit back or give up.

Thinh Liet enjoyed a period of relative calm after the final raid of October 1967. This peace was shattered with the Christmas Bombings from December 18 to 29 1972. These bombings left a tremendous impression on the memories of those present in Hanoi for the eleven days of the campaign. Not only were American B-52s striking targets in Hanoi for the first time, but a number of the American bombs missed their targets and hit populated sections of the city, notably Kham Thien street, which was levelled at 10:45 p.m. on December 26, killing 283 and wounding 266 (Nguyen Vinh Phuc and Tran Huy Ba 1979: 245). Thinh Liet suffered as well. During those eleven days, American planes dropped bombs on Thinh Liet five times. Two raids stand out in particular. In one, a bomb from a B-52 landed directly on a shelter on the commune's northwest side, killing eight people, including several mothers with their children. In another, a bomb from a B-52 landed directly on the main building in the compound of the local Buddhist temple. As I discovered during an interview at the temple in 1991, many residents are still furious that the temple was destroyed. Other bombs fell within residential areas, destroying homes and killing residents. Similar to what had taken place in 1967, residents were outraged by the random destruction of sacred property and the loss of innocent lives. Thinh Liet's approximately 5,000 residents lost what might seem to be a relatively small 54 people during the air campaigns, but the commune's close quarters and ubiquitous kin relations, as well as the deaths of innocent children, left no one untouched.

Caring for the Dead

While death in an air strike represented a periodic fear for Thinh Liet residents, the one fear that haunted residents throughout the war was the death of their loved ones in the military. When young men from Thinh Liet left for the front, many went with heavy hearts and the conviction that they probably would never return. A total of 347 Thinh Liet men served in the military during the American War. Of these, 82 were killed in battle (23.6 percent), 19 were permanently disabled, and a small number of others died from disease, accidents, or other causes. Given the poor communications between the front and rear areas, many families did not hear from loved ones in the military for many years. At wars' end there were cases of families receiving news that their loved one had died many years before, as well as the rare cases of people returning home when their family members had long taken them for dead. Although the approximately one hundred Thinh Liet men who died occupied a small percentage of the local population, their fate and the question of how to appropriately honor and care for them became and remains a dominant focus of social concern, though often for different reasons for the actors involved.

One of the main entities concerned about war dead has been the Vietnamese government. As noted above, the government had long sought to maintain positive relations with the families of those who fought and also to establish the nobility of war death. One of their earliest and most important innovations on this point was the creation of the new social category of the "revolutionary martyr" (*liet si*). The word *liet si* predated the revolution, but in revolutionary discourse the term took on the meaning of one who died for the revolutionary cause. For example, the term applied to Communist guerrillas executed by the French, but the dominant meaning it carries in social life today is one who died in combat. Thus, one sees throughout Vietnam monuments dedicated to war dead, all of which are adorned with the term *liet si*. To become a *liet si*, one must "sacrifice" (*hi sinh*) one's self for the cause. Like *liet si*, *hi sinh* also predated the revolution, and though it does to a certain extent retain the general meaning of giving up something for something else, its dominant quality now is to give up one's life for the revolution. Both of these terms regularly feature in conversations about the war and they carry with them a great deal of honor and nobility. One of the most important characteristics of the terms is that they are the product of official deliberations as only the state has the authority to determine who is a revolutionary martyr. When a soldier died while in the military, authorities investigated his death to conclude whether he had sacrificed himself for the cause. If he had, the proper paperwork would be issued to confirm that status.

The confirmation of revolutionary martyr status marked only the beginning of the state's involvement with the war dead. Once the determination was made, the government informed the administration of the soldier's native commune, who then had the responsibility to organize an official memorial service for the deceased (*le truy dieu*). This rite represented a unique innovation of the American War. Like the categories of revolutionary martyr and sacrifice, the government created it in order to show official support for the family and also to restate the glory of dying for the revolution. The dominant feature of the rite, which took place in the deceased soldier's home, was the presence of officials from the communal administration. The Social Policy Officer led the ceremony and was usually accompanied by the President of the People's Committee, the Village Militia Commander, the chairman of the agricultural cooperative, the secretary of the commune's Communist Party cell, the secretary of the residential cell in which the family resided, and at least one person from each of the party's mass organizations, such as the Women's Association or the Youth Association. On some occasions every member of the executive committees of the administration and the party cell were also in attendance. The ceremony was also heavily attended by kin, friends, and co-villagers.

In Thinh Liet, the commemorative rite normally took place in the early afternoon and lasted approximately one hour. The ceremony began with the placement of flowers on an altar for the dead soldier by the officials. The Social Affairs Officer then, after a minute of silence, delivered a eulogy for the soldier that declared how the soldier had sacrificed himself for the good of the war effort and restated the inherent nobility of that act. Following his speech, the family received three items that formalized the state's recognition of the soldier's sacrifice. The first was an official "Death Announcement" (*Giay Bao Tu*) that would be needed in future interactions with the government administration. The second was a certificate, approximately twelve by fifteen inches, upon which was inscribed in large red lettering, *To Quoc Ghi Cong*, which can be rendered as "The Fatherland Remembers Your Sacrifice." This certificate recorded the name, natal commune, and death date of the slain soldier. Finally, the family also received a gift of approximately one hundred and fifty dollars. This sum was a one time form of immediate assistance given to the family. At the ceremony's conclusion, a family member stood up and thanked the officials. Although it was an official ceremony, people openly wept throughout.

Thinh Liet families were grateful for the official commemorative ceremony. It provided a public context to remember those that had fallen, and it also helped to reiterate both the nobility of their sacrifice and the state's gratitude for having done so. In a number of cases it took years before the official confirmation of death, thus it also provided an opportunity to end a difficult period of doubt and waiting. The government ceremony nevertheless suffered from a critical shortcoming. Socialist North Vietnam was officially an atheist state. Therefore, while the ceremonies it organized for war dead did glorify those who had fallen, it did nothing to address the most fundamental concern that family members had for the war dead, the fate of their soul. The most basic function of Vietnamese funerary rites is for the living to facilitate the transition of the deceased's soul from this world to what the Vietnamese call the "other world" (*the gioi khac*), a spiritual realm that is identical to our own world. According to Vietnamese understandings, every body is animated by a set of "life spirits" (*via*) and a "soul" (*linh hon*).[1] At death, the life spirits cease to exist, but the soul lives on. The period right after death is extremely dangerous because the soul has left the body, but it has not crossed to the other world. While in this liminal phase, the living must perform funeral rites in order to remove the soul from this danger and send it on its journey. Funeral rites are also important because they establish a new relationship between the living and the dead soul. Following their completion, the living assume the obligation to regularly provide, through other mortuary rites, the food, clothing, money, and other things that the soul needs to survive in the other world. If funeral rites are not properly performed, the deceased's soul will become a "wandering soul" or "ghost" (*con ma*) that is condemned to forever roam this world. Furthermore, since it does not have anyone to provide it with the things it needs to survive, it will opportunistically prey upon the living, particularly by interfering in funeral rites for other souls, so that it can obtain the things it needs to survive.

At death every soul has the potential to become a wandering soul, but the danger diminishes if the deceased dies what people consider to be a good death. Definitions of a good death include a number of factors, such as dying at home, dying peacefully in a non-violent manner, and dying at an advanced age with many descendants. The combination of these mean that one quietly slips away and will always be cared for afterwards. Death is not a trauma that produces anger. And given the familiarity of the surroundings, the soul can easily find the altar where the funeral rites will be conducted and therefore can more easily travel to the other world. People who die a good death have a greater likelihood, with the proper funeral rites, to become benevolent and well cared for ancestors. Those who die a bad death face the strong likelihood that they will become wandering souls. The reasons for this are simple. Definitions of a bad death involve dying at a young age without children, dying away from home, dying in a violent manner, and dying in a manner that involves the mutilation of the body. All of these make it difficult for the soul to cross to the other world. A violent death, particularly at a young age, is held to provoke anger and rage in the soul because it was prematurely taken from the world of the living. To alleviate this rage, the soul seeks to wander and prey on the innocent so they too can share in misfortune. Death of a young childless person also makes it difficult for others to care for the soul after death. Vietnamese mortuary rites are structured such that descendants care for their forebears in the other world, thus the childless have no one to fill this role. Death away from home makes it difficult to coax the soul back to the altar for the funeral rites. And the mutilation or dismembering of the corpse theoretically prevents the soul from traveling to the other world.

The combination of these factors puts the soul in great danger, but as one can easily infer from the description, it also represented the common form of death for soldiers. Young, childless men died violent deaths far from home in which their bodies were mutilated or dismembered. The souls of war dead, therefore, were by definition in extreme peril. This peril only added to the poignancy of war death for those who remained behind because it created the strong possibility that the soul of their loved one, violently taken from the world, would itself never be able to find peace nor be properly cared for by the living. Instead, the world would be populated with an invisible army of lost souls condemned to forever roam the earth in search of sustenance. In order to respond to this concern, Thinh Liet residents created a new type of funeral rite, known as the "commemorative rite" (*le tu niem* or *le tuong niem*) that had the exclusive purpose of putting the souls of dead soldiers to rest. This innovative rite was similar to normal funerals in that it took place in the deceased's home, but it differed significantly because a younger sibling or spirit priest (*thay cung*) led the rites to put the soul at rest, and there was no feasting nor gift exchange as with normal funerals. Unlike the intensely social quality of regular funerals, the innovative rite was largely a private, family affair. The commemorative rite usually took place before the official ceremony. Given that official notification of death was extremely slow in coming, soldiers often asked comrades to write letters or visit their family in case of their death. When families received this informal notification, they immediately organized the commemorative rite. The sooner the rite was held the better because it meant that there was a greater likelihood that the soul could be sent to the other world. Other information, such as date and place of death, were also highly valued because family members could later perform mortuary rites on the proper date (ideally all dead have an annual ceremony organized on their death date) and go find the bones to bring them home so the soul could find lasting peace. Significantly, the performance of the family commemorative rite did not preclude a family's involvement in the official rites. On the contrary. The two rites focused on very different issues, the former being to find repose for the dead soul while the latter was a celebration of sacrifice for the revolution, but families welcomed the perform-ance of both types of rites. Each dealt with significant concerns of the families, thus the rites were complementary and not oppositional.

During the war years, the commemoration of war dead became a regular part of Thinh Liet life. Today, the war dead still remain an active focus of social life. In the 1980s, the Thinh Liet administration constructed a monument for war dead that recorded the names and years of death of the commune's "revolutionary martyrs." Every year on War Invalids and Martyrs Day (July 27), the administration organizes a ceremony at the war dead monument in which they once again express their gratitude to the dead and those families that lost loved ones. This ceremony is always well-attended by both the families of war dead and veterans. Afterwards, many families return home and conduct a commemorative rite for their loved one's soul that is followed by a group meal often for twenty people. The administration has also remained active in conducting official commemorative rites. Periodically, though increasingly rarely, the administration receives official confirmation of a soldier's death, some of which occurred almost three decades ago. Just as before, local officials organize a ceremony in the late soldiers' homes. One of the administration's most delicate responsibilities in recent years has been to resolve disputes that arose over the commune's war dead monument. This monument, which sits in Giap Nhi, represents all of the commune's war dead. Giap Tu objected to the fact that they did not have a monument to exclusively commemorate their war dead. The administration was reluctant to commit public funds to such a project, but ultimately allowed the village to use private funds to build an impressive new monument in their village. The old monument then began to attract other criticisms because many residents felt that its location was geomantically inauspicious and therefore an unsuitable location to remember war dead. People's dissatisfaction with the old monument became so great that the administration agreed in 1998 to move it to a new location. In each case, residents' concerns about showing proper respect to the war dead had been the dominant motivating factor.

The memory of the war dead also remains alive in their families. When one visits the homes of war dead families one always sees the framed "The Fatherland Remembers Your Sacrifice" certificates hanging on the wall and often a framed photograph or drawing of the deceased on the family ancestral altar. During the 1970s and 1980s government regulations limited families' abilities to organize large ceremonies for the dead on their death anniversaries, but in recent years these ceremonies have increased significantly in size. Whereas before they might have had only ten or twenty guests at the meal that followed the rites, many families now invite as many as fifty or sixty guests. These rites, combined with those conducted on War Invalids and Martyrs' Day, mean that many war dead families often hold two commemorative rites per year. The families that continue to face the most difficult situations are those who have never located the bones of their dead family members. Unlike most American soldiers whose remains were transported back to the US, the vast majority of North Vietnamese soldiers were buried where they fell. Some families have learned the location of their family member's remains, but many Thinh Liet families, like tens of thousands of others in Vietnam, never have. The Ministry of Labor and War Invalids and the Central Committee for War Veterans, through such publications as "War Veterans of Vietnam" (*Cuu Chien Binh Viet Nam*), circulate information to help families find the location of war dead graves, and families pursue informal sources as well, but accurate knowledge is often difficult to find. Several Thinh Liet families have organized trips to central and southern Vietnam to find remains, but most of these trips have been unsuccessful. Given that such trips often cost a great deal of time and money, most war dead families simply do not have the means to search for their loved one's remains. They must learn to live with the fact that the remains can never be brought home and will remain lost forever.

Thinh Liet After War

Even though the American War in Vietnam concluded over twenty five years ago, its reverberations still echo through Thinh Liet life. One of the most visible manifestations of this is the domination of the local administration by men who served in the military during the war. It is still a mark of pride and distinction for Thinh Liet men of that generation to have been in combat.[2] Those who were in the military but not in combat enjoy some measure of prestige, albeit less than actual combat veterans, while those who never served but were physically capable of doing so are sometimes subjected to indirect criticism for not having participated. A good number of veterans who returned after the war had become officers and therefore Communist Party members. Given their party membership, they became *de facto* members of the commune's party organization, and many began careers of public service from there. It is not impossible for a non-veteran to attain public office, but in the last twenty years the presidents of the commune have included one former lieutenant, one former captain, and one former colonel. Other administrative posts have also been staffed by former officers and veterans. The experience of having served in the military, for many, has become an important qualification for assuming leadership roles in the commune.

Perhaps the greatest way in which the war lives on, however, is in the complicated nostalgia about the war years. As mentioned earlier, the war years are considered by many to constitute a golden age for North Vietnamese society. The people showed unity and determination in the face of a more powerful opponent, but through the sheer force of their will and sacrifice, they were able to achieve victory. It is indisputable that to a very large extent the government has attempted to both define and monopolize this narrative of the heroic sacrifices of war in order to advance the regime's legitimacy. Their attempt to do so provides an important motivation for the continued construction of war dead memorials and the regular conduct of commemorative rites across the country. It is also true that many Vietnamese have ambivalent or even critical feelings about the war and its sacrifices and consequences, a trend visible in recent literature about the war (see the suggested further reading). But be that as it may, the war years, despite the many hardships people endured, and despite the many aspects they selectively choose to paper over, such as corruption, war-weariness, desertion, and draft evasion, still present an image or idea of what Vietnam was. And this image stands in stark contrast to what many feel Vietnam is today. Since the introduction of the Renovation Policy (*Doi Moi*) in 1986, Vietnam has experienced tremendous social, political, and economic change. Although the dissolution of the former collective economy, with its strong social and political controls, has brought about benefits for some, such as an increase in their standard of living, Vietnam has also experienced a number of less positive changes. In Thinh Liet, this has been manifest in an increase in crime, poverty, and what residents perceive as a breakdown in public morality and a heightening of social competition and conflict. Social life, many residents feel, has become more fractured and divisive than before, particularly when compared to the war years. It is again debatable whether the unity people project onto the past existed in the form they assert, but this image of what war time was has a powerful resonance in public life. The war may have brought death and suffering to their community, but it also brought a sense of unity, shared purpose, and ultimately victory. One man commented that the Vietnamese are splendid at uniting in times of war, but hopeless at doing so in times of peace. For many older Thinh Liet residents, this image of the war remains as both a critique of what contemporary society is not, and also an assertion of what it should be.

NOTES

1   Men have seven life spirits, women have nine.
2   Residents do not accord the same level of prestige to those who fought in Cambodia or against the Chinese. However, very few Thinh Liet residents actually served in these conflicts.

REFERENCES AND FURTHER READING

Bao Ninh 1991: *The Sorrow of War*. London: Secker and Warberg.
Duong Thu Huong 1995: *Novel Without A Name*. London: Penguin Books.
Ho-Tai, Hue-Tam 2001: *The Country of Memory: Remaking the Past in Late Socialist Vietnam*. Berkeley: University of California Press.
Lu Le 1997: *A Time Far Past*. Boston: University of Massachusetts Press.
Nguyen Vinh Phuc and Tran Huy Ba 1979: *Duong Pho Ha Noi: Lich Su Van Vat Thang Canh* (Hanoi Streets: Cultural and Scenic History). Hanoi: Nha Xuat Ban Ha Noi.

CHAPTER FIVE

The My Tho Grapevine and the Sino-Soviet Split

DAVID HUNT

I

Peasant voices are seldom heard in the literature on the Vietnam War. US adviser John Mecklin presents a view not far from the consensus. The Vietnamese, he declares, sought only "a full belly and an untroubled rest." Regarding "everything beyond fifteen kilometers" of the hamlet as "foreign" and hobbled by a vocabulary of only "a few hundred words," they could not fathom "terms like democracy, Communism, imperialism and cold war" (Mecklin, 1965, pp. 74–78). A population of this sort could not have risen up against the Government of Vietnam (GVN) and brought on the war. So it is not surprising that commentators have focused on "the organizational weapon" (Pike, 1966), employed by the Communist Party and the National Liberation Front (NLF) to foment rebellion in South Vietnam.

Materials gathered by the Rand Corporation in the Mekong Delta Province of My Tho in the mid-1960s offer evidence for a contrary reading. With funding provided by the Pentagon, Rand interviewed Vietnamese who had an interest in presenting themselves as "ralliers" (defectors) from the adverse camp. One might anticipate that responses elicited in such circumstances would be far from "the lived speech of human beings in their specific social relationships in the world" (Williams, 1977, p. 27). But when Rand "pushed" for military-related intelligence, interviewees "pushed back" with answers rooted in the everyday life of the countryside (the metaphor of subjects "pushing back" is found in Ortner, 1996, p. 298). The resulting compilation makes clear that peasants and peasant culture played a decisive role in the Vietnam War.

According to a rallier,

> the youths in the village liked to talk politics when they attended banquets or when they sat around drinking tea or when they conversed with each other about their daily work. They talked about the world situation, socialism, Russia and China. The old people didn't like to listen to this sort of thing because they thought the youths didn't even know what went on in the village let alone in the world, Russia and China. (257/15/19)

I draw inspiration from the youth, not content with hamlet citizenship, and from the elders, insisting that wisdom begins at home. Pictured by Mecklin and others as primitives, crouched over their rice bowls, country people of My Tho offer a thoughtful commentary on international relations.

The NLF and the Communist Party deserve credit for this cosmopolitanism. In study sessions and neighborhood meetings, they encouraged local people to see themselves as protagonists in a drama of universal significance, and peasants recruited to serve as cadres and soldiers were even more intensively schooled. At the same time, the Front and the Party did not exercise a monopoly on information reaching the hamlets and could not dictate how people thought and felt. When presented with interpretations of current events, villagers accepted, revised, questioned, and ignored aspects of what they had heard, they brooded in solitude, they debated with others around the banquet table.

Political consciousness in the Delta grew out of this interweaving of watchwords from above and cogitation at the base. The party line was not imprinted on a tabula rasa. The agrarian order of My Tho shaped the NLF and was shaped by it. Sometimes reinforced and sometimes contravened by the self-definitions of rural dwellers, the "organizational weapon" was balanced by popular culture.

Following the villagers in choice of subject matter, I focus on "socialism, Russia and China." The NLF did not know what to make of the dispute between the Soviet Union and the People's Republic of China, leaving space for "peasant intellectuals" (the term is borrowed from Feierman, 1990) to take the floor. In a debate then raging, and not just in Vietnam, what conclusions did they reach?

The My Tho grapevine informed this colloquy. Its roots were in the market place, a neutral ground where NLF quartermasters and government personnel stood in the same queues, a locus for sociability as well as for buying and selling. It was nourished by bulletins from Saigon, My Tho, and other towns, where villagers went to work, to shop, or to visit relatives. On the grapevine, the party line blended with speculation, anecdote, and gossip from many sources. Villagers did not distinguish between official and other informants, and, when asked by interviewers about "rumors," they were as likely to cite statements by "VC propagandists" (9/7/20) as the latest gleanings from the market place. "I suggest that GVN propagandists be sent to the markets to work," said a rallier, "because there were many women who could bring back to the village all they had learned" (28/11/27).

Calling to mind a diffuse, informal process, "grapevine" fits a situation where many were illiterate and print news circulated with difficulty, where travel was restricted and electronic media had made few inroads. The term is apt as well in denoting an organic network, one that would have withered if cultivators had not worked to maintain it. A chart of the grapevine would constitute a map of relations among villagers in My Tho and between them and a wider world. It would amount to a representation of popular culture in the Delta. There are many ways to study "communist insurgency" in Vietnam, but in my thinking, all roads lead toward social history.

II

In orientation meetings for Party members and Front cadres, instructors conducted seminars on international politics, and similar presentations were made to village assemblies. "As a rule," a platoon leader recalled, "before introducing the new policy to them, the village secretary always spoke of the international and home political situation so as to make the villagers become more enthusiastic about paying taxes to help the Front to feed the soldiers and to buy armaments" (108/10/21). In the early days of the NLF, international themes inspired local activists. According to a company commander, "They told us that the 13 socialist states in the world all supported the liberation war in South Vietnam. When they heard this," he continued, "all the cadres were very enthusiastic and encouraged because they knew that they were not alone in their struggle and that they were supported by their friends" (149/79/164). "The instructors demonstrated to us that the socialist orbit is stronger than the imperialist camp," a cadre reported, "because the first is an evergrowing force while the imperialists have retreated everywhere. They added that the Neutral Countries, moreover, were also leaning toward the socialist camp" (68/18/45). Borne along by the tide of history, the liberation movement was bound to win over a retreating enemy.

The USSR figured prominently among supporters of the NLF. "My assistant platoon leader used to tell us stories about the Soviet Union," a fighter remembered, "its modern weapons circling the earth, and its satellites" (58/13/64). "At the beginning of this century," an instructor explained to Party members, "the USSR had to fight alone against the imperialists and the feudalists, and the USSR won." Its triumph constituted a "brilliant example" for the Vietnamese (69/13/23). "It was due largely to the Russians that the Allies won [World War II] against the Germans and the Japanese," asserted a cadre (120/28/78). The Soviets "have retained great confidence in their strength" (69/13/23) and could be counted on to make their presence felt, even in faraway places.

The People's Republic of China was also seen as a formidable ally. "The Front propagandizes that China is a great nation, a strong nation with atomic weapons," declared a guerrilla; it was capable of destroying "the strongest imperialist country which was the United States" (97/4/9 and 10/19). According to a cadre, instructors "made a comparison between Red China's population and the United States' population to give us more confidence in the backing of Red China" (68/18/45). Another cadre testified that, as proof of good will, the PRC was planning to "return Yunnan Province to the North" (136/29/21). With such strong and generous friends, victory was assured.

US escalation in the mid-1960s threatened the NLF and raised the stakes for its allies. As American troops and equipment poured in and its planes filled the skies, Front personnel waited impatiently for the Socialist Bloc to retaliate. When "the socialist countries" realized "that the Americans are conducting a limited war in Vietnam," noted a fighter, surely they "would give assistance and participate directly in this war without having to do it furtively anymore" (70/19/94). Another combatant thought the situation was bleak "unless the socialist countries give the Front aircraft and artillery" (89/22/71). "If the socialist countries sent us their cars and planes," said weary soldiers on the march, "we would be much better off"; if they delivered "troops, battle ships and tanks," the tide of battle might be turned (85/31/78).

Many in the NLF continued to oppose the presence of foreign armies in Vietnam. "All the cadres approved of this line, because they said that we should be the masters of our own country, and that if there were foreign troops here, then we would lose our national sovereignty" (153/37/78). Nonetheless, activists and villagers were disappointed by Soviet caution. The exaggeration that prompted many to glorify the USSR as the most powerful country in the world now stimulated a backlash, as the Americans intervened and the Soviets did nothing to stop them. "Russia is a bloody coward," battalion and company commanders charged; "she's afraid to wage war." "The Liberation fighters are dying in large numbers," they raged, "and yet the most modern country in the Communist Bloc is acting as though she is deaf and blind" (149/90–91/188).

One senses within the NLF a greater reservoir of confidence in China. Russia might be a "shirker," asserted a cadre, but "I thought that Red China was wholeheartedly helping Vietnam" (182/54/205). "China provided the most aid to the Front," a soldier noted (52/25/150). While other nations of the socialist bloc equivocated, a platoon leader said, "it looks to me as if Communist China is the only one who wants to give assistance" (101/73/212).

Faith in the PRC took the form of a certainty that the Chinese stood ready to match US escalation. "The cadres were confident in China," a company commander remarked. If the Front asked for troops, "she would do so at once and she would send in as many troops as we needed" (149/91/189). "Red China would participate in this war but not right now," speculated a soldier; "the cadres said that Red China would fight the Americans if they resorted to nuclear and chemical weapons to kill the population" (113/12/44). Perhaps help was already on the way. "Although he didn't make clear that Red China would send its troops over here to fight the Americans," declared a platoon leader, the instructor "gave us the feeling that this was very possible" (160/15/57).

Hopes for Chinese intervention were often expressed in an apocalyptic register. "Most of the people wish that war would come to an end as soon as possible," asserted a POW; "so they want violent battles to occur" (145/31/71). Chinese troops would force the issue. "I think that the more American and allied troops are sent here the quicker the war will come to an end," reasoned a POW, "because if it reaches a certain point China will come in and will send troops here to fight against the Americans. And the war will be ended quickly" (130/35/70). Some were prepared to welcome globalization of the fighting, as in the case of the instructor who argued that Chinese troops would arrive in Vietnam with "the outbreak of the Third World War. He also added that when this occurred, the United States would be defeated within half an hour" (135/216/467).

Such expectations were doomed to disappointment. In the opinion of a cadre, "North Vietnam is a neighboring country of Red China, yet Red China has done nothing so far to help the North defend itself against the bombing" (3/14/94). "Many cadres of the district committee had told me that at the end of 1964 approximately, China would send 10,000 soldiers to South Vietnam to help the Front fight the GVN army," recalled an informant. "However, until now, many months after the start of the bombing of North Vietnam, no Chinese soldiers have appeared" (1/15/81). According to the cadres, China "promised to send soldiers to help the Front. This promise was made almost a year ago. However up till now there has not been any Chinese soldier in South Vietnam" (2/13/74). A Farmers' Association leader concurred. "The cadres also said that Chinese volunteers would come to the South to help the Front in 1966," he stated, "but we are now only 30 days from the end of the year and yet none of them have come" (148/127/264). "The people ask themselves why the Chinese Communists cannot even liberate their own miniscule island of Formosa," a guerrilla remarked, "and still are clamoring for the liberation of Vietnam" (97/4/9).

To sum up, Socialist Bloc aid appeared generous while the Americans stayed within the confines of special war. But when US escalation threatened to overwhelm the NLF, Soviet and Chinese support stood revealed in a less flattering light. As fighting intensified, a feeling of isolation gnawed at the villagers of My Tho.

III

The Sino-Soviet split heightened confusion within the Front and lent bite to discussions of who was to blame for stalemate on the battlefield. The Vietnamese were stunned when the Soviets and the Chinese traded insults formerly reserved for the imperialist camp. As the watchwords of proletarian internationalism degenerated into cynical epithets, NLF activists were forced to reassess the legitimacy of their cause.

"I once listened to Peking Radio," asserted a soldier, "which denounced Russia for taking sides with America against China. I was completely puzzled because I had always thought that Russia and Communist China were trying to accomplish the same purpose. How could they have come to such a split?" (176/47/115). According to a cadre, "the Party taught us that both Russia and Red China were the strongest countries." But lately, "If the instructors happened to speak about Russia, they only stated that Russia was a country which adopted the revisionist standpoint." Meanwhile, "Red China's broadcasts violently criticized Russia. That made me very sad and I could not understand the reasons for which these two countries were inimical to each other" (99/37/115). Internecine quarrels occasioned a deep disquiet among the Vietnamese.

How was "revisionism" to be explained? "I brought this matter up with some District cadres," stated an activist, "but perhaps since they did not know how to reply, they simply refused to discuss this matter with me" (114/13/47). According to a soldier, "when a district cadre passed through a village, and the village cadres asked him to explain revisionism to them, he didn't know what to say, and promised to study more about it and come back some other time to talk about it to the village Party Chapter" (205/64/128). It was the same in the army. "I was told by my comrades that something went wrong between the USSR and Red China," noted a fighter, "and that Khrushchev had been overthrown. This matter was brought up once in an indoctrination course but the instructor did not explain it in detail"

(123/9/42). When the subject was broached, a cadre affirmed, "the instructors usually cut off the discussion and stated that there were no dissensions, and that these differences were only slight disagreements on some points" (109/127/28). When it came to the Sino-Soviet split, the Front seemed at a loss.

The Communist Party tried to prevent discussion of this troubling subject. After local militants weighed in ("some said that Russia was right, and others said that Russia was wrong"), they "were told that the Communist Party of Vietnam hadn't dared conclude who was right and who was wrong, so how could they – lowly Party members, who were like grains of sand on a beach or pieces of garbage on a garbage dump – dare to condemn one side or the other" (205/64/129). But when asked if cadres discussed the schism "in private," an interviewee responded, "Of course they did" (135/203/438). "Between themselves the villagers talked about all kinds of taboo topics," recalled another informant (1/11/64). In the words of a third, "each cadre had his own opinion" on international politics (140/16/40). The villagers "listened to all kinds of news, but each one would have his own opinion about what he had heard" (19/8/19).

Theories on the split proliferated in the villages of My Tho. According to one informant, the Chinese only criticized "the revisionist group of the Soviet Communist Party and have not alluded to the Soviet Communist Party itself" (145/32/72). Another charged that, "The Socialist bloc, no less than the capitalist bloc, was placing personal interests above common cause" (146/64/110). Some thought Moscow put too much stock on victory through "economic competition with the Capitalist Bloc" (149/78/162), while others scorned the pessimism of revisionists who believed that "the economic system based on private property in imperialist countries is better than that of the Socialist countries" (135/201/431).

A Viet Minh veteran understood the quarrel as a tactical maneuver. "I think that Russia and China are like a velvet glove and an iron hand. China is the iron hand because it is determined to push the war strongly ahead, and Russia is the velvet glove because she has a flexible attitude. She uses softer and more conciliatory measures to bring victory to the Communist bloc" (136/31/24). In a similar vein, "the cadres said that it was difficult to tell whether the conflict was real or faked. They thought that since Russia and China were the main supporters of the Revolution in the South, these two countries might just be faking the feud to deceive the world. They might be in perfect understanding with each other, but outwardly, they pretend to fight with one another" (210/37/150).

A qualified sympathy for what critics called revisionism was sometimes expressed in the villages. A cadre reported that certain people, "coming from the upper social categories, such as former students and teachers in towns, used to complain about the acrimonious tone of the Peking [radio] broadcasts. They said this should be avoided because, despite the split, both Russia and China are on the same side." As for the regroupees, this informant continued, "most of them were more inclined to support Russian revisionism," or at least to counsel neutrality. For purposes of illustration, he cited a cadre who thought the Soviets were right to give more consideration "to the people's living standards," but wrong to neglect "building up a strong military force without which peace cannot be safeguarded" (135/203/438 and 204/439).

Soviet moderation frustrated revolutionaries who wanted to fight to the end, but it resonated differently with those who were weary of the war and anxious for a negotiated settlement. According to a district cadre, "everyone in the study meeting enjoys the idea of peace. No one of the six people in the Farmers' Association administrative committee in the district wanted to drag out the war." So, when an instructor declared that, "Russia was the only one for peace, and Red China wanted to fight, and to drag on the war," the reaction was unanimous; "everyone agreed to have peace, not war" (153/31/61 and 32/62).

On the other side, many cadres and fighters were ill-disposed toward the Soviet line and especially toward Nikita Khrushchev, widely identified in My Tho as the architect of revisionism. A soldier declared that, "When Stalin was still alive, he slapped Khrushchev once," and, in a fit of pique, "Khrushchev defamed his memory" (205/65/129). "Khrushchev was overthrown because he was a coward and was afraid to fight against the imperialists," a company commander explained (149/79/164). He had ordered North Vietnam to refrain from armed struggle in the South in the late 1950s, according to a cadre, who then "burst out crying and cursed Khrushchev. 'It's all because of him that so many organizations were destroyed and so many comrades killed between 1958 and 1960'" (135/201/432).

When, at a Moscow state function, Khrushchev asked for a moment of silence in memory of the recently assassinated President Kennedy, the Vietnamese delegation was not pleased. Back in Vietnam, "Diem was behaving so cruelly that every cadre hated the Americans intensely." On hearing about the moment of silence, an activist "stood up and said: 'If the Party allows me to go to the USSR, I will use a hammer to break Khrushchev's skull!'" (135/202/435).

Attempts to go beyond *ad hominem* explanations led to a deeper analysis of the Soviet Union. According to a soldier, "Most Front cadres side with China and think that the Russians have become capitalist and are now afraid of fighting" (176/47/115). The revisionist current arose "when the Soviets succeeded in completing the building of socialism, thus helping the Russians to become better off," a cadre speculated. "In a very natural way, when the people get happier, they don't worry about the struggle" (135/201/431). True enough, Soviet aid was reaching the North, but, another informant declared, this assistance was "only a symbolic gesture." The problem, he continued, was that Russia "is different from China. She is rich and could be considered as a bourgeois country. This is why she doesn't want to be in an armed conflict with the Americans" (140/60/127).

When viewed in material terms, the USSR appeared rather like the United States and therefore prone to seek an accommodation with the US at the expense of the Vietnamese. One informant heard that the "Russian revisionist policy was pro-American" and speculated that if the Soviets joined the American war effort, the NLF "would go to pieces" (148/97/194 and 195). "As leaders of the Communist world," reasoned another cadre, the USSR "should have helped Vietnam fight against the Americans instead of siding with them" (176/47/115).

According to an anecdote in the My Tho grapevine, at an NLF exhibit in Moscow documenting US/GVN attacks on civilians, "the Russians refused to believe that the Americans had committed atrocities." Khrushchev and his associates argued that "the U.S. was a wealthy country and the Americans are civilized people and it was inconceivable that the Americans thought of taking over Vietnam" or condoned massacres (135/81/177). Far from the Vietnamese inferno, the Soviets gravitated toward the United States. They simply could not grasp the nature of the war.

Villagers were prone to lose confidence in the Soviet Union because they imagined that it was a very different sort of country from Vietnam. In NLF propaganda, the USSR appeared a rich, comfortable place, superior "in the scientific and technical as well as economic fields" (109/90/358), and this prosperity made villagers think that the Soviets did not comprehend their plight and could not be trusted to stand by them. The moderate tone of the Russians, their efforts to arrange a compromise peace, seemed congruent with a view of them as satisfied with their lot in the world and reluctant to countenance destabilizing liberation struggles.

Attitudes toward the PRC also varied. A view of China as Vietnam's traditional enemy percolated among the people, as when village "elders" told a Farmers' Association member "that the Chinese had been very cruel and life under their yoke was very hard" (47/12/42). In another locale, a drunken young man was heard to predict "that this civil war between the VC and the GVN would simply weaken both sides to the advantage of Red China" (121/15/36). The Americans and the Saigon regime did their best to heighten suspicion. "I believe what you tell me," said a rallier to the Rand interviewer, that China is "the real aggressor" (153/37/79). In the words of another informant, the Chinese had "pushed North Vietnam to take over South Vietnam" (1/17/88).

At the same time, many cadres and fighters felt an affinity with China and found in the anti-revisionist campaign a validation of their revolutionary standpoint. The USSR and PRC were the "big brother allies" who had once worked in harmony to watch over Vietnam and the cause of socialism. To be sure, the kinship metaphor might lead to a pessimistic assessment of Chinese resolve, as in the case of the fighter who declared, "If the oldest brother is afraid to do something, the younger brothers are reluctant to do it also" (149/78/162). Elsewhere, it encouraged a more hopeful assessment. "China was now the mainstay of the Socialist Bloc and she would determine the future of all progressive mankind," a combatant recalled being told. "She was capable enough to depose Russia as the oldest brother of the Socialist Bloc and replace Russia in this role" (205/64/128).

Trading blow for blow with the enemy, My Tho activists were inclined to think that only the Chinese shared with them a certainty that they were fighting for their lives. Peking's anti-revisionism resonated especially among NLF intransigents, who believed that the two camps "were mortal enemies and were in a life and death struggle until one bloc disappeared. They shouldn't have any friendly relations with each other" (205/58/124). Racial solidarity reinforced this link. Peking radio broadcasts, declared a POW, "are very strong and ironical, and made in an Asian way, especially when it called the 'USA' a 'paper tiger,' and used the bitter phrase 'an eye for an eye, a tooth for a tooth.' I don't like to hear news broadcast from Moscow, since its comments are not so keen or ironical as those broadcasts from Peking and they are not made in an Asian way" (145/23/47).

A number of interviewees seconded this endorsement of Chinese propaganda. "We preferred Red China to the USSR," said a fighter, "because Peking broadcasts have always shown much sympathy towards our struggle" (123/9/43). In the words of another informant, cadres "preferred China, because they saw through radio broadcasts and through newspaper articles that China supported the Front more directly than the Soviet Union did. While China always denounced the U.S. without any reserve, the Soviet Union gave the Front verbal support, but little material aid" (140/37/83).

After discussion with Rand personnel, this interviewee adopted a rhetoric that was pro-US ("Americans were brave and fierce like tigers") and anti-PRC ("those damn Chinese") (140/37/83). "Throughout history," he asserted, "China had dominated Vietnam," making life "very difficult" for the people (140/16/40). But, then, borrowing from the idiom of high diplomacy, he noted that, "The two countries are like lips and teeth – and if the lips are open the teeth will get cold. This is why China has to do her best to help the North in all fields." Positing a domino theory in reverse, he added, China "is determined to help the North to the end, because if South Vietnam falls in the hands of the Americans, all of Southeast Asia will belong to the Americans" (140/59–60/126). To be sure, Chinese assistance had its limits, but the fault lay more with the Soviets than the PRC. "At present, even though China is doing all she can to persuade Russia to follow her course of action, Russia can't wholeheartedly oppose the Americans. Because of this, the Chinese do not dare to help the South unilaterally with all their might. Their help is more verbal than real" (140/60/127). Qualifications abound, but, in spite of Rand strictures to the contrary, the interviewee hints that he still "preferred China."

References to Cuba provide a counter-point to this discourse on big-power diplomacy, marked by ambivalence toward both the USSR and the PRC. In spite of the modesty of the material assistance they delivered to Vietnam, the Cubans were cited with warmth and gratitude. "Taking Cuba and Korea as examples," noted a cadre, "the instructors showed us that the Americans had failed to vanquish these countries. He stressed the American failure in Cuba, stating that despite their forces, the Americans had been forced to respect the Cuba people's self-determination even though Cuba is quite near American territory" (69/11/23). Seconding this view, a military instructor declared that "the Americans were suffering many defeats," most especially because "small countries like Cuba...dared to fight the Americans. Cuba was close to the United States and yet the Americans couldn't defeat it. Because of this, the small countries in the world which had always been afraid of the Americans now dared to fight them" (205/66/131).

Cuban solidarity constituted a battlefield asset. A company clerk in the 514th Battalion affirmed that the unit was "called by Castro the Giron Battalion," and that Ap Bac, where My Tho fighters won a great victory in 1963, "became the name of a village in Cuba" (107/20/56). "Cuba sent us a flag and a pistol to serve as a prize for the unit that scores the most achievements during the year," stated a platoon leader in the 261st Battalion; "the Cuban flag is carefully kept, and every time a difficulty is encountered, it is brought out" (101/43/135). In this affection, binding Vietnamese to comrades far

away, with no capacity and no desire to be anyone's "big brother," one senses the pulse
of an authentic internationalism.

IV

Interview commentaries on the Sino-Soviet split demonstrate the limits of "the
organizational weapon." The NLF commanded an audience, and the audience
heeded what it said. But listeners did not accept everything they were told. Because
it had encouraged the population to be curious about world affairs, Front organizers
were partially responsible for this outcome. When dilemmas arose, they might
attempt to bully villagers into passivity ("grains of sand on a beach or pieces of
garbage on a garbage dump"). But such efforts collided with their need for a
politicized peasantry. Unable to turn critical thought on and off at will, higher
echelons were obliged to leave space for rural dwellers to make up their own minds.

In any case, no political authority was strong enough to impose unanimity on the
countryside. Like the experiment where a whispered message is passed around a
circle, only to emerge in unrecognizable form at the end, policy crafted at the top
was relayed down the chain of command, with embellishments along the way.
Perhaps Ho Chi Minh ordered soldiers in My Tho to study "the proletarian ideological standpoint." It seems less likely that he was responsible for the suggestion,
attributed to an instructor, that Khrushchev should have said to President Johnson,
"In the name of the peace loving people in the world, I want to cut your head off and
let you join Kennedy" (205/58/124). As reflected in My Tho study sessions,
Communist Party policy appears to lack consistency, because instructors did not
precisely restate orders from above and because their audiences selectively responded
to what they were told. Unable to catch a strategic nuance, subject to wishful
thinking, or perhaps just stubbornly attached to their own interpretations, they
construed directives according to their own lights.

The persistent belief that the Chinese were coming testifies to the power of rumor
in the Delta. When asked why Front activists in Cai Be District thought "China
was about to send its troops into the South to help the Front," a cadre from
Chau Thanh District stated, "this viewpoint grew out of the erroneous leadership
of the head of the Cai Be Propaganda and Indoctrination Section. Either he misunderstood the Party line, or he said so to bolster the cadres and the people's morale"
(135/217/470). Elsewhere in the same interview, the Chau Thanh cadre himself
fell under the spell of a rumor, relayed by the "Head of the Region Propaganda
and Indoctrination Section," to the effect that "Red China would send 130,000
soldiers into the North in order to assume the defense of the North." In turn, "every
battalion of the South is to leave Central Vietnam to the Northerners and to
withdraw to the South" [in this context, the Mekong Delta] (135/216/468).
In the same vein, a province-level official enjoined others to stop talking about
Chinese intervention, because "the NLF must sustain itself first" – this after declaring, a few pages earlier, "that Communist China will send its armed forces to South
Vietnam" (145/27/59 and 26/57) (for more on "rumor," see Lefebvre, 1973, and
Turner, 1993).

Lower-level cadres who did not understand or who lacked the discipline to stay within guidelines were not alone responsible for the problem. At the top of the hierarchy, among members of the Central Committee of the Communist Party, disagreement ran so deep that strategic coherence was unattainable, as in the cobbling together of "neutralism" and "socialism" in 1962 or the tortured rationale for "protracted war" in 1965. Some leaders simply ignored directives they did not support ("Nguyen Chi Thanh never accepted the new protracted war strategy," Brigham, 1999, p. 50).

In 1966, Hanoi decided to remain neutral in the Sino-Soviet quarrel, to appeal for more Soviet aid, while dispatching NLF representatives to the PRC to join the anti-revisionist chorus. "There was a little something for everybody," a Communist Party official explained after the war. "We would bend toward Moscow and then send the NLF to China to sing its praises" (cited in Brigham, 1999, p. 61). But a compromise of this sort, which sounds clever enough in the abstract, tended to come unstuck as it descended from one level to the next, thereby opening the way for "erroneous" readings at the grassroots.

NLF activists and fighters were confused by official glosses on the schism and did not hesitate to formulate their own views. Observing such efforts in the transcripts, one gets a sense of villagers consulting evidence from the most rudimentary sources. When asked if the NLF could "rely on the support of other countries," a guerrilla replied, "I quite often used bullets with Chinese characters on them" (26/40/54). Commonly seen in the hamlets of My Tho, red stock rifles also conveyed a message. "The privates said among themselves, 'This red-stock rifle must come from a foreign country. How could our people be able to fabricate it?'" They had heard that the red-stocks "were given by Red China" (62/15/49), while others thought the guns had been sent by the Soviet Union (32/29/170).

The same curiosity prompted scrutiny of unfamiliar figures, as in the case of possible Chinese advisers, spotted in Hoi Cu Village. When speaking Vietnamese, "they had an accent like the Cho Lon Chinese," hazarded a cadre. "When they spoke to each other, they used a foreign language that sounded like Chinese." But the mysterious strangers "did not have any contact with the village cadres or with the villagers" (109/125/24). They disappeared without providing the answers sought by local people.

Radios also brought news of the outside world. To be sure, sets were expensive, and GVN and NLF personnel caused problems for villagers listening to the wrong station. Even so, the broadcasting medium was virtually impossible to regulate. NLF cadres tried to enforce a boycott of Radio Saigon, but were outflanked when listeners tuned in to Radio Peking, whose attacks on Soviet revisionism were just as unsettling as the psychological warfare contrived by the GVN and the US. While the Party recommended abstention, Chinese commentators, with their "acrimonious attacks on Moscow" (109/90/357), invited the Vietnamese to take sides.

To learn more, people consulted the grapevine, in which the NLF itself was entwined. Anxious to block demoralizing rumors or enemy propaganda while enforcing a monopoly for its own messages, the Front was trapped in a dilemma. By enlisting villagers, sending them here and there on assignment, and gathering them in district, province, and regional study sessions, it increased contacts and sources of information. Military recruitment further accelerated the circulation of news, given that units were quartered on the population, so that exchanges between peasants and fighters were an everyday occurrence. According to a soldier, troops "heard about current events from the villages we came across during our frequent moves" (72/16/56). Another reported that, "The radios in the civilians houses only picked up Radio Saigon, so that's what we listened to" (66/7/38).

Prominent among informants were the regroupees who had moved North at the time of the Geneva Accords in 1954, then returned to the South after 1960. These itinerants had seen more of the world than most villagers, and some had visited the USSR or the PRC (for example, the cadre who had studied in the People's Republic from 1952 to 1963, 149/83/175). Their observations, such as the report that Soviet advisers in the North were "arrogant and aloof" (101/75/215), enjoyed a special currency and are often cited in the transcripts. An activist ignored orders to refrain from discussing the schism, "because many regroupee cadres had told me that, in North Vietnam, the people were free to criticize and vilify the USSR" (109/127/28). The regroupees played on the widespread perception that they were privy to classified information, as in the case where several claimed to know that Chinese intervention in Vietnam "has already begun, but that this was still kept secret" (109/125/24). Regroupees, along with other cadres and fighters, served as intermediaries in an increasingly open society.

The Party line was positively received by many, and it insistently worked on fence sitters and skeptics. No doubt it had a huge impact on rural opinion. But it remained a human artifact, and the people who absorbed and transmitted it were enmeshed in a popular culture, which, by the nature of their political work, they tended to inform and enlarge. In its everyday activities, the Front watered the grapevine, insuring that it would flourish in a manner that no one could anticipate or control. Here as elsewhere, interaction between the political and the social shaped the way villagers experienced the Vietnam War.

V

The My Tho commentary on the Sino-Soviet split yielded mixed results. When a cadre says, "After Khrushchev was eliminated from the Russian government, the Party stopped talking about Russia and from then on, it only boasted about Red China's strength" (99/37/115), one might object that Khrushchev's removal opened a phase during which the Vietnamese moved closer to, not farther away from, the Soviets. Many of the claims put forward – that Stalin had slapped Khrushchev, that the Chinese planned to hand over entire provinces to the Vietnamese – were not seconded in My Tho or elsewhere. The attempt to deconstruct "revisionism" did not achieve closure.

At the same time, the shrewdness and analytic bent of the participants command respect. They were not alone in being confused by a phenomenon that remains difficult to grasp. No greater insight was achieved in the White House, where "the profundity of the Sino-Soviet schism was never fully understood" (Kolko,

1994, p. 403). In its turn, the scholarly literature is far from conclusive (Floyd, 1963; Smith, 1985; Zagoria, 1967). The Rand materials show a popular culture doing its work, as peasants gathered information and weighed the choices they faced. Theirs was a discourse of more than "a few hundred words."

In trying to figure out what the Soviets and the Chinese were up to, the Vietnamese were also seeking to define themselves. When the materials are examined in this light, two impressions emerge. First, humble villagers, scanning the horizon for deliverers, implore "big brothers" to intervene on their behalf. Elsewhere, a heroic note is sounded, with revolutionaries lining up against revisionism and proclaiming their determination to stay the course. Soldiers said, "When we defeat the Americans, North and South Vietnam will be reunified, but then we'll be influenced by revisionism. When other national liberation movements appear in other countries, we'll be afraid to fight, and we'll just sit and look. What's the use to fight and then to become revisionists?" (149/91/188). In such meditations, hope ("Vietnam will be united") and discouragement ("What's the use?") find expression. Lofty ambitions were reaffirmed, but an awareness of limits would not go away. Daring to struggle for all humanity, people of the NLF came to doubt if they possessed the means to change the world.

Both the youth and the elders around the banquet table were right. However utopian it may seem to outsiders, the heartfelt internationalism of cadres and fighters drove the Vietnam War. At the same time, the USSR was physically far away, and its relative development and security made it seem farther still. The truculence of the PRC struck a chord, and bullets marked with Chinese characters appeared to signal good will. But China could not shield the peasants of My Tho. Inquiry into the Sino-Soviet split circled around and brought them back to their villages, where they lived and fought alone.

REFERENCES

Most citations in this article are from "Series DT: Activities of Viet Cong Within Dinh Tuong Province," a subset of the Rand Corporation project on "Viet Cong Motivation and Morale" (Santa Monica: Rand Corporation, 1971). The Government of Vietnam and the Americans referred to My Tho as Dinh Tuong Province; hence the acronym "DT" in "Series DT." The notational system employed in this essay refers to interview number/page number/question number in the DT Series. Eighty-five percent of interviewees were defectors from the National Liberation Front; the rest were prisoners of war.

Other works cited include:

Brigham, Robert 1999: *Guerrilla Diplomacy: The NLF's Foreign Relations and the Viet Nam War*. Ithaca: Cornell University Press.

Feierman, Steven 1990: *Peasant Intellectuals: Anthropology and History in Tanzania*. Madison: University of Wisconsin Press.

Floyd, David 1963: *Mao Against Khrushchev: A Short History of the Sino-Soviet Conflict*. New York: Praeger.

Kolko, Gabriel 1994: *Anatomy of a War: Vietnam, the United States, and the Modern Historical Experience*. New York: New Press. First edition 1985.

Lefebvre, Georges 1973: *The Great Fear of 1789: Rural Panic in Revolutionary France*, trans. Joan White New York: Vintage. First edition 1932.

Mecklin, John 1965: *Mission in Torment: An Intimate Account of the U.S. Role in Vietnam*. Garden City: Doubleday.

Ortner, Sherry 1996: "Resistance and the Problem of Ethnographic Refusal," *The Historic Turn in the Human Sciences*, ed. Terrence Mcdonald. Ann Arbor: University of Michigan Press, 281–304.

Pike, Douglas 1966: *Viet Cong: The Organization and Techniques of the National Liberation Front of South Vietnam*. Cambridge, MA: MIT Press.

Smith, R. B. 1985: *An International History of Vietnam, Volume II, The Struggle for Southeast Asia, 1961–65*. New York: St. Martin's.

Turner, Patricia 1993: *I Heard It Through the Grapevine: Rumor in African–American Culture*. Berkeley: University of California Press.

Williams, Raymond 1977: *Marxism and Literature*. Oxford: Oxford University Press.

Zagoria, Donald 1967: *Vietnam Triangle: Moscow/Peking/Hanoi*. New York: Western.

Chapter Six

"Vietnam" as a Women's War

Karen G. Turner

The platoon of sappers from Battalion 33 commanded by Nguyen Thi Nha fought heroically...west of a frontier post and Road 20. There Nha and four of her mates died fighting on January 4, 1968. Nha was replaced by her second in command, Mai Lien. This platoon has been fighting since the early days of building Road 20 and the [women's] determination to fight enhanced the morale of the men of Line 559.

Vietnamese field report submitted from the Ho Chi Minh Trail, 1968

Strategists in Washington learned from Air Force intelligence reports that hordes of "coolie" laborers worked day and night, thwarting their plans to destroy the roads that made up the Ho Chi Minh Trail. But invisible to them were thousands of teenage women volunteers whose expertise with shovels, hoes, and guns kept the Trail open. US military planners wondered why it took seven years of steady bombing to finally destroy the Thanh Hoa Railroad and Highway Bridge, a strategic link between the supply depots of the north and the battlefields in the south. They would have been surprised indeed to discover that a nineteen year old Vietnamese militia woman's superhuman actions inspired artillerymen and villagers on the ground to keep fighting. American soldiers south of the DMZ learned from hard experience that village women who appeared gentle and harmless could be armed and dangerous. But they didn't know that a woman served as one of the most respected, experienced commanders of Viet Cong forces.

An accurate history of the war the Vietnamese call the "American War" must recognize Vietnamese women's contributions to Hanoi's victory in 1975. The material is so rich and women's roles so complex that a full accounting is yet to come. In this essay, I have kept two main goals in mind. First, I want to correct the notion, largely the legacy of the post-war American media, that Vietnamese women simply responded, as hapless victims, to American aggression. To be sure, Vietnamese women had no choice but to make the best of a ten year bloody conflict fought on their homeland, and many lost their lives, their health and their hopes for a normal family life to the war. But women did not expect men to fight on their behalf. They chose in a variety of ways to take action against the enemy, motivated not only by intense propaganda campaigns to draw the civilian population into a total people's war, but by a desperate need to protect their homes from annihilation. Their actions took on legitimacy as well because they could see themselves as part of a long tradition of women who had taken up arms to defend the nation from outside aggressors. Some women fought the war on familiar ground, serving in local militias and self-defense forces, maintaining production in factories and fields all the while. But many women severed their connections with home and family to work as sappers, gunners, liaison workers, road-builders, engineers, reporters, combat entertainers and medics in the battlegrounds south of the DMZ and in the jungles and mountains that framed the Ho Chi Minh Trail.

My second goal here is to show how the Vietnamese case challenges the enduring conviction that women's presence in combat inevitably diminishes the morale and capabilities of their male comrades. Evidence from Vietnamese military reports, documentary films, and male and female veteran's oral histories and writings reveals that women bore their fair share of the physical and psychic burdens of war with a competence and courage that lifted the morale of their male comrades. Though women had to negotiate with men for acceptance when they took the lead, they were almost never denigrated as burdensome distractions from the work at hand, especially by the men who worked closely with them. It was the higher officers in the rear, freed from the rank and file's day to day struggle to survive, who tended to underrate the fighting women.

Disregarding women during the war threw off US calculations about the true strength of Vietnamese military potential. The same mistake should not be made again as American scholars revisit the war, with better access to Vietnamese materials and scholars and an increased willingness to incorporate information about strategic planning and decisionmaking on both sides. A full reckoning of the extent of women's military service is only gradually emerging in Vietnam itself, however, as the regime's commitment to a masculinized heroic ideal recedes and writers and reporters turn toward assessing the human costs of the war. How many young people fought in the youth brigades on the Ho Chi Minh Trail is a matter of dispute in Hanoi today, since many contemporary observers believe that the government has deliberately underestimated their numbers. Official estimates state that between 1965 and 1973, at least 170,000 young people joined through their youth unions. Military historians in Hanoi today calculate that the volunteer youth kept open 2,195 kilometers of the roads that made up the Ho Chi Minh Trail, guarded over 2,500 key points under constant bombardment, built six airstrips, neutralized tens of thousands of bombs, shot down 15 enemy planes and transported on their pack bicycles tens of thousands of kilograms of cargo, weapons, and food. At least 70 percent of these youth were women. Reliable statistics about women in local self-defense and militia units are harder to pin down, but estimates range to almost 1 million. Their role was of particular importance, since in the coastal areas and other strategic sites, female anti-aircraft units formed the first line of defense. Most of the female volunteers and militia women were farmers, usually with at most a primary school education. Around

70,000 professional women – doctors, engineers, reporters – were recruited or volunteered to support NVA. After 1969 women who had the talent and temperament for military life could join the regular forces, but their numbers remained relatively small, less than 10,000. In the south, the NLF claimed more than one million women among its members by 1965 and as the war progressed, more women joined the guerilla units that bore the brunt of the war. Women made up about one-third of these units and many were combatants, skilled in the use of weapons and willing to fight.[1]

In late 1990s Vietnam, the militarized woman served as a powerful symbol – of the heroism of ordinary people and the high price they paid for their service. In 1996, veteran and Hanoi-based military historian, Nguyen Quoc Dung, called on feminine imagery to describe North Vietnam's wartime anti-aircraft defense system.[2] "The American pilots never knew that beneath them, our Vietnamese women had woven a fine hairnet of opposition." Relishing the contrast, he boasted that it was "the simple, modest activities of Vietnamese women . . . who used their small guns to shoot and their delicate hands to defuse bombs who defeated well-fed American pilots in their big heavy planes." Clearly Professsor Dung aimed his assessment of women's activities to reassert the official line that Vietnamese morale counted for more in the end than American technology. When queried about the impact of the war on these young women, he admitted that the volunteer youth who worked on the Trail had been poorly supplied during the war, and left without proper veteran's compensation when it ended. But he argued that the military life offered many young people the chance to learn new skills and so enhanced their post-war opportunities. In popular culture, however, much more attention is directed today to the postwar disappointments of women veterans than to their wartime exploits. The brave woman who returns home after years in the jungles so old and sick that she can never attract a man, so desperate for a child that she ensnares unsuspecting men to impregnate her, willing to defy convention to raise a child outside of marriage, has become a stock character in recent film and fiction.

The old Vietnamese adage, "When war comes close to home, even the women must fight," attests to a longstanding ambivalence about women's proper place, for it suggests that a woman's duty includes military service to the nation, but only when all else fails. Legends surrounding the most famous historical women fighters, the Trung sisters who raised a rebellion against the Chinese in 40 AD, and Lady Trieu, who continued the fight two centuries later, betray ambivalence about the martial woman. Male scholars over the ages have not questioned that these women acted with almost foolhardy bravery, but they have attempted to twist the scant historical sources to show that the Trung sisters fought not because they were angry that they lost lands and power under Chinese dominance but rather because they were bound to avenge a husband who had been killed by the invaders – a far more acceptable reason for taking up arms. The flamboyant Lady Trieu has proved more troublesome because she cannot be molded into the Confucian image of the good woman. A superwoman, riding proud on her war elephant, frightened Chinese soldiers tumbling before her sword, so stubborn that she refused marriage and housework and so charismatic that men followed her into battle, Lady Trieu seems to personify the matriarchal culture that mitigated Confucianized patriarchal norms in Vietnam. But she is also painted as something of a freak, a grotesque caricature, with her three-foot long breasts and savage, violent streak.[3] Moreover, like the Trung sisters and the many martial women whose valor would earn them a place in historical memory, Lady Trieu was defeated and killed in the end, never able to translate her military prowess into a voice of authority in a civil society. Women coming of age in Vietnam during the French and American Wars heard a mixed message from these legends: a woman should be willing to temporarily enter the masculine world of violence and death to save the nation, but she must not lose sight of her larger duty to produce sons, who would take their rightful place as the family and state's true citizens.

With all of this cultural and historical baggage, and in light of the official calls for women to link their fates with the nation during the French and American wars, it is no wonder that contemporary Vietnamese women's life histories inevitably echo prevailing official and social concerns. But imbedded in their remembrances are the details that matter. Women had choices. Some elected to fight from home while others left their families and communities; some resisted serving the Communist government while others identified their welfare with its promises for women's liberation; some fought for equal treatment with men while others accepted their subordinate status; some tried to maintain their femininity while others gloried in taking up men's work. And once the war ended, the survivors figured out as best they could how to use the resources available to them to regain a normal life.

"It takes a lot of power to turn a man into a soldier and a woman into the wife or mother of a martyr,"[4] as Cynthia Enloe has so astutely observed. It takes even more power to militarize a woman, especially in a society that places a high value on women's duties to the patriarchal family. Retired artillerywoman, movie star, and Hanoi-based film director, Duc Hoan, recalled in 1996 that it was the French who radicalized her – "I left my home to join the anti-French resistance when I was ten. Bigger than other girls of my age, I was able to convince the authorities for a time that I was old enough. Why did I, a sheltered, bourgeois girl, take such a chance with my life? Because I hated the way that my French Catholic school teachers looked down on the Vietnamese students. Because when my mother died, home had no meaning for me anymore. You see, I was the youngest of six daughters and my father was a traditional Confucian man. In 1948, at age 60, he remarried and had a son, and after that, my sisters and I were pretty much on our own." For Duc Hoan, the fact that traditional culture offered alternative models made a great difference as she assessed her future. "The stories of Vietnam's women heroes, the Trung sisters and Lady Trieu, were sung as lullabies by our mothers. We took the fact that women would fight for granted. Our heroines were not always successful in the long run – but they weren't sad, crazy figures like Joan of Arc!" She found the historic French maiden's male attire strange. "Why would a woman want to dress up like a man?"

Duc Hoan's life course would follow both martial and traditionally feminine paths. She studied Chinese and interpreted for high level military and Party officials, and put her French education to use by serving as a village teacher in the northern resistance areas during the late 1940s – allowed to work so far from home "because I didn't have family to worry about me." She learned to shoot a gun and handle combat situations with the E367 Artillery Unit in 1953 as the Viet Minh armies prepared to oust the French from Dienbienphu, and then joined the government's film production unit to play a variety of roles in the service of nationalist causes. During the American War, she used her talents as an entertainer to boost morale in some of the most dangerous spots in the south. And like women of her generation who played a part in the wars against colonial rule, Duc Hoan served as a role model for younger women: "I wasn't surprised when my teenage daughter put on a straw hat and carried a gun." She acknowledged that men always got the upper hand in the end, and noted that she had been neglected by her first husband, a career military man. But she had gained confidence and independence from her years in the field and she passed that legacy to her daughter. Duc Hoan distinguished French colonial rule from US attacks: "The French ate away at our souls, but the Americans threatened to destroy the very body of our country." She pointed out that during the French wars women could decide whether or not they would take action. But during the American War, women had no choice, because the nation, and with it women's hopes for a normal family life in the future, was in danger of total obliteration.

Other women's life histories confirm that while the heroines of old justified women's decisions to fight, it was the anti-French resistance in the 1930s and 40s that taught them how to stand up to a modern adversary. Like Duc Hoan, Vietnam's most famous contemporary woman warrior, Nguyen Thi Dinh, by the time of the American War a deputy commander and the highest ranking woman in the PLAF, left her farm family to join the anti-French resistance while still a teen. But while Duc Hoan's enduring power rests in her art, Nguyen Thi Dinh was a warrior to the core. Her memoir reads like an Indiana Jones story: from 1940 to 1943 she led rebellions against the French colonial armies in Ben Tre Province, her home area in the Mekong Delta, and resisted the Japanese occupation army in 1945. After reporting to Ho Chi Minh himself in 1946, she smuggled a large shipment of weapons through a dangerous French blockade to supply the revolutionary Viet Minh in the south. She gained her most important experience when she took charge of another uprising in Ben Tre Province in 1960, which initiated a sustained armed movement against the Diem government in the south. By that time, she was a seasoned fighter and strategist.

In her memoir, Dinh describes how her personal and military lives coalesced. In 1940, soon after her husband was taken to prison where he would die, she too was imprisoned for organizing against the French. When she entrusted her seven-year old son to her mother's care, she cried, as any mother would. But her maternal instincts never got the best of her when she faced down an oppressor. After her plans to organize the women themselves against brutal French prison guards failed, she persuaded the male prisoners to do the job. "Our women's cell talked over things with the [male] prisoners and suggested that they kill the corporal to set an example for the others." After describing the brutal killing, she informs her readers that she kept her spirits up in the most conventional female way, by embroidering pillowcases for her family.

The French wars propelled some one million women into the resistance and countless others followed their men to the Viet Minh resistance base areas. Very few women joined the regular forces, but women resistants by no means fought as disorganized, ragtag bands. Only with careful planning could they maximize their meager resources to accomplish their goals, as shown in the memoir of another famous woman revolutionary, Nguyen Thi Hung, a young peasant woman who joined the Indo-Chinese Communist Party to escape an arranged marriage. Hung describes how a group of local women plotted their strategy to attack a Japanese rice depot. "We had to discuss in detail the whole field of battle: the morale of the people, the strength of the guard at the depot...A staff [member] took charge of the leadership of the struggle, the organization of the people coming from the adjacent villages and the formation of specialized units for rice transportation, distribution and defence. And finally, the watchword and the time of action and the itinerary of the demonstrations were decided and the final battle plan . . . drawn up."[5]

Women did not hesitate to use any means at their disposal, including their own bodies, if it did the job. When French colonial soldiers tore off the clothing of one woman demonstrator during the Nghe-Tinh uprisings in the 1930s, her comrades all proceeded to strip to show solidarity and shame their oppressors.[6] A history of women published in Hanoi in 1966, a year after US troops had landed in Vietnam, summed up the legacy of the French wars for women: "Sixteen years ago, our women combatants were armed merely with large knives. At present, facing a much stronger and more ferocious enemy, they are much more numerous, are armed with machine guns and anti-aircraft guns, not to mention thousands of rifles. Twenty years of continuous struggle against the French colonialists and now the American imperialists have hardened the arms of our women who are certain of final victory."

In 1966–7, a French journalist interviewed young militia women in the villages of the north. He heard from angry women who wanted to avenge the death of their kin to US bombs, determined women who knew how to make good use of their anti-aircraft weapons, proud women who bragged that they could best the old men in shooting down American planes, and hopeful women who believed that their service would win them a better place in a new, more open civilian society when the conflict ended.[7] In light of what we know twenty years later, they were probably not exaggerating their prowess. But as the story of one of the most famous militia-women in the north reveals, their hopes for a better life after the war were far too optimistic.

It is precisely because she literally embodies the suffering of everyone who sacrificed their personal well-being to the war that a militiawoman, Ngo Thi Tuyen, has become one of the most beloved heroines in northern Vietnam today. Ngo Thi Tuyen won fame in 1965 for shouldering 95 kilograms of ammunition – twice her body weight – to supply artillery defending the strategic Thanh Hoa Bridge, known locally as the Dragon's Jaw Bridge, which was located in her hamlet outside Thanh Hoa city. The bridge itself stood as a powerful symbol of resistance for it stood fast in the face of almost continuous American air attacks from 1965 until 1972. Hanoians remember how they listened in on their radios to learn the fate of the bridge, believing that if the Dragon could stand, somehow the country itself would prevail. The famous poet and writer, Nguyen Duy, recalled over thirty years later that he and other artillerymen in the hills around the Bridge knew about this young woman and felt that if she could fight on so could they.

When it came time to receive her medals, the officials seemed more interested by her simple country ways than her military accomplishments. A description of her demeanor at the May Day celebration in Thanh Hoa in 1965, as she sat beside other heroes who had distinguished themselves, played up her youth and innocence: "This nineteen-year old young woman still looked like a little girl, with her round and innocent face and childlike features. She shunned public attention. Her big dark eyes fought shy of admiring gazes and she did not know what to do with her arms, now laying them on the great table before her, now crossing them on her chest."[8]

A mature Colonel Tuyen understands that her story has always served multiple purposes, but she is quite able to sort out the personal from the political. She talked openly with an admirer from Hanoi who visited her in 1991:[9]

> In 1965, just a few hours after our marriage, my husband was sent to area B [the southern battlefields]. As a militiawoman, I was in charge of transporting ammunition to the regular forces. That very night, April 3, the American planes poured bombs into the area and twenty-two of my comrades in arms were killed. But we had to defend the Dragon's Jaw Bridge at all costs on that terrible night – and we had to keep the trucks going over it on their way to the south. I don't know why I was able to carry those big boxes of ammunition that time. More than once, my strength came from anger and the need to avenge my dead comrades. Later I was interviewed by many journalists. I had to pose for their photos. I was young then and proud of myself. I was even invited to Hanoi to make a speech. It was so nice to be there. But they made me wear the traditional Vietnamese long dress, the *ao dai*, and it was too complicated for me and the high heeled shoes tortured my feet. So I had to hold up my dress to keep it from flopping around and walk barefoot when I finally retreated back to my room in the guest house. And I didn't know how to talk to people in Hanoi – I did not have a high level of education, you know.

Ironically, the serious physical injuries this young woman sustained stemmed more directly from her duties as a postwar icon than from her wartime exploits. "Many foreign journalists from the socialist countries wanted to interview me, and one East German television team didn't believe that I had carried ammunition twice my weight. So to prove it, I had to repeat the feat for them, right in front of the provincial guest house. After that, my back felt funny."

Today, Ngo Thi Tuyen is a lieutenant colonel in the regular army, in charge of veterans affairs for her area. She is disillusioned with corrupt local officials, angry about neglected veterans, and willing to speak out about these problems. An official dream girl during the war for her unstinting urge to sacrifice herself to the cause and her uncritical acceptance of authority, today she unnerves the Party bureaucrats. Not only is she honest but she has gained a certain charisma because of her heroism. It matters to ordinary people that she is childless, a result she thinks of those back-breaking exploits. And so her importance to her countrymen and women has changed. Now it is her barren, broken body that compels pity, and her shabby treatment at the hands of local Party cadre that arouses anger – her run-down house, for example, was in the late 1990s something of a minor local tourist attraction. Yet, Lieutenant-colonel Ngo Thi Tuyen reminds visitors to her hamlet, now the site of a museum commemorating the dead, that she and her team shot down their fair share of planes, not out of simple good luck, but because they were well-trained, disciplined fighters. Despite all of her private disappointments, she is still proud of what she and her fellow villagers accomplished.

For Ngo Thi Tuyen, as for most women in both the North and the South, the war was fought on home ground. Other young women in the North made a different choice, to leave home to fight. The Party's first appeal to northern youth came on June 21, 1965, when the government issued Directive 71 to establish an "Anti-US National Salvation Assault Youth Unit." Historians estimate that at least 50,000 young men and women signed on at that time. It was Ho Chi Minh's personal appeal on July 16, 1966, when the bombing campaign known as "Rolling Thunder" moved closer to the Northern urban areas, that brought young people into the war in large numbers.[10] When Colonel Le Trong Tam, who directed personnel on the Ho Chi Minh Trail after 1959, remembered the women who entered military service at that time, he brooded over the wartime deaths of his first girlfriend and his sister, reminding listeners that he too had suffered personal grief from the war and knew first-hand the price women paid for helping out in a national emergency. "We had never planned to use women on the Trail, and we knew very well the risks and hardships for women. In fact, our late President, Ho Chi Minh, cautioned us to watch out for women's welfare and special health needs. But we couldn't spare our able-bodied men after the U.S. expanded the land and air war after 1965." These youth worked under the direction of Line 559, a separate military division which was directed and supplied by the Ministries of Defense and Transportation. The young volunteers who made up the bulk of the units were subject to military discipline and regulations but could leave service after three years – if they survived and their health held out. In fact, many elected to extend their stays. They marched to the dangerous spots on the Trail with only rudimentary training and primitive equipment to become cogs in a huge conveyer belt with a single purpose that superseded the needs of any individual – to keep the supply trucks and marching soldiers on the move to the south.

Why did the young women volunteers, some as young as thirteen years, leave the relative safety of their homes to enter an unknown world of violence and death? Some of their reasons for joining echo those expressed by young people anywhere. The pull of adventure, the lure of freedom from home and village supervision, became all the more attractive if their choice served a higher cause in to the bargain. Some young-sters hoped that their families would be relieved of yet another mouth to feed in hard times and others went simply because "Uncle Ho" had asked for their help. Not all responded so quickly or positively to Ho Chi Minh's appeal. Educated women, who had more to lose, weighed carefully whether they should stay in school or on the job or support the military. A family's politics made the difference for some. One woman, educated by the French and bitter about the loss of her status and property under the socialist regime, stated that she had been coerced into using her talents as a trained engineer during the war. But other members of her family made different choices and she still seemed surprised, over three decades later, that one of her sisters had volunteered for the youth brigades. Some women did not want to deal with guns and elected to bolster the cause in other ways, by burying the dead, or putting out fires in the bombed villages around the cities. But it was the bombs, more than any other factor, that drove women to a turning point in their lives. Many young women who in normal times would be dreaming of a husband and children in the near future figured that they had to leave home to save home. As one woman veteran recalled in an interview in Hanoi in 1996,

I was born in Thai Binh Province. My family were farmers. In 1948 my father was killed in the French War. My mother was with child when he died and she raised us four children alone. In 1968, I volunteered to be a soldier, and I spent five years in the field during the most terrible time of the war. Why? Four people in my family died when the Americans bombed the Hanoi suburbs. I was angry and I believed that what men could do, I could do too. Life was hard. In the jungle, we kept the telephone lines open, and at first, I was homesick and afraid. But I wanted to avenge my family, to kill Americans for what they did. I survived, and when the war was over, my spirits soared. But life was still not easy. My husband is a career military man who served in the south during the American War and then in Cambodia. He carries a bullet in his body and he is not well after so many years in the battlefields.

When assessing her life, however, she places more value on her family than her military record. "We are lucky, because we have two children, a boy and a girl." And to a question about whether it had been hard to return home to domestic life after so much independence during the war, she responded indignantly, "Why would I not treasure my home? Sure my family would never be the same again. Some were dead, some wounded and sick. But the hope that I would one day raise children in a safe place kept me alive. It was what I was fighting for. And I was lucky. I survived when so many others died. I have children, when so many stay alone."

How women fared once they left home and how they got along with their male comrades were a few of the topics that the survivors of volunteer youth troop C814 talked over one Sunday in May 1996. Originally about 200 strong, their numbers are dropping as ill-health and poverty take a toll. Mostly poor farmers living outside Hanoi, they had ridden rusty bicycles or walked to the meeting place. A few of the women were so ill from goiter that they could not speak. Others were shy and at first the men dominated the conversation, with poetry about loss and stories about hard times together. But finally, the women began to speak, about the passage from home to the jungles, from all that was familiar to terrible hardship.

We left from a place near here – it was farm land then – on July 17, 1966. We were provided with a knapsack, two sets of uniforms, a pot, and a tin can. When they gave me a shovel and a hoe, I knew we would be road builders. We took the train to Thanh Hoa and started marching from there. We rested by day and walked by night, to avoid the bombs. It was so dark that we had to hold on to the shirt tail of the one in front of us, just like the game we played as children, "dragons and snakes make a ladder to the clouds."

After twenty-one days, the troop of two hundred teenaged girls and boys reached their destination in Quang Binh Province, their feet bloody and infected. And there they saw a side of war that was far more systematically destructive than the sporadic attacks they had witnessed in their northern villages.

We cried. We were so frightened by the bombs, constantly falling down on us, everywhere. We came upon a woman about to give birth. We were all young girls, and we
knew nothing about it. There was no one else to help her. When the baby came out
the cord was wrapped around its neck. We cut it and the woman stood up, bleeding. The
American flares helped us to see. We don't know what happened to her or the baby. As
we got closer to the battlefields, sometimes we came upon dead women, still holding on
to dead babies.

Once they reached their destinations, in many cases areas deep in the jungles where
the Ho Chi Minh Trail was being enlarged from a network of footpaths to full-scale
system of roads, they set about their work. Isolated in the jungles and highlands of
the Truong Son mountain range that borders Laos, the young people learned quickly
to place the needs of the truck drivers and the marching soldiers first, even if that duty
meant skimping on their own food and supplies. Equipped only with the barest
essentials, forced to forage for food and at times to manufacture their own shovels
and hoes, women tried to maintain decent hygiene and appearance in the wilderness
against all odds. Even simple ornaments could prove lethal, one woman remembered:
"When we worked in the daylight, we had to paint our hair ornaments black, because
the gleaming metal could attract air fire. We couldn't even dry our white underwear
for the same reason so we had to wear damp clothes in that wet jungle. We had no
thread to mend our clothes and only two sets of clothing to begin with. When they
had worn out, we got down to one set and the men gave us their clothes to wear
when we washed our own in the streams."

The men remembered that they had worried at the time about women's health in
harsh conditions:

> We men felt sorry for the women. It was harder for them. Sometimes they had to work
> underwater, moving stones. I was in charge of logistics. I went to find the women one
> day. I had to be careful to warn them, so they wouldn't be surprised, because they had to
> take their clothes off to work. These long stretches underwater harmed their health and
> now they have women's diseases. I know, I am a married man. Some of these women got
> sick during the war and now they are old and still they have no medicine. Some couldn't
> marry later, like Mau here.

His female comrade, Nguyen Thuy Mau, however, did not want to emphasize
her physical vulnerability, but her endurance and competence with guns and
bombs:

> Most of us carried AK 47s. One time when a bridge had been bombed and there was no
> time to rebuild it, we used our bodies to hold the planks so the trucks could keep
> moving. Sometimes people drowned in the mountain streams and rivers...We had
> different educational levels and we were young, A few had finished secondary school,
> but the majority were still in primary school. We were divided up along the same lines as
> the regular army, working in squads of fifteen to twenty people. We had to protect our
> fifteen kilometers of road and that was it. The road came first. We had orders not to run
> for cover when the bombs came, but to keep on working and to stand up and shoot at
> the planes.

Mau had more schooling than the others and so was trained on the spot to defuse bombs and land mines. She described how hard it was to learn to deal with each new kind of bomb the US developed, but that like typical teenagers the volunteers made a game out of this dangerous work, playing with the "baby bombs," sleeping in coffins, making toys out of leftover hardware. She was especially proud of her decision to join a squad of thirty people who volunteered to defuse particularly lethal bombs: "We had a service, and we asked our comrades to tell our families we had done our duty if we were killed and couldn't tell them ourselves." The women of C814 wanted it to be known that they had performed men's work with competence. And although the men declared that women suffered because they were women, they did not remember their female comrades-in-arms as creating undue burdens or tensions when they were all under fire. In fact, working with women who handled weapons and danger with poise served to deepen the resolve of men to act with similar courage.

Most of the US-Vietnam war was not waged in a conventional fashion, with a distinct battlefront where combat action took place and a rear that remained safe. In a people's war fought on the homeland, when death so often came from bombs dropped without warning, everyone became both a potential victim and combatant.[11] Moreover, if one were to argue that the Vietnamese women who lived in tunnels operating communication equipment, or jungle hospitals tending the wounded, or defusing bombs on the Ho Chi Minh Trail, did not really face combat and were therefore not "real" soldiers, then we must agree as well that most of the American men who served in Vietnam cannot be considered soldiers. There is in Vietnam, however, special honor paid to those who served in dangerous spots where the fighting was most fierce – the area around the Dragon's Jaw Bridge, the battlefields south of the DMZ and the hotly contested choke points on the Ho Chi Minh Trail, for example. Many of the memoirs penned by male veterans and reporters focus on the young men and women who worked in these areas.

Volunteer Youth Troop C814 spent the war years in one of the most dangerous spots along the Trail, Road 20. Constructed through rough mountain terrain in Quang Binh Province as an alternative route through the mountain passes on the borders of Laos, it was named for the average age of the youth who built it. Military writers extolled in their reports and memoirs the courage of the teenagers who lived and worked on the road and it became a favorite stop for journalists in search of a heroic story to inspire the people back home. These observers were particularly intrigued by the young women volunteers, who seemed so out of place in this remote outpost. A reporter painted a vivid picture of young women working together, singing, standing fast as US planes fired rockets. One woman who had defied orders that she remain behind because of illness impressed him: "Judging by way she held her rifle and the look on her face, I imagined that she thought she could defend the whole . . . area with her small rifle."[12] A newly arrived soldier reacted strongly to the presence of women in so dangerous a place. "They were young maidens, and I felt a deep pity for them. Anyway, they are women, just out of seventh grade. They have been here only seven months. Their skin is still smooth and not yet tanned. How beautiful and how youthful they are." Later, he begins to admire them for more than

their looks – as he witnesses how they work on construction using makeshift materials, laughing in the face of hardship. But he cannot forget that they are women after
all when he notes that they are beginning to look pale and ill and no longer
menstruate.

Women themselves often remembered their efforts to maintain dignity and nor-
malcy while under fire. Le Thi Linh, who spent almost ten years underground with a
small team of men operating radio equipment, remembered her own efforts to keep
sane and clean: "I tried to maintain some feeling of order and routine in these
conditions, which were terrible, especially for women. There were no sanitary supplies, but women's menstrual periods often stopped anyway because of bad diet
and stress." She recalled that male–female relationships were based on mutual respect
and pragmatic needs: "I lived this way from the age of eighteen to twenty-four. The
men did the harder physical work and they got sick more easily than the women.
We made our own clothes and helped the men with their sewing. Some people
couldn't live this way and went mad. Women seemed better able to endure because
they are naturally more patient. We gave the men our best rations, because we felt
sorry for them. The most terrible time came when two of my male comrades-in-arms
starved to death. We couldn't take time out to cook rice because the smoke would
attract the planes. Their diet of freshly picked grass wasn't enough to keep them
alive." Mrs. Linh had a boyfriend at home, and said that she and her teammates
would read the one letter he had sent over and over again, because it was the only
token they had of the world outside. Another woman, a veteran of the regular NVA
army described how her all-female platoon hated leeches and snakes, ate out of tin
cans with branches for utensils and yet tried to preserve a normal life: "We carried
books and we read. At night we would try to forget, and write home or read.
Sometimes we would put flowers in our hair, to try to look nice for a while. We
sang a lot, because we believed that our songs were louder than the bombs."

Military historian Nguyen Quoc responded to questions about sexual tensions
among men and women in the field by dismissing such concerns as irrelevant to the
Vietnamese situation. "We had no comfort women like the Japanese. People were
sick, tired, just trying to survive." Colonel Le Trong Tam is a bit more realistic,
pointing out that in the decade of peace after the defeat of the French in 1954 and
before the Americans invaded in 1965, young people were able to get an education,
to read literature and develop romantic ideas. He admitted that romantic liaisons
developed and some women did become pregnant, but contended that their commanders sent them home, with marriage certificates in some cases, to protect them
and their children from ostracism by conservative villagers. Other acccounts suggest
that Communist puritanism, which preached that men and women could not focus
on duty when distracted by romance and sexual activity, led to more serious punish-
ments for young people who broke the rules and engaged in sexual relations.[13]

It is difficult to elicit information from Vietnamese sources about the issue of sexual
harassment during the war. Some people admit that men did take advantage of
vulnerable young women, but declared that these cases usually occurred behind the
lines and almost always when a power differential existed. Written evidence from
the war and memoirs written afterward reveal that erotic sentiments about women

were more likely to be expressed by visitors to the battlefields than the rank and file. For example, one of the highest military commanders on the Ho Chi Minh Trail, Major General Phan Trong Tue, rhapsodized in his memoir of life on the Trail over the "poetic sight" of the young volunteers' underwear and penned a poem celebrating their "pink brassiers," "frail heels" and "sweet songs."[14] Similarly romantic memories focus on young females guiding the truck drivers through difficult terrain by "floating" through the jungle paths in their white blouses, encouraging the tired drivers with their smiles.[15] Despite these hints that young women's sexuality both intrigued and troubled the men they encountered in the field, anecdotes and interviews suggest that serious sexual harassment was not a significant problem among equals in the armies. As one woman stated, the morale of the armies and the people back home would have been endangered if young women were routinely harmed by men in the field, and morale was what the Vietnamese armies depended on above all. But everyone who had lived through the war in the field agreed that life was simply too hard, privacy so rare, and health problems so acute, that simply surviving became a constant preoccupation, and romance a luxury few could afford.

Women who took leadership roles had to contend with resistance from men. Despite their spectacular accomplishments, Deputy Commander Nguyen Thi Dinh and her female comrades, for example, had to endure less than equal treatment. In Dinh's memoir she describes how once she asked a female comrade why she needed to disguise herself as a man. "I followed the decision to disguise myself to deceive the enemy but also to put the minds of the men in my unit at ease. They despise us women, you know." The two women then joked about how much trouble the men made for them. In a post-war interview, Dinh seemed resigned to second-class status when asked how she felt about being omitted from Neil Sheehan's biography of John Paul Vann, the American military officer whose area of operations had overlapped with hers: "Oh, I understand. Men do not like to talk about women generals. Even Vietnamese men, and we have a history of famous women generals."[16]

Women at lower levels also had to struggle to gain respect when they took the lead. Many women worked in all female squads and platoons, but others fought with men and sometimes took leadership positions. There is no hard data about how many women commanded these small units, but Party documents and anecdotal evidence suggest that resistance to women leaders was a serious problem. For example, an article in the Party organ, *Nhan Dan* from March 6 1966, exhorts male Party members to overcome their belief that "women cannot lead but must be led."[17] A Party notation on the life history of a woman guerilla fighter who mobilized and commanded seven battles and taught school when not fighting admits that she is "brave and diligent," but that she is hot-tempered, quarrelsome and incapable of seeing the larger picture.[18] Some women overcame these prejudices through persistence and competence. A veteran who enlisted, along with tens of thousands of youth, in 1972 after Nixon renewed bombings in the North, gave up her chance of a university education to join the army. Lieutenant Phan Ngoc Anh, now a military librarian and a war widow with a child to raise, declared that her heroes were the young women who had joined the armies and youth corps in 1965 and 1966 during the darkest years of the war. She made it known that she could never be considered a heroine by their standards. But she had no doubts about her own capabilities in the field. "In all of the companies, there were women like me, between seventeen and eighteen years old. I thought I would fight. That was why I joined the army. But I was assigned to be a cook. I was angry and disappointed. But after a month, I became a sapper, working with dynamite, filling craters, and rebuilding bridges along Highways 9 and 14. I became the head of a company. There were twelve people under me, all in charge of explosives. We worked in teams of three and we did everything by hand. Most of the time I did not have trouble with the men." Eventually, her teams worked so well that she did not have to give orders. Her recollections echo those of veterans everywhere, that soldiers in the field begin to work for each other rather than a distant ideal or policy. "Each of us understood that our life depended on the actions of each and every one of us." A member of the women's Union in Thanh Hoa province remembered how men in her platoon had been initially disgruntled when she was ordered to take command, but finally accepted her because she had the ability to get people to work together.

In the Vietnamese armies, good morale mattered more than physical strength and so women's abilities as peacemakers were valued at times. Some men, however, remained intransigent about women's capabilities under fire. In a very telling account from the field in 1968, a newly arrived male commander reveals how his conception of women's place in war differed from the convictions of the young women in his charge. He met with resistance when he tried to convince a group of seasoned women volunteers to retreat to safer ground when the fighting grew close. "I decided to keep only the fittest and to transfer the girls back to the second line. Girls could be good at bookkeeping, handling freight, or even manning anti-aircraft guns. But they would be no match for the Saigon infantry. Sometime earlier, in fact, areas south of Highway 9 had been declared off-limits to women. And several all women units there had gone on strike against the decision." The women in his area also refused to retreat, but in the end, he forced them to leave. Most telling, however, are the terms in which they protested his decision: "As human beings, we are not inferior to other people. We are members of the Youth Union. We want to know if you really have a bias against us."

This story demonstrates how the dichotomy between the male warrior and the female "protectee" blurs when women work with men as equal partners in war. When women discovered that they could do men's work, they began to believe that they should enjoy men's rights and responsibilities. Even more troubling for conservative men, these women lost their awe of male authority figures. One intriguing report from a greenhorn new to the Trail describes his shock when a young female volunteer dressed in men's clothing and scolded her superior officers during a play that he organized for the troops. He never quite understood that her comrades tolerated her insolence because she was famed as an unusually brave fighter. More than one woman commented during interviews in 1996 that she would never be afraid of anything again after what she had endured during the war. The well-known writer, Le Minh Khue, a road-builder, engineer and reporter during the war, related how her feelings about stern, authoritarian military commanders changed when she heard them calling for their mothers as they died.[19]

The war temporarily altered traditional gender roles. Men turned to women for support in their weakest moments. Women expressed vengeful threats and carried weapons with the intent of killing an enemy that thwarted their hopes for a peaceful domestic life. Indeed, evidence from the Vietnamese side of the American War suggests that the most dangerous threat to the conception of male valor was not the disruptive presence of women under fire but the evaluative gaze they directed to their male comrades-in-arms. At work as well was worry that military women might lose their femininity and future reproductive capacities. A journalist on the Trail, for example, noted that soldiers taunted young women volunteers pushing heavily loaded pack bicycles up steep trails – "Be careful or you'll destroy your sex." Just after the end of the war, the Vietnamese Women's Union reassured readers in a tract called *Glorious Daughters of Vietnam* that the military authorities had not neglected their duty to properly socialize women in the field.[20] One story, of a brigade named after the famous historical heroine, Lady Trieu, was fashioned to show how even the toughest women, who made their own shovels and hoes, and built a road by moving massive amounts of hard rock, paid attention to domestic skills. "Classes are regularly held for brigade members, at which they can acquire a general education and learn sewing and embroidery. Brigade 609's idea of a good woman is one who works diligently, fights courageously, shows good morals and is likely to become a good wife and mother." Here, the official organization that represents women to the state places women in a vexing dilemma, making certain that their military skills, so necessary in war that they had to give up their youth and their health to the cause, will not in the end compromise their feminine duties.

As Cynthia Enloe has written so perceptively, "Wars have their endings inside families."[21] In Vietnam after 1975 veterans returned to decimated families and local communities to rebuild their lives in a nation now politically unified but isolated from global events, economically fragile, and culturally divided. As the focus of attention shifted from outside aggression to mending internal divisions, the notion of the ideal woman mutated as well. Women fighters remained symbols of past heroism, but it was now the unselfish mother, who would literally replenish the nation through her reproductive power and engender peace within family and community through her moral force, who became the more valuable citizen. This post-war preoccupation with motherhood as women's essential role is vividly displayed in the Women's Museum opened by the Vietnam Women's Federation in Hanoi in 1995. In the vestibule, the Amazonian statue holding a baby that stands under a breast-shaped conical ceiling with an elaborate chandelier, is described by a young Vietnamese guide as "the mother of Vietnam, whose milk brings peace and unity to all of her people." Obsession with motherhood is not simply the product of an official propaganda effort. Discussions about how a woman must give birth to fulfill her natural function percolates through daily conversation with men and women alike. "She might be crazy because she has never had a child," is a common observation of the childless woman. The problems faced by barren veterans is the topic of many television stories, fictional accounts and reportage.[22] In the face of official and popular messages that glorify the mother, women veterans cannot forget that no matter what their wartime accomplishments, in civilian society, they will be measured by their reproductive success. These outside pressures coincide with most women's personal desires and the terrible irony for so many of the young women who gave their youth, their most fertile years to the war, is that they cannot realize their dream of forming a family in peacetime. It would be a mistake, however, to see women as passive respondents to social constructions of the ideal woman or popular messages about their limited choices. Some women use the shared assumption that motherhood is a sacred right to challenge government policies and conservative notions of family. Veterans in the countryside admit proudly to having more children than official population control policies dictate. Data is beginning to emerge from Vietnam that documents the large numbers of women, many of them veterans or childless war widows, who are opting to have children outside of marriage. Sociologists who have studied the practice of "asking for a child" write about single women who pay healthy men who will likely contribute good genes to inseminate them and then sever ties with him once pregnant.[23] Some of these single mothers live in all-female communes in remote areas in conditions of extreme deprivation. Others, however, live within communities in which the fathers of their children are known. Married women view single women in search of a child with pity, empathy and unease, for they don't want their own husbands involved in these liaisons.[24] The government has been forced to recognize the social problems single mothers' children will face. In fact, in 1986 the state passed a law guaranteeing that the children of these women be treated as legitimate, full citizens.

It is no accident that it is a militiawoman, Ngo Thi Tuyen, who has become so important a heroine in the north. Her accomplishments were indeed extraordinary. But other women faced similarly terrible conditions with similar fortitude. Even the feat that earned her fame, carrying a load heavier than any woman should, was not completely unknown. Women who regularly carried heavy loads along the Trail gradually developed unusual stamina over time. But unlike women in the jungles, Tuyen performed her feats within the confines of her family and community. Unease about the virginal women who left home just as they came of age sexually surfaces in a variety of venues in the late 1990s. The female film director, Duc Hoan, said in 1996 that even the Vietnamese didn't understand how terrible it had been for the women who worked on the Ho Chi Minh Trail until a documentary about them came out in the early 1990s. "We cried when we saw their sick, dark-eyed faces, their thin bodies bent under heavy burdens, their feet almost bare and often bleeding." Without a great deal of solid evidence about what really went on among the youth in the jungles, recent Vietnamese creative literature and media productions are recreating an imagined wartime community of men and women playing out their lives far from the civilized world. A recent adaptation of a short story for television that featured lonely women trapped in the jungles for three rainy seasons hinted of madness, rape and lesbianism. The sensationalistic tone of the film raised the ire of many middle-aged Vietnamese, who felt that the loneliness, survival skills and patriotism that marked so many real women's service was diminished in the production. But no one disputed the portions of the story that focused on a woman whose urban boyfriend rejects her, with guilt because he admires her courageous sacrifice, because she has lost her beauty. He marries instead a younger, healthier girl who could give him the children he deserved. The volunteer youth who have never been officially recognized or recompensed for their war service have been taken up by writers who see them as living reminders of the human costs of war and the heartlessness of a corrupt bureaucracy. Their plight also offers male writers a safe venue for raising larger, politically sensitive issues about the Party's duties to the generation that sacrificed their well-being to save the nation. Women veterans today serve as symbols of the disenfranchised rather than the heroic spirit of the nation at war.

Vietnamese women fought the French and the Americans not only for personal security but to purge their country of outside forces that harmed women's well-being. It is especially galling for them to realize that Vietnam's market-oriented global economy has allowed trafficking in women and prostitution to increase. Vietnamese feminists today express disappointment that women are still treated poorly in the workplace and that domestic violence persists in so many families.[25] But they have not yet begun to press for full gender equality within the family in large part because the family still stands as their only bulwark in a very uncertain political and economic system and in part because the effects of half a century of almost continuous war have not been erased. Western feminists might well express disappointment that Vietnam's women warriors have not claimed their rights to full equality within the family with more vigor, but their choices must be respected in the context of a culture that still views the experience of motherhood as an essential rite of passage to adulthood, a country still so poor that a child is her only security, and a culture that values a woman's sacrifices far more than her personal accomplishments. We can only watch with empathy and respect as women in post-war Vietnam develop their own strategies to find a measure of personal satisfaction just as they so effectively put their ingenuity and quiet courage to work during the war.

And so Nguyen Thi Dinh became the head of the Women's Union after the war, using her skills to try to raise the position of women in peacetime. Duc Hoan won some of her battles with the censors and has directed a series of films that document the human emotions involved in war. She took the almost unheard of step of divorcing her soldier husband and marrying a man fifteen years younger – with the approval of all who know and admire her. Some of the women of Volunteer Youth Troop C814 who were able to marry broke the rules about population control deliberately and with social approval, to bear three or more children. Allowing these veterans to have children is one way to repay their service, for only recently has the government begun a program to offer some health benefits to the volunteer youth. Teacher Mau found that her fiancee had married another woman and that her family could not take her in when she returned home sick with malaria, so she lived for a time in an all-woman's commune. Eventually she returned to Hanoi and now teaches in a rural school. She tried to adopt a child, but had to return the girl when her birth parents needed her at home. Recent travelers to Thanh Hoa report with satisfaction that local officials have been shamed into repairing Ngo Thi Tuyen's house.

NOTES

1   These statistics come from interviews in 1996 with a military historian, Professor Nguyen Quoc Dung, and for the south from Sandra Taylor's superb new book, *Vietnamese Women at War: Fighting for Ho Chi Minh and the Revolution*. Kansas: University of Kansas Press, 1999.

2   I want to acknowledge my debt to my friend and colleague, Hanoi journalist and writer, Phan Thanh Hao. Much of the material I use here comes from our book, *Even the Women Must Fight: Memories of War from North Vietnam*. New York: Wiley, 1998. Some of the material I use in this essay has appeared in a collection, *A Soldier and a Woman: Women in the Military after 1945*, ed. Gerard de Groot and Corinna Peniston-Bird. London: Addison, Wesley, Longman. Unless otherwise noted, interview material comes from my meetings in northern Vietnam, collected in three research trips from 1993–7.

3   Contemporary Vietnamese female writers are deconstructing these legends. See for example, "The Makings of the National Heroine," by Cong Huyen Ton Nu Nha Trang in *Vietnam Review* 1, Autumn–Winter, 1996, pp. 388–435.

4   Quoted in Constance Sullivan, ed. *Feminism, Nationalism, and Militarism*. Association for Feminist Anthropology, 1979, p. 73.

5   In *Women in Vietnam*, Mai Thi Tu and Le Thi Nham Tuyet, eds. Hanoi: Foreign Languages Publishing House, 1978, p. 123.

6   In David Marr, *Vietnamese Tradition on Trial*. Berkeley: University of California Press, 1981, pp. 244–5.

7   See Gerard Chaliand, *The Peasants of North Vietnam*, trans. Peter Wiles. Baltimore: Penguin Books, 1969.

8   From an appendix at the end of *Vietnamese Studies*, No. 10, Hanoi, 1966.

9   From an interview with Phan Thanh Hao in Thanh Hoa, 1991.

10   Information is from Nguyen Van De. Than *Thanh nien xung phong: phuc vo giao thing van tai thoi chong my.* Hanoi: Nha xuat ban giao thong van tai, 1995 and Nguyen Thi Thap, ed. *Lich su phong trao phu nu viet nam.* Vol. 2. Hanoi: Nha xuat ban phu nu, 1981.

11   See Miriam Cooke, *Women and the War Story.* Berkeley: University of California Press, 1996; Cynthia Enloe, *The Morning After: Sexual Politics at the End of the Cold War.* Berkeley: University of California Press, 1993.

12   In the memoir of Do Vu, who traveled with the armies during the dry seasons after 1967. I have used a translation in manuscript taken from the original publication in *Tap chi van nghe quan doi* [Military Literature and Art Review]. Hanoi: Military Publishing House, 1990. When I refer to "Memoirs" it is to this version unless I state otherwise. These memoirs were in part taken from war diaries and were compiled to show the heroic determination of the men and women who worked on the Trail. But if read carefully, they are valuable sources of information.

13   *Vietnamese Women at War*, pp. 63–4.

14   In a diary entry dated 1965.

15   See the short story, "The Sound of Night," by Cao Tien Le, for example. In *Writing between the Lines*, ed. Kevin Bowen and Bruce Weigl. Amherst, MA: University of Massachusetts Press, 1997, pp. 46–50.

16   In Taylor, *Vietnamese Women at War*, p. 47, taken from Christine Peltzer White, "Love, War, and Revolution: Reflections on the Memoirs of Nguyen Thi Dinh." *Indochina Newsletter*, Mar.–April, 1991, p. 8.

17 The author is Vu Dung.
18 Document preserved in the Captured Documents Exploitation Center, and dated as 1967. This was taken from a 35 year old woman.
19 From an interview in Hanoi in 1996.
20 Published by the Vietnam Women's Union, Hanoi, 1975.
21 See "Women after Wars: Puzzles and Warnings," p. 306. In *Vietnam's Women in Transition*, ed. Kathleen Barry. London: Macmillan Press, 1996, pp. 299–313. Barry's compilation of short articles mostly by Vietnamese scholars is a very useful source for seeing the sorts of problems that concerned Vietnamese women in the 1990s.
22 See for example, Ngo Ngoc Boi, "The Blanket of Scraps." In Rosemary Nguyen, ed. and trans. *Lac Viet*, Vol. 16, 1997, pp. 96–123.
23 See for example, "Remarks on Women Who Live Without Husbands," in Barry, ed. *Vietnam's Women in Transition*, pp. 87–92.
24 Sociological studies by conservative women academics, for example, are remarkably tolerant of this practice. Interview data confirms the impression that a general feeling that childless women veterans are owed a debt that can be partially repaid by allowing them to have children out of wedlock prevails in the north. Harriet Phinney, a University of Washington doctoral student, is writing a dissertation based on extensive fieldwork on this phenomenon.
25 See for example Le Thi Quy, "Domestic Violence in Vietnam and Efforts to Curb It," in Barry, ed. *Vietnam's Women in Transition*, pp. 263–74.

PART II

The Americans in Southeast Asian Context

Before the War: Legacies from the Early Twentieth Century in United States–Vietnam Relations

ANNE FOSTER

The history of US interactions with Vietnam before 1945 shaped the options which all participants perceived after World War II. Three important legacies of these earlier years molded the views US officials had of Vietnam, and limited the choices which they perceived as available to them. The first legacy stemmed from the mutual perceptions of Americans, French, and Vietnamese. These images were often formed on the basis of little experience, but proved remarkably resilient throughout the first half of the twentieth century. The early role of communism in Vietnam's anti-colonial struggle, and activities of US officials to combat communism in Southeast Asia form the second legacy, and suggest that even Ho Chi Minh's nationalistic communism would never have been acceptable to US officials. The shifting strategic importance of Vietnam, which sometimes was tied to its position in Asia and other times was linked to its status as a French colony, form the third legacy. Vietnam itself was rarely important strategically, which made it difficult for the Vietnamese to attempt to influence US policymakers.

Mutual Perceptions

The perceptions the Americans, French and Vietnamese had of one another reveal primarily what each group hoped or feared about the future of the region and the colony. Historian Mark Bradley has argued that Vietnamese at the turn of the century were interested in learning about the major intellectual and political trends of Europe and the United States, but that their knowledge of the United States usually came secondhand. The young men who founded the Reform Movement in the early

I would like to thank Shawn McHale, Sara Abreu, and Emily Quartararo for helpful comments on an earlier draft of this essay. Responsibility for errors or lack of clarity remains mine.

twentieth century, with the intention of preparing Vietnam to regain its independence, were the most knowledgeable about the United States. These young men had watched their fathers' tradition-inspired efforts to expel the French fail, and wanted to learn from outside sources about modern ways to resist. They were inspired by reform movements in Japan and China, but found that these movements often borrowed from European and American ideas. The American example seems to have been more compelling to young Vietnamese intellectuals than it was in China or Japan, perhaps because of the taint of European colonialism in Vietnam.

The Vietnamese reformers extolled the talents of American heroes such as Thomas Edison, and enjoyed reading biographies of American political figures like Benjamin Franklin, George Washington, and Abraham Lincoln. They urged Vietnamese to consider such men as models. Phan Chu Trinh, one of the most important, early anti-French activists, wrote a poem celebrating the American Revolution. He praised the heroism of George Washington and his men during the difficult battle after crossing the Delaware River, and suggested that the sacrifices of these men demonstrated how civilized the Americans were. The conclusion of the poem reads

> That was why they opposed the oppressive English,
> Improved their schools, developed industry and commerce,
> And built a rich and powerful country,
> Everywhere on the four horizons the words peace and security were radiant.[1]

Phan Chu Trinh's praise would resonate with any American who read his poem, but notice that Phan Chu Trinh did not praise or even mention the democratic nature of the new government. Rather, the poem suggests that the appeal of the American example was that Americans had overcome colonial rule to build a strong, independent nation. If they could succeed, so could the Vietnamese. But the appeal surely also stemmed from the relative remoteness of the United States. Vietnamese could project their own values onto the American story, which came via Chinese, Japanese and sometimes French authors into Vietnam, and then was adapted to meet the expectations of Vietnamese reformers. The reformers knew a surprising amount about the United States and its history, but that knowledge was sufficiently vague that they could shape this history to their own ends.

Since the French colonial government conscripted Vietnamese laborers to work in France during World War I, some less well-educated Vietnamese returned to Vietnam with concrete experiences of Europe, and sometimes of Americans. An American missionary in Vietnam, Edwin Irwin, complained that the efforts of the Christian Missionary Alliance (CMA) to evangelize in Vietnam were hampered by rumors that converts would be "given twenty dollars and sent to school in America" by the American missionaries. Irwin was not sure which of the mission's "enemies" was spreading the rumors, but noted that the appeal of the United States stemmed from "extravagant stories . . . of the beautiful kingdom . . . their term for America" told by Vietnamese returned from Europe after World War I.[2] The stories claimed that in the United States, one could receive an education, and improve one's life. The CMA did not want to reinforce the idea that converts would be sent to America, but did send a few for theological education, perhaps feeding the rumors. This direct experience of Vietnamese with Americans was limited; only a few dozen CMA missionaries lived in Vietnam at a time. It did, however, seem to reinforce a vague sense among Vietnamese that Americans might offer a better situation than the French did.

The generation of anti-French activists who followed the Reform Movement was unlikely to be attracted by any message from the CMA. They were beginning to reject the fusion of traditional and modern ideas which earlier reformers had hoped would revitalize Vietnam, in favor of socialist, eventually communist ideologies. Ho Chi Minh is the best-known among these activists, but many young men explored similar ideas after 1920. Their view of the United States was conflicted. They saw the United States as an imperialist nation, and one of the strongest capitalistic nations of the world. Ho Chi Minh and many activists of his generation were coming to believe that capitalism was part of the explanation for colonialism, and that struggle against the latter also meant struggle against the former. How could they continue to have any admiration for the United States? At one level, they condemned the United States. Ho Chi Minh, who may have traveled to New York in 1912, wrote articles for communist publications, condemning racism and lynching in the United States, and noting the exploitation of American factory workers. He also, however, praised those Americans who worked to end racism. His only praise for Europeans, by contrast, was reserved for members of the Communist Party.

In the training manual Ho prepared for potential communists in Vietnam, however, he demonstrated his more subtle approach to the United States. Ho emphasized, to the dismay of party officials in the Soviet Union, the importance of the "national question" rather than "social revolution." In other words, he placed more stress on Vietnam becoming independent than on Vietnamese joining a worldwide movement to overthrow existing class relations. Ho used the American Revolution as an instructive example. His training manual explained the causes of the American Revolution in predictably materialist terms: Americans wanted to control their economic development, and so overthrew the British. In explaining the meaning of the American Revolution for Vietnamese, however, he emphasized the courage and unity of the American people. Ho demonstrated that he had been influenced by ideas from the Declaration of Independence, especially its initial pledge that people should be free to pursue their living and happiness with minimal interference from government. He did question whether Americans still adhered to these values, but lauded the ideals nonetheless. Mark Bradley's assessment that Ho found America an "imperfect guide" for the Vietnamese revolution captures the reserved enthusiasm Ho displayed about the United States.[3]

If the Vietnamese found American ideals appealing, but had little concrete experience with the United States or its people, the French in Vietnam were more likely to find American ideals potentially threatening, but to be reassured by contact with Americans. Towards the end of World War I, the French Vice Consul in Manila wrote that the United States was likely to grant independence to the Philippines at the end of the war. This report played to the worst fears of all regional colonial powers, whether French, Dutch or British. Officials in the region worried that the United States, through the concrete steps it was taking to provide more self-government for

Filipinos and continual discussion of independence, would prompt Vietnamese, Indonesians, and Burmese to expect similar change in status. The growing economic power of the United States exacerbated this fear, since some French officials believed that in Asia a nation's political influence stemmed from its economic power. French officials therefore were concerned to keep news of political developments in the Philippines from the Vietnamese, and to maintain the trade and investment restrictions for Vietnam which guaranteed French capital the preeminent place.

Contact with US officials tended to assuage these French fears. The US Consul in Vietnam for the late 1920s and the early 1930s, Henry Waterman, complained vociferously to Washington about discriminatory French trade practices, but he believed that French rule in Vietnam was both proper and necessary. He had almost no contacts with Vietnamese, and his reports on Vietnamese political activities drew exclusively on French sources. In addition, he had close relationships with French people in the colony. The French Governor General, Pierre Pasquier, demonstrated that he well understood Waterman's pro-French leanings when he used Waterman to convey his desire to visit the Philippines. Pasquier and the Governor General of the Philippines, Dwight B. Davis, exchanged visits in 1931–2. Pasquier found the exchange a complete success. He reported significant talks with Davis, which revealed that French and American colonial policies were not so far apart after all. Davis and Pasquier also agreed to exchange information about communists in the region. Throughout the interwar period, French officials continued to worry about the unsettling impact of American economic activity in the region, and political developments in the Philippines. Gradually, however, the French came to believe that many Americans, especially those in Southeast Asia, had only a minimal commitment to overturning colonialism.

American views of French colonial rule in Vietnam were shaped by comparing France with both the United States and other regional colonial powers. In neither case did the French come out well. US officials based their perceptions of French colonialists on first, French adherence to an open trading system and second, the value of French colonialism to the Vietnamese. In the minds of many Americans, these two characteristics were linked; a Vietnam open to foreign trade and investment would be a richer Vietnam, which would benefit the people. French colonial policy, however, emphasized tight links between the economies of France and Vietnam, to the exclusion of most other foreign trade. US officials in Vietnam complained that this policy was discriminatory and anti-American, and that the French tried to eliminate foreign competition. The judgments of US officials about economic policy probably constituted the most important element in their image of French colonialists. In this area they found the French weak, needlessly depressing the Vietnamese standard of living, and perhaps undermining their own goal of remaining a colonial power.

French colonial officials would have been surprised by this last assessment, but American observers believed that a colony with a developed, open economy was beneficial to both colonizer and colonized. US observers judged French success in part on the benefits French colonialism provided to the Vietnamese. Here again, the assessment was mixed. The French were praised for building roads, railroads, and schools, and reforming the justice system. Such improvements were not enough, however, and

France received criticism for trying to make the colony pay its own expenses plus provide profit. Davis, whose visit had so pleased Pasquier, judged French rule harshly. The French, he thought, provided a minimum standard of living for the Vietnamese only so that they would be available as profitable workers. The whole purpose of French rule was to enrich the French, not to develop the Vietnamese people. US officials in the region were only marginally impressed with French colonial rule in Vietnam, while they often noted their admiration for aspects of Dutch and British colonial rule. The French were less willing than the Dutch to encourage foreign trade and investment, and less willing than the British to take concrete steps toward greater indigenous participation in education and governing. The criticisms of French rule were not criticisms of colonialism, but only a criticism of how the French ruled Vietnam.[4]

US images of the French in Vietnam were shaped, then, by the American belief that the Vietnamese were not capable of ruling themselves. The French deserved criticism, many thought, for not taking all possible opportunities to improve the Vietnamese through education, economic development, or political tutelage. Such criticisms did not mean, however, that the Vietnamese deserved to rule themselves. A community of interest among those with white skins was ultimately more important than any assessment that French colonialism was not as effective as it should be. This sense of racial solidarity is the context in which criticisms of French colonialism should be placed. To say, as President Franklin D. Roosevelt did, that the French had "milked" Vietnam "for one hundred years" did not mean that he believed the Vietnamese deserved independence.[5]

The racism which informed US attitudes toward the Vietnamese is easily discernible in the images presented in both official and popular American sources before 1940. Most Americans knew little about Vietnam or the Vietnamese. Even those US officials living in Vietnam had only marginal contact with the Vietnamese people themselves. Waterman wrote voluminous reports on radical Vietnamese political movements and other aspects of Vietnamese culture without consulting any Vietnamese sources. Waterman's approach was not unique; a US consul had reported in 1924 that Vietnamese had very little influence in commercial matters. Other US reports emphasized that the Vietnamese were lazy and not ambitious. One could not trust the Vietnamese to remain docile, however, since they might also become menacing revolutionaries. Although US consular officers were required to report on Vietnamese political parties and movements, these activities were most often portrayed as sudden, violent, and irrational uprisings rather than a planned attempt to achieve goals, or an understandable response to grievances. Even when US officials spent several years in Vietnam, their images of the Vietnamese changed little from the stereotypes they brought with them from the United States. Reports by these officials, then, did little to change images held back in Washington.

If US consuls posted to Vietnam read about the country before they left, they were unlikely to receive a nuanced or informed view about the Vietnamese either. Articles and books about Vietnam did appear steadily throughout the 1910s to 1930s, but tended to exoticize the country, presenting it as a land of tigers, ancient ruins, and people who could be savage, childlike, devious, or sensuous. Writings on Vietnam fall into two general categories: the missionaries who wrote to attract both financial support and new volunteers, and travel/adventure writers. The first group emphasized the state of "heathen darkness" in which the Vietnamese lived, and how conversion transformed people with poor hygiene, tendencies to lie, and a lax attitude toward work into the embodiment of the Protestant work ethic.[6] These missionaries still could not imagine their Vietnamese co-religionists, however, as fully equal. When an American missionary asked a group of Vietnamese whether they wanted to be free, by which the missionary meant free of superstition, or Christian, he received an unexpected answer. They replied they wanted to be free of French rule. The missionary doubted whether these "poor people" could prosper without the help of the French.[7]

The travel writers also emphasized the exotic nature of the Vietnamese, although in a voyeuristic way that Americans were supposed to savor rather than attempt to change. As Harry Franck wandered through Vietnam during the 1920s, he noted all that was intriguing: the tooth filing rituals of people who lived in the upland areas of Vietnam, the religious ceremonies of Hindu moneylenders, or the amusing observation, accompanied by a photograph of a small naked boy piloting a boat, that one of the reasons the Vietnamese were such good boatmen was that they learned their craft before they learned that they should wear clothes.[8] So that Americans would better comprehend the people of Vietnam, however, Franck made analogies between the different ethnic groups he encountered there and ethnic groups familiar in the United States. He called the upland people savages, and compared them to the Native Americans of the United States. Both lacked civilization, he claimed, and remained relatively free of central government control. The Vietnamese he compared, favorably, with the Chinese: the former were cleaner, more accepting of foreigners, and worked harder. Books like Franck's were how most Americans learned about the Vietnamese, and the image they received during the 1920s reinforced the sense that colonial rule was generally beneficial to tropical peoples, as they were often called. Under colonialism, detrimental characteristics could be gently corrected but their picturesque qualities could be preserved for the delight of tourists.

By the 1930s, American travel writers were becoming more critical of French rule. The French were not mitigating the effects of the worldwide Depression for the Vietnamese and Japan's expansionistic behavior threatened the region. The Vietnamese remained exotic in these later books, but their customs and habits could no longer be considered simply amusing. They had to be considered within the context of how the French were responding to world crises, and what the United States might have to do if the French response proved inadequate. Mona Gardner's *Menacing Sun* makes these points explicitly, as she traveled around Southeast Asia after Japan attacked China in 1937. In Vietnam, she encountered Japanese who ran camera shops that seemed to have few customers, but plenty of photographs displaying the attractions of their towns: ports, oil installations, and other militarily important sites. French officials did not ban such businessmen from the colony, but instead carefully followed them. Gardner seemed unsure whether this measure would be sufficient, but implied that the French could expect no help from the Vietnamese in watching the Japanese. Virtually every time she encountered a Vietnamese person, she observed what she believed was an underlying hatred lurking behind polite dealings. She did not trace the hatred to French colonial rule, but believed it had been formed over centuries. Accompanying the hatred was a listlessness, she believed, observable in the thin bodies and slow movements of those Vietnamese she met. Several times, too, she mentioned that she had difficulty in telling apart men and women, which also suggested a certain lack of vigor, with men and women not capable of fulfilling appropriate gender roles. As President Theodore Roosevelt had argued years earlier about the Chinese, Gardner suggested that these characteristics did not mean that the Vietnamese were uncivilized. Rather, they were over civilized. They had already passed through the height of civilization that they as a people were likely to achieve, and were on a downward slope. Gardner believed that little assistance in meeting the growing Japanese menace could be expected from such people.[9]

Early Actions against Communism

One of the most important legacies of the interwar period was the assessment that US officials made about the role of communism in the anti-colonial movements of Southeast Asia, and Vietnam particularly. In the late 1940s, Secretary of State Dean Acheson did much to elucidate US policy toward Vietnam when he claimed that it was useless to attempt to distinguish between communists who followed Moscow slavishly and nationalists who took some inspiration from communism; all communists, he claimed, merely used nationalism to serve their ultimate goals. Acheson's views drew on a broadly shared and long-held characterization. As early as 1925, Washington received a warning to watch out for one "Iguen-Ai-Kwak" (a phonetic rendering of Nguyen Ai Quoc, Ho Chi Minh's name at that time) who was supposed to be attending a meeting of the Anti-Imperialist League in Mexico, and who might then travel to the United States. This warning came because US officials abroad were instructed to report on any communists or communist organizing. Officials in Washington believed that communism was a worldwide movement, directed from Moscow, which meant that their efforts against it also had to be worldwide.[10]

Although the effort to combat communism began in Europe, since many officials believed the threat of communism was not confined to Europe and the United States, anticommunist efforts should not be either. The Dutch colony in Indonesia had the first communist party in Southeast Asia, founded in 1920, and Dutch officials were the first to talk with US officials about the threat of communism in Asia. The concern remained at a low level for a few years, but by 1925, the French also began talks with the other countries in the region about sharing information, in part because Thanh Nien, predecessor to the Indochinese Communist Party, was founded that year. Aristide Briand, the French Foreign Minister, believed that Britain, the Netherlands, Siam, and Portugal had no objections to sharing information about communism, but that the United States would not be interested in joining such an agreement. Briand observed that communism was not a big problem in the US colony, the Philippines, and that US public opinion tended to be anti-imperialist, so US officials were reluctant to cooperate openly with other colonial governments.

Cooperation among the European powers remained informal but regular after 1925. They exchanged reports made by their secret police, allowed personnel from those secret police in one another's colonies, and sometimes arrested and deported suspected revolutionaries. The US government never officially agreed to cooperate, but by 1926, most US officials in Asia were fully informed about secret police intelligence, and rendering such assistance as they could. A large part of the impetus for US involvement stemmed from the Indonesia's 1926–7 revolt, the first apparently communist rebellion in the region. Although disorganized and easily crushed, it was also widespread and utilized symbols of communism which made colonial officials nervous. One leader of the Indonesian Communist Party, Tan Malaka, fled to the Philippines. Americans in Manila tracked him down, although he had committed no crime in the Philippines, and deported him. They let him go to China, but first informed Dutch authorities where his ship would dock, so Dutch officials could meet it and arrest him. The scheme did not work as planned, since Tan Malaka fled the ship while it was still in harbor and escaped. He remained in China for a few years, but while there was monitored by French police, who shared information on his whereabouts with the Dutch authorities.

Tan Malaka's case demonstrates that officials from the Southeast Asian colonial powers had begun to see communism as a regional threat, requiring a regional response. Information sharing and personnel exchanges among intelligence services increased during the late 1920s. Although no communist rebellion had yet occurred in Vietnam, these measures extended to that colony, including sharing of information between the French government and US officials there which reinforced this notion of a regional communist threat. Waterman reported that the French police were monitoring a society called "Cong Sanh" (meaning Communistic Society, according to Waterman). It had branches throughout Asia, including the Philippines, was directed from Moscow and Canton, and its regional head was Nguyen Ai Quoc. Since "cong san" means "communist", and the Dang Cong San Viet Nam (Vietnamese Communist Party) was formed in February 1930, Waterman's information was nearly correct. Although Waterman believed the French government was following an effective policy to combat this group, he also stressed that it could recruit easily among peasants since members could point to grievances not addressed by the French government. Waterman's reports served effectively to portray communism as a serious, external, and growing threat to colonial rule in Southeast Asia.

When a rebellion broke out in northern Vietnam soon after Waterman's report had been sent, marked by symbols of communism such as red flags painted with hammers and sickles, the assessment of a regional communist threat seemed to have been realized. The Indonesian rebellion had been small and easily crushed. This 1930–1 rebellion in Vietnam, called the Nghe-Tinh rebellion, involved thousands of peasants, lasted eighteen months, and required massive French efforts to crush it, despite the fact that the peasant rebels often were armed with only sharpened sticks and some swords. Waterman's reports to Washington on this rebellion emphasized its communistic aspects: when successful in overthrowing a village government, the rebels set up "xo-viet" governments in their place and slogans used by the rebels drew on communist principles. Not everyone in Washington was convinced, and scholars since have pointed to the early effects of the Depression as equally important in explaining Nghe-Tinh. One of Waterman's superiors complained that he accepted French explanations too easily, rather than investigating possible economic or nationalistic causes. Still,

Waterman was never reprimanded for his analysis, and other US officials were allowed to read Waterman's reports in order to assess the likely impact of the rebellion on trade conditions. The reservations held by some Washington officials about the communist nature of the rebellion were overshadowed by their greater concern to discover possible connections between Moscow and Southeast Asian political movements. Also in the late spring 1930, one State Department official commented that the government was not concerned with the methods used to obtain information about communist activities so long as the information was received. Washington officials showed some skepticism about Waterman's analysis, but on the topic of communism and its threat to the region, they expected him to report any suspicions.

Although Waterman did echo closely the assessment made by French officials of the Nghe-Tinh rebellion, and although many in Washington accepted at least the premise that communism was a threat to the region, US officials still believed the United States had a different role in Southeast Asia from that of the Europeans. The dilemma stemming from this contradictory approach to policy in the region was highlighted during the visit of Philippine Governor General Davis to Vietnam in 1931. Davis believed communism's threat could be met effectively by formal, regular exchanges of information with other colonial governments, and US Consuls in the region sharing information directly with the Philippine government. Davis, in private meetings with the French Governor General, Pasquier, proposed that the two share mutually interesting political information. Davis also asked Waterman if he would send directly to Manila any political reports of importance for the Philippines, particularly those on communism in Vietnam. Both Pasquier and Waterman were enthusiastic about these proposals, and believed them important in combating communism.

The reaction in Washington was subdued. All agreed that communism posed a serious threat, but as Assistant Secretary of State William R. Castle suggested, the measures currently in place allowed US officials to share information with each other or representatives of foreign governments when necessary. Castle saw no benefit to more explicit instructions. Others in the State Department were, privately, more blunt. The US position in the region, they argued, depended in part on Southeast Asians viewing the United States as different from other colonial powers. In other words, US officials wanted to act as both an anticommunist and an anti-colonial power in the region. To accomplish the first, they would cooperate fully but secretly with European governments in tracking, arresting, and deporting communists. To accomplish the second, they would maintain strict secrecy about their cooperation with the Europeans and continue to progress steadily, if gradually, toward self-government for the Philippines. The discussion about how to handle the Davis proposals ranged to the top of both the State and War Departments, but since no decision to formalize cooperation was made, the prevailing system of informal cooperation continued throughout the 1930s.

US officials may have believed during the 1930s that they had succeeded in their attempt to present the United States as an anti-colonial power to Southeast Asians, and as an anti-communist power to Europeans. In 1935, the Philippines became a Commonwealth, with substantial self-government. US officials believed this action was inspirational for Southeast Asians, and a model for how Europeans should treat their colonies. During 1936, the US Consul General in Singapore learned about communist activities in that British colony through secret interviews with the head of Singapore's Secret Police. These two contradictory tendencies in US policy could co-exist during the 1930s for some particular reasons. First, anti-colonial movements in most of the colonies, communist-inspired or not, were relatively young and weak. Most of their leaders had little expectation of achieving independence soon, and did not demand assistance from the United States as they would after World War II. Second, European governments were worried about the influence of US policies in the Philippines on their colonies, and expressed that fear. European complaints tended to convince some Southeast Asians that the differences between Americans and Europeans were important, which ironically may have made Southeast Asians more admiring of US policy than they would otherwise have been.

Finally, Southeast Asia was not a critical strategic area for the United States during the 1930s, so a contradictory policy had fewer consequences. US officials did not care as much as they would after 1945 about disappointing either Southeast Asians or Europeans. The strategic importance of Southeast Asia, especially Vietnam, increased by the end of the 1930s and during World War II, but the major threat to US interests in those years was Japan. After World War II, when US officials believed their rival in the region was the Soviet Union, it would be more difficult for them to convince the Vietnamese that anti-communism and anti-colonialism were compatible.

Vietnam's Growing Strategic Interest for the United States

Soon after the United States acquired the Philippines, US military officials recognized that the most likely war scenario in the Pacific Ocean was a struggle between the United States and Japan for control of the region. As a result of this concern, US military planners drew up War Plan Orange, which guided US strategic thinking about a war between the United States and Japan until 1940. War Plan Orange focused on defending the Philippines, using the US presence there to defeat the Japanese, and on control of the Pacific Ocean. The war situation which developed in Asia, however, required a different response. Japan invaded China in 1937, effectively beginning World War II in Asia. World opinion, including in the United States, tended to see China as the victim, and Japan as the aggressor in the early years of the war, but no country was then willing to go to war against Japan to help China. Still, US policymakers began to take a second strategic look at the region, since the likelihood that the United States would be involved in a war there had increased.

Vietnam's importance to the United States grew after 1937, because US policymakers discovered that only one accessible re-supply route, through northern Vietnam, existed for the parts of China still controlled by the Chinese. Travel writer Mona Gardner observed crates of "pianos" being sent from Hanoi to China's Yunnan province. When she remarked that the Yunnanese must be very musical, the customs official whispered to her that these "pianos" would surely play a death song for the Japanese. It did not take her long to figure out that the crates contained machine guns.[11] US officials in Saigon and Washington were watching this supply route, as well, noting that it was important to keep it open.

The concern in Washington grew once the European war began. Immediately, consuls throughout Southeast Asia were instructed to report on what impact the war would have on shipments of vital goods to the United States from the region, such as rubber, tin, and oil. The news was not good: European governments wanted to reserve these vital resources for their own war efforts. With the fall of France to Germany in June 1940, the situation became even more problematic. Would France be able to continue holding its colonies, even while occupied by a foreign power? The French certainly hoped so, and stated their intention to do so. Japan, however, cast covetous eyes at Vietnam. Its designs on the country began to be realized in September 1940, when Japan, Germany, and Italy signed the Tripartite Pact creating the Axis powers. That same month, Japan issued an ultimatum to Vietnam's French government. It demanded that Japanese troops be stationed in Vietnam, and that Japan be allowed to use airfields and transit lines in the fight against China. Unable to defend the colony, and receiving no words of encouragement from France, the French Governor General, Jean Decoux, had no choice but to acquiesce. Japan moved troops into northern Vietnam by the end of September 1940.

Decoux had attempted to get assistance from both Britain and the United States. Their refusal might be seen as a sign that Vietnam held little strategic importance, but should not be. In September 1940, Britain was fighting Germany alone in Europe and had its hands more than full. The United States was not yet in the war, and President Franklin D. Roosevelt knew full well that if Americans had not been ready to fight on behalf of the Chinese, they would not want to fight to protect the Vietnamese, or French colonial rule. Roosevelt did, however, cut off steel and iron exports to Japan, a move which stunned the Japanese. Roosevelt recognized that Japan's move into northern Vietnam was likely to be the beginning of a broader campaign in Asia, which would touch American interests more directly than previous Japanese actions. He also recognized that the Tripartite Pact made the war global, and US entry was probably inevitable.

Although the United States moved steadily, if often secretly, toward entering the war, the developing situation in Vietnam prompted one of the next major turning points in the potential war with Japan. In July 1941, after Germany had launched its invasion of the Soviet Union, the officials in Tokyo who wanted a "southern strategy" prevailed; Japan would expand southward, into Southeast Asia instead of north toward the Soviet Union. The first step in this plan was a new demand on the French government in Vietnam – to allow Japanese troops in the southern half of the country. Decoux again could not resist, and Roosevelt's reaction was swift. Japanese assets in the United States were frozen, imposing an effective embargo on US exports to Japan. The Japanese again seem to have been surprised at the response, but US officials saw that with Japanese troops and naval vessels in southern Vietnam, European and American colonies in the region were vulnerable to surprise attack. The Japanese offered to leave southern Vietnam in return for an end to the embargo, but the US position had hardened. Japanese officials began to worry, since their supplies of vital raw materials, especially oil, were running low while the United States had begun to reinforce its troops in the Philippines and re-build the navy.

The Japanese responded by deciding to attack Pearl Harbor, in hopes of knocking out a substantial portion of the US Pacific Fleet, bringing the United States into the war before it was ready, perhaps demoralizing Americans with the surprise attack, and providing further reason for Japan to move southward in Asia. The attack on Pearl Harbor came on December 7, 1941; the attack on the Philippines, Singapore, and Indonesia was launched only a few hours later. A few hours before, the Japanese Army General in Vietnam, Chō Isamu, demanded that Decoux provide Japan with broad assistance, including access to military facilities and support for economic activities necessary for conduct of war. Chō essentially demanded that the French retain the outward signs of ruling in Vietnam, but rule completely at the behest of Japan. Decoux tried to delay his response, but events of the next few hours made resistance futile. Although neither the Vietnamese nor the French had played an active part in convincing US officials that the United States should enter World War II, Japanese actions in Vietnam had been important factors in convincing US officials, from Roosevelt down, that US entry was necessary for the defense of US interests.

The United States and Vietnam during World War II

Strategic interests remained the most important factor in US thinking on Vietnam during World War II, but not all US officials shared a common assessment of those interests. During the war, these different understandings of Vietnam's potential role did not conflict. After the war, when the strategic importance of Vietnam had faded, the earlier perceptions Americans had of Vietnamese, and the concerns with communism would reassert themselves. The combination of these legacies would help US policymakers decide to support the return of French colonial rule, despite assistance and encouragement given to Ho Chi Minh by US military officers during the war.[12]

Once the United States had formally entered in the war, Vietnam's strategic importance stemmed from the potential that Allied troops would attack Japan from China through Vietnam. US officials then had several decisions to make. Would it be best to cooperate with the French, in hopes of receiving assistance in any such attack from French soldiers remaining in Vietnam? Or, would it be better to encourage anti-colonial Vietnamese, in hopes that they would rise up to provide assistance? For most of the war, US policy tended toward the latter solution, but US support for Vietnamese anti-colonial movements was always weak, and undermined by promises to France that one Allied war goal was to return France to all its colonies. A large part of the reason for the contradictory policy was that although Roosevelt had several times expressed his opinion that the French had not been effective colonial rulers and therefore did not deserve to regain their colony, he also was willing to compromise this principle when important military goals required it. For instance, in 1942, Roosevelt told the Pacific War Council that France should not regain its colony in Indochina, and even hinted that France itself might be in need of a trusteeship. In the fall of that year, however, as delicate negotiations occurred over the planned Allied landing in North Africa, especially the hope that the Vichy French government there would remain neutral, Roosevelt's personal representative assured the French that the

Allies planned to see France regain its lost colonies. Roosevelt rebuked the representative, but let the French and British continue to believe this pledge.

Roosevelt's assertion that the French should not continue to govern Vietnam does not indicate he was a committed anti-colonialist. Rather, Roosevelt, like many Americans, saw colonialism as inefficient and old-fashioned. He believed that after the war, colonialism would gradually fade away, and Roosevelt simply wanted to control that process to the advantage of the United States. This sentiment explains his emphasis on a trusteeship for Vietnam, which he pushed consistently from 1943 to early 1945. Roosevelt's model for Vietnam was what he perceived had been US policy for the Philippines: a benevolent, disinterested and developed country ruled over another country, but for the sole purpose of educating its people for self-government. The trustees for Vietnam would be China and the United States, with the former taking a lead role. Not even the leader of the Chinese Nationalist government, Chiang Kai-Shek, was enthusiastic about this plan. He called the Vietnamese difficult people. Not for the last time, US policy would neglect to take into account the centuries-long antagonism between Vietnam and China.

The French obviously did not favor the trusteeship plan, but neither did the British, who saw it, probably quite rightly, as Roosevelt's model for how all colonies should be governed at the end of the war. The British, too, wanted to return to their colonies at the end of the war. The Vietnamese, however, also had no reason to like the trusteeship plan, since one of its primary, although unemphasized, tenets was that the Vietnamese were not yet capable of governing themselves. Here was the limit to Roosevelt's anti-colonialism: he believed colonial rule was outmoded, but also that Asians and Africans still needed decades of guidance before they would be able to govern themselves. Even this limited anti-colonialism was shared by few other US officials at the time. Some, especially in the State Department, actively worked in support of French interests even when Roosevelt was attempting to set a different policy.

Other US officials, of course, believed in the ability of Vietnamese to govern themselves, and supported Vietnamese anti-colonial movements. The operatives of the Office of Strategic Services in China during World War II met Ho Chi Minh and became impressed with him personally and with his potential to organize both anti-Japanese and anti-French resistance within Vietnam. Several OSS officers traveled inside Vietnam towards the end of the war, visited Ho Chi Minh at Viet Minh headquarters, and provided supplies, a few weapons, and some training to Ho's followers. These OSS officers, initially wary of Ho's communism, often became his ardent supporters. Back in Washington, however, support for Ho Chi Minh never materialized. During the spring and summer of 1945, the minimal assistance of the OSS was justified as part of the war effort. After the Japanese surrender, however, it became clear that the three legacies, of mutual perceptions, anti-communism, and broader strategic importance had again combined to eliminate any possibility that the United States would support the new Democratic Republic of Vietnam, which Ho Chi Minh declared on September 2, 1945.

The successful island-hopping campaign waged by the United States in the Pacific made clear by early 1945 that the invasion of Japan at the end of the war would come from the Pacific Ocean, rather than from China through Vietnam. The strategic importance of Vietnam declined precipitously, as did US concern with who there might give assistance to the Allied war effort. To those planning for the postwar, Vietnam remained of some strategic importance. New threats to the region would require that the United States have access to military bases in stable countries, and Vietnam's strategic location between Southeast Asia and China meant that a base there would be welcome. The strategic importance of Vietnam became subsumed in a broader context, however. US officials became worried in 1945 about the strength and political orientation of France after the war. With the defeat of Germany, US officials increasingly perceived a threat from the Soviet Union. General Charles de Gaulle, leader of the Free French, played into this worry as early as March 1945, exclaiming to Roosevelt that any attempts to strip France of its colonies would weaken the country and perhaps force it into the Soviet orbit. Roosevelt immediately ordered the OSS in China and Vietnam to work with any French who opposed the Japanese, as well as with Vietnamese. Before Roosevelt's death, he had essentially abandoned even the trusteeship idea for Vietnam, declaring that France could voluntarily put Vietnam under international trusteeship if it wished.

Persistent sentiment among many Americans that the Vietnamese were not capable of self-government drew on the images of the Vietnamese formed during the 1920s and 1930s. Exacerbating this negative assessment of Vietnamese capabilities was a renewed concern during 1945 with communism, which also drew on the legacies of the 1920s and 1930s. As during the earlier time period, US officials viewed the battle against communism as global. For the Vietnamese, this view had two unfortunate consequences. First, the need to shore up France in Europe as a bulwark against communist expansion there meant that the strategic importance of Vietnam was tied to continued colonial rule. Second, despite the assessment by OSS officials who had spent time with him that Ho Chi Minh's communism was tempered by an even greater commitment to an independent Vietnam, Washington officials did not believe they had the luxury of making such distinctions. Although in 1945, the future still held several chances for the United States to avoid the devastating war it waged in Vietnam during the 1950s through 1970s, the legacies of the pre-World War II era made it unlikely that such chances would be seized.

NOTES

1   Mark Bradley, "Imagining America: The United States in Radical Vietnamese Anticolonial Discourse," *The Journal of American-East Asian Relations* 4 (1995), 299–330, poem on 307.
2   Edwin F. Irwin, *With Christ in Indo-China: The Story of Alliance Missions in French Indo-China and Eastern Siam* (Harrisburg, 1937), 69.
3   Bradley, "Imagining America," 321.
4   This argument is developed more fully in Anne L. Foster, "Alienation and Cooperation: European, Southeast Asian, and American Perceptions of Anti-Colonial Rebellion, 1919–1938" (Ph.D. diss, Cornell University, 1995) chapter 3.

5   Stein Tønnesson, *The Vietnamese Revolution of 1945: Roosevelt, Ho Chi Minh and de Gaulle in a World at War* (London, 1991) 40.
6   Grace Cadman, *Pen Pictures of Annam and Its People* (New York, 1920) 124.
7   Gordon H. Smith, *Light in the Jungle* (Chicago, 1946) 40.
8   Harry A. Franck, *East of Siam* (New York, 1926).
9   Mona Gardner, *Menacing Sun* (London, 1939).
10 This section draws on Foster, "Alienation and Cooperation," chapter 3 and Anne L. Foster, "Secret Police Cooperation and the Roots of Anti-Communism in Interwar Southeast Asia," *The Journal of American-East Asian Relations* 4 (1995) 331–50.
11 Gardner, *Menacing Sun*, 20.
12 This section draws on Walter LaFeber, "Roosevelt, Churchill, and Indochina, 1942–1945," *American Historical Review* 80 (1975) 1277–95; David G. Marr, *Vietnam 1945: The Quest for Power* (Berkeley, 1995); Tønnesson, *The Vietnamese Revolution*.

REFERENCES

Bradley, Mark 1995: "Imagining America: The United States in Radical Vietnamese Anti-colonial Discourse," *The Journal of American-East Asian Relations*, 4, pp. 299–330.

Cadman, Grace 1920: *Pen Pictures of Annam and Its People*. New York.

Foster, Anne L. 1995: "Secret Police Cooperation and the Roots of Anti-Communism in Interwar Southeast Asia," *The Journal of American-East Asian Relations*, 4, pp. 331–50.

Foster, Anne L. 1995: "Alienation and Cooperation: European, Southeast Asian and American Perceptions of Anti-Colonial Rebellion, 1919–1938," Ph.D. diss, Cornell University.

Franck, Harry A. 1926: *East of Siam*. New York.

Gardner, Mona 1939: *Menacing Sun*. London.

Irwin, Edwin F. 1937: *With Christ in Indo-China: The Story of Alliance Missions in French Indo-China and Eastern Siam*. Harrisburg.

LaFeber, Walter 1975: "Roosevelt, Churchill, and Indochina: 1942–1945," *American Historical Review*, 80, pp. 1277–95.

Marr, David G. 1995: *Vietnam 1945: The Quest for Power*. Berkeley.

Smith, Gordon H. 1946: *Light in the Jungle*. Chicago.

Thorne, Christopher 1988: "Indo-China and Anglo-American Relations, 1942–1945," *Border Crossings: Studies in International History*, ed. Christopher Thorne. New York, pp. 86–106.

Tønnesson, Stein 1991: *The Vietnamese Revolution of 1945: Roosevelt, Ho Chi Minh and de Gaulle in a World at War*. London.

CHAPTER EIGHT

Franklin Roosevelt, Trusteeship and US Exceptionalism: Reconsidering the American Vision of Postcolonial Vietnam

MARK BRADLEY

Just a few months after the Japanese attack on Pearl Harbor, President Franklin D. Roosevelt expressed doubts about French colonial rule in Indochina and initiated plans to place Vietnam under some form of international trusteeship. By mid-1942, discussions were underway within the State Department on possible forms of international supervision for the development of indigenous political and civil society in postwar Vietnam. From 1942 onward, Roosevelt vigorously pressed members of the wartime alliance to support trusteeship, winning the support of Chiang Kai-shek and Stalin. At the same time, American officials in southern China were increasingly drawn into discussions about trusteeship for Vietnam. By the spring of 1945, however, the United States had retreated from these efforts, abandoning plans for the international supervision of Vietnam's transition to independence and acquiescing to the return of the French to Indochina.

Franklin Roosevelt's dogged pursuit of trusteeship for Indochina during World War II has often been viewed as a peculiarly quixotic personal crusade.[1] While scholars debate Roosevelt's culpability for the quiet death of trusteeship in the spring of 1945, most wistfully agree that postwar American diplomacy toward Vietnam marked a sharp break with FDR's wartime plans for Indochina. But if Roosevelt's advocacy of trusteeship ended in failure, its significance lies not in a story of what might have been. Rather than a didactic parable of a pacific alternative to the increasingly bellicose character of the subsequent Cold War in Vietnam, trusteeship marked the full articulation of a persisting American vision that transcended FDR's personal crusade.

Not all American policy makers shared Roosevelt's certainty that trusteeship was the best tool to realize America's imagined postcolonial Vietnam. But they did embrace the assumptions that underlay his larger vision. Roosevelt and the wartime American policy makers in Washington and southern China who framed the American vision of postwar Vietnam believed that the Vietnamese were innately incapable of self-government, that French rule had done almost nothing to correct these deficiencies and that the dislocations of the Pacific war offered the opportunity to arrest the stagnation of Vietnamese's civil society by providing the Vietnamese with tutelage in American political, economic and social models.

Embedded in the harsh judgments of World War II era American policy makers was a broader discourse on the proper relationship between what was seen as the backward character of nonwhite peoples and the more progressive West. American images of Vietnamese society reflected a fundamental belief in racialized cultural hierarchies that had underlain the American encounter with nonwhite peoples at home and abroad since the mid-nineteenth century.[2] Much of the vociferous critique of French colonialism rested on the widespread notion of the unique success of the American colonial project in the Philippines and the superior claims of American models to reshape the lives of backward peoples.

But if their assumptions were in part rooted in a domestic context, Roosevelt and wartime American policymakers also displayed strong commonalties with the patterns of perception and behavior of European colonialists. Notwithstanding the anti-French rhetoric of wartime policymakers, their deprecating assessment of Vietnamese society was grounded in a wider Orientalist discourse on the non-Western "other" through which, as Edward Said and others have argued,[3] Western imperial powers used a culturally constructed conception of the negative essence of colonized peoples to denote Western superiority and reinforce imperial military and economic dominance. Although wartime Americans often celebrated what they saw as their own exceptionalism as a colonial power, their apprehensions of Vietnam and visions for its future point toward the shared rather than antithetical nature of colonial discourse and practice in Europe and the United States. If the transformation of the incipient American vision for Vietnam eventually encountered serious and ultimately insurmountable obstacles, these efforts and the assumptions that guided them reveal the centrality of a shared Euro-American colonial discourse in the American construction of a postcolonial Vietnamese state during World War II and in its aftermath.

"Benefiting the Owner:" Roosevelt and Trusteeship

At a July 21 1943 meeting of the Pacific War Council, the inter-allied working group that oversaw military operations in the Pacific theater, President Roosevelt addressed the members of the Council assembled in the Cabinet Room of the White House:

> Indo-China should not be given back to the French Empire after the war. The French had been there for nearly one hundred years and had done absolutely nothing with the place to improve the lot of its people . . . Probably for every pound they got out of the place they put in only one shilling . . . [W]e ought to help these 35,000,000 people in Indo-China. Naturally they could not be given independence immediately but should be taken care of until they are able to govern themselves . . . [I]n 1900 the Filipinos were not ready for independence nor could a date be fixed when they would be. Many public works had to be taken care of first. The people had to be educated in local, and finally, national governmental affairs. By 1933, however, we were able to get together with the

Filipinos and all agree on a date, namely 1945, when they would be ready for independence. Since this development worked in that case, there is no reason why it should not work in the case of Indo-China. In the meantime, we would hold Indo-China as a trustee. This word cannot even be translated into some languages. It means to hold for the benefit of the owner.[4]

Roosevelt's remarks before the Pacific War Council were not his first mention of plans for international trusteeship in Indochina. But the sentiments they convey aptly characterize his approach to the creation of a postcolonial Vietnamese state. Roosevelt saw French rule in Vietnam as a particularly egregious example of colonial failure. Traveling with his son Elliott to Casablanca, a journey which brought him intimate views of the poverty and disease in French Morocco, Roosevelt reflected on French colonial rule in Vietnam: "Why was it a cinch for the Japanese troops to conquer that land? The native Indo-Chinese have been so flagrantly downtrodden that they thought to themselves: Anything must be better than to live under French colonial rule!" In his remarks before the Pacific War Council, Roosevelt argued that the French acted solely in their own economic self-interest in Vietnam and had done nothing to "improve the lot of the people." It was a refrain that he would repeat many times in wartime discussions of trusteeship for Indochina with the Chinese, the British and the Soviets. In a meeting with Stalin at the Tehran conference in November 1943 where he won the support of the Soviet leader for trusteeship, for instance, Roosevelt told Stalin, "that after 100 years of French rule in Indochina, the inhabitants were worse off than they had been before."[5]

Underlying Roosevelt's hostility toward French policy in Indochina was not so much opposition to colonial rule itself as a sense that the French had not upheld the obligations of a colonizing power. In one of his earliest statements on French colonialism in Vietnam, Roosevelt observed that "the French did not seem to be very good colonizers." French conduct in Indochina, he suggested, "was at considerable variance with general practice of Great Britain and the United States to encourage natives to participate in self-government to the limit of their abilities."[6] Roosevelt made explicit some ten months later the critical role French failure to reform Vietnamese society played in his assessment of Indochina's future, arguing "that we must judge countries by their actions and that in that connection we should all avoid any hasty promise to return French Indo-China to the French."[7]

Roosevelt was also certain that the Vietnamese were unable to govern themselves, an assumption that rested in part on his belief that the failed policies of the French had left the Vietnamese unprepared for independence. But his use of the word "naturally" to introduce his assertions before the Pacific War Council that the Vietnamese were not yet ready for self-government and required external improvement suggests his perception of Vietnam's political immaturity was also refracted through a prism of racialized cultural hierarchies. Roosevelt's direct knowledge of indigenous Vietnamese society was extremely limited. In one of the few instances in which he described the Vietnamese, Roosevelt called them "people of small stature, like the Javanese and Burmese" who were "not warlike," a comment that recalled contemporary American perceptions on non-Western societies as feminized, weak and permeable to outside influence.[8] In presenting Vietnamese society as analogous to the Philippines before American colonial rule, Roosevelt linked his vision of Vietnam to the broader and familiar American beliefs that posed a natural division between the stasis of non-Western societies and the dynamism of the West. The reductionist analogy Roosevelt used to join Vietnamese and Filipino societies may have seemed particularly compelling because he viewed Vietnam as another backward Asian society in need of development on more progressive Western lines.

The interconnections Roosevelt drew between Vietnam and the Philippines were central to his conception of Vietnamese development under trusteeship. Roosevelt's brief before the Pacific War Council that the success of American policy in the Philippines demonstrated there was "no reason why it should not work in the case of Indo-China" illustrates his oft expressed faith in the universality of American models and the ease of their cross-cultural transfer. But his emphasis on gradual evolution toward full independence in the Philippines suggests he saw the process of political and social development in Asia as very slow. In Roosevelt's view some forty-five years would elapse between the coming of American rule to the Philippines and independence. Roosevelt argued that in 1900, not only were the Filipinos unprepared for independence, but a date could not "be fixed when they would be." Even after thirty-three years of efforts to build public works and provide education in "local, and finally, national governmental affairs," Roosevelt continued, both American and Philippine elites agreed that the Philippines would not be "ready for independence" until 1945.

Roosevelt's description of American efforts to guide the Philippines toward independence at the Pacific War Council indicates that he envisioned the transformation of Vietnamese society under international trusteeship would be guided by the same gradualism and moderation that had characterized US colonial policy in the Philippines. These lessons from the American experience in the Philippines certainly informed Roosevelt's presentation of a timetable for trusteeship in Vietnam. In conversations with Chiang Kai-shek and Stalin later in 1943, for instance, Roosevelt raised the Philippine analogy to suggest that trusteeship "would have the task of preparing the people for independence within a defined period of time, perhaps 20 to 30 years."[9]

Roosevelt's emerging vision of postcolonial Vietnam was not, however, as sharp a departure from prevailing colonial norms as his rhetoric sometimes suggested and he himself appeared to believe. The easy links Roosevelt drew between his plans for Vietnam and American policy in the Philippines should not obscure the failure of the American colonial project in its own terms. As one leading scholar of American colonialism in the Philippines argues, the three central policies undertaken to transform Philippine society in the American image – preparing the Filipinos to exercise governmental responsibilities, providing primary education for the masses and developing the economy – "failed . . . to bring about fundamental change," challenging "the widely held myth . . . of the United States as an essentially successful colonial power."[10] Nor did Roosevelt's views, shared by many who would make wartime American policy on Vietnam, acknowledge the inherent similarities in American and European colonial aims and practices. What Americans celebrated as "benevolent assimilation" in the Philippines both sanitized the violence of colonial conquest and presumed the backwardness and inferiority of their Filipino beneficiaries. If American colonial tutelage in the Philippines was a transitional stage to independence, as another scholar recently argued, "self-rule was not the product of a social compact among equals but the result of sustained disciplinary measures requiring the colonized to submit unstintingly to a pedagogy of repression and mastery."[11] Despite Roosevelt's belief that trusteeship in Vietnam marked a revolutionary break from the colonial past, the shared Euro-American beliefs that underlay the American approach to the Philippines and Vietnam belied his exceptionalist claims.

Debating the Instruments of Change: Postwar Planning and Vietnam

As President Roosevelt worked in 1943 to advance his plans for international trusteeship in Indochina, members of the State Department's postwar planning staff began to craft their own proposals to prepare Vietnam for independence and self-government. The final recommendations of State Department planners favored a more limited role for the United States in Vietnam's future development than the one envisioned by Roosevelt, but their deliberations on the necessity for political, economic and social change in Vietnam were infused by the same broader assumptions that guided Franklin Roosevelt's plans for trusteeship as well as his insistence that American models could best direct Vietnam's future development.

The most sustained wartime discussion in Washington of Indochina policy took place in the Subcommittee on Territorial Problems, one of the many committees in the State Department's labyrinth postwar planning apparatus. In meetings held in November of 1943, the subcommittee took up the question: "Should Indo-China be restored to French sovereignty, with or without conditions?" For these discussions, its regular membership was supplemented with representatives from the Division of Far Eastern Affairs and several members of the policy planning research staff who were to serve as area specialists. None of these specialists had particular training on Vietnam, but three of them – Kenneth P. Landon, Amry Vandenbosch and Melvin K. Knight – did bring some knowledge of Southeast Asia and French colonialism. Landon, a former missionary in Thailand for ten years, had recently joined the State Department's Division of Southwest Pacific Affairs. Vandenbosch, a University of Kentucky political scientist who was the leading American scholar on the Dutch East Indies, and Knight, an economic historian who had published works on French colonial rule in North Africa, were members of the research staff. Isaiah Bowman, a noted Johns Hopkins geographer and an important advisor to President Roosevelt on colonial issues chaired the subcommittee.[12]

The subcommittee initially took up a review and discussion of working papers prepared by Vandenbosch and Knight on French colonial practices in Indochina and the capabilities of indigenous peoples to govern themselves. In their critical assessments of French colonialism and Vietnamese society, which met with general agreement among the members of the subcommittee, Vandenbosch and Knight echoed the views of President Roosevelt. Subcommittee members believed that French practices in Vietnam "fell short of the standards set by most of the other Western European powers." The committee also shared Roosevelt's views that the

Vietnamese were not yet ready for independence. Their impressions of Vietnamese political immaturity, like those of FDR, were partially grounded in perceptions of the failures of French colonial rule. French unwillingness to prepare the Vietnamese for eventual self-government, subcommittee members argued, represented a sharp departure from what they believed to be prevailing colonial norms. Vandenbosch told the subcommittee that the "Dutch had done much better by their colonies than had the French" as "the Indonesians had made more rapid progress in the direction of self-government under the Dutch than had the populations of Indo-China under the French." A sense of the superiority of American policies in the Philippines also shaped the subcommittee perception that French failure to guide Vietnamese political development had violated a fundamental obligation of colonizing powers. Assistant Secretary of State Adolph A. Berle, another subcommittee member, observed, "self-government, as was indicated by our experience in the Philippines, depended . . . on the policy which the government pursued."[13]

The subcommittee's perceptions of Vietnamese political immaturity also rested upon assumptions of Vietnam as an inferior society, although it emerged more elliptically in their deliberations. In a discussion of Vietnam's "backward political development," Melvin Knight told subcommittee members "it was doubtful whether the Annamites . . . would have been any better off had the French not taken them in hand." Vandenbosch called French rule the "glue" that held Vietnam together, adding "it would not be possible to conduct any government in this area" without it. The subcommittee's contemptuous perceptions of Vietnamese nationalism did not reassure them that Vietnam was capable of self-government. Members of the sub-committee expressed sympathy with the frustrations that had produced nationalist sentiment in Vietnam, as they believed French colonial policy had done little to advance Vietnamese political or socioeconomic welfare. But their unfavorable impressions of nationalist politics reinforced their sense that the Vietnamese lacked the abilities necessary to immediately govern themselves. As Vandenbosch told the sub-committee, the nationalist movement was "limited" to a small number of educated elites who were unable to win the support of the peasant masses.[14]

The idea that indigenous political traditions or abilities might permit the Vietnamese to govern themselves in the postwar period was almost inconceivable to the members of the subcommittee as a revealing exchange between Melvin Knight and the subcommittee chair, Isaiah Bowman, illustrates. Despite his derisive portrait of Vietnamese political culture, Knight somewhat timorously suggested that the Vietnamese might be capable of self-government without external direction. Bowman, with the apparent assent of the committee, immediately pressed Knight to elaborate. Did Knight really believe the chances of self-government in Vietnam were good? When Knight replied "it would be a good bet," Bowman questioned him further. Under Bowman's continuing pressure, Knight began to back away from his initial assertion, suggesting "it was probably difficult for an old culture to be reformed along modern lines." But he added the "case was still open as to whether it was governable." Not satisfied, Bowman pressed him again. Finally, Knight conceded "while at some future time Indo-China might be made self-governing" that time had not yet arrived.[15]

There was considerable debate and disagreement, however, over the appropriate policy to promote Vietnam's eventual movement toward independence, with advocates of international trusteeship pitted against supporters of a vaguer international accountability for the restoration of some form of French colonial rule. A minority of the subcommittee embraced President Roosevelt's proposal for international trusteeship in "recognition of the failure of France to provide adequately for the welfare of the native population." A majority of the subcommittee members raised a number of objections to international trusteeship for Indochina. Several members questioned the efficacy of employing an international administrative agency to affect reform in indigenous society. Trusteeship, one member argued, would be "experimental in character and of doubtful effectiveness." Although French administration "was maintained at a low level of competence," he continued, "the long experience of the French in the colony could be utilized to good advantage during the period of postwar development." Several members also asked how France could be required to relinquish its sovereignty over Indochina when the British and the Dutch were likely to maintain their colonies in Southeast Asia. Advocates of trusteeship argued that France was a special case as it had not been able to protect itself and its colonies at the outset of the war. Moreover, they suggested, "the difference of physical strength was so great between France on the one hand and Great Britain on the other" that France could only retake Indochina with the assistance of allied military forces and would thus be bound by the wishes of the other powers.[16]

While the uncertainties of the wartime situation prompted it to reject the form of international trusteeship, the subcommittee remained committed to the goals of reforming French colonial practices and preparing the Vietnamese for eventual self-government. In place of trusteeship, the majority of the subcommittee supported a combination of incentives and constraints aimed at placing postwar French colonial rule under "international accountability." Confident in the powers of international suasion, they believed the establishment of a regional commission in Southeast Asia, a colonial charter for Vietnam and the preparation of annual reports by the French would reform French colonial practices in Indochina and hasten the emergence of a self-governing Vietnamese state in a more realistic manner than the "idealism" of international trusteeship.[17]

More important than the debates over the mechanisms by which to guide Indochina toward postwar independence, however, were the common assumptions that informed proposals for trusteeship and commissions, charters and reports. Both proposals shared Franklin Roosevelt's unwavering belief in the applicability of American political values and institutions for organizing the postwar Vietnamese state and tutoring the Vietnamese in principles of self-government as well as the moderation Roosevelt believed had marked America's successful policy in the Philippines. Advocates within the State Department for international trusteeship wholly reflected this Rooseveltian vision. The fullest extant outline of American plans for trusteeship in Indochina, contained in a March 1944 working paper drafted mainly by the Division of Southwest Pacific Affairs, went far beyond Roosevelt's somewhat cryptic vision of how trusteeship would actually work. Its calls for the establishment of an executive, a legislative and a judicial branch under joint control of the Vietnamese and international trustees; for the creation of a civil service board to oversee training in local and national governmental affairs; for immediate voting rights for indigenous peoples; and for a constitutional convention demonstrate the depth of American faith in the cross-cultural transfer of its political institutions. The twenty year period of trusteeship before granting Vietnam full independence recommended in the working paper also suggests the persistence of the gradualist Philippine model in shaping State Department policy toward Indochina.[18]

But the combination of a regional commission, colonial charter and annual reports that increasingly dominated State Department planning for postwar Indochina also firmly rested upon the use of American models to slowly correct the perceived weaknesses in French colonialism and Vietnamese society. Discussion of the ways in which the colonial charter and annual reports would serve as conditions for a return of French colonial rule most fully reflected the American vision of political and economic liberalization in Vietnam. State Department planners suggested that the French be asked to promise to establish local and national representative institutions, provide for indigenous suffrage, expand educational and occupational opportunities and develop local industries. The shared assumptions joining Roosevelt's advocacy of trusteeship and the deliberations of State Department planners were also fully reflected in American reporting on Vietnam from southern China and the recommendations of field officers concerning Vietnam's future development.[19]

"Subservient Annamites": Wartime American Reporting on Vietnam from Southern China

In a December 1942 cable to Washington, the American Ambassador to China Clarence E. Gauss reported that he had seen a letter protesting the arrest by Chinese authorities of a Vietnamese nationalist leader. A year would pass before Gauss and his embassy staff realized whom the Chinese had arrested. Gauss relayed a letter in a December 1943 dispatch to the State Department from the Central Committee of the Indochina Section of the International Anti-Aggression Association. The letter asked Gauss for assistance in the "immediate and unconditional" release of "Hu Chih-minh . . . in order that he may lead the members of the Association in activities against the Japanese." The "Annamite" in question, Gauss told the department, "was apparently" the same person whose arrest he had reported the previous December.[20]

Gauss's December 1943 dispatch, the first mention by any US policy maker of Ho Chi Minh, reveals the limitations on American wartime reporting on Vietnam and its dismissive perceptions of the Vietnamese. The embassy staff did make inquiries into the reasons for Ho's continued detention, apparently unaware he had been released by the Chinese some four months earlier. But the name Ho Chi Minh meant nothing to Gauss and the embassy's political officers. Nor did Gauss see the need to reply to the "Annamite organization" or further investigate its activities. The French delegation at Chungking, who were a primary source of information about the Vietnamese for American officials in southern China, had assured him it "was of little importance," probably one of the "Annamite organizations under the auspices of the

Kuomintang" representing nothing "more than an attempt by the Chinese to make a show of their friendly feelings for subject peoples in Asia."[21]

Gauss and the US Embassy in Chungking were one of several critical sources of American political reporting on Vietnam from wartime China. While Indochina remained occupied by the Japanese, American diplomatic, military and intelligence personnel responsible for following developments in Vietnam did so largely from Chungking or Kunming in southern China. Planning documents from the Office of Strategic Services' Morale Operations (MO), designed to discredit the Japanese and disseminate pro-American propaganda to the Vietnamese, offer one important and typical example of appraisals from the field of Vietnamese society and its perceived receptivity to American models. Because MO planners saw their task as an extension of psychological warfare, they sought to identify what they termed "Annamite mentality." The starting point for these analyses was the assumption that "Annamite reasoning" was fundamentally different than "our own," reflecting the division between Western and Asian thought processes inherent in the prevailing beliefs in racialized cultural hierarchies. As one member of the MO planning team for Indochina remarked: "The stimuli from . . . reality can and do produce stereotypes in the minds of the natives quite different from those produced in our own minds."[22]

In the discussions of the Vietnamese role in American psychological warfare strategies by MO planners, the characteristics most commonly ascribed to the "Annamite mind" were almost always negative and condescending. One MO report noted, it was "futile" to attempt to win over the Vietnamese to the allied cause by "propagandizing" them that a Japanese defeat would ultimately benefit Vietnam as it was "part of the fundamental psychology of Annamites to be interested only in ventures which promise a quick turnover." Reports that presented the "individual Annamite" as "a rather vain person" and urged MO campaigns to "[f]latter the pride of the Annamites by telling them that without their co-operation the Japs would not be able to do a thing" were lauded by MO senior planners as raising "an excellent, and well-taken, point."[23]

Another MO planning document suggested that the "subservience" and "mercenary proclivities" inherent in Vietnamese society were barriers to the successful establishment of an indigenous underground organization:

> The Annamites have been a subject race for so many years, by the French, and the Chinese before them, that they have no organizing ability or initiative . . . They are quite incapable of developing an organization of any kind, certainly not an underground. Being suspicious of each other and practicing trickery among themselves, any organization they have ever attempted to create has always broken down from the incapacity of its members to pull together. An underground organization would fall apart before it ever got going . . . The mercenary proclivities of the Annamites is another hindrance to the development of a successful underground. The Annamites will do anything for money but they cannot be expected to take risks from ideological motives.[24]

Propaganda leaflets were potentially more effective strategies, MO planners argued, because "Annamites love to talk," "enjoy lengthy discourses or lectures," and responded best to "emphatic" or "exaggerated words which qualify force."[25]

These deprecatory images of Vietnamese society also shaped the assertions of MO planners that Vietnam would be highly receptive to American direction. "The Annamites are used to obeying," one report argued. "Instructions, advice, pleas or recommendations coming from Americans would be effective because they are authoritative. The Annamites recognize authority." Another report suggested that because the "Annamites are very much impressed by physical strength, courage and skill," they particularly enjoyed American films about "cowboys" and "test pilots." The report also stressed "they are *very much impressed by mechanical perfection* [emphasis in original], such as frigidaires, reconditioning units, guns, plants, etc., and for them the word 'American' is synonymous with perfection in all that is modern industry."[26]

In late summer of 1944, as Americans in southern China began to encounter for the first time representatives of the Viet Minh, the organizational vehicle through which Ho Chi Minh and the Vietnamese communists would seize power in Vietnam in August 1945, their perceptions remained very unfavorable. A Viet Minh delegation in Kunming met with American officials in August and September 1944 and provided the basis for the first American reports on the existence of the Viet Minh, its organizational structure and its program for national independence. Their American audience was unimpressed with what it learned. William Powell, the representative of the Office of War Information in Kunming, reported on several meetings with the Viet Minh and called them "rather naïve politically" and "not too well organized." Commenting on the history of Vietnamese anticolonialism that representatives of the Viet Minh had given him along with appeals for American assistance, Powell patronizingly remarked:

> The whole document . . . certainly is a touching appeal. Any coherent appeal from an oppressed people who wish to rule themselves is touching. However, from conversations with these leaders themselves, and with well-informed foreigners here, I think there is little doubt but what they are not ready for complete independence. They've had little experience in modern government . . . and probably will require quite a bit of tutelage before they can completely run their country themselves in as responsible a manner as a modern post-war government must be run.[27]

William Langdon, the US consul at Kunming, was even more critical of the Vietnamese, dismissing the Viet Minh as a group of "no real importance in the Indochina questions" after his own meeting with their representatives in September 1944. Langdon reported to Washington that they "lacked the spirit and aggressiveness one would expect of revolutionaries" and "did not impress [him] as having proper knowledge of the world or a sufficient grasp of the international situation." They were not, he argued, "far enough advanced politically to maintain a stable society or familiar enough with administration, jurisprudence, science, industry, finance, communications operation, and commerce to run a state on modern lines."[28] The tenor of Langdon's recommendations, which closely followed diplomats in Washington who argued for a conditional restoration of French rule in Vietnam, fully reflected the prevailing American assumptions of French colonial failure, Vietnamese inadequacies and the promise of American models. While he lauded trusteeship as "ideal at this stage for Indochina," he questioned if it was "within the realm of practical politics" as "it would be most certain to be opposed and obstructed" by France and Great Britain. The "only logical proposition for Indo-China," Langdon argued, was a period of tutelage under continued French rule. Reflecting American confidence in its abilities to reform both French colonialism and Vietnamese society, Langdon suggested the "commanding position" of the United States ought to make it possible to impose "certain conditions" on the French "to obtain for Annamites some substantial political rights." The American ambassador in Chunking Clarence Gauss shared Langdon's views, telling Washington the time had come "to formulate a clear and definite policy" for the making of postcolonial Vietnam.[29]

With Franklin Roosevelt's death in April 1945 came the end of the US advocacy of international trusteeship in Vietnam. When Harry Truman moved into the Oval Office, he undoubtedly knew little, if anything, of American postwar planning on Vietnam. Confronted by a host of more pressing issues, Truman only nominally oversaw two decisions that severely limited US ability to influence immediate postwar developments in Vietnam. In May, Truman offered no opposition to State Department assurances to France that the United States recognized French sovereignty over Indochina. In July, at the Potsdam Conference, Truman endorsed the expansion of the British-led Southeast Asia Command (SEAC)'s borders. Northern Vietnam remained in the American dominated China theater, but Vietnamese territory south of the sixteenth parallel became the responsibility of SEAC that was sympathetic to French efforts to regain control of Indochina in the postwar period. By early September, French troops had joined British forces in occupying Saigon and accepting the surrender of Japan.

Despite the US decision to move away from trusteeship, a number of contemporary French and British observers viewed US support for the French return to Indochina with caution, remaining uneasy about future American intentions in Vietnam. While the European powers were right to be skeptical of a fundamental transformation in US thinking about Vietnam, their lingering suspicions should not obscure the critical commonalities that united American and European perceptions toward Vietnam. Much of the existing scholarship on trusteeship minimizes or ignores those similarities. Along with viewing trusteeship as Roosevelt's personal crusade, these works often ruefully render it as a lost opportunity for acting on US historical identification with the principle of self-determination.[30] The few departures from this tack, which depict trusteeship as an example of a peculiarly American manifestation of empire, also remain bounded by an exceptionalist explanatory framework for wartime US policy in Vietnam.[31] But whether mourning the declension of US anticolonial ideals or recovering a suppressed empire with uniquely American values and forms, these works emphasize essential US differences from European colonial norms and the historical novelty of an American approach to colonialism. Like the policy makers they analyze, they do not pause to critically interrogate the contradictions in US self-conceptions as an anticolonial power. Nor do they explore the revealing ways in which American discourse on colonized peoples closely followed that of most European powers.

The central place of time in American thinking about trusteeship for Vietnam is particularly revealing of the shared Euro-American norms out of which US policy arose as well as how it would complicate relations with the French and the Vietnamese after 1945. Whether posed as the almost half-century of US colonial rule in the Philippines or the quarter-century of trusteeship envisioned for Vietnam, the virtually unanimous perception among wartime American policy makers of the necessity for an exceedingly long period of tutelage in US political, social, and cultural models signaled an underlying certainty of the vast chasm that separated the stasis of backward Vietnam from the dynamism of the United States. The conscious ordering of time in plans for trusteeship in Vietnam – premised on a gradual, unilinear, and progressive path to human development – sought to provide a temporal framework to guide the Vietnamese toward political and social change in the American image. By attempting to engineer the processes of change in Vietnam through the manipulation of the meaning and passage of time, trusteeship represented a variation, rather than a sharp departure, from the hierarchical conceptions of racial difference and the exercise of power at the heart of European colonialism.[32] In this sense, European suspicions about US intentions in Vietnam might be seen not so much as fears that a crusading US anticolonialism sought to overturn the colonial order but as a more nationalistic reaction against the emergence of a powerful rival who sought to challenge Europeans' own efforts to control colonial time and space.

Significantly, however, the temporal order embedded in trusteeship was also an effort to retard the passage of time, indicating doubts that lurked beneath the supreme confidence through which American and Europeans appeared to approach the colonial project. The compression of time was an essential element in the dual character of the conceptions of modernity that animated Euro-American understandings of their own societies and those they encountered in the colonized world. On one hand, the embrace of modernity reflected assurance of the universal and enduring virtues of contemporary Western society. But the telescoping of time, an inevitable result of the competitive and speculative rhythms of capitalism that accompanied the rise of modernity, also produced an overwhelming fear of fragmentation, transience, and chaotic change.[33] This prevailing sensibility was reinforced for both American and European policy makers of the World War II era, whose historical experience was shaped by two world wars, the rise of fascism, and the worldwide economic depression.

The palpable doubts and fears over what the uncontrolled acceleration of time could produce framed the temporal order that informed US plans for trusteeship in Vietnam. The dislocations of World War II quickened the pace toward decolonization in Vietnam and much of the colonized world, producing a sense among both the colonizers and the colonized of time rushing forward. For both the French and the Americans, the quickening pace of change was viewed with alarm. If the French would have preferred to arrest completely the temporal movement toward decolonization, US plans for trusteeship, with the twenty-year timetable for Vietnamese independence, were also profoundly conservative. Emblematic of the fears upon which the faith in modernity rested, trusteeship aimed to retard the passage of time in order to wrest control over temporality and reassert the centrality of rational, orderly, and gradually progressive paths to Vietnam's future development.

With the movement away from trusteeship, and the related notions of colonial commissions and charters, Americans abandoned their efforts to manipulate so closely the processes of change in Vietnam. Moreover, the accelerating movement toward decolonization in Vietnam made an extended period of tutelage in advance of independence moot. Ironically, the Vietnamese revolutionaries who joined Ho Chi Minh in proclaiming Vietnam free of French colonial rule in 1945 enthusiastically embraced the modernist conception of quickening time. But the American vision of postcolonial Vietnam that emerged during the World War II period remained an essential starting point for US attitudes toward Vietnam in the postwar period.

Like their counterparts during World War II, America policy makers after 1945 seldom paused to explicate the premises that lay behind their perceptions of the Vietnamese and the role they believed US models should play in the construction of a new political community in Vietnam. Nor were these ideas ever fundamentally challenged. America continued to classify and define the Vietnamese in a way that signaled US power and superiority. At the same time, the growing American sense of mission to remake Vietnamese society in its own image continued to join US policy in Vietnam to the broader Euro-American project to transform the immutable, stagnant, and primitive "oriental."

As the Cold War came to dominate American policy, the idiom of modernization rather than cultural hierarchies informed US discourse toward the postcolonial world, including Vietnam. In its conceptual underpinnings, however, modernization theory reflected many of the central assumptions of the racialized cultural hierarchies that had shaped US efforts to identify and manipulate social change in non-Western societies throughout the century, including a sharp distinction between the "backward" and the "modern" and the insistence that "stagnant societies" ought to move in a gradual, linear path toward the universal evolutionary endpoint represented by the United States.[34]

The significance of these ideas in mediating and framing the Cold War imperatives that brought Vietnam to a central position for US foreign policy in the 1960s is perhaps best revealed in Lyndon Johnson's thinking about Vietnam at the time of his decision to send US ground troops to South Vietnam. Johnson's attitude toward the Vietnamese was derisive, as his often-expressed sense of North Vietnam as a "piss-ant" nation or "a raggedy-ass little fourth-rate country" suggests.[35] But for Johnson, the escalating war in Vietnam held meanings beyond the need for Soviet containment. In a key speech on Vietnam delivered at Johns Hopkins University in April 1965, Johnson coupled his expression of US resolve against communism with an offer of $1 billion to support an immense project under the auspices of the United Nations to build dams along the Mekong River in Thailand, Laos, Cambodia and Vietnam to foster regional economic development, a project Johnson believed could include Ho Chi Minh's government. "The vast Mekong River," Johnson said in the speech, "can provide food and water and power on a scale to dwarf even our own TVA."[36]

The connection Johnson made to the New Deal Tennessee Valley Authority, a project one scholar of Johnson's policy in Vietnam has aptly termed the internal colonization of a backward America, suggests that the interconnections between US models of development and their universal applicability continued to exert a powerful hold on America's imagined Vietnam.[37] As Johnson said after the speech, "I want to leave the footprints of America on Vietnam. I want them to say when the Americans come, this is what they leave – schools, not long cigars. We're going to turn the Mekong into a Tennessee Valley... Old Ho can't turn me down."[38]

NOTES

1   For the existing scholarship on Roosevelt's plans for trusteeship in Indochina, see Lloyd Gardner, *Approaching Dien Bien Phu* (New York: W.W. Norton & Company, 1988): 21–53; Gary R. Hess, "Franklin Roosevelt and Indochina," *Journal of American History* 59.2 (September 1972): 353–68; Hess, *The United States' Emergence as a Southeast Asian Power, 1940–1950* (New York: Columbia University Press, 1987): 47–158; Walter LaFeber, "Roosevelt, Churchill and Indochina: 1942–1945," *American Historical Review* 80.5 (December 1975): 1277–95; and Christopher Thorne, "Indochina and Anglo-American Relations, 1942–1945," *Pacific Historical Review* 45.1 (February 1976): 73–96.

2   The most important analysis of the place of racialized cultural hierarchies in American thinking is George W. Stocking, Jr., *Victorian Anthropology* (New York: Free Press, 1987).

3   Edward W. Said, *Orientalism* (New York: Vintage, 1979); and Said, *Culture and Imperialism* (New York: Alfred A. Knopf, 1993).

4   Minutes of the Pacific War Council, July 21 1943, Folder: "Naval Aide's Files, Pacific War #2," Box 168, Map Room File, Franklin D. Roosevelt Papers as President, 1941–1945, Franklin D. Roosevelt Library, Hyde Park, New York.

5   Elliott Roosevelt, *As He Saw It* (New York: Duell Sloan and Pearce, 1946): 115; Roosevelt–Stalin–Churchill Meeting, November 28 1943, *Foreign Relations of the United States [FRUS]: The Conferences at Cairo and Tehran, 1943* (Washington, DC: US Government Printing Office, 1961): 485.

6   Minutes of the Pacific War Council, May 23 1942. The recollections of participants in the May 1954 Princeton Seminar, which gathered together wartime and Cold War policy makers, also suggest that Roosevelt's critique of French rule in Vietnam was less an attack on colonialism than on France's inadequacies as a colonial power. See Transcript of May 15 1954, Folder Title: "Reading Copy III: Princeton Seminars May 15–16, 1954 (Folder 2)," Box 84, Papers of Dean Acheson, Harry S. Truman Library, Independence, Missouri: Reel 5, Track 1, Page 8.

7   Minutes of the Pacific War Council, March 17 1943. See also Edward R. Stettinius, Jr., *Roosevelt and the Russians* (Garden City: Doubleday and Company, Inc., 1949): 237; and Elliott Roosevelt, *As He Saw It*: 115, 165, 251.

8   Roosevelt–Stalin Meeting, February 8 1945, *FRUS: The Conferences at Malta and Yalta, 1945* (Washington, DC: US Government Printing Office, 1955): 770.

9   Roosevelt–Stalin Meeting, November 28 1943, *FRUS: The Conferences at Cairo and Tehran, 1943*: 485.

10   Glenn Anthony May, *Social Engineering in the Philippines: The Aims, Execution and Impact of American Colonial Policy, 1900–1913* (Westport: Greenwood Press, 1980): xvii.

11   Vincete L. Rafael, "White Love: Surveillance and Nationalist Resistance in the US Colonization of the Philippines" in *Cultures of United States Imperialism*, edited by Amy Kaplan and Donald E. Pease (Durham: Duke University Press, 1993): 216. See also Michael Salman, "The United States and the End of Slavery in the Philippines,

1898–1914: A Study of Imperialism, Ideology and Nationalism (Ph.D. diss., Stanford University, 1993): 605–17.

12   Biographical information on Kenneth P. Landon is contained in *Biographic Register of the Department of State: September 1, 1944* (Washington, DC: US Government Printing Office, n.d.): 125. Landon's wife, Margaret, is the author of *Anna and the King*, which served as the basis of the Broadway musical "The King and I." Amry Vandenbosch's best known work was *The Dutch East Indies: Its Government, Problems and Politics* (1933). Melvin King's critiques of French colonialism emerge in his *Morocco as a French Economic Venture* (1937). The geographer Isaiah Bowman's writings on Africa reflected the framework of racialized cultural hierarchies that animated American perceptions of Vietnam; on Bowman see Thomas Borstelmann, *Apartheid's Reluctant Uncle: The United States and Southern Africa in the Early Cold War* (New York: Oxford University Press, 1993): 11.

13   T Minutes, 56, November 11 1943; T Minutes 55, November 5 1943; Indochina: Political and Economic Problems (T-398); Subcommittee on Territorial Problems, Division of Political Studies, Box 59, Records of the Advisory Committee on Post-War Foreign Policy (Harley Notter Files, 1939–45), Record Group 59, National Archives, Washington, DC.

14   T Minutes 56, November 11 1943; T Minutes 55, November 5 1943.

15   T Minutes 56, November 11 1943. Prevailing skepticism of Vietnamese ability to immediately undertake self-government is also reflected in a November 2 1943 memo from John Carter Vincent, Assistant Chief of the Division of Far East Affairs, to Assistant Secretary of State Berle. Vincent argued that the Vietnamese were "capable of self-government" only after a post-war administration had trained them to assume "the responsibilities of self-government." The memo was initialed by Joseph W. Ballantine, Chief of the Division of Far Eastern Affairs and a member of the subcommittee. See Memo from Vincent to Berle, November 2 1943, *FRUS: 1943 China* (Washington, DC: US Government Printing Office, 1957): 886.

16   Indo-China: Political and Economic Factors (T-398), November 2 1943; T Minutes 56, November 11 1943.

17   Indo-China: Political and Economic Factors (T-398), November 2 1943.

18   "Draft Outline of an International Trusteeship Government for Indochina," CAC-114, March 13 1944, Box 109, Notter Files.

19   CAC Document 89, March 1 1944, Box 109; T Minutes 56, November 11 1943, Notter Files.

20   Gauss to Secretary of State, December 31 1942, 851G.00/81 and Gauss to Secretary of State, December 23 1943, 851G.00/95, Box 5065, State Department Decimal Files, Record Group 59.

21   Gauss to Secretary of State, December 23 1943, 851G.00/95.

22   "Outline of MO Objectives and Operations in Indo-China," n.d.; "Indo-China MO Mission," October 30 1943; "Indo-China-MO Unit," December 13 1943, Folder #1864, Box #138, Entry #139, Records of the Office of Strategic Services, Record Group 226, National Archives.

23   Memo from R. P. Leonard to Harley C. Stevens, May 16 1944; "Propaganda and the War in Indo-China," n.d.; "Comments re Memorandum of Mr. Leonard," May 23 1944; Memo from Harold C. Faxon to Betty MacDonald, November 17 1944, Folder #1863, Box #138, Entry #139, Record Group 226.

24   "Determining a Policy for MO Operations in Indochina," n.d., Folder #1863, Box #138, Entry #139, Record Group 226.

25   "Suggestions for Leaflets to French Indo China," December 7 1944, Folder # 1863, Box #138, Entry #139, Record Group 226.

26   "Suggestions for Leaflets."

27   "Political Conditions in Indo-China," William J. Powell, OWI Air Liaison, Kunming, August 28 1944, 851G.00/9–944, Folder 273, Box 35, Entry 35, Record Group 226.

28   Langdon to Secretary of State, September 9 1944, 851G.00/9–944; Memorandum of Conversation, September 9 1944, 851G.00/9–944; Langdon to Secretary of State, September 20 1944, 851G.00/9–2044.

29   "Indo-China Question," William R. Langdon, August 3 1944, 851G.00/8–344; Gauss to Secretary of State, July 26 1944, 851G.00/7–2644.

30   Robert J. McMahon has most recently made this argument in his *The Limits of Empire: The United States and Southeast Asia since World War II* (New York: Columbia University Press, 1999), 9–13, 28, but it is more fully developed in Hess, *United States' Emergence*, 47–158. Similar interpretations emerge in two broader accounts of US wartime attitudes toward decolonization; see Warren F. Kimball " 'In Search of Monsters to Destroy': Roosevelt and Colonialism," in his *The Juggler: Franklin Roosevelt as Wartime Statesman* (Princeton: Princeton University Press, 1991): 127–57, and Wm. Roger Louis, *Imperialism at Bay: The United States and the Decolonization of the British Empire, 1941–1945* (Oxford: Oxford University Press, 1977).

31   See, for example, LaFeber, "Roosevelt, Churchill, and Indochina."

32   My discussion of time as a critical element for the exercise of power is shaped by Johannes Fabian, *Time and the Other: How Anthropology Makes Its Object* (New York: Columbia University Press, 1983); Pierre Bourdieu, *Outline of a Theory of Practice* (Cambridge: Cambridge University Press, 1977): 159–97, and Arjun Appadurai, *Modernity at Large: Cultural Dimensions of Globalization* (Minneapolis: University of Minnesota Press, 1996): 66–85 and 178–99.

33   My discussion on the interrelationship of modernity and the telescoping of time draws on David Harvey, *The Condition of Postmodernity* (Cambridge: Blackwell, 1990), 201–83, and more broadly, Karl Polanyi, *The Great Transformation* (Boston: Beacon Press, 1943).

34   The best-known proponent of modernization theory is Walt Rostow, from whose work these commonalties are drawn; see Rostow, *The Stages of Economic Growth: A Non-Communist Manifesto* (Cambridge: Cambridge University Press, 1960). For a thoughtful discussion of modernization theory and its relationship to Kennedy policy toward Latin America, see Michael E. Latham, "Ideology, Social Science, and Destiny: Modernization and the Kennedy-Era Alliance for Progress," *Diplomatic History* 22.3 (Spring 1988): 199–229.

35   David Halberstam, *The Best and the Brightest* (New York: Random House, 1972), 512, 564.

36   Lyndon Baines Johnson, speech of April 7 1965, reprinted in US Senate, Committee on Foreign Relations, *Background Information Relating to Southeast Asia and Vietnam*, 90th Cong., 2nd sess. (Washington: DC: US Government Printing Office), 148–53.

37   My reading of the Johns Hopkins speech and the notion of internal colonization relies on a wonderful essay by Lloyd Gardner; see his "From the Colorado to the Mekong," in *Vietnam: The Early Decisions*, edited by Lloyd C. Gardner and Ted Gittinger (Austin: University of Texas Press, 1997): 37–57, and his *Pay Any Price: Lyndon Johnson and the Wars for Vietnam* (Chicago: Ivan R. Dee, 1995).

38   Doris Kearns Goodwin, *Lyndon Johnson and the American Dream* (New York: Harper and Row, 1976): 267, and Stanley Karnow, *Vietnam: A History* (New York: Viking Press, 1983): 416, cited in Gardner, "For the Colorado": 53.

CHAPTER NINE

Dreaming Different Dreams: The United States and the Army of the Republic of Vietnam

ROBERT K. BRIGHAM

Introduction

Nearly thirty years after the end of the Vietnam War, much of that conflict remains an enigma to scholars, military leaders, and policy makers. Perhaps one of the most perplexing issues is why Vietnamese Communist forces seemed to out perform their counterparts in the South Vietnamese army, the Army of the Republic of Vietnam (ARVN). From its inception in the 1950s, until its inglorious defeat on April 30, 1975, the ARVN was constantly criticized by friend and foe alike. To the Communists, the ARVN was the puppet army of foreigners, a thinly-veiled shield to disguise US intervention. Ironically, the ARVN also suffered at the hands of its allies. Most US reports conclude that the ARVN was a "paper tiger," riddled by corruption, inefficiency, and a lack of patriotism.[1] "They didn't want to fight," one former US Marine recently complained, "the average ARVN soldier lacked courage and ran away from contact with the Communists."[2] These sentiments are also reflected in scores of "After Action Reports" written by US military advisors during the war. Several contend that the ARVN "lacked the willingness to engage the enemy fully on the field of combat."[3] According to journalist Neal Sheehan, the ARVN indeed had an "institutionalized unwillingness to fight."[4]

Still, there are others who suggest that we know so little about the ARVN and the people they were fighting for that it may be too early to draw such conclusions. According to historian George C. Herring, the South Vietnamese have been conspicuously absent in most histories of the war.[5] Indeed, in our collective rush to find explanations for the US failure in Vietnam, we may have accepted negative stereotypes of the ARVN that do not fully explain the conduct and outcome of the war. It has been too easy to blame the ARVN for the Communist victory in Vietnam, and, therefore, US policy makers have ignored some of the war's basic lessons. Most US studies on the war claim that it was lost because "our Vietnamese" were somehow culturally or socially inferior to the Communists. With or without a strong ally, however, it is likely the US nation-building effort in Vietnam would have met the same fate. Instead of a critical post-war examination of US policy in Southeast Asia during the Cold War, most in the West simply blamed the ARVN and its government in Saigon for the ignominious defeat.

This essay, utilizing the latest Vietnamese-language sources and interviews with former ARVN soldiers in the United States and in Vietnam, is one attempt to show a fuller history of the war by examining South Vietnamese morale and motivation. I argue essentially that the ARVN's performance was in part the result of poor morale caused by inadequate pay, food, and housing, an arbitrary leave and rotation system, and a refractory conscription policy. Perhaps this is why the ARVN faired so poorly against its Communist adversaries in Vietnam despite overwhelming technological superiority. Simply put, the daily concerns of the ARVN infantry soldier were not met, nor were the government's policies sympathetic to the life of a Vietnamese peasant. The result was a high desertion rate, low morale, and misunderstanding between the ARVN and its American allies. "It was as if we and the Americans were sleeping in the same bed," reported an ARVN infantry soldier, "but we were dreaming different dreams."[6]

According to most military experts, an army's morale is the key to victory. Napoleon believed that "morale is to the physical as three is to one." During the Second World War, Great Britain's General Bernard Montgomery warned, "We must be very careful what we do with British infantry. Their fighting spirit is based largely on morale and regimental esprit de corps. On no account must anyone tamper with this."[7] Carl Von Clausewitz, one of the modern world's most influential military thinkers, suggested that morale was the responsibility of good leaders.[8] West Point cadets are taught today that leadership is the key to accomplishing tough missions. A good leader respected and trusted by the troops, can overcome any "quality of life" issue. He can lead them into attack under hostile fire where the "quality of life" is not so great. Still, few can doubt that troop morale can also be tied to a soldier's basic needs: housing; pay; food; extended leaves; and a fair conscription and rotation policy.[9] For many ARVN enlisted men, poor leadership and an ineffective government in Saigon forced them to take responsibility for their basic requirements and this may have distracted them from their assigned missions.

The ARVN infantry soldier constantly complained about "quality of life" requirements, especially in relationship to his American counterparts. "There were serious shortcomings in some very fundamental areas of life," complained Nguyen Hue, an ARVN infantry soldier from II Corps.[10] Another ARVN captain, Tram Buu, described the problem this way:

> US soldiers are leaving, and you want the Vietnamese soldiers to take their place. But look at the US soldier: he is well-paid, well-fed, well-supported, gets good housing, doesn't have to worry about the safety of his wife and family while he's away, gets R & R trips and sometimes a trip home, and he can leave for good in one year. The average ARVN soldier is not well-supported, makes very little money, and may live in squalor

even when he is on leave, and knows he will be in the army for many years to come. Look at the soldiers' housing . . . pitiful.[11]

Many American officers who served in Vietnam thought that the ARVN spent too much time complaining about "quality of life issues," and not enough time fighting the Communists to ensure that South Vietnam survived. "The real problem in Vietnam was not whether the ARVN soldier had enough to eat and decent housing" explained one former US Army Colonel, "but whether they were willing to fight to ensure that all South Vietnamese had enough to eat and decent housing . . . that was the task in Vietnam."[12] Still, most ARVN enlisted men thought these quality of life issues were important to their performance on the battlefield and to morale. In any event, problems with essential requirements translated into unusually high ARVN desertion rates. According to one official US report, the ARVN desertion rate for 1968 was an average of 17.7 per one thousand assigned.[13] If these figures are accurate, ARVN desertion rates are among the highest in the history of modern warfare.

Desertion

Military historians often use desertion rates to determine an army's effectiveness and morale. In Vietnam, however, the desertion rate among the ARVN is one of the war's most misleading statistics. According to a report issued by Brigadier General John W. Barnes, the Deputy Senior Advisor in II Corps, there were often extenuating circumstances that led ARVN soldiers to desert. General Barnes protested that the average ARVN soldier faced severe shortages and inadequacies in housing. There was also insufficient transportation for ARVN soldiers going on leave and returning to duty. Finally, he found that the ARVN leave system did not match the reality of life in Vietnam. The official policy permitted the ARVN infantry soldier only fifteen days of leave per year, and required that these be taken in two seven to eight day periods. This hardly met the needs of many peasants who had to return to their families and villages to help harvest crops for the year.[14] Furthermore, contact with family members was a constant problem facing the ARVN soldier. "We never got mail when we were away from our home province," complained an ARVN enlisted man, "in two years, I only received one letter from my wife."[15]

In 1968, the US Army Advisory Group conducted a survey of ARVN enlisted men to surface the contributing factors that led to such high desertion rates. Overwhelmingly, ARVN infantry soldiers pointed to the lack of contact with their families, prolonged operations away from the home base, poor pay distribution, unsatisfactory housing, and unrewarded service as the main causes for leaving their unit.[16] According to one official State Department report, American advisors clearly understood that many of the peasants conscripted into the armed services left routinely to "return to their families for brief visits, especially during peak periods of farming activity, and later return to their original units or other units nearby."[17]

An official US military study completed in 1971 confirms the State Department summary. In a special Rand Report entitled, "A People's Army For South Vietnam:

A Vietnamese Solution," Brian Jenkins argued that the ARVN deployment policy ran counter to the character and scope of its mission. Furthermore, Jenkins suggested that a new deployment strategy would help with desertions. He wrote:

> Almost one-half of South Vietnam's able-bodied men are already soldiers, not counting those who serve part-time in the People's Self-Defense Force. Because of the high casualty rate and even higher desertion rate, the annual net loss to the armed forces exceeds the potential influx of young men who reach draft age each year. The armed forces maintain their present size only by not allowing the release of any soldiers and by dipping deeper into the manpower pool of 18 to 38 year olds who have not already served ... desertion rate of Regional Forces who serve in their home provinces is considerably lower than that of the regular army, and the desertion rate of Popular Forces who serve in their own villages, is lower yet.[18]

Jenkins' primary concern was, of course, that ARVN deployment and desertions had a negative impact on manpower utilization, morale, and effectiveness. Surprisingly, his concerns are unfounded if we examine the way desertion statistics were compiled in Saigon.

Beginning in 1957, the ARVN command and the Saigon government listed as a deserter any infantry soldier who failed to answer the morning muster. Using this standard, Saigon routinely listed annual desertion figures at over 100,000. This was a highly unusual practice and probably added to the public relations and morale problems the ARVN faced. Few armies in history have used such stringent rules for desertion. In sharp contrast, the US Military Assistance Command-Vietnam (MACV) listed any US soldier failing to answer the morning muster as Absent Over Leave (AOL) or Absent Without Leave (AWOL). Furthermore, as reported above, a large number of the Vietnamese deserters soon returned to their units.[19] Many soldiers who did not return to their units were later found serving in another unit closer to home. According to one unofficial survey, over sixty percent of ARVN infantry soldiers listed as deserters in 1967 were actually serving with other units closer to their villages.[20] While exact figures are not available, US military advisors estimated that only 20 to 30 percent of the total listed as deserters were actual deserters.[21] "We often left our units to go home to take care of sick relatives ... only to return to a unit nearby," explained one ARVN infantry soldier after the war. According to Phan Thuy, an ARVN artillery expert in I Corps, "I did whatever I could to be near my family. I always returned to the fighting, but closer to my home. After all, that is how Vietnamese had fought for centuries."[22] Indeed, there was historical precedent in Vietnam for fighting near one's home village or in one's own province. [23] We now know, for example, that North Vietnamese soldiers often complained about going South to fight and confronted many of the same problems facing the ARVN. As more sources from the North become available, we may be able to compare morale factors between those fighting for the revolution and those who supported the Saigon government.

Still, desertion accounted for seventy-seven percent of the ARVN's total manpower losses and the Saigon government thought it had to respond somehow.[24] Typically, Saigon used a "carrot and stick" approach that often created more problems than it solved. After 1966, ARVN soldiers found a new and improved award and decoration policy, and a more liberal leave program. To discourage desertions, however, MACV introduced a new fingerprinting identification system and established a desertion control board with unprecedented authority to make decisions on a soldier's status.[25] In addition, the US agreed to provide $200,000VND per quarter for a deserter apprehension program.[26] In August 1966, Saigon published its strongest decree, authorizing long prison terms and the death sentence for desertion. South Vietnamese civil-military courts tried over 12,000 deserters in the first two years of this "get tough" policy. A common sentence for an ARVN enlisted man convicted of desertion was five years imprisonment at hard labor.[27]

After four years of record high desertions, South Vietnamese President Nguyen Van Thieu announced, in July 1970, a decree outlining a new role for the ARVN soldier. The new plan relocated ARVN combat units far from their "previously accustomed operational areas near population centers – and thus separated the soldier from his family, friends, familiar surroundings, and, in some cases, sources of additional income (e.g., part time jobs in nearby communities)."[28] The result of this policy was, of course, a general increase in desertions "coupled with considerable difficulty in maintaining a sufficiently high level of recruiting to offset desertions, casualties, and attrition."[29] According to Nguyen Van Hieu, who served seven years with the ARVN, "They thought that taking us far away from our families would keep us with our units, but this had the reverse impact. Some of my friends simply refused to go and took cover. Instead of having them fighting, the government forced them into hiding. It was ridiculous."[30] Increasing desertion rates in the face of government policies to produce the opposite effect forced Saigon to take drastic measures that had a further negative impact on ARVN morale.

Conscription

To effectively fight a war, a nation must have firm control and direction over all its manpower resources. When it could not reduce desertions, Saigon saw as its only option increasing overall manpower numbers to field the size army it thought was required. To accomplish this task, Saigon passed one of the most repressive conscription and rotation policies in the modern era. By 1968, one in six adult males in South Vietnam fought in the ARVN.[31] The total figure for men under arms soared past 700,000 early in that same year.[32] According to one official State Department report, if the United States mobilized the same proportion of its adult male population, it would have sent over eight million men per year to Vietnam.[33] In 1968, the Saigon government passed its most encompassing mobilization decree. The new law tightened deferment policies, broadened conscription rules, and expanded reserve status, all to add 65,000 men to the military rolls by the end of the year.[34] Specifically, the proclamation extended the conscription age from eighteen to thirty-three; requisitioned technical support services at all levels from those between the ages of thirty-four and forty-five; and recalled all veterans within either age limits. Furthermore, the new law abolished all deferments and exemptions for occupational reasons, foreign travel, education or religion.[35]

Despite the new conscription policy, desertions continued to plague the Saigon government. Furthermore, by 1967, total ARVN combat losses approached 55,000, adding significantly to the morale and manpower problems.[36] Why did desertions continue to increase? It now seems clear that official policies and programs did little to improve the life of and care for the ARVN soldier. This was especially true in the areas of food, pay, and housing. Falling short in each of these areas meant that the ARVN infantry soldier had to rely on his own skills and family to survive. This led him away from his unit and to his own village and household. Despite US efforts to rectify the situation, the Saigon government remained aloof and unresponsive to the ARVN's most basic needs.

Food

An army's food supply has often determined the scope and course of battle. Ancient armies fought relatively short battles at short distances from their food supply because a soldier had to eat at least one meal per day to remain effective. In the nineteenth century, railroads and canned foods released the army to further fields of combat, but it was still dependent on complicated logistics for re-supply.[37] During the Vietnam War, the Communists gained a legendary reputation for their ability to move quickly and deeply into the jungles and highlands, and away from enemy ground forces by "living off the land." What this usually meant was Communist cadres secured food locally from sympathetic villagers or took food and supplies by force. For long journeys, Communist guerrillas often took rice balls stuffed inside the inner tubes of bicycle tires. One rice ball per day was often the only meal for those traveling at high speed under adverse conditions.[38]

In his recent memoir, Truong Nhu Tang, a former member of the National Liberation Front (NLF, derogatorily called the Viet Cong by its enemies), described life on the run this way:

> In addition to rice, each man's personal larder was rounded out by a small hunk of salt, a piece of monosodium glutamate, and perhaps a little dried fish or meat. The rice ration for both leaders and fighters was twenty kilos a month.[39]

Bui Tan, a colonel with the People's Army of Vietnam (PAVN), made the long journey down the Ho Chi Minh Trail on several occasions. Each time, he reports, food was found locally:

> We woke every morning at 4 o'clock to cook rice, which we ate with roasted sesame mixed with salt. Sometimes we were able to catch fish in streams. We dried and salted them, although often there was more salt than fish. Then when we ran out of salt, we licked the banana leaves used to wrap the dried fish. What we really lacked was vegetables and fruit. Occasionally we would find an orange tree close to a deserted house and really treasured its fruit. In the same way, whenever we saw any edible leaves we stopped to pick them to make a soup for the evening meal.[40]

Despite these hardships, the Communists never suffered from serious morale problems because of food. "We always knew that we could find food if we needed it," reported General Nguyen Dinh Uoc, of the People's Army. "Local villagers were always willing to give us what they had, and the diet was familiar to us. We never ate food outside of the normal Vietnamese diet and this helped us keep our strength and good spirits."[41] Indeed, malnutrition was rarely reported in Communist field hospitals.[42]

For the ARVN, however, food was always a problem. Throughout the war, an inadequate field ration weakened the ARVN's ability to conduct sustained combat operations. According to one MACV report, the number of non-combat related illnesses was unusually high in the ARVN because of poor nutrition in the field. [43] Although ARVN rations changed over time and according to each unit's position in the field, most South Vietnamese infantry soldiers consistently complained of poor food quality and quantity. "Didn't Napoleon say an army travels on its stomach?" asked one ARVN soldier in a recent interview. "We never had enough to eat and the distribution system forced us to spend much of our time searching for food."[44] Several US "After Action Reports" confirm this problem. According to a December 1967 report, ARVN battalions often supplemented their Vietnamese ration with US rations acquired through the "buddy system." Apparently, US infantry units often gave the ARVN extra food rations "in the interests of harmony and in the spirit of the combined operation."[45] However, this type of sharing and cooperation was not official US policy, and, therefore, it depended largely on the initiative of individual American units. "If it were not for the kindness of our American friends . . . privates, corporals . . . the enlisted men," one former ARVN soldier told me recently, "we would have been in a terrible fix."[46] The sharing of US rations also meant that the ARVN soldier did not venture into the local market to supplement his own food supply. This had multiple benefits, including denying the enemy intelligence based on food purchase patterns and making more ARVN infantry soldiers available for duty.

When ARVN units were forced to rely on their own rations, they habitually used Class A rations instead of operational rations. Class A rations were fresh local products, purchased by a supply officer in the Vietnamese market, whereas operational rations were canned goods. According to one official US report, the ARVN found the operational ration unappetizing. "The ARVN soldier does not like the operational ration because it is not palatable to him, does not contain fresh meat and vegetables which he considers essential to his diet, and he loses his advance ration allowance (36 Vietnamese dollars per day) when this ration is issued."[47] The daily diet was extremely important to southern Vietnamese who had always had an abundant food supply, even during the French War. "The South has traditionally been the bread basket of Vietnam," a former ARVN officer explained after the war, "and we had always considered our diet part of what made us Vietnamese. We were used to the high protein foods like *bun thit heo nung* [rice vermicelli with grilled pork] and *tom xao xa ot* [shrimp with lemon grass on rice], but then we were forced to eat meat from a can made in the United States. It made me sick."[48] Another former ARVN soldier complained, "we could see our traditional foods all around us, but we were forced to eat imported food in the field. It made no sense to me or any of my friends. We would have been better off without the ration system."[49] To combat this problem, many US advisors simply allowed the purchase and use of Class A rations to replace the standard operational ration, even though there were security risks attached to large purchases in local markets.

Another difficulty facing the ARVN was food rations for attachment forces. When extra military personnel, such as Kit Carson Scouts, interpreters, or local guides were attached to regular ARVN units, official food rations for them were often not authorized in advance. This situation existed throughout the 1960s, and only in late 1970 was there an official attempt to rectify the problem.[50] "Because of my skills as an interpreter of mountain people languages," reported Nguyen Hue, an ARVN volunteer, "I was often moved from unit to unit. My food ration never seemed to find me and I often had to buy food from local villagers."[51] Nguyen Co Huong, a Kit Carson Scout in II Corps, also reported problems receiving his food ration while in the field. "For most of 1968, my ration of food goods was never quite right. I also had problems with the ration tickets."[52] In addition, the ARVN infantry soldier had meals deducted from his pay.[53]

Corruption in the food distribution system was also a common occurrence. Graft in the rationing system often led ARVN soldiers to work outside established protocol, and this created severe tensions between the South Vietnamese and their American advisors. "We had to make sure that the ARVN weren't alienating the local population by stealing their food," explained one US advisor.[54] Another concern was that assigned food rations were not making their way to ARVN soldiers. According to an official US report, MACV introduced a system of supported supplies during combat operations on July 1, 1967 to fight corruption. These supported rations consisted of an A-Pack of 800 grams of dehydrated rice, and a B-Pack consisting of canned meat, pork, or fish, plus an accessory package of salt, pepper, and candy. Indications were, however, "that rations were not reaching the troops. Most were being held at corps level where administrative red tape made it improbable that the units in combat operations were able to obtain them when required."[55]

Another significant problem with ARVN rations was the replacement of the traditional Vietnamese *nuoc mam* [fish sauce] with soy sauce. *Nuoc mam* is a high protein fish sauce and a staple of the Vietnamese diet. Together with rice, it provided the Vietnamese with the perfect mixture of protein and carbohydrates, and was readily available. The move to replace *nuoc mam* with soy sauce came about apparently because US supply officers attached to ARVN units believed that the foul smelling *nuoc mam* spoiled too easily in the field. In over three hundred interviews with ARVN soldiers who used rations, all complained that their daily diet had a dramatic impact on morale.[56] Several former ARVN infantry soldiers told me that they actually left their units for long periods of time to search for decent food. "We needed to eat in order to fight," explained one foot soldier, "but we could not bring ourselves to eat those American rations." Another explained, "I know I was listed as a deserter, but actually I left to get food from some cousins in a nearby village. I eventually came back to my unit, but it took me weeks to clear my name with my commanding officer."[57] If an army does travel on its stomach, the ARVN clearly did not want to stray far from home.

Pay

Equally troubling to the ARVN soldier was inadequate pay. Throughout the war, US advisors complained that pay and allowances for the ARVN had not kept pace with the cost of living.[58] The ARVN did receive regular pay increases, and, in fact, from 1964 to 1968, Saigon increased salaries through forty-six different redress actions in the form of adjustments, refinements, and general pay raises.[59] Still, most US officials agreed that Saigon habitually underpaid its troops. Part of the problem, of course, was that pay increases did not keep up with inflation. The cost of basic foodstuffs and household supplies continued to rise in the 1960s, as the introduction of Americans and their money had an inflationary impact on the South Vietnamese economy. Furthermore, attempts to rectify the situation always involved increasing pay, but little was done to control costs, and this too meant that ARVN salaries were inadequate. "We could never buy the basic goods we needed because the prices for everything kept going up," complained the wife of an ARVN soldier.[60]

US attempts to create a new pay and allowance system also met with disaster. On June 1, 1967, MACV authorized a "rice allowance" of $200VND for ARVN soldiers and each dependent. Under this new policy, an ARVN private with three years of service and five dependents earned a base pay of $1,680VND per month, a family allowance of $1,012VND per month, and cost of living allowance of $2,212VND per month, a rice allocation of $1,200VND, and a temporary pay raise for $1,471VND per month for a total of $7,575VND per month.[61] The problems of introducing pay increases into an inflationary economy became apparent rather quickly, however, as prices continued to increase dramatically throughout 1967. Furthermore, price supports and pay increases created a certain dependency on the US that the Saigon government and its soldiers found hard to shake. "We used to be an exporter of many agricultural products," explained one former Saigon official, "but the Americans introduced a system that made us buy what we used to grow ourselves. Our soldier's pay could never keep up with the rising costs of imported goods. I don't buy the argument that the war made it necessary to import goods. The Viet Cong didn't import food and clothing."[62] Indeed, there may have been a systemic problem and certainly the procurement policy handcuffed the ARVN and thereby had a debilitating impact on morale.

Throughout the war, the Saigon government routinely spent fifty percent of its budget on non-defense related items. The US supported these expenditures directly, but never provided enough maintenance to meet rising needs or costs. By 1965, the South Vietnamese deficit had mushroomed to unmanageable proportions and the inflation rate approached unprecedented levels. According to US Army historian Jeffrey Clarke, consumer prices in South Vietnam rose 900 percent between 1964 and 1972. The cost of rice during this period rose an unbelievable 1400 percent.[63] Of course, military personnel on fixed salaries felt these economic strains intensely. During the war, salaries of enlisted men rose only 500 percent. On the surface, incremental and periodic pay raises appeared necessary, but these presented the Saigon government with a host of problems. Salary increases only added to the South Vietnamese deficit and increased the money supply, contributing to further inflation.

The growing number of ARVN enlisted men added significantly to the cyclical nature of the inflation dilemma. With each new recruitment year, the overall size of the ARVN increased, and therefore, so did the salary budget. More soldiers on the payroll meant growing inflation and higher prices as individuals competed with each other for limited supplies.

The official exchange rate between the US dollar and the Vietnamese piaster also created inflationary pressures that had a devastating impact on ARVN morale. From 1964 to 1972, the exchange rate rose from $35VND to $420VND, decreasing the actual value of ARVN pay. For example, an ARVN private saw his pay in real terms drop from $77USD to $30USD per month.[64] With rising prices and lower salaries, it is no wonder that so many ARVN supplemented their incomes with part-time jobs or returned to their families for food, clothing, and shelter. Of course, when they tried to take care of themselves, the enlisted men were cited as deserters. "I felt like I could not do anything but return to my family," Nguyen Van Hieu explained after the war. "I was forced to go home for food and work to support my wife and three kids. No one told us how we were supposed to fight the Communists and take care of our families at the same time."[65] In her recent memoir, Duong Van Mai Elliot remembers life in Saigon in those inflationary days. "The upshot of billions of dollars circulating in a country the size of Texas was that people had more money to spend. Supply could not keep up with demand, and prices shot up."[66] Indeed, serious inflationary problems plagued experts in Washington and Saigon throughout the war.

Housing

Another major obstacle facing government officials in Washington and Saigon was securing suitable housing for the ARVN. In 1965, MACV estimates suggested that the ARVN needed 200,000 family units for regular forces. By the end of 1966, there were less than 60,000 built, and budget figures from 1967 suggest that less than 4,000 were added to the total figure that year. [67] By the time of the Tet Offensive in 1968, therefore, less than thirty percent of the 1965 needs were met. Of course, the ARVN continued to increase its overall troop strength annually, making the 1965 housing needs obsolete by 1966. There were several problems associated with ARVN housing: graft, corruption, budgeting procedures, and short supplies. Saigon's inability to solve these problems suggests it never had the full confidence of the South Vietnamese. "If we could not meet our most basic requirements," reported Nguyen Van Hieu, "how could we mobilize our entire society for the war effort?"[68] Indeed, corruption and budgeting problems shackled the various dependent housing programs, adding to ARVN morale problems.

A look at some of the programs for dependent housing illustrates the difficulties faced by MACV and the ARVN. In 1965, IV Corps received a $10 million grant from the US to construct housing for enlisted dependents, but not one single unit was ever built. Local commanders and South Vietnamese officials siphoned money and supplies off to rent-seeking construction projects that promised them personal rewards. To combat this system of corruption, General Westmoreland used US funds to support a self-help housing system that bypassed the Saigon government and the

ARVN command. The plan required ARVN enlisted men to use US supplies to build their own temporary housing. US advisors and construction engineers would monitor the progress and utilization of resources.[69] This self-help program was first established in base areas near Saigon, and if successful, would quickly spread to other provinces. Unfortunately, the program was quickly abandoned as one obstacle after another reduced its effectiveness.[70] Land purchases from the Saigon government proved troublesome and individual ARVN soldiers were never given the time to construct the units. In 1967, a frustrated Westmoreland announced the transfer of responsibility for ARVN dependent housing construction to the Engineer's Office with MACV's Central Logistics Command. According to the general's new plan, MACV would directly purchase all of the land and pay private contractors to construct nearly 200,000 housing units at a cost of $7.6 million.[71]

Westmoreland's revised plan for dependent housing also failed to produce the desired results. By the end of 1968, Westmoreland's replacement at MACV, General Creighton Abrams, complained bitterly that the self-help and dependent housing programs were a complete failure. He suggested that at the current construction rate, it would take fourteen years to finish the limited self-help program near Saigon.[72] Of course, the ARVN continued to increase its total numbers annually, adding to Abrams' frustration. For two years, the dependent housing program languished while MACV tried to find a solution. In early 1969, the new Secretary of Defense, Melvin Laird, approved $8 million in funds to provide supplies and materials for construction of 1,160 additional family shelters in FY 1969.[73] Furthermore, Laird announced an eight-year plan to house 40,000 ARVN and their dependents in vacated American facilities and to construct an additional 200,000 new housing units. Under Laird's plan, the US would provide $6 million per year for new ARVN housing and cost sharing with Saigon at an annual level of $13.2 million.[74]

Despite good intentions, Laird's plan also failed to meet the ARVN's increasing needs. Saigon's archaic annual budgeting procedures meant that funds were never available when needed to purchase building materials. As a result, by the end of 1970, less than half of the anticipated shelters had been built. By 1972, Saigon had only constructed 1,690 units as events on the ground took precedence over housing. Laird's own policies had an impact on ARVN housing, and often times contradicted his stated goals. In 1971, he announced that the ARVN was no longer going to be tied to base camps, that it would now be a mobile fighting force.[75] Laird had been impressed by the ARVN's 1970–1 offensives into Cambodia and believed the time had come to cut the "umbilical cord" between the soldiers and their families near the base camps. From the early 1960s, ARVN dependents routinely lived near base camps. With the war raging in the villages, many ARVN family members tolerated poor conditions in exchange for the perceived security that the base provided. As a result, clusters of "relatives' villages" sprang up near most ARVN base camps. This arrangement made it less likely that the ARVN would want to venture far from the base camp. As Westmoreland reported, "When the fighting began, the soldiers were often torn between defeating the enemy and looking after their wives and children."[76] Laird's new mobility initiative did little to raise ARVN morale, however, and infantry soldiers still complained bitterly about poor housing and pay.

Conclusion

Since Thucydides, military historians have wondered why individuals will endure the sight of combat and eventually throw themselves before the weapons of their enemy. Most conclude that bravery in battle has little to do with idealism, patriotism, or treasure. Instead, they suggest that "soldiers fight to protect their comrades at their side."[77] William Manchester, writing of his World War II experience in the Pacific, put it this way:

> Those men on the line were my family, my home. They were closer to me than I can say, closer than any friends had been or would ever be. They had never let me down; and I couldn't do it to them. I had to be with them rather than let them die and let me live with the knowledge that I might have saved them. Men, I know now, do not fight for flag, country, for the Marine Corps, or glory or any other abstraction. They fight for one another.[78]

Indeed, since the Greek hoplite battles of the fifth century BC, bravery has been associated with camaraderie. Within the ARVN, however, morale and camaraderie were in such short supply that it was almost impossible to field an effective army. What plagued the ARVN most was that it was never more than a collection of individuals. As John Keegan writes, "inside every army is a crowd struggling to get out . . ."[79] The ARVN were never allowed to develop the esprit de corps that usually can hold an army together in difficult times because, as individuals, they were always worrying about food, shelter, pay, and their families. Deficiencies in these basic requirements were highlighted by the fact that the Americans seemed to "have things so much better."[80] Poor ARVN morale led to high desertion rates and constant manpower problems for Saigon and its US allies. In the end, however, little the US or the ARVN could do was going to change the outcome of the war. But blaming the ARVN alone for the failure in Vietnam ignores the complicated reality of that conflict and focuses attention away from a critical examination of US policy toward Southeast Asia past, present, and future.

NOTES

1   William Gibbons, *The US Government and the Vietnam War: Executive and Legislative Roles and Relationships* Part III (Princeton: Princeton University Press, 1989), p. 367.
2   Author interview with George Jones, former US Marine, Boston, June 1999.
3   "Combat After Action Report, May 11, 1970," Records of the US Forces in Southeast Asia, MACV, Assistant Chief of Staff of Operations (J3), Evaluation and Analysis Division (MAC J3–05), Report 26–70, Box 43, Folder MACV J3 #40–70, National Archives, College Park, Maryland (Hereafter NA).
4   Neal Sheehan, *A Bright Shining Lie* (New York: Random House, 1988), p. 90.
5   George C. Herring, "Peoples Quite Apart: Americans, South Vietnamese, and the War in Vietnam, *Diplomatic History* 14 (Winter 1990), pp. 1–24.
6   Author interview with Tran Van Do, Los Angeles, June 1999.

7   As cited in Victor Davis Hanson, *The Western Way of War*, p. 117.
8   Michael Howard and Peter Paret, eds., *On War* (Princeton: Princeton University Press, 1976).
9   John Keegan, *A History of Warfare* (New York: Vintage Books, 1993).
10 Author interview with Nguyen Hue, Ho Chi Minh City, March 1996. South Vietnam was divided into four corps tactical zones, each under the command of an army corps headquarters. I Corps ran from the Demilitarized Zone at the 17th parallel south to the city of Quang Ngai. II Corps encompassed the entire central highlands and the central seacoast provinces. South Vietnam's capital, the city of Saigon, was at the heart of III Corps. It stretched from the South China Sea westward to Cambodia. Finally, IV Corps was the southernmost part of South Vietnam, from My Tho to the Ca Mau peninsula.
11 "Memorandum to C. E. Mehlert from Lacy Wright, April 24, 1970, Conversation with Captain Tram Buu, Interpreter for Generals Nguyen Viet Thanh and Nguyen Huu Hanh, April 23, 1973, Can Tho, Vietnam," The Francis N. Dawson Papers, US Army Military History Institute, Carlisle Barricks, Carlisle, Pennsylvania.
12 Author interview with a former US Army Colonel who requested anonymity, Washington, DC, June 1999.
13 RVNAF Assessments, 1970, "Assessment of ARVN/VNMC Operations, February 1970," 4, Center for Military History, Washington, DC (Hereafter CMH).
14 "Draft Report-Deputy Senior Advisor, II Corps Tactical Zone," US Army Advisory Group, John W. Barnes, Brigadier General, USA Commanding, CMH.
15 Author interview with Huong Thuy, New York, June 1999.
16 "Causes for ARVN Desertion," US Army Advisory Group, October 7, 1968, as reported in "Draft Report-Deputy Senior Advisor, II Corps Tactical Zone," US Army Advisory Group, John W. Barnes, Brigadier General, USA Commanding, CMH.
17 *State Department Briefing Book on Vietnam*, Section Two (February 1968), p. 5.
18 Brian M. Jenkins, "A People's Army for South Vietnam: A Vietnamese Solution," R-897–ARPA, November 1971, (Santa Monica: Rand Corporation, 1971), pp. 5–9.
19 "Desertions Not Defections from ARVN, July 1967," Office of Media Services, Bureau of Public Affairs, Department of State Publication #260, East Asian Pacific Series 163, US Government Printing Office, 1967.
20 Author interview with Nguyen Van Hieu, Los Angeles, June 1999.
21 "Desertions Not Defections from ARVN, July 1967," Office of Media Services, Bureau of Public Affairs, Department of State Publication #260, East Asian Pacific Series 163, US Government Printing Office, 1967.
22 Author interview with Phan Thuy, San Francisco, June 1999.
23 Truong Buu Lam, *Patterns of Vietnamese Response to Foreign Intervention, 1858–1900* (New Haven: Yale University, Southeast Asia Studies, Monograph Series, No. 11, 1967), *Cuoc Khang Chien Chong My, Cuu Nuoc, 1954–1975: Nhung Su Kien Quan Su* [The Great Anti-American Resistance War for National Salvation of the Fatherland, 1954–1975: Military Events] (Hanoi: Nha Xuat Ban Quan Doi Nhan Dan, 1988), and Nguyen Khac Vien, *Vietnam: A Long History* Revised Edition (Hanoi: The Gioi Publishers, 1999).
24 "1966 Evaluation of RVNAF: The Desertion Problem," pp. 103–105, CMH.
25 RVNAF Assessments 1970, "Assessment of ARVN/VNMC Operations, February 1970," p. 4, CMH.
26 RVNAF Assessment 1967, "Desertion Control Report, Republic of Vietnam Armed Forces," CMH.

27 RVNAF Assessment 1967, "Quality Improvement of RVNAF, January 9, 1968," pp. 2–4, CMH.

28 Records of US Army Commands 1942–Records of HQ, US Army, Pacific Military Historians Office, Command Reporting Files, 1963–1972, RG 338, Box 204, Folder: BG D. P. McAuliffe, Deputy Senior Advisor MR3, Debriefing Reports, NA.

29 Records of US Army Commands 1942–Records of HQ, US Army, Pacific Military Historians Office, Command Reporting Files, 1963–1972, RG 338, Box 204, Folder: BG D. P. McAuliffe, Deputy Senior Advisor MR3, Debriefing Reports, NA.

30 Author interview with Nguyen Van Hieu, Los Angeles, June 1999.

31 Tran Ngoc Nhuan, *Doi Quan Ngu* [Life in the Army] (Westminster, California: Van Nghe, 1992), pp. 600–5.

32 Dong Van Khuyen, *The RVNAF* (Washington: Center for Military History, Monograph Series, 1980). See also Nguyen Vu, *12 Nam Linh* [Twelve Years of Being a Soldier] (Westminster, California: Van Hoa, 1990).

33 *State Department Briefing Book on Vietnam*, Section Two (February 1968), pp. 4–9.

34 Cao Xuan Huy, *Thang Ba Gay Sung* [The March of the Broken Rifles] (Westminster, California: Van Khoa, 1986).

35 *Dai Dan Toc* [Greater National Community], March 3, 1969.

36 *State Department Briefing Book on Vietnam*, Section One (February 1968), p. 4A.

37 Keegan, *A History of Warfare*, pp. 301, 305–6.

38 Author interview with Vu Huy Phuc, Hanoi, June 1992.

39 Truong Nhu Tang, *A Viet Cong Memoir: An Inside Account of the Vietnam War and Its Aftermath* (New York: Vintage Books, 1985), p. 158.

40 Bui Tin, *From Cadre to Exile: The Memoirs of a North Vietnamese Journalist* (Chiang Mai, Thailand: Silk Worm Books, 1995), p. 51.

41 Author interview with General Nguyen Dinh Uoc, Hanoi, June 1997.

42 Author interview with Dr. Hoang Quang Ho, Hanoi, June 1992.

43 "Combat After Action Report, September 12, 1968," Records of the US Forces in Southeast Asia, MACV, Assistant Chief of Staff of Operations (J3), Evaluation and Analysis Division (MAC J3–05), Report 981–1022, Box 28, Folder MACV J3 #1002–1008, NA.

44 Author interview with Nguyen Van Hieu, Los Angeles, June 1999.

45 "Combat After Action Report, December 1, 1967," Records of the US Forces in Southeast Asia, MACV, Assistant Chief of Staff of Operations (J3), Evaluation and Analysis Division (MAC J3–05), Report 531–560, Box 9, Folder MACV J3 #544, NA.

46 Author interview with Nguyen Van Hieu, Los Angeles, June 1999.

47 "Combat After Action Report, June 24, 1969," Records of the US Forces in Southeast Asia, MACV, Assistant Chief of Staff of Operations (J3), Evaluation and Analysis Division (MAC J3–05), Report 155–169, Box 41, Folder MACV J3 #168–169, NA.

48 Author interview with Nguyen Hue, Ho Chi Minh City, March 1996.

49 Author interview with Phan Thuy, San Francisco, June 1999.

50 "Combat After Action Report, May 11, 1970," Records of the US Forces in Southeast Asia, MACV, Assistant Chief of Staff of Operations (J3), Evaluation and Analysis Division (MAC J3–05), Report 26–70, Box 43, Folder MACV J3 #40–70, NA.

51 Author interview with Nguyen Hue, Ho Chi Minh City, March 1996.

52 Author interview with Nguyen Co Huong, San Francisco, June 1999.

53 RVNAF Assessment 1967, "Quality Improvement of RVNAF, January 9, 1968," pp. 2–4, CMH.

54 Author interview with George C. Davis, Washington, DC, July 1999.
55 Westmoreland Study, "Support of RVNAF, 1965–1967," CMH.
56 Interviews conducted by the author in Vietnam and the United States between 1989 and 1999.
57 Author interview with former ARVN soldier who requested anonymity, Las Vegas, November 1997.
58 "Memo for the Secretary of Defense, JCS, Briefing for Secretary of Defense, August 7, 1968," CMH.
59 Westmoreland Study, "Support of RVNAF, 1965–1967," CMH.
60 Author interview with Nguyen Thi Thuy, Los Angeles, June 1999.
61 "Westmoreland Study, Support of RVNAF, 1965–1967," CMH.
62 Author interview with former Saigon official who requested anonymity, Washington, DC, June 1996.
63 Jeffrey Clarke, *Advise and Support: The Final Years*, p. 503.
64 Dong Van Khuyen, *The RVNAF*, pp. 252–3.
65 Author interview with Nguyen Van Hieu, Los Angeles, June 1999.
66 Duong Van Mai Elliot, *The Sacred Willow: Four Generations in the Life of a Vietnamese Family* (New York: Oxford University Press, 1999), p. 314.
67 Westmoreland Study, "Support of RVNAF, 1965–1967," CMH.
68 Author interview with Nguyen Van Hieu, Los Angeles, June 1999.
69 Clarke, *Advise and Support: The Final Years*, p. 156.
70 Westmoreland Study, "Support of RVNAF, 1965–1967," CMH.
71 Ibid.
72 Clarke, *Advise and Support: The Final Years*, p. 320.
73 Westmoreland Study, "Support of RVNAF, 1965–1967," CMH.
74 USMACV, *Command History, 1969* 2: VI-64, CMH.
75 USMACV, *Command History, 1972–1973* 2: E-33 to E-34, CMH.
76 General William Westmoreland, *A Soldier Reports* (Garden City: Doubleday, 1976), 253.
77 Victor Davis Hanson, *The Western Way of War* p. 118.
78 William Manchester, *Goodbye Darkness* (New York: Random House, 1979), p. 391.
79 John Keegan, *Face of Battle* (New York: Penguin, 1976), pp. 173–4.
80 Author interview with Nguyen Van Hieu, Los Angeles, June 1999.

SELECT BIBLIOGRAPHY

Bui Diem 1999: *In the Jaws of History.* Bloomington: Indiana University Press.
Butler, David 1985: *The Fall of Saigon: Scenes from the Sudden End of a Long War.* New York: Dell.
Clarke, Jeffrey 1988: *Advice and Support: The Final Years, The US Army in Vietnam.* Washington: The Center for Military History.
Duong Van Mai Elliot 1999: *The Sacred Willow: Four Generations in the Life of a Vietnamese Family.* New York: Oxford University Press.
FitzGerald, Frances 1972: *Fire in the Lake.* Boston: Little, Brown, and Company.
Nguyen Cao Ky 1976: *Twenty Years and Twenty Days.* New York: Stein and Day.
Nguyen Tien Hung and Jerrold L. Schecter, 1986: *The Palace File: Vietnam Secret Documents.* New York: Harper and Row.
Prados, John 1995: *The Hidden History of the Vietnam War.* Chicago: Ivan Dee.

Race, Jeffrey 1972: *War Comes to Long An: Revolutionary Conflict in a Vietnamese Province.* Berkeley: University of California Press.

Scigliano, Robert 1964: *South Vietnam: Nation Under Stress.* Boston: Houghton Mifflin Company.

Sheehan, Neal 1988: *A Bright Shining Lie: John Paul Vann and America in Vietnam.* New York: Random House.

Snepp, Frank 1977: *Decent Interval: An Insider's Account of Saigon's Indecent End.* New York: Random House.

Spector, Ronald 1985: *Advice and Support: The Early Years of the US Army in Vietnam, 1941–1960.* New York: The Free Press.

Tran Van Don 1978: *Our Endless War: Inside Vietnam.* San Rafael, California: Presidio Press.

CHAPTER TEN

JFK and the Myth of Withdrawal

EDWIN E. MOISE

Most Americans are at least vaguely aware of the theory suggested in Oliver Stone's film *JFK*, that powerful elements of the American "military-industrial complex" assassinated President John F. Kennedy. The suggestion is that these people wanted Lyndon Johnson in the White House because Kennedy would not go along with their desire for a big war in Vietnam and the big military budgets it would bring, while Johnson would give them the war and the spending they wanted. The disputes over this theory have centered mainly on the issue of conspiracy. People have argued about whether the evidence indicated Kennedy had been killed by a conspiracy or a lone gunman, and about whether the military-industrial complex was made up of the sort of people who might engage in a murderous conspiracy. More attention needs to be placed on the underlying nature of Kennedy's and Johnson's policies. Was Johnson in fact more inclined to large-scale military spending, and more inclined to fight a war in Vietnam, than Kennedy had been? These questions remain important even when the notion of Kennedy having been killed because of such a difference in policies and attitudes is discarded.

Kennedy, Johnson, and Military Spending

Many people assume too readily that the Vietnam War did raise the military budgets of Lyndon Johnson's administration, fighting a war in Vietnam, far above the levels of the peacetime years under the Kennedy administration. America's wars had always done this in the past. World War II had lifted spending on national defense from just under $1.5 billion in Fiscal Year 1940, to more than $63 billion in Fiscal Year 1943, and more than $81 billion in Fiscal Year 1945. Even the much smaller Korean War had almost quadrupled national defense spending, from $13 billion in Fiscal Year 1950 to $50 billion in Fiscal Year 1953.[1] Looking at the amount of military hardware Lyndon Johnson was using in Vietnam in the late 1960s, most people assumed, without thinking much about the matter, that purchasing all this hardware must have required a huge increase in military spending, compared with the levels in peacetime in the early 1960s. There had not, however, been a growth in military spending remotely comparable to that in previous wars.

The last year for which Kennedy set the budget, Fiscal Year 1964, was also the last that was effectively a peacetime year for the United States – the last during which the United States was not bombing North Vietnam and did not have significant ground troop units in South Vietnam. Kennedy's budget allocated $55.4 billion to the military that year. Fiscal Year 1965, the first for which Lyndon Johnson set the budget, was a transitional year. The first battalions of regular ground troops arrived, but they did not see much combat. The scale of US bombing in Indochina became substantial, but was not yet really large – about 27,900 tons of air munitions were expended during the fiscal year. During the last four of the years for which Johnson set the budgets, Fiscal Years 1966–9, the United States was clearly at war.

The average amount spent on the military in Johnson's five budget years was only $67.8 billion, or 22 percent above the amount in Kennedy's last peacetime budget. The maximum level of military spending during the Vietnam War, that for Fiscal Year 1969, was $81 billion – not even 50 percent above Kennedy's last peacetime budget.

But if we are trying to find the effect on the military budget of Lyndon Johnson's having become president, we need to factor in the amount spending would have been likely to grow even had Kennedy remained president. Military spending had always risen from one year to the next under Kennedy, even without a major war. The average growth had been about 5.3%. Kennedy's last budget, that for Fiscal Year 1964, had been 4.9% above that for the previous year. If we assume that with Kennedy remaining in office the military budget would have continued to grow at the lower of these rates, 4.9% per year, it is possible to project the Kennedy administration's pattern of spending forward onto the years Johnson was president, and compare these figures with what Johnson actually spent. All figures are in billions of current dollars, and come from the presidents' annual budget messages to Congress.

	FY 64	FY 65	FY 66	FY 67	FY 68	FY 69
Projected	$55.4	$58.1	$61.0	$63.9	$67.1	$70.4
Actual	$54.2	$50.2	$56.8	$70.1	$80.5	$81.2
Difference	−$1.2	−$7.9	−$4.2	+$6.2	+$13.4	+$10.8

The total spending for all six fiscal years is only $17.1 billion higher in the actual figures than in the ones that project forward the pattern of Kennedy's military budgets. This is not an impressive difference. It is, in fact, astonishingly small. Doesn't a war cost more than that?

A large part of the explanation can be found in the first three columns of the table. Kennedy's budget for Fiscal Year 1964 had called for $55.4 billion in military spending. Kennedy was assassinated, and Johnson became president, toward the middle of that fiscal year. Johnson immediately began cutting back on military spending; he simply left unspent $1.2 billion of what Kennedy had budgeted for the military. In Fiscal Year 1965, despite the way US involvement in the war was expanding, military spending dropped much farther, down to $50.2 billion. Johnson was shifting military resources to Vietnam from other areas of the world, not giving the military additional resources. Even in Fiscal Year 1966, by the end of which the United States had 268,000 men in Vietnam, the amount spent on the military was barely above what Kennedy had budgeted for Fiscal Year 1964.

The "procurement" section of the military budget, the one that pays for weapons purchases, was especially hard hit in Johnson's first months in office. Kennedy had planned to spend $16.3 billion on military procurement in Fiscal Year 1964. Johnson left a billion of that unspent, and cut procurement for the following fiscal year to $11.8 billion. Even in Fiscal Year 1966, with huge amounts of equipment and ammunition being used in Vietnam, procurement spending was only $14.3 billion – well below the level in Kennedy's last peacetime budget.[2]

Lyndon Johnson was a domestically oriented president. The programs he wanted to dominate the budget were the domestic ones collectively known as the "Great Society." When he came into office he immediately took a meat axe to the military budget, especially the procurement budget (which is where the big defense contractors got most of their profits), in order to free up money for things about which he cared much more. The Vietnam War later forced him to make substantial increases in military spending, especially procurement, but the increases began not from the level of Kennedy's military budgets, but from the considerably lower level to which Johnson had cut military spending in Fiscal Year 1965.

For anyone to have killed Kennedy under the impression Johnson would be more enthusiastic about military spending than Kennedy had been, they would have had to be remarkably confused about Johnson's actual priorities.

Johnson and Vietnam

When Johnson became President, he did not make major changes among the top officials in defense and foreign policy. Robert McNamara remained Secretary of Defense, Dean Rusk Secretary of State, John McCone Director of Central Intelligence, and McGeorge Bundy the President's Special Assistant for National Security Affairs (National Security Advisor). Maxwell Taylor only remained Chairman of the Joint Chiefs of Staff for half a year, but when he left that post, it was to become Ambassador to the Republic of Vietnam, so he remained a key member of the team that advised the President on Vietnam policy. The consensus of these men, in 1964, was that the war in Vietnam should be escalated. The Joint Chiefs of Staff unanimously urged bombing of North Vietnam. The highest-ranking "dove" among the men Johnson had inherited from Kennedy was distinctly a second-level figure, Under Secretary of State George Ball.

Johnson was less enthusiastic about escalation than any of his top advisors. Partly this was because he mistrusted assurances that escalation in Vietnam could be kept under control, not triggering a war with China or possibly even the Soviet Union. He remembered Douglas MacArthur's assurances to President Harry Truman in 1950, that the United States could invade North Korea without triggering a major Chinese intervention. But Johnson was also concerned with the obvious fact that wars cost money. If he fought a major war in Vietnam, he could not expect to hold the military budget at a level below what Kennedy had spent on the military even in peacetime.

Some officials were hoping that Johnson was simply delaying escalation until after the 1964 presidential election. McGeorge Bundy implied as much when he went to Ray Cline, the CIA's Deputy Director for Intelligence, and asked for President Johnson whether the United States could afford to wait until after the election to escalate the war. Would South Vietnam by that time already be irretrievably lost? Cline replied that it would just barely be possible to put off a major expansion of the US role in the war until after the election; "you're going to have your back to the wall."[3] During the campaign, Johnson's advisors warned him not to get too carried away, in rhetoric about not getting into a big war in Vietnam, because the words might come back to haunt him. But he did get carried away, talking of the policy he wished he would be following, when he should have been taking more account of the policy he knew he would probably be forced into.

Joseph Califano, at that time Special Assistant to Secretary of Defense McNamara, later recalled that officials in the Defense Department had expected Johnson to take prompt action once the election was behind him, but that the decision still did not come. "We were poised to increase military activities there and bomb North Vietnam. But Johnson just kept asking more and more questions. In the eyes of the Pentagon he was a querulous wallflower, disappointingly reluctant to join the war dance in Southeast Asia."[4]

Even more important than Johnson's delay in authorizing the actual beginning of a major escalation of the war was his failure to order the preparations for one. He had probably decided by late 1964 that he was going to have to order a major escalation in Vietnam, but he kept hoping to figure out some way of avoiding this. As long as he kept hoping, he didn't take any action to ensure that the military would have the personnel necessary for escalation. During Fiscal Year 1965, as the United States moved toward a major war, the Selective Service System was not even drafting enough men each month to hold the military at constant size. In the last days of the fiscal year, in June 1965, as the US ground troop units that had been defending air bases in South Vietnam began to move away from those bases for offensive operations – the 173rd Airborne Brigade launched a probe into War Zone D, a guerrilla stronghold northeast of Saigon – the total strength of the United States armed forces was *32,000 less* than it had been a year earlier. The number of young men drafted each month remained at peacetime levels until September.

The way Johnson had postponed both escalation of the war and the strengthening of the military it required, as long as he thought he could, unmistakably reflects an overall lack of enthusiasm for the war. John Kennedy's attitude to the war, however, is a subject about which there has been much more dispute and uncertainty.

Kennedy and Vietnam

It had been Kennedy who took the United States beyond provision of advice and training to the Republic of Vietnam, and began to put Americans into combat – the Army Special Forces soldiers who trained and led the Civilian Irregular Defense

Groups in the Highlands, the Army and Marine Corps helicopter pilots, and the Air Force pilots who flew air strikes against the guerrillas under the code name FARMGATE. But he kept the American combat involvement small enough so that it would not draw too much attention; the fiction that the Americans were just there as advisors was preserved to the extent possible. And the men he sent were mostly volunteers; the 120 Americans killed in action in Vietnam between 1961 and 1963 included only a single draftee.[5] Keeping US combat participation low-key would have made it easier to end that participation, if the president had chosen to do so.

By now it is well known that Kennedy, during the last year of his life, had been planning to withdraw at least a large proportion of the US military personnel in South Vietnam in 1965. Two very different types of withdrawal plans, however, have been reported.

What shows in the documentary record is that during the second half of 1962 and most of 1963, senior US military officers were reporting that the Communist forces in South Vietnam were being defeated. Military Assistance Command, Vietnam (MACV) was established in February 1962, under the command of General Paul Harkins. In December, when Senate Majority Leader Mike Mansfield came to look at the situation in Vietnam, General Harkins told him that the war could be won in a year.[6] Early in 1963, MACV issued a "Summary of Highlights" of its first year, which included the claim that ". . . barring greatly increased resupply and reinforcement of the Viet Cong by infiltration, the military phase of the war can be virtually won in 1963."[7] General Harkins told the Chairman of the Joint Chiefs of Staff in August 1963 that an end to the war was "not far off if things continue at present pace."[8] Higher-ranking officers were slightly more cautious, but Admiral Harry D. Felt, who as Commander in Chief, Pacific (CINCPAC) was Harkins' immediate superior, said in a press conference at the Pentagon on January 30, 1963, that the war would be won within three years.[9] Chairman of the Joint Chiefs Maxwell Taylor, in a letter to Ngo Dinh Diem dated October 1, said he was convinced that if Diem would take the appropriate steps to end political turmoil in Saigon and get his government focused once more on the war in the countryside, the insurgency in the northern and central part of South Vietnam could be "reduced to little more than sporadic incidents by the end of 1964." He expected the southernmost part of the country to take a bit longer, but even there the war "should be completed by the end of 1965."[10]

President Kennedy also read much more pessimistic evaluations. These were written mostly by civilians – some by officials in the State department, others by journalists like Malcolm Browne and David Halberstam. Kennedy did not openly commit himself to either the optimists or the pessimists. The fact that he encouraged subordinates to draw up plans based on the optimists' projections should not be taken as proof that he believed the optimists were correct. It is not at all unusual in Washington for people to write plans based on a "best-case" scenario. It also seems possible that when Kennedy based plans on the optimists' projections, he was using this as a way of putting pressure on senior military officers to be realistic in their reports. They might be less inclined to write inflated claims of progress if they were clearly told that such claims would be treated as justifications for troop pullouts.

Secretary of Defense McNamara issued a directive in July 1962, calling for the formulation of a plan directed to the goal that by the end of 1965, the insurgency should be sufficiently under control, and the government of the Republic of Vietnam sufficiently strengthened, that the US could begin phasing out its special military assistance at that time.[11] General Harkins, commander of MACV, submitted a plan in January 1963, according to which MACV would no longer be needed after Fiscal Year 1965, and the strength of the US Military Assistance Advisory Group could be reduced by half.[12] When top officials met in Honolulu on May 6, 1963, General Harkins "did not attempt to predict a date when the insurgency would be broken, but did feel that we are certainly on the right track and that we are winning the war in Vietnam." McNamara said that the assumption for planning purposes was that the back of the insurgency would be broken by Fiscal Year 1965, and that he believed the plans for a US withdrawal were too slow; US forces should be reduced to a minimal level before Fiscal Year 1966. He ordered that a plan be prepared to begin the withdrawal before the end of 1963.[13] Admiral Felt came up with a plan for withdrawal of 1,000 men in four installments. Admiral Felt and the JCS seem to have believed that the purpose of the withdrawal was the impact it would have on American public opinion; the chairman of the JCS commented that doing it in four installments had the virtue of allowing "news prominence and coverage over an extended period of time."[14]

These plans were clearly contingent on continued success. McNamara's directive on May 6 had been that withdrawals could begin toward the end of the year "if the situation allows."[15] At a National Security Council meeting on October 2, President Kennedy indicated he did not want to get so locked into withdrawal plans that it would be difficult to cancel them if the war did not go so well after all (see below). On November 20, at a meeting in Honolulu, Ambassador Henry Cabot Lodge told other senior officials "we should continue to keep before us the goal of setting dates for phasing out US activities and turning them over to the Vietnamese...We can always grant last-minute extensions if we think it wise to do so."[16]

A few people associated with Kennedy have described something very different: a plan for withdrawal that was based on the expectation of failure rather than of success. These accounts suggest that Kennedy had given up hope of victory, but wanted to get through the 1964 election before acknowledging defeat in the struggle for South Vietnam. The first, the most detailed, and probably the most influential such story came from Kenneth O'Donnell, an aide to Kennedy, who published in 1970 and 1972 two slightly different versions of a statement he said Kennedy had made to him in private in 1963: "In 1965, I'll [*become one of the most unpopular Presidents in history. I'll*] be damned everywhere as a Communist appeaser. But I don't care. If I tried to pull out completely now [*from Vietnam*], we would have another Joe McCarthy red scare on our hands, but I can do it after I'm reelected."[17] It is hard to believe, however, that Kennedy as a politician would not have cared about spending his last three years in the White House politically crippled, one of the most unpopular presidents in history. It is hard to believe that Kennedy as a man who had spent so much effort cultivating an image of *machismo* and youthful vigor would not have cared about being thought a Communist appeaser.

There are worse problems with another story O'Donnell has told, that Kennedy had tried to get a strong statement about withdrawal released to the press, but failed:

> On October 2 [1963], when Defense Secretary Robert McNamara and General Maxwell Taylor came to a meeting of the National Security Council to report on a trip to Saigon, President Kennedy asked McNamara to announce to the press after the meeting the immediate withdrawal of one thousand soldiers and to say that we would probably withdraw all American forces from Vietnam by the end of 1965. When McNamara was leaving the meeting to talk to the White House reporters, the President called to him, "And tell them that means all of the helicopter pilots, too."
>
> McNamara discreetly softened the President's prediction of a complete withdrawal in his on-the-record statement to the press; he merely said that in his judgment "the major part of the US military task" in Vietnam could be "completed by the end of 1965."[18]

Kennedy did direct, at the October 2 meeting, that a statement be made to the press about withdrawal of soldiers from Vietnam. But Kennedy did not assign McNamara to make this statement, on the basis of verbal instructions. Kennedy went over a written draft at the meeting, and when he was satisfied with the text, he had it presented to the press not by McNamara but by White House Press Secretary Pierre Salinger. The minutes of the meeting indicate that the original draft had said the president expected to withdraw 1,000 men from Vietnam before the end of the year. It was President Kennedy, not McNamara, who wanted this watered down.

> The President objected to the phrase "by the end of this year" in the sentence "The US program for training Vietnamese should have progressed to the point where 1000 US military personnel assigned to South Vietnam could be withdrawn." He believed that if we were not able to take this action by the end of this year, we would be accused of being over optimistic.
>
> Secretary McNamara said he saw great value in this sentence in order to meet the view of Senator Fulbright and others that we are bogged down forever in Vietnam . . . .
>
> The draft announcement was changed to make both of the time predictions included in paragraph 3 a part of the McNamara–Taylor report rather than as predictions of the President.[19]

The revised draft of the portion of paragraph 3 under discussion, as approved by Kennedy as this meeting and then presented to the press, read:

> Secretary McNamara and General Taylor reported their judgment that the major part of the US military task can be completed by the end of 1965, although there may be a continuing requirement for a limited number of US training personnel. They reported that by the end of this year, the US program for training Vietnamese should have progressed to the point where 1,000 US military personnel assigned to South Viet Nam can be withdrawn.[20]

A few days later, the President formally directed "that no formal announcement be made of the implementation of plans to withdraw 1,000 US military personnel by the end of 1963."[21] On November 14, in what was to be his last press conference, Kennedy was asked whether he was still expecting to withdraw 1,000 men before the end of the year. He replied that he was planning to withdraw "several hundred" but that the exact number had not been decided.[22] The US military, however, continued using the figure of 1,000 men for a few more weeks. On November 15, Major General Charles Timmes announced in Saigon that the United States was planning to withdraw 1,000 servicemen in December, which would bring the number down to about 15,500.[23] The figure of 15,500 would in fact have represented a drop of more than a thousand from the level of October 1963, which had been 16,732.[24] On December 2, after Kennedy's death, General Harkins announced that 1,000 men were being withdrawn that month.[25]

The projected 1,000–man withdrawal was not actually carried out in full. In October, the US had had 16,732 military personnel in Vietnam. The number did drop by the end of December, but not by 1,000. A later US government estimate that it went down to about 16,300[26] has been widely accepted, though some sources give lower figures. The lack of a precise and reliable figure may result partly from embarrassment about the failure to withdraw the whole of the projected 1,000, and partly from embarrassment about the fact that the withdrawal that did occur was partially spurious. In a normal month, there were considerably more than 1,000 US military personnel leaving Vietnam, either through normal rotation or for medical reasons, and a similar number of personnel arriving to replace them. In December, the arrival of replacements was delayed, so the number of men in the country was artificially low at the end of the month.[27]

O'Donnell's suggestion that Kennedy had wanted the government firmly and publicly committed to a withdrawal, but that his subordinates had not issued the clear statement Kennedy had wanted, is so contradicted by the contemporary written record that it can safely be discarded.

There is other and more credible testimony, however, to strong private statements from Kennedy. When O'Donnell's story first appeared in 1970, Senator Mike Mansfield immediately said that Kennedy had told him also that he intended to withdraw from Vietnam after the 1964 election: "He had definitely and unequivocally made that decision . . . ."[28] Another friend of Kennedy's, the journalist Charles Bartlett, quoted him as having said in April 1963, "Those people hate us. They are going to throw our asses out of there at almost any point. But I can't give up a piece of territory like that to the Communists and then get the people to reelect me."[29]

Roger Hilsman, Director of the Bureau of Intelligence and Research at the State Department, had been much more realistic about supposed progress in Vietnam than the senior military officers were. Early in 1963, President Kennedy made Hilsman Assistant Secretary of State for Far Eastern Affairs. Kennedy told Hilsman that he himself had doubted ever since the mid 1950s the long-term viability of Ngo Dinh Diem's regime. He said Hilsman's principal job, as Assistant Secretary for Far Eastern Affairs, would be to keep Vietnam from becoming an American war.[30]

In the summer and fall of 1963, Kennedy's pessimism was deepening, and Hilsman says Kennedy was pushing Robert McNamara, hard, to get a plan drawn up for a withdrawal of US military personnel from South Vietnam. Kennedy was much more assertive on this in private than he was in formal meetings of the National Security Council. He was not ready for a fight over this; he especially did not want to tell the Joint Chiefs of Staff how eager he was to withdraw from Vietnam. What was discussed in the National Security Council was a plan to withdraw US troops when the Communist forces in South Vietnam had been so weakened that there was no longer a need for so many US personnel in Vietnam. In other words, withdrawal following from victory. What Kennedy told Hilsman in private was that he did not expect victory, and that he intended to withdraw anyway. He wanted Hilsman to be alert to prevent things from happening that would commit the United States more strongly to Vietnam, and thus make such a withdrawal more difficult.[31]

Kennedy did not say such things to very many people, certainly never at a meeting of his top defense and foreign policy officials. It is not merely that there is no available record of his having notified them of such a decision. If he had done so at some meeting for which no record is now available, this would dramatically have altered the tenor of discussion of Vietnam at the meetings for which records *are* available.

There are enough witnesses so that it is reasonable to believe that Kennedy did say he would pull out of Vietnam even without a victory. But to accept that he said this does not necessarily resolve the question of what he was thinking, because there were a number of occasions, far better documented, on which he indicated pretty clearly that he would not withdraw on any basis but victory.

In a press conference on July 17, 1963, asked about the struggle in Vietnam, he replied: "We are not going to withdraw from that effort. In my opinion, for us to withdraw from that effort would mean a collapse not only of South Viet-Nam, but of Southeast Asia. So we are going to stay there."[32] One passage in a televised interview September 2 has often been quoted: "in the final analysis it is the people and the Government [of South Vietnam] itself who have to win or lose this struggle. All we can do is help, and we are making it very clear." Less often quoted are the sentences that came immediately after: "But I don't agree with those who say we should withdraw. That would be a great mistake. . . . Forty-seven Americans have been killed in combat with the enemy, but this is a very important struggle . . ."[33] By including the direct participation of Americans in combat in his description of the policy from which he was saying he did not intend to withdraw, abandoning the pretense that they were just there as advisors, President Kennedy was himself doing what he had told Hilsman to prevent other officials from doing: significantly deepening his administration's rhetorical commitment to the war. On September 25, in a speech in Montana, he went a step further by exaggerating the scale of American military involvement, saying that in Vietnam there were "over 25,000 of your sons and brothers bearing arms."[34] The following day, he added:

> We are the keystone in the arch of freedom. If the United States were to falter, the whole world, in my opinion, would inevitably begin to move toward the Commuist bloc.
>
> So when you ask why are we in Laos, or Viet-Nam, or the Congo, . . . we do so because we believe that our freedom is tied up with theirs, and if we can develop a world in which all the countries are free, then the threat to the security of the United States is lessened. So we have to stay with it. We must not be fatigued.[35]

Was Kennedy lying when he told a few people he would abandon Vietnam? Or was he lying when he told far more people he would not do so? There is no need to assume he was lying in either set of statements.

The typical pattern of behavior, for an American leader faced with a choice between very unpalatable alternatives, is to put off making a firm choice for as long as possible, in the hope that some tolerable option will become apparent. Lyndon Johnson could see clearly in 1964 that he was faced with a choice between losing the Vietnam War and escalating it, but he was horrified by both alternatives so he waited until 1965 to escalate. Some of the decisions he may have made as early as October 1964, but these were tentative – he was still hoping to find some excuse not to carry out his plans for escalation.

Kennedy had not shown himself to be dramatically unusual in this regard. And if Kennedy once were going to make a firm decision long in advance to take an action that he knew would have very unpleasant consequences, the abandonment of South Vietnam seems a particularly odd choice. There seemed no possibility that this could be done without very high political costs. But the costs of *not* abandoning South Vietnam would not have seemed so clearly predictable. The political situation in Saigon was in flux; Kennedy could not know in 1963, *and does not seem to have thought he knew*, who would emerge in control of the government of South Vietnam. Why would he have assumed that there was no possibility someone worthy of continued support would rise to the top in Saigon? The situation in the Communist bloc, which would affect the amount of external support available to Hanoi, was also unpredictable.

Hilsman states very firmly that if faced with the choice Lyndon Johnson faced in 1965 – withdraw and let the Communists take Vietnam, or else make Vietnam an American war, first by the systematic bombing of North Vietnam, and then by the commitment of large US ground troop units – Kennedy certainly would have chosen to withdraw, because he did not believe the use of direct American military force would be capable of winning the war there.[36] This is a completely reasonable position. It can also be buttressed by other arguments. Fredrik Logevall, for example, has pointed out that Kennedy was more open than Johnson was to advice from allied governments that thought escalation was a mistake, such as those of England and France.[37]

The suggestions that have sometimes been made that Kennedy would not have had to make any decision in 1965, because he had already in 1963 committed himself to withdraw in 1965, is less reasonable. To have reached a firm decision to withdraw, so long in advance, he would have to have felt that no possible new development, between 1963 and 1965, might create a prospect of an acceptable outcome of a continued struggle. To have thought the situation was such an unmitigated and unmitigatable disaster, he would have had to think that most of what was being said about the Vietnam War in the National Security Council was nonsense, and that his top military and foreign policy advisors were fools or liars. If he felt that way, he did an extraordinary job of concealing it, and the tensions such a feeling would have generated. The record from 1963 in fact shows considerably better agreement between Kennedy and senior military officers, in regard to the size and role of US military forces in Vietnam, than there was between Lyndon Johnson and the same officers in 1964 and 1965. There is no sign that senior military officers were horrified by the idea of pulling 1,000 men out of Vietnam by the end of 1963; indeed, as was described above, the military continued public announcements about this plan even after Kennedy had backed away from it.

Kennedy was faced in 1963 with wildly divergent reports from his subordinates, some optimisitic, some pessimistic, about a very confusing and rapidly changing situation. Sometimes he himself spoke optimistically about it and said he would carry the struggle to victory; sometimes he spoke pessimistically and said he would pull out. It seems far more likely that this variation reflected variations in the way he felt about the war than that only the pessimistic statements were sincere, and that the optimistic ones were a tissue of lies in which he concealed that whole pattern of his thinking on Vietnam even from his top advisors. And if we do not accept such a picture of systematic and massive deception on Kennedy's part, we are left with the Kennedy who was described by his brother, probably his closest confidant, in an oral history interview in 1964. Robert Kennedy said that his brother as President had been determined not to lose Vietnam, and determined to keep it a Vietnamese war, not put Americans on the ground to fight it. Asked what John Kennedy would have done if he had been faced with a choice, if the Vietnamese were clearly losing and the only way to rescue the situation was to put Americans on the ground, Robert Kennedy said "We'd face that when we came to it."[38] If John Kennedy had remained President he would have faced that choice no later than 1965. He well might have decided to pull out, but if so it would have been a difficult decision for him, as difficult as Lyndon Johnson's decision to escalate.

We are left, in short, with a John Kennedy who was more inclined to large-scale military spending than Lyndon Johnson was, and not a lot less enthusiastic about the Vietnam War.

NOTES

1 *Statistical Abstract of the United States, 1966* (Washington: Department of Commerce, 1966), p. 252.

2 *Statistical Abstract of the United States, 1964* (Washington: Department of Commerce, 1964), p. 254; *Statistical Abstract of the United States, 1970* (Washington: Department of Commerce, 1970), p. 247.

3 Ray S. Cline, Oral History 2, May 31, 1983 (LBJ Presidential Library), pp. 21–2. Ted Gittinger, ed., *The Johnson Years: A Vietnam Roundtable* (Austin: Lyndon Baines Johnson Library, 1993), pp. 24–5.

4 Joseph Califano, *The Triumph and Tragedy of Lyndon Johnson* (New York: Simon & Schuster, 1991), p. 32.

5 *Statistical Abstract of the United States, 1970*, p. 258.

6 Theodore Heavner, Memorandum for the Files, December 27, 1962, in *Foreign Relations of the United States, Vietnam* (referred to hereafter as *FRUS*), 1962, p. 798.

7 Quoted in *United States–Vietnam Relations, 1945–1967*, (Washington: US Government Printing Office, 1971), Book 3, IV-B-4, p. 11.

8   Harkins to Taylor, August 22, 1963, in *FRUS*, January–August 1963, p. 608.

9   *New York Times*, January 31, 1963, p. 4.

10 Quoted in *United States–Vietnam Relations, 1945–1967*, Book 3, IV-B-4, p. 20.

11 Ambassador Nolting to Department of State, March 26, 1963, in *FRUS*, January–August 1963, pp. 178–9.

12 General Paul Harkins, "Comprehensive Plan for South Vietnam", January 19, 1963, *FRUS* January–August 1963, p. 45.

13 Memorandum for the Record of the Secretary of Defense Conference Honolulu, May 6, 1963, *FRUS* January–August 1963, pp. 265, 267–8, 270.

14 *FRUS* January–August 1963, pp. 591–3.

15 Memorandum for the Record of the Secretary of Defense Conference Honolulu, May 6, 1963, *FRUS* January–August 1963, p. 270.

16 *FRUS*, August–December 1963, p. 610.

17 Kenneth O'Donnell, "LBJ and the Kennedys," *Life*, August 7, 1970, pp. 51–2. The words in italics were added in the version of the quote in Kenneth P. O'Donnell and David F. Powers, with Joe McCarthy, *Johnny, We Hardly Knew Ye: Memories of John Fitzgerald Kennedy* (Boston: Little, Brown, 1972), p. 16.

18 O'Donnell, *Johnny*, p. 17.

19 Summary Record of the 519th Meeting of the National Security Council, October 2, 1963, in *FRUS*, August–December 1963, p. 351.

20 *FRUS*, August–December 1963, p. 353; full text also in *Department of State Bulletin*, October 21, 1963, p. 624.

21 National Security Action Memorandum 263, October 11, 1963, in *FRUS*, August December 1963, p. 396, reporting a decision Kennedy made in a meeting October 5.

22 *Public Papers of the Presidents*, 1963, p. 852.

23 *New York Times*, November 16, 1963, p. 1.

24 *United States–Vietnam Relations, 1945–1967*, Book 3, IV-B-4, p. 30.

25 *FRUS*, August–December 1963, p. 652.

26 *Statistical Abstract of the United States, 1967*, p. 264.

27 *United States–Vietnam Relations, 1945–1967*, Book 3, IV-B-4, p. 30.

28 *Washington Post*, August 3, 1970, A1 (I am indebted to Scott Mathias and Bryan Schmuck for this reference).

29 Fredrik Logevall, *Choosing War: The Lost Chance for Peace and the Escalation of War in Vietnam* (Berkeley: University of California Press, 1999), pp. 38–9. For another version of the quote, different in phrasing but not in substance, see Seymour M. Hersh, *The Dark Side of Camelot* (Boston: Little, Brown, 1997), p. 418.

30 Roger Hilsman, personal communications.

31 Roger Hilsman, personal communications.

32 Quoted in *United States–Vietnam Relations, 1945–1967*, Book 7, V-A-1-C, p. 37.

33 Ibid, pp. 40–1.

34 Ibid, p. 42; see also press conference, September 12, 1963.

35 Ibid, pp. 43–4.

36 Roger Hilsman, personal communications.

37 Logevall, p. 396.

38 Edwin O. Guthman and Jeffrey Shulman, eds., *Robert Kennedy In His Own Words: The Unpublished Recollections of the Kennedy Years* (New York: Bantam, 1988), p. 394–5. I am indebted for this reference to Douglas Macdonald.

CHAPTER ELEVEN

The Politics of Escalation in Vietnam During the Johnson Years

ROBERT BUZZANCO

In an extraordinary August 1967 meeting of the Joint Chiefs of Staff [JCS] America's military leaders, frustrated and angry over what they perceived as the civilian-imposed military policy of the Vietnam War, apparently discussed and agreed to resign *en masse* to protest President Lyndon Johnson's handling of the war. Though not carried out, the chiefs' plan demonstrates the depths to which civil–military relations had sunk and the extent to which politics had come to dominate military affairs regarding Vietnam.[1]

Since that time, however, US military leaders, politicians, and scholars critical of Lyndon Johnson's conduct of the war have in large part rehabilitated the US role in Vietnam. American military forces in Indochina, these conservative revisionists argue, had performed well enough to achieve victory, but had been forced to fight with "one hand tied behind their back" by craven politicians, an adverserial press, and the Peace Movement. The war then was lost in Washington, DC rather than in Vietnam.[2]

The revisionists are correct. American leaders – both civilian and military – did base their approaches to the war in Vietnam on considerations of politics within the United States as well as in the Republic of Vietnam [RVN] in the south and the Democratic Republic of Vietnam [DRVN] in the north. Especially during Lyndon Johnson's presidency, from late 1963 until the crisis of the 1968 Tet Offensive, political concerns conditioned US policy in Vietnam. The White House was more concerned with its Great Society programs at home and hoped to avoid a wider war in Southeast Asia, and thus it committed American resources and soldiers to a war that it would contradictorily expand and restrain at the same time.

US service leaders developed military policy with politics in mind as well. They continually recognized the parlous situation in Vietnam but consistently pressed for more troops and escalation of the war, even though it was clear from the beginning to many military and political officials that such expansion would neither bring progress nor be forthcoming. Consequently, civil–military relations – already damaged by the reorganization and budget battles of the 1940s and 1950s and the Bay of Pigs debacle in 1961 – became even more politicized and strained. Such developments had a clear impact on policy for Vietnam as civilian and armed forces leaders created a cycle of recognizing deterioration in Vietnam, military requests for total escalation, and White House denial of such proposals.

· Neither side really attempted to break the cycle and seek new ways to end the war. The military, since it would not gain authorization to fight the type of war it wanted, forced the president to make hard decisions regarding the future of the war. For his part, Lyndon Johnson, who was aware of the military's often bleak evaluations and concerned about the political implications of US intervention, kept waiting for the military to turn the corner in Vietnam. After Tet 1968 the president finally took decisive action – rejecting another massive escalation of the war – but his hesitation and vacillation to that point would provide the basis for the revisionist critique which has created so much political currency since then.[3]

The military's reservations regarding combat in Asia antedated the massive US commitment to Vietnam of the 1960s. As Bruce Cumings points out in his study of the origins of the Korean War, "presumably 'conservative' military figures dragged their feet" while "liberal" political leaders expanded American participation in the Korean and Vietnamese conflicts. Similarly, more than any other institution the US Armed Forces worked against an American military role in the First Indochina War in the early 1950s.[4] And, notwithstanding John Newman's and Oliver Stone's arguments that the JCS pressured President John F. Kennedy into deeper commitments to the RVN despite his grave reservations, there is ample evidence that even in the early 1960s the military did not feel compelled to intervene in Indochina.[5] Thus, as Lyndon B. Johnson assumed the presidency in late 1963, there was no military imperative driving the United States into Vietnam.

Indeed, reports from Vietnam indicated continued deterioration, with the enemy Viet Cong [VC] holding the military initiative, the government of the RVN experiencing political turmoil, the RVN's Armed Forces [RVNAF] vulnerable to the enemy, passive and suffering from poor morale, and pacification efforts such as the Strategic Hamlets program failing.[6] More directly, Marine General and incoming Commandant Wallace M. Greene, Jr., speaking to fellow officers in 1963, feared that American troops were already "mired down in South Vietnam ... and we don't seem to be able to do much about it." The Marines, Greene continued, "do not want to get any more involved in South Vietnam because if we do we cannot execute our primary mission ... and we've got enough business right now."[7]

A March 1964 report by General Richard Stilwell, the Assistant Chief for Plans in the Military Assistance Command, Vietnam [MACV], seemed to confirm that the Americans were mired down in Vietnam. In analyzing counterinsurgency in the RVN, Stilwell discovered that poor training, an unenthusiastic population, and ineffective leadership had undermined the southern government's efforts to increase its political appeal. While arguing that more US resources – money and equipment – could improve the situation, Stilwell admitted that crucial problem areas such as intelligence, effective combat operations, command and control, military initiative and motivation, and popular support for the government required more than increased funding. Perhaps because of this recognition, Stilwell's recommended action did not include the introduction of US combat troops to Vietnam.[8]

By August 1964, in the aftermath of the Gulf of Tonkin incident, new MACV Commander William C. Westmoreland expected VC infiltration and operations to increase and thus urged the White House to prepare to deploy additional US forces to Vietnam (Da Nang specifically) in the event of enemy action beyond the RVNAF's capability to contain. Westmoreland, however, was also aware that such reinforcement, as well as operational planning to cut enemy infiltration via pursuit into Cambodia and Laos and massive air strikes, ran the risk of provoking the northern People's Army of Vietnam [PAVN] and the People's Republic of China [PRC] into the war in southern Vietnam.[9]

In the coming months Westmoreland, the MACV staff, and the Ambassador to the RVN, General Maxwell D. Taylor, would more directly confront the issue of a widening war as the United States deployed combat troops to Da Nang in March 1965. In January, however, the MACV staff, with Taylor's concurrence, opposed the introduction of such ground forces. Although Westmoreland and his planners observed that the US advisory effort had stalled and the war was going badly, they assumed that the use of US combat personnel carried great disadvantages, including increased American responsibility for the war, mounting casualties, and Communist propaganda equating Americans with French imperialists. To Taylor and the MACV, combat intervention "would at best buy time and would lead to ever increasing commitments until, like the French, we would be occupying an essentially hostile foreign country."[10]

In a separate cable, General Taylor bluntly added that the White House had to choose between supporting the current government in the RVN, or refusing to do so and accepting the consequences, "which might entail ultimate withdrawal" as he saw it.[11] Taylor's reservations, as Larry Berman has documented, continued throughout early 1965 and he consistently opposed the introduction of combat troops into Vietnam.[12] His influence waned, however, and in late February the president and his advisors decided to deploy two Marine battalions to Da Nang to provide base security and hopefully stem the continued deterioration in the south. The Marine presence notwithstanding, the service chiefs doubted that the new troops would do much to improve the situation, while the JCS chair, General Earle Wheeler, feared that the VC might have already progressed to the point that it could cause the RVN to collapse regardless of US action against the enemy.[13]

Westmoreland discounted such worries but notified Wheeler and the Commander-in-Chief of Pacific Forces [CINCPAC], Admiral US Grant Sharp, in early June that the Army of the RVN [ARVN] was plagued by mounting casualties – "several battalions had been decimated by the VC," the MACV lamented – and high desertion rates and thus would not realize its planned expansion for 1965.[14] Worse, as Marine General Fredrick J. Karch assumed command at Da Nang he found the MACV staff "dismal" over US prospects in the war, the VC still holding the politico-military initiative, and the ARVN still passive, defensive and corrupt. Vietnam, Karch would later charge, "was just one big cancer."[15] And it was metastasizing as officials in Saigon and Washington continued to recognize their imperiled position in Vietnam throughout the spring and early summer of 1965. Nonetheless in late July President Johnson increased the US troop level from 75,000 to 125,000 and agreed to send additional forces to Westmoreland "as requested."[16]

The military's response to the growing crises of 1965 reflected its awareness of both military problems in Vietnam, and the politics of war. Despite recognizing the obstacles to success inherent in a military campaign in Indochina, neither military nor civilian officials seriously considered alternatives to expanding the US manpower base and escalating the war. The Johnson administration, as George McT. Kahin observes, made a "political calculation" that the fall of the RVN to the Communists would open the Democrats to a Vietnamese version of the "loss of China" charges of the 1950s. Then Johnson, as previous Democrats had been, would be vulnerable to "serious domestic political attack" if he "lost" Vietnam.[17]

For its part, the military's reports and analyses clearly demonstrated that success would be elusive at best. Yet America's generals also understood that the political will of the Johnson administration to fight in Vietnam was strong, and accordingly began to pressure civilian leaders to expand the war.[18] From the beginning, however, the military understood that it would not receive authorization to fight the type of totally unrestrained war for which it asked. Politics and public opinion – as well as the objective conditions of Vietnam – would invariably mitigate against escalation and limit the war. Nonetheless the MACV and JCS continued to advocate the same policies – essentially more troops for attrition warfare and totally unrestricted air strikes – from 1965 until the end of the Johnson presidency. If they would not win the war, US military leaders would at least force the White House to bear responsibility for the outcome. Meanwhile the president, equally concerned with the political implications of the situation, waited for Westmoreland to create enough success to provide a way out of Vietnam with the least damage to all parties.

Such political considerations were evident early in the Johnson years. In a frank November 1964 memo to the president, his advisor Jack Valenti recommended that the White House "sign on" the JCS before making any final decisions regarding Vietnam. By bringing the military into the process, Valenti pointed out, the Chiefs "will have been heard, they will have been part of the consensus, and our flank will have been covered in the event of some kind of flap or investigation later."[19] Similarly, Assistant Secretary of Defense John McNaughton, only days after the Marines landed at Da Nang, contended that seventy percent of the US objective in Vietnam was "to avoid a humiliating...defeat," both internationally and at home. "[D]omestic political considerations [were] so ingrained" in the president's and his advisor's minds, George Kahin explains, that they were "taken for granted and require[d] no explicit articulation" in McNaughton's memorandum.[20]

During simultaneous May 1965 trips to Vietnam, both Maxwell Taylor and the Marine Corp's Pacific Commander, General Victor H. Krulak, recognized that domestic politics would constrain the US effort. Taylor, as Krulak reported, feared that, "however successful we are, it is still going to take a long time to win, and...the nation at large may not have the requisite patience." General Wallace Greene was more blunt. The American attitude toward this "unwanted, undesired, miserable war" was getting worse, and at least half of Americans, as the Commandant saw it, "don't want anything to do with it."[21]

Obviously the president recognized such domestic concerns as his advisors debated Westmoreland's plea for more troops in June and July 1965. To Johnson, public dissent at home, trouble on the battlefield in Vietnam, and the threat of intervention by the PRC meant that the US had to deter the enemy "as much as we can, and as simply as we can, without going all out." By approving Westmoreland's troop request, the president made clear, "we get in deeper and it is harder to get out....We must determine which course gives us the maximum protection at the least cost."[22] Admiral Sharp, was also concerned about the coming escalation of the war, warning Westmoreland that – although he had authority to commit US forces to combat – he had to "realize that there would be grave political implications involved if sizable US forces are committed for the first time and suffer a defeat."[23]

Those implications notwithstanding, the president's major advisors – with General Taylor and undersecretary of state George Ball dissenting – came to a consensus on the need for more troops and the need to limit the war in July 1965.[24] Accordingly, Westmoreland himself, though clamoring for more forces and a fully unrestrained bombing campaign, understood that any plans to operate beyond the RVN's borders to cut infiltration "was not in the cards in the foreseeable future because of complex political and other considerations."[25] Although US military leaders would direct great efforts toward expanding the war from July 1965 until Tet 1968, they could see from the beginning that unlimited escalation was never a politically viable option, yet it was a choice they kept presenting to the president.

At the same time the military continued to recognize its problems in Vietnam. In a September 1965 directive on US force employment and strategy, the MACV acknowledged enemy domination of much of the RVN, and also understood that American forces could not destroy the insurgents without unduly risking the lives, and hence political approval, of non-combatants in regions of VC influence. Such warfare, MACV officers admitted, "requires an extremely high caliber of leadership plus the exercise of judgment and restraint not formerly expected of soldiers."[26] Even Westmoreland's chief for planning, General William DePuy, a strident advocate of American firepower use in Vietnam, understood the grave politico-military dangers facing the Americans in Vietnam. In a remarkable briefing at Marine Headquarters in October, DePuy admitted that there was no end in sight for the war. "The thing that's going to keep US troops in Vietnam for a long, long time," he explained, "is the fact that the government of [southern] Vietnam is really bankrupt."[27]

The US forces in Vietnam would have to overcome a dedicated and impressive enemy as well. The VC "fight like tigers," DePuy observed, "and the discipline they display on the battlefields is fantastic." During the much-publicized Operation STARLITE in August, the VC "maneuvered in the jungle, maintained tactical integrity, withdrew their wounded, lost practically no weapons, and did a first class job. We'd be proud of American troops of any kind who did as well against such a large force [in this case the 173d Airborne division] that surprised them in the middle of the jungle." The general also recognized that such conditions were likely to continue. The RVN's political leadership was likely to remain unstable for an indefinite time, and the enemy was not likely to shift to a big-unit war where it would be vulnerable to US firepower. On top of that analysis – which the MACV's planners essentially disregarded in developing their conventional strategy – DePuy recognized that civilian officials would put limits on the US commitment. Although the MACV hoped to add two additional divisions in its plans for 1967, "only time will tell whether the manpower base will be able to support it. It won't unless there's been progress." It was more likely, DePuy concluded, that "we'll be forced to win the war by attrition and penny packets [a derisive term for incremental reinforcement]."[28]

Westmoreland was equally candid in a late November meeting with Robert McNamara, telling the Defense Secretary that the war so far "had been characterized by an underestimation of the enemy and overestimation of the [presumably southern] Vietnamese." Accordingly, the war was assuming "an attritional character with heavy losses on both sides," and American leaders would have to "take a good hard look at our future posture." The MACV Commander, however, realized that the future was uncertain at best. In December 1965 he told Ambassador Henry Cabot Lodge that he would like to request extended terms of enlistment and an activation of reserves for Vietnam, but he already knew that such an authorization "might require drastic action that could be politically difficult for the President."[29]

By late 1965, then, chaos in the government of the RVN, continued VC success, and political considerations in Washington were damaging US efforts in Vietnam. Worse, the MACV itself began to feel the strains of an interservice rivalry which would be a serious irritant throughout the war. In September, Westmoreland recognized that the Air Force was pressuring its leaders in Vietnam to "push the Air Force party line" and emphasize the air war over northern Vietnam.[30] But it was against the Marines – who were responsible for I Corps Tactical Zone in the northern RVN – that Westmoreland and the Army had its biggest battles. Since deploying to Vietnam in March, the Marine leadership had stressed a strategy of civic action, or pacification, as the means to provide security and coopt the VC's political appeal. Such an approach, however, ran directly contrary to the MACV reliance on firepower and "search and destroy" tactics. However, the Marines, as well as Army mavericks like John Paul Vann and others, contended that the resulting destruction from such conduct would alienate the Vietnamese people and thus strengthen the enemy's position.[31]

Westmoreland on the other hand saw the Marines' emphasis on civic action as a diversion from the need to eradicate the enemy and concentrate their offensive punch against VC strongholds. In fact, the MACV Commander charged, American forces in I Corps had become dangerously dispersed and were hesitant to conduct offensive operations other than coastal maneuvers when naval gunfire was available.[32] For the Marines, General Krulak led the counterattack against Westmoreland and the Army leadership within the MACV. In a December 1965 strategic appraisal Krulak urged a strategy quite unlike any proposed at military headquarters in Saigon. In addition to continuing attacks on the enemy's material resources, the Marines' Pacific Commander argued that it was imperative to "shift the thrust of the GVN and US ground effort to the task of delivering the people from guerrilla oppression, and to protecting them adequately thereafter." Thus Krulak wanted Westmoreland to "put the full weight of our top level effort into bringing all applicable resources – US and GVN – into the pacification process."[33]

The Marine Commandant reinforced Krulak's views during a January 1966 visit to Vietnam. American and ARVN forces, General Wallace Greene noted, "could kill all [the] PAVN & VC [in the south] & still lose the war" unless pacification was given priority. Greene then compared Westmoreland's strategy of attrition to "a grindstone that's being turned by the Communist side, and we're backing into it and having our skin taken off of...our entire body without accomplishing a damn thing because they've got enough to keep the old stone going." The Commandant also presciently understood that the VC could withstand losses twenty or thirty times greater than America "because in the end, although their casualty rate may be fifty times what ours is, they'll be able to win through their capability to wage a war of attrition." Yet, Greene concluded, "this is a thing that apparently the Army doesn't understand." Krulak added that the JCS Chair "doesn't understand it" either, whereas US congressmen, presumably more attentive to public opinion and obligated to vote on war-related issues, were aware of the perils of Westmoreland's strategy. Krulak, citing Wheeler's recent pleasure with operations in which the VC suffered about seven times more casualties than America, then wondered "just how...did that bring us nearer to winning the war?...[T]his is not the strategy for victory."[34] Such candid and often bleak comments clearly showed that high-ranking military officials, fully two years before the crisis of the Tet Offensive, understood the US military and political dilemma in Vietnam.

After barely two years in the White House, then, Lyndon Johnson had committed increasing amounts of resources and troops to Vietnam with a full understanding of the troubles that lay ahead and the limits to future expansion of the war. At the same time, Westmoreland, Wheeler, Marine leaders, and other military figures were equally aware of obstacles to future progress and the political constraints on military policy, yet they continued to seek more forces and bombs. Thus, for both the White House and the US military, political considerations would increasingly determine the course of the war. Johnson and the service chiefs, in their crucial 1965 decisions to commit to and expand the American combat role in Vietnam, had determined the nature and limits of military policy, while also establishing patterns of civil–military relations which would continue, and disintegrate, throughout the rest of their time in Vietnam.

From 1966 until the Tet Offensive the military would take an increasingly sanguine view of the war, yet consistently recognize serious shortcomings in the RVN's political and military institutions, the enemy's strength, and the political factors which were invariably restraining the war. Rather than seek a new approach to Vietnam, however, the MACV and JCS kept pressuring the White House for more soldiers, activation of reservists, and approval of new bombing targets even though they knew that Johnson was never likely to authorize the levels of escalation which the brass was urging. As a result, American continued its war of attrition in Indochina, the president continued to avoid decisive action while incrementally expanding the US commitment, and the MACV, in addition to fighting the VC and PAVN, had to manage both an interservice feud, in Saigon, and political battles over its conduct of the war, in Washington.

The situation in Vietnam at the beginning of 1966 had not changed appreciably from the previous year. Westmoreland, who was lobbying to be named Ambassador in addition to Commander of the MACV, urged that the various American efforts in Vietnam – political, military, economic, and internal security – be merged in order to support the "greatly weakened" RVN. The Communists, on the other hand, had "learned this lesson well. Their integration of effort surpasses ours by a large order of magnitude."[35] Whatever hopes Westmoreland may have had for integration and stability were dashed barely two months later when the Buddhist-led "Struggle Movement" – which included ARVN officers and units – conducted large-scale anti-government demonstrations in Hue, Da Nang, and elsewhere in I Corps.

The impact of such political turmoil on the US effort was obvious. The MACV Deputy Commander, General John Heintges, feared that "our people back home are going to get their dander up and want to wash their hands of this mess over here." Krulak was, if anything, more bleak. "Repressive measures are all that is left" to quash the domestic dissent, he wrote to Admiral Sharp, "and you will recall what happened after Diem launched his repressive measures." Krulak also admitted that, "despite all our public assertions to the contrary, the South Vietnamese are not – and never have been – a nation."[36]

Wheeler's outlook from Washington was just as alarming. "Several key congressmen," he informed Sharp and Westmoreland, believed that America was now "overextended in our military commitments . . . and will be unable to support adequately our present forces and surely cannot support additional forces." The JCS Chair also reported that civilian officials had expressed concern over not only the inchoate political situation in the RVN but also the "very low level of Vietnamese military activities" during the Buddhist crisis, and the RVNAF's casualty rates, which were lower than those of US forces. More directly the president, satisfied that Westmoreland was "sufficiently understanding" of the constraints imposed on him, told the MACV commander at Honolulu in February 1966, "General, I have a lot riding on you. I hope you don't pull a MacArthur on me."[37]

By late May Wheeler found the reaction in Washington to the "continuing political turmoil . . . far more adverse than heretofore" experienced. With 250,000 troops in Vietnam, American prestige on the line, and US casualties mounting, the American people "rightly or wrongly" saw developments in Vietnam as "proof positive" of antiwar leaders' charges that American soldiers were fighting and dying while RVN officials "squabble pettily among themselves to achieve political advantage." Wheeler also realized that even a "farfetched" – to use his description – proposal by Senator Jacob Javits to stop the air war and cease offensive ground operations would have "distinct appeal," both to political doves and "even more importantly, to the relatives of our men in South Vietnam whose lives are at risk." And Wheeler himself admitted "much sympathy" for the latter group.[38]

Time, then, was not on Earle Wheeler's side in early 1966, as public opinion at home, the continued enemy build-up in southern Vietnam, and interservice friction were conspiring to seriously hamper the American military campaign.[39] Even if, as Westmoreland was claiming, the media had exaggerated the gravity of US problems in the war, the perception among Americans of stasis in Vietnam could not be ignored.[40] Wheeler seemed to understand this, citing Gallup Poll statistics on rising antiwar sentiment and observing that press reports, though tending to be "highly colored," would "if true...indicate a far more serious situation, both current and impending, than you and your officers on the scene believe to be the case."[41]

But Westmoreland and his staff were aware of many of the problems in the RVN. A MACV study pointed out that the RVN's primary manpower pool – 20 to 30 year old men – would be exhausted by 1968, and the secondary group – those 16 to 19, 31 to 45, and others previously considered unqualified for service – would run out by mid-1969. Along with its manpower problems, the RVN lacked the material resources to sustain its economy, thus creating serious inflation and "diluting the focus of the war effort." To Westmoreland it was "obvious...[that] the RVN has failed to organize itself to meet the heavy demands placed upon its manpower and its economy by the pressures of war." Accordingly the southern Vietnamese would have to fully mobilize their human and material resources for the war effort, but, the MACV Commander understood, such moves would carry "serious implications" for the governments of the RVN and United States.[42]

In addition to planning for mobilization, the MACV also understood that it had to confront serious corruption within the ARVN, which could not be overcome by "changing a man or two or by other half-way measures." As one of Westmoreland's deputies put it, "the entire administrative system must be overhauled."[43]

Amid the recognition of such structural problems in the RVN, the military also had to confront its future in Vietnam and the political limits of the war. Writing to the Army Chief of Staff Harold K. Johnson, Westmoreland hoped for a "maximum buildup" to bring "an earlier successful conclusion," but added that "considerations of quality, including morale, may well justify a smaller force" than the maximum envisioned. Such considerations, the MACV chief understood, "include the assumption that there will be no major call up of reserves." Nevertheless Westmoreland would continue to make that very request throughout the war.[44]

In Washington, Harold K. Johnson did not have good news for Westmoreland. The more he deliberated over the MACV's force requests, "the more uncertain I am as to my ability to give you a [satisfactory] answer." With voluntary enlistments lower than expected, draft calls inadequate for Westmoreland's needs, too little time to train new troops, and congressional criticism that the Army was overextended in Southeast Asia, the Army Chief saw "no indication here to carry the war outside South Vietnam." In fact, "the tendency to limit the war to South Vietnam is hardening." Westmoreland in fact claimed to be shocked by Washington's response to the MACV's plans, replying to General Johnson that "your analysis of the impact on forces requested by this command is far greater than my wildest assumptions."[45]

There is some question, however, regarding the genuineness of Westmoreland's astonishment. At a debriefing with Marine leaders the MACV Commander and Admiral Sharp reported that Defense Secretary McNamara had informed them that US force levels would "have to be consistent with political, psychological and economic factors, as they impact on the GVN." There was a "definite limit," Westmoreland and Sharp realized, to the amount of money – and hence the number of US troops – that could be put into the RVN. Accordingly, General Krulak observed, the MACV would have to contend with a new limitation on US military policy – "one that cannot be related to shortages back home." Westmoreland understood the situation, admitting that "we have really crossed the Rubicon. We are involved deeply in what is almost certain to be a long war. Everyone knows this, and what we need now is to settle down with a professional force that our country can support for the long pull, without calling up reserves." Westmoreland then estimated that a US force of 480,000 would be adequate for Vietnam, which was exactly the number which McNamara had earlier urged. Their agreement "seems remarkable," Krulak sarcastically observed, "and convenient too."[46]

Westmoreland's upbeat evaluation notwithstanding, Harold K. Johnson confessed his "continuing concern with the level and tempo of combat activity that we can support." Concern over inflation in the RVN had forced McNamara to limit US expenditures to about 44 billion piasters and, the Army Chief expected, a ceiling on US deployments was likely as well. "We are already overcommitted in maneuver battalions for the level of support that is available for them," Johnson warned Westmoreland, and limits to piaster expenditures would continue to directly affect US combat capability in Vietnam.[47]

McNamara made that precise argument to Wheeler, observing that economic stability in the RVN was essential for political stability and military progress. "Runaway inflation," the secretary warned, "can undo what our military operations accomplish."[48] Westmoreland understood such worries, telling US congressmen that "we had to prepare the American people for a long war in Vietnam. I frankly could not see an early ending." In this war of attrition, US leaders would thus have to create a force which could be "sustained indefinitely."[49]

The civilian leadership, however, had its own frank appraisal of the war. Various officials, Wheeler reported to Westmoreland, were beginning to raise questions about the conduct of the war "which may in a fairly short time cause us difficulty." Specifically, Washington remained troubled by the lack of emphasis given to pacification, the continuing lack of ARVN military activity, and growing Communist infiltration into the south, which was offsetting the VC's huge losses.[50] But thwarting the enemy's movement into the RVN, Westmoreland conceded, was difficult because the MACV lacked "any precise means to differentiate between the North … and South Vietnamese."[51]

In evaluating pacification in I Corps, Westmoreland found Marine Commander Lewis Walt confident of future success, but the MACV Commander expected continued deterioration in the northern provinces in 1967. In fact, the enemy had the potential to disrupt the US effort throughout the RVN. The VC or PAVN "can attack at any time" in I, II, and III Corps in divisional strength, and in IV Corps with regimental strength, local forces and guerrillas, while simultaneously continuing harassing attacks at points of their choosing. In addition, Chinese and Soviet aid to the insurgency in Vietnam would likely increase, as would infiltration into the RVN and training of political cadre already in the south.[52]

The MACV leadership continued to cite the ARVN's deficiencies as well. The rapid expansion of the RVN's military establishment, Westmoreland noted, had "negate[d] concurrent efforts" to increase the level of armed forces leadership. And that situation was nearing a crisis point. Future success would thus require "immediate and substantial qualitative improvements in all aspects of RVNAF capabilities and operations."[53]

Despite such forthright evaluations, the military continued to emphasize its accomplishments and to expect progress. In a January 1967 evaluation, the MACV stressed that the American and ARVN forces were routing the enemy, many VC and supporters were rallying to the RVN, and pacification was likely to improve markedly in the coming year. While the enemy's determination had not weakened, "the conflict has taken a decided turn for the best."[54]

The JCS had a more ambivalent view of the war. In a report for McNamara on future courses of action, the Chiefs pointed out that they had consistently requested a greater bombing effort over the north, mining of ports, cross border operations, a reserve callup, and extended terms of service for US soldiers. While the JCS sought to "break the [White House's] pattern of slow escalation and apparent vacillation," it recognized that "fundamental parts" of the military's planning for an expanded war "have never been accepted." The Chiefs nonetheless put forth the same recommendations that they had been sending to the civilian leaders in Washington for over two years.[55]

Rather than adapt to the political–economic–military realities of the war, US military leaders were, in essence, forcing the president to choose between a politically difficult – if not impossible – escalation, or continued stasis. Since Johnson was no more likely than the brass to reevaluate the war, and was if anything more aware of the domestic ramifications of both expansion and failure, the JCS had put the ball into the White House's court. If Lyndon Johnson's limited war in Indochina failed, then at least he would be responsible for it.

In the early months of 1967 the US military seemed to be involved in battles in Vietnam and Washington, DC. Wheeler warned Westmoreland that the debate over the air war had "heightened in intensity, with critics of bombing most vocal." The JCS Chair's report could hardly have come at a worse time, for just weeks later the MACV Commander admitted "without hesitation" that the war on the ground – due to intelligence problems and inadequate helicopter support, as well as uncertain troop availability – "cannot be significantly accelerated" beyond current and projected levels. Westmoreland shortly thereafter added that the VC's "strength, armament, professionalism and activity" were increasing; thus America could "ill afford" to withhold available military from Vietnam, especially air power.[56]

The military, however, pointed out the dilemma the MACV faced in escalating the war. Westmoreland recognized, as he later put it, that "even had Washington adopted a strong bombing policy, I still doubt that the North Vietnamese would have relented." "The influx of men and materials" into the south, Admiral Sharp admitted, "has increased despite considerable air effort expended to hinder infiltration." But Sharp also knew that the White House's reluctance to remove even more restrictions was "based primarily on political considerations." The JCS Chair, however, thought that those political factors might work to the military's benefit. In addition to citing damage done to the VC and PAVN by US air strikes, Wheeler contended that growing antiwar sentiment might induce the president to grant broader authority to conduct the bombing campaign. Johnson, Wheeler believed, valued the military's advice above all others. Accordingly, "the only obstacle which could impede additional authority for military action would be one created by us."[57]

Although the obstacle to which Wheeler referred was public criticism of the president by military leaders, another appeared just days later. In revising its statistics on enemy action, the MACV found that the number of VC initiated major unit attacks was actually about 400 percent higher than originally estimated. Upon receiving the new numbers an obviously alarmed Wheeler cabled Westmoreland that "if these figures should reach the public domain, they would, literally, blow the lid off of Washington." He thus directed the MACV to do "whatever is necessary" to avoid disclosure of the new information.[58]

The JCS leader, as Larry Berman makes clear, understood the political impact of such appraisals. "I cannot go to the President and tell him," Wheeler observed, "that contrary to my reports and those of the other chiefs as to the progress of the war . . . the situation is such that we are not sure who has the initiative in South Vietnam." Surely the president was not ignorant of that reality. Johnson, as Berman contends, "never intended" to escalate the war as the military was urging, and developments in Vietnam in early 1967 had reinforced that position. Nonetheless as the president and military officials met at Guam in late March, Westmoreland – whom Johnson had told to produce a "coonskin on the wall" only months earlier – was, as National Security Advisor Walt W. Rostow put it, "conservative and non-promissory." The MACV Commander did, however, request reinforcement of up to 200,000 additional forces. But Defense Secretary McNamara, among others, had soured on the war, and believed that attrition would ultimately fail, as Berman wrote, "as a military strategy as well as a presidential policy for political survival."[59]

The president himself had made such concerns clear to Westmoreland and Wheeler when the MACV Commander claimed that US/ARVN forces had eroded enemy strength to the "crossover point" at which its losses exceeded input into the south. In response, Johnson wondered, "when we add divisions, can't the enemy add divisions? If so, when does it all end?" Moreover, the Commander-in-Chief asked, "at what point does the enemy ask for [presumably Chinese] volunteers?" The generals' answers were not reassuring. The insurgents had eight divisions in the RVN already and could add four more, Westmoreland reported. With current US troop levels of 470,000 "we would be setting up a meat grinder." With 100,000 additional forces the war "could well go on for three years," and even with reinforcement to bring US manpower to 665,000 it could continue for another two years. Wheeler added that such a buildup would have international repercussions, expecting diversionary pressure from North against South Korea, Soviet moves in Berlin to force America to reinforce its European force structure, Soviet, Chinese and Korean "volunteers" going into the RVN, or even overt PRC intervention into Vietnam or elsewhere in Southeast Asia. The JCS Chair also admitted that the air war – the military's fundamental answer to the problems of Vietnam – "is reaching the point where we will have struck all worthwhile fixed targets except the ports."[60] As a result of such evaluations, on top of the blunt military reports coming out of Saigon, the president's patience grew thin and he accordingly rejected the upper-limit request in April 1967.

The White House, however, did not interpret the events of early 1967 as proof of US failure in Vietnam and it continued to seek ways to revitalize the war. The civilian leadership directed Wheeler to find new ways to increase the South Vietnamese manpower contribution, "thereby reducing the need for US troops." Thus the JCS asked Westmoreland to consider extending ARVN tours of duty, reenlisting previously released veterans, or reducing the draft age. The MACV Commander too recognized that the "increasing tempo and scale of the VC/NVN aggression" in the RVN would "dictate a concomitant increase in the combined military effort." Such escalation, however, would inevitably be tempered by growing public dissent at home as West-moreland visualized increasing opposition to the American commitment, especially to any substantive troop reinforcement. In May, then, the US "political climate ... militates against further substantial troop augmentation," at the very least until the Vietnamese themselves demonstrated their own contribution to the war.[61]

The importance of the early 1967 political maneuvering and decisions regarding the future of the war cannot be overestimated. Almost a year prior to the Tet Offensive, the White House and the JCS and MACV had clearly drawn the lines over which civil–military battles would be fought. The civilian leadership had recognized that success was hardly imminent, but it continued to reject unre-strained warfare. The military had too recognized the continued peril of war in Vietnam and was aware that it would not receive authorization to fight without restrictions. The JCS and MACV knew that the Pentagon would "avoid the explosive congressional debate and US reserve call-up" included in Westmoreland's planning. Admiral Sharp, still pressing for an unlimited air campaign, neverthe-less admitted that "recent strikes in the Hanoi area have raised the temperatures of the war in a manner which could elicit additional Soviet assistance to the North Vietnamese." Wheeler added that, short of population bombing or closing inter-national ports – "neither of which would be politically acceptable" – the air war could not reduce infiltration into the south or coerce the DRVN into negotiations. Earle Wheeler was more bleak, lamenting the White House's understanding that "the Main-Force war ... is stalemated ... and there is no evidence that pacification will ever succeed in view of the widespread rot and corruption of the government, the pervasive economic and social ills, and the tired, passive and accommodation prone attitude of the armed forces of South Vietnam."[62]

Given such bleak judgments it would take a rather great stretch of imagination to expect success in Vietnam. Yet the war continued, with the White House and military as concerned about avoiding responsibility for failure as with actually improving the situation in Vietnam. Army Chief Harold K. Johnson admitted as much, telling Wheeler that the war was being lost and the military would "take the fall." Indeed, the service chiefs, as Mark Perry puts it, "now believed that they had been betrayed by their civilian leaders, that the war could not continue without an irrational loss of American lives, and that ... there was little reason to hope for an eventual American victory." Accordingly the military decided that it had to have a greater voice in determining US policy.[63]

For the remainder of 1967, then, public relations became an even more critical factor in developing the US approach to Vietnam. While being careful to "avoid charges that the military establishment is conducting an organized propaganda campaign, either overt or covert," Westmoreland found it imperative to counter media reports of military inaction or stalemate. But, despite challenging a Peter Arnett report that the RVNAF was essentially paralyzed, Westmoreland admitted that leadership problems still plagued the ARVN, "corruption is everywhere," night operations were unproductive, US advisors were having difficulty working with their Vietnamese counterparts, and the desertion rate remained high.[64] In addition, Westmoreland, Sharp and acting JCS Chair Harold K. Johnson were all concerned with the heavy casualties American forces were suffering in the northern provinces, both because of the political impact of such casualties and the limited operational benefits which were "not consistent with the losses incurred."[65]

Nor were they compatible with the political heat the MACV was taking. In a *New York Times* article, an unnamed US general charged that Westmoreland's continued need for reinforcements "is a measure of our failure with the Vietnamese." The president seemed to agree. At his weekly luncheon meeting with advisors in mid-September, Johnson directed the JCS to "search for imaginative ideas . . . to bring this war to a conclusion." The military, the president told Harold K. Johnson, should not "just recommend more men or that we drop the Atom bomb" since he "could think of those ideas" himself.[66]

Imagination was apparently in short supply in Washington and Saigon. As Johnson continued to lament the "deteriorating public support" for the war and again complained to Wheeler that the ARVN was avoiding its share of military action, the president, Westmoreland understood, "wanted bad news like a hole in the head."[67] In Saigon, however, bad news seemed to be spreading. Although the MACV Commander had claimed to have reached the "crossover point," a new Order of Battle study in the Autumn of 1967 found the VC and PAVN numbers in the south increasing. Westmoreland, several MACV intelligence officers would later charge, ordered the new figures suppressed because, he apparently told his intelligence chief General George McChristian, they would create a "political bombshell" in Washington.[68]

Such allegations and Westmoreland's denial are not as important as the political realities underlying such developments. By late 1967 Lyndon Johnson had to have good news; not only the war but his political future depended on it. But given his refusal to escalate, the military saw little reason to accept responsibility for the situation in Vietnam or develop a way out of the war that might benefit the president. However, in order to meet the president's expectations and make him ultimately accountable when things worsened, Westmoreland, during a visit to the United States in late November, offered a rosy view of the war. Citing enemy losses and RVNAF improvements, the MACV leader anticipated that the Vietnamese themselves would increasingly take responsibility for the war and, within two years, some US troops would begin to withdraw. Although he expected tough times ahead, Westmoreland could see "some light at the end of the tunnel."[69]

That light, the general's critics later joked, was a train headed toward Westmoreland, and at the end of January 1968 it thundered through the RVN. Taking advantage of a Tet New Year cease-fire, the VC and PAVN struck virtually every military and political center of importance, even invading the US embassy grounds.

Within sixty days, Tet would bring down a president, finally force a reassessment of the war at the highest levels, and bring to a climax one of the gravest crises in civil–military relations in US history. Tet, as it were, became the US obituary in Vietnam.

Since 1968 the Tet Offensive has attained near-mythic status. Analysts of virtually every ideological position now agree that Tet was – as William Westmoreland and Lyndon Johnson, among others, claimed at the time – a decisive American military success but even greater psychological and political defeat.[70] In doing so, however, they neglect the military's own outlook on the war in February and March 1968. Indeed, throughout the Tet crisis, officials in the MACV and JCS – as well as political leaders – recognized America's perhaps intractable dilemma in Vietnam. Despite Westmoreland's publicly sanguine statements, his director of the Combat Operations Center, General John Chaisson, elaborated on the impact of Tet at a February 3 press briefing. "We have been faced with a real battle," he admitted, "there is no sense in ducking it." Because of its audacity, intensity and coordination, Chaisson had to give the Communists "credit for having engineered and planned a very successful offensive in the initial phases." Although suffering huge losses, the enemy, as Chaisson and the MACV Commander understood, had withheld many of its main force and PAVN units in many areas. Thus, Westmoreland pointed out, the Communists, "continue . . . to maintain a strong capability to reinitiate attacks country-wide at the time and place of [their] choosing."[71]

Days later Westmoreland reported to Wheeler that, "from a realistic point of view, we must accept the fact that the enemy has dealt the GVN a severe blow," bringing the war into cities and towns, inflicting heavy casualties and damage on the population, interrupting the supply and distribution of necessary items, and disrupting the economy. The Vietnamese, he observed, "have felt directly the impact of the war." As a result, the RVN faced a "tremendous challenge" to achieve stability, aid those who were suffering, and rebuild damaged areas. Westmoreland did end on an upbeat note, claiming that the enemy's losses and failure to provoke the overthrow of the government in the south constituted the failure of the offensive. But he also recognized that the enemy's objectives "were primarily psychological and political."[72]

Such evaluations would continue throughout the Tet crisis. American military officials would repeatedly point out the military problems exposed, exacerbated, or caused by the offensive. Amid reports of enemy initiatives, RVNAF desertions, a troubled logistics system, and a PAVN siege at Khe Sanh, an unnerved president wondered on February 9, "what has happened to change the situation between then [initial optimistic reactions] and now?" Johnson's military advisor, General Taylor, was more direct, interpreting Westmoreland's cables as proof that "the offensive in the north is against him [Westmoreland]."[73]

At the same time Westmoreland, expecting another series of Communist attacks, asked for reinforcements, "*which I desperately need*" both to protect Khe Sanh and because he had diverted forces to I Corps until it contained over half the US troops in Vietnam. Because of Tet, the MACV Commander explained, "we are now in a new ballgame where we face a determined, highly disciplined enemy, fully mobilized to achieve a quick victory."[74] Such analyses obviously dismayed the president, who thus dispatched Wheeler to Saigon to review the situation. In juxtaposition to Westmoreland's public optimism, Wheeler told reporters that he saw "no early end to this war." The JCS Chair, Defense Secretary Clark Clifford later noted, had lost confidence in the MACV leader and presented an "even grimmer" assessment of the war than Johnson had been receiving from Vietnam.[75]

In his well-documented report, Wheeler found the enemy strong and capable of continuing its attacks. The ARVN meanwhile had lost about one-quarter of its pre-Tet strength. The pacification program had been badly undermined. And the government's effectiveness was obviously in question, especially as it confronted massive problems of refugees and reconstruction. "In short," Wheeler concluded, "it was a very near thing." Harold K. Johnson was more blunt. "We suffered a loss," he cabled Westmoreland, "there can be no doubt about it."[76]

Those bleak evaluations notwithstanding, US military officials continued to claim victory because of the huge losses the enemy suffered. Although the VC and PAVN did suffer staggering casualties, US policymakers based their decisions regarding Vietnam on their evaluations of the war in February and March 1968. Post-Tet evaluations were thus moot. But questions of victory and defeat took a back seat in late February 1968 anyway when Wheeler and Westmoreland stunned Washington by re-submitting their old request for 206,000 more troops and the activation of about 280,000 reservists. The proposal "simply astonished Washington," as Clark Clifford put it. If – as Westmoreland and others claimed – Tet had been a conclusive US triumph – why would the MACV need 200,000 more forces in Vietnam?[77]

Within the context of civil–military relations during the Vietnam War, however, the reinforcement request had a certain logic. It was consistent with long-term White House and MACV patterns of behavior toward the war. By February and March 1968 military and civilian leaders understood that the political environment in the United States had made reinforcement, especially in such vast numbers, impossible. But the military, rather than change course after Tet, sent notice that it would continue its now discredited war of attrition. In so doing, however, the service leaders forced Lyndon Johnson finally to take decisive action regarding Vietnam and bear responsibility for the war's failure.

Westmoreland himself later admitted that he and Wheeler "both knew the grave political and economic implications of a major call-up of reserves." But the MACV Commander also suspected that the JCS Chair had become "imbued with the aura of crisis" in Washington, and had thus adopted an alarmist tone to pressure for the additional forces. Westmoreland also recognized, however, that "the request may have been doomed from the first" due to long-standing political pressure to de-escalate.[78]

Wheeler, whose concern for the depleted strategic reserve was a factor in the reinforcement proposal, nonetheless understood that the MACV's immediate needs "could very well be jeopardized by adding...longer range requirements at this time." The JCS, he told Westmoreland, "can handle only one major problem at a time," and proposals for major new programs could "derail any urgent requirements you may be thinking about submitting." Similarly, Harold K. Johnson spent a "grueling day on the hill" in mid-February lobbying for extended terms of service in Vietnam, but doubted that it would receive favorable consideration. Indeed, some of Army Chief's proposals regarding redeployment of units to Vietnam were "dismissed out of hand." Likewise General Dwight Beach, the Army's Pacific Commander, had become aware of the reinforcement request and, according to General Bruce Palmer, "had commented that it would shock" government officials.[79]

The military had good reason to expect such a reaction from Washington. Not only had the White House consistently rejected Westmoreland's plans for major reinforcement and escalation, but the president on February 2 had told reporters that the US troop goal was 525,000, just above then present strength, and "there is not anything in any of the developments that would justify the press in leaving the impression than great new overall moves are going to be made that would involve substantial movements in that direction." At the same time, Secretary of State Dean Rusk argued against the proposed increase and even senate hawks like John Stennis and Henry Jackson wavered as they recognized the hopelessness of the war.[80]

More pointedly, the president confronted his advisors with charges that "all of you have counseled, advised, consulted and then – as usual – placed the monkey on my back again . . . I do not like what I am smelling from those cables from Vietnam and my discussions with outside advisors [the so-called Wise Men]." Johnson was especially concerned that his advisors were harboring serious doubts about the war, and feared that the military might exploit the situation. "I don't want them [Westmoreland and Wheeler] to ask for something," the president worried aloud, "not get it, and have all the blame placed on me." Although he was not expecting such a huge reinforcement request, it was obvious that Johnson understood the political implications of any future moves in Vietnam. Philip Habib, a State Department specialist in East Asian affairs, similarly reported that there was "serious disagreement in American circles in Saigon over the 205,000 request." And Ambassador Ellsworth Bunker, Neil Sheehan reports, had warned Westmoreland against asking for the troops, explaining that such reinforcement was now "politically impossible" even if the president had wanted it, which was also more unlikely than ever.[81]

Indeed it was. Put on the defensive by both the enemy offensive and his own military's huge reinforcement proposal, Johnson thus directed incoming Secretary of Defense Clark Clifford to reassess the war. Throughout March 1968, as the Clifford group pondered the US future in Vietnam, the president continued to receive alarming information from various advisors. In addition to advice to deescalate from the Wise Men, Johnson met with the incoming MACV Commander Creighton Abrams – who sought to "divorce myself from the somewhat more optimistic reports coming out of Saigon" – in late March, and he received another candid evaluation of the enemy's capabilities and America's problems.[82] Upon receiving such appraisals the president lamented that *"everybody is recommending surrender."*[83]

But it was Johnson himself who surrendered. At the end of a March 31 broadcast in which he announced only some minor new deployments and a bombing halt in Vietnam, the president stunned his national audience by withdrawing from the 1968 presidential campaign. Finally forced to confront his failure to determine a consistent policy on Vietnam by the twin shocks of Tet and the reinforcement proposal, the president knew that time had run out on both his political career and the US experience in Vietnam.

Lyndon Johnson had spent the better part of four years waiting for William Westmoreland to achieve success in Vietnam without expanding the US commitment there to levels that would damage the president's political goals at home or prompt greater international conflict. For their part, Westmoreland and other military leaders recognized the barriers to progress in Vietnam and knew early in the war, as early as 1965 and 1966, that they would not receive authorization for a wholly unrestrained war. The military, as William DePuy understood in October 1965, would have to rely on a war of attrition and incremental reinforcement. Yet the MACV and JCS leadership never pursued alternative strategies in Vietnam. Indeed, only Marine officers had even presented a plan different from the reliance on attrition that Westmoreland had devised, but effective pacification – which could not ensure victory in any case – was too time consuming and its progress could not be gauged empirically. Clearly, both the civilian and service sides were aware that the war was not going well. Thus the president's tentativeness and vacillation and the military's pleas for expansion were equally disingenuous and damaging. Earle Wheeler and his fellow chiefs may have reconsidered their decision to resign in that fateful 1967 meeting, but they – and civilian leaders as well – had given up on the war nonetheless.

NOTES

1   Mark Perry, *Four Stars* (Boston, 1989), 163.
2   On conservative revisionism on Vietnam see Walter LaFeber, "The Last War, the Next War, and the New Revisionists," *democracy* 1 (1981): 93–103; Bob Buzzanco, "The American Military's Rationale Against the Vietnam War," *Political Science Quarterly* 101:4 (Winter 1986): 559–76. On the continuing political use of Vietnam by conservative political figures see George Bush's speech to America as the Gulf War began and his claim that the US victory over Iraq meant that the "Vietnam syndrome" was over. *Washington Post*, January 17 and March 2 1991. See also Bob Woodward, *The Commanders* (New York, 1991), especially pages 163, 167, 306–7, 339, and 347.

   One of the more recent and publicized works to develop such themes was H. R. McMaster's *Dereliction of Duty: Lyndon Johnson, Robert McNamara, the Joint Chiefs of Staff, and the Lies that Led to Vietnam* (New York, 1997), which contends that the war was lost in Washington DC *even before* the American air and ground commitments of the mid-1960s.

   US civilian policymakers, McMaster contends, were arrogant and deceitful, and the military was excluded from the decision-making process. The emphasis in *Dereliction of Duty* is on individuals, acting almost independently of larger forces like the Cold War, politics, interservice rivalries, or the needs of the military–industrial complex. Moreover, as this article shows, American policymakers, were fundamentally candid about the problems they faced in Vietnam, the nature of the war there, and the dim prospects for success. Yet, America's war leaders, civilian and military both, continued and escalated a military intervention that was destructive and futile. Rather than a dereliction of duty, their actions should be considered a violation of international law and morality.
3   See note 2 above.

4   Bruce Cumings, *The Origins of the Korean War, Volume II: The Roaring of the Cataract,
    1947–1950.* (Princeton, 1990): 59; Robert Buzzanco, "Prologue to Tragedy: U.S.
    Military Opposition to Intervention in Vietnam, 1950–1954," *Diplomatic History* 17,
    (Spring, 1993).

5   John M. Newman, *JFK and Vietnam: Deception, Intrigue, and the Struggle for Power*
    (New York, 1992).

6   Report by Col. F. P. Serong to Gen. Paul D. Harkings, COMUSMACV, sub: Situation in
    South Vietnam Following Change of Government, November 1963, in Record Group
    319, Papers of William Childs Westmoreland, Washington National Records Center,
    Suitland, MD., folder 498 [2 of 2]: #1 History Backup, March 30 1962–November
    1963. Hereafter cited as Westmoreland Papers, with appropriate filing designations.

7   Wallace M. Greene, Jr., "A Marine Corps View of Military Strategy," 1963 Speech, Tape
    #6276, Oral History section, Marine Corps Historical Center [MCHC], Washington
    Navy Yard. This tape, and all others, transcribed by the author.

8   Stilwell, ACS, J-3, MACV, Report, sub: Counterinsurgency Vitalization, March 10 1964,
    Westmoreland Papers, folder 460 [2 of 2]: #3 History File, December 20 1965–January
    29 1966.

9   Westmoreland MACJ3 8149 to US Grant Sharp and Earle Wheeler, August 15 1964, sub:
    Improvement US Posture SVN, Westmoreland Papers, folder 504: #7 History Backup,
    July 27–August 31 1964.

10 Taylor to Secretary of State, January 6 1965, in *The War in Vietnam: Classified Histories by
    the National Security Council,* University Publications of America microfilm edition, Reel
    2, "Deployment of Major US Forces to Vietnam: July 1965. Hereafter cited as NSC
    History – The War in Vietnam, with appropriate reel number. This document can also be
    found in *Declassified Documents Reference System* 1983, #002793. Hereafter cited as
    DDRS with appropriate year and document number.

11 Taylor to Secretary of State, January 6 1965, in NSC History – The War in Vietnam,
    reel 2.

12 Larry Berman, *Planning A Tragedy: The Americanization of the War in Vietnam* (New
    York, 1982).

13 MACV Command History, 1965, p. 31.

14 Ibid., 35.

15 Karch interviews, January 15 1972, in Oral History Transcript, MCHC, 58–62.

16 See Maxwell Taylor's cables from Saigon throughout the NSC History – The War in
    Vietnam, reels 2 and 3 *passim;* Berman, *Planning A Tragedy;* and George McT. Kahin,
    Intervention: How America Became Involved in Vietnam (Garden City, N.Y., 1987),
    especially chapters 12–15.

17 Kahin, *Intervention,* 313; for a different view on the politics of strategy in Vietnam, see
    George Herring, " 'Cold Blood': LBJ's Conduct of Limited War in Vietnam," Paper
    Presented at the Military History Symposium, Colorado Springs, CO., October 1990.

18 The president's advisors were pressuring him to expand the US role in Vietnam in early
    1965. National Security Advisor McGeorge Bundy wrote to Johnson that he and Defense
    Secretary Robert McNamara were both "pretty well convinced that our current policy can
    lead only to disastrous defeat." Accordingly Bundy and McNamara concluded that the
    proper response would be to "use our military power in the Far East and . . . force a change
    of Communist policy" in Vietnam. Few military leaders were so strident about the use of
    US power at that time. Bundy to Johnson, January 27 1965, sub: Basic Policy in Vietnam,
    NSC History – The War in Vietnam, reel 2.

19   Valenti to Johnson, November 14 1964, in Lyndon B. Johnson Papers, C.F., CO 312, Vietnam, Box 12, folder: CO 312, Vietnam, 1964–65.

20   McNaughton, "Action for South Vietnam," March 10 1965, in NSC History – The War in Vietnam, reel 2; Kahin, *Intervention*, 313.

21   "Miscellaneous Vietnam Comments," in FMFPac, CG's Trip Summary, WestPac Visit, 14–21 May 1965, FMFPac Trip File, MCHC; Conference between CMC/FMFPac, at FMFPac Headquarters, April 23–29 1965, tape #6298, MCHC, my transcription.

22   Summary Notes of 552d NSC Meeting, June 11 1965, by Bromley Smith, in LBJ Library, National Security File, NSC Meetings File, Box 1, folder: V.3, tab 34.

23   Sharp memorandum to Westmoreland quoted in NMCC to White House, June 13 1965, NSC History – The War in Vietnam, reel 3.

24   Kahin, *Intervention*, 348–52; Larry Berman, who has produced the most thorough study of the policy debates leading to the July expansion of the war, contends that Johnson's policy of limited reinforcement meant that the US "decided to lose the war slowly." Berman, *Planning A Tragedy*.

25   General Westmoreland's History Notes, August 29 1965, in Westmoreland Papers, folder 458 [2 of 2]: #1 History File, August 19–October 24 1965.

26   General William B. Rosson, Chief of Staff, MACV, Directive 525–4, September 17 1965, sub: Tactics and Techniques for Employment of US Forces in the Republic of Vietnam. Westmoreland Papers, folder 458 [2 of 2]: #1 History File, August 19–24 October 1965.

27   General William DePuy, J-3, Briefing on Plans and Force Requirements, October 21 1965, Marine Corps Headquarters, tape #6173, MCHC, my transcription.

28   Ibid.

29   General Westmoreland's History Notes, entries of November 29 and December 9 1965, Westmoreland Papers, folder 459: #2 History Files, October 25–December 20 1965.

30   General Westmoreland's Historical Notes, entry of September 5 1965, Westmoreland Papers, folder 458 [2 of 2]: #1 History File, August 19–October 24 1965.

31   On the Marines's view of the need for pacification, see, *inter alia*, Jack Shulimson and Charles M. Johnson, *US Marines in Vietnam: The Landing and the Build Up, 1965* (Washington, DC, 1978); Victor H. Krulak, *First to Fight: An Inside View of the US Marine Corps* (New York, 1991); Neil Sheehan, *A Bright Shining Lie: John Paul Vann and America in Vietnam* (New York, 1988).

32   General Westmoreland's History Notes, entries of October 20 and December 8 1965, Westmoreland Papers, folder 458 [2 of 2]: #1 History Files, August 19–October 24 1965, and folder 459: #2 History Files, October 25–December 20 1965.

33   Krulak, "A Strategic Appraisal – Vietnam," December 1965, Victor H. Krulak Papers, Box 2, envelope: Point Papers, Briefings, Trips, Reports, 1965, MCHC. Hereafter cited as Krulak Papers with appropriate filing information.
       Ironically, DePuy – in his October briefing for the Marines – had also recognized problems in providing and maintaining security and gaining the allegiance of villagers, but, unlike Krulak, did not conclude that a priority on pacification was needed. See note 27 above.

34   Greene notes, in Wallace M. Greene Papers, Box 39, folder 415–1: Notes on trip to WestPac, January 3–15 1966, MCHC. Hereafter cited as Greene Papers with appropriate filing information. Greene and Krulak in FMFPac Briefing for CMC, Headquarters, FMFPac, Camp Smith, HI., January 1966, tape #6278, MCHC, my transcription.
       For further development of the Army–Marine rift over strategy, see Sheehan, *A Bright Shining Lie*; Krulak, *First to Fight*; Jack Shulimson, *US Marines in Vietnam: An*

Expanding War, 1966 (Washington, DC, 1982); and Greene's and Krulak comments in *Vietnam Comments File, 1966*, MCHC.

35 Westmoreland MAC 0117 to Collins, January 7 1966, Record Group 407, Records of the Adjutant General, *Westmoreland v. CBS*, Litigation Collection, Box 14, folder: MACV Backchannel messages from Westmoreland, January 1–31 1966. Unless otherwise noted, future references will come from Litigation Collection, and hereafter cited as Westmoreland v. CBS, with appropriate filing information.

36 Heintges MACJ01 to Westmoreland, March 23 1966, sub: Demonstrations in I Corps, Westmoreland Papers, folder 462: #5 History File, March 13–April 23 1966; Krulak to Sharp, March 31 1966 and Krulak to Navy Undersecretary Robert Baldwin, April 20 1966, Krulak Papers, Box 1, folder: Correspondence, March–July 1966, MCHC.

37 Wheeler CJCS 1974–66 to Sharp and Westmoreland, April 13 1966, Westmoreland v. CBS, Box 15, folder: MACV Backchannel messages to Westmoreland, April 1–30 1966; Wheeler CJCS 2644–66 to Westmoreland and Sharp, May 12 1966, Westmoreland v. CBS, Box 15, Folder: MACV Backchannel messages to Westmoreland, May 1–31 1966; Westmoreland quoted in Herring, "Cold Blood," 8–9.

38 Wheeler CJCS 2837–66 to Westmoreland and Sharp, May 20 1966, Westmoreland v. CBS, Box 15, folder: MACV Backchannel messages to Westmoreland, May 1–31 1966.

39 For details see, among others, Wheeler to Westmoreland, May 18 1966, Westmoreland Papers, #6 History File, April 24–May 28 1966; Westmoreland 16210 to Sharp and Wheeler, May 11 1966, sub: Arc Light Forces Reaction Capability, Westmoreland v. CBS, Box 28, folder: Message, dated May 2 1966.

40 Westmoreland MAC 4081 to Wheeler and Sharp, May 22 1966, Westmoreland v. CBS, Box 28, folder: Message, MAC 4081.

41 Wheeler JCS 2844–66 to Westmoreland and Sharp, May 23 1966, Westmoreland v. CBS, Box 15, folder: MACV Backchannel messages to Westmoreland, May 1–31 1966.

42 Westmoreland Memorandum for Henry Cabot Lodge, June 15 1966, sub: Mobilization of the RVN, Westmoreland v. CBS, Box 13, folder: Memo May 16 1967.

43 Gen. John Freund, Memorandum for the Record, June 25 1966, sub: Discussion with General Tran Van Don, June 24 1966, Westmoreland Papers, folder 463a: #7 History File, May 29–July 16 1966.

44 Westmoreland MAC 7720 to Johnson, September 5 1966, Westmoreland v. CBS, Box 16, folder: MACV Backchannel messages from Westmoreland, September 1–30 1966.

45 Johnson WDC 10846 and 10849 to Westmoreland, September 13 1966, in Westmoreland v. CBS, Box 16, folder: MACV Backchannel messages to Westmoreland, September 1–30 1966; Westmoreland MAC 8710 to Johnson, October 6 1966, Westmoreland Papers, folder 362 (1): Eyes Only Message File.

46 Krulak to Wallace M. Greene, October 16 1966, sub: CINCPAC/COMUSMACV Debriefing, HQMC Message File [Eyes Only Messages], 1966–7, MCHC.

47 Johnson WDC 12415 to Westmoreland, October 20 1966, Westmoreland Papers, folder 362 (2): COMUSMACV Message File.

48 McNamara Memorandum for CJCS, November 11 1966, sub: Deployments to Southeast Asia, LBJ Library, Papers of Paul Warnke – John McNaughton File, Box 7, folder: VNS 1 [VN, 1966–8] (2).

49 General Westmoreland's Historical Briefing, November 25 1966, Westmoreland Papers, folder 467: #11 History File, October 30–December 12 1966.

50 Wheeler CJCS 7859–66 to Westmoreland and Sharp, December 21 1966, Westmoreland Papers, folder 362(2): Eyes Only Message File.

51 Westmoreland 53846 to Sharp, December 19 1966, sub: Enemy Strength in South Vietnam, Westmoreland v. CBS, Box 29, folder: Message, Dated December 19 1966.

52 General Westmoreland's Historical Briefing, January 1 1967, Westmoreland Papers, folder 468 [2 of 2]: #12 History Files, December 13 1966–January 26 1967; Westmoreland 00160 to Sharp, January 2 1967, sub: Year End Assessment of Enemy Situation and Enemy Strategy, Westmoreland v. CBS, Box 29, folder: Message, Dated January 4 1967.

53 Westmoreland MACJ311, January 16 1967, sub: Improvements within RVNAF, Westmoreland Papers, folder 424: Top Secret COMUSMACV Signature File, January 1967.

54 Measurement of Progress Briefing, given by Lt. Col. A.M. Robert Dean, MACJ34, n.d., Westmoreland Papers, folder 468 [2 of 3]: #12 History File, December 13 1966–January 26 1967.

55 Third Working Paper, Report by the J-3 to the Joint Chiefs of Staff on Courses of Action for Southeast Asia, January 13 1967, Enclosure: Draft Memo for Secretary of Defense, sub: Future Conduct of the War in Southeast Asia, Westmoreland Papers, folder 579: Joint Chiefs of Staff, January 13 1967.

56 Wheeler JCS 0979–67 to Westmoreland and Sharp, February 3 1967 and Westmoreland MAC 1658 to Sharp and Wheeler, February 17 1967, both in Westmoreland Papers, folder 363: Eyes Only Message File; Westmoreland MACJOO 6127 to Sharp and Wheeler, February 27 1967, Westmoreland Papers, folder 469 [2 of 3]: #13 History File, January 27–March 25 1967.

57 Westmoreland, *A Soldier Reports*, 113; Sharp to Wheeler and Westmoreland, February 16 1967, sub: Restrictions on Operations in Southern Laos, Westmoreland Papers, folder 363: Eyes Only Message File; Wheeler JCS 1691–67 to Sharp and Westmoreland, March 6 1967, folder 363: Chief of Staff Message File.

58 Wheeler CJCS 1810–67 to Westmoreland, March 9 1967, Westmoreland v. CBS, DA/ WNRC Files, Box 2, folder: Suspense; figures reproduced in Wheeler CJCS 1843–67 to Westmoreland and Sharp, March 11 1967, Westmoreland Papers, folder 363: Eyes Only Message File.

59 Berman, *Lyndon Johnson's War*, 24, 31–4, 37.

60 "Notes on Discussion with the President," April 27 1967, LBJ Library, Papers of Paul Warnke – McNaughton Files, Box 2, folder: McNTN Drafts 1967 [2].

61 Wheeler JCS 3332 to Westmoreland and Sharp, May 5 1967, Westmoreland v. CBS, Box 18, folder: MACV Backchannel messages to Westmoreland, May 1–31 1967; Westmoreland to Ellsworth Bunker, May 16 1967, sub: Mobilization of the Republic of Vietnam, Westmoreland Papers, folder 428: Signature File, May 1967.

62 Wheeler JCS 3891 to Westmoreland and Sharp, May 26 1967, Westmoreland v. CBS, Box 18, folder: MACV Backchannel messages to Westmoreland, May 1–31 1967; Wheeler JCS 4200 to Sharp and Westmoreland, June 6 1967, Westmoreland v. CBS, Box 18, folder: MACV Backchannel messages to Westmoreland, June 1–30 1967.

63 Perry, *Four Stars*, 163.

64 Westmoreland MAC 7180 to Wheeler, Johnson, Sharp, 2 August 1967, Westmoreland v. CBS, Box 18, folder: MACV Backchannel messages from Westmoreland, August 1–31 1967; Westmoreland MAC 8875 to McConnell and Sharp, September 20 1967, Westmoreland Papers, folder 478: #22 History File, September 10–30 1967.

65 Johnson JCS 7987 Sep 67 to Sharp and Westmoreland, September 25 1967, and Sharp to Westmoreland, September 26 1967, both in Westmoreland v. CBS, Box 25, folder: Backchannel traffic July 1966–June 1968 [1 of 2]; Westmoreland to Johnson and

Sharp, September 27 1967, Westmoreland Papers, folder 365: COMUSMACV Message File.

66   *New York Times* quote in Wheeler JCS 6336 to Westmoreland and Sharp, August 8 1967, Westmoreland Papers, folder 372: Eyes Only Message File; Jim Jones, Memorandum to the President, September 11 1967, sub: Weekly Luncheon, Meeting Notes File, Box 2, folder: September 12 1967, LBJ Library.

67   Wheeler JCS 9298 to Westmoreland and Sharp, October 31 1967, Westmoreland v. CBS, Box 19, folder: MACV Backchannel messages to Westmoreland, October 1–31 1967; Westmoreland in transcript of CBS Reports – "The Uncounted Enemy: A Vietnam Deception," broadcast January 23 1982, Westmoreland v. CBS, DA/WNRC Files, Box 1.

68   "The Uncounted Enemy," see note above.

69   Westmoreland HWA 3445 to Abrams, November 26 1967, Westmoreland v. CBS, Box 19, folder: MACV Backchannel messages from Westmoreland, November 1–30 1967.

70   See, for example, the writings of Johnson, Westmoreland, Maxwell Taylor, Douglas Pike, or Herbert Schandler on the conservative side, or liberals such as Frances FitzGerald, Sandra Taylor, or Loren Baritz. For conflicting interpretations, see Gabriel Kolko, Neil Sheehan, or Andrew Krepinevich.

71   Chaisson briefing in Westmoreland Papers, Folder 9; Message, COMUSMACV 29/68 to VMAC, February 4 1968, Westmoreland Papers, folder 389: COMUSMACV Outgoing Message File.

72   Westmoreland to Wheeler, February 4 1968, NSC History – The War in Vietnam, "March 31st Speech," reel 6; Westmoreland to Wheeler, February 4 1968, Declassified and Sanitized Documents from Unprocessed Files [DSDUF], Vietnam, Box 4, folder: Vietnam, Box 69, 2C (4), GMA, LBJ Library; Westmoreland cable, February 8 1968, *DDRS*, 85, 001576.

73   Notes of President's Meeting with Senior Foreign Policy Advisors, February 9 1968, *DDRS*, 85, 000747; Notes of President's Meeting with JCS, February 9 1968, Tom Johnson's Notes, Box 3, LBJ Library [Box numbers of Tom Johnson's Notes have changed since original research in 1988]; Notes of President's Meeting with Senior Foreign Policy Advisors, February 11 1968, Papers of Clark Clifford, Box 4, folder: 2d Set [Memos on Vietnam: February 1968], LBJ Library.

74   Emphasis in original, Westmoreland to Wheeler and Sharp, February 12 1968, Papers of Clark Clifford, Box 2, Folder: The White House [Vietnamese War], Memos on Vietnam, February-August 1968, LBJ Library; *DDRS*, 79, 369A.

75   Wheeler's report is in various sources, including Papers of Clark Clifford, Box 2, folder: Memos on Vietnam: February-March 1968, LBJ Library; *DDRS*, 79, 382B; and the Gravel and *New York Times* editions of the *Pentagon Papers*. Wheeler quote in *New York Times*, February 26 1968. Clifford with Richard Holbrooke, "Annals of Government (The Vietnam Years – Part II,") *The New Yorker* (May 13 1991), 58.

76   Wheeler report in above; Johnson WDC 3166 to Westmoreland and Abrams, March 1 1968, Westmoreland Papers, folder 380: Eyes Only Message File.

77   Clifford, "The Vietnam Years," 58.

78   Westmoreland paper, "The Origins of the Post-Tet 1968 Plans for Additional Forces in the Republic of Vietnam," April 1970, Westmoreland Papers, folder 493 [1 of 2]: #37 History Files, January 1–June 30 1970; Westmoreland, *A Soldier Reports*, 469.

79   Wheeler JCS 1589 to Westmoreland, February 9 1968, Westmoreland v. CBS, Box 20, folder: MACV Backchannel messages to Westmoreland, February 1–28 1968; Johnson WDC 2515 to Palmer, February 17 1968, same as above; Beach in record of Fonecon

with General Palmer, 0850, February 25 1968, sub: Discussion, Westmoreland Papers, folder 450: Fonecons, February 1968.

80 Johnson in *New York Times*, February 3 1968; Dean Rusk with Richard Rusk, *As I Saw It*, edited by Daniel S. Papp (New York, 1990), 478; Stanley Karnow, *Vietnam: A History* (New York, 1983), 557; Clifford, "The Vietnam Years," 70.

81 Notes of President's Meeting with NSC, January 24 1968, LBJ Library, Tom Johnson's Notes, Box 2, folder: January 24, 1968–1 p.m.; Notes of President's Meeting with Senior Foreign Affairs Advisory Council, February 10 1968, same as previous citation, folder: February 10, 1968–3:17 p.m.; Habib in Clifford, "The Vietnam Years," 54, 60; Sheehan, *A Bright Shining Lie*, 720.

82 Clifford, "A Vietnam Reappraisal: The Personal History of One Man's View and How It Evolved," *Foreign Affairs* 47,4 (1969), 601–22; Abrams MAC 03966 to Wheeler, Westmoreland, and Sharp, March 22 1968, Westmoreland Papers, folder 380. Eyes Only Message File; Notes of President's Meeting with Generals Wheeler and Abrams, March 26 1968, Tom Johnson's Notes, Box 3, LBJ Library.

83 Emphasis in original. CIA DOD Briefing by General DePuy and George Carver, March 27 1968, Tom Johnson's Notes, Box 3, LBJ Library.

Australian diplomat and historian Milton Osborne agrees that the *Newsweek* piece enraged Sihanouk and "triggered" the break. Historian David P. Chandler concurs. The article, he writes, was the "last straw for Sihanouk in his dealings with the United States."[9]

At the time, however, American officials believed that the offending article was only a pretext, for relations were near the breaking point well before the demonstration.[10] Some officials felt that the demonstration was related to Sihanouk's campaign to block a proposed Geneva conference to guarantee Cambodia's neutrality, a conference that the prince had long wanted but that he was no longer supporting. An official unpublished history of US-Cambodian relations offered another explanation: an armed incursion into Cambodian territory from South Vietnam in April was to blame.[11]

No single factor caused the break, although the official history was closest to the truth. Rather, it was the cumulative effect of several issues that increasingly strained the relationship. The war in neighboring Vietnam was of central importance. The demonstration at the embassy came shortly after the United States had begun bombing North Vietnam in a sustained way and had sent its first combat units to South Vietnam. The war was on the verge of escalating out of control, and Sihanouk feared that the hostilities would engulf his own small country. As Bergesen put it at the time, the demonstration resulted from "the Prince's frequent and increasingly vituperative criticism of American policy, especially in Viet-Nam." More generally, the overarching Cold War and Sihanouk's militantly neutral posture underlay the break. The Krisher article was only a contributing factor, and probably a minor one at that. In the end, the demands of the Cold War – particularly the desire to contain China and defeat the Communist-led insurgency in neighboring Vietnam – revealed the limits of American acceptance of neutralism in Cambodia. Although internal Cambodian factors contributed to the break in relations, in the final analysis in Southeast Asia the United States was simply unable to find a way to support anti-communism and neutralism at the same time.[12]

The Cambodian–American relationship was never an easy one. It had always required delicate and astute diplomacy to keep it on a more or less friendly footing. Ever since the nation acquired independence from France in 1953–4, Sihanouk had pursued a determinedly neutral international course. At the height of the Cold War, the United States looked askance at those countries that were unwilling to align themselves with the West. Still, as historian H. W. Brands has demonstrated, American policy toward neutral countries could be remarkably nonideological – despite the overheated rhetoric emanating from high officials in Washington. Although Cambodia was not among the countries included in Brands' study, the American approach to Cambodia during the 1950s and early 1960s *was*, in some respects, unusually flexible. Cambodian neutrality was, after all, preferable to a Cambodia allied with North Vietnam or "Red" China. Some Americans considered maintaining Cambodia's independence – even a neutral independence – absolutely vital to saving all of Southeast Asia. The country was the "hub of the wheel in Southeast Asia," wrote one military official.[13] And so throughout the 1950s the United States provided Cambodia with economic aid. The shining example was the Khmer–American Friendship

Highway, which connected Phnom Penh with the newly built port of Kampong Som. Completed in 1959, this road allowed Cambodia to import goods without having to rely on the Mekong River route through Vietnam. Even today Cambodians remember the highway as an example of constructive American assistance.

The United States also muscled its way past the French and began to provide arms and other military supplies to Cambodia. By the early 1960s the United States was paying for 30 percent of the country's military budget and providing most of its arms and supplies. Even more remarkable, the United States stationed a Military Assistance Advisory Group (MAAG) in Cambodia – the only professedly neutral country in the world where this was done.[14]

But even as the United States provided economic and military aid, it increasingly disliked – and challenged – Sihanouk's foreign policy. A central concern for Sihanouk (and most Cambodians) was a deep dislike of more powerful and populous neighbors, Thailand and Vietnam. Although these animosities were long standing and had little directly to do with the Cold War, the fact that Thailand and South Vietnam were Cold War allies of the United States made good relations between the United States and Cambodia difficult to maintain. Sihanouk was both suspicious of American intentions – believing that the United States supported and even encouraged Thai and Vietnamese incursions into his country – and jealous that the aid provided to his neighbors was considerably more than was provided to Cambodia. Particularly harmful to the relationship was Sihanouk's belief – amounting to virtual certainty – that the United States (and in particular the Central Intelligence Agency) was supporting dissident Cambodians, the Khmer Serei, led by a Cambodian patriot and former official San Ngoc Thanh, who operated from bases in Vietnam and Thailand.

The Prince's perception was not entirely fanciful. Particularly after Sihanouk recognized the People's Republic of China and sought aid from Soviet bloc countries, the United States covertly supported South Vietnamese and Thai efforts to undermine his government. In 1959 the United States was implicated directly in the abortive Dap Chhuon plot against him. "The importance of this development in shaking Cambodian confidence in US motives cannot be over-emphasized," wrote one State Department official a few months after the event. Relations were so tense in 1959 that American officials in Phnom Penh dubbed it "a Year of Troubles."[15]

Thereafter the State Department determined that because Sihanouk was widely popular in Cambodia, that the army was loyal to him, and that he was suppressing Communists and other leftists at home, anti-Sihanouk actions were counterproductive. Thus, during the John F. Kennedy administration, the Americans attempted to keep Thai and Vietnamese plotting under control and quickly informed the Cambodian government of conspiracies that came to their attention. On balance, relations between the two countries during most of the Kennedy period were reasonably good, not the least because of the able work of Ambassador William C. Trimble, one of the very few Americans whom Sihanouk trusted.[16]

Trimble left Phnom Penh in 1962, however, and during the summer of 1963 South Vietnamese forces entered Cambodian territory on several occasions in pursuit of the Viet Cong. In August Khmer Serei clandestine radio broadcasts suddenly began, originating from South Vietnam. Sihanouk broke relations with South

Vietnam and began to charge that the CIA was once again supporting his opponents. Early in November the American supported overthrow and assassination of South Vietnam's president Ngo Dinh Diem and his brother Ngo Dinh Nhu badly shook the prince. Although his dislike of Diem had been "deep and visceral," he feared that the Americans might have similar plans in store for him. As David Chandler put it, "Their deaths confirmed the prince's suspicion that America could never be trusted as an ally." In mid-November two former Khmer Serei publicly testified that the Americans were supporting the anti-Sihanouk movement, and shortly thereafter, only two days before Kennedy's assassination, the Cambodian leader informed the United States that he would expel the MAAG and henceforth accept no more American aid. He had concluded that American aid could no longer protect him from his enemies and that, in fact, close ties to the United States would be detrimental should the Communists prevail in Vietnam, as increasingly he thought they would.[17]

Relations quickly went down hill. On December 8 1963 Sihanouk's antagonist Prime Minister Sarit Thanarat of Thailand died, and Sihanouk called for a national celebration, which Undersecretary of State for Political Affairs W. Averell Harriman called "barbaric."[18] But what particularly angered the United States was Sihanouk's broadcast assertion that the deaths of Ngo Dinh Diem, Sarit Thanarat, and John F. Kennedy resulted from divine intervention to save Cambodia. "We had only three enemies, and the leaders of these three countries all died and went to hell, all three, in a period of a month and a half," he allegedly stated. "They are meeting there in a conference of the Free World's SEATO."[19]

The United States protested strongly. Sihanouk reacted angrily, denied that he had made the broadcast, and closed his embassy in Washington. The United States considered cutting its staff in Cambodia to a bare minimum, and Ambassador Philip Sprouse prepared to return to Washington.[20] Although the Cambodian–American relationship lay in tatters, neither side broke relations.[21]

For a time both the United States and Cambodia held out some hope that the breach could be repaired. Despite the fact that both ambassadors had been recalled, each country allowed its ambassador to remain for several weeks. The Cambodians wanted the United States to withdraw its "barbaric" comment (they even suggested that Charles Yost, who had delivered the protest to Cambodia's ambassador Nong Kimny, could personally apologize) and stop the Khmer Serei broadcasts. They also indicated that a positive response to Sihanouk's proposal for an international conference to guarantee Cambodia's neutrality would have done much to restore the relationship. The United States for its part hoped that the Cambodians would accept their contention that Americans were not involved with the Khmer Serei and had attempted to influence the Vietnamese and the Thais to stop the broadcasts. They also thought that the cost of ending American aid would begin to sink in and that the armed forces and other internal Cambodian influences might moderate Sihanouk's position.

In January 1964 both sides agreed to accept Philippine President Diosdado Macapagal's offer to extend his good offices to try and repair the breach, and by mid-January Sihanouk said that he was "very hopeful" that the mediation effort would succeed and that the United States and Cambodia would be friends again.[22] But before the mediation could succeed, a number of strains emerged. Son Ngoc Thanh surfaced in South Vietnam, the Khmer Serei broadcasts continued, and serious incidents took place along the Cambodian–South Vietnamese border. As Sihanouk said in a news conference at Siem Reap on February 11, "there were too many 'things' between USA and Cambodia" for a successful mediation,[23] and in the end Macapagal's efforts came to naught.

Cambodian assertions that the United States was collaborating with Thailand, South Vietnam, and his arch enemy Son Ngoc Thanh, to destabilize his country constituted an important irritant in the relationship. In January and February 1964, for example, the Cambodians made at least three serious charges of American involvement with their enemies. On January 25 they provided information to the co-chairs of the Geneva Conference about American involvement with Son Ngoc Thanh. A little later testimony in a spy trial in Phnom Penh implicated an American agent. Later that same month Cambodia accused the United States of helping the Khmer Serei form commando units to infiltrate into Cambodia.[24] In May the well known journalist Marquis Childs claimed that the Pentagon was advocating that Sihanouk be overthrown, an article which naturally fueled the Prince's suspicions of American intentions.[25]

Almost surely Sihanouk's charges were essentially accurate. In March the South Vietnamese government acquired a copy of an investigative story written by a *Time Magazine* reporter (but not yet published), and gave it to the American embassy. Intended as a cover story for the popular news weekly, the reporter, who had managed to arrange a special interview with Son Ngoc Thanh, reported that about half of the 1,000 Khmer Serei troops served in the Civilian Irregular Defence Groups (CIDG) funded by the CIA and were led by American and Vietnamese Special Forces teams. They operated along the Cambodian border. The other 500 Khmer Serei operated independently.[26] If the journalist's information was correct, Sihanouk's charges that the Khmer Serei served with the American Special Forces was entirely accurate.

At about the same time Military Assistance Command, Vietnam (MACV) conducted its own investigation of reports that American personnel were training Khmer Serei forces, which corroborated some of the reporter's findings. Of the 1677 soldiers of Cambodian descent in the "strike force companies," about 1,000 were believed to be Khmer Serei. These forces were trained by American personnel who were said to be unaware of their political affiliation. The investigation discovered other Khmer Serei units operating near Loc Ninh; American advisors there "consider them to be by far the most effective of the three Strike Force Companies operating out of Minh Thanh."[27] A little later the state department expressed its concern "that Khmer Serei personnel who have been trained in US sponsored or GVN camps might engage in activities inimical to resolution of Cambodian–GVN differences."[28] In sum, there is little doubt that at least some of the Khmer Serei forces were integrated into South Vietnamese military, notably the CIDG units, which were paid for by the United States, and which were trained by Americans.

Equally, if not more, damaging were allegations that the United States had sanctioned and participated in military raids on Cambodian border villages launched from

South Vietnam. This was not a new charge. But as the war in Vietnam heated up, the number of incidents involving Cambodia increased in number and seriousness. Sihanouk was infuriated when on February 5 1964 South Vietnamese aircraft attacked the village of Mong (or Muong) two kilometers inside Cambodia, killing five and wounding six.[29] He accused the South Vietnamese, with American support, of trying to provoke war. Sihanouk protested to the Geneva Conference co-chairs and asked that the conference be convened to consider his charges against South Vietnam and the United States. He also sent a telegram to President Lyndon B. Johnson deploring the attack on Mong and calling on him to support the positioning of several International Control Commission (ICC) posts along the border. If the attacks continued, he stated, he might have to end his policy of neutrality and gain the protection of "certain large friendly countries."[30] The United States considered Sihanouk's message offensive in tone and objected to its immediate publication. In his response Johnson deplored the loss of life but rejected Sihanouk's implications of American responsibility and suggested that talks be resumed with South Vietnam.

Contributing to Sihanouk's irritation with the United States was the American reaction to his renewed interest in an international conference to guarantee his country's neutrality and borders. In December, prior to Sihanouk's remarks about Kennedy's death, Secretary of State Dean Rusk had been inclined, if reluctantly, to attend a conference, in part because the French and British wanted one. But Sihanouk's comments about Kennedy, along with strong opposition in the National Security Council, from some sectors of the state department, and from the Thais and Vietnamese caused the secretary to back off. The new American tactic was to try to negotiate the issues diplomatically, in full consultation with the Thais and South Vietnamese, and to have a conference, if at all, only to ratify agreements already reached.

This ultimately required a very unilateralist approach, since both the British and French wanted to move ahead. The Soviet Union wanted to issue invitations for a conference to be held in April. But Rusk told the British bluntly that the United States would not attend a conference unless the results were agreed upon before hand, and indeed that he was not even very happy at the prospect of a conference called merely to sign an agreement.[31]

In February, however, Sihanouk moved close to the American position. Rather than a Geneva Conference, he would agree to a quadripartite conference of Thailand, South Vietnam, the United States, and Cambodia which would settle the boundary issues. The United States found the proposal constructive and urged its Southeast Asian allies to attend. But the Americans probably sabotaged the idea inadvertently when they presented to Sihanouk a proposed settlement which, in the words of an Australian analysis, was "rather derogatory in tone" and, by advocating mixed boundary commissions to determine border questions, "appeared to ignore the various treaties" concerning the border.[32] When Sihanouk read the American draft he was incensed. As Australian officials in Washington put it, "the United States' drafts were never intended to be a 'bombshell' although they apparently had the effect of a bombshell upon the highly emotional Sihanouk."[33] The Prince called it an "immense deception" that was absolutely unacceptable; he saw the American proposal as a rejection of his own settlement proposal. Kimny later explained that because the American draft did not accept the international treaties that defined Cambodia's boundaries and had used the word to "delimit" the borders, it was interpreted to mean that the present borders would be changed. This had upset the Cambodians "beyond belief."[34] The Americans later admitted that it was a mistake to have sent their draft to Sihanouk. Instead it would have been better to have simply gone to the conference.[35] This was surely a correct assessment, for a day after the Cambodians rejected the American draft the mob attacked the American embassy.

Recognizing that Sihanouk had in fact moved close to the American position of bilateral diplomacy, the United States had genuinely tried to respond positively to Sihanouk's proposed quadrilateral conference. But in the end the United States could not convince Sihanouk that it seriously wanted a solution that would preserve his territorial integrity in the face of challenges from his regional enemies who were America's allies. Although the quadripartite conference did not take place, in a sense the United States won the larger diplomatic game because the Geneva Conference it did not want was not held. But its "victory" was at a considerable cost to its relations with Sihanouk.

Some, however, including French Foreign Office officials, thought the Americans had been entirely too rigid.[36] But the Americans, although they acknowledged that showing the American draft proposal to Sihanouk had been a mistake, believed that in the final analysis there was nothing they could reasonably have done that would have improved the relationship. Sihanouk's actions, they believed, resulted ultimately from his conviction that China's strength was growing and that the National Liberation Front (NLF) would prevail in Vietnam. Consequently, they concluded, he had decided to cut the best deal with them that he could. Offers of reasonable American concessions, therefore, would be futile. There was, in sum, little the US could do to influence events. It could only keep a low profile and be patient – or so American officials believed.

Ultimately most American officials believed that they had to choose between Sihanouk and its obstreperous allies Thailand and South Vietnam, and they chose the latter. Relations with Thailand and South Vietnam were "far too important to be jeopardized by concessions to Sihanouk which, even if they should prove acceptable, are unlikely [to] purchase any lasting benefit as long as he is convinced of forthcoming victory communist forces in SEA,"[37] asserted Herbert Spivack, the American chargé in Phnom Penh. The Australian ambassador in Phnom Penh caught the American perspective well. In a personal note to a colleague about "the complete bankruptcy of American policy in Cambodia," he asserted that the Americans had never considered Cambodia or its problems important. Rather, they always viewed the country as part of some larger issue. Even Spivack regularly reminded his staff that in the larger framework of American objectives Cambodia was unimportant. "If the man on the spot thinks so," Deschamps wrote, "the attitude of the State Department becomes more comprehensible."[38] Deschamps' insight was entirely accurate. As Roger Hilsman put it in a telegram to Henry Cabot Lodge, "our fundamental objective is to cope with the problem of Cambodia in such a way as to meet security interests of the Free World in Southeast Asia."[39]

Even as the parties were adjusting to the new situation and trying to determine what to do next, on March 19 – only nine days after the violent demonstrations at the embassies – aircraft from South Vietnam attacked the Cambodian village of Chantrea using napalm and machine guns. The attack lasted over two hours. Seventeen Cambodians died, and nineteen were wounded. South Vietnamese troops on the ground with American advisers also participated. In an unusual move, the ICC commissioners went immediately to the scene (almost becoming casualties themselves when their helicopter crash landed). The Canadian commissioner described the chilling devastation:

> We first saw fresh traces of numerous track vehicles (reported to have been twelve) which had obviously just gone through village. We saw at least twenty of reported 40 killed bulls and buffaloes; some were still dying. We were being prepared slowly to see on actual spot where they had just died thirteen villagers including pregnant women and children. Death was so recent blood had not rpt not yet dried. Some had died from bullet wounds other from shells and three at least had been run over by very heavy vehicles. [Cambodians claimed that wounded people had been deliberately run over.] Later in hospital we saw two children who had died half hour earlier as result of burns when incendiary bombs had completed destroyed their huts. In fact cinders were still smoldering when we looked at site of huts and picked up pieces of napalm bombs which French M[ilitary] A[ttaché] identified. We found tank caps which read twenty USA gallons. We saw numerous bullet holes and later spent cartridges with inscription 20mm Nessco which French MA said were used on Sky Raiders planes which SVN army uses . . . . [Back in Svay Rieng] we saw 14 wounded two of whom were children reaching delirious stage . . . . Violence of attack has shocked Cambodians and I admit Commissioners who saw results.[40]

The American military attaché, who went to Chantrea the next day, confirmed the devastation and reported that Americans had been seen in the armored personnel carriers (M-113s) and that one American pilot was reported to be on a plane that was shot down and landed in South Vietnam. The report was true. The plane (a Vietnamese L-19) was shot down by Cambodian planes (T-28s supplied by the United States), probably over South Vietnam. The Vietnamese observer was killed and the American pilot seriously wounded.

Michael Forrestal informed President Johnson that American personnel had penetrated Cambodian territory, allegedly because they were, in the language of official military double talk, "deficient in determination of their geographical position."[41] South Vietnam immediately apologized for the incident. Johnson was also inclined to apologize but was persuaded that to do so would play into Sihanouk's long standing contention that the United States controlled South Vietnam.[42] In the end, the United States officially regretted the Chantrea incident, acknowledged that American advisers were present (though it insisted they did not do any of the shooting), and ascribed it to an error in map reading; but it did not accept responsibility; that was left to the South Vietnamese. The Cambodians, however, insisted that the United States shared responsibility for the incident.

The seriousness of the incident led some to question if the raid had deliberate political implications. It occurred just as a high level team from Saigon, led by General Cao, was arriving in Phnom Penh to conduct negotiations with Cambodian officials. Deschamps reported that the "synchronization of action with the arrival of General Cao's mission to Cambodia is incomprehensible, unless it was a deliberate attempt to sabotage negotiations." Cao himself said that he had "been stabbed in the back."[43] Lodge, never a proponent of improving relations with Sihanouk, reacted to news of the raid with a cold and unsympathetic dispatch that blamed the incident on Cambodia's harboring of Viet Cong. The incident "should be viewed in prospective [sic] of total GVN [Government of Vietnam] effort to survive communist avowed objective of crushing and eventually dominating South Vietnam," he wrote. He did not believe a strong representation to the Vietnamese government was warranted,[44] and he tried to water down the final American note of regret to Cambodia. Furthermore, the initial American military report of the incident was incomplete and evasive.[45] The French foreign office believed that such border raids "were probably deliberately planned at some level of GVN."[46] Although none of this proves that the Chantrea attack was deliberately intended to sabotage prospective negotiations, it would not be the last time that a major border incident interfered with efforts to improve relations.

Whether deliberate or not, the incident illustrated the unimportance of Cambodia to the Johnson administration. American policy toward Cambodia, wrote Deschamps, was characterized by "unimaginativeness, rigidity, indifference and plain stupidity. How, otherwise," he wrote, "in the present tense and potentially dangerous situation, could American officers have been involved in the worst and most blatant and inexcusable Vietnamese aggression against Cambodia on record?"[47]

Some Americans shared Deschamps' perspective, at least to the extent of demanding that steps be taken to insure that this sort of incident would not occur in the future. Even Rusk pointed out that current restrictions on military actions near the Cambodian border had been violated in several respects. But Lodge and the military resisted. Lodge and General Paul Harkins, the commander of American forces in Vietnam, in fact, wanted to reduce the current restrictions on border operations.[48] Maxwell Taylor refused to ask Harkins what steps were being taken to prevent a similar incident in the future, and Forrestal said that directives from Washington had no effect in the field anyway. "If there is to be an effect," he wrote, "some sort of action has to be taken to bring home to the officers involved that this kind of mistake could affect their careers."[49] In the administration's view, Cambodian considerations took second place.

There was understandable concern that the situation in Phnom Penh could turn violently against the Americans and the British. Both embassies began a measured evacuation of some dependents. There were also efforts to revive the quadripartite idea, and Rusk was even willing to attend a Geneva Conference under certain conditions. The United States worked intensively for a time with the French and the British on these matters. But angry responses, especially from Lodge who argued hyperbolically that a conference would destroy South Vietnam, derailed the idea. Sihanouk angrily accused the United States of sabotaging the conference – which was not far from the mark.

Fortunately for the Americans, Sihanouk's venture to strike a bargain with North Vietnam on border guarantees went sour at precisely this time, and the Prince accused the North Vietnamese of acting just like the Thais.[50] Consequently the danger of a complete break with the United States faded. For the time being Sihanouk decided not to pursue either the quadripartite meeting or the Geneva Conference and ignored previously issued ultimata saying he would break relations if the conference was not called. He would now, he said, devote himself to his family and internal matters and visit France.[51] The immediate crisis had passed. Sihanouk's various gambles had failed, and the Prince was prepared for the time being to watch and wait.

Now some state department officials thought it would be wise to be more conciliatory toward Cambodia. Secretary Rusk prepared a friendly letter to the Cambodian foreign minister and even raised the possibility of inviting Sihanouk to visit the United States on his way to France. But due to opposition within the government, Rusk's letter remained undelivered, and the Prince was not invited to visit Washington.[52]

That Sihanouk had for the moment given up on the Geneva Conference and was temporarily focusing on domestic matters did not mean the tension between the two countries had ended. On the contrary, as Deschamps reported, this would "not be a period of calm" but rather "one of increasing tension during which any incidents could precipitate a crisis."[53] In May, in fact, Spivack reported that Sihanouk's anti-American campaign was not "ebbing in any way. Accusations are becoming even more virulent," he wrote.[54] Indicative of Sihanouk's attitude toward the United States at the time was his letter to *Time Magazine* in response to a story critical of him. The article, he said, had implied that he was mad. On the contrary, the Prince retorted, American policy in Asia was insane, even in the view of many American allies. "Wherever your go," Sihanouk concluded, "you spread war, revolution and misery."[55]

To mention two of the many irritations in the next few months, in May 1964 Sihanouk accused the United States of sabotaging road machinery that Cambodia had purchased to repair the Khmer–American Friendship Highway and charged that an American scientific expedition searching for the rare wild cattle, the kouprey, had killed the animals and ravaged the forests.[56] Particularly dangerous were the many border incidents in which American personnel were often present. Among the more serious were those at Taey and Thlork (also in May), which involved several deaths. (Whether the American or Americans present in these cases actually crossed the border was a matter of dispute.) One thousand people demonstrated in the streets of Phnom Penh; Cambodia characterized the incidents as "acts of war" and made a formal complaint against the United States and South Vietnam to the United Nations Security Council.[57]

Late in July Sihanouk returned to Phnom Penh after several weeks in France for rest and medical care. He was relaxed, jovial, and in good humor and went out of his way to be friendly to the American chargé. The very next day, however, reports arrived that seventy-seven villagers (a number later raised to 107) in Ratanakiri Province had died from "yellow powder" dropped, it was said, by South Vietnamese planes. (A similar incident occurred in Svay Rieng Province shortly thereafter.) Both the United States and South Vietnam denied any involvement in the incident, stating that no herbicide operations had crossed the border and that in any case herbicides did not form powder under any circumstances. (The United States also noted that the herbicides used in Vietnam were "completely harmless to humans.")[58] This incident, however, insured that relations would continue to be hostile, as Sihanouk soon accused the Americans of responsibility for the deaths. The American embassy referred to "a torrent of invective" emanating from Cambodia.[59]

In late August and early September another important series of border incidents occurred, in which South Vietnamese planes strafed the village of Koh Rokor and Cambodian boats on the Mekong River; ground troops also attacked. These raids, along with renewed reports of chemical attacks and the first American bombing of North Vietnam in response to the Gulf of Tonkin incident, deeply angered Sihanouk. After the United States protested Sihanouk's anti-American remarks made at a gathering where the American chargé was present, the Cambodian government suggested that the chargé be recalled. Sihanouk then refused to accept the credentials of the newly-appointed American ambassador, Randolph Kidder, who was already in Phnom Penh. Rusk ordered Kidder to return to Washington; he never went back to Cambodia.[60]

In October yet another major border incident occurred, this time at Anlong Kres in Kompong Cham province, which was attacked twice: on October 20 and October 24. Fire from South Vietnamese aircraft killed eight villagers (including two women and four children).[61] In another incident the Cambodians shot down an American transport plane over Dak Dam. Eight crew members died. The Cambodians removed the wrecked C-123 to Phnom Penh where they put it on display. By the end of the month there had been at least eight cross border raids, for which an angry Cambodian government held the United States jointly responsible with South Vietnam.[62] Sihanouk threatened to break relations with the United States and recognize North Vietnam and the NLF if any more violations of Cambodian territory occurred; the United States quietly evacuated dependents from Cambodia.[63] The White House also ordered tighter controls over air operations along the border until an investigation could be completed.

By this point Alf Bergesen, the new American chargé in Phnom Penh who had taken over when Herbert Spivack left and who, in the opinion of one Australian official, was "much more helpful and cooperative than Spivack,"[64] had become convinced that American policy was becoming counterproductive. Detecting a "distinct hardening" in American policy since the C-123 had been shot down, Bergesen wrote to Thomas J. Hirschfield, the state department's officer in charge of Cambodian affairs, that the United States appeared to be "naive or hypocritical" in criticizing the action of Cambodian soldiers. The United States underestimated "the fear on the part of the people in the border areas of strange aircraft," he wrote. All in all, Bergesen continued, "after 12 years of trying, American policy in Cambodia has failed." Sihanouk was "simply *sui generis*, a fact which we are apparently unable to accept. For this reason many of our finest and most polished three cushion shots wind up on the floor as far as achieving the effect here that was sought." Anything resembling a threat must be avoided, Bergeson advised, because they would "not do any good," would "not change Cambodian policy," and would be, in a word, "counterproductive." As for the border area, Bergesen wondered why it was necessary to have any Americans there. "The question remains whether the presence of American advisers in the frontier areas is worth the cost," he wrote, "and I have yet to see any evidence that it is."[65]

Whether Bergesen's letter had any impact on American policy is not clear, but shortly after he wrote it Rusk asked the French if they thought a "discreet, unpublicized meeting between specially designated US and Cambodian representatives" might help alleviate the problems.[66] Just how sincere the United States was in making this gesture is open to question, since the state department informed the American embassy in Phnom Penh that it doubted if such a message would postpone a break in relations and that it was largely to have the American offer on the record.[67] But to the great surprise of the Americans, the Cambodians accepted the offer with "surprising swiftness" and suggested New Delhi as the venue, which was acceptable to the United States since the respected former ambassador to the United States, Nong Kimny, was now stationed there.[68] In explaining his decision, Sihanouk stated that the government had been examining whether to break diplomatic relations with the United States. But, moved by the plight of the victims of the Anlong Kres attack, he did not want to take actions that might increase the cross border attacks, particularly since there was now a lull in border action.[69] Deschamps, in fact, thought that the American offer of talks thwarted a left wing bid within Cambodia to break relations, a bid which had come very close to success.[70]

The proposal for talks in New Delhi was the one constructive effort made to confront the issues during this entire period. The most likely candidate to head the American delegation was Averell Harriman, since the Cambodians had appointed Son Sann who, next to Sihanouk, was the most influential Cambodian politician. But the state department decided (over objections from Bergesen in Phnom Penh who wanted someone of higher rank) to appoint veteran diplomat Philip Bonsal.

The Cambodians wanted primarily to discuss an end to attacks on Cambodian villages, an end to accusations that they harbored the Viet Cong, and the withdrawal of South Vietnamese claims from certain islands (although they eventually withdrew the third objective). Secondarily they sought indemnification for those killed and injured in the border raids, an end to Khmer Serei broadcasts, and the freeing of Cambodians whom the South Vietnamese had arrested. The Americans hoped to resume normal diplomatic relations with Cambodia, convince Cambodia that a take over of South Vietnam by the Viet Cong was not going to happen, to reassure Cambodians that the United States did not support Cambodian dissidents and did not seek to overthrow their government, to warn the Cambodians that if they recognized the NLF or North Vietnam this would cause the United States to reexamine its position and make it more difficult to restrain South Vietnam, and explore the possibility of resuming Cambodian–South Vietnamese talks which had been broken off following the Chantrea incident the previous March.[71]

Neither side was very optimistic that the talks would succeed. Bonsal and the Cambodian delegation, headed by Son Sann, nevertheless made considerable progress toward the compromise settlement. But the American government soon ordered Bonsal to end the talks, stating that the Cambodian proposals for compromise required more extended study. Sihanouk, too, in some very negative public comments appeared to disown the proposed compromise, although this may have been a tactical ploy.[72]

The talks did succeed in preventing a rupture in diplomatic relations, permitted a relaxed exploration of issues, allowed Sihanouk to "get out of the corner into which he had been cleverly maneuvered by [the] left wing," and served Sihanouk's purpose by demonstrating to China and Hanoi that he had options.[73] But none of the issues was resolved. In the end, the two sides could not even agree on a joint communique, as each side issued its own final statement to the press. At a personal level, however, the talks did not end in acrimony as both sides jointly hosted a dinner honoring their Indian hosts.

There was certainly some blame on both sides for the inability to reach any agreements. Since neither side had held out much hope for success, neither side had been especially imaginative in its proposals. Sihanouk's statements that appeared to disown the compromise proposals were provocative, and his efforts to undertake simultaneous negotiations with the Chinese and North Vietnamese irritated the Americans. Bonsal did, however, think an agreement was possible (as apparently did Son Sann) and was making progress when the American government ordered him to stop the talks. Indeed the American delegation felt, as James C. Thomson, Jr. told Averell Harriman in 1966, "that they came within a day or so of success but were undercut by Washington."[74]

American officials feared that the collapse of the talks might result in violent demonstrations at the American embassy or perhaps in a diplomatic break. Relations were so poor that when the Polish representative on the International Control Commission was gravely injured in an automobile accident near the Phnom Penh airport, local people at first refused to assist him, thinking he was an American.[75] By the end of the year the US presence in Cambodia numbered only twelve individuals,[76] down from over 300 a year earlier.

After the breakdown of the New Delhi talks, there were some efforts to resume discussions and improve relations. Senator Mike Mansfield (D-MT), a respected authority on Asia, wrote the President a lengthy and eloquent memorandum (which the President read) about the dangers of an increasing American commitment in Southeast Asia. With respect to Cambodia, he recommended keeping American forces clear of the border and using American influence to insist that the South Vietnamese "abstain from exacerbating their border difficulties." There could easily be a ten to fifteen mile pull-back zone along those portions of the boundary where it was not well defined, he stated. He also gave Johnson his unsolicited opinion about Sihanouk, which was very contrary to the accepted wisdom: "We have consistently underestimated Sihanouk's astuteness and ability and overrated his naivete and instability," he told the President. "In my judgment," he continued, "he and his principal advisors are exceptionally able and are playing their cards totally in terms of Cambodia's independent survival and other interests."[77] James C. Thomson, an official on the National Security Staff, also urged South Vietnamese concession and American pressure on both them and the Thais to stop the Khmer Serei broadcasts.[78]

At the end of the year Sihanouk hinted that he wanted to improve relations with the United States, and Son Sann, too, made at least two efforts to get the talks going. The state department urged Ambassador Chester Bowles in New Delhi to keep open a channel of communication with the respected Cambodian ambassador, Nong Kimny. But in the end, nothing came of these (and other) efforts to resume serious discussions.

A very basic problem facing those who wanted to improve relations with Cambodia was that at this very moment the United States was in the process of choosing war in Vietnam, and the idea of improving relations with Cambodia was even more a secondary concern than before. There were, therefore, almost no significant steps in the first months of 1965 to improve their relations. Sihanouk continued to criticize the United States, often in angry tones, for any number of lapses: providing aid with strings, criticizing his non-aligned posture, allowing American journals to publish unflattering stories about him and Cambodia, and for the new sustained bombing of North Vietnam. In February Sihanouk told an Indian journalist that the United States "was today hated more than the French were in the worst phase of the colonial war."[79]

Cross border raids on Cambodia continued to be a major source of anger and were particularly dangerous to the US–Cambodian relationship. In January Son Sann had pleaded with the United States to avoid any border incident. If one more Cambodian were killed, it was likely that Sihanouk would break relations with the Americans, he said.[80] But the incidents did not stop. In mid-February 1965, after an upsurge in incursions (most of them relatively minor) from South Vietnam, Sihanouk said that he would declare war against the United States and South Vietnam if any more bombing of Cambodian villages took place and threatened to appeal to China for support.[81] Sihanouk's threat made no difference. The very next week there were thirteen minor incidents, and a US helicopter also landed briefly inside Cambodia.[82]

In Phnom Penh Bergesen argued that the cross border raids, as well as continued Khmer Serei activity aimed at overthrowing Sihanouk, were counterproductive. Despite his erratic behavior and anti-American outbursts, Bergesen believed that the Prince was "unquestionably the most effective Khmer leader" and that Cambodia had prospered under his leadership. Therefore the United States should try to "keep the wild men in Bangkok and Saigon from getting out of control and attempting to 'liberate' Cambodia. We do not believe that in the long run the best interests of the Free World would be served by an attempt to unseat him."[83]

Such advice was not heeded. Every week there were more reports of raids on Cambodian villages. After an attack on Kompong Trach, a village in the province of Kampot, Sihanouk issued what he said was his final warning. "I launch a last and solemn notice to imperialist Americans in warning them for the last time, that my country will break diplomatic relations with the U.S. upon the next attack upon a Cambodian life," he stated in a speech on 26 March.[84]

But the attacks did not let up appreciably. On April 3 1965 ARVN (South Vietnamese) forces reportedly killed a Cambodian in Bavet, Svay Rieng province. A week later they attacked another village in Takeo, seriously wounding one person. In addition there were reports of aircraft from Thailand spreading poisonous chemicals in the area of Pailin. Bergesen once again warned his government of the consequences of continued incidents and suggested some assurances be passed to the Cambodian government about continued American concern about the border incidents and detailing measures which the United States was taking to minimize them.[85]

If there was no progress on resolving these matters separating the United States and Cambodia, there was some movement on Sihanouk's long demand for a Geneva Conference on Cambodia. A new call for a conference emerged from a Sihanouk-sponsored Conference of Indochinese Peoples. Having failed in 1964 to get satisfactory pledges from the United States and its Southeast Asian allies to respect Cambodian neutrality and territorial integrity, the Prince convoked the conference late in February 1965. Sihanouk hoped to find a way to limit the fighting in the region and secure long sought guarantees for his own country's neutrality and territorial integrity. The most important conference participants were the Fatherland Front of North Vietnam and the NLF. But nearly forty other groups from Cambodia, Laos, and Vietnam, all of them leftist or neutralist, attended.[86]

Since the North Vietnamese, the NLF and perhaps China were then uninterested in negotiating a settlement in Vietnam short of a total American withdrawal, the conference failed to call for a new Geneva Conference to settle the war or in other more limited ways to move toward peace in Vietnam. This was a disappointment to Sihanouk who found the communist delegations rigid, for despite his vigorous anti-Americanism he feared the consequences of a total North Vietnamese victory. As far as Cambodia was concerned, Sihanouk said to reporters, North Vietnamese communism was the worst kind, "worse than [the] Chinese or Russian" varieties.[87]

The Americans gloated over the conference's apparent failure. Was this not a "salutary lesson for Sih[anouk]?" Bergesen told American diplomats gathered in the Philippines.[88] However, the conference did support another of Sihanouk's goals: the calling of a new Geneva Conference to deal with Cambodia.[89]

Bergesen's initial response to the renewed call was that it seemed "to have less steam behind it than was the case several times in the past."[90] But on April 3 in response to Cambodia's request of March 15 to the Geneva co-chairs, Great Britain and the USSR, the Soviet Union endorsed the idea. The British soon agreed in principle as well, although they did not immediately accept the specific Soviet proposal to issue invitations.[91]

The serious possibility that a new Geneva conference on Cambodia would be called deeply divided the American diplomatic community. From the American embassies in Saigon and Bangkok came the usual dire warnings that American acceptance of such a conference would be seen as a sign of weakness,[92] while the Saigon government itself was strongly opposed. In Phnom Penh, on the other hand, Bergesen was cautiously supportive of a conference.[93] Canada and France also favored the conference, as did Britain, although the British saw it primarily as an opportunity through side conversations to deal with Vietnam rather than Cambodia.

Lower level officials, including William Bundy, twice presented a negative recommendation to Rusk,[94] but George Ball and Averell Harriman weighed in on the other side, and in the end the Secretary of State seemed inclined to give the conference his blessing. Particularly important in this respect was President Johnson's television address on April 7 at Johns Hopkins University in which he had offered to engage in "unconditional discussions" on Vietnam. Could the United States refuse to discuss the less difficult Cambodian situation? A conference might, as the British hoped, also provide the communists with a face-saving way "through corridor talks" to respond to Johnson's offer on Vietnam. It also provided a face-saving way of excluding from the talks the NLF, which had not been a participant at the Geneva Conference of 1954.[95]

Still, the United States was cautious. As in the past, it hoped that agreement on the major issues could be reached informally ahead of time so that the conference itself would do little more than ratify previously reached understandings. As it happened, the British government was then just about to send Patrick Gordon-Walker to Southeast Asia to explore whether a conference on Cambodia or Laos might be a way to open talks on Vietnam. The United States suggested that his mission be altered to include soundings of interested states to see if understandings could be reached about Cambodia's "border difficulties."[96]

Even this suggestion elicited criticism from Ambassador Graham Martin in Bangkok who found the idea of Gordon-Walker speaking to the Thais about the boundary positively dangerous.[97] In Saigon, Ambassador Taylor was unenthusiastic about any movement toward a conference but favored the Gordon-Walker mission because it was in effect a delaying tactic.[98] The next day Rusk and McGeorge Bundy discussed the mission with Prime Minister Harold Wilson, who was then in Washington, and other British officials. Gordon-Walker, they agreed, would "explore attitudes in Phnom Penh, Bangkok, and Saigon," always making it clear the he did not speak for the United States. This meant that a firm American decision on the conference itself would be delayed by at least two weeks,[99] thus allowing time for further reflection and debate.

Despite the fact that Rusk and Bundy had discussed the Gordon-Walker mission with Prime Minister Wilson, the British Foreign Office found the American position "disquieting." Foreign Secretary Michael Stewart immediately understood that the United States was once again stalling (to the distress of Harriman and Ball) and feared that the Soviets might withdraw their proposal. He "stressed that we did not have time in which to play with conference idea," reported the American minister in London.[100] Stewart was right about the need for haste; an early and positive American response just might have forestalled the subsequent break in relations.

American caution was evident when Rusk met with the British ambassador on April 19. Britain wanted the United States to at least approve a Cambodia conference in principle. But Rusk would only say that "we wanted to do everything possible to avoid saying no to a conference." In addition, Rusk made five specific suggestions for Gordon-Walker, two of which, if adopted, meant additional delay. His most important suggestion was that Gordon-Walker see if the parties might consider British draft proposals made in January 1964 "as [the] basis for [a] Cambodia settlement."[101] As the British immediately pointed out, both the USSR and Sihanouk had rejected the earlier drafts, and bringing them up again "would queer any prospects for a conference."[102] Rusk backed down.

Meanwhile Gordon-Walker had begun his mission. In Thailand Ambassador Martin, given permission to be frank in his views, was almost hostile. Gordon-Walker, he concluded, wanted to see a "unified Titoist-type Socialist state" in Vietnam, an outcome that would, in Martin's view, "be regarded as [a] shattering American defeat" which would only encourage wars of national liberation in Africa and Latin America. Gordon-Walker's suggestion that American military actions in Vietnam, particularly the bombing of North Vietnam, be curtailed, also irritated the ambassador. With respect to Cambodia specifically, Martin predicted that if the Thais felt threatened by the proposed conference, they would probably lift their restraints on Khmer Serei activities and work to "bring about a change of regime in Cambodia."[103]

Others, though, including the French ambassador in Washington, urged the United States to embrace the conference. From New Delhi Ambassador Bowles cabled that American support of a Cambodian conference might help heal the very tense relations with India.[104] In Burma General Ne Win implied that the Chinese saw a Cambodian conference as the first step in settling the Vietnam War.[105] The following day, April 22, even Thailand indicated that it might agree to a conference, doubtless to Martin's chagrin.[106]

Now the momentum clearly favored those who wanted the United States to support a conference. Still, Rusk held back. He agreed that Gordon-Walker could now go to Saigon and speak with the Prime Minister Phan Huy Quat. But he was "not optimistic about what a conference might achieve" and was not yet committed to it. Nevertheless, the pressures were strong. An added factor favoring American support was that the Johnson administration needed support for the expansion of the American war in Vietnam. "We would have difficulty in saying 'no' to a conference in relation to our own need to mobilize international and domestic support for what seems to be an inevitable increase in our effort in South East Asia," Rusk acknowledged.[107]

When South Vietnam fell into line after Gordon-Walker "twisted Quat's arm very hard,"[108] and Sarit Thanarat agreed that he would "acquiesce" in a Cambodian conference if the United States thought it important,[109] all seemed poised for an American announcement accepting the conference. President Johnson himself apparently agreed to support a conference in principle.[110] But on April 24 Taylor asked for a forty-eight hour delay so that Quat would have time to persuade elements in his government, including the military, that the conference was necessary.[111] Quat did not get his forty-eight hours, for on April 25 Rusk announced that the United States would gladly participate in a conference on Cambodia if one were called. Averell Harriman, the secretary told the press, would represent the United States.[112]

Why, after weeks of foot-dragging, had the United States suddenly moved at this particular time to full support of the conference?[113] The reason lay with Sihanouk. On April 23 in a speech dedicating USSR Avenue in Phnom Penh, the Prince asserted that the United States was considering attending a conference only because it might lead to progress on Vietnam. The Americans, who constantly referred to Cambodia as "tiny" and "backward," had no interest in Cambodia itself. It "is the least of their worries," he stated. Any conference, he insisted, must deal only with

Cambodia.[114] Even more troubling, the next day at a ceremony opening a new grocery store, Sihanouk indicated that he now did not want Thailand, South Vietnam, or the United States to attend. He appeared to be fed up with American stalling. The United States, he stated accurately, "without saying 'no', do not say 'yes' either." Sihanouk even appeared to be saying that he no longer wanted a conference at all. "This conference interests us today much less than at [the] time when we were demanding [it] and when [the] Anglo-Saxons were obstructing it," Sihanouk told his audience. "[The] Conference, to tell the truth is outdated... because things have evolved in such [a] fashion that it [is] no longer necessary to convene it."[115]

Sihanouk's remarkable about-face forced the American action. As Rusk explained to American diplomats in Bangkok and Vientiane:

> By Sunday we were confronted with the fact that Sihanouk's remarks at grocery store opening had been published.... Gordon Walker was on point of leaving Saigon for Phnom Penh. There seemed some reason to hope that, by announcing US and GVN [Government of Vietnam] agreement beforehand, we could forestall official Cambodian response to Gordon Walker that US and GVN attendance at conference unacceptable. It was thought that announcement might equally forestall RKG [Cambodian Government] demand for Liberation Front representation. These factors seemed to us to warrant risks that announcement might, on the contrary, get Sihanouk's back up, and precipitate official confirmation as well as disadvantage seeming to be unduly anxious about conference.[116]

Why, at a time when the British and the Americans were finally willing to support a conference, when Thailand and South Vietnam had fallen in line, and when China, the Soviet Union, North Vietnam, and the NLF had also voiced support, did Sihanouk throw a fatal wrench into the works? He may have been convinced, as he stated, that the Americans had simply stalled too long; and in any event if they were finally interested it was only to speak with their opponents about Vietnam. He no doubt believed that, as he told the French ambassador, "at least 'certain circles' " in the American government were anti-Sihanouk. The Americans, he asserted, "remained afraid of spread of neutralism" and believed that Sihanouk, as a leading defender of neutralism, "was somehow [a] danger to U.S. policy."[117]

To the extent that Sihanouk's perception of American policy explains his decision to sabotage the conference, an early, positive American response might have produced positive results. But Sihanouk also acted for reasons not directly related to American stalling. In his biography of Sihanouk, Australian scholar and diplomat Milton Osborne asserted that at a conference in Jakarta scheduled shortly before the demonstration at the embassy took place (the conference was to celebrate the tenth anniversary of the Bandung Conference), China's Premier, Zhou Enlai (Chou En-lai), personally asked Sihanouk not to go ahead with the conference he had so long championed because it might work to the disadvantage of China's Vietnamese allies. "Faced with this request," Osborne writes, "Sihanouk, who only the year before had been accorded a place of honour beside Mao Zedong at the celebration of the fifteenth anniversary of the Chinese Revolution in Peking, could only oblige."[118]

Though Osborne provided no evidence to support his assertion, American and Australian documents indicate that his point was valid. On April 25 the Australian embassy in Phnom Penh reported that the Chinese had told Sihanouk that they would not attend a conference where Vietnam was discussed and that they were prepared to give Cambodia the assurances it sought, thus making a conference unnecessary.[119] The next day a CIA report concluded that, while the USSR and North Vietnam wanted a conference (supposedly because it would make it more difficult for the United States to escalate the war in Vietnam and continue the bombing of North Vietnam), Chinese support for the conference had always been a façade because they feared it would increase Soviet influence in Hanoi. Thus they engaged in "intensive efforts . . . to sabotage the conference by convincing the Cambodian premier that negotiations are unnecessary."[120] Two weeks later the French ambassador in Phnom Penh conveyed remarkably similar information to Bergesen. "Almost certainly . . . Chou En-lai told Sihanouk in Djakarta that Chicoms did not wish to have conference at present time," he told the American, "and Sihanouk was willing to oblige his friends."[121] In any event, the day after Rusk's announcement that the United States was prepared to attend the conference, the demonstrators attacked the American embassy in Phnom Penh.

It appears likely that once Sihanouk had determined that the conference could not be held, he allowed the demonstration at the American embassy to take place – the result of his long standing anger at American support for the Khmer Serei, continuing cross-border military operations from South Vietnam, American stalling on the conference, his general irritation at what he regarded as a patronizing attitude toward himself and Cambodia, as well as internal political pressures. He used the offensive Krisher article in *Newsweek* as the excuse.

However important the conference issue may have been in forming Sihanouk's general anti-Americanism or in bringing about the demonstration, it was not the most important cause of the break in diplomatic relations. Indeed, it is not even certain that Sihanouk intended the demonstration as a prelude to a break in relations. As late as April 30 – four days after the demonstration – the Cambodian cabinet was reportedly uncertain about breaking relations.[122]

Almost certainly the most immediate reasons for the break was yet another border incident. On April 28, two days after the demonstration, four planes, thought to be South Vietnamese Skyraiders, bombed the Cambodian village of Phum Chantatep (or Cheam Tatep) and Moream Tiek in Kompong Cham province. The villages were about four kilometers from the Vietnamese border. One thirteen year old boy was killed, and others were seriously injured. American military attachés who went to the scene the same day confirmed the death and counted thirty-five bomb and rocket craters. Bergesen predicted that Sihanouk would break relations over the border incidents, not the *Newsweek* article. As a last ditch attempt to salvage the situation, he suggested an immediate South Vietnamese apology and compensation to the victims.[123]

The situation was actually worse than Bergesen first thought. An investigation quickly determined that the planes in question were *American*, not South Vietnamese. Consequently, in an effort to prevent a break Bergesen urged that the United

States immediately apologize and offer compensation. A note along these lines was prepared and sent to the White House on May 1, but it was never sent.[124] Had it been, it might have prevented a break in relations. After the break, an unidentified Cambodian Foreign Ministry official speculated to a CIA agent that the reason Sihanouk broke relations "was that no acknowledgement of the error in bombing a Cambodian village on 28 April had come from the GVN."[125] Probably because relations were soon broken, the United States government never officially acknowledged that it was at fault, although privately it understood that American planes were responsible for the incident.

When Sihanouk broke relations, an aide told President Johnson that the Prince based his action on two grounds: the Krisher article and the border bombing. McGeorge Bundy also told him that "the Cambodians have put the burden *equally* on *NEWS-WEEK* and on the air attacks." Bundy thought it was "good" that the Cambodians based their decision on the two grounds. Sihanouk's action made an apology "irrelevant," and the government would claim (inaccurately) that the bombing incident was still being investigated.[126] Johnson's aides had misled him, for the actual note breaking relations referred only to the attack on the villages (which the Cambodians still assumed had been a South Vietnamese action). No other factors, including the Krisher article, were mentioned, something which John Dexter, the Cambodian desk officer in the state department, pointed out to Australian diplomats at the time.[127]

Any initial confusion about the primacy of the border attacks as the cause of the break soon disappeared, for Cambodian officials made it clear that an end to the cross border actions was the only condition for restoring relations. Sihanouk himself told French officials that the break resulted from "repeated border incursions," and "he would be happy to restore relations if US put [a] stop to" them.[128] One foreign ministry official indicated that Cambodia could even live with some border incidents, as long as Vietnam would immediately accept responsibility, apologize, and offer compensation.[129]

In sum, the American bombs and rockets that hit Phum Chantatep and Moream Tiek were the immediate cause for the break in relations. The hundreds of such incidents involving South Vietnamese and/or American personnel were the most important underlying cause as well. Alleged American support for Sihanouk's bitter enemies, the Khmer Serei, also contributed to the break, as did American stalling on the Geneva Conference. Less tangible factors, such as patronizing American attitudes toward Cambodia and unflattering stories in the American press, helped produce a general anti-American atmosphere in Cambodia. Sihanouk's own assessment of the future of Indochina, as well as his concern with domestic politics, also affected his decision.

At the heart of it was the war in Vietnam, which seriously exacerbated pre-existing tensions between Cambodia and its neighbors and consequently with their ally, the United States. Even more fundamental was the Cold War thinking that deeply affected American policy makers. Though not unaware of the regional character of Cambodia's problems, they generally viewed developments through a Cold War lens. Even when regional factors were recognized, the United States almost always subordinated them to Cold War considerations. It was too bad that Sihanouk would be angered, but opposing the spread of international communism took first place.

The break in relations starkly revealed the limits of American acceptance of neutralism in Southeast Asia. It was also tragic in that it was an important part of a chain of events that ended in tragedy for Cambodia. Diplomatic relations were not restored until 1969, a period during which the United States attempted to destabilize the Sihanouk government.[130] In 1969 the United States began the secret bombing of Cambodia. Then in March 1970 Lon Nol and Sisowath Sirik Matak overthrew Sihanouk in a pro-American (and possibly American-supported) coup. Sihanouk, greatly angered at this turn of events, appealed to the people to support the opposition Khmer Rouge. The next month American and South Vietnamese forces invaded Cambodia in an attempt to destroy the Communists' Central Office for South Vietnam (COSVN). Both of these actions further destabilized Cambodian society. Five years of civil war followed, with devastating consequences. In 1975 the Khmer Rouge took over the country and ruled so harshly that perhaps two million Cambodians (out of a population of less than eight million) perished. Had the United States and Cambodia been able to resolve their differences constructively, Cambodia might have been spared the holocaust it endured.[131]

NOTES

1 Alf Bergesen to Secretary of State, April 26 1965, Tels. 636 and 637, General Records of the Department of State, Record Group 59, Central Foreign Policy Files, 1964–66, box 1970, folder POL 23, National Archives II, College Park, Maryland.

2 For a complete report on the demonstration and the damage caused, see Bergesen to Department of State, May 11 1965, Airgram A-235, RG 59, CFPF 1964–66, box 1970, folder POL 23, NAII. Bergesen to Secretary of State, April 26 1965, Tels. 638 and 639, RG 59, CFPF 1964–66, box 1970, folder POL 23, NAII. Demonstrators managed to break a heavy plate glass door, but folding metal doors held.

3 "Sihanouk Apologizes for Riots But Says West Provoked Them," *New York Times*, March 12 1964. Peter Murray, British Embassy Phnom Penh, to R. A. Butler, March 11 1964, Series No. A1209/112, Control symbol 1964/6181 Part A, National Archives of Australia, Canberra. Deschamps, Australian Embassy Phnom Penh, to External Affairs Department (EXAF), March 12 1964, Tel. 97, Series No. A1209/112, Control symbol 1964/6181 Part A, NAA.

4 Milton Osborne, *Sihanouk: Prince of Light, Prince of Darkness* (Honolulu: University of Hawaii Press, 1994), 163.

5 Australian Embassy Phnom Penh to EXAF, March 16 1964, Tel. 107, Series No. A1209/112, Control symbol 64/6181 Part A, NAA. Deschamps, Australian Embassy Phnom Penh to EXAF, March 17 1964, Memorandum 142, Series No. 1838/280, Control symbol 3016/2/1 Part 16, NAA. Interview with Ambassador Noël St. Clair Deschamps, June 19–20, 1999, at the Commonwealth Club, Canberra, ACT, Australia, by Kenton J. Clymer. Institute of Oral History, University of Texas at El Paso, El Paso, TX.

6 Bergesen to SS, April 29 1965, RG 59, box 1970, folder POL 23. Bergesen to SS, April 28 1965, Lyndon Baines Johnson Papers, Cambodia Cables, Vol. III, 8/64–6/65, NSF-Country File, box 236, Lyndon Baines Johnson Library, Austin, Texas. Bergesen to USDS, April 30 1965, Airgram A-228, RG 59, box 1967, folder POL 2–1.

7   Bergesen to SS, May 3 1965, Johnson Papers, Cambodia Cables, Vol. III, 8/64–6/65, NSF – Country File, box 236. Bergesen to SS, May 7 1965, Airgram A-233, RG 59, box 1967, folder POL 2–1.

8   Bergesen to USDS, May 14 1965, Airgram A-236, RG 59, box 1967, folder POL 2–1.

9   Osborne, *Sihanouk*, 164. David Chandler, *The Tragedy of Cambodian History: Politics, war, and Revolution since 1945* (New Haven, 1991), 146.

10 Bergesen to SS, April 26 1965, Tel. 640, RG 59, box 1970, folder POL 23. Bergesen to USDS, May 11 1965, Airgram A-235. American officials noted that the demonstration took place three weeks after the article appeared, suggesting that it was only a pretext. An ironic sidelight to this affair is that later Krisher collaborated with Sihanouk in writing a book. Osborne, *Sihanouk*, 165.

11 "Cambodia," Administrative History – State Department, Chapter 7, Part I (East Asia), Johnson Papers, box 3.

12 Bergesen to USDS, May 11 1965, Airgram A-235, RG 59, box 1970, POL 23. American containment policy on the periphery and toward neutralism has begun to see some significant historical treatment. See, for example, Robert J. McMahon, *The Cold War on the Periphery: The United States, India, and Pakistan* (New York, 1994), and H. W. Brands, *The Specter of Neutralism: The United States and the Emergence of the Third World, 1947–1960* (New York, 1989). On the other hand, discussion of American policy toward Cambodia has been largely limited to the period of the American invasion of Cambodia in 1970. See William Shawcross, *Sideshow: Nixon, Kissinger, and the Destruction of Cambodia*, rev. ed. (New York, 1987), and Harold Isaacs, *Without Honor: Defeat in Cambodia and Vietnam* (Baltimore, 1983). American military operations during this period are ably discussed in Wilfred Deac, *Road to the Killing Fields: The Cambodian War of 1970–1975* (College Station, TX, 1997), while the most recent treatment of the *Mayaguez* affair of 1975 is John F. Guilmartin, Jr., *A Very Short War: The Mayaguez and the Battle of Koh Tang* (College Station, TX, 1995.) American policy during the Jimmy Carter administration is investigated in Sheldon Neuringer, *The Carter Administration, Human Rights, and the Agony of Cambodia* (Lewiston, NY, 1993) and Michael Haas, *Cambodia, Pol Pot, and the United States: The Faustian Pact* (New York, 1991). For the earlier years see Kenton J. Clymer, "Decolonization, Nationalism, and Anti-Communism: United States Relations with Cambodia, 1945–1954," *Journal of American-East Asian Relations*, 6 (Summer/Fall 1997): 91–124. American policy toward Cambodia also receives some attention in three important recent works on Cambodia itself: Ben Kiernan, *How Pol Pot Came to Power: A History of Communism in Kampuchea, 1930–1975* (London, 1985); Chandler, *The Tragedy of Cambodian History*; and Osborne, *Sihanouk*. An earlier work on Cambodian foreign policy is Michael Leifer, *Cambodia: The Search for Security* (New York, 1967).

13 Brands, *The Specter of Neutralism*. Brands limits his discussion to India, Yugoslavia, and Egypt. Memorandum of Conversation, Walter S. Robertson et al., August 5 1958, US Department of State, *Foreign Relations of the United States, 1958–1960* (Washington, 1992), 16: 244.

14 Osborne, *Sihanouk*, 166. By the terms of the agreement, the United States was only to supply the Cambodian armed forces; French military advisers were to do the training. Gradually, however, the United States took over some of the training responsibilities as well.

15 Richard E. Usher to John M. Steeves, March 11 1960, *FRUS 1958–1960* 16: 355. Richard E. Usher to John M. Steeves, March 11 1960, *FRUS, 1958–1960* 16: 255. For

Sihanouk's own account see Norodom Sihanouk, *My War with the CIA: The Memoirs of Prince Norodom Sihanouk as related to Wilfred Burchett* (New York, 1972).

16   See Kenton J. Clymer, "Ambassador William Cattell Trimble and Cambodia, 1959–1962," in *The Human Tradition in the Vietnam Era*, ed. David H. Anderson (Wilmington, DE: 2000), 23–42.

17   Osborne, *Sihanouk*, 151. Chandler, *The Tragedy of Cambodian History*, 130–4; Kiernan, *How Pol Pot Came to Power*, 205–6. Renunciation of American aid also fit in with Sihanouk's growing concerns about foreign domination of the nation's economy. See Osborne, *Sihanouk*, 160–1.

18   Memorandum of a telephone conversation between Averell Harriman and Dean Acheson, December 9 1963, *FRUS 1961–63* (Washington, 1994), 23: 282. During the celebration civil servants were allowed to come to work two hours later than normal. Phnom Penh Domestic Radio Broadcast, December 9 1963, ibid., 280–1.

19   Sihanouk speech, given on December 9 and broadcast on December 10 1963, ibid., 281–2.

20   Philip D. Sprouse to USDS, December 17 1963, ibid., 288–90. George Ball to US Embassy Phnom Penh, December 19 1963, ibid., 295–6. Sprouse to USDS, December 22 1963, ibid., 299–301.

21   Later, in justifying his decision to terminate American aid, Sihanouk recalled all of his problems with the Americans in the 1950s and early 1960s: American support for various Cambodian opposition movements; the failure of the United States to prevent raids by South Vietnamese forces into Cambodia; the American refusal to allow him to use American equipment to repulse the Vietnamese and Thai incursions; the huge amounts of aid given to Laos, when compared with what was given to Cambodia; the interminable time it took to get four "*avions à reaction*" (and then they came incompletely equipped); and in general the humiliating way he felt Cambodia had been treated. In the event of aggression, he said, he would now turn to the Soviet Union or China. *Le Reject de l'aide Américaine: Trois Exposés de S.A.R. Le Prince Norodom Sihanouk* [*The Rejection of American aid: Three Presentations by His Royal Highness Prince Norodom Sihanouk*] (Phnom Penh, n.d. [1963]), copy in Fonds "Affaire Etrangere" (No. 2), Boite 58, Cambodian National Archives, Phnom Penh, Cambodia. The Cambodian National Archives contain French colonial records and some newer foreign policy material, mainly published. See Kenton J. Clymer, "The Cambodian National Archives," *Cold War International History Project Bulletin*, 6–7 (Winter 1995–96), 260, 265.

22   "Cambodian Chief Hopeful of Early Accord with U.S.," *New York Times*, January 15 1964.

23   Sprouse to SS, February 12 1964, Tel. 776, RG 59, CFPF 1964–1966, Box 1974, folder POLITICAL AFFAIRS & RELS CAMB-US 1/1/64, NAII.

24   US Embassy Phnom Penh, to USDS, February 6 1964, Airgram A-423, February 6 1964, RG 59, CFPF 1964–1966, Box 1967, folder POL 2-1. Philip D. Sprouse to USDS, February 11 1964, Airgram A-434, RG 59, Box 1970, folder "POL 23 CAMB." Bergesen to USDS, February 27 1964, Airgram A-451, RG 59, CFPF 1964–1966, Box 1967, folder POL 2-1, NAII

25   US Embassy Phnom Penh, to USDS, May 19 1964, RG 59, CFPF 1964–1966, Box 1974, folder POL 1 General Policy 1/1/64, NAII. US Embassy Phnom Penh, to USDS, May 22 1964, RG 59, CFPF 1964–1966, Box 1967, folder POL 2-1, NAII. The *Washington Post* published a similar story.

26   Lodge, US Embassy Saigon, to SS, March 28 1964, Tel. 1852, RG 59, CFPF 1964–1966 Box 1967, folder POL 2-1, NAII.

27 Lodge, US Embassy Saigon, to SS, April 11 1964, Tel. 1956, RG 59, CFPF 1964–1966 Box 1977, folder POL 32–1 CAMB-VIET S 4/1/64, NAII.

28 George Ball to US Embassy Saigon and CINCPAC, April 17 1964, Tel. 1715, RG 59, CFPF 1964–1966 Box 1977, folder POL 32–1 CAMB-VIET S 4/1/64, NAII.

29 US Embassy Phnom Penh to USDS, February 14 1964, Airgram A-438, RG 59, CFPF 1964–1966 Box 1977, folder POL 32–1 CAMB-VIET S 2/1/64, NAII.

30 Sihanouk to Johnson, February 8 1964, RG 59, CFPF 1964–1966, Box 1974, folder POLITICAL AFFAIRS 7 RELS CAMB-US 1/1/64, NAII.

31 Department of State Memorandum of Conversation, Nigel Trench, Dean Rusk et al, January 24 1964, RG 59, CFPF 1964–1966, Box 1971, folder POL 27–CAMB 1/1/64, NAII.

32 "SEATO Brief – *Cambodia*," n.d., Series No. A1838/280, Control symbol 3016/2/ 1 Part 16, NAA.

33 Australian Embassy Washington DC to EXAF, March 12 1964, Series No. A1838/280, Control symbol 3016/2/1 Part 15, NAA.

34 Department of State Memorandum of Conversation, Nong Kimny, Harriman, William J. Jorden, March 14 1964, RG 59, CFPF 1964–1966, Box 1974, folder POLITICAL AFFAIRS & RELS CAMB-US, NAII.

35 Australian Embassy Washington DC to EXAF, March 13 1964, Tel. 754, Series No. A1838/280, Control symbol 3016/2/1 Part 15, NAA.

36 Lyon to SS, March 12 1964, Tel. 4297 (Paris), RG 59, Box 1968, folder POL 8. France was disappointed "by U.S. inability or unwillingness to give Sihanouk the little that he wants despite clear Western interest in Cambodia."

37 Sprouse to USDS, February 28 1964, Airgram 456, RG 59, Box 1968, folder POL 2–3. Spivack to SS, March 13 1964, Tel. 929, RG 59, Box 1970, folder POL 23.

38 Deschamps to Keith Waller, March 24 1964, Series No. 1838/280, Control symbol 3016/2/1 Part 16, NAA.

39 Rusk to US Embassy Saigon, January 9 1964, Tel. 1050, Johnson Papers, NSF-Country File, Box 236, folder Cambodia Cables, Vol I.

40 [Canadian ICC Commissioner] Phnom Penh to Canadian Department of External Affairs, Ottawa, March 20 1964, Series No. 1838/280, Control symbol 3016/2/1 Part 16, NAA.

41 Michael V. Forrestal, Memorandum for the President, March 21 1964, Johnson Papers, WHCF, Confidential File, Box 7, folder C0 40 – Cambodia. Bergesen to USDS, March 27 1964, Airgram A-487, RG 59, CFPF 1964–1966, Box 1967, folder POL 2–1, NAA.

42 Recorded telephone conversation, Michael Forrestal and Lyndon Johnson, March 21 1964, Johnson Papers, WH 6403.14, PNO 10.

43 Deschamps, Australian Embassy Phnom Penh, to EXAF, March 21 1964, Series No. 1838/280, Control symbol 3016/2/1 Part 16, NAA.

44 Lodge, US Embassy Saigon, to SS, March 20 1964, Tel. 1792, RG 59, CFPF 1964–1966, Box 1977, folder POL 32–1 CAMB-VIET S, NAII.

45 British Embassy Saigon to Foreign Office, March 21 1964, Tel. 274, Series No. 1838/ 280, Control symbol 3016/2/1, NAA.

46 Lodge, US Embassy Saigon, to SS, May 14 1964, Tel. 2198, RG 59, CFPF 1964–1966, Box 1977, folder POL 32–1 CAMB-VIET S 5/1/64, NAII.

47 Deschamps to Keith Waller, March 24 1964, Series No. 1838/280, Control symbol 3016/2/1 Part 16, NAA.

48   Lodge, US Embassy Saigon, to SS, March 24 1964, Tel. 1818, RG 59, CFPF 1964–1966, Box 1977, folder POL 27–Military Operations CAMB-VIET S 1/1/64, NAII.

49   Michael V. Forrestal to McGeorge Bundy, April 1 1964, "Luncheons with the President" folder, Vol. 1, Part 2, NSF-McGeorge Bundy Papers, Box 19, Johnson Library.

50   Spivack to SS, March 18 1964, Tel. 956, RG 59, CFPF 1964–1966, Box 1968, folder POL 8. Spivack characterized Sihanouk's frankness about Hanoi as "more 'cards *on* table' diplomacy."

51   US Embassy Phnom Penh to SS, March 31 1964, RG 59, CFPF 1964–1966, Box 1968, Folder POL 8. By this time too Sihanouk was cracking down on domestic communists, many of whom had fled to the forests. This was in part Sihanouk's way of reacting to the American presence in Vietnam. Though he believed the NLF would win in the end, for the moment the Americans were going to be in Vietnam for some time, and his options were therefore narrowed. See Kiernan, *How Pol Pot*, pp. 210–19.

52   Rusk to US Embassies Saigon, Bangkok, London, Paris, April 1 1964, Tel. 1580 (Saigon), RG 59, CFPF 1964–1966, Box 1968, folder POL 8. Dean Rusk to William Bundy, April 2 1964, ibid. Bundy to Rusk, 6 April 1964, ibid.

53   Deschamps, Australian Embassy Phnom Penh, to EXAF, April 13 1964, Tel. 157, Series 1838/387, Control symbol 3016/11/161 Part 16, NAA.

54   Spivack, US Embassy Phnom Penh to USDS, May 1 1964, Tel. 1149, RG 59, CFPF 1964–1966, Box 1977, POL 32–1 CAMB VIET S 5/1/64, NAII

55   Sihanouk, letter to *Time*, in USDS to US Embassy Phnom Penh, RG 59, CFPF 1964–1966, Box 1969, POL 15–1 CAMB 4/1/64, NAII.

56   US Embassy Phnom Penh to USDS, May 1 1964, Airgram A-542, RG 59, CFPF 1964–1966, Box 1967, POL 2–1, NAII

57   The incidents, admitted the American embassy in Phnom Penh, furnished Sihanouk with a "propaganda bonanza to use . . . in his current anti-American campaign". US Embassy Phnom Penh to USDS, May 15 1964, Airgram A-561, RG 59, CFPF 1964–1966, Box 1967, Folder POL 2–1. In his response at the UN, Ambassador Adlai E. Stevenson regretted the incidents, denied that American advisers were present, and blamed Viet Cong terrorism in South Vietnam as the underlying cause. Stevenson's remarks are found in Department of State Press Release No. 249, May 21 1964, Box 21, Folder "Southeast Asia, General, Cambodia 1959–1966," James C. Thomson, Jr. Papers, John F. Kennedy Library, Boston, MA..

58   Maxwell Taylor, US Embassy Saigon, to SS, July 29 1964, Tel. 250, Johnson Papers, NSF-Country File, Box 236, folder Cambodia Cables Vol. II 3/64–7/64.

59   US Embassy Phnom Penh to USDS, August 24 1964, Airgram A-52, RG 59, CFPF 1964–1966, Box 1975, Folder POL 27–10, NAII. An Australian embassy report concluded that the allegations were probably false, that the people more likely died of an outbreak of cholera and other diseases. Ian E.Nicholson, Australian Embassy Phnom Penh, to Secretary EXAF, August 19 1964, Memorandum 473, Series No. 1838/280, Control symbol 3016/2/9 Part 2, NAII.

60   Australian Ambassador Deschamps believed that Sihanouk's refusal to receive Kidder was the direct result of the American protest. An oral protest, Deschamps believed, would have been much better than a written, rigid one and might not have resulted in Kidder having to leave Cambodia. Deschamps, Australian Embassy Phnom Penh, to Secretary, EXAF, September 21 1964, Memorandum 555, Series No. A1838/280, Control symbol 3016/7/1 Part 4, NAA.

61 US Embassy Phnom Penh to USDS, October 23 1964, Airgram A-109, RG 59, CFPF 1964–1966, Box 1967, Folder POL 2–1, NAII. In Saigon Ambassador Taylor blamed the attack on the South Vietnamese who, given the uncertainties (and small value) of their target, should never have attacked. Taylor, US Embassy Saigon, to SS, October 26 1964, Tel. 1267, RG 59, CFPF 1964–1966, Box 1977, Folder POL 31 Air Space. Boundaries CAMB-VIET S 1/1/64, NAII. The official note of regret, however, mentioned only inaccurate maps.

62 US Embassy Phnom Penh to USDS, October 30 1964, Airgram A-111, RG59, CFPF 1964–1966, Box 1967, Folder POL 2–1, NAII.

63 US Embassy Phnom Penh to USDS, November 6 1964, Airgram A-113, RG59, CFPF 1964–1966, Box 1967, Folder POL 2–1, NAII.

64 Ian E. Nicholson, Australian Embassy Phnom Penh, to Secretary EXAF, February 10 1965, Memorandum 84, Series No. 1838/334, Control symbol 3016/11/161 Part 6, NAA.

65 Alf E. Bergesen to Thomas J. Hirschfeld, November 6 1964, RG59, CFPF 1964–1966, Box 1974, folder POLITICAL AFFAIRS & RELS CAMB-US 7/1/64, NAII.

66 USDS to US Embassy Paris, November 15 1964, Tel. 2817, RG59, CFPF 1964–1966, Box 1974, folder POL 1 General Policy CAMB-US 1/1/64, NAII.

67 USDS to US Embassy Phnom Penh, November 15 1964, Tel. 265, Johnson Papers, NAF-Country File, Box 236, folder Cambodia Cables, Vol III.

68 Bergesen to USDS, November 20 1964, Airgram A-121, RG59, CFPF 1964–1966, Box 1967, Folder POL 2–1, NAII.

69 "Translation of Text of Official Cambodian Press Agency Report of the Working Meeting Presided by Monsigneur The Head of States in the Evening of the 16th November 1964," Series No. 1838/334, Control symbol 3016/11/161 Part 6, NAA.

70 Australian Embassy Phnom Penh to EXAF, November 18 1964, Tel. 384, Series No. 1838/334, Control symbol 3016/11/161 Part 6, NAA.

71 Harriman to US Embassies Bangkok et al, December 3 1964, Circular Tel. 1081, RG59, CFPF 1964–1966, Box 1974, Folder POLITICAL AFFAIRS & RELS CAMB-US 12/1/64, NAII.

72 Deschamps, Australian Embassy Phnom Penh, to EXAF, December 17 1964, Tel. 422, Series No. A1838/334, Control symbol 3016/11/161 Part 6, NAA.

73 Deschamps, Australian Embassy Phnom Penh, to Secretary EXAF, January 13 1965, Memorandum 22, Series No. A1838/334, Control symbol 3016/11/161 Part 6, NAA.

74 James C. Thomson, Jr. to Harriman, August 4 1966, Thomson Papers, SEA, Box 21, folder SE Asia Cambodia 1959–1966, Kennedy Library. The official report of the Bonsal mission is in Bonsal and Henry L. T. Koren to Harriman, January 4 1965, RG59, CFPF 1964–1966, Box 1974, Folder POL POLITICAL AFFAIRS & RELS CAMB-US 1/1/65, NAII.

75 US Embassy Phnom Penh to USDS, December 24 1964, Airgram A-148, RG59, CFPF 1964–1966, Box 1967, Folder POL 2–1, NAII. The representative, Mieczyslaw Gumkowski, was eventually taken to a hospital but died on the way.

76 US Embassy Phnom Penh to USDS, December 18 1964, Airgram A-143, RG59, CFPF 1964–1966 Box 1967, Folder POL 2–1, NAII.

77 Mansfield to Johnson, December 9 1964, Johnson Papers, WHCF-Confidential File, Box 44, folder CO 312–Vietnam (1964–1965).

78 James C. Thomson, Jr., Memorandum for the President, December 28 1964, Thomson Papers, NSF-Country File, Box 236, folder Cambodia Vol. 3, Kennedy Library.

79 L. Douglas Heck to USDS, February 11 1965, Airgram A-844, RG59, Subject Numeric File 1964–1966, Box 1970, Folder POL 15–1, NAII.

80 Bergesen, US Embassy Phnom Penh, to SS, January 7 1965, Tel. 447, RG59, SNF 1964–1966, Box 1979, Folder POL 32–1 CAMB-VIET S 12/1/64, NAII.

81 Bergesen to USDS, February 12 1965, Airgram A-184, RG59, SNF 1964–1966, Box 1967, Folder POL 2–1, NAII. Bergesen to USDS, February 19 1965, Airgram A-187, RG59, SNF 1964–1966, Box 1967, Folder POL 2–1, NAII.

82 Bergesen to USDS, February 26 1965, Airgram A-191, RG59, SNF 1964–1966, Box 1967, Folder POL 2–1, NAII.

83 Bergesen to USDS, March 9 1965, Airgram A-200, RG59, SNF 1964–1966, Box 1967, Folder POL 2–1, NAII.

84 US Embassy, Phnom Penh, to SS, March 30 1965, Tel. 583, RG59, SNF 1964–1966, Box 1970, Folder POL 15–1, NAII. In the same speech the Prince alleged that the Khmer Serei ("contemptible servants" of the Americans) had "resumed their aggression."

85 Bergesen to USDS, April 16 1965, Airgram A-222, RG59, SNF 1964–1966, Box 1967, Folder POL 2–1, NAII. Bergesen to USDS, April 6 1965, Tel. 593, RG59, SNF 1964–1966, Box 1979, Folder POL 32–1 CAMB-VIET S 4/1/65, NAII.

86 A longer term goal was the formation of a "League of Indochinese States" (which might later be expanded to include other Southeast Asian states), with a permanent secretariat.

87 Sihanouk quoted in Douglas R. Perry to SS, March 7 1965, Tel. 558, RG 59, SNF 1964–1966, Box 1970, Folder POL 15–1 CAMB, NAII.

88 James C. Thompson, Jr. Handwritten notes of proceedings of Baguio Conference, March 1965, Thompson, Papers, Box 19, Folder Far East 1961–1966 Baguio Conference, Baguio II, 3/65 Thompson Handwritten Notes, Kennedy Library.

89 Douglas R. Perry to USDS, March 12 1965, Airgram A-203, RG 59, SNF 1964–1966, Box 1967, File POL 12–1, NAII.

90 Bergesen to SS, March 25 1965, Tel. 581, RG 59, SNF 1964–1966, Box 1969, folder POL 8 Neutralism. Non-Alignment CAMB, NAII

91 George Ball, Circular Telegram 1921, RG 59, SNF 1964–1966, Box 1969, Folder POL 8 Neutralism. Non-Alignment CAMB, NAII.

92 Maxwell Taylor to SS, April 10 1967, Tel. 3311, RG 59, SNF 1964–1966, Box 1968, Folder POL 8 Neutralism Non-Alignment CAMB, NAII. Graham Martin, US Embassy Bangkok, to SS, April 10 1965, Tel. 1516, RG 59, SNF 1964–1966, Box 1969, Folder POL 8 Neutralism Non-Alignment CAMB, NAII.

93 Bergesen to SS, March 25 1965, Tel. 581, RG 59, SNF 1964–1966, Box 1969, folder POL 8 Neutralism Non Alignment CAMB, NAII.

94 Keith Waller, Australian Embassy Washington DC, April 13 1965, Tel. 1273, Series No. A1838/280, Control symbol 3016/7/1/1 Part 1, NAA.

95 Dean Rusk, Circular telegram 1953, April 13 1965, Johnson Papers, NSF-Country File, Box 236, folder Cambodia Cables Vol. III. Graham Martin and Maxwell Taylor both excoriated the state department's reasoning. See Martin, US Embassy Bangkok, to SS, April 15 1965, Tel. 1555; and Taylor, US Embassy Saigon, to SS, April 15 1965, Tel. 3398; both in RG 59, SNF 1964–1966, Box 1969, Folder POL 8 Neutralism Non-Alignment CAMB, NAII.

96 Dean Rusk, Circular telegram 1953, April 13 1965, Johnson Paper, NSF-Country File, Box 236, folder Cambodia Cables Vol. III.

97 Martin to SS, April 15 1965, Tel. 1555, RG 59, SNF, 1964–1966, Box 1969, Folder POL 8 Neutralism Non-Alignment CAMB, NAII.

98 Taylor to SS, April 15 1965, Tel. 3398, RG 59, SNF, 1964–1966, Box 1969, Folder POL 8 Neutralism Non-Alignment CAMB, NAII.

99 Rusk to US Embassy London, Bangkok, Phnom Penh, Saigon, and Vientiane, April 16 1965, Tel. 6629 (to London), RG 59, SNF 1964–1966, Box 1968, Folder POL 8 Neutralism Non-Alignment CAMB, NAII.

100 Kaiser to SS, April 18 1965, Tel. 5045, RG 59, SNF 1964–1966, Box 1969, Folder POL 8 Neutralism Non-Alignment CAMB, NAII.

101 Dean Rusk, Circular Telegram 1992, April 19 1965, RG 59, SNF 1964–1966, Box 1969, Folder POL 8 Neutralism Non-Alignment CAMB, NAII. Rusk's other suggestion that would have caused a delay was to have Gordon-Walker hedge on British support for a conference and to say only that the "UK is urgently exploring the convening of a conference."

102 Kaiser to SS, April 20 1965, Tel. 5063, RG 59, SNF 1964–1966, Box 1969, Folder POL 8 Neutralism Non-Alignment CAMB, NAII. The Foreign Office subsequently agreed with the United States that the earlier British drafts had not in fact been formally rejected. But, said the Foreign Office, they had been disregarded and vitiated. Kaiser to SS, April 21 1965, Tel. 5079, RG 59, SNF 1964–1966, Box 1969, Folder POL 8 Neutralism Non-Alignment CAMB, NAII.

103 Martin to SS, April 19 1965, Tel. 1581, RG 59, SNF 1964–1966, Box 1969, Folder POL 8 Neutralism Non-Alignment CAMB, NAII. Martin also feared that Gordon-Walker would at least tacitly imply that the United States supported his mission, which would "delay recognition by DRV and Chicoms that American commitment to SVN [is] firm."

104 Chester Bowles to SS, April 21 1965, Tel. 2983, RG 59, SNF 1964–1966, Box 1969, Folder POL 8 Neutralism Non-Alignment CAMB, NAII.

105 US Embassy Bangkok to SS, April 22 1965, Tel. 1619, RG 59, SNF 1964–1966, Box 1969, Folder POL 8 Neutralism Non-Alignment CAMB, NAII. Ne Win made his comments to Gordon-Walker. He expressed very little interest himself in the proposed conference.

106 Martin to SS, April 22 1965, Tel. 1614, RG 59, SNF 1964–1966, Box 1969, Folder POL 8 Neutralism Non-Alignment CAMB, NAII.

107 Rusk, Circular Telegram 2025, April 22 1965, RG 59, SNF 1964–1966, Box 1969, Folder POL 8 Neutralism Non-Alignment CAMB, NAII.

108 Taylor to SS, April 24 1965, Tel. 3523, RG 59, SNF 1964–1966, Box 1969, Folder POL 8 Neutralism Non-Alignment CAMB, NAII. According to Taylor, Gordon-Walker told Ambassador Sullivan in Vientiane that the conference could not "accomplish anything on Cambodia" and that its primary purpose would be to discuss Vietnam. Taylor to SS, April 20 1965, Tel. 3459, RG 59, SNF 1964–1966, Box 1969, Folder POL 32–1 CAMB-VIET S 4/1/65, NAII.

109 Martin to SS, April 24 1965, Tel. 1633, RG 59, SNF 1964–1966, Box 1969, Folder POL 8 Neutralism Non-Alignment CAMB, NAII.

110 Canadian High Commission, London, to EXAF Ottawa, April 22 1965, Tel. 1351, Series No. A1838/280, Control symbol 3016/7/1/1 Part 2, NAII.

111 Taylor to SS, April 24 1965, Tel. 3523, RG 59, SNF 1964–1966, Box 1969, Folder POL 8 Neutralism Non-Alignment CAMB, NAII. A subsequent telegram the same day suggested that the United Kingdom and South Vietnam agree on the timing of an announcement and that, depending on what was decided, the United States could then issue its own statement. Taylor to SS, April 24 1965, Tel. 3524, RG 59, SNF 1964–1966, Box 1969, Folder POL 8 Neutralism Non-Alignment CAMB, NAII.

112 Rusk, Circular Telegram 2041, April 25 1965, RG 59, SNF 1964–1966, Box 1969, Folder POL 8 Neutralism Non-Alignment CAMB, NAII.

113 Although the United States had been stalling, the announcement, when it came was so hurriedly prepared that Gordon-Walker was "surprised and somewhat embarrassed," for the United States had made its announcement even before the two Geneva co-chairs had formally issued invitations. Edwin Reischauer to SS, April 28 1965, Tel. 3493 (Tokyo), RG 59, SNF 1964–1966, Box 1969, Folder POL 8 Neutralism Non-Alignment CAMB, NAII.

114 Bergesen to SS, April 24 1965, Tel. 630, Johnson Papers, NSF-Country File, Box 236, Folder Cambodia Cables, Vol. III.

115 Bergesen, US Embassy Phnom Penh, to SS, April 24 1965, Tel. 631, and Bergesen, US Embassy Phnom Penh, to SS, April 25 1965, Tel. 632; both in Johnson Papers, NSF-Country File, Box 236, Folder Cambodia Cables Vol III 8/64–6/65. By some accounts Sihanouk said American attendance was optional.

116 Rusk to US Embassies Bangkok and Vientiane, April 26 1965, Tel. 1794 (to Bangkok), RG 59, SNF 1964–1966, Box 1969, Folder POL 8 Neutralism Non-Alignment CAMB, NAII.

117 Bergesen to SS, May 12 1965, Tel. 704, RG 59, SNF 1964–1966, Box 1969, Folder POL 8 Neutralism Non-Alignment CAMB, NAII.

118 Osborne, *Sihanouk*, 171.

119 Australian Embassy Phnom Penh to EXAF, April 25 1965, Tel. 122, Series No. A1838/280, Control symbol 3016/7/1/1 Part 1, NAA.

120 Central Intelligence Agency, Office of Current Intelligence, Intelligence Memorandum 1201/65, April 26 1965, NSF-Country File, Box 236, Folder Cambodia Cables, Vol. III, Johnson Papers. Presumably drawing on this account, Bergesen reported the same day that the Chinese had expressed their concerns about a conference while at the Jakarta meeting, although he wasn't certain how adamant they were. He also reported that advance publicity about possible corridor talks on Vietnam might have convinced the Chinese that to attend a conference would be construed as a sign of weakness. Bergesen to SS, April 26 1965, Tel. 634, ibid. See also Bergesen to SS, April 27 1965, Tel. 641, RG 59, SNF 1964–1966, Box 1970, Folder POL 23 Internal Security. Counter-Insurgency. CAMB.

121 Bergesen to SS, May 12 1965, Tel. 704, RG 59, SNF 1964–1966, Box 1969, Folder POL 8 Neutrality. Non-Alignment. CAMB.

122 Bergesen to SS, April 30 1965, Tel. 651, Johnson Papers, NSF-Country File, Box 236, Folder Cambodia Cables Vol III.

123 Bergesen to SS, April 28 1965, Tels. 643 and 645, and May 2 1965, Tel. 659, Johnson Papers, NSF-Country File, Box 236, folder Cambodia Cables Vol. III.

124 Bergesen to SS, April 30 1965, Tel. 651, Johnson Papers, NSF-Country File, Box 236, Folder Cambodia Cables Vol. III 8/64–6/65. Draft telegram, USDS to US Embassy Phnom Penh, April 30 1965, attached to Benjamin H. Read to McGeorge Bundy, May 1 1965, Johnson Papers, NSF-Country File, Box 236, Folder Cambodia Cables Vol. III 8/64–6/65. A handwritten note on the draft indicates that it was not sent. When the break came, McGeorge Bundy wrote to the President, "the initial recommendation for a prompt apology on the accidental air attack was based on a hope that it might marginally affect this Cambodian decision, but my own judgment is that relations were about to break anyway."

125 Intelligence Information Cable 314/06205–65, May 5 1965, Johnson Papers, NSF-Country File, Box 236, Folder Cambodia Cables Vol. III.

126   Arthur McCafferty to Johnson, May 3 1965, Johnson Papers, NSF-Country File, Box
      236, Folder Cambodia Cables Vol. III 8/64–6/65. McGeorge Bundy to Johnson, May
      3 1965, Johnson Papers, NSF-Country File, Box 236, Folder Cambodia Cables Vol. III
      8/64–6/65. My emphasis.
127   Bergesen to SS, May 3 1965, Tel. 668, Johnson Papers, NSF-Country File, Box 236,
      Folder Cambodia Cables Vol. III. Australian Embassy Washington DC to EXAF, Tel.
      1510, Series No. A1838/280, Control symbol 3016/7/1/1 Part 1. Seymour Topping
      of the *New York Times* got the story right. Although he presumably had no access to the
      Cambodian note announcing the break, he correctly stated that Sihanouk was breaking
      relations because of the attack. In his speech, Topping reported correctly, Sihanouk did
      mention the Krisher article, but the story made it clear that even in the speech the border
      attacks were much more important than the article. "Cambodia Breaks Tie with the
      U.S.," *New York Times*, May 4 1965, 1, 4.
128   Bohlen to SS, May 13 1965, Tel. 6451, RG 59, SNF 1964–1966, Box 1969, Folder
      POL 8 Neutralism Non-Alignment CAMB, NAII.
129   Intelligence Information Cable 314/06205–65, May 6 1965, Johnson Papers, NSF-
      Country File, Box 236, Folder Cambodia Cables Vol. III 8/64 – 6/65.
130   Ben Kiernan, *The Pol Pot Regime: Race, Power, and Genocide in Cambodia under the
      Khmer Rouge, 1975–79* (New Haven: Yale University Press, 1996), 16.
131   In his recent book, historian Ben Kiernan asserts that American intervention in Cambo-
      dia was crucial to Pol Pot's success. While the revolution was indigenous, it "would not
      have won power without U.S. economic and military destabilization of Cambodia,
      which began in 1966." Ben Kiernan, *The Pol Pot Regime: Race, Power, and Genocide
      in Cambodia under the Khmer Rouge, 1975–79* (New Haven, 1996), 16.

ACKNOWLEDGMENT

This chapter is a substantially revised version of "The Perils of Neutrality: The Break in U.S.-
Cambodian Relations, 1965," *Diplomatic History* 23 (Fall 1999): 609–31 and is included with
permission. The author thanks the staffs of National Archives II in College Park, MD, and in
particular Milton Gustafson, and the National Archives of Australia in Canberra, especially Gay
Hogan, for their very helpful assistance. The author also wishes to thank the following people
who offered suggestions for improvement or provided information: Charles Ambler, Marlee
Clymer, Cary Fraser, Bill Herod, Bradford Perkins, David Schalk, and Pamela Sodhy.

CHAPTER THIRTEEN

The Last Casualty? Richard Nixon and the End of the Vietnam War, 1969–75

LLOYD GARDNER

In preparing his final questions for a famous set of television interviews, the British journalist David Frost pondered about asking Richard Nixon how Vietnam had led to the destruction of his hopes for a transition from the Cold War to what the president had sometimes called, "A Structure of Peace."[1] Frost was anxious not to make it appear that Nixon had simply been the victim, the inheritor of an impossible situation, neither did he want to make Watergate the cause.

As posed, the question asked whether if the Vietnam War had not gone on so long would the "so-called abuses of power ... have occurred, or come to light, or been necessary. In that sense, someone has said – I wonder if you agree – that in that sense, perhaps, you were the last American casualty of the Vietnam War?"[2]

Nixon's face became a mask of pain, Frost wrote later, as if an old wound had been reopened. Finally, he answered. "A case could be made for that, yes ... it could be said that I was, ah, if I, that I was one of the casualties, or maybe the last casualty in Vietnam. If so, I'm glad I'm the last one ...."[3]

The war went on after Nixon's resignation in August, 1974, of course, and Vietnamese continued dying until Saigon was "liberated" at 12:30 p.m. on April 30, 1975. Half a world away, a visitor to Henry Kissinger's office in the State Department found Nixon's principal policy aide in a saddened, but philosophical mood. Vietnam was a great tragedy, the secretary of state said. "We should never have been there at all. But now it's history."[4]

Richard Nixon lived that history almost start to finish. It is startling to remember that Nixon played more roles in the Vietnam War over a longer time than did any other American policymaker. Reporting to the National Security Council on December 23, 1953, the then vice-president offered to President Eisenhower's inner circle what he had learned on a fact-finding mission to Southeast Asia. It was not, he began, an optimistic picture. Even if the French achieved a military victory in the forthcoming spring campaigns, that was absolutely no guarantee the Vietminh or some other group would not rise again. The core problem was China. "About Indochina we must talk optimistically; we have put good money in, and we must stick by it."[5]

There were some Asian leaders, he went on, who recommended an all-out campaign to overthrow the Communist regime in China, but that was as impossible as going to the other extreme by offering Mao's government diplomatic recognition and a seat in the United Nations. The question therefore became how to hold matters in check until the Vietnamese could build up their own "power and leadership" to resist Communist subjugation. His "plan" to end the first Vietnamese War was almost as much of a surprise then as would be his diplomatic overtures two decades later. Stop opposing trade with China by America's allies, he suggested. That would quiet criticism of Washington's policy in Europe, and it might give the Chinese a stake in – what he would call many years later – the "structure of peace."[6]

But in the first year of the Eisenhower administration, with the siege of Dienbienphu already in the headlines, the vice-president's strategy held little appeal. Nor would it have halted the war under more favorable circumstances, for the route to peace in Indochina always led straight to Hanoi – and not through Moscow or Beijing. True enough, Hanoi counted on aid from their "comrades" sitting in the great capitals of the Communist world, and roundly criticized their "appeasement" policies toward Washington, but it was the determination of the Vietnamese to decide their own fate that decided the issue – a lesson never learned by Eisenhower or any of his successors.

Simply put, the Cold War idea was too deeply imbedded in American minds to be dislodged. That idea postulated an agent theory of revolution, whether it was Korea or Vietnam or Nicaragua. The agent theory was essential, of course, to mobilizing public opinion behind policy decisions – and was considered essential to countering the supposedly ever-present isolationist tendencies that shoot up in the great plains between the Appalachians and the Rockies. Lest policymakers ever lose sight of the idea, there were always Cold War intellectuals to remind them that the source of all the world's difficulties was Moscow. Thus the Harvard professor Henry Kissinger in 1957:

> Each successive Soviet move is designed to make our moral position that much more difficult: Indo-China was more ambiguous than Korea; the Soviet arms deal with Egypt more ambiguous than Indo-China. . . .[7]

Presumably, Kissinger had in mind the cheshire cat in *Alice in Wonderland*, whose grin remained after the rest of it had vanished. That grin was the most dangerous threat, because it was the most ambiguous of all. "Well! I've often seen a cat without a grin, but a grin without a cat! It's the most curious thing I ever saw in my life!" commented Lewis Carroll's Alice.

Nixon was chasing the whole cheshire cat in 1968, still pessimistic. On one occasion, indeed, at the outset of the 1968 presidential campaign, he even told an aide, "I've come to the conclusion that there's no way to win the war. But we can't say that, of course. In fact, we have to seem to say the opposite, just to keep some degree of bargaining leverage."[8] Yet he still also believed the road to peace would pass through ancient Cathay, where a traveling American president could entice or cantilever Mao into believing China had a huge stake in a peaceful settlement of the Vietnam War – a settlement that would at least allow the beleaguered American-sponsored regime in Saigon a decent chance for survival.

It would be wrong, however, to conclude that Nixon always believed his most pessimistic appraisals of the situation in Vietnam. He wavered back and forth – as did most other policymakers – throughout "America's Longest War." There was plenty of time, as T. S. Eliot had put it in a famous poem: "...time yet for a hundred indecisions, And for a hundred visions and revisions."

Indeed, four months after he had offered an early version of his "China card" plan to Eisenhower's National Security Council Nixon appeared to take the lead in advocating a rescue mission by putting American troops into Vietnam to lift the siege of Dienbienphu. Controversy remains over whether he was floating a trial balloon, trying to shape the debate within the administration, or, as he said, only seeking to educate the people to the importance of saving Indochina from the Red Menace.

In any event, during an address to the American Society of Newspaper Editors on April 16, 1954, a time when it had become obvious that the French were finished in Indochina, at least without large scale military aid, the vice-president declared that if American efforts to secure a united front with its allies against the Communist enemy failed, then it would have to act alone – or "go right down the road to disaster."

Almost immediately, however, President Eisenhower ordered the State Department to put out a disclaimer that sending troops was not on the immediate agenda. And Nixon suffered criticism elsewhere. Colonel Robert McCormick, owner and publisher of the *Chicago Tribune*, had been present at the speech. Long known as the leading isolationist journal in America, the *Tribune* also had a strong Cold War focus. But McCormick had no taste for fighting the wrong war in Southeast Asia. "He talks like a gibbering idiot," McCormick growled, "we should stay out of Indochina, no matter what happens."[9]

Ironically, given later events, it was the *New York Times* that came to the vice-president's aid. Reciting the supposed series of defeats America had suffered in Asia since the end of the war, the *Times* writer argued that the stakes at Dienbienphu were nothing less than "a question of survival in a free world, for us as well as for the Indochinese. This is the reason that the Vice-President and our Administration take the case seriously and the reason why we must do likewise."[10]

Meanwhile, Nixon had backed off his exposed limb, declaring in speeches in Ohio and Iowa that the purpose of the administration was to "avoid sending our boys to Indochina or anywhere else to fight."[11] But Vietnam had already become inextricably and fatefully linked with his political career. Defeated for the presidency in 1960, and humiliated in the 1962 California gubernatorial election, losing by nearly 300,000 votes, Nixon vowed he would leave politics forever.

He blamed biased coverage for his defeat, convinced that the "liberal" media had never forgiven him for exposing the establishment-bred Alger Hiss as a Communist agent. In an eerie early-morning "concession speech," the twice-defeated candidate lashed out at his foes. "You won't have Nixon to kick around anymore," he said in darkly sibilant tones, "because, gentlemen, this is my last press conference."[12]

The Hiss case had launched the young California Congressman's career in national politics early in the Cold War. Overnight he had become a controversial figure, and he remained controversial throughout his vice-presidential years. Ike had picked him as his running mate, but seemed at times to try to distance himself from the partisanship of Republican politics, which Nixon represented in full passion.

He might just as easily have blamed Eisenhower for assigning him the "heavy's role" in his administration, but Nixon needed Eisenhower even after California. Once the searing pain of this humiliating defeat eased, Nixon began his climb all over again. His animus against press and television journalists never really left him, but he hid it well during the "exile" years, showing himself able to banter like a Kennedy with Jack Paar on the late night show. Could Kennedy be defeated in '64, Paar asked mischievously? "Which one?" Nixon answered back, a snappy reference to the Kennedy clan's seeming determination to monopolize national politics for the next decade and longer.[13]

The next phase of his phoenix-like career was just beginning. He moved his base from California to the "fast-track" of New York City, where he found a place in a Wall Street law firm. Nixon's experiences in dealing with world statesmen made him a valuable asset to corporations seeking assistance in the world market. And the New York experience introduced the former vice-president to visionary themes of the post-Cold War world as one giant marketplace, integrating both the second-world, the Communist superpowers and their client states, and the third-world of LDCs (Less Developed Countries), where the Cold War superpowers kept getting involved in local struggles.

The godfather to Nixon's career as Wall Street lawyer, for example, was Elmer Bobst, head of the huge pharmaceutical company, Warner-Lambert. It was Bobst who convinced Milton Rose to take on Nixon as a full partner to create the new firm of Nixon, Mudge, Rose, Guthrie and Alexander.[14] Soon after Nixon took up residence in the metropolis, however, there was something more challenging to think about in the aftermath of oddly-paired deaths.

On November 1, 1963, Washington's once-favored, but now increasingly disliked, and increasingly stubborn ruler, Ngo Dinh Diem, was overthrown and murdered. Three weeks later President Kennedy was killed by an assassin's bullet in Dallas, Texas. Though conspiracy theories of Kennedy's death continue to find a wide audience – in part, certainly, because of arguments that he planned to get out of Vietnam as soon as it was politically possible – none have real explanatory power for what happened that pre-Thanksgiving Friday in Dallas. If Oswald acted alone, however, Diem's killers had not. They were part of a conspiracy. And it took no privileged access to secret documents to conclude that the generals would not have acted without at least a wink or nod from the American Embassy. If Washington had continued to support Diem, the generals would have had no recourse but to go along because only

American aid could offer them a chance at victory. Not so the Buddhist protestors against Diem, of course, but their actions provided added reason for the conspirators to act to prevent chaos. Kennedy had sent more than 10,000 "advisers" to Indo-china, after all, and, as Henry Kissinger would write in his memoirs, by sending troops the question of whether Vietnam was a "vital interest" to American security had been settled.[15]

Kennedy was upset, not at the coup, but at the murder of Diem and his brother. Nixon was genuinely upset by it all. He refused his old rival any forgiveness for the deeds carried out in Saigon. "The Diem murder," he wrote a Republican senator, "was the most disgraceful deed to date in our mixed-up foreign policy record."[16] Over the next several years, accordingly, Nixon took over the role of chief critic of the Vietnam policy. The blackest moment in the history of the war, he repeated in a 1964 article, was the murder in Saigon. The United States, he asserted, had disgraced itself by showing it "will use a friend until he no longer serves our purposes and then let him be liquidated."[17]

Lyndon Johnson inherited the burden of Diem's death, and, like Nixon, he put the blame on misguided "liberals" for expecting perfection. That was not why the coup had taken place, but it was a way to get a political handle on the war. And Nixon eagerly grasped it. Watching Kennedy's successor enmesh himself in Vietnam's coils, he waited for the right moment to drive home his point that the "liberals" lacked the will to win the war. This assertion was a bit of a stretch, given that Nixon had charged the "liberals" with Diem's murder – a pretty strong example of will to win it would seem. But never mind. Nixon's moment came in the 1966 Congressional campaign, when Lyndon Johnson emerged from a conference of nations with fighting forces in Vietnam waving a new "peace" offer. American troops, LBJ said after the Manila Conference, would be out of Vietnam six months after a cease-fire. Speaking in Chicago, Nixon pounced on that statement. What the president was really saying, he asserted, was that the United States would leave Saigon unprotected against a resurgence of the subversion. It was a formula for disaster. He could not resist adding a personal barb. "This is the first time a President may have figured the best way to help his party is to leave the country." Johnson's aides quickly responded that there was an added phrase in the Manila Communique Nixon had ignored; the promise to withdraw was qualified by the clause, "and the level of violence thus subsides."[18]

But Nixon had hit a vital spot in LBJ's self-image as America's great political genius. Johnson took out his frustrations on Nixon at a press conference, declaring it was the Republican's penchant for finding fault with his country during October every two years. "Why would we want to stay there if there was no aggression, if there was no infiltration and the violence ceased? We wouldn't want to stay there as tourists. We wouldn't want to keep 400,000 men there just to march up and down the runways at Cam Ranh Bay."[19]

Whatever else, Nixon had succeeded in drawing Johnson into a treacherous swampy area. The publicity given to the fine-print in the Manila Communique was unwelcome as the president needed to placate a growing number of dissenters, even within the "Establishment," while the artful quip about phantom soldiers marching up and down the runways at Cam Ranh Bay reminded everyone of how the American presence had grown from 15,000 to 400,000 and upwards without a resolution of the conflict anywhere in sight.

But more than making Johnson seem peevish and un-presidential, Nixon wanted to appeal to restless constituencies, normally Democratic voters since Franklin Roosevelt's day, but now increasingly disenchanted with Great Society programs. Vietnam took its full measure of blood from the black ghettoes in the cities, but also from lower class whites without college deferments, the so-called ethnics, and from small rural communities which had never before questioned the wisdom of an American war.[20]

Even for families relatively untouched by Vietnam, the war symbolized something very wrong in American politics, whether it was middle-class resentment at the War on Poverty, or alarm at the "radical" protest movements including civil rights, feminism, and counter-culture experiments with psychedelic drugs and sex. "The Age of Aquarius" could become a hit on Broadway, but nudity and long hair did not, as Nixon knew, play well in Peoria. The Republicans made significant gains in the 1966 by-year elections for Congress, and Nixon took full credit for fashioning the victory out of LBJ's dilemma with the Vietnam War. On the very eve of the election, Nixon drafted a point-by-point critical analysis of the Manila Communique that the *New York Times* printed in full. Did the Manila Communique mean that we would stand aside to allow South Vietnam's fate to be decided by a struggle between the Viet Cong and the Saigon Government, he asked? How many more troops did the Administration plan to send? "Does the Johnson Administration, as is widely predicted, intend to raise taxes after November 8 to pay the rising costs of the war? Or will the President follow the proposed Republican route of cutting nonessential spending to provide funds for this conflict?"[21]

It was a brilliantly conceived attack, with something to think about for both conservatives and dissidents within the president's own party. Although the paper had switched positions dramatically on Vietnam, this was the second boost, intentionally or not, that the "Establishment's" premier news organ had given the putative candidate for the 1968 Republican nomination.[22]

Years later Nixon recalled the moment with great relish:

> After the last returns were in and our victory was confirmed, I rounded up a small party to go to El Morocco for a victory supper of spaghetti and red wine. There was a lot for me to celebrate. The first major hurdle had been met, faced, and surmounted in style. There were more hurdles ahead, but this was an auspicious start. It was gratifying to know that I had played a major part in this Republican victory – a prerequisite for my own comeback.[23]

If the Republican electoral victory in the 1966 contest had demonstrated the potential for a new political alliance to replace the fast fading New Deal/Great Society system that had dominated national politics since the Great Depression, Nixon had given several hostages to a commitment to "victory" in Vietnam that would come back to haunt him later. In an interview with Eric Sevarid, Nixon made a strangely self-revealing comment. He wanted, he said, to identify "with the middle class, the middle-aged and the Middle West, not with Boston, the mind of America, or with New York, its adrenalin glands."[24]

It was self-revealing because it was not true, except in the special sense that Nixon, like the first Republican leader, Abraham Lincoln, was arriving from another place. In the meantime, however, his efforts to attract Boston and New York to reconsider their views and see a "new" Nixon met with great success. Perhaps – no, certainly – he never felt at home with the "leadership class" he often disparaged as a worn-out volcano, but he could speak the language now of the table-talk found at elite club lunches; his writings were now to be found in the soundest and most sophisticated of quarterlies, no longer confined to middle-brow outlets like the *Reader's Digest*.

Nixon's arrival at this level was announced with quiet understatement when *Foreign Affairs* printed his article "Asia After Vietnam."[25] From the opening sentence it was a stunner. "The war in Vietnam has for so long dominated our field of vision," he wrote, "that it has distorted our picture of Asia. A small country on the rim of the continent has filled the screen of our minds; but it does not fill the map." After some standard assertions about how the American stand in Vietnam had prevented China from sweeping up the dominoes all across Asia, Nixon came back to his theme and variations: The United States could not continue the role of world policeman, nor could the world continue to risk a nuclear holocaust because the superpowers became involved in what were essentially local contests.

He said it much plainer a year-and-a-half later in what became known as the "Nixon Doctrine." But even here one could see how his thoughts were shaping themselves into concrete proposals. If another world war – a nuclear holocaust – was to be prevented, it would be necessary to "minimize the number of occasions on which the great powers have to decide whether or not to commit themselves."

Much of the rest of the article concerned finding ways to "contain" China, thereby obliging it to change its domestic policies, but it was placed within the framework of getting China back into the family of nations while also avoiding the impression in Beijing that the West (plus the Soviet Union?) was ganging up on the Chinese. The most famous sentence in the article read, "Taking the long view, we simply cannot afford to leave China forever outside the family of nations, there to nurture its fantasies, cherish its hates, and threaten its neighbors."

Like his commentary on the Manila Communique there was something for everyone in this article. It was in deep code, and code that had (or could have) several meanings at once. Read one way it offered an even more militant containment policy *vis-à-vis* China; but there were enough original phrases (starting with the opening sentence) to pique Beijing's interest, particularly as Nixon had been dropping hints here and there – in Bucharest for example – about the need to open contacts with China.

In another section of the article, the putative Republican candidate discussed the Asian awakening from centuries of stagnation and poverty:

> Poverty that was accepted for centuries as the norm is accepted no longer. In a sense it
> could be said that a new chapter is being written in the winning of the West: in this case, a

winning of the promise of western technology and Western organization by the nations of the East. The cultural clash has had its costs and produced its strains, but out of it is coming a modernization of ancient civilizations that promises to leap the centuries.

Though Richard Nixon styled himself the "middle-man's candidate," Middle Western, middle aged, middlebrow, and all the rest, "Asia After Vietnam" was anything but. A close associate wrote later that the article had been intended as a statement to China that "*every responsible* leader in this country" agreed that there could be no withdrawal from Vietnam. Even more pointedly, it was supposed to send a signal that a Nixon presidency would not wait for China to become a full-fledged nuclear superpower, but would strike quickly by bombing and naval blockades to end the stalemate. In short, it was intended as a cover to protect strong actions in Vietnam by preparing Beijing for the shock of a leader who would not take defeat for an answer.[26]

Well and good. No doubt that was one meaning, but there was more, more that the editors of *Foreign Affairs* recognized in accepting the article, and more that readers in Moscow and Beijing understood. Flying over snowy Wisconsin in February of 1968, Nixon chatted with Garry Wills, not about the Tet offensive that had at last blown apart the Administration's optimistic predictions based on bodycounts and what Defence Secretary Robert McNamara had once called other favorable "quantitative measurements" to indicate approaching victory, but about far-reaching post-Vietnam objectives.

Actually, Wills had asked if Nixon felt he could handle the presidency "in this period." But Nixon ignored the presumption that either he was not the man for the times, or that no man who had not taken leave of his senses would want to face the twin battlefield crises in Vietnam and in the cities from the Oval Office over the succeeding four years. Instead, he launched into a full-blown restatement of America's world mission. "Yes," he replied, he could handle it. "It is a time when a man who knows the world will be able to forge a whole new set of alliances, with America taking the lead in solving the big problems. We are now in a position to give the world all the good things that Britain offered in her Empire without any of the disadvantages of nineteenth-century colonialism."[27]

Nixon finally found exactly the right exemplar for his global vision in Benjamin Disraeli, the prime minister who had presented Queen Victoria with the scepter that symbolized her rule as Empress of India. That was not what moved him to emulate Disraeli, however. "My approach is that of a Disraeli conservative," he would declare, "a strong foreign policy, strong adherence to basic values that the nation believes in and the people believe in, and to conserving those values, and not being destructive of them, but combined with reform, reform that will work, not reform that destroys."[28]

The Disraeli comparison came up again and again during his presidency, in good times and bad: in good times like the citation above, in bad times as a kind of totem to ward off negative thoughts about becoming a "burnt out volcano" as in Disraeli's description of his equally famous opponent, William Gladstone, had become after exhausting his reform agenda.[29] The whole thing seemed to be coming true – Nixon as authentic reincarnation of Disraeli – in February, 1972, when the first American president to visit Beijing stepped off Air Force One. The "Star Spangled Banner" had never sounded so stirring to him, recalled Nixon, as on that moment he descended onto the tarmac to be greeted by Zhou En-lai and a Chinese band playing the American anthem.[30]

From this historic airport scene, almost as if a few more hours or even minutes should not go by without an end to the years of mutual antagonism, Nixon was taken for his first meeting with Mao. Sitting side by side with the Chinese leader in Mao's book-strewn study, the two exchanged quips about Henry Kissinger's "girl friends" and American party politics. Then Mao said: "I like rightists ... I am comparatively happy when these people on the right come into power." He could have given Nixon no better opening. "I think the most important thing to note is that in America, at least at this time, those on the right can do what those on the left can only talk about."[31]

Four years earlier, however, he thought he might never get the chance. As the 1968 presidential campaign entered its final days, he was convinced Lyndon Johnson would – however reluctantly – pull Hubert Humphrey's rabbit out of the hat so that the Democratic candidate could squeak into the presidency. The 1968 election must certainly be remembered for the campaign that all but ignored the most burning issue, Vietnam, until its last stages – when both sides grew desperate. Nixon had let it be known he planned on giving a speech describing the need to put the war into the broader negotiating context of Soviet–American relations, but when the day arrived for the speech he was preempted by LBJ's surprise announcement on March 31, of a partial bombing halt, and his renunciation of a quest for a second full term. "I shall not seek, and I will not accept," Johnson intoned, "the nomination of my party for another term as your President."[32]

Nixon was unsettled – along with everyone else including both the North and South Vietnamese – by LBJ's sudden turn-about from speculations about plans for new troop escalations up to 200,000 additional men. Facing the crucial New Hampshire primary contest, the Republican candidate did his own turn-about, explaining to the press that he would observe a "moratorium" on Vietnam "in order to avoid anything that might, even inadvertently, cause difficulty for our negotiators."[33]

After the tumultuous Democratic convention, Hubert Humphrey faced a long uphill climb if he were to somehow break out of LBJ's shadow. Finally, on September 30 in Salt Lake City, the vice-president delivered a carefully crafted speech that, while it barely went beyond Johnson's stated position on a full halt to the bombing, left the impression Humphrey had taken the leap to free himself from White House control. He would stop the bombing, he said, "as an acceptable risk for peace...." But before taking such action, he went on, he would place key importance on evidence that the Communists were willing to restore the demilitarized zone between North and South Vietnam. If Hanoi showed "bad faith," moreover, Humphrey would reserve the right to resume bombing.[34]

As noted, the speech itself hardly went beyond Johnson's position on stopping the bombing, but reporters were clued in that the vice president had made the break with the White House. From that time forward, Nixon expected LBJ himself to take the initiative to declare a halt. He was furious nevertheless when the president did indeed act on October 31. Nixon had been preparing for a nationally televised rally at Madison Square Garden that afternoon when a White House operator called: the president was placing a conference call to Humphrey, George Wallace, and himself. Johnson informed them that there had been a breakthrough in the Paris negotiations, and, without giving the candidates the details of that breakthrough, informed them that his advisers believed it warranted a total bombing halt over North Vietnam.

He had been expecting it – no matter how many indications LBJ had given of his dissatisfaction with Humphrey and the wavering Democrats in general. But Nixon felt Johnson had flummoxed him even so. Anger still burned through his words as he wrote his memoirs a decade later – anger that he had lost a chance, not simply for election, but to set his own terms for negotiations to end the war:

> The telephone call over, I could feel my anger and frustration welling up. Johnson was making the one move that I thought could determine the outcome of the election. Had I done all this work and come all this way only to be undermined by the powers of an incumbent who had decided against seeking re-election?[35]

His anger and frustration led Nixon to start down a very dubious path that, in fact, initiated a pattern of deception which continued throughout his struggle to end the war on "honorable terms." Using intermediaries from his campaign staff, Nixon made contact with South Vietnamese leaders to urge them to drag their feet in agreeing to go to the peace table – assuring them Saigon would receive better treatment from a Nixon administration than if Humphrey were elected.[36]

Johnson knew about the ploy, but decided the state of American political life was so fragile that exposing the Republicans for interfering with the negotiations could not be risked. One might speculate about likely sequences to a Johnson announcement that Nixon's representatives had broken the law by engaging in private negotiations with a foreign state, but for Johnson to have done so would mean revealing illegal acts by his own agencies. William Safire would write that, "Nixon probably would not be President were it not for [South Vietnamese President Nguyen Van] Thieu." Safire also wrote, "Nixon remembered."[37]

It is doubtful that Thieu would have agreed to go to the Paris talks in November of 1968 whether or not Nixon had contacted him in secret with implied promises of a better deal. It simply was not in his interest to knuckle under to Johnson's pressure, nor, indeed would things be different four years later when Nixon applied the same sort of pressure to get Saigon to accept the terms of an agreement negotiated by Henry Kissinger. Thieu could well have thought that the Republican's overture offered him a surprisingly easy way to gain leverage with a Nixon Administration by appearing to respond to such a plea. He may have thought that, indeed, as Safire indicated, Nixon would remember. If so, he was to be bitterly disappointed.

Nixon would write in his memoirs that "almost everything involving a Vietnam settlement was negotiable except for two things: I would not agree to anything that did not include the return of all our POWs and an accounting for our missing in action; and I would not agree to any terms that required or amounted to our overthrow of President Thieu." He would, he said, have to prepare public opinion for the reality that "total military victory was no longer possible" and the "only possible course was to try for a fair negotiated settlement that would preserve the independence of South Vietnam."[38]

Read carefully these statements indicate precisely what Nixon hoped for – a "decent interval" between American withdrawal and the fall of Saigon. Now, it is certainly true that Nixon entertained fantasies of a "total military victory," and sometimes tested reality to see if it would support such dreams, but from the beginning he was determined to use Vietnam to provide a foundation on which to cantilever Moscow and Beijing into his scheme for a post-Cold War vision of a *Pax Americana*. In this regard it is significant that the first letter Nixon sent to Thieu did not come until 1972, and, even more important, after he had convinced the South Vietnamese leader that he would have to begin withdrawing American troops in July, 1969, he did not tell him that he was sending National Security Adviser Henry Kissinger to Paris to begin secret negotiations with the North Vietnamese.[39]

Kissinger's efforts did not succeed – despite an offer that went considerably beyond anything Johnson had put on the table earlier. Indeed, it is hard to imagine Hubert Humphrey making a more serious opening bid for peace had the election gone the other way. And Nixon had in fact told the nation in a speech on May 14, 1969 what he was prepared to do to achieve an early peace. It will be remembered that he had criticized the 1966 Manila Communique, with its promise of a withdrawal six months after a truce was signed as leaving the South Vietnamese at the mercy of the Vietcong. Now he offered a mutual withdrawal immediately after a signed peace agreement. He also made more explicit than ever the Johnson Administration's latter day concession that "each significant group" in South Vietnam would have "a real opportunity to participate in the political life of the nation."[40]

Secretary of State Dean Rusk had once vowed that the Vietcong would never be allowed to shoot its way into power, or even a share of power, a position that gradually softened as the war dragged on; but Nixon's May 14, 1969 statement went beyond previous concessions by showing a willingness to determine when South Vietnamese elections would be held, and who would be allowed to participate – notwithstanding any provisions of the South Vietnamese constitution stipulating dates or banning Communists from voting.

To be sure the May 14 statement did not stand by itself. Nixon had always hankered after a dramatic gesture, such as he thought Eisenhower had made to end the Korean War. The so-called atomic threat Ike had employed to bring the North Koreans to terms in 1953 remains something of a historical problematic, but whatever message was conveyed to Beijing had to do with an end to the war – not military victory.[41]

Nixon's imagined version of the Eisenhower threat went this way as he explained it to aide Robert Haldeman:

> I call it the madman theory, Bob . . . I want the North Vietnamese to believe I've reached the point where I might do anything to stop the war. We'll just slip the word to them

that, "for God's sake, you know Nixon is obsessed about Communists. We can't restrain him when he's angry – and he has his hand on the nuclear button," and Ho Chi Minh himself will be in Paris in two days begging for peace.[42]

The real version was much milder. When Kissinger went to Paris in the summer of 1969 he carried a personal letter from Nixon to Ho that warned of dramatic action if the peace negotiations stalled beyond November, the first anniversary of the bombing halt. In the meantime, however, the president had demonstrated that he was anything but irrational.

Nixon wrote in his memoirs about the constraints on his freedom of action that removed total victory as an option, and his intention "to try for a fair negotiated settlement" that would preserve South Vietnam's independence – but he had not said for how long, or under what kind of government. And the first offer he made in May, 1969, far from narrowing discussion on those most salient questions only made American terms more ambiguous.

It would be well to reconsider for a moment the context of Nixon's Vietnam "choices." The Vietnam War had become far too costly, not only in terms of American lives, but as a powerful factor in the increasing balance of payments difficulty that had grown to crisis proportions. Economic historian Robert Collins has argued persuasively that the March 31, 1968 decision for a partial bombing halt and to initiate peace negotiations "was as much economic as it was political or military... In 1968, growth liberalism came a cropper and the American Century came to an end."[43]

Nixon thought he could re-arrange alliances and somehow get the American Century back on track, as we have seen, but he was fully aware of the economic constraints. Ike's atomic diplomacy was something to fantasize about, but Nixon was far more concerned to mull over the meaning of Eisenhower's letter of endorsement in July, 1968. "It meant a great deal to me," Nixon wrote of Eisenhower's statement. "I feel," it concluded, "that the security, prosperity, and solvency of the United States and the cause of world peace will best be served by placing Dick Nixon in the White House in January 1969."[44]

Solvency is the key word here. Eisenhower had not changed since 1953, when he feared that a perpetual war economy meant disaster sooner or later. The Great Society and Vietnam together, or even Vietnam itself, had gotten the nation into deep trouble, especially as Johnson had waited so long to ask for an increase in taxes. Another elder statesman, Dean Acheson, who had a strong claim to being the doyen of American Cold War diplomats, had issued a similar warning to Johnson in the wake of the Tet offensive. No two Americans had shared a greater dislike for one another, save perhaps Burr and Hamilton, than Dean Acheson and Richard Nixon, dating back to the Hiss Case in the Truman years. In all those years they had never met face-to-face, a situation that changed when Truman's secretary of state congratulated the new president at a Washington dinner on his handling of Congressional opposition to the Safeguard anti-ballistic missile system. An invitation to the White House followed. Acheson arrived, of course, as no stranger to the Oval Office on March 19, 1969. They quickly discovered a mutual enemy on whom to whet their condemnation,

Senator J. William Fulbright, and, by extension, the rest of the "doves" in Congress, and thus left themselves free to make the most of their personal "detente."[45]

Acheson urged a quick end to the stalemate. But Nixon, while confessing he was frustrated and puzzled as to what to do, said he opposed the overwhelming opinion of the business, financial and legal world in New York, which, he added, favored "scuttling Vietnam at any price." Acheson changed tack, arguing that the president should seek to reduce the level of belligerency, so that "with minimum, competent help from us the South Vietnamese could survive in an attempt to reach a political modus vivendi with the Vietcong." He was adamant against a resumed bombing campaign, and repeated that the withdrawal of American troops should begin as soon as possible so as to signal Moscow that Washington was serious about deescalating. To his surprise, the president said he agreed completely.[46]

The signal was sent up from Midway Island on June 8, 1969, where Nixon met with Thieu and the American commander in Vietnam, General Creighton Abrams. Neither man was at all happy about the president's decision to announce a 25,000 man reduction in American forces, nor about Nixon's added twist that he was responding to their suggestions! According to one account, Abrams "seethed with contempt as he listened to Nixon's plan." However sugarcoated, here was the beginning of "a sad rearguard action by the American military." Thieu heard Nixon plea for an understanding of his domestic difficulties, and put aside (for the moment) his fear of betrayal to endorse the step. Back in Washington, meanwhile, Henry Kissinger watched amazed as the president then told a press conference that he hoped to beat former Defense Secretary Clark Clifford's timetable for a rapid disengagement. "Thieu will consider it a betrayal," the national security adviser complained loudly, "as will all of South East Asia, and it will be interpreted as unilateral withdrawal."[47]

Only a month later, finally, the president announced the "Nixon Doctrine" while on a trip through Southeast Asia after greeting the returning astronauts from their journey to the moon. Speaking to reporters in an off-the-cuff fashion on Guam, Nixon promised the United States would meet its obligations under the SEATO Treaty, but went on to say that "we must avoid that kind of policy that will make countries in Asia so dependent upon us that we are dragged into conflicts such as the one that we have in Vietnam." Presumably the United States had been "dragged" into Vietnam to halt the Red Tide of Communism, but Nixon's suggestion here was that it was instead a certain "kind of policy" that had produced the entanglement. Quite a startling difference. A reporter asked about future challenges? And the answer – " . . . It will not be easy. But if the United States just continues down the road of responding to requests for assistance, of assuming the primary responsibility for defending these countries when they have internal problems or external problems, they are never going to take care of themselves."[48]

Except for a nuclear threat by a major power, he ended, the United States had a right to expect Asian nations to handle their own security problems. There are several things to note about this remarkable performance. First, it came close to suggesting that the original involvement had been a mistake. Second, it sent a clear signal to *all* the interested parties – Saigon, Hanoi, Beijing, Moscow, and *New York* – that Nixon wished to set new ground rules for competition in the "Third World." Third, there was a special signal to Hanoi that his emphasis on the "internal" threat pointed to a policy of political reconciliation through Vietcong participation in the electoral process. Indeed, two days earlier in Manila, Nixon had declared, "Peace in Asia cannot come from the United States. It must come from Asia. The people of Asia, the governments of Asia, they are the ones who must lead the way to peace in Asia."[49]

Defense Secretary Melvin Laird, who also hoped that Clifford's timetable would be met or bettered, labeled the deescalation policy "Vietnamization," and the name stuck. Henry Kissinger, meanwhile, had to face North Vietnamese negotiators in Paris who did indeed understand the signals – and told him why they could be ignored. From the outset, he was filled with doubts. "I myself pursued the ambiguities of our complex policy with a heavy heart and not a little foreboding." Describing his first encounter with Le Duc Tho, Kissinger wrote:

> He cut to the heart of the dilemma of Vietnamization. All too acutely, he pointed out that our strategy was to withdraw enough forces to make the war bearable for the American people while simultaneously strengthening the Saigon forces so that they could stand on their own. He then asked the question that was also tormenting me: "Before, there were over a million U.S. and puppet troops, and you failed. How can you succeed when you let the puppet troops do the fighting? Now, with only U.S. support, how can you win?"[50]

Given the continuing torment of Vietnamization, why did Nixon allow himself to become the second White House victim of the war? Why not follow de Gaulle's policy of cutting free from Algeria? Senator George McGovern asked Kissinger that question. You are in a fortunate position, the future Democratic nominee told Kissinger a few months after Nixon came into office, because there was a growing consensus that the war was a disaster. You aren't responsible for it, so why not just announce you are getting out? Kissinger's reply pointed to dilemmas of "Vietnamization" at home, no less tortuous than the Paris negotiations, and scarcely more manageable. "I think it is clear now that we never should have gone in there, and I don't see how any good can come of it. But we can't do what you recommend and just pull out, because the boss's whole constituency would fall apart; those are his people who support the war effort: the South, the blue-collar Democrats in the North.... If we were to pull out of Vietnam, there would be a disaster, politically, for us here, at home."[51]

McGovern thought Kissinger's argument an abomination, commenting that never afterwards would he have any respect for the Vietnam policy; but if "us" is taken to mean the general problem of political stability, the comment becomes less cynical – if more depressing as a description of the terrible *denouement* of the war, and more generally of how the Cold War had distorted political thinking.

But neither Nixon's May offer nor his letter to Ho Chi Minh induced Hanoi to budge from its demand that the Thieu Government must be replaced before serious negotiations could take place. The president had set November 1, 1969, as the deadline, after which he would put into action some version of the "madman" thesis to force the issue. Actually, he had already authorized a secret bombing campaign against Vietcong/North Vietnamese redoubts in Cambodia. Fearful of domestic reaction to a "widening" of the war, the White House had engaged in a deception that quickly built upon itself when Nixon reacted to a *New York Times* story revealing the bombings by ordering wiretaps on Kissinger's aides in the National Security Council, and, eventually on private citizens as well to plug supposed leaks.[52]

It was a bad omen of far worse things to come, and it created early on a byzantine atmosphere of intrigue and back-stabbing even up to the very doors of the Oval Office. Kissinger learned, he wrote in his memoirs, not to obey certain orders from Nixon – at least not until the president had a chance on his own to give second thoughts to a rash action. He did not stop the wiretaps, but he did manage to evade an instruction that he convey to Soviet Ambassador Anatoly Dobrynin that Nixon was "out of control" on Vietnam. "I knew that Nixon was planning to take no action on November 1. To utter a dire threat followed by no action whatever would depreciate our currency."[53]

Nixon did tell Dobrynin on October 20 – eleven days before the supposed deadline – that if there was no progress, the United States would have to pursue its own methods for bringing the war to an end. On the other hand, if Moscow helped out in Hanoi, he was prepared to "do something dramatic" to improve Soviet–American relations. According to Kissinger, Dobrynin pretty much ignored what the president had said about Vietnam, but he gave Nixon a positive answer to an earlier Washington request to begin strategic arms limitations talks. This "concession" of sorts, wrote Kissinger, was beautifully timed, as it took advantage of the recent antiwar demonstration, the October Moratorium, to pinion Nixon on a dilemma: he could not very well jeopardize the chance for serious arms negotiations by a sudden escalation of the war.[54]

A much longer precis of this conversation appears in Nixon's memoirs, however, which emphasizes how tough he had been with the Soviet ambassador. "You may think that you can break me," Nixon recalled his words. "You may think that the American domestic situation is unmanageable. Or you may think that the war in Vietnam costs the Soviet Union only a small amount of money while it costs us a great many lives." On and on he went, berating Dobrynin for Soviet failures to do anything about Hanoi's recalcitrant behavior. Throughout this harangue the ambassador heard Nixon repeat his personal stake in a successful conclusion of the war so many times that it appeared the president's *amour-propre* and America's national interest were one and the same. "I can assure you," Nixon said, "the humiliation of a defeat is absolutely unacceptable to my country. I recognize that the Soviet leaders are tough and courageous. But so are we." And again, "I . . . want nothing so much as to have my administration remembered as a watershed in American and Soviet relations. But let me repeat that we will not hold still for being diddled to death in Vietnam."[55]

In Nixon's account, Kissinger saw Dobrynin to his car, and then returned to exclaim, "I wager that no one has ever talked to him that way in his entire career! It was extraordinary! No President has ever laid it on the line to them like that." Nixon's recollection of Kissinger's praise in such detail appears to fall somewhere between braggadocio and a summons to Harry Truman's ghost to stand beside him as he confronted the latest crisis in the Cold War. Nixon's close paraphrasing here of an incident in Truman's memoirs suggests the latter. Truman recorded that on April 23, 1945, he had faced down Soviet Foreign Minister V. M. Molotov over Poland's future in the first Cold War crisis. According to Truman, an astonished Molotov gasped, "I have never been talked to like that in my life." "Carry out your agreements," Truman supposedly retorted, "and you won't get talked to like that."[56]

For all of Truman's bravado, however, and his later reputation for plain speaking, Poland soon became part of the Soviet "Empire" in Eastern Europe – until it liberated itself four decades later with only moral support from the West. There was little Nixon could do about North Vietnam, either, even though he invoked another presidential spirit in his "Silent Majority" speech to the nation on November 3, 1969. "Fifty years ago," Nixon intoned, "in this very room and at this very desk, President Woodrow Wilson spoke words which caught the imagination of a war-weary world during World War I." Wilson's dream had been shattered by the realities of power politics. He was not promising that Vietnam would be the war to end all wars. "I do say that I have initiated a plan which will end this war in a way that will bring us closer to that great goal of a just and lasting peace to which Woodrow Wilson and every President in our history has been dedicated."[57]

According to Bob Haldeman, Nixon had spent an "incredible" number of hours drafting and re-drafting the speech. He had ordered a search for Wilson's desk in order to make the occasion as authentic as possible. As it turned out, the White House searchers had ferreted out the wrong desk from a basement storeroom. But that was only a minor flaw in a speech the president regarded as the best he had given since the "Checkers" speech in 1952, when his position on the Eisenhower ticket was put in jeopardy by reports of a secret slush fund.[58]

The burden of the speech had to do with an appeal to the "great silent majority" to support his efforts to bring peace to Vietnam. Revealing that he had ordered 60,000 Americans, 20 percent of the combat force, out of Vietnam by December 15, he asked for the support of the nation to stick it out. His policy, he promised, was not Johnson's policy. "In the previous Administration, we Americanized the war in Vietnam. In this Administration, we are Vietnamizing the search for peace."

Divisions at home – like those promoted by the antiwar movement and its now monthly marches on Washington – only slowed the peace process. As always, he (like his predecessors) put the issue as a matter of choice between an honorable exit from Vietnam, and a humiliating bug out. But he had proof he was actually ending American participation in the war. "North Viet-Nam cannot defeat or humiliate the United States. Only Americans can do that."[59]

It was a risky ploy, this deliberate playing up of the divisions in the country in order to gain some time. But it worked – for a while. The marches on Washington ceased to be major events, and Nixon's standings in the Gallup Polls soared to highs for his first term. In his memoirs, Nixon complained that his original plan for this speech was undercut by the first march on Washington in mid-October. Instead of a preemptory warning to Hanoi, it became instead an appeal for unity at home. As Nixon put it: "Although publicly I continued to ignore the raging antiwar controversy, I had to face the fact that it had probably destroyed the credibility of my ultimatum to Hanoi."[60]

Like so many Nixon pronouncements, this statement repays very careful reading. Throughout the memoirs of so many figures in that administration runs the theme that the peace movement, combined with Watergate later on, turned victory into defeat. At the same time, the "Silent Majority" speech is presented as an effective answer to the protestors and Hanoi's play off American dissent – but if it was as successful as the "Checkers" speech in saving Nixon's political future, perhaps that is the standard by which it should be judged, not whether it actually helped keep open the options in Vietnam.

Indeed, by making promises to the "silent majority" – and then declaring himself their agent – the president actually reduced his negotiating options. He was hostage to his own rhetoric.[61] Worse, he acted out the false logic of the reaction to the "Silent Majority" speech six months later with the Cambodian "incursion." The struggle for a safe exit from Vietnam now became, in Nixon's mind, a contest between the "Establishment," which had always scorned him, and his personal creation, the "Silent Majority." Near the end of January, 1970, *Time* and *Newsweek* cast doubts on Vietnamization. Nixon commented, "K-[issinger] – this shows the Establishment *is* for peace at any price and they all go together. H-[aldeman] Have your ltrs team give them Hell – *we must keep our Silent Majority group involved.*"[62]

By late April, 1970, the president's staff was discussing among themselves the waning of Nixon's euphoria over the reaction to the speech. Added to the continuing Vietnam imbroglio, Nixon felt sorely aggrieved by the Senate's refusal to confirm his two proposed appointments to the Supreme Court, Clement Haynsworth and Harrold Carswell. There were other challenges. The Senate Foreign Relations Committee voted to repeal the Gulf of Tonkin Resolution, and, personally the most painful, a forced decision not to attend his daughter's graduation exercises. "It was just at this time," notes biographer Stephen Ambrose, "that he started watching the movie *Patton*. Patton, one could hardly doubt, would have ignored the doubters and seized the opportunity."[63]

The opportunity, such as it was, came after Cambodia's long-time "neutralist" Prime Minister, Prince Norodom Sihanouk, was overthrown by a rightist, General Lon Nol. In the weeks following, ARVN (South Vietnamese) forces began conducting hit-and-run raids against the "Ho Chi Minh Trail" in Cambodia. This caused a reaction from the NVA (North Vietnamese Army), and fears that the Communists would seize the Cambodian capital of Phnom Penh.

As Nixon laid plans for the ARVN–US attack on the supposed Vietcong stronghold in the Parrot's Beak, an area where Cambodian territory jutted eastward into Vietnam, even Kissinger felt he was moving "too rashly without really thinking through the consequences." "Quite a discussion in staff this morning," Bob Haldeman recorded on April 24, 1970, "about P's loss of momentum and leadership in public eyes."[64]

Kissinger had good reason to worry. Nixon had telephoned him several times the night before – each call filled with vituperation at one of his old enemies. In one he attacked the "senators" who thought they could push him around. In another he said, "The liberals are waiting to see Nixon let Cambodia go down the drain the way Eisenhower let Cuba go down the drain."[65]

All these late night phone calls, the repeated White House screenings of *Patton*, the rambling self-justifications, bespoke a leader determined, indeed, *desperately determined*, to tempt fate. On April 20, 1970, Nixon addressed the nation on "Progress Toward Peace in Vietnam." The enemy had failed in all its objectives, he averred, because of basic errors in their strategy:

> They thought they could win a military victory. They have failed to do so. They thought they could win politically in South Vietnam. They have failed to do so. They thought they could win politically in the United States. This proved to be their most fatal miscalculation.[66]

After reminding his audience that it was "your stamina that the leaders of North Vietnam are watching tonight," the president announced that 150,000 more Americans would be out of Vietnam before another year had gone by. Having successfully outflanked the antiwar movement, Nixon conveyed the impression he had Vietnam under control. Yet only ten days later he was back before the nation to explain that the remaining Americans in Vietnam faced risks that he must take action to counter. What followed began with a spurious claim that the United States had "scrupulously" respected Cambodia's neutrality despite the provocations provided by North Vietnamese actions, and, now, by the intolerable threat to Phnom Penh. Cambodia had issued a plea for help, he said, building a grandiose argument on this false premise, and the United States dare not risk refusing to come to Lon Nol's rescue. "Tonight, American and South Vietnamese units will attack the headquarters for the entire Communist military headquarters in South Vietnam."[67]

Something approaching a wave of pandemonium swept across the country, even up to the National Security Council itself. Three of Kissinger's top aides resigned almost immediately. The antiwar movement sprang back to life on college campuses across the country. At Kent State University in Ohio and Jackson State in Mississippi confrontations with national guardsmen and state police resulted in the deaths of several students. Nixon, meanwhile, had made two famous trips, first to the Pentagon, where, after a conference with his military advisers, he pronounced himself determined to go after all the sanctuaries in Cambodia, and thence a few days later after Kent State, to an eerie late night/early morning meeting with arriving student protestors on the steps of the Lincoln Memorial.

In the Pentagon briefing room he declared the military should have *carte blanche*, "I want to take out all of those sanctuaries. Make whatever plans are necessary, and then just do it. Knock them all out...." Emerging from the meeting, Nixon responded to a reporter's question by denouncing the war protestors. If they didn't have Vietnam as an excuse, he claimed, it would be something else. "You see these bums, you know, blowing up the campuses. Listen, the boys that are on the college campuses today are the luckiest people in the world ... and here they are burning up the books...." The word "Bums" was in every headline the next morning.[68]

Oddly enough, perhaps, a well-known hawk turned dove appeared in Kissinger's office at the peak of furor and put on his desk a list of ten prominent Americans, saying quietly, "You pick five, and I'll call the other five, to get their support." Kissinger's visitor was the President of the World Bank, Robert McNamara, LBJ's secretary of defense, who had left the office in a virtual state of despair about the futility of the war. His mission may have been prompted by a fear that Nixon's action would fatally divide the nation, rather than a feeling of sympathy for the Cambodian operation. Certainly the shootings at Kent State made many others besides McNamara fearful of such an outcome.[69]

Nixon's visit to the Lincoln Memorial suggested he was worried as well. In a long rambling discourse with students camping out in the Memorial, Nixon tried to suggest that he was as concerned for peace as they were – and to have them see Vietnam as he did, a necessary war to prevent a repetition of Chamberlain's popular, but tragically misguided, policy of appeasement. He had tried to reach out to them in a comradely fashion, he told Haldeman. They could only see the president on television, but here was a chance, "to try to lift them a bit out of the miserable intellectual wasteland in which they now wander aimlessly around."[70]

Extravagant claims would be made for the success of the Cambodian invasion, citing numbers of weapons captured, and so on; but while it no doubt did set back Hanoi's timetable, Cambodia made it plainer than before that there were definite limits on American military initiatives – if only because it showed the mandate from the "Silent Majority" did not cover a widening war. He might treat the students with friendly condescension, but at a news conference on May 8, Nixon responded to a question about Cambodia's future in a highly qualified manner. The United States was interested in restoring Cambodia's neutrality, he said: "However, the United States, as I indicated in what is called the Nixon or Guam Doctrine, cannot take the responsibility in the future to send American men in to defend the neutrality of countries that are unable to defend themselves."[71]

Less than a decade earlier, John Kennedy had proclaimed that the United States would bear any burden, pay any price, to defend the cause of freedom. Richard Nixon had discovered that path ended in the jungles of Southeast Asia. A feeling – stronger than ever before – set in that the government was under siege. Charles Colson, a key figure in Watergate, remembered the scene in the basement of the Executive Office Building across from the White House, where a battalion of soldiers waited in full battle dress to quell any efforts by protestors to storm the White House grounds. "It was hauntingly reminiscent of what I had seen twice before in Central American countries: uniformed troops guarding the palace against its enemies. But here – in the strongest democracy in the world?"[72]

"Within the iron gates of the White House," Colson continued in partial explanation of all that was to come about because of Vietnam, "quite unknowingly, a siege mentality was setting in. It was now 'us' against 'them.' Gradually as we drew the circle closer around us, the ranks of 'them' began to swell."[73] Dissatisfied with the intelligence agencies' inability to demonstrate that war protestors were supported by external Communist forces (as Johnson had been before him), Nixon acted to correct the situation by attempting to reorganize them all under J. Edgar Hoover's chairmanship, and with a staff directed by a young conservative "hot shot" Tom Charles Huston, who, ironically, kept a portrait of John C. Calhoun over his desk. No one feared extension of federal powers more than Calhoun had, but Huston devised a plan to spy on presumed "enemies" that boggled even Hoover's mind.

The problem was, Nixon explained to the assembled intelligence officials, that the American people, "perhaps as a reaction to the excesses of the McCarthy era, are unwilling to admit the possibility that 'their children' could wish to destroy their country." Therefore, he went on, "We must develop a plan which will enable us to curtail the illegal activities of those who are determined to destroy our society."[74]

When Huston presented his plan, however, Hoover balked at implementing it without a written order from the president. Whatever the FBI director's motives, jealousy, fear, or possibly even scruple, Nixon refused to put his signature to such a document. Despite the appearance of a large "hard hat" prowar mobilization in Washington, and although Nixon would refer to the will of the silent majority in his 1972 campaign speeches, Cambodia undermined the Administration's faith in itself.

The Laos incursion a year later undermined faith in the success of Vietnamization. This time no American troops accompanied the ARVN forces as they moved into Laos, again in search of the elusive nerve center of the North Vietnamese/Vietcong war effort. The result was a rout. Between Cambodia and Laos, the American negotiating position had changed. Kissinger had offered a ceasefire in place, with no demand that the North Vietnamese withdraw their forces. After Laos, Kissinger offered a ceasefire in place, plus a unilateral American withdrawal after six months, and the resignation of President Thieu thirty days before a plebiscite was held on the political future of South Vietnam.[75]

The DRV counterproposal dropped the demand that the US replace Thieu as a precondition to negotiations, and only called upon Washington to "stop supporting" Thieu in the elections scheduled for later in the year. Nixon and Kissinger chose to portray this proposal as nothing more than the same old demand that Thieu be overthrown. In fact, it was a proposal that had been worked out in Hanoi to make it possible for the United States to disengage without seeming to retreat from its earlier position.

Months earlier Nixon had given answers in his press conferences that indicated the United States would not support Thieu's insistence that Communist candidates be barred from participation, but in the event the American Embassy, the CIA, and other agencies helped rig the election to make it appear as though the Vietnamese popular will had been expressed, while assuring Thieu's victory. This was accomplished by bribing the legislature to disqualify one candidate, likely to give trouble, and attempting to bribe another to stay in to preserve the appearance of legitimacy.

Nixon's bluff had been called. But the summer of 1971 had a crowded agenda that impinged on the president's willingness to force Thieu into an election he probably could not win. There was the *Pentagon Papers* battle that Kissinger told him had to be waged or it would appear he was not in charge of his own government. The outcome of that battle went against him. There were negotiations over the status of Berlin – long a crisis point in the Cold War. There the outcome was more favorable. Tough decisions had to be made about international economic policy to meet the ever-increasing balance of payments problem. What was under consideration was a momentous departure from the postwar gold standard, along with a tariff surcharge, and wages and price controls.

These took much attention away from serious consideration of difficult peace terms for Vietnam. Still, the president had another card to play. Cambodia and Laos had been trumped. But there was no higher card than what he was about to play. On July 11 a one word message was received from Henry Kissinger. It read "Eureka." The one word had been sent from Beijing. And it meant that Nixon had been invited to China to discuss "a normalization of relations between the two countries and also to exchange views of concern to the two sides."[76]

Both sides in the Vietnamese struggle, Hanoi and Saigon, were quick to grasp the meaning of Nixon's startling announcement. A rapprochement with China would permit the president to cut loose from Saigon by – in effect – repealing the Gulf of Tonkin resolution on his terms. LBJ (and his predecessors) had fought the war on the basis of a Chinese Communist-sponsored effort to knock over newly independent Asian countries like dominoes. The Gulf of Tonkin Resolution was, therefore, cognate to the Truman Doctrine. Remove the Chinese threat, and the rationale ceased to compel victory in Vietnam.[77]

Just as important, the president's fabulous journey to Beijing would permit China to cut loose from Hanoi – or so Nixon hoped – and would put into play a triangular situation in which both Russia and China were bidding for America's favor. Moscow listened to Hanoi's complaints that the Nixon–Mao summit would strike a deal at Vietnam's expense, but its response was less than comforting to the Vietnamese comrades. Informed as early as May, 1971 that Hanoi planned a military offensive to break the stalemate at Paris, Soviet diplomats were alarmed by the situation, especially after the announcement of Nixon's impending visit to China. And while the Soviets continued to insist to the Americans that they had no capability – or intention – to interfere, Moscow did caution Hanoi that it was "necessary to turn the matter toward a settlement. . . ."[78]

Hanoi's spring offensive of 1972 had long been planned. But the "re-election" of Thieu and Nixon's China diplomacy provided inescapable arguments that it was now necessary to strike a powerful blow against "Vietnamization" to force Washington to recognize that there were no circumstances, not Moscow's disapproval, not Beijing's pressure, nor yet both together, that would turn back the quest. "Never Munich again, in whatever form," North Vietnam's Pham Van Dong had vowed in 1966. The Vietnamese had a keen sense of being duped in 1946 and again in 1954 with promises of independence and free elections. But what a shock those words were coming from Pham Van Dong – at least to Americans, who thought *they* were fighting to avoid the consequences of another Munich![79]

Hanoi's move came between Nixon's February visit to Beijing, which had produced no apparent changes in China's policy toward the war, and a planned trip to Moscow to complete negotiations on an arms treaty. In not quite the way Hanoi had imagined, the offensive that began at the end of March did prove to be the catalyst that finally, albeit through a tortured route, produced a "peace" agreement. Nixon blamed the Russians for the invasion, either because they fomented it in cooperation with Hanoi, or because they did nothing to stop it. He was especially angry because, he told Haldeman, he could not go to a summit "during a Soviet sponsored invasion of South Vietnam."[80]

But maybe there was a way to finesse that situation to his advantage. Ever since Johnson's decision to send the first 100,000 troops to Vietnam, conservative critics of the war had argued for a "knockout" blow against North Vietnam. Nixon saw an opportunity now to try out the "madman thesis," having already announced in January yet another troop withdrawal of 70,000 men, he had, in a way, reduced the "hostage" problem, for it could not be argued that using air and sea power to force Hanoi to give up its attempt to settle the issue by military means would require casualties in the ground war.

Still, he held his breath for a time after his May 8 speech announcing the mining of Hanoi, and a bombing campaign to interdict supplies coming by rail from China – held his breath waiting to see if the Kremlin would cancel the summit. To Henry Kissinger, he said the real question was whether Americans gave a damn anymore. If he had failed to act, then the US would cease to be a military and diplomatic power – would withdraw into itself, leaving every non-Communist nation in the world living in terror.[81]

Addressing the nation, Nixon said that there were three choices, to withdraw, to continue to try to negotiate, or to strike a "decisive" military blow to end the war. Then he did an abrupt turn toward Hanoi, lecturing its leaders that their people had already suffered too much in "pursuit of conquest." "Do not compound this agony with continued arrogance; choose instead the path of a peace that redeems your sacrifices, guarantees true independence for your country, and ushers in an era of reconciliation." It was an odd appeal, phrased in condescending language, but suggesting that the military and political issues could indeed be separated. And, finally, he addressed his opposites in Moscow. Let all great powers, he said, help our allies, but only for purposes of defense. "Let us not slide back toward the dark shades of a previous age."[82]

Kissinger was later heard to quip that the antiwar movement protested the bombing and mining more than did the Soviets, who voiced only some diplomatic complaints about Russian ships in Haiphong harbor. Nixon could exhale. The summit was on. In a revealing passage in his memoirs, Ambassador Dobrynin explained how Moscow came to that decision. Hanoi, he wrote, had not taken Moscow into its confidence about either the offensive or what was happening in the negotiations in Paris. Indeed, the Kremlin learned more from the Americans about the latter situation than it did from the Vietnamese:

> As a result, their actions often were a surprise to us and put us in difficult positions. Actually they did not pay much attention to how they affected our relations with Washington. On the contrary, they did not mind spoiling them. . . . All that aroused irritation in Moscow. The final verdict of the Politburo was to go ahead with the summit, because its members recognized that the alternative would amount to handing Hanoi a veto over our relations with America.[83]

Obviously, Dobrynin's account shades toward his own preoccupation with improving Soviet–American relations, but that does not diminish the general implication of his comment: that the China policy and the May 8 speech did in fact loosen the comradely ties between Moscow and Hanoi. Kissinger had told the ambassador on his return from Beijing that Nixon had pressed the Chinese on Vietnam – to no avail. The president had made it clear, said the national security adviser, that "if North Vietnam showed some flexibility and understanding, Hanoi would essentially get what it wanted within two or three years." The Chinese had responded to this overture by turning it aside with "the observation that it was not Beijing but Moscow that had a stake in the military operations in Vietnam."[84]

Whatever had gone on in China, who said what to whom, this was the sort of high stakes diplomacy that Kissinger, the admirer of "restoration" politics in the early nineteenth century, loved to play out on the modern international stage.[85] The day after the May 8 speech, Nixon sent President Thieu a long letter advising him that the mining and bombing would go on until Hanoi agreed to an internationally supervised truce agreement. What he did not tell the South Vietnamese leader was that the United States had agreed in pre-summit conversations with Soviet diplomats, to allow the 200,000 North Vietnamese soldiers to remain in the South after the fighting stopped. Nor was Thieu informed that during the summit conference in late May, Kissinger explained to Andrei Gromyko that the US was prepared to accept a three-part electoral commission in South Vietnam that would include the Saigon government, neutralists, and the Viet Cong. Washington did not consider itself tied to any government in South Vietnam, he said. In the course of events a Communist government might come to power. "The U.S.A. will not stand in the way of it," Kissinger ended. "However the U.S.A. cannot do this now by its own hands."[86]

These were essentially the terms Kissinger discussed with North Vietnamese negotiator Le Duc Tho throughout the summer of 1972. Nixon's re-election campaign against the hapless George McGovern was going well. In foreign affairs the summits in Beijing and Moscow substantiated the president's claim that, "I think I have learned how to negotiate. I think I know what we want and what they want. I think I know the next steps that can be taken."[87]

In 1964 Lyndon Johnson had tried to solidify his standing with a Cold War gesture, the Gulf of Tonkin Resolution. Senators who voted for it had no idea they were voting to send 500,000 men to Southeast Asia. Eight years later, Richard Nixon wanted to beat Johnson's record plurality. And again, Vietnam became the object to be manipulated. As the election neared, Nixon wavered between playing the hawk or the dove. His opponent, George McGovern, was hopelessly behind. The Democrats were in disarray, still, four years after debacle at the Chicago convention. Vietnam was no longer the issue to determine an election. Nixon did not need a "peace offer" in the same way LBJ had maneuvered from the time of his March 31, 1968 "farewell" speech. But Nixon had wanted to make peace quickly, end the war within a year if possible. Instead, he had had to settle for the agonizingly slow process of "Vietnamization." He had hoped to isolate Hanoi from its Communist allies – and had succeeded in his cantilevering strategy – but the war continued. It continued despite the hints Nixon had strewn through his speeches even from the Silent Majority speech, and Kissinger's comments in private directly to Le Duc Tho and to Soviet leaders, that Washington would not stand in the way of a political change in South Vietnam.

On September 15, both sides exchanged new offers in Paris. Le Duc Tho agreed that Thieu could remain in power, administering areas under his control, until elections brought a new government to power. The North Vietnamese offer also called on the United States to pay $9 billion in reparations, divided equally between north and south. Kissinger's offer did not mention reparations, but it provided for an election commission, to be called the Committee of National Reconciliation, to review the constitution, and under whose auspices an election would be held. The offers appeared to narrow the differences between the two sides enough so that the negotiators agreed to set a date for ending the war – October 15.[88]

But it did not end, of course. Kissinger's task in moving all parties to an actual signing ceremony proved impossible. The negotiations had been kept secret from Thieu, who certainly would object to the two most important American concessions: those that allowed the North Vietnamese to retain their forces inside South Vietnam, and the role of the Committee of National Reconciliation as an inevitable precursor to a coalition government. Nor was Nixon sure he wanted peace before the election. After all that he had put up with from the old "Establishment" because the war had continued throughout his whole first term, to pull an "October surprise" like LBJ's bombing halt did not appeal to his sense of what he wanted to do in his second term. Haldeman recorded on the day after the September 15 meeting in Paris, when Nixon learned of Le Duc Tho's suggestion the war be ended in a month, that the president began ruminating about Disraeli and Gladstone again. Gladstone had left office an exhausted volcano, and with the British people tired of wanting to be "improved" by reforms. "He's doing a lot of talking about the approach to policy for the second term, in that context. That not only do we clear out our enemies and build our own establishment, that we clear out the bad programs and so on, too."[89]

Kissinger played his hand skillfully, insinuating to Saigon that its obstinacy played into the hands of Hanoi and those who wanted to drive a wedge between Thieu and Nixon, and carefully maneuvering to convince Nixon, on the other hand, that the South Vietnamese were trifling with him. Nixon's fragile *amour propre* was a tricky business, however, for all those who dealt with him. By early October, for example, he seemed convinced that a negotiated settlement would hurt him in the election, not defeat him, but detract from the chances to build on his accomplishments with an overwhelming mandate for four more years.[90]

On October 8, Le Duc Tho made his final "offer." Even though the North Vietnamese had tried to make the language more acceptable, and played around with new titles such as a National Council of Reconciliation and Concord, the basic conditions remained the same – with the ultimate objective of reunification stated in plain language. Kissinger thought that Le Duc Tho had given him what he needed all along, a plan for a decent interval. The sticking point about POWs, a powerfully symbolic issue (even today), had been removed with a North Vietnamese agreement to their return immediately after a peace document was signed.[91]

With the offer in hand, Kissinger rushed home, got the president's imprimatur to go ahead with "RN's settlement," and left for Saigon. He carried with him a letter from the president:

Were you to find the agreement to be unacceptable at this point and the other side to reveal the extraordinary limits to which it has gone in meeting demands put upon them, it is my judgment that your decision would have the most serious effects upon my ability to continue to provide support for you and for the government of South Vietnam.[92]

Thieu was unyielding. At the end of their acrimonious sessions, Kissinger agreed to take back a list of Saigon's demands. As Nixon had predicted, Hanoi then released the draft agreement in a radio broadcast. Embarrassed, Kissinger scheduled a press conference in Paris at which he attempted to cover over the situation with a statement that peace "was at hand." This pleased none of the principals, neither Hanoi, nor Saigon, nor, especially, Richard Nixon.

Le Duc Tho presented his own revised conditions for peace, and the negotiations dragged on for weeks after the American election without getting anywhere. Finally, on December 13, the North Vietnamese negotiator announced that he was going home for consultations — in effect breaking off that phase of the talks. Le Duc Tho's decision to return to Hanoi provided Nixon with a "reason" to initiate the "Christmas Bombings," massive B-52 raids against North Vietnam. Afterwards, Nixon and Kissinger both claimed that the bombing had driven the North Vietnamese back to the peace table to sign an accord that brought – at long last – peace with honor.

The "Christmas Bombings" caused an uproar in the press, but it was not "war by tantrum," as the president's critics charged. Rather it was a calculated and coolly cynical measure whose real target was Saigon, not Hanoi. In 1965 the American bombing of North Vietnam had begun as a measure to boost South Vietnam's morale, without any real hope the war would be decided by such a method. The idea had been to convince both sides that the United States was committed to seeing it through to the end. The "Christmas Bombings" and the huge military build-up offered South Vietnam, "Operation Linebacker," were designed to buy off Thieu, or, at least, to convince hawks at home that the war had been "won" in something like a traditional outcome.

Nixon would argue that the North Vietnamese had come hat in hand to ask that the talks be resumed. But in his memoirs he casually comments that, "On December 22 we sent a message to the North Vietnamese requesting a meeting for January 3. If they accepted, we offered to stop the bombing north of the 20th parallel in December and suspend it for the duration of the meeting." On December 26, he went on, the North Vietnamese "sent the first signal that they had had enough."[93]

On December 20, however, only a few days after the bombing started, Nixon told his aides that he was "very concerned" about the rate of loss the B-52s were sustaining and the reaction to those casualties. He wavered back and forth saying one minute the bombing had to go on, and the next, saying that the rate of loss was "going to be very tough to take. . . ." Then Nixon vented his anger against Thieu. The South Vietnamese leader was ignoring his letters and stating his own demands. Kissinger joined in the denunciations: "over and over" again as the meeting went on, he "really blasted Thieu as a complete SOB." Finally it was agreed, "If Hanoi accepts the January 3 meeting, we should meet, settle, and put it to Thieu. . . . We should now treat Thieu with total silence, not give him another chance."[94]

The wording changes from the draft of mid-October to the final document signed on January 27, 1973, did not change Thieu's mind, did not improve the contradictory and anomalous future status of South Vietnam, and did not warrant any serious claims of victory. Chapter IV of the January 27 agreement, for example, guaranteed the right of the people of South Vietnam to self-determination "through genuinely free and democratic elections under international supervision." Chapter V stated, however, that, "The reunification of Viet-Nam shall be carried out step by step through peaceful means on the basis of discussions and agreements between North and South Viet-Nam, without coercion or annexation by either party, and without foreign interference. The time for reunification will be agreed upon by North and South Viet-Nam."[95]

Nixon had promised the North reparations, the South, retaliation if the agreement was violated. He had a good idea even then, before Watergate swallowed up his foreign policy initiatives, that decisions on these matters would be rendered not by him alone, but in conjunction with a Congress determined to end American participation in Vietnam's struggles. If that were so, then, having gotten the prisoners back, he would be satisfied to blame the legislators if Vietnamization failed. It was not the best ending, but, after all, blaming the Democratic "doves" for "losing" the war could redound to his benefit by making him the champion of the new majority of his imagination, destined to remove the debris left by the old "Establishment" and thence to move on to a Disraeli-like settlement of the Cold War.

Nguyen Van Thieu understood the real target of the "Christmas Bombings" all too well. "The Americans let the war become their war," he told his cabinet in explanation of why he must sign the peace accord, "when they liked the war, they carried it forward. When they want to stop it, they impose on both sides to stop it. When the Americans wanted to enter, we had no choice, and now when they are ready to leave we have no choice." After the bombings, he added sardonically, "If Kissinger had the power to bomb the Independence Palace to force me to sign the agreement, he would not hesitate to do so."[96]

A Kissinger aide put it somewhat differently. Believing that the bombings had actually put the United States in a military position to demand better terms, John Negroponte complained privately, "We bombed the North Vietnamese into accepting our concession."[97] He may not have been right about the first, but he certainly understood how American participation in the war ended.

On the day the accord was signed Nixon announced the peace in a televised address. Those who had not been so close to the situation took him at his word. John Ehrlichman met Kissinger accidentally the next day. He congratulated him, hoping the national security adviser would give him some assurances. "Instead he told me the truth," the presidential aide recounted, "and it shook me badly."

"I think that if they're lucky," Kissinger told him, "they can hold out for a year and a half." Kissinger missed the date of Saigon's fall by about six weeks.[98]

NOTES

1   The more familiar word that Nixon and his National Security Adviser Henry Kissinger often used was, of course, *detente*, but, as Nixon himself understood, *detente* had too many ambiguous connotations, suggesting that the Cold War had somehow been replaced by an era of "Good Feelings." "Structure of Peace" was no doubt a better way of conveying their idea of countervailing forces achieving an equilibrium in an age of rough nuclear parity, and (in a somewhat coded fashion), the obligations of the superpowers in checking client state misbehavior. Whether this more descriptive phrase actually described anything different from what had been going on during the Cold War is, obviously, a different matter altogether, for it is arguable that from the time of the Yalta Conference in 1945 to the fall of the Berlin Wall in 1989 that the major preoccupation of the "superpowers" was how to maintain their joint global hegemony – and that they made necessary adjustments all along during those years to that end. Even so, however, Nixon's early pronouncements on Soviet–American relations reflected a serious rethinking of Cold War issues, and how they might evolve into a safer "Structure of Peace." See Raymond L. Garthoff, *Detente and Confrontation: American–Soviet Relations from Nixon to Reagan* (Washington: The Brookings Institution, 1985), chap. 2, especially pp. 27–9.

2   David Frost, "*I Gave Them a Sword,*" *Behind the Scenes of the Nixon Interviews* (New York: William Morrow & Co., 1978), pp. 141–2.

3   Ibid.

4   Arnold R. Isaacs, *Without Honor: Defeat in Vietnam and Cambodia* (Baltimore: Johns Hopkins Press, 1983), p. 485.

5   Lloyd C. Gardner, *Approaching Vietnam: From World War II Through Dienbienphu* (New York: W. W. Norton & Co., 1988), p. 163.

6   Ibid., 164.

7   *Nuclear Weapons and Foreign Policy* (New York: Harper & Bros., 1957), p. 428.

8   The comment was made in private to an aide helping him to prepare a major foreign policy address just two days before Lyndon Johnson announced that he would not seek re-election to dedicate himself to finding an end to the war. Johnson's surprise announcement re-set the stage for the campaign, causing Nixon to abandon his plan temporarily for a far-reaching discussion of his proposed approach to superpower negotiations. Richard Whalen, *Catch the Falling Flag: A Republican's Challenge to His Party* (Boston: Houghton Mifflin Co., 1972), p. 137.

9   Gardner, *Approaching Vietnam*, pp. 230–1.

10 Ibid., 232.

11 Ibid.

12 Cited in Christopher Matthews, *Kennedy & Nixon: The Rivalry that Shaped Postwar America* (New York: Simon and Schuster, 1996), p. 218.

13 Ibid., 221.

14 Elmer Holmes Bobst, *Bobst: The Autobiography of a Pharmaceutical Pioneer* (New York: David McKay, 1973), p. 327.

15 This essay is no place to delve into the full literature on the question of American responsibility for the coup, but certainly Anne Blair's *Lodge in Vietnam: A Patriot Abroad* (New Haven: Yale University Press, 1995) esp. chap. 3, resolves the issue for all but the most fervent apologists for Washington's policy. Like Richard Nixon, Lyndon Johnson, who also did not see all the cables, never doubted what had happened and why.

16   Matthews, *Kennedy and Nixon*, p. 232.

17   Quoted in Lloyd C. Gardner, ed., *The Great Nixon Turn-Around: America's New Foreign Policy in the Post-Liberal Era* (New York: New Viewpoints, 1973), p. 24.

18   William Safire, *Before the Fall: An Inside View of the Pre-Watergate White House* (Garden City: Doubleday & Co., 1975), p. 35; Lloyd C. Gardner, *Pay Any Price: Lyndon Johnson and the Wars for Vietnam* (Chicago: Ivan R. Dee, 1995), p. 318.

19   Ibid.

20   See Christian Appy, *Working-Class War: America's Combat Soldiers and Vietnam* (Chapel Hill: University of North Carolina Press, 1993).

21   Safire, *Before the Fall*, p. 37.

22   Ibid., 40. The article and a radio broadcast projected him into the limelight, Safire notes, as "official party spokesman, the number one campaigner, the man who acted like a President when the President did not."

23   Richard Nixon, *RN: The Memoirs of Richard Nixon* (New York: Grosset and Dunlap, 1978), p. 277.

24   Henry Brandon, *The Retreat of American Power* (New York: W. W. Norton & Co., 1973), p. 16.

25   "Asia After Vietnam" originally appeared in *Foreign Affairs*, October, 1967. It is reprinted with commentary in Gardner, *Nixon Turn-Around*, pp. 74–92.

26   See Safire, *Before the Fall*, pp. 367–8. Safire here reprints notes Nixon dictated while the article was being drafted. Garry Wills comments that the article was pretty much the product of Ray Price, who worked on long-range ideas and projects, but Wills sees it as merely a hodge-podge of specifics, slogans, and evasions. Garry Wills, *Nixon Agonistes: The Crisis of the Self-Made Man*, (Boston: Houghton Mifflin: 1970), p. 15. The interpretation presented in this article is obviously at variance with these views.

27   Wills, *Nixon Agonistes*, p. 20.

28   Stephen E. Ambrose, *Nixon, Volume Three: Ruin and Recovery* (New York: Simon & Schuster, 1991), p. 13.

29   H. R. Haldeman, *The Haldeman Diaries: Inside the Nixon White House*, with an introduction and afterword by Stephen E. Ambrose (New York: Putnam: 1994), pp. 246, 505, 506, 532; Safire, *Before the Fall*, pp. 534, 535, 542, 564, 596, 654, 671, 692. The man who suggested Disraeli as a model to Nixon was Pat Moynihan, the former LBJ policymaker and thinker who got into trouble with his description of the ails of the black family as dysfunctional. Moynihan gave Nixon a biography of Disraeli by Robert Blake. "Intelligent conservatives like Disraeli and Nixon, Moynihan argued, were in the strongest position to carry out the best *liberal* ideas – ideas for which liberals themselves would be unable to muster the support necessary to overcome orthodox conservative opposition." Tory men with liberal ideas could win working class support, which, in America, had left the Democratic Party. See, Tom Wicker, *One of Us: Richard Nixon and the American Dream* (New York: Random House, 1991), p. 535.

30   Nixon, *RN*, p. 559.

31   Ibid., 562.

32   For events leading up to this speech see, Gardner, *Pay Any Price*, pp. 443–58.

33   Whalen, *Catch the Falling Flag*, pp. 143–4. Whalen notes that once the shock wore off, Nixon was pleased that he was able to avoid a possible mis-step because of Johnson's action, and laid the groundwork for a nonaggression pact between the White House and the Nixon campaign. But Whalen, a speechwriter and aide, was disgruntled, "All in all, Nixon's withdrawal into silence was a brilliantly executed political stroke – and a cynical

default on the moral obligation of a would-be President to make his views known to the people." Ibid.

34 The context of Humphrey's speech and the way his aides, including George Ball, manipulated the situation to make it appear that the vice-president had gone much further, is discussed in Gardner, *Pay Any Price*, pp. 490–3.

35 Nixon, *RN*, pp. 322–3.

36 For details, see Stephen Ambrose, *Nixon: The Triumph of a Politician, 1962–1972* (New York: Simon & Schuster, 1989), pp. 207–13; and Bui Diem, *In the Jaws of History* (Boston: Houghton Mifflin Co., 1987), pp. 235–46.

37 Safire, *Before the Fall*, p. 88.

38 Nixon, *RN*, pp. 348–9.

39 See Nguyen Tien Hung and Jerrold L. Schecter, *The Palace File* (New York: Harper & Row, 1986), pp. 40–1.

40 "Address to the Nation on Vietnam," May 14, 1969, in Office of the Federal Registrar, *Public Papers of the Presidents of the United States: Richard Nixon, 1969* (Washington: G.P.O., 1971), pp. 369–75. (Hereafter: PP, followed by year.)

41 See Edward C. Keefer,, "President Dwight D. Eisenhower and the End of the Korean War," *Diplomatic History*, 10 (Summer, 1986): 267–89.

42 Quoted in Marilyn Young, *The Vietnam Wars, 1945–1990* (New York: Harper Collins, 1991), p. 237.

43 "The Economic Crisis of 1968 and the Waning of the 'American Century,'" *American Historical Review* (April, 1996): 396–422.

44 Nixon, *RN*, p. 307.

45 Douglas G. Brinkley, *Dean Acheson: The Cold War Years, 1953–71* (New Haven: Yale Univ. Press, 1992), pp. 268–9.

46 Ibid., 270.

47 Walter Isaacson, *Kissinger* (New York: Simon and Schuster, 1992), p. 235; Hung, *Palace File*, p. 40; Haldeman, *Diaries*, p. 65.

48 "Informal Remarks on Guam with Newsmen," July 25, 1969, *PP, 1969*, pp. 544–56.

49 Brandon, *Retreat*, p. 80. For a discussion of the Nixon or Guam Doctrine, as it was variously called, see, Lloyd C. Gardner, *A Covenant with Power: America and World Order from Wilson to Reagan* (New York: Oxford University Press, 1984), pp. 181–3.

50 Kissinger, *White House Years* (Boston: Little, Brown & Co., 1979), pp. 311, 444.

51 Gerald S. and Deborah H. Strober, *Nixon: An Oral History of His Presidency* (New York: Harper Collins, 1994), p. 171.

52 For details, see Seymour M. Hersh, *The Price of Power: Kissinger in the White House* (New York: Simon & Schuster, 1983), pp. 61–5, 85–8. The greatest irony was that William Beecher's story had not been a leak at all, but simply something that was picked up out of observations in Cambodia itself. The story was not especially critical, either, "but did say that the missions were designed to 'signal' Hanoi that the Nixon Administration would be tougher and far more willing to take military risks for peace." It was true, however, that Beecher had also written a story about inside debates on how to deal with a North Korean shoot down of an American reconnaissance plane. Ibid., 87.

53 Kissinger, *White House Years*, pp. 305–6.

54 Ibid., 305.

55 Nixon, *RN*, pp. 406–7.

56 Quoted in Walter F. LaFeber, *America, Russia and the Cold War, 1945–1992* (New York: McGraw-Hill, 1993), p. 17. LaFeber notes that "this precise exchange was possibly

created by Truman's imagination," as the words were not recorded in official records of the conversation. The quotation was famous, however, in all the annals of Cold War presidential sayings, and was no doubt familiar to Nixon, making the exchange with Kissinger even more intriguing as a study in the search for a usable past. Dobrynin's memoirs, on the other hand, do not mention that Vietnam was even discussed on October 20, 1969, perhaps because he came away from that meeting with a commitment to begin strategic arms talks – an indication that Nixon's assertion that he would do something dramatic for Soviet–American relations only in exchange for progress in the peace negotiations came apart at the very moment he uttered those words. Anatoly Dobrynin, *In Confidence: Moscow's Ambassador to America's Six Cold War Presidents* (New York: Random House, 1995), p. 202.

57 The speech in context is discussed in Safire, *Before the Fall*, pp. 174–9.

58 Haldeman, *Diaries*, p. 105.

59 "Address to the Nation on the War in Vietnam," November 3, 1969, *PP, 1969*, pp. 901–9.

60 Nixon, *RN*, p. 401.

61 William Safire's astute tracing out of the implications of the "Silent Majority" speech makes the point very well that it had an impact on "his political philosophy," another way of saying that he was captive to his own creation, or supposed creation, because the silent majority had no real existence beyond a temporary rallying around the flag. Belief in the silent majority, and himself as its chosen agent, had immediate consequences in the Cambodian "incursion" and through the rest of the war. Safire calls attention to a 1972 campaign speech, "as remarkable as it was unremarked." In this speech, Nixon said, "On November 3, 1969, I came before my fellow Americans on radio and television to review our responsibilities and to summon up the strength of our national character. The great silent majority of Americans – good people with good judgment who stand ready to do what they believe to be right – immediately responded. The response was powerful, nonpartisan, and unmistakable. The majority gave its consent, and the expressed will of the people made it possible for the Government to govern successfully." *Before the Fall*, p. 178.

It was indeed a remarkable statement, this assertion that the speech had brought out the "expressed will of the people" and "made it possible for the Government to govern successfully." Conservatives would have great difficulty, to say the least, in squaring such an assertion with a strict construction of the Constitution. What other echoes can be heard here will have to be discussed in another place.

62 Ambrose, *Nixon: The Triumph*, p. 325.

63 Ibid., 337. Ambrose's treatment of the events leading up to the Cambodian incursion is the most useful in print.

64 Haldeman, *Diaries*, p. 154.

65 Ambrose, *Nixon: The Triumph*, p. 341.

66 Nixon, *PP, 1970*, pp. 373–7.

67 "Address to the Nation on the Situation in Southeast Asia," April 30, 1970, ibid., 405–10.

68 Hersh, *Price of Power*, p. 193.

69 Safire, *Before the Fall*, p. 192.

70 Ibid., 211.

71 Nixon, *PP, 1970*, p. 420.

72 Charles W. Colson, *Born Again* (Old Tappan, N.J.: Chosen Books, 1976), p. 39.

73 Ibid., 41. Bob Haldeman also noted that Cambodia "marked a turning point for Nixon; a beginning of his downhill slide...." Ambrose, *Nixon: The Triumph*, p. 361.

74 Ambrose, *Nixon: The Triumph*, p. 361.
75 This discussion of the events in the summer of 1971 is drawn largely from, Jeffrey P. Kimball, "Nixon and the Diplomacy of Threat and Symbolism," in David L. Anderson, ed., *Shadow on the White House: Presidents and the Vietnam War, 1945–1975* (Lawrence: University of Kansas Press, 1993), pp. 162–83; Luu Doan Huynh, "The Seven-Point Proposal of the PRG (July 1, 1971) and the U.S. Reaction," in Jayne S. Werner and Luu Doan Huynh, eds., *The Vietnam War: Vietnamese and American Perspectives* (Armonk: M.E. Sharpe, 1993), pp. 198–202; and Young, *Vietnam Wars*, pp. 263–5.
76 Ambrose, *Nixon: The Triumph*, p. 453.
77 For Thieu's reaction, see Hung, *Palace File*, p. 20.
78 Ilya V. Gaiduk, *The Soviet Union and the Vietnam War* (Chicago: Ivan R. Dee, 1996), p. 232.
79 Isaacs, *Without Honor*, p. 491.
80 Haldeman, *Diaries*, pp. 445–6.
81 Kissinger, *White House Years*, p. 1185.
82 "Address to the Nation on the Situation in Southeast Asia," *PP, 1972*, pp. 583–7.
83 *In Confidence*, p. 248.
84 Ibid., pp. 241, 246.
85 The best discussion of the diplomacy of the May 8 speech is by Tom Wicker, in *One of Us*, pp. 602–7.
86 Hung, *Palace File*, pp. 60–4; Gaiduk, *Soviet Union and the Vietnam War*, p. 240.
87 "Remarks on Arrival in San Clemente," August 24, 1972, *PP: 1972*, pp. 817–20.
88 Hersh, *Price of Power*, pp. 577–8.
89 Haldeman, *Diaries*, p. 505.
90 On Kissinger's handling of the two sides, see Hersh, *Price of Power*, pp. 580–3.
91 Kimball, "Nixon and the Diplomacy of Threat and Symbolism," pp. 170–1.
92 Ibid., and Hung, *Palace File*, p. 101.
93 *RN*, p. 738.
94 Haldeman, *Diaries*, p. 558.
95 The Paris Peace Accords can be found most easily in Stanley I. Kutler, ed., *Encyclopedia of the Vietnam War* (New York: Scribners, 1996), pp. 657–78.
96 Hung, *Palace File*, p. 145.
97 Ibid.
98 John Ehrlichman, *Witness to Power: The Nixon Years* (New York: Simon & Schuster, 1982), p. 316.

CHAPTER FOURTEEN

Remembering Nixon's War

CAROLYN EISENBERG

On the first day of my undergraduate Nixon class, I ask the students to write down their impressions of his Presidency. Few know much about him but most report mixed opinions. The typical response is that Nixon did "something very wrong" in Watergate, but that he was "a great foreign policy President." "What great things did he do?," I inquire. From across the room, many chime in: "He opened relations with China" and "He ended the war in Vietnam."

One of the ironic effects of the Watergate scandal is that it has become the controversy for which Nixon is most famous. Among young people, it is widely known that there was some kind of burglary at Democratic Headquarters and an associated cover-up, which forced the President out of office. As exemplified by the recent satirical movie "Dick," Watergate details have filtered into popular culture and continue to shape the public's image of Richard Nixon.

For those old enough to remember, it is remarkable to contemplate the resulting eclipse of the four years of ferocious domestic struggle over Nixon's Vietnam policies. It was that struggle which dominated his Presidency and established the context in which the Watergate scandals occurred. To supporters and critics alike, the defining feature of Nixon's White House years was his controversial decision to prolong the war in Southeast Asia.

Indeed, Richard Nixon was the only President in American history to engage in sustained military action against three nations without a mandate from the public, the press, the government bureaucracies or the foreign policy elite. From this circumstance flowed disaster: for the people of Indochina and America, and ultimately for the Nixon administration itself.

Yet if Watergate now overshadows Nixon's record on Vietnam, it has also yielded rich materials for comprehending it. The collapse of Nixon's Presidency produced an outpouring of memoirs and diaries that are unprecedented in their detail and candor. From these sources, one can assemble an amazingly clear picture of decision-making at the highest levels. Many of the disturbing practices in the Nixon White House reflected longstanding trends in national security policy. But in charting a course for Southeast Asia, Nixon brought to the task a degree of rage and irrationality that bore his own mark.

I

Richard Nixon had risen to national prominence on the strength of his anticommunist credentials. Early in his career he had defeated Democratic opponents for the House and Senate by impugning their patriotism. And while serving in Washington, he had made a name for himself by uncovering the sensational evidence that linked former State Department official Alger Hiss to a Soviet spy-ring. Later as Dwight Eisenhower's Vice President, Nixon had stood up to rock-throwing, leftist mobs in Caracas and he had garnered widespread admiration for his hard-hitting "kitchen debate" with Soviet Premier Nikita Khrushchev.

However, in seeking the Presidency in 1968 this Cold War background was of no direct use. Following the Tet offensive, the American public had turned sharply against the Vietnam War and was not receptive to further anticommunist crusades. Nixon's best hope for victory was that popular antipathy towards Lyndon Johnson's war policy would adhere to the Democratic candidate Vice President Hubert Humphrey. With this in mind, he softened his Cold Warrior image and made frequent promises on the campaign trail of a "secret plan for peace."

Electoral prospects seemed bright when, in late October, word came from Paris of a diplomatic break-through between American and North Vietnamese negotiators. The Johnson Administration had agreed to a complete bombing halt over North Vietnam, in exchange for a promise of military restraint and the inclusion of the government of South Vietnam in forthcoming peace talks. This provided an immediate and dramatic boost to Hubert Humphrey's standing in the polls.

Richard Nixon was not surprised, having been privately kept abreast of Paris developments by Harvard Professor Henry Kissinger, a consultant to the US delegation. Conveniently warned of the impending break-through, Nixon had sent a secret message to the South Vietnamese President Nguyen Van Thieu indicating that he would receive a better deal under a Republican Administration. The intervention bore fruit on November 2, when Thieu publicly refused to participate in the peace talks under the existing terms. His recalcitrance dampened hopes for an early end to the war and slowed the last minute boom for Humphrey.

Three days later Richard Nixon was elected President of the United States with 43.5 percent of the popular vote. In taking office, he assumed leadership of an angry, divided country that could not agree on how to end the war in Vietnam. But if there was a mandate in 1968 – from the public, from the media, from the academy and from within the "foreign policy establishment" – it was that the United States must somehow extricate itself from the conflict.

Whoever became President in 1969 would have encountered a searing choice. The only way to rapidly exit the war was to lose it. A small minority of those who protested believed that a victory by the Viet Cong would improve the lives of the Vietnamese, but most critics of the war had not accepted the reality of defeat. It would have taken a special kind of leader to absorb the loss on his own watch, and to insist that this was the only alternative to continued bloodshed.

This was not Richard Nixon's intent. From the outset his primary goal was the same as his predecessors: to maintain South Vietnam as an independent non-communist entity. Together with his National Security Advisor Henry Kissinger, Nixon firmly believed that American credibility remained at stake. Indeed the very duration of the American involvement in Vietnam made it especially important to demonstrate to allies and adversaries alike that the United States would honor its commitments there.

There was nothing novel in this outlook. Such reasoning had undergirded American policy for the past decade. However, by the late 1960s, many of their Cold War colleagues had come to believe that this essentially symbolic struggle had reached the point of diminishing returns. With rising US casualties, a serious drain on the domestic economy, furious criticism abroad, a multiplying anti-war movement and no clear strategy for winning, was not the symbolism the exact opposite of the intention?

Nixon expected to ameliorate many of these problems by a policy of rapid troop withdrawals. This approach would cut costs, mute public dissatisfaction and enhance his personal popularity. The obvious liability was that it would weaken the American ability to coerce the enemy. His solution was "Vietnamisation," an American-funded increase of the Army of South Vietnam (ARVN) from 850,000 men to over a million, and the provision of large quantities of new equipment, everything from rifles and grenade launchers to helicopters, ships and planes.[1] He also planned a more ambitious use of American air-power, both in Laos and in South Vietnam, ordering a sharp increase in the number of B-52 bombing sorties over previous levels.[2] While these measures might not produce a decisive victory on the battlefield, the combination of brute force and skillful diplomacy would induce North Vietnam to accept a negotiated settlement.

In February 1969, Nixon encountered his first challenge when South Vietnamese insurgents launched a spring offensive that abruptly doubled American casualties. Viewing this as a "deliberate test, clearly designed to take the measure of me and my administration," his response was to order the secret bombing of enemy enclaves inside Cambodia. There the neutralist leader Prince Norodom Sihanouk was maintaining a delicate equilibrium by allowing NLF forces to establish base camps in the border areas, in tacit exchange for which the North Vietnamese government had denied support to the small group of Cambodian communists (Khmer Rouge), who were trying to overthrow his government.

For years the Joint Chiefs of Staff had asserted the military usefulness of eliminating these safe areas, claiming as well, that the North Vietnamese Central Headquarters for South Vietnam (COSVN) would be found there. For Nixon and Kissinger, however, the main appeal of bombing Cambodia was that it would quickly demonstrate the Administration's willingness to act boldly. As the National Security Advisor explained, the Soviets, the North Vietnamese and the Chinese would be watching: "If we strike back, even though it's risky... they will say 'This guy is becoming irrational – we'd better settle with him.'"[3]

Within the government, both Secretary of Defense Melvin Laird and Secretary of State William Rogers viewed this escalation as inflammatory and potentially destabilizing to the Sihanouk government. The effect of this dissension inside the two Departments was to strengthen Nixon's reliance on Kissinger and the National Security Council(NSC) staff. At an early meeting at the NSC, the President commiserated with their need to deal with "the impossible fags" in State and encouraged them to ignore the bureaucrats.[4]

Nixon's decision was to initiate the MENU bombings – BREAKFAST, LUNCH, DESSERT, SNACK and DINNER. Over the course of the next fourteen months, American planes executed 3,875 bombing runs over Cambodia, dropping 108,223 tons of bombs. Yet despite the massive effort, COSVN was never found and the Vietnamese forces moved deeper into Cambodia.

Apart from the destruction in Cambodia, MENU had other harmful effects. Because of the opposition within the government, Nixon decided to keep the MENU bombings secret both from the public and his own bureaucracies. Under orders from the White House, the American command in Vietnam falsified the flight records, logging the missions into Cambodia as attacks on South Vietnam. Over Laird's objections, the President refused to inform the Secretary of the Air Force or to notify Congress of his decision. When in May, NY *Times* reporter William Beecher broke a story about the Cambodian air war, Nixon became enraged over leaks. With Kissinger's help he ordered the Federal Bureau of Investigation to place wire-taps on members of the NSC staff and selected journalists.

By spring, it was evident that the Cambodian operation was having little impact on North Vietnam's willingness to accept US terms. Nixon's publicly announced conditions for peace featured a mutual withdrawal of American and North Vietnamese forces from South Vietnam. Through intermediaries, the North Vietnamese rejected the parallel between their indigenous troops and those of the United States.

Although Hanoi was unyielding, both Rogers and Laird continued to insist that the US troop withdrawals proceed. An exasperated Kissinger contended that if the United States continued to pull out forces unilaterally, this would deprive North Vietnam of any incentive to make concessions. However, this was one instance when the President backed his Cabinet Secretaries, understanding the perils of disappointing the American public.

To Kissinger, this all signified a maneuver by Rogers to undermine his standing with the President. According to White House Chief of Staff HR "Bob" Haldeman, he "feels that P has made a decision to reverse Vietnam plan and . . . hasn't discussed with him . . . he feels that maybe the P has lost confidence in him. Swore me to tell him if this ever happens . . . "[5]

The concern was misplaced. In mid-July Nixon told Kissinger to "go for broke" – to make it clear to the North Vietnamese that they must quickly sign a peace agreement or the US would accelerate its military effort.[6] In a secret meeting in Paris, Kissinger informed North Vietnamese representative Xuan Thuy that "if by November 1 no major progress has been made toward a solution, we will be compelled – with great reluctance – to take measures of the greatest consequences."[7]

But what might these measures be? In a meeting of NSC staffers in September, Kissinger stressed his disbelief that "a fourth-rate power like North Vietnam doesn't have a breaking point."[8] To devise "a savage, punishing blow" against

North Vietnam, a group from the National Security Council collaborated with representatives of the Joint Chiefs of Staff on a plan of attack they called Duck Hook, which included the mining of the port of Haiphong, a naval blockade and intensive bombing raids on North Vietnamese military targets and population centers.

With his eye on the November 1 deadline, Kissinger insisted to Haldeman that "we only have two alternatives, bug out or accelerate, and that we must escalate or the P is lost."[9] Yet he was again thwarted by Secretary of Defense Laird, who argued convincingly to Nixon that while the projected strikes would be dramatic, they would not relieve the military pressure in South Vietnam.[10] Though instinctively drawn to Duck Hook, the President also worried that he could "not hold the country" for the six to eight months it might take to implement Kissinger's strategy.[11]

A key factor in Nixon's attitude was the resurgent peace movement, which had organized a nation-wide Moratorium Day for October 15. With public impatience mounting, antiwar activists had scheduled teach-ins, memorial services, rallies and marches across the country. Although the President projected an image of indifference, behind the scenes Haldeman noted a "Lot of concern plans for Moratorium day as.... heat builds."[12]

On the day itself, millions of Americans stayed home from work or school to demand that Nixon end the war. An estimated 250,000 people marched on Washington, another 100,000 in Boston Common. Nixon was furious, believing that the demonstrators had undermined his ultimatum to Hanoi. There were certainly no signs of movement from North Vietnam, which continued to insist that the conditions for peace were the removal of American forces from South Vietnam and the replacement of the Thieu regime with a coalition government.

One idea was to involve the Russians. Kissinger had been holding "back channel" meetings with their Ambassador Anatoly Dobrynin since early in the year, but had insisted that, until Vietnam was settled, progress on such vital questions as nuclear arms control, economic relations and the German settlement would be frozen. Though eager to pursue these other items, Dobrynin claimed that North Vietnam did not take instructions from Moscow.

In late October Nixon leaned harder, warning the Ambassador that, "You may think you can break me ... You make think our domestic situation is unmanageable ... I want you to understand that the Soviet Union is going to be stuck with me for the next three years and three months and I will keep in mind what is being done right now, today."[13] On the other hand, if the Russians helped to end the war, "we might do something dramatic to improve our relations." While Dobrynin made no concession, Kissinger was impressed: "It was extraordinary! No President has ever laid it on the line to them like that."

Meanwhile, Nixon needed a quick antidote to the powerful antiwar movement. In a major policy address on November 3, broadcast on national television, he asserted that "Precipitate withdrawal would ... be a disaster of immense magnitude ... It would not bring peace, it would bring more war."[14] Vietnamisation was working. US troops were coming out and the war was going better. But people must be patient. Calling upon "the silent majority" for support, he admonished the audience,

"North Vietnam cannot defeat or humiliate the United States. Only Americans can do that."

The speech was a huge success. Where public opinion polls had been showing 58 percent disapproval rates for Nixon's handling of the war, in the aftermath of the speech approval sky-rocketed to 68 percent Some of the enthusiasm was manufactured. Bob Haldeman was set to work generating favorable calls and wires, creating pressure on the TV networks, and meeting "a plea" from the President, "if only do one thing get 100 vicious, dirty calls to New York *Times* and Washington *Post* about their editorials."[15] Yet there was no doubt that Nixon had swung the majority of his listeners by appealing to their patriotic idealism and persuading them that he was implementing a viable policy for ending the war.

Exuberant over the reception of his speech, Nixon was unfazed by the Moratorium in November. As demonstrators gathered in the dark, each person carrying a candle and a placard with the name of an American killed in the war, Haldeman recorded that "the P was not interested, spent two hours in the bowling ally."[16] On the second night, Nixon learned that violence had broken out as the marchers made their way to the South Vietnamese Embassy, for which he offered "helpful ideas such as using helicopters to blow their candles out."[17]

Despite his effective public relations, at the end of 1969 the the President was without a coherent strategy for getting North Vietnam to accept his agenda. In this first year of what was now Nixon's War, 11,527 American servicemen had died, along with 22,000 South Vietnamese soldiers. There was no accurate count of the thousands of Vietnamese and Cambodian civilians who had perished during this period.

II

In early 1970 Henry Kissinger began pressing Nixon for authority to resume secret negotiations with the North Vietnamese. The skeptical President instructed: "I don't know what those clowns want to talk about, but the line we take is either they talk or we are going to sit it out."[18] In Paris, Kissinger restated the American desire for a mutual withdrawal of troops to be followed by a political settlement that would be negotiated by the two Vietnamese governments. This was unacceptable to the new Vietnamese negotiator Le Duc Tho, who insisted that the North would not withdraw its armies while Thieu remained in power.

Yet the National Security Advisor detected signs of movement, reporting to Haldeman in mid-March that he was playing "a tough, uneager role, and they keep going for the next step."[19] If the President could hold the country for two to four months, he could get a deal. He was therefore disappointed, when on April 5 Le Duc Tho unequivocally rejected the American position. This confirmed for both Nixon and Kissinger the need for an overwhelming use of force to compel North Vietnamese cooperation.

Towards that end, Nixon had accelerated the secret air war in Laos by authorizing B-52 strikes against civilian inhabited areas in the Plain of Jars. This generated a storm of editorial protest in the press, and from legislators of both parties. The State Department had objected to the attacks from the beginning, and when Rogers sought a meeting to reopen the question, Nixon admonished Kissinger "to go ahead and bomb, don't make announcement or notify state, just do it and skip the argument."[20]

By spring, Kissinger's rivalry with the Secretary of State was careening out of control. With Nixon's blessing, the National Security Advisor had taken over large areas of American foreign policy, keeping Rogers in the dark about such crucial items as negotiations with North Vietnam and the Soviet Union. While deploring Kissinger's "psychopathic obsession" with this competition[21] Nixon was impelled to rely on him, in part because of the State Department's disaffection from the war.

Problems with State were especially acute on Cambodian matters. The American B-52 attacks on North Vietnamese sanctuaries had driven enemy forces deeper into the country, where their presence proved de-stabilizing. In response, the pro-American Defense Minister Lon Nol staged a successful coup against Prince Sihanouk, ordering the Vietnamese forces to leave Cambodia immediately. Nixon's decision was to send immediate aid, overriding the objections of both Rogers and Secretary of Defense Melvin Laird, who warned that Lon Nol's abandonment of Cambodian "neutrality," would align the North Vietnamese with the Khmer Rouge.

As the fighting inside Cambodia escalated, the US Commander in Vietnam General Creighton Abrams pressed the President for new action against the sanctuaries. Abrams had been upset by the news that Nixon would be withdrawing 175,000 American troops by year's end. Charged with the daunting task of winning the war with constantly diminished forces, he hoped to reduce the pressure on his troops by curtailing enemy movement across the border. This dovetailed with the President's own wish to make a fresh display of military might.

Nixon's decision was to dispatch the South Vietnamese Army (ARVN) into the Parrot's Beak section of Cambodia, a small strip of land located thirty-three miles from Saigon. At the same time, a joint US–ARVN operation would head into the Fishhook area, where Nixon believed they could find and destroy the Communist command post for all South Vietnam (COSVN). Once again the President had overruled Rogers and Laird, who argued that the incursion would cause large numbers of casualties without significant gains. Laird also challenged the quest for COSVN, stressing that "the damn thing moves all the time."[22] The discord even reached inside Kissinger's NSC staff, where four of his top aides resigned in protest.

Yet Nixon's orders were not entirely irrational, given his lack of concern about casualties. Once this was factored out, then even the remote gamble that the Cambodian operation could help the war was worth taking. However, the mood in the White House was tense and embattled to a degree that alarmed Kissinger, who later reflected that "in the days before announcing this most fateful decision … Richard Nixon was virtually alone, sitting in a darkened room in the executive Office Building, the stereo softly playing neo-classical music – reflecting, resenting, collecting his thoughts and his anger."[23]

On April 30, as South Vietnamese troops streamed into the Parrot's Beak, the President went on national television to explain his decision. He had sought peace but the enemy was intransigent and was now poised to take over Cambodia. Ignoring the thirteen months of MENU bombings, Nixon maintained that both the United

States and South Vietnam had so far refrained from moving against the sanctuaries "because we did not wish to violate the territory of a neutral nation." But the stakes were too large for inaction, for if "when the chips are down, the world's most powerful nation, acts like a pitiful helpless giant, the forces of totalitarianism and anarchy will threaten free nations . . . throughout the world."

In the aftermath of the speech, the President prepared the White House staff for the inevitable criticism. "Don't play a soft line," he warned them. "I don't want to see any aid and comfort to anybody here. The big game is to pull this off. It's a bold move, imaginative and it's no more of this screwing around."[24] He hoped nobody would worry about polarization, "Hit 'em in the gut. No defensiveness."

The storm was even greater than imagined. Across the country students went out on strike and engaged in furious demonstrations, some of them violent. With tempers rising, Ohio National Guardsmen were called on to the Kent State campus where they shot into a peaceful crowd of students, wounding eleven and killing four. The murders at Kent State, and two subsequent slayings at Jackson State, sent tens of thousands of students pouring into Washington DC to protest the war at home and abroad.

Nixon was momentarily shaken by Kent State, fearing that "his decision had set this off."[25] In the early morning hours of May 8, a sleepless President summoned his valet and drove to the Lincoln Memorial to talk with some of the surprised students who had gathered there. Affirming his desire for peace, he observed that ending the war or cleaning up the environment "was not going to solve the spiritual hunger which all of us have and which . . . has been the great mystery of life from the beginning of time."[26] From there he moved to the virtues of foreign travel and expressed enthusiasm for the Syracuse football team.

To the protestors, the greatest mystery of their collective lives was the futile Vietnam war which would not end. Yet Nixon was ill-equipped to understand this, shielded as he was from the human suffering engendered by his policies. Above him, the marble president in the white chair had experienced the deaths of America's soldiers with anguish. But Nixon did not inhabit this realm of feeling – not for America's youth, certainly not for the Vietnamese.

Meanwhile in an unprecedented display of independence, two hundred and fifty foreign service officers signed a letter of dissent, while the Viet Cong flag was raised over the Peace Corps building. On Capitol Hill, moderate Republicans joined together with hostile Democrats to offer new legislation barring US military action in Cambodia and setting a time limit on the American presence in Vietnam.

As on previous occasions, the excesses of the protestors had drawn the wrath of middle Americans, boosting Nixon's ratings in the polls and generating some counter-demonstrations of support. Yet the President was plainly rattled and despite his bravado, announced his intention to have all the troops out of Cambodia by the end of June.

As American and South Vietnamese troops turned up large quantities of weapons, food and supplies, Nixon persuaded himself that the Cambodian incursion had saved Lon Nol's regime and prevented a fresh communist offensive within South Vietnam. The Pentagon's civilian research office was less sanguine, maintaining that the captured supplies could be re-constituted in seventy-five days.[27] Unless the two armies remained in the border areas, the enemy could easily return. The elusive COSVN had not been found.

As for the damage, 130,000 Cambodians had become refugees, 344 Americans and 818 South Vietnamese soldiers had died. Meanwhile Cambodia itself was continuing to disintegrate, as the invasion sealed a partnership between the government of North Vietnam and the indigenous Khmer Rouge, thereby igniting a more ferocious civil war.

In the aftermath of the Cambodian crisis, the bruised President was more determined than ever to shut off domestic dissent. Bob Haldeman later reflected that this was "a turning point for Nixon; a beginning of his downhill slide."[28] Dissatisfied with the performance of both the FBI and CIA, the President called in all his top intelligence people, and demanded more aggressive action to be handled by a new coordinating agency lodged in the White House.

Meanwhile the war continued. Any notion that the attack in Cambodia would make North Vietnam more tractable had dissipated by Fall. As the mid-term elections approached, Nixon was under pressure from Laird and the Joint Chiefs to accelerate troop removals and reduce the bombing. There were also fresh problems in Congress, where moves were afoot to cut off funding for the war.

To minimize Congressional losses, Nixon barnstormed the country campaigning against the antiwar movement. Despite public doubts about his Vietnam policy, the polls consistently showed substantial hostility to the often disheveled and sometimes crude protestors. For Nixon, a high point was San Jose, where thousands of enraged demonstrators ringed the auditorium in which he was speaking. According to Haldeman, "We wanted some confrontation and there were no hecklers in the hall, so we stalled departure a little so they could zero in outside."[29] To rile the crowd Nixon stood up and gave the V sign, eliciting "rocks, flags, candles, . . . as we drove out." This turned into "a huge incident and we worked hard to crank it up."

Such theatrics notwithstanding, the election results were inconclusive as the Republicans lost nine seats in the House of Representatives, while picking up two in the Senate. By the beginning of 1971, Kissinger was anticipating that the impending dry season might be the last opportunity for a major South Vietnamese offensive that would be backed by American forces. At the urging of General Creighton Abrams and Ambassador Ellsworth Bunker, he recommended a major ARVN move into Laos to halt the massive supply operations coming down through the Ho Chi Minh trail.

Kissinger was buoyantly optimistic about the prospects for this campaign, assuring Haldeman that if successful "it would in effect end the war because it would totally demolish the enemy's capability."[30] However, General Abrams had indicated that the Laotian operation was a high-risk gamble because ARVN would be marching into rugged country, where they would be outnumbered by a superior enemy force and dependent on tight coordination with American air power.[31]

On February 3, 1971 as the 1st ARVN Division massed at the Laotian border, news of the campaign broke in the American press. This provoked new objections from Rogers, Laird and CIA Director Richard Helms. Undaunted, Nixon and Kissinger decided to proceed on the grounds "that if the P now allowed himself to be talked out of it, in effect by the press reports leaked from State and Defense that he would lose any hope of controlling the bureaucracy."[32]

Yet once launched, Operation Lam Son 719 proved disastrous. Bad weather prevented American helicopters from transporting the South Vietnamese troops into the approved places and fighter bombers could not provide the anticipated support. As in the past, the South Vietnamese forces were poorly commanded on the ground, taking up foolish positions and falling back quickly. After seizing the crossroads town of Tchepone, where they continued to meet heavy fire, General Thieu abruptly ordered their withdrawal from Laos. Outnumbered and outgunned, the terrified soldiers sought rescue by US helicopters and when shoved aside some held on to the skids for dear life.

These disturbing scenes were broadcast back in the United States, mocking the very concept of "Vietnamisation." Once again the South Vietnamese seemed unwilling or unable to fight for their own cause. Despite the debacle, Nixon managed to find redemptive features in Lam Son 719. As described by Haldeman, "the P has a sort of mystic feeling about the Laotian thing and says so. He is not sure what it is or why, but he has the feeling that there may be more involved here than meets the eye."[33]

In the spring of 1971, what met the public's eye was a failed policy. Fresh polls showed that 71 percent of Americans considered the war a mistake, and that 58 percent thought it immoral. Nixon's approval ratings for his handling of the conflict were at the lowest point since he had entered office. Especially problematic for the Administration was the demoralization of the American military. Drug use was rocketing out of control, with as many as 20 percent of the troops suffering from serious addiction. The attacks on officers ("fraggings") grew more common, as were desertions and outright acts of insubordination.

In the United States, there were dozens of anti-war coffee houses around military bases and a new organization Vietnam Veterans Against the War (VVAW) had been formed, which aligned itself with the national protest movement. During dramatic Winter Soldier hearings in Detroit, men who had returned from Vietnam testified to the war crimes they had witnessed or performed: rapes, torture, the bombing of villages, the murder of civilians.

The spring weather brought mass marches in Washington and San Francisco. In an escalation of tactics, an organization known as the May Day Tribe invited thousands of demonstrators to disrupt traffic and shut down the government in Washington. When the police expelled the protestors from their campgrounds along the Potomac River, many found shelter in the Georgetown homes of the Washington elite. If their hosts did not approve of law-breaking, they were sufficiently alienated from the President's policies to offer hospitality to those who did.

On June 13, the first installment of the "Pentagon Papers" appeared in the *New York Times*. This was a study commissioned by former Secretary of Defense Robert McNamara, tracing the path by which the United States had become steadily embroiled in the Vietnam War. Consisting of a narrative and thousands of pages of classified documents, it had been photocopied by Daniel Ellsberg of the RAND corporation and released to the press.

While the exposure was chiefly embarrassing to the Democrats, it infuriated Nixon, who saw this as another egregious example of press irresponsibility and the treachery of the foreign policy establishment. The President immediately went to court to block the *Times* and *Washington Post* from printing further classified material and obtained an indictment of Ellsberg for violation of the Espionage Act. When the judiciary upheld the freedom of the press, Nixon's determination to nail Ellsberg grew even stronger.

In what would prove to be a fateful decision, the President authorized a Special Investigative unit in the White House to ferret out leakers and find new links to Ellsberg. Dubbed the "Plumbers," the group could expand wire-taps and burglarize places where important information might be found. One early target was the Los Angeles office of Daniel Ellsberg's psychiatrist.

Though accelerating his attack on domestic dissenters, by the summer of 1971 Nixon was in deep gloom about the war. With the 1972 Presidential election on his mind, he recognized that the US could not stay in Vietnam indefinitely. ARVN's abysmal performance in Laos had shattered his confidence in Vietnamization and he was pessimistic about the prospects for negotiations. In a grim session with Kissinger, he reflected that if the next round of talks failed, the United States would withdraw from Vietnam "with a total bombing of the North to eliminate their capability of attacking."[34]

III

Then quite suddenly the Administration's fortunes looked up, when an important secret initiative finally bore fruit. On July 15, Henry Kissinger issued the stunning announcement that he had just returned from Beijing and that the President would visit there early next year.

For a man, who had begun his political career flagellating a Democratic Administration for "its loss of China," this was a startling turn-about. Yet it had been long in the making. Since the mid-60s American policy-makers had been aware of a deepening Sino-Soviet rift. By 1969 the conflict had erupted in fighting along the border of the two nations. The fracture of the Communist world had stimulated Chinese interest in a rapprochement with the United States and created the possibility that by skillful diplomacy, the United States could play off the two Communist superpowers against one another. Among the benefits Nixon and Kissinger hoped to garner was Chinese help with their Vietnam problem.

While in Beijing, the National Security Advisor had gently probed the possibility of linking a resolution of the Taiwan issue with a settlement of the war.[35] Although Chinese Premier Zhou Enlai showed no willingness to pressure the North Vietnamese, Kissinger remained optimistic. For the short term, there was a great surge in the President's approval ratings as a war-weary public welcomed this surprising move towards international reconciliation. Moreover, the opening to China generated enormous anxiety in Moscow, where Soviet leaders began pressing for an early summit. On October 12, the White House proudly announced that the President would be going to Moscow the coming spring. These two developments cast Nixon in a whole new light – the first American President to visit the capitals of his communist adversaries in search of peace.

In the preparations for the Beijing meetings, American representatives were unusually accommodating. During the Fall, the United Nations had admitted the People's Republic of China without significant opposition from Washington. As important, Kissinger indicated the American intent to "normalize" relations with the Mainland and his understanding that Taiwan and China were one nation. Meanwhile he unsuccessfully pressed for Beijing's help with the Paris Peace talks and for an invitation to Le Duc Tho to meet with Nixon in China.[36]

When the President finally arrived in Beijing on February 21, 1972, he received warm greetings but no solace on the war. Zhou Enlai strongly advised the United States to withdraw. Nevertheless, Nixon continued to be forthcoming on Taiwan. While the two sides could not find common language for the communique, the American version called for a peaceful solution and promised that "it will progressively reduce its forces . . . on Taiwan as the tension in the area diminishes."[37]

One of the sub-plots of the China visit was Kissinger's exclusion of Secretary Rogers from any important business. When State Department officials finally saw the Communique, they were appalled to discover that Kissinger had not mentioned America's treaty obligation to Taiwan.

Though he had made no progress on the war, the gain for Nixon was a seven-day television pageant in which millions of Americans watched him tour the sites of China and exchange friendly toasts with its highest dignitaries. Just prior to the President's departure, Kissinger learned that the North Vietnamese were seeking high level talks, which he interpreted as a sign of their worry about the incipient Sino-American friendship. As related by Haldeman, "Henry was particularly ecstatic because it would be for lunch. They have never had any American official for any meal before."[38] The National Security Advisor was hopeful that "there would be no major offensive, as we've been fearing." Even Nixon allowed himself to believe that North Vietnam might finally buckle.

Heartened by the China trip, neither man was alarmed by Hanoi's request for a six-week delay in the negotiations nor did they heed the intelligence reports about the massing of enemy troops near the Demilitarized Zone. On April 1 Nixon and Kissinger were shocked by the news of a powerful North Vietnamese offensive in which twelve divisions equipped with Soviet-made field tanks and heavy artillery were attacking South Vietnam from across the DMZ and from the sanctuaries inside Laos and Cambodia.

Although vastly outnumbering the enemy forces, ARVN's initial performance was dismal. Within days North Vietnamese units had seized control of much of Quang Tri Province in the north and in the south they were advancing on the town of An Loc, just sixty miles west of Saigon. Finally appreciating the dimensions of the attack, Nixon was furious. Only 95,000 American troops were left in the South, with less than 6,000 in combat units to back up ARVN. The President's immediate instinct was to deploy massive air power against the North, telling Haldeman that "the bastards have never been bombed like they are going to be bombed this time."[39]

Yet the American military was reluctant to comply. The Air Force did not wish to fly in the poor weather conditions that obtained, while Creighton Abrams was insisting that any available planes be targeted in the South to relieve the pressure on ARVN. However, Nixon and Kissinger insisted that the invasion was an act of desperation and that by striking North Vietnam they could gain a favorable peace settlement. Ignoring the views of the Defense Department and the CIA, on the weekend of April 15–16, they ordered American B-52 bombers to hit targets north of the DMZ. After leaving church on Sunday, the elated President informed Haldeman that the strikes had been "exceptionally effective, the best ever in the war . . . We really left a good calling card."[40]

The more difficult issue from Nixon's perspective was how to handle the Soviets. The upcoming summit scheduled for late May was to have been his crowning diplomatic achievement in the run-up to the November elections. Yet here were North Vietnamese armies, equipped with up-to-date Soviet weapons sweeping through the South. Could the United States continue its friendly initiatives in the face of this frontal challenge? And what if the Soviets themselves took umbrage at the American air-strikes on their North Vietnamese ally and chose to cancel the summit?

For months Henry Kissinger had been secretly negotiating with Soviet Ambassador Dobrynin on a comprehensive agreement that would incorporate both anti-ballistic missile defenses (ABM) and offensive nuclear weapons. This was to have been the centerpiece of the Nixon–Brezhnev meeting. In conducting these negotiations, the National Security Advisor was going behind the back of the official American arms control delegation that was talking with the Soviets in Helsinki. On his own, Kissinger made concessions to Dobrynin that the Helsinki group had not been permitted and which left the United States in a relatively weaker position *vis-à-vis* the Soviets.[41]

Indeed one of the most remarkable features of Nixon and Kissinger's "Triangular Diplomacy" was their willingness to compromise with old adversaries to boost the Administration's popularity at home and to get their help with Vietnam. Ostensibly, Americans were fighting and dying in Southeast Asia to show the Soviets and Chinese that the United States had an implacable will. Yet with Nixon's blessings, Kissinger was trading off long held positions on arms control and Taiwan.

However, since the inception of the Cold War "credibility" had always had a dual aspect. While American Presidents publicly stressed the need to impress the Communist superpowers, the undiscussed underside was the effort to intimidate indigenous revolutionary movements and to preserve pro-capitalist regimes. These aims were normally intertwined, but the American failure in Vietnam was forcing a choice. By moving towards detente, Nixon and Kissinger were conjuring up a new approach to international relations in which the conciliation of Moscow and Beijing would give them a freer hand in the Third World.

Yet Hanoi's Spring Offensive cast this into doubt. Kissinger remained eager to fly to Moscow on April 20 to complete the plans for the summit. But Nixon was more reluctant, acceding only on the condition that Kissinger press the Soviets on Vietnam. In his first session with Brezhnev the National Security Advisor took a tough line, warning that a continuation of the offensive would jeopardize the improvement in East-West relations.[42] He wished to see Le Duc Tho back at the negotiating table and expected him "to change his negotiating habits."

The Russian leader made no promises, but agreed to transmit American peace proposals to Hanoi. In conjunction with his silence about the American bombing of the North, Kissinger was reasonably satisfied. Back in Washington, Nixon was fuming. He considered the Soviet position on South Vietnam to be "frenzied and frivolous"[43] and wanted Kissinger to come home. Defending the Russians, Kissinger fired back," I do not believe that Moscow is in direct collusion with Hanoi."[44] They had other global concerns, for which Vietnam had become an obstacle. "What in God's name are they getting out of this?" he queried.

Nixon was especially agitated because the lifting of the weather and the subsequent large-scale use of American air power in South Vietnam had brought no improvement on the battlefield. Saigon remained at risk as control over An Loc shifted back and forth. Then on May 1 came the shattering news that the city of Quang Tri had fallen and panicky ARVN units were fleeing towards Hue. General Abrams now thought it possible that the South Vietnamese "had lost their will to fight . . . and that the whole thing might be lost."[45]

Nixon was in an emotional state as he observed the unraveling of his "Vietnamization" policy. After claiming success in the Cambodian and Laotian operations, the North Vietnamese had come marching across those same borders with apparent impunity. And despite the great infusion of American dollars and equipment, ARVN was not doing the job. At this late hour, the President privately acknowledged what his predecessors had painfully learned: "the enemy is willing to sacrifice in order to win while the South Vietnamese aren't willing to pay that much of a price . . . to avoid losing."[46]

Nixon's antidote was to revive the old plans for Duck Hook – the mining of Haiphong harbor, the blockade of the coastline and sustained, draconian bombing raids on the North. His problem was that the Departments of State and Defense were still opposed to massive bombing of North Vietnam. With fresh battles shaping up outside Hue and Kontom, General Abrams was pleading for every plane he could get. In a blistering memo, the President demanded that the military get "off its backside."[47] For years, his administration had failed to follow through on its dire threats. Now the enemy had "gone over the brink *and so have we*. We have the power to destroy his war-making capacity. The only question is whether we have the *will* to use that power . . . I have the *will* in spades."

Would he then go to Moscow? At this crucial juncture, Nixon was relying for political advice on Secretary of the Treasury John Connelly and Chief of Staff Bob Haldeman, both of whom urged that he proceed. From a policy standpoint, it might be absurd to clink glasses with Brezhnev while the United States was fighting off their client's invasion. But the polls showed clearly that most Americans wanted the meeting, and there was no reason to assume that the Russians would cancel.[48]

Inside the Politburo, there was intense debate about what to do.[49] Finally on May 12, Dobrynin brought Kissinger the welcome news that Nixon was expected in Moscow as scheduled. The Soviet government intended to give the President a hydrofoil and hoped that Brezhnev could receive a sports car.[50] For Kissinger, this was proof that his strategy of detente was paying off. Triangular Diplomacy had impelled the Kremlin to "cut loose from its obstreperous small ally on the other side of the globe,"[51] enabling the Nixon Administration to "neutralize our domestic opposition."

By the time the President arrived in Moscow on May 20, the American air operations had enabled ARVN to stabilize its lines in the Central Highlands and north of Saigon. More relaxed, Nixon began the meetings in high spirits. Much of the practical work was already complete. Each day, Nixon and Brezhnev had agreements to sign on scientific and technological cooperation, on cultural exchange, on avoiding incidents at sea and for a commission to develop commercial relations. Little was said about Vietnam, except for one tense session at Brezhnev's dacha, where President Nikolai Podgornyi emotionally exclaimed, "There is the blood of old people, women and children on your hands. When will you finally end this senseless war?"[52] Then the matter was abruptly dropped.

The real work in Moscow centered on arms control. The two sides had already agreed on an ABM treaty limiting the Soviet Union and the United States to one anti-ballistic defense system apiece. The avowed purpose was to stabilize deterrence by insuring that both powers would remain vulnerable to a nuclear attack. Still unfinished was the five-year Interim Agreement on long-range nuclear missiles. Bored by the subject, Nixon left the matter to Kissinger who continued to shut out experts from the State and Defense Departments.

Functioning under intense time pressure, Kissinger made significant concessions on many unresolved questions.[53] Indeed, considered in its entirety, the very structure of the agreement on offensive strategic weapons seemed disadvantageous to the United States. Its central provisions froze the Soviet lead in land-based ballistic missiles (ICBM) and allowed them to build-up their sea-based missiles to a number exceeding that of the American arsenal.[54] Both Nixon and Kissinger were relying on the new MIRV technology, which was enabling the United States to put independently targeted war-heads on individual missiles, thereby nullifying the Soviet lead in launchers.[55] However, arms control experts had regularly cautioned that the Soviets would soon be able to MIRV their own missiles, which would restore significance to the imbalance.

It was a strange irony that the two people whose anxiety about Superpower appearances was supposedly leading them to order thousands of bombing raids on Vietnam, were casually conceding a surface inferiority in the nuclear competition. Yet success at the summit had become essential to Nixon's re-election prospects. In the posture of international peace-maker, the President paid a dramatic visit to the museum in Leningrad, where he was moved by the tragic diary of twelve year-old Tanya who had died in the siege.[56] In a final television address to the Soviet people, Nixon stressed the urgency of cooperation and proposed that, "As we work toward a more peaceful world, let us think of Tanya and . . . let us do all that we can to ensure that no other children will have to endure what Tanya did . . ."

As Vietnamese youngsters perished under the relentless pounding of B-52 air-strikes, the American President stretched out his hand of friendship to the Soviet people. It was a brilliant performance, which according to John Ehrlichman had all the right ingredients – "the picture was great, great setting, another historic event, big buildup."[57] Nixon wanted to be sure that the Tanya segment was re-broadcast in the United States, because that was "the most important part."

IV

By the summer of 1972, the war had reached another stalemate. Hanoi's spring offensive had failed to topple the South Vietnamese government. But American Linebacker operations had not been fully successful either. Although US planes had flown a total of 9,315 sorties, dropping 17,876 bombs on the North, the CIA reported that "The bombing and mining program probably will not, of itself, pose unmanageable difficulties to the North Vietnamese regime – either now or through 1973."[58]

American air strikes in the South had been more effective. They had enabled ARVN to finally withstand the assault, inflicting as many as 100,000 casualties on enemy troops. However by early Fall, 140,000 North Vietnamese soldiers remained in South Vietnam, holding more territory than previously and enabling the National Liberation Front (NLF) to reconstitute itself in the Delta.

Both sides now felt pressure to settle. Hanoi had no prospect of launching a fresh offensive in the near future, while the upcoming elections in the United States made an agreement seem desirable. Nixon's summitry had gained him renewed popularity with the voters and the campaign of Democratic peace candidate George McGovern was stumbling badly. However, Democrats were expected to pick up more Congressional seats, increasing the likelihood that all funding for the war would soon be cut off.

In early October Kissinger resumed talks with Le Duc Tho. By now both he and Nixon considered it inevitable that the North Vietnamese troops would stay in the South. Meanwhile North Vietnam had offered a fresh concession: it would no longer insist on the removal of Thieu and the creation of a coalition government as a precondition for a cease-fire. To Kissinger this represented the long awaited capitulation, although Nixon was more skeptical.

The outlines of a deal were rapidly struck. There would be a rapid cease fire across Vietnam, to be followed within sixty days by the departure of all American military forces. During the same period all prisoners of war would be returned. North Vietnamese troops would continue in the South, administering the territory they controlled. Both the South Vietnamese and the Provisional Revolutionary Government (PRG) would remain in place with a tripartite Council of Concord and Reconciliation, charged with organizing new elections.

On October 12 Kissinger returned to Washington in high excitement, telling the President "you've got three for three."[59]. The United States had achieved a far better deal than was expected. The fighting would end, Thieu could stay in power and a requirement of unanimity would constrain any practical interference by the tripartite Council. Nixon was sufficiently excited by the news to call in Haldeman, and to break out a special bottle of his '57 Lafite-Rothschild wine in celebration.

However, in the ensuing days Nixon began to worry about the reaction of General Thieu. On October 20 he directed Kissinger that "we must have Thieu as a willing partner in making any agreement. It cannot be a shotgun marriage."[60] Yet Thieu was outraged, as Kissinger soon discovered when he arrived in Saigon. The South Vietnamese leader insisted that the accord was an obvious sell-out. The Americans would be going home, with the enemy troops still in place. Kissinger might delude himself that the agreement was a victory, but the South Vietnamese leader knew only too well that absent American power, his army would crumble.

Infuriated by Thieu's intransigence, Kissinger wanted to halt the bombing of North Vietnam and proceed to Hanoi on schedule. He warned Nixon that "we have played a tough, ruthless game of using our election deadline as blackmail against the other side," and now the US had its best chance for peace. These were "fanatics who have been fighting for twenty-five years" and there was no guarantee that in future months "they will be willing to settle on the terms that are now within our grasp."[61]

Yet Nixon was determined to prevent confrontation before the election and he was beginning to have second thoughts about the merits of the accord. Kissinger was sent back to Paris with a list of sixty-nine amendments demanded by South Vietnam, many of them substantive.[62] Feeling betrayed, Le Duc Tho refused to cooperate and began to retract previously ceded points. Kissinger later acknowledged in his memoirs that "the list was so preposterous . . . so far beyond what we had indicated publicly and privately"[63] as to deserve Hanoi's wrath. But he prudently muted this opinion at the time.

Although Nixon swept the Presidential contest by an overwhelming 60 percent vote, the mood in Washington was ominous. Watergate problems were beginning to envelop the President, as the *Washington Post* provided daily revelations about White House schemes to spy on and sabotage political enemies. The jailed burglars were beginning to squeeze the Administration for money, and Nixon was turning against his former friends. On the morning following his election, the President called in the entire White House staff, followed by the Cabinet to demand the signed resignations of everyone. People would be notified in a month whether they would be retained.

In this foul temper, Nixon was again attracted to the idea of intensive bombing. Thieu was obviously correct in claiming that the peace agreement jeopardized his regime, but if there were massive attacks on North Vietnamese targets before it was implemented, this could delay a Communist victory for a long period. Briefly undecided, Nixon issued contradictory instructions to Kissinger, at one point insisting "that we have no choice but to reach agreement along the lines of the October 8 principles"[64] and at another that he halt the negotiations as a prelude to air strikes.

Inside the White House, Kissinger's personal standing was eroding and the President was seriously contemplating his replacement. Since the opening towards China the National Security Advisor had achieved celebrity status in his own right. As Nixon and others in his administration were fending off new criticisms about Watergate, Kissinger's reputation as a brilliant and dedicated public servant continued to grow. All of this had stoked intense jealousy and an eagerness to blame him for a floundering diplomacy.

Aware of these currents, Kissinger was negotiating in Paris in a state of extreme agitation. When the new round of talks failed to dislodge Le Duc Tho from his position, Kissinger returned to Washington in a rage: "They're just a bunch of shits. Tawdry, filthy shits. They make the Russians look good..."[65] Nixon and Kissinger quickly agreed that the best course of action was to bomb the North. However, they were mindful that "there was no support for military action anywhere in the administration" and that there would be devastating criticism in the press.[66] With the backing of the Joint Chiefs of Staff, Secretary Laird had written Nixon urging him to stop the war. The November elections had increased the number of antiwar Senators who would soon block all funds. Why should more American pilots die in the interim?

Nixon was prepared to be ruthless. Although Kissinger preferred to use fighter-bombers to attack the cities of Hanoi and Haiphong, the President thought this too cautious. His Administration would take "the same heat for big blows as for little blows," so it made sense to get the shock value of using the B-52s against the North Vietnamese cities. To do anything less would "only make the enemy contemptuous."[67]

Kissinger was still holding out prospects for significant North Vietnamese concessions, but Nixon had no such illusions. Once the American air strikes ceased, the two sides would return to something close to the October agreement. What he would have accomplished in the interim was to preserve his own reputation for toughness, to assuage some of Thieu's doubts about the peace accords, and to further handicap the enemy through large-scale destruction.

Nixon ordered that every available B-52 be brought to Vietnam for a series of relentless daily attacks. To Admiral Moorer, Chairman of the Joint Chiefs of Staff, he snapped "I don't want anymore of this crap about the fact that we couldn't hit this target or that one. This is your chance to use military power effectively to win the war, and if you don't I'll consider you responsible."[68]

The President was fed up with the military and its unwillingness to take losses. In his diary he compared himself to Winston Churchill, who understood that a leader must choose between audacity and caution and that it was "disastrous" to attempt both policies at once. The United States had "now gone down the audacious line and we must continue until we get some sort of break."[69]

On December 18, American planes began their fierce assault on North Vietnamese targets. Flying high over Hanoi and Haiphong, the B-52s struck several residential districts, destroying the Bach Mai hospital and damaging eight foreign embassies. As the US military had feared, enemy air defenses were sufficiently effective to bring down thirteen tactical aircraft and fifteen B-52s with the resulting loss of more American crewmen.

There was a storm of denunciation in the press. Writing in the *New York Times*, Tom Wicker lamented, "There is no peace. There is shame on earth, an American shame, perhaps enduring, surely personal."[70] The headlines were damning, "New Madness in Vietnam" (*St. Louis-Post Dispatch*), "The Rain of Death Continues" (*Boston Globe*), "This Will End the War?" (*Chicago Daily News*).

International reaction was also severe. Pope Paul the VI called the bombing "the object of daily grief." The London *Daily Mirror* proclaimed that the bombing "made the world recoil in revulsion." The Hamburg *Die Zeit* called it "a crime against humanity." The governments of Denmark, Finland, Holland and Belgium lodged official protests. Indeed not a single NATO ally rallied to the American side.

While the criticism rattled Kissinger, Nixon was oddly peaceful. The day before Christmas, he mused in his diary, "It is God's great gift to me to have the opportunity to exert leadership not only for America but on the world scene..."[71] The only time the United States had exercised so much power was in the aftermath of World War II. But then there had been other world leaders of great stature. Now he was the only one. This imposed an enormous responsibility but...at the same time the greatest opportunity an individual can have." He resolved to approach the new year with "as much excitement, energy, and...real joy that I can muster."

From the inception of the December bombings, Nixon had intended them to be of brief duration. He did not wish to start his second term with Congress forcing him out of Vietnam. After withering attacks on the enemy, he expected to make peace along the lines of the October agreement. Early in the new year, Nixon dispatched Kissinger to Paris for the resumption of formal peace talks. The latter worried that the United States might now appear weak, but was reassured by Nixon that despite returning to the earlier accord "there will be alot of details that will have been ironed out so that we can claim some improvement over that agreement."[72]

Once the United States accepted the previous agreement, negotiations were rapid. By January 11, Kissinger had sealed the bargain and flew triumphantly to Key Biscayne where the President was vacationing. Despite earlier tension, the personal hostility abated as the two men celebrated the President's birthday with an end to the war. Nixon walked Kissinger to his car, assuring him "that the country was indebted to him for what he had done." Kissinger responded that without the President's "courage to make the difficult decision of December 15...we would not be where we are today."[73]

Yet apart from some minor changes,[74] little had been achieved by the Christmas bombings. Indeed, not much was accomplished by the four additional years of war. Hanoi had abandoned its demand for the immediate resignation of Thieu and for the formation of a coalition government. In other respects, Saigon was in a weaker position than it had been in 1969. There were more North Vietnamese troops in the South than previously, and by accepting the peace accords the United States had implicitly acknowledged the existence and legitimacy of the Provisional Revolutionary Government of South Vietnam.

For these obvious reasons General Thieu continued to resist. But Nixon would brook no further complaints, observing to Kissinger that, "Brutality is nothing... You have never seen it if this son-of-a-bitch doesn't go along, believe me."[75] Finally grasping that he had no choice, America's South Vietnamese ally capitulated.

On January 23, the President went before the Cabinet with the announcement that peace had been achieved. According to Nixon, "All our conditions have been completely met."[76] It had been a difficult haul but "the fact that we stood firm as a country...has had a decisive effect on the world." Without that resolve, "the Chinese and the Russians would have no interest in talking to us. Europe wouldn't consider us as a reliable ally, despite their bitching about the war." The United States had an obligation to preserve freedom in the world and "that's what this peace was about."

At midnight, Nixon phoned Kissinger from the Lincoln Sitting Room to say that "every success brings a terrific let-down...I should not be discouraged. There were many battles yet to fight. I should not weaken."[77]

Between January 1969, when Richard Nixon first took office, and January 1973, when he signed the peace accords, 15,315 Americans, 107,504 South Vietnamese and an estimated 400,000 North Vietnamese/NLF soldiers had died. Hundreds of thousands of civilians in the two Vietnams, Cambodia and Laos had also perished.[78]

Two years later, a victorious Khmer Rouge swept to power in Phnom Penh. Within weeks, General Thieu had abdicated as the communist armies consolidated their control of South Vietnam. It was no surprise to anybody that the Paris Peace Accords had not held. At the time of their signing John Ehrlichman had asked Henry Kissinger, "How long do you think the South Vietnamese can survive under this agreement?" "If they're lucky," replied Kissinger, "they can hold out for a year and a half."[79]

NOTES

1   George Herring, *America's Longest War* (New York: McGraw Hill, 1986), 231.
2   Jeffrey Kimball, *Nixon's Vietnam War* (Kansas, University of Kansas Press, 1998) 137.
3   Richard Nixon, *RN: The Memoirs of Richard Nixon* (New York: Grosset & Dunlap, 1978) 384.
4   Cited in Richard Morris, *Uncertain Greatness : Henry Kissinger and American Foreign Policy* (New York: Harper & Row, 1977) 156.
5   H. R. Haldeman, *The Haldeman Diaries* (New York: Berkeley Books, May 1994) June 19 & 20, 1969.
6   Nixon, 393.
7   Ibid., 396.
8   Morris, 164.
9   Haldeman, October 3, 1969.
10 Morris, 165.
11 Haldeman, October 9, 1969.
12 Haldeman, October 13, 1969.
13 Nixon, 407.
14 Cited in Stephen Ambrose, *Nixon: The Triumph of a Politician 1962–1972* (New York: Simon and Schuster, 1989), 309.
15 Haldeman, November 3, 1969.
16 Ibid., November 13, 1969.
17 Ibid., November 14, 1969.
18 Kimball, 186.
19 Haldeman, March 15, 1970.
20 Haldeman, March 20, 1970.
21 Cited in Kimball, 196.
22 Cited in Walter Isaacson, *Kissinger: A Biography* (New York: Simon & Schuster, 1992), 255.

23   Henry Kissinger, *White House Years* (Boston, Little, Brown & Co., 1979) 503.

24   William Safire, *Before the Fall* (New York: Doubleday & Co., 1975), 190.

25   Haldeman, May 4, 1970.

26   Nixon, 465.

27   William Bundy, *A Tangled Web* (New York: Hill & Wang, 1998) 157–8.

28   Cited in Ambrose, 361.

29   Haldeman, October 29, 1970.

30   Haldeman, January 21, 1971.

31   "Looking at the situation in cold objectivity, it did look very much like sending a boy to do a man's job in an extremely hostile environment." General Bruce Palmer Jr., *The 25-Year War America's Military Role in Vietnam*) (Kentucky: The University Press of the University of Kentucky, 1984), 110.

32   Haldeman, February 3, 1971.

33   Ibid., March 25, 1971.

34   Ibid., June 26, 1971.

35   Qiang Zhai, *China & the Vietnam Wars* (Chapel Hill: University of North Carolina Press, 2000), 196.

36   James Mann, *About Face: A History of America's Curious Relationship with China, From Nixon to Clinton* (New York: Vintage Books, 1998) 39.

37   Cited in Ambrose, 516.

38   Haldeman, February 14, 1972.

39   Cited in Kimball, 303.

40   Haldeman, April 16, 1972.

41   In Helsinki, the Americans were insisting on a freeze of both land-based (ICBM) and sea-based ballistic missiles (SLBM). The latter were of particular concern because this was a category in which the Soviets were making their greatest gains. To Dobrynin's surprise, Kissinger indicated a willingness to leave the sea-based missiles out. There was also strong support in the American delegation for a ban on MIRV (Multiple Independently targeted Re-entry Vehicles) because once the Soviets achieved the technology to place independently targeted warheads on a single rocket, their heavy ICBMs could carry a greater number than the American missiles. Yet Kissinger ignored this danger, opting instead for a freeze on land-based missiles that would put the US arsenal at a disadvantage in a still-spiraling nuclear competition.

42   Kissinger, 1144–5.

43   Ibid., 1160.

44   Ibid.

45   Nixon, 594.

46   Ibid., 600.

47   Ibid., 606.

48   Haldeman, May 3, 1972.

49   Anatoly Dobrynin, *In Confidence* (New York: Random House, 1995) 252–4.

50   Haldeman, May 12, 1972.

51   Kissinger, 1201.

52   Cited in Kimball, 317.

53   Among the unresolved questions was the deployment of mobile missiles, the conversion of "light" to "heavy" missiles, and the size of the silos. See discussion in Tad Szulc, *The Illusion of Peace* (New York: Viking Press, 1978), 561–80.

54 For this reason the Pentagon's subsequent support of the SALT I agreement was conditioned on Congressional funding of a new B-1 bomber, the MX missile, cruise missiles and Trident submarines. In this way SALT I ultimately spurred on an intensified nuclear competition.

55 Moreover in counting offensive weapons, whole categories had been excluded, among them the forward-based systems of the American allies, bombers of every type and cruise missiles. For Nixon and Kissinger, these omissions justified the final numbers set in SALT.

56 Nixon, 616–17.

57 Haldeman, May 28, 1972.

58 Cited in Kimball, 325.

59 Haldeman, October 12, 1972.

60 Nixon, 597.

61 Nixon, 599.

62 These included the proposal that North Vietnam remove some of its troop from the South and that any direct reference to the presence of the Provisional Revolutionary Government (PRG) be stricken from the text. See discussion in Kimball, 350.

63 Kissinger, 1417.

64 Ibid., 1421.

65 Nixon, 733.

66 Kissinger, 1447.

67 Nixon, 734.

68 Ibid., 734.

69 Ibid, 736.

70 Critical comments cited in Isaacson, 471.

71 Nixon, 739.

72 Nixon, 743.

73 In his diary, Nixon later observed that "It is not really a comfortable feeling for me to praise people so openly… On the other hand Henry expects it, and it was good that I did so." Ibid.

74 One such detail was the status of the DMZ, which had been a source of contention for months. Kissinger had insisted on a clause stating that following the cease-fire, the two Vietnamese sides would decide how to regulate "civilian passage" across the line, which to him meant that all military passage was forbidden. Le Duc Tho was amenable to the wording, although probably not the spirit of Kissinger's suggestion. Since North Vietnamese troops controlled both sides of the DMZ, this gave the American formula little practical difference. Moreover, Kissinger had made the larger concession by agreeing that DMZ would be considered a temporary demarcation line rather than a boundary between sovereign states.

   The other changes were also minor. The phrase "administrative structure" was dropped from the description of the National Council of Reconciliation, and the International Control Commission was expanded to 1600 members, improving its ability to police the cease-fire. References to the People's Revolutionary Government (PRG) were stricken from the text of the agreement, although retained in the Preamble and the signing procedures.

75 Kissinger, 1459.

76 Haldeman, January 23, 1973.

77 Kissinger, 1475.

78 Figures given in Marilyn Young, *The Vietnam Wars* (New York: Harper-Collins, 1991), 280.
79 Cited in Isaacson, 486.

BIBLIOGRAPHICAL NOTE

The scholarly literature on Nixon's Vietnam policy remains sparse. Especially useful are Stephen Ambrose, *Nixon The Triumph of a Politician 1962–1972* (New York: Simon and Schuster, 1989), Jeffrey Kimball, *Nixon's Vietnam War* (Kansas, University of Kansas Press, 1998) and Keith Nelson, *The Making of Detente: Soviet–American Relations in the Shadow of Vietnam* (Baltimore: Johns Hopkins Press, 1995).

Some of the best writing on this subject is that of journalists, notably Seymour Hersh, *The Price of Power: Kissinger in the Nixon White House* (New York: Summit Books, 1983), Arnold R. Isaacs, *Without Honor Defeat in Vietnam and Cambodia* (Baltimore: Johns Hopkins University Press, 1983), William Shawcross, *Kissinger, Nixon and the Destruction of Cambodia* (New York: Simon and Schuster, 1987), Tad Szulc, *The Illusion of Peace: Foreign Policy and the Nixon Years* (New York: Viking Press, 1978) and Tom Wicker, *One of Us: Richard Nixon and the American Dream* (New York: Random House, 1991).

For a valuable discussion of the Chinese role see Quiang Zhai, *China and the Vietnam Wars* (Chapel Hill: University of North Carolina Press, 2000) and of the Soviet role, Ilya V. Gaiduk, *The Soviet Union and the Vietnam War* (Chicago: Ivan R. Dee, 1996).

CHAPTER FIFTEEN

America's Secret War in Laos, 1955–75

ALFRED W. MCCOY

Introduction

For nearly fifteen years, the US Central Intelligence Agency (CIA) fought a secret war in Laos that remains one of the most significant and least understood aspects of the Vietnam War. Even now, nearly three decades later, the nature of this covert warfare and Laos's role in the wider Vietnam conflict are little understood. Since few beyond those Washington policy makers with access to classified studies are privy to its secrets, the legacy of American intervention in Laos remains obscure.

Nonetheless, the war in Laos is, through the presence of Hmong refugees, gradually slipping into American consciousness, albeit from a partisan perspective. To cite one example, the November 8 1993 edition of my local newspaper, *The Wisconsin State Journal*, carried two obituaries of American war veterans – one telling the story of a war that we all know, and the other revealing a history that, for most Americans, never happened. In the back pages of the paper's third section, we read of Joseph J. "Jim" Daggett of Monona, Wisconsin, who died at 73. Born here in Madison, Wisconsin and educated in our local schools, Jim served as a sergeant in the US Army in World War II, fighting in the major battles of the European campaign – Normandy, the Bulge, the Rhineland crossing, and Central Europe. Returning home to Madison after the war, Jim married "the former Grace Ostrowski" on October 19 1946 and worked for the next thirty years as a sergeant with the Dane Country Traffic Department. "He was a past commander and life member of VFW Post Number 7591, life member of the Disabled American Veterans, member of the Battle of the Bulge, member of the Cooties (VFW Hospital Division), member of the Wisconsin Professional Police Association, and also a member of the Immaculate Heart of Mary Catholic Church."

Further down the same page, is the obituary of Chia Vue Vang, also of Madison and also dead at 73. Her life reveals the broad outlines of this hidden history. Born in Ban Thia, Xhieng Khouang Province, Laos, Chia "was a great mother who worked very hard as a farmer and raised seven sons . . . while her husband served in the CIA." During the Vietnam War, "six of her sons served with the CIA, fighting against the Communists. Meanwhile, Chia and the rest of the family hid in the jungles, going from place to place, avoiding the Communists." After 1975, "when the Communists took over the country," the Vang family fled to Thailand without any money. There, people had little to offer, "so the Vang family flew to the United States to start a new life safe from the Communists."

The war in Laos remains one of the most disturbing aspects of the wider Vietnam war. From 1965 until 1973, Laos absorbed more bombs per square mile than any country in the history of warfare. From 1960 to 1975, the Hmong people – non-literate, migratory hill farmers in the most remote reaches of northern Laos – suffered one of the highest mortality rates of any people in any modern war. Yet, as an ethnic minority, the Hmong had little to gain from the outcome of this conflict. In effect, they absorbed these exceptional casualties as pawns in a superpower struggle, a twentieth-century version of what British imperialists had once called "the great game."

In studying this secret war in Laos, we are thus forced to confront one of the most unpleasant aspects of the Vietnam War and one of the ambiguous applications of American power during the whole of the Cold War. While the United States had genuine ties to Britain, France, or even China, Laos remained, throughout our twenty years' intervention, little more than an arena of geopolitical conflict. Since Americans had no attachments to Laos and no real empathy for its peoples, Washington felt no restraint in the application of the technology of mass destruction and the tactics of covert warfare to its terrain. By the time combat ceased in 1974, the US Air Force had dropped 2.1 million tons of bombs, making tiny, impoverished Laos the world's most heavily bombed nation. For the sustained bombing of populated areas in northern Laos, the United States was probably guilty of war crimes under the 1949 Geneva Convention on protection of non-combatants.

During the first decade of American intervention (1955–65), Washington used the CIA and its new tactics of covert-action to intervene in Laotian politics – dividing local factions and stoking the tensions that led to civil war. During the 1950s, Laos was, in Washington's view, a "finger" pointing into the heart of Southeast Asia that would allow an eventual communist Chinese invasion. In the early 1960s, Laos thus became a testing ground for toughness in the global conflict between the USA and USSR. During America's second decade in Laos (1965–75), the White House combined CIA covert action with the technology of tactical bombing to fight a full-blown secret war in Laos. In this latter decade, Laos was home to the Ho Chi Minh trail – a strategic enemy supply route from North to South Vietnam that, from an American perspective, had to be destroyed at all costs. Throughout these twenty years, this alliance between the world's richest nation and its poorest was thus marked by an extreme imbalance of power that made it a most problematic relationship. The destruction of Laos during the Vietnam conflict is one of the saddest chapters in the history of the larger Cold War – a tragic interaction of American geopolitics and Lao internal politics.

Washington Intervenes

During the early years of the Cold War, Laos, a French colony for the previous sixty years, joined the community of nations as a strategic territory whose fate would be determined by geopolitical conflicts elsewhere in the region or on the globe. In the early 1950s, as it moved from partial to full independence, Laos had a fragmented society and factionalized politics that left it open to manipulation by foreign powers. In forming the Kingdom of Laos out of four lowland principalities and dozens of highland societies, the French had created a new nation that was the sum of its divisions – ethnic, factional, and ideological. During the late 1950s, this small, mountain kingdom became a major flash-point of Cold War confrontation under presidents Dwight Eisenhower and John Kennedy.

During the early years of the First Indochina War (1946–54), the Lao nationalist movement, or *Lao Issara*, split three ways – communist, neutralist, and right wing. In August 1950, Prince Souphanouvong. a member of the royal family with socialist sympathies, broke away to form the *Pathet Lao*, a left-nationalist coalition allied with the Vietnamese revolutionary movement. In November 1951, his half-brother, the political moderate Prince Souvanna Phouma, became the prime minister of what was still a French client state. When Vietnam's People's Liberation Army swept across northern Laos in March 1953 during an offensive against the French army, it installed the pro-communist Pathet Lao in the provincial capital of Sam Neua – an area adjacent to northern Vietnam that was to remain a liberated zone for the next twenty years. In October 1953, France granted Laos its independence, and the Royal Lao government emerged from the 1954 Geneva accords with its territory intact. Through French and American pressure, there were no territorial concessions to the Pathet Lao guerrilla forces.

Seeking to block the influence of the Pathet Lao and thereby hold this strategic flank of South Vietnam securely in the Western camp, the US Central Intelligence Agency, acting on White House instructions, backed the right-wing in seizing power in the late 1950s. Mindful of Laos's strategic position, the Eisenhower administration made this poor, highland nation a major focus of its Southeast Asian policy, at times appearing even more committed to Laos than South Vietnam. Under the Manila pact that created the Southeast Asian Treaty Organization (SEATO) in late 1954, Laos, like South Vietnam, became a "protocol" nation that would be defended from communist aggression by the signatory powers like Thailand and the United States. During a visit to Bangkok for the inaugural SEATO meeting in February 1955, Secretary of State John Foster Dulles signaled the seriousness of US commitment to Laos by visiting Vientiane to urge attacks on the Pathet Lao territory. Under a diplomatic agreement between Vientiane and Washington in July, the US funded formation of a 25,000 man Royal Lao Army (RLA) – a comparatively large standing army beyond the means of a poor nation of less than three millions. Convinced that the RLA would serve as "trip wire" to block a communist invasion of Southeast Asia, the US Secretary of State invested 80 percent of US foreign aid to Laos in building a new army from the ground up.

But in November 1957, after months of talks, neutralist Prime Minister Souvanna Phouma and the communist Pathet Lao agreed to form a coalition government. Without consulting American officials, the neutralist Souvanna Phouma remained prime minister and Pathet Lao leader Souphanouvong became his finance minister. In February 1958, the Pathet Lao guerrilla forces were formally integrated into the Royal Lao Army, a development that aroused concern in Washington.

With the left on the edge of power, the CIA began to intervene actively in Lao politics through its clients in the army and the right wing. In the parliamentary elections of February 1958, the Agency provided clandestine funding for the right-wing parties but they polled badly – capturing only seven of the twenty-one seats contested. Nonetheless, backed by CIA funding, a new conservative coalition, which included the CIA's client Colonel Phoumi Nosavan, emerged in parliament to oust the neutralist Prime Minister Souvanna Phouma in August 1958. With the support of the CIA, Laos's new right-wing leader, Phoumi Nosavan, seized power in April 1960.

In August 1960, however, an obscure paratrooper, Captain Kong Le, angered at this blatant foreign intervention, led a neutralist coup that brought Souvanna Phouma back to power and forced Phoumi Nosavan from the capital. From his base further south along the Mekong in Savannakhet, Phoumi, with substantial CIA funding, rallied his forces and allied with Hmong leader Touby Lyfoung. In December, Phoumi's troops marched on Vientiane – capturing the capital after three days of artillery shelling and driving Kong Le's neutralists out of the city. Supplied by Soviet aircraft flying out of Hanoi, Kong Le retreated north, capturing the strategic Plain of Jars in January 1961. As North Vietnamese "volunteers" joined Kong Le and Pathet Lao forces, Soviet transport aircraft became a constant presence on the Plain of Jars, delivering supplies and ferrying troops. This operation represented the first projection of Soviet power into Southeast Asia, arousing deep concern in Washington and prompting formal diplomatic protest from the United States. Simultaneously, a Hmong force of 9,000 guerrillas – trained and armed by CIA operatives – seized control of mountains ringing the Plain of Jars for Phoumi and his new right-wing government.

As Laos descended into a three-way civil war, the great powers backing each faction came to the brink of nuclear war and then pulled back through summit negotiations. During these two years of tensions that led eventually to neutralization, tiny, impoverished Laos – through its remoteness and deeply divided politics – proved a dangerously volatile flash point of Cold War confrontation. In March 1961, the Pentagon, frustrated by the failure of the Royal Laotian Army to advance, had tried to convince the Kennedy White House to send a force of 10,000 marines to the Plain of Jars. When Kennedy seemed unwilling to support such a massive intervention, the Chair of the Joint Chiefs of Staff told the National Security Council in April 1961 that: "If we are given the right to use nuclear weapons in Laos, we can guarantee victory."

Instead of such a massive response with conventional or nuclear forces, President Kennedy agreed, while meeting Soviet leader Nikita Khrushchev at Vienna in June 1961, to consider a negotiated end to superpower confrontation over Laos. At the urging of the great powers, all Laotian factions agreed to a cease-fire. For the next 14 months, the negotiations over Laos continued, searching for an internal settlement that would lessen global tensions.

Then in May 1962, General Phoumi Nosavan, apparently concerned at the way diplomacy seemed to diminish US support, used a clash with communist Pathet Lao forces at Nam Tha Province in the country's remote northwest to claim, apparently falsely, that Chinese Communist forces had crossed the border – just as they had in Korea a decade earlier. Lacking accurate intelligence about this obscure quarter of the globe, the Kennedy White House, convinced that its mettle was being tested by the Soviets, went into crisis mode. Over a thousand US Marines advanced to the Lao border. The US Navy's Seventh Fleet took up battle stations off Thailand. A strategic reserve of four thousand more US troops arrived in Thailand. In case these forces failed, the White House planned nuclear attacks on China.

This crisis demonstrated the dangers when superpowers attached global significance to the volatile internal politics of such a fragile nation. Within weeks, the Kremlin expressed its support for neutralization, the Lao parties began to talk, and the world pulled back from the brink of nuclear war. On July 23 1962, the US delegation, led by the distinguished diplomat Averell Harriman, joined the Soviet Union and other parties to the conflict in signing an agreement at Geneva to respect Laos' neutrality and end all military operations inside the country. If observed, this agreement should have exempted Laos from any further role in the Cold War. The country's leading neutralist, Souvanna Phouma, again assumed office as prime minister with his authority now legitimated by this international agreement. With the signing of this neutralization accord, it became, within the loose fabric of international law, illegal for the United States to conduct any military operations in Laos.

In retrospect, Kennedy's withdrawal from Laos was a major strategic miscalculation. At the start of US intervention in Indochina in 1955, the Eisenhower administration, mindful of the region's geopolitical imperatives, had made Laos its primary bastion against communist infiltration into Southeast Asia. Reversing this policy, Kennedy pulled back from Cold War confrontation by neutralizing Laos in 1962 and then relied on aggressive counterinsurgency inside South Vietnam to contain communism. This policy change in Laos was, of course, part of Kennedy's global shift away from reliance upon conventional forces to contain communism in favor of his new "special warfare" doctrine of using US advisers to train local allies for counterinsurgency. But when counterinsurgency failed and the Vietnam War started two years later, there was no longer any restraint on North Vietnamese infiltration through Laos into South Vietnam. Now treaty-bound to respect Laos's neutrality, Washington, was in an ambiguous, even contradictory, position – forced to intervene in a country where it could no longer intervene. Ambiguity forced improvisation, leading the US to develop a new covert-warfare strategy that combined tribal mercenaries and massive air power as a substitute for the regular troops that it could no longer use inside Laos.

Covert War

Within months of signing the Geneva agreement on Laos, the White House began practicing a policy that defied its spirit. On the surface, US foreign policy respected the neutrality of Laos and the Geneva accord. But still seeing Laos as one of four

"roads" for a Communist China invasion of Southeast Asia, the Kennedy administration decided that Vientiane had to be held in the Western camp at all costs – no
matter what the Geneva agreement might say. Instead of backing the right wing as
Eisenhower had done, the Kennedy administration decided to regain its influence in
Laos by slowly pressing the neutralist government to adopt a more sympathetic
position to the US military presence in Laos. Instead of trying to stigmatize Souvanna
Phouma, the US courted him with aid and support. Simultaneously, communist
forces defied the Geneva agreement and strengthened their forces inside Laos.
Though the Soviet aircraft quickly left the Plain of Jars, the North Vietnamese troops
remained inside Laos with the Pathet Lao, soon supplemented by several thousand
more Vietnamese troops.

As the war inside Vietnam escalated, the neutralization of Laos under the Geneva
accord of 1962 would force the United States to use covert air and ground operations
to conceal its intervention. Neutralization thus fostered many of the contradictions
and contortions for the US presence in Laos – the clandestine bombing, the CIA's
reliance on its "Secret Army" of Hmong guerrillas, and the concealment of these
operations from the American public. After agreeing at Geneva in 1962 to end all
military operations inside Laos, Washington soon found that the escalating war along
the Vietnam–Laotian border made intervention in Laos a military imperative. Covert
warfare became Washington's solution to this diplomatic conundrum. Thus, by mid
1964 the White House, working through the CIA, was again intervening in Laos
through covert operations that maintained the facade of "plausible deniability."

Soon after his inauguration in 1961, President Kennedy had ordered the CIA to
support the right-wing military factions through covert operations. Using US Army
Special Forces as trainers, the Agency began to expand its clandestine force of Hmong
irregulars commanded by Major Vang Pao, a middle-ranking Hmong officer in the
Royal Lao Army. In the months after Geneva, particularly in 1963–4, the CIA
sparked local conflict between its Hmong irregulars and Pathet Lao forces around
the strategically-sited Plain of Jars in northeastern Laos. As the fighting in South
Vietnam escalated, right-wing factions in the Royal Lao Army, backed by the CIA,
launched a coup in April 1964, forcing Prime Minister Souvanna Phouma into a
coalition government. Simultaneously, the CIA began transforming its 9,000 strong
Hmong militia into the Secret Army, or *Armée Clandestine*, with 30,000 men, using
this covert-action asset to harass the Pathet Lao forces on the Plain of Jars.

These tensions soon erupted into conflict. In mid May, the Pathet Lao forces,
reacting to the right-wing's April coup, drove Kong Le's neutralist forces off the Plain
of Jars and installed a local revolutionary regime. Within days, the CIA's "A Team,"
civilian American pilots flying T-28 propeller-aircraft painted with Lao Air Force
markings, began bombing communist positions on the Plain of Jars. In June, Pathet
Lao gunners shot down two US jets on reconnaissance flights, sparking a sporadic US
bombing of the plain. By early 1965, the United States had started its secret bombing
of Laos and the CIA's Secret Army were fighting Pathet Lao forces around the Plain
of Jars.

The history of CIA's long covert alliance with the Hmong people of northern Laos
is perhaps the most complex and morally ambiguous relationship between the United

States and any of its Indochina allies. When the CIA began to intervene in Laos during the late 1950s, there were an estimated 290,000 Hmong people living in the mountains of northern Laos – about eight percent of the country's population of three million. Divided into tribes and clans, the Hmong were the most isolated of Laos's ethnic groups. Instead of living on the plains or upland valleys like the Lao or Tai, the Hmong clung to the mountain peaks, building their villages of plank-houses at elevations of 3,000 to 5,000 feet. From the green valley floors of northern Laos, cliffs soar skyward – with silvery threads of water falling down and tiny trees reaching up from limestone faults to ridges and peaks where the Hmong built their houses.

The Hmong economy was a mix of subsistence and cash crops. For subsistence, their farmers grew sticky rice through slash-and-burn cultivation. For cash, they cultivated the opium poppy – scraping the sap and selling the bundles of jelly-like narcotic to itinerant Yunnan Chinese merchants who moved through the mountains leading strings of pack horses. Within this mix of cash and subsistence, there was a gender-based division of labor. Men felled trees with axes and burned off the brush to clear the fields, while women planted the crops and did most of the harvesting, whether cutting the rice stalks or scraping the poppy bulbs.

But to portray the Hmong as tribal innocents, some of Rousseau's latter-day "noble savages" in the hills of Southeast Asia, would do them an injustice – in effect, to deny them a role in the making of their own history. To summarize very broadly, the Hmong alliance with America served the interests of certain elements in both societies that controlled the relationship. In allying with the Hmong, the CIA acquired tribal warriors ideally suited to clandestine warfare in a remote and extraordinarily difficult terrain where there were few alternative allies. As natives of these rugged mountains, Hmong males had the habit of long journeys for hunting and warfare that made them ideal guerrillas. Since they were a tribe, not a nation, CIA operatives could negotiate with Hmong leaders without incurring any formal diplomatic obligations.

Instead of a rigid hierarchy of nobles or king, the Hmong had a decentralized social structure of tribes and clans that engendered intense, protracted local rivalries. Since the prime political objective of Hmong clan leaders was to defeat internal rivals, they actively sought alliances with powerful external patrons who could reinforce their local power. From the Hmong perspective, the CIA was just another foreign patron, like the French, who could provide guns and food in exchange for soldiers and support.

What the Hmong did not understand, however, was that the CIA was not just another foreign ally. Through its growing expertise in covert warfare, the agency was developing techniques for the manipulation of tribal mercenaries to extract maximum casualties for minimum payment. In sum, the Americans could manipulate the Hmong more effectively than any of their previous patrons – whether Chinese, French, Vietnamese, or Lao – paying less silver for more blood than ever before.

Hmong involvement in the Indochina conflict had began in the final months of World War II when French commandos operating from India established a guerrilla *maquis*, or liberated zone, among the Hmong of northern Laos. When the French had first conquered Laos in the 1890s, the leading Hmong factions at the eastern edge of the Plain of Jars, the Ly and the Lo clans, had aligned themselves with the new regime, seeking external support in their struggles against local rivals. For several decades before the war, the Ly influence grew steadily from French patronage and the Lo lost power – their rivalry intensifying through a host of incidents, petty and substantial. When French commandos parachuted into the Plain of Jars at the end of World War II, they soon found allies among their former political clients, the Ly clan, now led by a rising French-educated politician named Touby Lyfoung. Once one or two Hmong clans took up arms to aid a few French commandos, the tribe became inextricably enmeshed, through internal divisions and external alliances, as partisans in an escalating Indochina conflict.

Just as one Hmong faction led by Touby Lyfoung sided with the French, so the rival Lo clan, under an ambitious young chief named Lo Faydang, allied with the communist Pathet Lao during the France's Indochina War (1946–54). When the Viet Minh attacked Laos in 1952, the Hmong of eastern Xieng Khouang Province, led by Touby Lyfuong, enlisted on the side of the French and later served them as local guerrillas in the losing battle at nearby Dien Bien Phu in 1954.

Only four years after the French withdrawal in 1954, the CIA recruited the Hmong as an effective, anticommunist force in northern Laos. Instead of dealing exclusively with Touby Lyfuong as the French had done, the CIA found a new leader in Vang Pao, then an obscure Hmong officer in the Royal Lao Army who compensated for his lack of traditional status with an extraordinary enthusiasm for combat. Through a complex process that we do not fully understand, Vang Pao would use the CIA's arms, finance, and air support to recruit many Hmong villages into a Secret Army that numbered 30,000 tribal guerrillas by the mid 1960s.

Overview of War

As fighting in South Vietnam intensified in 1964–5, the White House authorized clandestine bombing inside neutral Laos to interdict the communist lines of communication between North and South Vietnam. Accordingly, in March 1965 the Johnson administration approved two distinct air operations in Laos with separate command structures: "Operation Steel Tiger" to block enemy infiltration along the Ho Chi Minh Trail in southern Laos; and "Operation Barrel Roll" to support ground forces in northern Laos.

By late 1965, these decisions had created four main elements to America's secret war in Laos. Most importantly, in southern Laos the US Air Force launched a massive strategic bombing campaign against the Ho Chi Minh trail, seeking desperately to slow the flow of North Vietnam's men and material into South Vietnam. In the north, US Air Force tactical fighters, flying from bases in northeastern Thailand, engulfed the mountains surrounding the Plain of Jars in a spreading fire storm. Backed by this tactical air support, the CIA's Secret Army of 30,000 Hmong guerrillas fought most of the battles for the ridges of northeastern Laos following the ebb and flow of the monsoon rains – the CIA hill-tribe militia advancing under air cover in the wet season and the communist Pathet Lao and their North Vietnamese allies recovering lost ground in the dry months. On nearby battlefields in northern Laos, the Royal Lao Army fought a conventional war against the Pathet Lao forces, usually mounting desultory defense of the main roads or royal capital.

By the end of the Vietnam War, Laos had become the world's most heavily bombed nation. Between 1965 and 1971, Laos, an impoverished country with only three million people, absorbed 1,600,000 tons of bombs – 10 times the 160,000 tons dropped on Japan throughout World War II. By the time the bombing stopped in April 1973, the US Air Force, after nine years of bombing, had dropped an unimaginable 2.1 million tons on Laos – a figure equal to the total Allied tonnage of 2.1 million tons of conventional bombs dropped on both Germany and Japan in all of World War II.

As the Vietnam War escalated, the US Air Force expanded its air operations over southern Laos until they became a massive air war with 3,000 sorties per month by late 1967. For the next five years, the US Air Force conducted a high-tech, electronic bombing campaign against the truck convoys on the Ho Chi Minh Trail. At a peak cost of $800 million per annum, the US Air Force dropped thousands of electronic sensors across the mountains of southern Laos camouflaged as plants to detect the sound, vibration, or heat that might indicate North Vietnamese trucks moving south with men and material. As these sensors broadcast their electronic noise, a computer bank under "Operation Igloo White" at the US Air Force base in Nakhon Phanom, in northeastern Thailand, processed the acoustic and seismic pulses to create a line of light called "the worm" on the visual monitor of an US Air Force technician. After computations to determine the worm's position, its coordinates were then fed to US fighter bombers that, night after night, dropped tons of bombs on the supposed truck convoys moving down the Ho Chi Minh Trail. From October 1970 to May 1971, US Air Force claimed destruction of 25,000 North Vietnamese trucks in southern Laos. The Igloo White computers said there was a truck, Air Force night bombers reported dropping bombs where the truck was supposed to be, and the US Air Force reported that this invisible truck must have been destroyed. Indeed, it had been destroyed. But there was only one problem with this impressive yield: the US Air Force could never produce the visual evidence, photographs or sightings, that proved such destruction. If a small area like southern Laos had been, in fact, littered with the charred, smoking ruins of 25,000 trucks, it should have produced visual evidence of a spectacular visibility.

Within this extraordinary total of 2.1 million tons, some 500,000 tons were concentrated inside a narrow, hundred-mile corridor in northern Laos that reached from North Vietnam's border, across the communist-controlled Sam Neua Province, to the Plain of Jars. From 1964 to 1971, the Plain of Jars region became the main battlefield between the CIA's Secret Army and the Pathet Lao guerrillas. At the start of this massive bombardment, this plain had a population of some 50,000 peasants, villages made of bamboo and thatch, a few market towns with medieval Buddhist temples, and clusters of massive stone jars on the hillsides hinting at the ancient origins of the local Lao Phoueun civilization. The plain is a diamond-shaped plateau, 3,500 feet in elevation, with rolling grasslands 40 miles wide and encircled by ragged ridges, covered with heavy forests and scattered Hmong villages, that soar upward to peaks of 5,000, 8,000, and 9,000 feet elevation. The old French colonial Route 7, the main road from northern Laos to North Vietnam, crosses the plain from west to east, while smaller roads lead north and south to adjacent Laotian provinces and trails climb up the ridges to Hmong villages. Within the often impenetrable mountains of northeastern Laos, the Plain of Jars was thus a cross-roads, a strategic prize for both the communist forces in the caves of Sam Neua Province just to the northeast and the CIA secret army based at Long Tieng valley just to the southwest.

Thus, the ultimate aim of US air operations was to block the communist advance across the Plain of Jars towards the Royal Lao government's capital at Vientiane only a hundred miles further south. If the communists had somehow captured the capital while the war in Vietnam raged, then they could, under the 1962 Geneva agreement, demand an end to the US bombing campaign against the Ho Chi Minh trail in southern Laos and end any possible chance of an American victory in Vietnam.

After the Pathet Lao captured the Plain of Jars in mid 1964, the White House made it a free-fire zone and expanded the air war – increasing its own tonnage and arming the Laotian Air Force with an additional T-28 fighter-bombers and C-47 gunships. By late 1964, the US Air Force stationed seventy-five fighter-bombers in northern Thailand for "Operation Barrel Roll," the sustained but still clandestine bombing of northeastern Laos. Four years later, as the fighting for the Plain of Jars intensified, US bombers flying out of Thailand dropped some 230,000 tons of bombs on northern Laos. By 1969, the US Air Force was flying 300 bombing sorties a day over northern Laos in support of the CIA's Secret Army. Following the pace of ground warfare, the bombing intensified in 1970–1, with the first use of B-52 strategic bombers, and then tapered off until the cessation of US combat operations in 1973. By war's end, this Plain of Jars, a small region with poor highland farms and no infrastructure, received over three times the total dropped on industrial Japan, becoming the most intensely bombarded place on the face of the planet.

As the air war intensified from 1964 to 1971, the US embassy in Vientiane, without effective oversight from the White House or Pentagon, controlled this massive bombardment and managed to conceal it from the US Congress and the public. After US military operations in South Vietnam escalated in 1964, President Johnson appointed William Sullivan, a career diplomat who had negotiated the neutralization of Laos two years before, as his ambassador in Vientiane. During his five years in his post, Sullivan, known as the "Field Marshall" among senior US military in Saigon, took command of the air war and expanded it from a few clandestine CIA bombing runs into the largest aerial bombardments in military history. Under instructions from the White House, Sullivan won Prime Minister Souvanna Phouma's tacit consent for a clandestine bombing of Laos in December 1964 and then assembled an *ad hoc* command structure that placed the US Embassy at the epicenter of this air war. While the US Air Force directed the strategic bombing of the Ho Chi Minh trail in southern Laos, Ambassador Sullivan and his successor, G. McMurtrie Godley, controlled the tactical bombing against communist forces in the northern mountains around the Plain of Jars.

In this tight command structure designed for maximum secrecy, US Air Force Forward Air Controllers known as "the Ravens," flying at low elevations, radioed possible targets to the main CIA base Long Tieng; inside the Embassy the US Air

Force attaché, Colonel Robert Tyrell, and the CIA station chief endorsed the targets to Ambassador Sullivan; and, once he approved, Colonel Tyrell contacted the 7/13 Air Force command across the Mekong River at Udorn, to dispatch the fighter-bombers. As bombing sorties rose from 4,658 in 1965 to 7,316 in 1966, the costs escalated and the White House kept Congress ignorant by shifting funds from other military and intelligence accounts. For nearly six years, the US Embassy directed one of history's largest air wars, concealing it from both Congress and the international community to preserve the fiction of US compliance with Laotian neutrality.

The truth did not emerge until October 1969 when Senator Stuart Symington chaired closed-door hearings in the Senate Foreign Relations Committee that remained, like the war itself, secret for another six months until heavily-edited transcripts were finally released. In their testimony, American officials claimed that great care was taken to avoid civilian casualties. Called to explain his management of the bombing, Ambassador William Sullivan minimized its extent: "The United States Air Force contribution was limited to striking at the logistic routes ... or at points of concentration which into the area where the actual ground battling was taking place ... it was the policy not to attack populated areas." His Air Force attaché Colonel Tyrrell was even bolder: "Villages, even in a freedrop zone, would be restricted from bombing." Congress was not satisfied, and two years later Senator Symington won passage of legislation setting a $350 million ceiling on all US aid to Laos, effectively re-asserting legislative control over this secret war and its financial legerdemain.

Viewed in retrospect, it would seem that managing such a massive air war outside the regular Air Force command, with only a small staff of attachés and CIA agents to clear targets and conduct post-attack assessments, probably allowed a wide latitude for error – particularly as the sorties climbed into the hundreds every day. In late 1971, the US Senate Subcommittee on Refugees reported that "the sheer volume and constancy of bombing activity since 1968 makes effective control of these strikes almost impossible." Taking a bleaker view of the US air war, the few American journalists covering the war generally agreed, as reporter Robert Shaplen put it, that the aim of the US bombing in northern Laos was "to destroy the social and economic fabric of Pathet Lao areas."

During its ten years of full combat, the CIA's Secret Army relied upon a relatively simple structure to maintain a remarkably efficient army suited to the harsh mountain warfare in northern Laos. From its secret base at Long Tieng valley, just south of the Plain of Jars, the CIA controlled a largely Hmong guerrilla army under the operational command of General Vang Pao, a Hmong career officer in the Royal Lao Army. Through a self-contained radio net and a shuttle service of helicopters and light aircraft, the CIA ferried men and material from Long Tieng to over 200 air strips near Hmong villages on ridges and mountains scattered across northeastern Laos. To avoid Congressional scrutiny, the entire CIA operation was concealed within the large US Agency for International Development (USAID) bureaucracy as an humanitarian relief operation for war refugees.

To mask the scale of the CIA's military operations at Long Tieng, USAID maintained an refugee relief center at nearby Sam Thong where journalists and official visitors from Washington could tour hospitals, schools, and food distribution centers under the gruff gaze of its legendary director, Edgar "Pop" Buell, an Indiana corn farmer who gave his life to this anticommunist cause. Hmong villages that provided recruits were rewarded with regular rations of rice and protein, delivered by USAID which contracted the CIA's own airline, Air America, to drop the goods from C-130 cargo aircraft. CIA officers, many seconded from the US Army's Special Forces, worked with the Hmong guerrillas, training them in weapons, tactics, communications, and sabotage.

This Secret Army, or *Armée Clandestine*, was charged with three main missions: to fight the Pathet Lao advance in northern Laos, thus maintaining a covert US military presence without violating the country's neutrality; conduct intelligence operations along the border with North Vietnam; and, finally, to defend critical American installations such as the secret guidance facility at Phou Pha Thi near the North Vietnamese border.

Although this secret war was fought on the ground by tribal guerrillas, it was held together by one of the most remarkable air armadas in the history of warfare. To tie these scattered mountain-top villages into people armed, the CIA's Air America had a fleet of agile U-10 Heliocouriers, an aircraft designed by the Swiss to land on Alpine peaks. As the war expanded, the CIA brought in helicopter gunships and cargo aircraft to increase Hmong air mobility and provide tactical air support. To air drop supplies to the Hmong villages, the CIA used C-130 transports with rear doors and cargo kickers – the working grunts of this air war. The Royal Lao Air Force operated squadrons of antiquated T-28 propeller trainers that were effective in close support bombing. Flying out of bases in nearby northeast Thailand, wings of US Air Force fighter bombers pounded Laos during daylight hours. Later, after 1970, B-52 strategic bombers unleashed massive attacks on critical war zones, notably the Plain of Jars. After dusk, "Puff the Magic Dragon" replaced the jets and the bombers. By cutting gun-doors in the side of C-47s, a World War II vintage, two engine-transport, and arming them with rapid-fire naval machine guns, the US Air Force created the AC-47 gunship, known as the "Puff-the-Magic Dragon ship" – a killing machine with "people sniffers" that could detect concentrations of ammonia in mammal urine and guns that could unleash a hail of six-thousand rounds per minute upon the monkeys, water buffalo, guerrillas, or farmers in the darkness below. By 1971, one US diplomat, speaking with what scholar Charles Stevenson called "quietly expressed pride," felt that the United States had discovered a new strategic doctrine of using bombs as a replacement for ground forces in foreign intervention: "The Lao have shown us a new way of fighting a war."

Hiking in the hills of western Xieng Khouang Province in mid-1971, this historian became an accidental witness to the air war. As I reached Hmong villages in mountains at the western edge of the Plain of Jars, the intensity of this airwar etched a cat's cradle of bomber contrails into the azure blue of the highland sky above. Out of sight at 35,000 feet were the command-and-control craft that coordinated the air operations. Beneath them at 30,000 feet, the B-52s strategic bombers periodically dropped their racks of five-hundred pound bombs in fiery boxes. Next, still invisible to the naked eye, were the tankers hovering at 20,000 feet for refueling. During daylight hours, the contrails of the fighter bombers were always visible, flying to and from their bombing runs at 10,00 feet. Hovering just above the plain at 2,000 to 5,000 feet were the "Raven" forward air controllers who spotted targets and radioed coordinates for suggested strikes. At night, as I slept in a Hmong village on the edge of the free-fire zone, the sound of the C-47 engines faded almost out of hearing, then became stronger as "Puff the Magic Dragon" passed nearby – a droning punctuated by occasional bursts as machine guns fired 6,000 rounds per minute whenever the "people sniffers" detected mammals in the dark. While this layered air armada hovered above the plain, night and day, for over five years, there were no US troops in the area and even the CIA's Hmong guerrillas only occasionally penetrated the Plain of Jars. Out of sight of Congress and the American people, the CIA and the US Air Force had created a new kind of mechanized battlefield that, in defiance of conventional military doctrine, had made air power alone an effective strategic weapon that took and held ground without any infantry.

After that night of listening to the droning gunships, I woke the next morning to find a group of twenty refugees, sitting dirty and tired midst bundles of their worldly goods, who had somehow emerged from that hail of gunfire. They were the remains of a larger group of villagers who had fled from the Moung Soi area on the Plain of Jars two weeks before to escape an air war that had forced them to live in caves and farm in the dark when the skies were free of the US fighters. Unable to survive in such conditions, some ninety villagers had started hiking west towards government territory. Twice at night during their march, the gunships had found them and fired. These twenty whom I met that morning, almost all women and children, were the only survivors.

Refugees from the Plain of Jars reacted to the air war with a mix of shock, displacement, and grief. In 1972, an American volunteer working in Laos, Fred Branfman, collected memoirs from ordinary refugees who had fled from the Plain of Jars and published them in a slender volume titled *Voices from the Plain of Jars*. In a hand-written statement, a twenty-one year-old farmer from the Plain of Jars expressed a wrenching sadness: "Before my village had prosperity and good homes for Laotian rice farmers.... But then came the present time, as we and our rice fields were hit by the planes and burned; our homes were hit and burned, our belongings completely lost. I think back and within me tears want to fall. But there are not enough. For I have fled from the village of my birth." A thirty-three year-old woman recalled the terror of living under the massive US bombing: "I saw this in the village of my birth, as every day and every night the planes came to drop bombs on us. We lived in holes to protect our lives ... I saw my cousin die in the field of death. My heart was most disturbed and my voice called out loudly as I ran to the houses. Thus, I saw life and death for the people on account of the war of many airplanes in the region of Xieng Khouang. Until there were no houses at all. And the cows and the buffaloes were dead. Until everything was leveled and you could see only the red, red ground. I think of this time and still I am afraid."

From meeting refugees and compiling their memoirs, Branfman concluded that the US bombing campaign destroyed human society on the Plain of Jars. Prior to the start of the air war in 1964, the Plain of Jars had been, in his words, a "picturesque and prosperous rural society of some fifty-thousand people" that had "long been the largest fruit-producing and cattle raising area of Laos." Then, for over five years, the US Air Force launched a systematic assault upon this society, bombarding the plain with "white phosphorous, fragmentation, ball-bearing and flechette anti-personnel bombs, immediate and delayed-action high explosives." In 1970–1, the United States Information Service (USIS) interviewed 213 civilian refugees from the Plain of Jars and found that 96 percent had their villages bombed, 75 percent suffered damage to their homes, and 61 percent had seen a person killed by the bombing. While communist soldiers usually eluded the air attacks, it was these civilians who suffered heavily. In interviews with over a thousand refugees, Fred Branfman established the bombing took a "heavy toll on the civilian population" because they "could not survive on the run and had to remain near the villages: which were the targets most often hit." Under this unrestrained US bombing campaign, "village after village was leveled, countless people buried alive by high explosives, or burnt alive by napalm and white phosphorous, or riddled by anti-personnel bomb pellets." By 1969, "after a recorded history of 700 years," human civilization on the Plain of Jars had, in Branfman's view, "disappeared."

Twenty years after the end of the bombing, my own visit to the Plain of Jars in 1994 seemed to confirm Branfman's bleak assessment. Every vista was marked by bomb craters – criss-crossing the hills, scarring the valleys, and marching across the countryside through towns and villages. In Xiengkhouangville, the region's capital, Buddhist temples were still roofless rubble, as was the modest palace of the region's royal family. Population had not recovered, the maimed were omnipresent, and countless unexploded bombs and antipersonnel bomblets were still causing new casualties.

Shrouded in secrecy until 1971, the bombing of civilian targets could not arouse public opposition and became a model for later US intervention in Cambodia. In 1969, President Richard Nixon ordered secret B-52 bombing raids against communist sanctuaries in eastern Cambodia. After the US openly intervened in 1970, massive B-52 bombing raids on extensive, heavily-populated areas of central Cambodia became the main US weapon in blocking the communist capture of the capital. In short, the tactics of air warfare under the pressures of covert warfare in Laos became a standard military doctrine that the US Air Force applied in Cambodia and elsewhere.

Tides of War

Although this clandestine war in northern Laos continued for ten years, it received almost no press coverage and remains, even a quarter-century later, the least understood chapter in America's Vietnam debacle. After the communist Pathet Lao forces attacked Captain Kong Le's neutralists and captured the Plain of Jars in 1964, two overlapping armies would battle for northeastern Laos – not a war of territory but of elevations. In the upland valleys, the Pathet Lao controlled much of the territory from North Vietnam's border to the Plain of Jars. Above them on the ridges and peaks, the CIA's Hmong guerrillas, supplied by Air America, clung to mountain peaks across the breadth of northern Laos all the way to the border of North Vietnam.

For eight years, this see-saw battle for the rugged northeast raged back-and-forth across a narrow 200-mile span of mountains from the capital at Vientiane, across the Plain of Jars, to North Vietnam's border. If the Pathet Lao had captured the capital in one of its annual offensives, then a new coalition government could have invoked the 1962 Geneva accords to force a suspension of all US air operations, particularly the massive bombing of the Ho Chi Minh trail in southern Laos. North Vietnam's unmolested transit of men and material through Laos to South Vietnam would have been a critical blow to any American chances of victory in Vietnam. Though conducted in secrecy for over five years, this war for control of Laos's remote, rugged northeast was not a backwater or a sideshow. It was, in fact, central to the whole American war effort. Its battles were thus fought with an intensity that made them a maelstrom consuming all in its path – the Hmong militia, the Pathet Lao guerrillas, and the hapless civilians of the Plain of Jars. Even though this mountain warfare was also critical for the survival of the non-communist government in Vientiane, its lowland Lao conscripts in the regular Royal Lao Army units seemed to see these mountains as an alien terrain and simply refused to fight, often breaking ranks after brief contact with the enemy. Thus, the Hmong soldiers of General Vang Pao's Secret Army did almost all the fighting and all of the dying in this brutal mountain warfare.

In retrospect, there seem two distinct phases in this decade of war for control of northeastern Laos. From 1964 to 1968, the CIA used the Hmong Secret Army as defensive guerrilla forces to hold the highland ridges above the Plain of Jars and collect intelligence about communist operations. From 1969 to 1974, by contrast, the CIA deployed its Secret Army like conventional infantry and provided them with the tactical air support to launch offensives against the communist forces on the Plain of Jars.

During the initial guerrilla phase, the Hmong guerrillas performed reasonably well. But they could not stem the relentless pressure of disciplined communist infantry, a combined force of Pathet Lao guerrillas and regular North Vietnamese units. One-by-one, the CIA's mountain-top bastions ringing the Plain of Jars fell to determined communist attacks. In February 1964, 5,000 North Vietnamese troops captured the Hmong base on Phou Khe, a 7,000 foot mountain southwest of the plain, after a bloody fifteen-hour assault that routed the CIA's tribal allies. Two years later, a combined Pathet Lao–North Vietnamese assault overwhelmed Hmong defenders at Na Khang, an important CIA base northeast of the plain used to launch helicopter rescue missions for downed pilots inside North Vietnam.

The most important defeat came at Phou Pha Thi, a 5,800-foot eagle-nest mountain located just 17 miles from North Vietnam's border and 160 miles from Hanoi. When the US bombing over North Vietnam intensified in 1966, the US Air Force installed a sophisticated Tactical Air Navigation System (TACAN) on this mountain that proved capable of accurate, all-weather guidance for jets striking within 60 miles of Hanoi. The Air Force also used the base to launch helicopters into North Vietnam to rescue downed American pilots. To protect the system and its sixteen Air Force technicians, the CIA assigned 300 Secret Army guerrillas to guard the mountain and protected its approaches with an elaborate net of anti-personnel mines. During the 1968 Tet offensive in South Vietnam, the People's Liberation Army of Vietnam and Pathet Lao launched a major offensive against the Secret Army's bases in Sam Neua Province.

The battle for this mountain was particularly bloody. As a high, eagle's nest plateau near the Vietnam border, Phou Pha Thi allowed US Air Force radar to "look down" over the whole Red River delta – greatly increasing the accuracy of the US bombing of North Vietnam. Determined to capture the installation, on March 11 1968 North Vietnamese soldiers scaled the mountain and attacked the installation, scattering the defenders and killing or capturing eleven American technicians. The CIA rescued three Americans by helicopter and then called in air strikes to destroy the valuable TACAN radar system.

Such combat was like placing a human hand on an anvil – with the hammer blows of Vietnamese and Pathet Lao offensives smashing the Hmong fingers against the rock face of these mountains. With nearly a thousand dead between January and March 1968, General Vang Pao's forces faced certain defeat in the northeast. Rather than let the Hmong villages remain under Pathet Lao control, the US Air Force increased its bombing and the CIA conducted a mass evacuation of all Hmong northeast of the Plain of Jars to refugee camps in the mountains further south. In retrospect, it seems that it was only the massive escalation in air operations that saved the Secret Army from defeat. Though many Hmong and Lao refugees were evacuated by air, others were forced into long, unplanned marches through mountain terrain that killed some ten percent of the villagers, usually the very old and very young.

As communist offensives intensified in 1969–70, the CIA converted General Vang Pao and his Hmong guerrillas into conventional ground troops and supplied them with massive tactical air support to mount a series of hard-fought offensives against communist forces on the Plain of Jars. When President Johnson proclaimed a bombing halt over North Vietnam in October 1968, the US Air Force used its now surplus bombing capacity to support the CIA's covert operations in northern Laos. After flying only fifteen or twenty sorties a day for four years, US fighter-bombers based in northern Thailand expanded operations to 300 sorties a day in 1969 and 1970, dropping some 230,000 tons of bombs on northern Laos. Gradually, the number of sorties dropped to around 100 a day until the bombing ended in mid 1973.

In the first of these conventional offensives in September 1969, the CIA, ignoring the high cost to the Hmong soldiers, threw these ill-trained tribal guerrillas into "Operation About Face," an assault against the battle-hardened North Vietnamese 316th Division dug in on the Plain of Jars. Backed by massive US air support reaching 200 sorties per day, General Vang Pao and his Secret Army temporarily captured much of the plain. After the bombing drove the Pathet Lao out of the provincial capital at Xieng Khouangville, Vang Pao's troops flew in, occupied the town, and seized massive communist supply caches. In anticipation of an enemy offensive, the CIA evacuated some 20,000 civilians from the Plain of Jars to refugee camps near the capital Vientiane. In early 1970, the communist forces counter-attacked, recapturing Xieng Khouangville and pushing south towards the main CIA base at Long Tieng. To blunt the attack, the US Air Force used B-52 strategic bombers in northern Laos for the first time, dropping over a thousand tons of bombs on the plain in "boxes" up to two-miles long that incinerated all in their path. Undeterred by the massive bombing, the North Vietnamese pushed Vang Pao's forces off the plain in March 1970 and threatened Long Tieng. Their advance hit the heart of the Hmong army, forcing 110,000 refugees around the main CIA bases to evacuate further south into a forty-mile wide strip between Long Tieng and the Vientiane plain. After a massive air attack by gunships and bombers, the communist forces pulled back to the Plain of Jars within a few weeks.

In May 1971, General Vang Pao launched "Operation About Face II" and, again backed by massive US air power, managed to re-capture the Plain of Jars. These battles were his last victories. Henceforth, his Secret Army would be on a long, slow slide into defeat. Some six months later, the communist forces counter-attacked. Using 130 mm artillery to crush the Secret Army's defenses, some 12,000 Pathet Lao and North Vietnamese troops re-captured the Plain of Jars despite massive B-52 bombing and then forced Vang Pao's army further south, capturing the center of USAID refugee operations at Sam Thong and threatening the main CIA base at nearby Long Tieng. With over 50,000 Hmong refugees at their rear, General Vang Pao's 8,000 irregulars fought desperately, and successfully, for four months to defend the ridges surrounding Long Tieng. Although the US Air Force flew thousands of missions and used "smart bombs" to blast enemy artillery, the communist forces hung on until the onset of the monsoon rains again forced their withdrawal to the Plain of Jars. This fighting drove many of Hmong villagers further south, compressing some 150,000 refugees into that narrow crescent between Long Tieng and the Vientiane Plain. Since these evacuations were often ill-planned marches through mountains and jungle, the weakest Hmong, infants and elderly, died in great numbers. Hmong elders feel that each forced migration brought a heavy death rate to their villages – about 10 percent when the marches were orderly and up to 30 percent when refugees became lost in the forest.

During this second phase of conventional combat, the Hmong took casualties that strained their limited population which had numbered little more than a quarter million at the war's start. By late 1971, Vang Pao's army of 30,000 had been decimated with an estimated 3,300 killed and 5,400 wounded – about one-third of his combat forces. According to a US Air Force study: "By 1971, many families were down to the last surviving male (often a youth of 13 or 14), and survival of the tribe was becoming a major concern." As the Secret Army's ranks thinned, the CIA filled the depleted Hmong ranks with boy soldiers and Thai regulars – allowing Vang Pao's army to fight on.

As the devastating force of the US bombing campaign slowed and finally stopped in 1973, the war turned definitively against General Vang Pao and his Hmong infantry. In the war's final months, it was only the US Air Force that saved his forces from defeat. At the close of their final dry-season offensive in April 1972, the communist forces remained in the hills just north of Long Tieng, blocking Vang Pao's offensive when he then tried to advance under the cover of the annual monsoon rains. Six months later, as the communist forces mobilized from these nearby positions for an assault on Long Tieng, US Air Force's new F-111 fighters, deployed in Laos for the first time, used their night and all-weather instrumentation to bomb enemy forces in the dark, while F-4s and B-52s continued their daylight attacks. Under such extraordinary round-the-clock bombardment, the communist forces finally pulled back to the Plain of Jars in December to wait for the expected cease-fire.

After the United States and North Vietnam signed the Paris Peace Accords in January 1973, the chief US negotiator, Henry Kissinger, advised Prime Minister Souvanna Phouma that American support for his government was winding down. A month later, the Royal Lao government and the communist Pathet Lao agreed to end the fighting and rule the country jointly. In April, after US B-52s bombed the Plain of Jars for the last time to support Vang Pao's forces, all US bombing in Laos ended. After the communists joined a coalition government at Vientiane that same month, the last CIA operatives flew out of Laos – leaving the Hmong crowded around Long Tieng without food or ammunition.

A year later, the Pathet Lao and North Vietnamese forces launched a major attack on General Vang Pao's base at Long Tieng. Unwilling to risk his shaky coalition with the communists, Prime Minister Souvanna Phouma refused to support Vang Pao with his small Royal Laotian Air Force. On May 10 1975, Vang Pao and twelve Hmong elders issued a statement reminding the CIA of its past promises of protection and appealing for a mass evacuation of their Hmong followers to Thailand. But the Agency refused to mount a massive air lift. Finally, four days later, as Pathet Lao forces closed in on Long Tieng, the CIA flew Vang Pao and his family to Thailand – their first step on the road to exile in America. In December, the Lao People's Revolutionary Party dropped its nationalist Pathet Lao facade, abolished the 600 year-old monarchy, and established a Marxist regime – the Lao People's Democratic Republic.

Despite these crippling losses in the last four years of war, Vang Pao was able to extract new recruits from the Hmong villages and kept fighting until the war's end in 1974. By 1969, 30 percent of Vang Pao's recruits were under the age of fourteen. By 1971, heavy casualties forced Vang Pao to draw almost all his recruits from the ten to fourteen age bracket. Faced with such heavy casualties, why did the Hmong continue to give their children to the CIA's Secret Army? The answer lies in the nature of the agency's relationship with Vang Pao and, in turn, his controls over the Hmong.

Dynamics of Covert War

Throughout fifteen years of secret war (1960–74), the CIA's relationship with Vang Pao was the key to its covert operations. Although the Hmong had allied with the French, their traditional leader, the *kaitong* or chief Touby Lyfoung, had been unwilling to take heavy casualties. Speaking with elderly Hmong commanders in the early 1970s, they recalled with fondness how Touby took the French arms but usually ordered retreat at the first sign of heavy combat. In this colonial exchange relationship, the Hmong, under Touby's leadership, paid little blood for a considerable reward in guns, silver, and rice.

Instead of a traditional leader with the political authority and autonomy to manipulate the alliance, the CIA selected an ordinary Hmong officer, Major Vang Pao, and used its influence to transform him into a powerful patron among the Hmong villages. Over the long years of their alliance, the CIA arranged Vang Pao's promotion from major to general in the Laotian Army, a rank that gave him a non-traditional kind of prestige. Invested with state authority and massive foreign resources, Vang Pao became an effective tribal broker who mobilized his people for protracted war. Since Vang Pao's authority came from his external patrons, rather than local prestige, he was more responsive to foreign pressure for combat and casualties. Under his leadership, the balance in clientelist exchange shifted markedly, and Hmong soldiers would now shed considerable blood to earn their guns, rice, and cash.

As the success of its secret war became dependent upon Vang Pao, the CIA used several tactics to raise his prestige among the Hmong – most importantly, by giving him the resources to become a powerful patron, and, secondarily, by encouraging his alliance with more traditional tribal elite, notably the Hmong cabinet minister Touby Lyfoung. In its initial report on the Hmong army to the White House in 1961, the CIA stated that "political leadership . . . is in the hands of Touby Lyfoung, who now operates mostly out of Vientiane" and "the military leader is Lt-Col Vang Pao, who is field commander." As CIA director William Colby later explained, the agency promoted Vang Pao as a "new breed of tribal leadership," but simultaneously encouraged "the expression of external deference to the old leaders." Accordingly, when the war intensified in the late 1960s Vang Pao acquired the vestiges of traditional legitimacy by arranging for his son and daughter to marry the children of Touby Lyfoung, who still had the authority of a traditional *kaitong* or chief. These maneuvers did raise Vang Pao's prestige, but it was the material and coercive aspects of his relationship with the tribe that would remain paramount.

To prosecute a war that offered the ordinary Hmong soldier little more than rice and death, the CIA gave its client General Vang Pao control over all air transport into tribal villages scattered across northern Laos. In effect, the general held power over the shipment of rice, the tribe's main subsistence commodity, into the villages; and the transport of opium, the tribe's only cash crop, out to markets in Vientiane and beyond. With a choke-hold over the economic essentials of every Hmong household, General Vang Pao imposed a centralized command over this disparate tribe, quickly elevating himself from a minor officer into a powerful tribal warlord who could extract boy soldiers for the slaughter in this hopeless war. Through these mechanisms, the CIA, through Vang Pao, transformed the Hmong from a scattering of clans and households into a unified people mobilized for war.

Until the start of the war, the traditional Hmong economy, as discussed above, had depended upon rice production for subsistence and opium cultivation for cash. Through its air power, the CIA allowed Vang Pao to take control of both. As the fighting withdrew Hmong males from the villages, the slash-and-burn rice fields soon lost their fertility after one or two harvests. The younger males, who in ordinary times would have cleared forests for new fields, were dead, wounded, or away at war. With each monsoon cycle of fighting and planting, the villages became increasingly dependent upon USAID air drops of rice – shipments that Vang Pao controlled. As fighting swept through the valleys and Chinese traders could no longer reach the villages with their strings of highland horses to buy the opium, Vang Pao also used the CIA's Air America to collect the bundles of raw narcotic from the villages and transport it to market. Though long a significant source of cash for the Hmong, the opium poppy's importance increased since its fields remained fertile for up to ten years and the harvest could compensate, in part, for the decline in household income from the loss of male labor.

Within this complex exchange relationship, Vang Pao won considerable authority and proved skillful in manipulating his CIA advisers. "CIA had identified an officer... originally trained by the French, who had not only the courage but also the political acumen...for leadership in such a conflict...," recalled retired director William Colby. "His name was Vang Pao, and he had the enthusiastic admiration of the CIA officers, who knew him...as a man who...knew how to say no as well as yes to Americans." Many CIA field operatives admired his ruthlessness. When agent Thomas Clines, commander of the CIA's secret base at Long Tieng, demanded an immediate interrogation of six prisoners, Vang Pao ordered them executed on the spot. Clines was impressed. "What I meant to say, general, is that I would *appreciate* it if you would *allow* us to interrogate prisoners, *please*."

Since opium reinforced Vang Pao's authority, pragmatism dictated that the CIA should tolerate the traffic. While this compromise might have been understandable at the outset in 1960 or even in 1965, it became less comprehensible when the Agency's Laotian allies began producing heroin for US combat forces fighting in South Vietnam. In 1968–9, CIA clients opened a cluster of heroin laboratories in the Golden Triangle – the tri-border region where Burma, Thailand, and Laos converge. When Hmong officers loaded opium on the CIA's own Air America and the commander of the Lao Army, General Ouane Rattikone, opened a major heroin laboratory to supply US troops in South Vietnam, the Agency was silent. In a secret internal report compiled in 1972, the CIA's Inspector General explained the reasons for the Agency's inaction: "The past involvement of many of these officers in drugs is well known, yet their goodwill...considerably facilitates the military activities of Agency-supported irregulars." Instead of trying to restrain drug trafficking by its Laotian assets, the agency engaged in concealment.

How did these political dynamics allow Vang Pao to extract boy soldiers from their families for near certain slaughter in a losing war, one in which the Hmong had, at best, an ambiguous stake? When the war turned against the CIA in 1968–9 and the secret army started suffering heavy casualties, the general held the economic and military levers to extract thirteen and fourteen-year old recruits from the villages to renew his ranks. In 1971, I hiked into Long Pot district, west of the Plain of Jars, where most able-bodied males between the age of 15 and 40 had been wounded or killed in seven years of guerrilla warfare. When the Hmong district leader refused Long Tieng's orders to deliver the fourteen year olds, Vang Pao sent a non-local team of intelligence operatives with a radio into the village to monitor this quiet revolt. Acting on his orders, USAID stopped its rice deliveries to the village even though they were supposed to be humanitarian relief goods. By the time I arrived, the village had been without rice deliveries for a month and hunger was evident in the distended bellies of the children. The pressure on the village was enormous – send the boy soldiers or starve. The same high casualties that forced Vang Pao to demand boy soldiers from Long Pot also denied the village the labor that it needed to remain self-sufficient in rice, creating a cruel demographic trap that forced most villages to deliver their children for slaughter in a war that was both endless and hopeless.

Aftermath

Although an effective CIA client, General Vang Pao left a troubled legacy for his Hmong. For over a decade, he pressed his soldiers to take heavy casualties in a war whose outcome would make little difference in their lives. When the fighting was over in 1975, Vang Pao fled Laos, leaving his Hmong followers to face retaliation by a victorious Pathet Lao government. Conflicts soon erupted between the remaining Hmong and the new socialist government, eventually forcing over 100,000 tribes-men to flee across the Mekong into a chain of Thai refugee camps where most were eventually processed for migration to America. While his followers lived under harsh communist rule or in bleak refugee camps, Vang Pao, with the help of a loyal CIA case officer, settled into the comfortable life of a gentleman farmer on a 400-acre cattle farm in Missoula, Montana that he bought for a half-million dollars.

Once established in the United States, Vang Pao used the militant anti-communism of the Reagan era to become the dominant leader of the exiled Hmong. Through Lao community organizations across America, Vang Pao collected tribute from Hmong immigrants, many then impoverished welfare recipients, to support the armed "resistance" inside communist Laos. Operating from refugee camps in Thailand, Hmong "freedom fighters" under his command began making raids into communist Laos, conducting sabotage by shooting up buses and trucks along mountain roads.

Looking back on this secret war in Laos a quarter-century later, there seem to be two pressing questions of legal and moral accounting. America's long alliance with the Hmong, which inflicted such devastating casualties on this tribe, raises issues of moral responsibility. More broadly, the US reliance on massive, indiscriminate bombing in populated areas may have been a violation of the 1949 Geneva Convention – in short, a war crime.

Although the CIA used the Hmong as cost-effective cannon fodder, outrage over America's abandonment of them at war's end seems somehow inadequate. The Hmong were never, in any legal sense, an American ally. They were simply pawns in a covert operation who proved remarkably appropriate for the agency's immutable principle of plausible deniability. The Hmongs' chief asset in this *de facto* alliance was their willingness to fight hard for remarkably little money. Since the Hmong were a tribe, not a nation, their sacrifice incurred no formal obligation from the United States. Under Vang Pao's leadership, the Hmong committed themselves to a military alliance in rituals that featured CIA agents making promises written in the wind. With America's commitments so recorded, the Hmong then fought battle after bloody battle for bullets and a few bags of rice. That Vang Pao led his people into such a hopelessly one-sided alliance adds an unsettling dimension to this man whom many, his American supporters and Hmong loyalists included, would anoint a hero. If we view the US involvement in Laos and its Hmong alliance from a geopolitical perspective, we might excuse both as a justifiable excess in defense of the Free

World. If, however, we view our involvement through the prism of bilateral Lao–American, or Hmong–American relations, then US policy seems manipulative, even exploitative.

Of more lasting importance, America's bombing of northern Laos seems a clear violation of the 1949 Geneva Convention on "the protection of civilian persons in time of war." Although silent on specific rules for air warfare, the Convention, as stated in Article 2, applies to "all cases of declared war or any other armed conflict," and requires, under Article 3, that "persons taking no active part in the hostilities . . . shall in all circumstances be treated humanely." Moreover, Article 3 specifically prohibits all "violence to life and person, in particular murder of all kinds, mutilation, cruel treatment and torture." Indeed, Article 16 provides that "the wounded and sick, as well as the infirm, and expectant mothers, shall be the object of particular protection and respect." When it signed the agreement on August 12 1949, the United States stated formally "it fully supports the objectives of this Convention" and "reserved the right to impose the death penalty" for any violations.

Within these protections of all non-combatants, the massive US bombing of the Plain of Jars and the consequent destruction of this society would seem a clear violation of the Geneva Convention. Since the United States remained the world's leading power at the end of the Vietnam War, and the victims from the Plain of Jars were among the world's very poorest, there were, of course, no complaints. Even if there had been, there was still no higher authority to investigate any American violations of the Geneva Convention. In answer to some hypothetical indictment, US Air Force commanders might have argued in their defense that the communist guerrillas lived in and among these innocent peasant farmers, making collateral damage an inevitability when using air power for counter-guerrilla operations. Such tactics and exculpatory logic, no matter how necessary they might seem to combatants in the heat of battle, are not, and were not, sanctioned within the 1949 Geneva Convention.

In the real world of the 1970s, there was no sovereign power nor any international body with the authority, much less the will, to call America to account for these crimes. Though perhaps more moral than most, the American state still acts as a state, maximizing its power and shirking accountability until pressed by some high authority within or without – whether an international tribunal or an aroused citizenry.

When a state fails to act morally, writers, acting as the voice of civil society, can sometimes stir a nation's collective conscience, forcing the state to correct its excesses. While the war still raged, a handful of activists and academics raised the moral and legal implications of the air war and its disproportionate force. Coming to Laos as a rural development worker with International Voluntary Services (IVS), a private Peace Corps, Walt Haney had first-hand contact with the impact of the air war on Lao villagers. In the summer of 1970, Haney led Lao students in working with refugees from the Plain of Jars. In these camps, he heard disturbing stories of their life under the bombs. After Haney wrote the US Ambassador, G. McMurtrie Godley, recounting how US aircraft "would shoot or bomb any people they saw," the ambassador called him for a private meeting that November, insisting that American jets "adhere to strict rules of engagement which proscribe the bombing of inhabited villages except under highly unusual circumstances." During his school vacation that December, Haney went back to the refugee camps for a systematic survey, discovering, significantly, that 58 of the 74 villagers interviewed had witnessed bombing attacks when no communist soldiers were nearby.

After returning to America, Haney became a staffer on the US Senate Subcommittee on Refugees, compiling its survey of civilian casualties on the Plain of Jars. In an essay on US involvement in Laos for the Beacon Press edition of *The Pentagon Papers*, Haney documented the secrecy and deception used to mount the secret air war over Laos. After immersion in these classified documents, he tried to reconcile their tough *realpolitik* with the suffering he had seen among refugees from the Plain of Jars: "Reading these things my mind goes back to some of the people I met in Laos. I recall a refugee named Xieng Som Di, who returned...from working in his rice fields only to find that his village had been bombed. His house and all his possessions were destroyed, and his mother, father, wife and all three of his children had died in the bombing raid." In an angry conclusion, Haney charged that "the U.S. Executive has rained down literally billions of dollars worth of bombs on a country with whom the United States is not at war and without Congressional or international sanctions."

Like his friend Walt Haney, Fred Branfman first came to Laos as an IVS volunteer and thus became another accidental witness to the air war, later returning home to write and speak about its devastation of Laos. Among his writings, *Voices from the Plain of Jars*, a collection of memoirs from the ordinary peasants who suffered this death and destruction, stands as an eloquent indictment of the US bombing campaign. The book's frontispiece features a crumpled wedding photo of a peasant couple from the Plain of Jars, the bride wearing the hand-woven cloth and hand-crafted silver belt of her culture, under the caption: "In memory of Sao Doumma, a twenty-five-years-old woman from the Plain of Jars, killed in a bombing raid in August, 1969...and all the others." He warned that this air war "marks a new era in the history of military conflict: war which is not fought by men but machines, war which can erase distant and unseen societies clandestinely, unknown to and unsuspected by the world outside." After carefully documenting the way the US Air Force had destroyed a peasant society of 50,000 people on the Plain of Jars, Branfman probed for the moral implications of this brutal bombardment: "what does it mean when leaders of the richest and most technologically advanced nation in history use all their weaponry short of nuclear arms against rice farmers who pose the most marginal of challenges to their interests?" Though distributed by Harper & Row, one of the country's largest publishers, the book was not well advertised, received few reviews, and disappeared after a small print run.

Similarly, a group of scientists at Cornell University, led by physics professor Raphael Littauer and astronomer Carl Sagan, formed Project Air War and mustered the available evidence on the US bombing in Indochina. In 1972 they published a dense, detailed academic monograph that documented, among other topics, the extraordinary scale of the US bombing operations in Laos. Significantly, after reviewing international law, the authors concluded that the legal basis for US bombing in South Vietnam was "tenuous at best," but that "the legal case for

American bombing in the rest of Indochina is untenable." In their view, US air operations violated, to varying degrees, three central principles of international law: (1) proportionality between the damage caused and the anticipated military gain; (2) a prohibition on attacks against enemy civilians, medical installations, and undefended towns and cities; and, (3) a prohibition on weapons that cause unnecessary suffering. Most importantly, American bombing violated the general principle "that a reasonable proportionality exist between the damage caused and the military gain sought." More specifically, US air operations often violated rules of war that "prohibit direct attacks on enemy civilians." After a careful rule of possible justifications, the authors found: "The impropriety of much of the American bombing . . . has been due to the absence . . . of a military objective important enough to justify the destruction of entire towns and villages."

In his introduction to this report, Neil Sheehan, a Pulitzer prize-winning reporter for the *New York Times*, found that the American bombing has "reached the level of calculated slaughter which may gravely violate the laws of war, laws the United States has pledged itself to uphold and enforce." Writing in the direct, non-academic style of a journalist, he concluded: "The air war may constitute a massive war crime by the American government and its leaders."

Rejecting any prosecution of culpable American commanders, the Cornell scientists noted that "air warfare has been left almost totally unregulated." After World War I, which saw the first use of both tactical and strategic bombing, some legal experts endorsed by the Hague had drafted a set of "Rules of Aerial Warfare" in 1923. But not a single nation ratified the proposed convention, and the issue of air war was not addressed in the drafting of the Geneva Convention in 1949. While there were elaborate rules under the Hague and Geneva Conventions for both land and sea warfare, aerial combat, "the most significant instrument of destruction in contemporary armed conflict," had no specific rules or restrictions. To correct this historical failing, these scientists called on the major powers to negotiate new "treaties and conventions that permit detailed application of restraining rules and precise coverage." Although they came to Washington for a press conference and meetings with Congress, their report attracted little public attention and was soon forgotten.

By contrast, the few American writers who have engaged Laos in the quarter-century since the war's end have avoided any detailed analysis of the bombing and remained mute on its moral implications. Through a mix of evasion and justification, postwar writers have helped erase the memory and meaning of this bombing, and its criminal excess, from American consciousness. To cite one important example, in 1995 a leading New York publisher, Simon & Schuster, published *Back Fire*, a history of US covert operations in Laos by a young freelance writer, Roger Warner. Though the book is well researched and adds many new actors and anecdotes to our collective knowledge of this secret war, Warner ultimately fails to engage the two issues that seem to lie at the heart of his war story – the massive US bombing campaign over Laos and the CIA's alliance with the Hmong. In the course of his narrative, Warner leaves a trail of clues that the air war over Indochina set the US policy agenda for its secret war in Laos. Indeed, as Warner tells us, the United States dropped more bombs on Laos than it did on Germany or Japan during the whole of World War II.

Aside from a few stories about the use of tactical air in support of General Vang Pao, we learn little about these operations and even less about the vast strategic bombing effort in southern Laos. Most importantly, Warner never deals with the human or moral implications of these slender facts. In our bombing campaigns against Germany and Japan we were attacking advanced, urbanized societies with legitimate industrial targets and elaborate civil defense capacities. Moreover, we were in a legally defined state of war. In Laos, by contrast, we were bombing a neutralized nation with a scattered rural population. The sheer tonnage of bombs dropped over Laos, and the loose rules of engagement in this covert war, inflicted indiscriminate damage upon Laotian civilians. In striking contrast to Branfman's earlier work, the voices of the Lao villagers who suffered under this air war are silenced in Warner's book. In the end, this author refuses to engage the possibility that, in the 10 years of the Cold War, if the United States were guilty of one war crime then that might well have been our secret bombing of northern Laos.

Although much of the book is taken up with the story of the CIA's relations with General Vang Pao and his army of 30,000 Hmong guerrillas, Warner does not offer us any analysis of the political dynamics at play in this remarkable alliance between the Agency and a Southeast Asian hill tribe. The author, as an honest and careful reporter, offers us anecdote after anecdote of General Vang Pao's cowardice, corruption, brutality, and military incompetence – yet he never deals with the implications of these details. Why did the CIA continue to deal with him if he were so venal and incompetent?

The answer seems to lie in the *realpolitik* of the CIA's doctrine of plausible deniability, the Agency's standard practice around the globe during the Cold War. Within the patronage dynamics of proxy warfare in Laos, Vang Pao was the only Hmong willing to lead his people to the slaughter year after in a war they could never win. Through his fifteen-year alliance with the CIA, Vang Pao, born a poor member a weak tribal clan, rose to become the unchallenged lord of the Hmong people – commander of a 30,000 man army with its own aircraft and a wealthy man with five wives. In this bargain of blood for power, the CIA operatives whom Warner celebrates did not feel moved to expend their political capital to restrain the general's use of torture, systematic corruption, or drug dealing. For example, CIA agent Vint Lawrence, Warner's culturally-sensitive Ivy League graduate, learned that Vang Pao "kept prisoners sleeved in fifty-five-gallon barrels in holes in the ground and . . . was not averse to summarily executing prisoners or even offenders . . . from his own tribe." The general's "violent, brutal side" was useful to the CIA and so nothing was done to restrain it.

In the end, Warner's work fails to engage the profound moral and legal issues raised by the secret war in Laos. Instead of reflecting on these issues himself, the author lets the secret warriors have the final word. General Richard Secord, who was CIA–Air Force liaison in Laos and later achieved notoriety in the Iran–Contra scandal, tells us that we could have won the war if "we had bombed Vietnam back to the stone age." Former US Ambassador to Laos William Sullivan (1964–9), who supervised the most intense bombing in military history, feels no "personal anguish" for Laos and blames that country's suffering on the North Vietnamese whose "intentions were evil."

After the Cold War was over, Laos, Warner concludes, went back to being "its own sweet, goofy self" and Laotians "didn't hold a grudge for the destruction of their country." The book ends with a final anecdote about the quiet Texan Bill Lair who quit the CIA to become an interstate truck driver. After thousands of hours on the road thinking about Laos, he came to feel that "everything was supposed to turn out the way it did." If Cold War were a road movie, the author seems to say, then Laos was so much road kill – a little blood on the tires but nothing much to worry about. We can bask in our Cold War victory and forget the uncomfortable national self-examination that history has forced upon our former enemies in Eastern Europe and Russia. With our past so sanitized, we can now march into the future leading the new world order assured of our moral righteousness.

While Warner skirts the bombing, military historian Timothy Castle meets the issue head on. Without any of the national guilt or moral angst of Walt Haney and Fred Branfman, Castle, in his 1993 history, *At War in the Shadow of Vietnam*, finds the US bombing fully justified. When describing combat between the CIA's Secret Army and the communist guerrillas in 1970, Castle notes that US B-52 strategic bombers were deployed over Laos for the first time, dropping "almost eleven hundred tons of munitions on the Plain of Jars." He then quotes, and apparently accepts, Fred Branfman's assertion that American bombing destroyed human society on the plain. Instead of analyzing such disproportionate force and its damage to non-combatants, Castle, ignoring the obvious superiority of US firepower, tries to make the communist forces equally culpable: "It should also be noted, however, that for many years the communist forces had bombarded the plain with substantial amounts of artillery and mortar fire." In his next paragraph, Castle recalls flying over the plain in September 1990 and being "startled" by the bombing scars still visible on the land: "I thought the water-filled craters resembled thousands of shiny coins. On the ground it seemed incongruous that such a quiet, cool, green plain could have been subjected to such a massive assault. But the steady stream of Vietnamese trucks that I saw headed down Route 7 were a quick reminder of why the area had been such an important target." Ignoring the 1949 Geneva Convention, Castle finds this massive, indiscriminate bombardment with heavy civilian casualties justified by the mere presence of enemy forces in the area.

Even the most experienced American war correspondent in Laos, Arthur J. Dommen, has failed to engage the full reality of the air war. Although he often exposed American excesses during his years of reporting Laos, Dommen's recent summing up of the secret war for Oxford's *Encyclopedia of the Vietnam War* seems a timid, even inadequate, engagement of the air war's enormity. In describing the fighting in northern Laos, Dommen remarks that the bombing was simply "another important factor in keeping the communists at bay." Summing up the terms of the 1973 cease-fire agreement that ended the US bombing, Dommen discusses the air war indirectly, almost parenthetically, as an operation "which had dropped almost 2.1 million tons of ordnance on Laos (more than the total tonnage dropped by the U.S. in the European and Pacific theaters in World War II)." In assessing the legacy of such destruction for postwar Laos, Dommen notes that the country faces problems of "political repression, lack of government funding for development projects, and leftovers from the war," notably "the unexploded bombs left scattered about the countryside, which continued to take a toll on civilians, particularly in the north." In another entry on the Plain of Jars, the target of US Air Force saturation bombing attacks, Dommen is sparse with his words: "The plain was heavily bombed by U.S. planes, and unexploded ordnance continues to kill people in the area." Such muted prose seems unequal to what happened when the world's most powerful nation unleashed history's heaviest bombardment upon this impoverished peasant society.

Through the failure of American society to examine the moral and legal meaning of this air war, Laos has left a troubling legacy. Under the peculiar conditions of secret war, the Pentagon seems to have conducted an experiment in the use of air power for foreign intervention. In defiance of established military doctrine that only infantry can take or hold ground, the US Air Force used massive tactical bombing in northern Laos *without* effective ground forces to fulfill these missions. Instead of providing tactical support for the main strategic force, infantry, as it had in past wars, in Laos the Air Force itself was the sole strategic force. But to compensate for the absence of ground forces, this new strategy required an aerial bombardment of unprecedented intensity, producing a level of indiscriminate destruction that defied international law on proportionality between damage and objective.

Significantly, this air-war strategy, born of necessity in a secret war that barred the US from using infantry, gained an additional advantage in the post-Vietnam era – the minimization of American casualties. After suffering 58,000 dead in Vietnam, the postwar American public proved intolerant of casualties in foreign conflicts. This new air-war doctrine allowed maximum fire power for minimum casualties, making it an ideal prescription for that postwar malaise known as the "Vietnam syndrome" – a fear of suffering another costly, demoralizing defeat. Tested in Laos and perfected in Cambodia, this air-war doctrine would become central to US force-projection doctrine during the next quarter century. Of course, reducing American casualties with massive bombardment often meant increasing the collateral damage inflicted upon foreign civilians. Though such a strategy proved militarily effective and met domestic political imperatives, it placed the United States at variance with international law which was moving rapidly, in an opposite direction, to ban all indiscriminate force against civilian society.

After the Vietnam War, Washington ignored the call of the Cornell scientists for a new Geneva Convention to set rules for air warfare. There is a striking, and instructive, contrast between Congress's reaction to press exposés about environmental warfare and air war. In July 1972, the American press reported that the US military had tried to block North Vietnamese infiltration of South Vietnam by manipulating the weather over Indochina to flood strategic areas. After hearings confirmed these reports, the US Senate passed a resolution urging a treaty to ban environmental warfare. Consequently, Washington and Moscow negotiated the terms directly, and, in December 1976, the UN General Assembly approved the "Convention on the Prohibition of Military. . . Use of Environmental Modification Techniques." A few months later, the United States signed the convention. Some 53 nations have ratified this treaty, effectively banning environmental warfare. Simultaneous press exposés also prompted several Senate committees to investigate the bombing of civilians in

Laos. An angry Congress did force the White House to reduce the bombing over Indochina. But there was no Senate resolution for a new international convention on air war.

Even without leadership from the United States, the world community recognized that the 1949 Geneva Convention was no longer adequate for contemporary conflict – particularly, in guerrilla warfare where combatants are often indistinguishable from civilians. Starting in 1969, the International Red Cross moved to amend the Convention and the Swiss government convened a major diplomatic conference at Geneva in the mid-1970s to draft two supplemental protocols. While the 1949 Convention had made no mention of air war, Protocol I of 1977 applies specifically to "any land, air or sea warfare which may affect the civilian population." The original Convention had established the individual rights of certain protected persons (such as women, children, and prisoners). But Protocol I is much broader, banning both attacks on "the civilian population as such" and attacks on civilian infrastructure – whether agricultural, industrial, environmental, or cultural. Although the United States participated in the negotiations and signed the protocols in 1977, it failed, for over a decade, to join the world community in ratifying this war-crimes treaty and adapting its military tactics accordingly.

Finally, in January 1987, President Ronald Reagan sent a strongly-worded message to the Senate condemning Protocol I to the Geneva Convention and urging its rejection. By this time, 68 other nations had already ratified this treaty, making these protocols a new international standard for the conduct of war. Although the United States, the president explained, "has traditionally been in the forefront of efforts to . . . improve the international rules of humanitarian law in armed conflict," Protocol I was "fundamentally and irreconcilably flawed." The Pentagon, he reported, had found that "a number of the provisions of the Protocol are militarily unacceptable." On a similar note, Secretary of State George Schultz explained that the Pentagon found the Protocol "unreasonably restricts attacks against certain objects that traditionally have been considered legitimate military targets." Since certain of its provisions reflected "customary international law," the Secretary assured the Senate that the United States would "consult with our allies" to incorporate these into the "rules that govern our military operations." Though his language hints strongly that the Pentagon objected to new restrictions on its right to bomb civilian infrastructure, its report on the protocol remained "classified." For the first time since World War II, the United States had failed to ratify an international treaty on the rules of war. In a sharply worded reply, the senior legal advisor to the International Red Cross, Hans-Peter Gasser, said the US rejection of the Protocol "would deprive the world of a common framework for the humanitarian rules governing armed conflicts." Moreover, this rejection would, he said, "weaken the United States in its policy of working actively to gain respect for humanitarian law worldwide." Long a world leader on humanitarian issues, the United States now lagged far behind.

Without an open public debate over the moral implications of mass tactical bombing and the manipulation of minorities for covert warfare, Laos has instead served as something of a model for subsequent US foreign policy crises. When

President Reagan's advisors reviewed their foreign policy options in the early 1980s, they found Vietnam a failure but Laos a success. During the Central America crisis, the Reagan White House used CIA veterans of this secret war to mobilize antic-ommunist Contra guerrillas against Nicaragua's left-wing Sandinista government, sparking a divisive public debate over this covert warfare.

Similarly, under President William Clinton, massive application of air power, divorced from any commitment of US ground forces, would again become an instrument of US foreign policy in Iraq, Bosnia, and Kosovo. In 1999, when the North Atlantic Treaty Organization (NATO) tried to end atrocities in Kosovo by expelling Yugoslav troops, the US Air Force, in the most extreme application of this strategy, led NATO's punitive bombing of Yugoslavia's economic infrastructure. The damage from "smart bombs" in Belgrade pales before the B-52 "carpet-bombing" on the Plain of Jars. Even so, Amnesty International charged that some of the US attacks on Yugoslavia constituted a war crime. Human Rights Watch expressed concern about NATO air strikes, particularly, in the words of the *New York Times*, over "the use of cluster bombs near populated areas, attacks on civilian targets like factories or a major power plant, the bombing of a bridge near a busy market during daylight hours and air strikes against mobile targets (among them a column of refugees) from 15,000 feet without solid assurances that the targets were military." The UN's prosecutor for the Balkan war crimes tribunal considered, and then rejected, filing charges against NATO for this bombing campaign, arousing a deep antipathy inside the Pentagon to any international oversight of its operations.

A year later, in July 2000, delegations from a hundred nations gathered at the United Nations in New York to draw up a criminal code for a new International Criminal Tribunal. Appalled by a decade of brutal warfare – ethnic cleansing in Bosnia, genocide in Rwanda, mutilations in Sierra Leone, unrestrained bombardment of Chechnya – the world community was establishing the first international court that could punish war crimes and crimes against humanity. After over a half-century of leadership in this field, the United States, apparently concerned that its military might be indicted for future air operations like Yugoslavia, played a reluctant role.

During his administration's last days in December 2000, President Clinton signed the UN Convention for the International Criminal Tribunal and turned the matter over to an incoming Republican President who seems reluctant to proceed with ratification. In the thirty years since the United States violated the Geneva Convention by bombing civilian targets in Indochina, Washington has made air power central to its global force-projection capabilities. If the American public had recoiled from the sustained, unrestrained bombing of civilians in Laos, Cambodia, and Vietnam, then Washington might have repudiated this strategy and taken the lead in drafting a new Geneva Convention on air war or ratified Protocol I and the International Criminal Tribunal. Instead, the American people remained largely ignorant of the secret US bombing of civilians during the Vietnam War, and have, in the decades since, forgotten the little they knew. Instead, Washington became wedded to a strategy of air warfare that violates the 1949 Geneva Convention and its later Protocols, weakening its leadership in the campaign for an international rule of law.

REFERENCES

Branfman, Fred 1970: "Presidential War in Laos, 1964–1970," in, Nina S. Adams & Alfred W. McCoy, eds., *Laos: War and Revolution*. New York: Harper & Row, pp. 213–80.

Branfman, Fred 1972: *Voices from the Plain of Jars: Life Under an Air War*. New York: Harper & Row.

Branfman, Fred 1978: *Village of the Deep Pond: Ban Xa Phang Mouk, Laos*. Amherst: University of Massachusetts at Amherst.

Brown, McAlister and Zasloff, Joseph J. 1986: *Apprentice Revolutionaries: The Lao Communist Movement, 1930–1985*. Stanford: Hoover Institution Press.

Castle, Timothy N. 1993: *At War in the Shadow of Vietnam: U.S. Military Aid to the Royal Lao Government 1955–1975*. New York: Columbia University Press.

Colby, William 1978: *Honorable Men: My Life in the CIA*. New York: Simon & Schuster.

Colby, William 1989: *Lost Victory*. Chicago: Contemporary Books.

Crossette, Barbara. 2000: "Parsing Degrees of Atrocity Within the Logic of Law," *The New York Times*, 8 July 2000, pp. A-15,17.

Dommen, Arthur J. 1971: *Conflict in Laos: The Politics of Neutralization*. New York: Praeger, pp. 293–317.

Dommen, Arthur J. 2000: "Laos," in Spencer C. Tucker, ed., *Encyclopedia of the Vietnam War: A Political, Social, and Military History*. New York: Oxford University Press, pp. 221–3.

Dommen, Arthur J. 2000: "Plain of Jars," in Spencer C. Tucker, ed., *Encyclopedia of the Vietnam War: A Political, Social, and Military History*. New York: Oxford University Press, p. 331.

Evans, Grant. 1983: *The Yellow Rainmakers*. London: Verso.

Gasser, Hans-Peter 1987: "An Appeal for Ratification by the United States," *American Journal of International Law* 81, no. 4 (October 1987), pp. 912–25.

Gunn, Geoffrey C. 1988: *Political Struggles in Laos (1930–1954): Vietnamese Communist Power and the Lao Struggle for National Independence*. Bangkok: Editions Duang Kamol.

Haney, Walt 1972: "The Pentagon Papers and United States Involvement in Laos," in Noam Chomsky and Howard Zinn, eds., *The Pentagon Papers: Volume Five*. Boston: Beacon Press, pp. 248–93.

Littauer, Raphael and Norman Uphoff, eds. 1972: *The Air War in Indochina*. Boston: Beacon Press.

McCoy, Alfred W. 1974: "The Politics of the Poppy in Indochina: A Comparative Study of Patron–Client Relations under French and American Administrations," in Luiz R. S. Simmons and Abdul S. Said, eds., *Drugs Politics and Diplomacy: the International Connection*. Beverly Hills, CA: Sage Publications, pp. 122–9.

McCoy, Alfred W. 1991: *The Politics of Heroin: CIA Complicity in the Global Drug Trade*. New York: Lawrence Hill Books.

Powers, Thomas 1979: *The Man Who Kept the Secrets: Richard Helms & the CIA*. New York: Alfred A. Knopf.

Quincy, Keith 1988: *Hmong: History of a People*. Cheney: Eastern Washington University Press.

Quincy, Keith. 2000: *Harvesting Pa Chay's Wheat: The Hmong and America's Secret War in Laos*. Spokane: Eastern Washington University Press.

Robbins, Christopher 1979: *Air America: The Story of the CIA's Secret Airlines*. New York: Putnam.

Robbins, Christopher 1987: *The Ravens: The Men Who Flew in America's Secret War in Laos.* New York: Crown Publishers.

Roberts, Adam, and Richard Guelff 1989: *Documents on the Laws of War.* Oxford: Clarendon Press.

Senator Gravel Edition 1972: *The Pentagon Papers: The Defense Department History of United States Decision Making on Vietnam, Volume II.* Boston: Beacon Press.

Stevenson, Charles A. 1972: *The End of Nowhere: American Policy Toward Laos Since 1954.* Boston: Beacon Press.

Stuart-Fox, Martin 1997: *A History of Laos.* Cambridge: Cambridge University Press.

Toye, Hugh 1968: *Laos: Buffer State or Battleground?* Oxford: Oxford University Press.

Warner, Roger 1995: *Back Fire: The CIA's Secret War in Laos and Its Link to the War in Vietnam.* New York: Simon & Schuster.

U.S. Senate, 100th Congress, 1st Session 1987: *Protocol II Additional to the 1949 Geneva Conventions, and Relating to the Protection of Victims of Noninternational Armed Conflicts.* Washington, DC: US Government Printing Office, in, *Senate Treaty Documents Nos. 1–10: United States Congressional Serial Set.* Washington, DC: US Government Printing Office, 1989, pp. iii–15.

Yang, Dao 1993: *Hmong at the Turning Point.* Minneapolis: World Bridge Associates.

PART III

Americans at Home and Abroad

CHAPTER SIXTEEN

Missing in Action in the Twenty-First Century

BRUCE FRANKLIN

The POW/MIA flag is the only one besides the Star-Spangled Banner that has ever flown over the White House, where it has fluttered yearly since 1982. As visitors from around the world stream through the Rotunda of the US Capitol, they pass a giant POW/MIA flag, the only flag that has ever been displayed amid the epic paintings and heroic statues, given this position of honor in 1987 by the Congress and President of the United States. The POW/MIA flag flies over every US post office at least several times each year, thanks to a law passed by Congress and signed by the President in 1997. During the 1980s and 1990s, the legislatures and governors of every one of the fifty states issued laws mandating the display of this flag over public facilities such as state offices, municipal buildings, toll plazas, and police headquarters. The POW/MIA flag also hangs over the trading floor of the New York Stock Exchange, waves at countless corporate headquarters, shopping malls, union halls, and small businesses, and adorns millions of bumper stickers, buttons, windows, motorcycle jackets, watches, postcards, coffee mugs, T-shirts, and Christmas-tree ornaments.

The flag thus symbolizes our nation's veneration of its central image, a handsome American prisoner of war, his silhouetted head slightly bowed to reveal behind him the ominous shape of a guard tower. A strand of barbed wire cuts across just below his firm chin. Underneath runs the motto: YOU ARE NOT FORGOTTEN.

This black and white banner implies that the Vietnam War may never end. It demonstrates to the world both the official United States government position since 1973 and a profoundly influential national belief: Vietnam may still secretly hold American prisoners of war. This was the official reason why every postwar administration – Nixon, Ford, Carter, Reagan, Bush, and Clinton – reneged on the 1973 treaty pledge that the United States would help rebuild Vietnam and instead waged relentless economic and political warfare against that nation for decades. Even when President Clinton announced in 1995 that Washington was finally establishing diplomatic relations with Vietnam, he claimed the primary motive was to further "progress on the issue of Americans who were missing in action or held as prisoners of war."[1]

To begin to understand what this all means, it is first necessary to recognize that there is simply no rational basis or evidence for the belief that Americans are still imprisoned in Vietnam. Indeed, it runs *counter* to reason, common sense, and all evidence.

None of the armed forces has listed a single prisoner of war (POW) or even a single person missing in action (MIA) from the war since 1994. There are, it is true, 1,945 Americans listed as "unaccounted for" but not one of these is classified as a prisoner, a possible prisoner, or even missing. Most of the "unaccounted for" were *never* listed as POW or even MIA because well over half were originally *known* to have been killed in action in circumstances where their bodies could not be recovered. Their official designation has always been "KIA/BNR" – Killed in Action/Body Not Recovered. All that is missing is their *remains*. This KIA/BNR category was never included with the missing in action during the Vietnam War; it was lumped together with the POW/MIA category only after the 1973 Paris Peace Agreement was signed.

The confusion thus created was quite deliberate. But the most brilliant device for creating public confusion was the POW/MIA concoction. In all previous wars, there was one category "Prisoners of War," consisting of those known or believed to be prisoners. There was an entirely separate and distinct category of those "Missing in Action." The Nixon Administration publicly jumbled the two categories together into a hodgepodge called POW/MIA precisely in order to make it seem that every missing person might possibly be a prisoner. Because this possibility cannot be logically disproved, the POW/MIA invention perfectly fulfilled its original purpose: to create an issue that could not be resolved.

In all major wars, many combatants die without being identified or having their bodies recovered. There are more than 8,100 unaccounted for from the Korean War and 78,794 still unaccounted for from World War II. So the total of 1,945 unaccounted for in the Indochina war is astonishingly small, especially since 81 percent of the missing were airmen mainly lost over the ocean, mountains, or tropical rain forest, many in planes that exploded. To get another perspective on these numbers, consider the fact that on the other side there are between 200,000 and 300,000 Vietnamese missing in action.

During the war, the Pentagon listed as a POW anyone reported as *possibly* being held prisoner anywhere in Vietnam, Laos, Cambodia, or China at any time from 1963 to 1973, whether or not there was credible evidence of capture and even if there was evidence of subsequent death. After the 1973 Peace Agreement, all but 56 men on the Pentagon's internal lists were either released or reported to have died in captivity. In the following years, intensive analysis resolved each of these remaining cases. Except for one man who had defected, all had died. The one defector, Robert Garwood, is the only captured person who survived the war and was not returned to the United States during Operation Homecoming in 1973.

Despite many investigations by congressional committees, federal agencies, and private organizations, there has yet to be a shred of verifiable or even credible evidence that any US POWs were withheld by Vietnam. Debriefing of all the returning POWs, ongoing aerial and satellite reconnaissance, covert raids, as well as interrogations of thousands of Vietnamese refugees and defectors including high-ranking military and intelligence officials all point to one conclusion: except for Garwood, there were no surviving POWs. Even offers of huge rewards – currently amounting to well over two million dollars – have produced nothing but waves of phony pictures, fake dog tags, and other bogus "evidence."

Then there is the question of motive. Why in the world would Vietnam keep US prisoners for years and decades after the war?

To torture them, of course, a perfectly plausible motive given the inscrutable cruelty of Asians – as depicted in a century and a half of Yellow Peril propaganda in American culture. Besides, these Asians are Communists, so add half a century of Red Menace propaganda, and no further explanation is needed. One ostensibly more rational motive is offered by POW/MIA evangelists: the prisoners are being used as "hostages" or "bargaining chips." But what good are hostages to a nation that denies holding any? How can you bargain with a chip that you swear doesn't exist?

A belief that runs counter to reason, common sense, and all evidence but that is widely and deeply held by a society is a myth – in the fullest and most rigorous sense. A myth is a story of ostensibly historic events or beings crucial to the world view and self-image of a people, a story that appears as essential truth to its believers, no matter how bizarre it may seem from outside that society or when subjected to rational analysis. Indeed myths must defy commonplace plausibility and transcend everyday logic. Myths are often central to cultures, and may be their most distinctive features, which is why many anthropologists and archaeologists find them so essential to understanding a society.

To comprehend the POW/MIA myth, we need to trace its history. For the first fifteen years of US covert and overt combat in Vietnam – that is, from 1954 to 1969 – there was not even a POW/MIA concept. Its seeds were sown in 1968, the year of the Tet Offensive and its aftermath, including President Johnson's withdrawal from the election campaign, the assassination of Martin Luther King and Robert Kennedy, the tidal wave of urban rebellions, the opening of peace negotiations, and the nomination of Richard Nixon as the Republican peace candidate. In his acceptance speech Nixon declared that "as we look at America, we see cities enveloped in smoke and flame," and then vowed that "if the war is not ended when the people choose in November," "I pledge to you tonight that the first priority foreign policy objective of our next Administration will be to bring an honorable end to the war in Vietnam."[2]

Richard Nixon had no intention of ending the Vietnam War without preserving a US client government in Saigon. But how many Americans in 1968 could have predicted that he would be able to continue the war year after bloody year until 1973? Perhaps even fewer than those who remembered that back in 1954 as Vice President he had been the first Administration official openly to advocate sending American troops to fight in Vietnam because, as he put it, "the Vietnamese lack the ability to conduct a war by themselves or govern themselves."[3]

Nixon, however, had several formidable problems. Negotiations had already opened in Paris. The Tet Offensive had convinced most Americans and even much of his own Defense Department that the war was unwinnable. The antiwar movement was growing ever more powerful, domestically and within the armed forces. There was certainly no enthusiasm for the war. What could he do?

What he needed was something to wreck the negotiations, shift the apparent goal of the war, counter the antiwar movement, and generate some zeal for continued combat. Soon after his inauguration, Nixon and an enterprising businessman named H. Ross Perot solved his problem by concocting a brand new issue: demanding a "full accounting" for Americans missing in action and the release of American prisoners as a *precondition* of any peace accord.[4]

This issue created, for the first time, sizable emotional support for the war. It deadlocked the Paris negotiations for four years. It counteracted the antiwar movement. It even neutralized another White House and Pentagon problem that had been building throughout 1968: American revulsion at the torture and murder of the prisoners of US and Saigon forces. And it later provided a basis for continuing economic and political warfare against Vietnam for decades after the war was supposedly over.

Domestically, the issue was a masterly stroke. After all, how else could any deeply emotional support for the war be generated? Certainly not by holding out the old discredited promises of military victory. And who would be willing to fight and die for the notoriously corrupt generals ruling Saigon? But supporting our own prisoners of war and missing in action was something no loyal Americans would dare oppose. It also seemed easy to understand, requiring no knowledge of the history of Vietnam and the war. One measure of the campaign's success was the sale of more than fifty million POW/MIA bumper stickers during the next four years.[5]

The Nixon administration's "go public" campaign, designed to "marshal public opinion" for "the prompt release of all American prisoners of war," was initiated in March 1969. Perot was put in charge of building mass support, and he was soon rewarded. Thanks to White House intervention, his EDS corporation got 90 percent of the computer work on Medicare claims, enabling Perot to become what one writer in 1971 dubbed "the first welfare billionaire."[6]

Perot's publicity maneuvers, each approved by the President and aided by the White House staff, included full-page ads in the nation's hundred largest newspapers and TV programs in 59 cities demanding the immediate release of all US POWs; sending two plane loads of reporters and Christmas presents for the POWs to Laos; and persuading Congress to place in the Rotunda of the Capitol a tableau, designed by him, of two POWs besieged by huge cockroaches and rats.[7] By the end of 1970, this tableau was being set up in state capitols across the country, TV networks were airing "POW/MIA Specials," President Nixon had created a national Prisoner of War Day, the Steve Canyon cartoon strip was featuring POW/MIA relatives, and the US Post Office had issued 135 million POW/MIA postage stamps.[8]

America's vision of the war was being transformed. The actual photographs and TV footage of massacred villagers, napalmed children, Vietnamese prisoners being tortured and murdered, wounded GIs screaming in agony, and body bags being loaded by the dozen for shipment back home were being replaced by simulated images of American POWs in the savage hands of Asian Communists.

Congress had fallen into line immediately. In December 1969 an obedient Senate and House unanimously passed a resolution demanding the release of US POWs.

The State and Defense Departments, the Republican National Committee, a host of politicians of both parties led by Republican Senator Robert Dole, and the White House staff meticulously choreographed every step in helping to create an organization named the National League of Families of American Prisoners and Missing in Southeast Asia.[9] The League, whose principal organizers and activists were wives or parents of career officers, would play crucial roles in the evolution of the POW/MIA issue from then through the rest of the century.

A militant prowar organization known as VIVA (originally Victory in Vietnam Association) decided to sell bracelets engraved with the names of POWs and MIAs to promote and fund the POW/MIA campaign. The first bracelets were produced just in time for VIVA's 1970 annual Salute to the Armed Forces Ball, where Governor Ronald Reagan was the keynote speaker, Bob Hope and Martha Raye were made co-chairs of the bracelet campaign, and H. Ross Perot was named Man of the Year. The bracelet idea quickly mushroomed into a propaganda coup for the POW/MIA campaign and financial bonanza for VIVA, which by mid 1972 was selling more than ten thousand bracelets a day. Bracelets were prominently worn by such luminaries as President Nixon, General William Westmoreland, Billy Graham, George Wallace, Charlton Heston, Bill Cosby, Pat Boone, Cher and Sonny Bono, Fred Astaire, Johnny Cash, Steve Allen, Princess Grace of Monaco, and Bob Hope, who personally distributed more than a thousand. The bracelet also became a kind of fetish for sports stars such as Willie Shoemaker, Don Drysdale, Lee Trevino (who claimed it saved his golf game), and Jack Kramer (who swore it cured his tennis elbow).[10]

By 1973, perhaps ten million Americans were wearing POW/MIA bracelets. The influence on the national imagination cannot be calculated. Each person who wore a bracelet vowed never to remove it until his or her POW/MIA was either found to be dead or returned home from Vietnam. Millions of people thus developed profound emotional bonds with the man on their wrist. Countless American schoolchildren went through their formative years linked to these amulets. How could they not continue to believe that their POW/MIAs were alive?

With both popular and unanimous congressional support on the POW/MIA issue, Nixon was able to stalemate the Paris talks for almost four years by demanding that Hanoi must account for America's missing in action and negotiate the release of American prisoners separately from the question of US withdrawal. When the other side insisted that the release of POWs depended on ending the war (the conventional position of warring nations), this was denounced by the Administration and the media as "unprecedented," "inhuman," and "barbaric."[11] When the other side suggested that they would set a date for the release of all POWs if the United States would set a date for withdrawal from their country, the administration accused them of "ransoming" the POWs and using them as "hostages" and "bargaining chips." These metaphors would become central to the postwar POW/MIA myth.

How is it possible to comprehend this truly astonishing position, which seemed ready to trade countless American and Vietnamese lives for several hundred prisoners who would presumably be released anyhow at the conclusion of the war? By early

1971, President Nixon could explicitly declare that US ground and air forces would remain in Vietnam "as long as there is one American prisoner being held prisoner by North Vietnam." Since North Vietnam was making the release of the prisoners contingent on US withdrawal, the logic of Nixon's position could be, as Tom Wicker put it, that "we may keep both troops and prisoners there forever."[12] If that seems absurd, what would follow if it could be made to appear that North Vietnam was concealing some of its prisoners? Then, since it could never be proved that some missing American was not "being held prisoner by North Vietnam," and since more Americans would be missing as the fighting continued, the war could literally go on forever.

Rationality, however, has never been a component of the POW/MIA issue. As Jonathan Schell observed, by 1972 "many people were persuaded that the United States was fighting in Vietnam in order to get its prisoners back," and the nation's main sympathy was no longer for "the men fighting and dying on the front," who "went virtually unnoticed as attention was focused on the prisoners of war," "the objects of a virtual cult": "Following the President's lead, people began to speak as though the North Vietnamese had kidnapped four hundred Americans and the United States had gone to war to retrieve them."[13]

Nixon's four-year campaign to secure the release of American POWs separate from US withdrawal was doomed, along with his other war goals, by the peace accord signed in Paris on January 27, 1973. The Agreement called for the complete withdrawal of all US forces from Vietnam within sixty days and the return of all POWs "simultaneously with and completed not later than the same day" as the US withdrawal. Hanoi had already delivered to Washington a complete list of its prisoners and those who had died in captivity. Within the stipulated two months, all the living prisoners were repatriated. Both Vietnam and Laos returned or accounted for *more*, rather than *fewer*, than those listed by the Pentagon and State Department as possibly captured in each country.

The Peace Agreement also guaranteed that "the United States will contribute to healing the wounds of war and to postwar reconstruction of the Democratic Republic of Viet-Nam." On February 1, Nixon wrote a secret letter to Hanoi Prime Minister Pham Van Dong, pledging this reconstruction aid to Hanoi would be at least $3.25 billion.[14] But when Henry Kissinger brought this document to Hanoi in early February, he simultaneously confronted the Hanoi government with "some 80 files of individuals who we had reason to believe had been captured." Because "we are extremely dissatisfied" with Hanoi's accounting for these MIAs, Kissinger concluded, "we cannot proceed" with the "economic aid."[15]

Why did Kissinger's list contain 80 names? The highest number of such cases then publicly claimed or secretly listed by the government was 56. The truth finally came out in 1992 when Roger Shields, head of Pentagon POW/MIA affairs in 1973, acknowledged that Washington had deliberately included on Kissinger's list a number of cases that the Vietnamese could not possibly account for.[16] Thus the Nixon Administration created an issue that could never be resolved.

Having no intention of honoring the US pledge of aid, Nixon made *accounting* for the *MIAs* the issue. But accounting is a meaningless issue unless there is some belief in the possibility of living *POWs*. Hence each postwar Administration tried to exaggerate this *possibility* of living POWs. But no administration could afford to claim there actually *were* POWs, because then it would be expected to rescue them. True believers, however, knew that reconnaissance, espionage, and the debriefing of defectors would have to reveal POWs to US intelligence. Hence by the late 1970s the POW myth was beginning to incorporate belief in a government conspiracy precisely the opposite of the real one. While the government was pretending that there might be POWs, the POW/MIA myth saw the government pretending that POWs might not exist.

Not all the machinations of the Pentagon, political opportunists, scam artists, the media, and presidents can create a true myth unless that myth resonates with deep psychocultural needs of a society. There are some fairly obvious needs being met by the images of American POWs tortured year after year by sadistic Asian Communists. We, not the Vietnamese, become the victims as well as the good guys. The American fighting man becomes a hero betrayed by his government and the antiwar movement, especially by unmanly types such as the bureaucrats in control of the government, "peaceniks," cowards, and those who would rather make love than war. This stab-in-the-back theme, with its loud echoes of the myth of national betrayal central to the rise of Nazism, is one way of convincing ourselves that *we* didn't really lose the war. It also suggests that American manhood itself is threatened and must be rescued if we are to restore America's military might and determination. So it is no surprise that the POW/MIA myth has been functioning as a potent agent of militarism. But this is also a myth of imprisonment, a myth that draws deep emotional power by displacing onto Vietnam the imprisonment, helplessness, and alienation felt by many Americans in an epoch when alien economic, technological, and bureaucratic forces control much of their lives.

Because the postwar POWs are imaginary beings, elaborating the myth and implanting it deep in America's collective imagination has been the job of art forms specializing in imaginary beings: novels, comic books, TV soaps, video games, and, of course, movies. Although the story of American prisoners abandoned in Southeast Asia could not become a major American myth until the dream factory geared up its assembly line for mass production of the essential images, Hollywood was actually involved in creating bits of the history that its POW rescue movies would soon fantasize.

The character central to the POW/MIA story as mythologized in the 1980s was retired Special Forces Colonel James "Bo" Gritz, who organized raids into Laos to rescue POWs he imagined as captives of Asian communists. Gritz claimed that he had to accept this mission because the only two other men capable of such intense "action" were unavailable: "Both Teddy Roosevelt and John Wayne are dead."[17]

But other men of action were available to help: Captain Kirk of the Starship *Enterprise*, Dirty Harry, and a Hollywood star who had just moved into the White House. William Shatner put up $10,000 and received movie rights on the Gritz story. Clint Eastwood contributed $30,000 and was assigned a crucial role in the adventure.[18] And Ronald Reagan's Administration was secretly arranging funding and logistics for Gritz, while creating within Laos an organization that fed back to the United States a stream of phony evidence of live POWs.[19]

By 1980, the POW myth envisioned a conspiracy high in the government to deny the existence of American prisoners. The villains were government bureaucrats, devious CIA operatives, and liberal politicians, personified by President Carter. With the inauguration of Reagan in early 1981, the myth evolved a new twist: the good President walled off by a cabal of scheming bureaucrats and liberals now known collectively as the "gatekeepers." There could be no doubt about the President's sincerity. After all, Ronald Reagan had been active with POW issues ever since he himself had actually been a POW of Asian communists during the Korean War – as the star of the 1954 movie *Prisoner of War*.

There was one man in America who could get by the all-powerful gatekeepers and bring the truth to the good President: Clint Eastwood. On the night of November 27, 1982, after Gritz's team had crossed into Laos, Eastwood was to fly from his Shasta, California, ranch to a prearranged meeting at Reagan's Santa Barbara ranch to inform his old friend the President, who was supposedly itching to send military forces to rescue the POWs. When the raiders returned from Laos to Thailand on December 3, they found this message from a team member in California:

CLINT AND I MET WITH PRESIDENT ON 27TH. PRESIDENT SAID: QUOTE, IF YOU BRING OUT ONE U.S. POW, I WILL START WORLD WAR III TO GET THE REST OUT. UNQUOTE.[20]

Gritz's raids, however, did not turn out like a Hollywood production. The American heroes encountered no POWs and were easily routed by the Laotians.[21] Yet three days before the news of Gritz's first raid burst upon the public, and while he was conducting a second raid, President Reagan, who had been kept closely informed, publicly declared that from now on "the government bureaucracy" would have to understand that the POW/MIA issue had become "the highest national priority."[22]

The first movie version began shooting amid the media hoopla about the Gritz raids. Starring Gene Hackman as a thinly-veiled counterpart of Gritz, *Uncommon Valor* made it to the screen for the Christmas season of 1983. Reviewers, who at first dismissed it as a "bore" with "comic-strip-level heroism," were soon trying to comprehend the startling audience response to what turned out to be the "biggest movie surprise" of the 1983–4 season. The best explanation seemed to come from "an ordinary moviegoer who said with satisfaction of the bloody ending in which dozens of the enemy are mowed down by the Americans, 'We get to win the Vietnam War.'"[23]

Uncommon Valor presents a tableau of a nation run by bureaucrats, politicians, and shadowy secret agents in business suits who revile and betray its true warrior heroes. Hackman is a retired colonel whose efforts to rescue his MIA son are continually menaced by "the politicians" and omnipresent government agents equipped with high-tech spy mikes and phone taps. The idealism, virility, martial powers, and heroism of his team of men who dedicate their lives to rescuing their abandoned comrades, sons, and fathers are presented as the alternative to a weak, decadent America subjugated by materialism, hedonism, and feminism.

The following year came *Missing in Action*, with Chuck Norris as retired Special Forces Colonel James Braddock, a fantasy version of retired Special Forces Colonel James "Bo" Gritz. Here the myth took more potent shape, with Norris as lone superhero – incarnate in a fetishized male body – replacing Hackman's team of macho warriors and graphically dramatizing how much more erotically exciting it is to make war, not love. The meaning and tremendous popular allure of *Missing in Action* were expressed in full-page ads showing Norris, sleeves rolled up to reveal bulging biceps, and a huge machine gun seeming to rise from his crotch, which is blackened by its great shadow. Below ran the message: "THE WAR'S NOT OVER UNTIL THE LAST MAN COMES HOME!"[24]

Because the power of these movies flows from some of deepest elements of American culture, they were able to transform the POW/MIA *issue* into a true *myth*. After all, one foundation of American culture is the mythic frontier, with its central images of white captives tortured by cruel non-white savages until they can be rescued by the first great American hero, the lone frontiersman who abandons civilized society to merge with the wilderness. The movies that transmuted what had been a fringe political issue of the mid-1970s into a central national myth did so precisely by using these primal cultural materials.[25] Hollywood moved us from seeing American POWs in Vietnam as quintessential symbols of betrayed American manhood in *The Deer Hunter* (1978) through the formative POW rescue movies *Uncommon Valor* (1983) and *Missing In Action* (1984) to the apotheosis of the myth in *Rambo: First Blood Part II* (1985). *The Deer Hunter* explicitly calls attention to its use of the mythic frontier and frontiersman, fleshed out in the early nation state by James Fenimore Cooper's Deerslayer. But it was *Rambo* that used the old mythic elements to turn Sylvester Stallone, as muscled as the giant he-men in Nazi propaganda posters, into the true American superhero of the post-Vietnam epoch.

At the beginning of the movie, Rambo himself is a prisoner in America. Thoroughly alienated from civil society by his experience in the Vietnamese wilderness – what GIs called "Injun country" – he is the only one who can rescue the tortured white captives from their savage captors. Rambo can do this by merging with the wilderness even more completely than the Vietnamese can. Why? Because he, like the mythic frontiersman, has coalesced with the Indian and the wilderness. Rambo is of "German-Indian descent," "a hell of a combination." His long, dark hair restrained by a headband, a necklace dangling above his bare muscled chest, armed with a huge caricature of a bowie knife and a bow that shoots exploding arrows, Rambo conceals himself behind trees and waterfalls and literally rises out of the mud and water to ambush the savages in their own primitive land.

Rambo's vast powers – both over his enemies and his audiences – derive also from other American mythic heroes. America's most popular author, Edgar Rice Burroughs, created two of Rambo's forebears: a martial arts expert and veteran of a defeated American army who fights for good causes in alien lands against seemingly insurmountable odds (John Carter); and a bare-chested muscular he-man who merges completely with the tropical jungle to carry out spectacular deeds of heroism (Tarzan). Rambo also incorporates one of America's most distinctive cultural products, the comic-book hero who may seem to be an ordinary human being but really possesses superhuman powers that allow him to fight, like Superman, for "truth, justice, and the American way" and to personify national fantasies, like Captain

America. No wonder Rambo can stand invulnerable against the thousands of bullets fired at him, many from point-blank range, by America's enemies.

Like the mythic frontiersman, Rambo confronts his antithesis not in the Indian but in feminized, devious, emasculating civil society as embodied by Murdock, the arch bureaucrat who represents the Washington administration and those who manipulate the computerized technology used to control the lives of everyday men. The climax comes when Rambo, after rescuing the POWs, hurls himself on top of the prostrate Murdock and forces this fake man to whimper and moan in terror of our hero's gigantic phallic knife.

Thus *Rambo* projects a fantasy in which the audience gets to violate the enemies of everyday life, the boss and his computerized control over work life, the bureaucrats and politicians who conspire to emasculate America's virility and betray the American dream. American men find their surrogates both in the POWs who embody humiliated, betrayed, enslaved American manhood and in the warrior hero who can rescue them when he escapes the imprisonment of post-Vietnam America.

Six weeks after the opening of *Rambo*, President Reagan projected himself into its star role – while hyping the film with a presidential plug – as he declared (ostensibly as a microphone test before his national address on the release of US hostages in Beirut): "Boy, I saw *Rambo* last night. Now I know what to do the next time this happens."[26] Two weeks later, members of Congress "signaled a new tough-minded attitude" on foreign relations by invoking the image of Rambo a dozen times in debating a foreign aid bill.[27] Rambo's political repercussions ricocheted around the world. For example, in 1990 President Saddam Hussein of Iraq defiantly responded to the US threat of war with his own bluster in the guise of cultural criticism: "The Americans are still influenced by Rambo movies, but this is not a Rambo movie."[28]

The advent of *Rambo* helped make the MIA religion not only a prominent feature of American culture but also a lucrative market. Rescuing POWs from the evil Vietnamese Communists now became almost a rite of passage for Hollywood heroes, as the formula degenerated through *P.O.W.: The Escape*, the 1986 Israeli production starring David Carradine, to *Operation Nam*, a 1987 Italian production starring John Wayne's son Ethan Wayne, which might be called the first spaghetti rescue movie. In 1987 appeared the first issue of *Vietnam Journal*, a comic book prominently displaying on every cover the POW/MIA logo next to a lead about an MIA feature. In 1985, Jack Buchanan published *M.I.A. Hunter*, the first of his fifteen wildly popular POW rescue novels featuring Mark Stone, a former Green Beret who "has only one activity that gives meaning to his life – finding America's forgotten fighting men, the P.O.W.s the government has conveniently labeled M.I.A.s, and bringing them back from their hell on earth."[29]

The cultural products that disseminate the MIA mythology in the popular imagination have tended increasingly to project a vast government cover-up and conspiracy. In the 1989 TV movie *The Forgotten*, starring Keith Carradine and Stacy Keach, high government officials actually conspire to torture and assassinate POWs held by Vietnam until 1987 so they won't reveal that these officials had colluded with North Vietnam to sabotage a POW rescue mission. Jack Buchanan's M.I.A. Hunter constantly battles against "Washington" and its sinister operatives; in *M.I.A. Hunter:*

Cambodian Hellhole he can pursue his quest only "after demolishing a C.I.A hit team sent to arrest him." So by the end of the 1980s, the POW/MIA myth had emerged from American popular culture in the shape of an ominous Frankenstein's monster beginning to haunt its ingenious creators in Washington.

The monster became a more serious problem as corporations from Europe and Asia staked out major investments in Vietnam, barred to US corporations by the US embargo. Pressure was building for normalization of relations.

On April 9, 1991 – one month after the defeat of Iraq led him to declare "By God, we've kicked the Vietnam syndrome once and for all!" – President George Bush handed Vietnam a "Road Map" toward normalizing relations within two years – contingent upon Vietnam's making what Washington deemed satisfactory progress in resolving "all remaining POW/MIA cases."[30] Instantly the smoldering POW/MIA issue was fanned into a firestorm.

In May, Senator Jesse Helms released, in the name of all Republicans on the Senate Foreign Relations Committee, a hundred-page pseudohistory alleging that five thousand US POWs had been abandoned in Indochina, and that some were still alive, betrayed by a vast Washington conspiracy. The report's principal author was later exposed as having falsified much of its "evidence" about abandoned POWs.[31] Senator Bob Smith, who had helped engineer the Helms document, next tried to set up a Senate committee to ballyhoo its thesis. But Smith's efforts seemed doomed because the Senate was due to recess on August 2, 1991.

Suddenly on July 17 began one of the most spectacular media coups in US history, orchestrated largely by Smith and associates. A photograph purportedly showing three US pilots shot down during the Vietnam War and still being held captive exploded as the lead story on the TV and radio networks. Newspapers across the country front-paged the picture under banner headlines. Within a week photographs ostensibly showing two more live POWs – identified as Daniel Borah Jr. and Donald Carr – hit the media. "Bring on Rambo" was a headline in the August 2 *Wall Street Journal*, which reported that 69 percent of the American people now believed that US POWs were being held in Indochina and 52 percent were convinced that the government was derelict in not getting them back. The same day a stampeded Senate unanimously passed Bob Smith's resolution to create a Senate Select Committee on POW/MIA Affairs – along with a resolution to fly the POW/MIA flag over federal buildings.

The photos that launched the Senate Committee later proved as bogus as all other "evidence" of postwar POWs. "Daniel Borah" turned out to be a Lao highlander who had happily posed because he never had his photograph taken before. "Donald Carr" was a German bird smuggler photographed in a Bangkok rare bird sanctuary. The picture of the three other alleged POWs was a doctored version of a 1923 Soviet photograph; the three men were actually holding a poster extolling collective farming (mustaches had been added and a picture of Stalin subtracted).

Bob Smith was made Vice Chairman of the Senate committee. Chairman John Kerry, who in 1971 had joined a thousand other antiwar Vietnam veterans in throwing their medals at the Capitol, now strangely seemed to accept the preposterous notion that the government during the war and ever since had been minimizing the possibility of

POWs being kept back. The Select Committee refused to permit testimony about how the POW/MIA issue was created and used by the government to legitimize hostilities against Vietnam from 1969 on. The only witnesses allowed to testify were either government apologists or POW/MIA movement partisans. Although the Committee found not a shred of credible evidence of postwar POWs, its final report asserted that the POW/MIA issue should continue to have the "highest national priority."[32]

While the Select Committee had the media spotlighting the POW/MIA issue in 1992, President Bush was fighting for his political life. The very man who had boasted about healing America's Vietnam wounds was now trying to win reelection by reopening them, turning what Bill Clinton had or hadn't done during the Vietnam War into the Republicans' main campaign issue. Meanwhile Ross Perot was campaigning as the wartime champion of the POWs and a Rambo-like hero who would rescue the dozens allegedly still alive in Indochina, and by extension, the nation itself.

Unlike Bush and Clinton, Perot had no national party apparatus. What he used as a remarkably effective substitute was a ready-made national infrastructure, a network of activists motivated by religious fervor and coordinated by grassroots organizations: the POW/MIA movement. Perot chose ex-POW James Stockdale as his running mate and ex-POW Orson Swindle as his campaign manager. At his typical rally, Perot sat with former POWs and family members on a stage bedecked with POW flags. POW activists and organizations were central to the petition campaigns that got Perot on the ballot in every state.[33]

Portraying himself as the lone outsider from Texas ready to ride into Washington to save us from its sleazy bureaucrats and politicians who had betrayed the POWs and the American people, Perot cut deeply into President Bush's constituency. Without the Perot candidacy, Bush probably would have beaten Bill Clinton in a one-on-one race. The POW/MIA issue was thus central to the election's outcome.

In the closing days of the presidential campaign, George Bush claimed he was on the verge of ending hostilities by forcing Vietnam into resolving the POW/MIA issue. He now presented himself as the man who was about to lead the nation to "begin writing the last chapter of the Vietnam War."[34]

The President was responding to two developments. One was Vietnam's all-out efforts to resolve the POW/MIA issue, including actions utterly unprecedented between hostile states, such as opening their military archives to US inspection, conducting joint searches throughout their country, and allowing short-notice US inspection of suspected prison sites. The other was the pressure from US corporations anxious not to lose lucrative business opportunities to foreign competitors already swarming into Vietnam.[35]

But neither corporate anxiety nor Vietnamese cooperation could overcome the potent forces wielding the POW/MIA issue, forces still including its original engineer, Richard Nixon. On December 30, 1992, Nixon sent a judiciously leaked memo to the Senate Select Committee, insisting that "it would be a diplomatic travesty and human tragedy to go forward with normalization" until Hanoi "fully accounts for the MIAs." As the *Los Angeles Times* observed, "Nixon's written statement provides the strongest evidence so far that he and officials of his former Administration constitute a powerful and determined, though largely hidden, lobby against normalization."[36]

So instead of following his own Road Map, Bush merely allowed US enterprises to begin negotiating for future business. This left a curious situation in the early months of the Clinton Administration: US corporate interests, which had supported and profited from the Vietnam War, furtively leaning on the former antiwar demonstrator to end the war. Even the *Wall Street Journal*, for decades one of the master builders of the POW/MIA myth, ran a major editorial headlined "President Clinton, Normalize Ties With Vietnam" and arguing that "by any account, the Vietnamese have more than met" all the conditions of the Road Map, including the requested "help in resolving the fate of American MIAs."[37] The Clinton Administration began tiptoeing toward normalization. "Bill Clinton may be on the verge of finally ending the Vietnam War," declared the April 12 *Wall Street Journal*, which went on to warn, however, of "an orchestrated campaign" to stop him.[38]

Right on cue, the same day's *New York Times* featured a sensational front-page story about a "top secret" document "discovered" in Moscow by "Harvard researcher" Stephen Morris and "authenticated by leading experts" (unnamed) as a Russian translation of a 1972 report to Hanoi's Politburo. This "smoking gun" the article said, "proves" that Vietnam withheld "hundreds" of US POWs. For an "expert" opinion, the *Times* turned to Zbigniew Brzezinski, who in 1978 had persuaded Jimmy Carter not to normalize relations with Vietnam. Since, as Brzezinski knew, there has never been any credible evidence of postwar US POWs in Vietnam, he offered an explanation that was sooner or later destined to become part of the POW/MIA mythology: "the Vietnamese took hundreds of American officers out and shot them in cold blood."[39]

In a replay of the phony photogambits of 1991, the "smoking gun" now exploded as the lead story on every TV network, including PBS, whose balanced coverage showcased a MacNeil/Lehrer panel on April 13 consisting of three disinterested "experts" – Brzezinski, Kissinger, and Morris himself. Brzezinski's massacre scenario was repeated in newspaper editorials across the country. Headlines blared "North Vietnam Kept 700 POWs after War: 'Smoking Gun' File Exposes '20 Years of Duplicity'"; "POWs: The Awful Truth?"; "We Can't Set Up Ties with Killers of Our POWs."[40]

Not one of the "facts" about POWs in this spurious document conforms to the historical record.[41] Yet this clumsy hoax helped maintain the trade embargo for almost a year. And when President Clinton finally did call off the embargo in 1994, he claimed that he was doing so to get more "answers" about the MIAs, because "any decisions about our relationships with Vietnam should be guided by one factor and one factor only – gaining the fullest possible accounting for our prisoners of war and our missing in action."[42]

A 1993 poll indicated that two-thirds of Americans believed that US POWs "are still being held in Southeast Asia."[43] The poll did not measure how many of the other third believe Brzezinski's fable of hundreds of American officers being massacred in "cold blood." Though conveniently disposing of the belief in live POWs – which eventually would be biologically impossible anyhow – this scenario has become a fantasy that may allow the POW/MIA myth to endure indefinitely.

When diplomatic relations with Vietnam were finally established in 1995, President Clinton deftly undercut the POW/MIA lobby by naming as the first US Ambassador Douglas ("Pete") Peterson, a former Air Force fighter pilot who had spent six-and-a-half years as a POW in Hanoi. In the years that have followed, joint US–Vietnamese search teams have combed every accessible site for possible remains; swarms of US visitors – including many veterans as well as businesspeople – have toured all parts of Vietnam; Hanoi has opened its secret records of those captured to American researchers. So we know with as much certainty as could ever be possible that there are not now, and never have been, American prisoners held in Vietnam after the war. So why are the POW/MIA flags still flying all over America?

NOTES

1   "Clinton on Vietnam's Legacy," *The New York Times*, July 12, 1995.
2   *Nixon Speaks Out* (NY: Nixon-Agnew Campaign Committee, 1968), 235.
3   *Vietnam and America*, ed. Marvin Gettleman, Jane Franklin, Marilyn Young, and H. Bruce Franklin (New York: Grove Press, 1995), 52.
4   Memorandum from Peter Flanigan, June 30, 1969, Nixon Presidential Materials Project, National Archives and Records Administration, White House Special Files, Haldeman Box 133, Perot Folder; H. Bruce Franklin, *M.I.A. or Mythmaking in America* (New Brunswick: Rutgers University Press, 1993), 50–6, 188–92.
5   *Final Report of the House Select Committee on Missing Persons in Southeast Asia*, 94th Congress, 2nd Session, December 13, 1976, 136.
6   Memorandum from Arthur Burns, April 9, 1969, and Memorandum from Peter Flanigan, June 30, 1969, Haldeman Box 133, Perot Folder; Robert Fitch, "H. Ross Perot: America's First Welfare Billionaire," *Ramparts*, November 1971, 42–51.
7   "Projects Proposed by Ross Perot," Memorandum from Butterfield to Haldeman, Ehrlichman, Kissinger, and Harlow, October 24, 1969, Haldeman Box 133, Perot Folder; "Message from Perot," Memorandum for the President from Alexander Butterfield, President's Handwriting Files, Box 4 (Nixon has written a big double-underlined "Good!" on this); *American Prisoners of War in Southeast Asia, 1970: Hearings before the Subcommittee on National Security Policy and Scientific Developments of the Committee on Foreign Affairs*, House of Representatives, 91st Congress, 2nd Session, April 29, May 1, 6, 1970, 66–79; "Exhibit to Stir Opinion on P.O.W.'s Open in Capitol," *New York Times*, June 5, 1970.
8   Jon M. Van Dyke, "Nixon and the Prisoners of War," *New York Review of Books*, January 7, 1971, 35; Richard A. Falk, "Pawns in Power Politics," reprinted in *American Prisoners of War in Southeast Asia, 1971: Hearings before the Subcommittee on National Security Policy and Scientific Developments of the Committee on Foreign Affairs*, House of Representatives, 92nd Congress, 1st Session, March 23–April 20, 1971, 474.
9   "POW Policy in Vietnam," Memorandum for the President from Henry A. Kissinger, October 2, 1969, President's Office Files, Series A: Documents Annotated by the President, Box 3; memoranda from Butterfield to Colonel Hughes, December 4 and December 8, 1969, Haldeman Box 55, Hughes folder; Lyn Nofziger to Butterfield, December 4, 1969, Butterfield Box 8; *M.I.A. or Mythmaking in America*, 190, 240–1.
10 Janet L. Koenigsamen, *Mobilization of a Conscience Constituency: VIVA and the POW/MIA Movement*, Unpublished Dissertation, Kent State University, 1987, 36–8, 44–50,

77–8; "Unit for P.O.W.s Has New Project," *New York Times*, February 26, 1973; "Reminder of Vietnam Stays on Hand," *Los Angeles Times*, February 13, 1989;

11   "U.S. Gives Enemy List of Missing," *New York Times*, December 31, 1969.

12   *Public Papers of the Presidents of the United States: Richard Nixon, 1971*, 541; Tom Wicker, "Illogic in Vietnam," *New York Times*, May 25, 1971.

13   Jonathan Schell, "The Time of Illusion IV: For the Re-election of the President," *New Yorker*, June 23, 1975, 76.

14   Nixon's letter is reprinted in *M.I.A. or Mythmaking In America*, 204–7.

15   Confirmation Hearings of Dr. Henry Kissinger as Secretary of State, September 7, 10, 11, and 14, 1973, as reprinted in "Americans Missing in Southeast Asia," *Hearings before the House Select Committee on Missing Persons in Southeast Asia*, Part 5, June 17, 25, July 21, and September 21, 1975, 175.

16   "Long Shadow of the M.I.A.'s Still Stalks a Pentagon Official," *The New York Times*, September 20, 1992.

17   Quoted in Charles J. Patterson and Colonel G. Lee Tippin, *The Heroes Who Fell from Grace* (Canton, Ohio: Daring Books, 1985), 102.

18   "Daring Search for POWs Told," *Los Angeles Times*, January 31, 1983; "'Star-studded' Raid Fails to Free POWs," *Star-Ledger* (Newark, NJ), February 1, 1983; "Private Raid on Laos Reported," *New York Times*, February 1, 1983; Patterson, 52.

19   *Report of the Select Committee on POW/MIA Affairs, United States Senate* (Washington: US Government Printing Office, 1993), 155, 221, 276–80, 302, 305–10, 334–5.

20   "Daring Search for POWs Told"; Patterson, 50, 70, 92–107, 146.

21   Patterson, 128–9, 147, 176.

22   "Remarks at a Meeting of the National League of Families of American Prisoners and Missing in Southeast Asia, January 28, 1983," *Public Papers of the Presidents of the United States: Ronald Reagan, 1983* (Washington, 1984), 131.

23   Review by Richard Freedman, *Star-Ledger*, December 16, 1983; Aljean Harmetz, "2 Holiday Movies Turn into Surprise Successes," *New York Times*, February 13, 1984.

24   Tony Williams, "*Missing in Action*: The Vietnam Construction of the Movie Star," in *From Hanoi to Hollywood* (New Brunswick: Rutgers University Press, 1990), 129–44; Louis J. Kern, "MIAs, Myth, and Macho Magic: Post-Apocalyptic Cinematic Visions of Vietnam," in *Search and Clear: Critical Responses to Selected Literature and Films of the Vietnam War*, ed. William J. Searle (Bowling Green, OH: Bowling Green State University Popular Press, 1988), 37–54.

25   Gaylyn Studlar and David Desser, "Never Having to Say You're Sorry: *Rambo*'s Rewriting of the Vietnam War," *Film Quarterly* 42 (Fall 1988), 9–16; Don Kunz, "First Blood Redrawn," *Vietnam Generation* 1 (Winter 1989), 94–111; Gregory A. Waller, "*Rambo*: Getting to Win This Time," in *From Hanoi to Hollywood*, 113–28.

26   "Reagan Cites 'Rambo' as Next-Time Example," *Star-Ledger* (Newark, NJ), July 1, 1985; "Reagan Gets Idea from 'Rambo' for Next Time," *Los Angeles Times*, July 1, 1985.

27   "'Machismo' on Capitol Hill," *New York Times*, July 14, 1985.

28   "Iraq Spurns 'U.S.-imposed' Council Solution," *Star-Ledger* (Newark, NJ), December 1, 1990.

29   Jacket copy, Jack Buchanan, *M. I. A. Hunter* (New York: Jove, 1985).

30   "'Road Map' to Renew Ties with Hanoi Could Lead to Some Trade by Year End," *Wall Street Journal*, April 15, 1991.

31   *Hearings before the Select Committee on POW/MIA Affairs*, Part I of II, November 5, 6, 7, and 15, 1991, 443–7.

32   *Report of the Select Committee on POW/MIA Affairs*, 164.

33   David Jackson, "MIAs' Kin Want Perot as President," *Dallas Morning News*, May 19, 1992; interview with David Jackson, May 18, 1992; telephone interview with John LeBoutillier, June 12, 1992; "It's Businessman Perot and Not War Hero Bush Who Attracts a Following Among U.S. Veterans," *Wall Street Journal*, July 2, 1992.

34   "Bush Sees Gain in Vietnam Ties," *Los Angeles Times*, October 24, 1992.

35   "Corporations Ask Bush to Lift Vietnam Ban," *The New York Times*, May 9, 1992; "Vietnam: The Big Buildup Begins," *Washington Post*, December 9, 1992.

36   "Nixon Opposing U.S.–Vietnam Normalization Policy," *Los Angeles Times*, January 9, 1993.

37   "President Clinton, Normalize Ties With Vietnam," *Wall Street Journal*, March 8, 1993.

38   "Clinton Prepares to Relax Policy on Vietnam As U.S. Business Urges Access to New Market," *Wall Street Journal*, April 12, 1993.

39   "U.S. to Press Hanoi to Explain '72 P. O. W. Report," *The New York Times*, April 13, 1993.

40   *Washington Times*, April 12; *USA Today*, April 12; *Washington Post*, April 15; *Jersey Journal*, April 18.

41   For exposés of the document, see Nayan Chanda, "Research and Destroy," *Far Eastern Economic Review*, 6 May 1993, 20, and H. Bruce Franklin, "M.I.A. sma," *The Nation*, May 10, 1993, 616.

42   "In Clinton's Words: 'Fullest Possible Accounting' of M.I.A.'s," *The New York Times*, February 4, 1994.

43   *Wall Street Journal*, April 23, 1993.

CHAPTER SEVENTEEN

African Americans and the Vietnam War

JAMES WESTHEIDER

Prior to the Vietnam War, African Americans had served with pride and distinction in all of America's wars, viewing military service as an opportunity to prove their patriotism, their worth as citizens and soldiers, and as a vehicle for social and economic advancement. Blacks compiled an impressive record of military service despite the fact this almost always meant serving under unequal conditions in segregated units with substandard equipment, and being detailed mostly to menial or fatigue duties. Vietnam, it was hoped, would be different. It was the first war in which the armed forces were totally integrated from the beginning, and the first in which African Americans ostensibly had the same opportunities as whites. But as the war progressed, many blacks became disenchanted with the personal and institutional racism still endemic in the services, and this dissatisfaction would eventually manifest itself in several ways. It would prove to be a major catalyst in the rise of black solidarity within the armed forces, but would also be a contributing factor to an epidemic of racial violence in the services beginning in 1968. Ultimately, it would force the chain of command to address seriously the problems of racism and discrimination in the American military establishment.

In the early 1960s the military enjoyed a reputation in the black community as one of the most integrated and racially egalitarian institutions in America. At a time when African Americans still faced legalized segregation and disenfranchisement in the South, and discrimination throughout the country, the armed forces seemed to offer the best chance for opportunity and advancement. Columnist Roscoe Drummond remarked that the military represented "the most completely integrated, successfully integrated segment of American society," a sentiment echoed by many African Americans in the service. Captain Sylvian Wailes, for example, believed that, "basically, the Army affords you as good an opportunity as you can find . . . there is at least a better, or more of an equal opportunity." (Grove, 1966, p. 7).

For many, this meant economic opportunity and a sense of belonging. Sgt. Charles Hall, married with three children, re-enlisted for six more years because, "the job opportunities outside just weren't that good. The Army is taking care of me and my family." (Grove, 1966, p. 7). Hall was typical. In 1967 the black unemployment rate was 7.3 percent, more than double the white rate of 3.4 percent. That same year 49 percent of blacks in the army eligible for re-enlistment did so, compared to only 16 percent of the whites.

Military service also provided African Americans with a sense of self worth and status largely unavailable to them in the civilian sector. It also gave them yet another chance to dispel the myth that blacks were inferior to whites on the battlefield. Consequently, many African Americans, especially those hoping to make a career out of the military, often welcomed their assignment to Vietnam in the early days of the war. As late as 1968, Major Beauregard Brown could state with confidence that Vietnam, "represented a greater chance for advancement of the Negro career military man than any place in the world." Some, like Major-General Frederick E. Davison, the first black to command a division in Vietnam, had to wage a bitter fight with his own superiors just to get a combat assignment. "I wanted to go very badly," he recalled, but, "there were no plans to take me. And I God damn nearly lost my family – lost my family because they couldn't see why the hell I had to volunteer to go to Vietnam." (Westheider, 1997, p. 16).

The dedication and efforts of men like Hall, Brown, and Davison did not go unnoticed. African Americans in Southeast Asia were proving themselves to be capable and courageous, finally putting to rest the racist stereotype of the lazy and cowardly black in uniform. Instead, a new, more flattering image was emerging, that of the "good soldier," one who was brave, patriotic, and the equal of his white counterpart. Civil Rights leader Whitney Young remarked in 1966 that "for all intents and purposes, race is irrelevant," in Vietnam, and that, "in spite of dangers and loneliness, the muck and mire of a war torn land, colored soldiers fight and die courageously as representatives of all America." General William Westmoreland, Commander-in-Chief of Military Assistance Command, Vietnam (MACV), found the performance of black soldiers under his command to be "particularly inspirational... They have served with distinction. He has been courageous on the battlefield, proficient, and a possessor of technical skills." Thomas Johnson of the *New York Times* reported in 1968 (p. 1) that "the Negro fighting man has attained a sudden visibility – a visibility his fore-fathers never realized while fighting in past American wars."

But African Americans were paying a high price for this new visibility in the form of disproportionately high casualty rates. Though blacks made up only about ten percent of the total active duty personnel assigned to Vietnam, they made up, on average, between a quarter and a third of the combat troops, and accounted for 12.6 percent of US fatalities by 1973, a death rate approximately thirty percent higher than their percentage of US forces in Southeast Asia. In all, out of the nearly 58,000 Americans killed in Vietnam, 7,241 of them would be black.

The high casualty rates were viewed by some as proof that African Americans were worthy, loyal, and willing to do their part. Milton Olive, II, the father of Medal of Honor recipient Army Private Milton Olive III, claimed that his son's sacrifice, and "the service the colored soldier has given in Vietnam has erased for all time the disparaging statements made about him." One of the highest ranking African Americans in the Army in 1968, Lt. Colonel George Shoffer even remarked that, "I feel good about it. Not that I like the bloodshed, but the performance of the Negro in Vietnam tends to offset the fact that the Negro wasn't considered of being a front-line soldier in other wars." (Stern, 1968, p. 37).

Unlike Shoffer, many African Americans did not consider the dead in Vietnam as vindication, but rather as evidence that blacks were being used by a racist military, and bearing an undue burden in an immoral war. As early as 1966, the normally moderate *Baltimore Afro-American*, called the high death rates "disturbing," and suggested racism as one of the reasons. An editorial in the *Black Panther* in October 1968, blasted racist "glory seeking" generals for the needless deaths of black marines. A few even voiced the fear that the war was a sinister attempt by the government to reduce the black population, "a totalitarian instrument used to practice genocide against black people," according to Student Non-Violent Coordinating Committee (SNCC) spokesperson Walter Collins.

The US government was not using the war to systematically exterminate young blacks, but African Americans had good reason for believing that racism was a major problem in the armed forces, and that they were being required to bear an undue share of the war effort. Despite optimistic claims by the Department of Defense in 1968 that racial discrimination had been "officially eliminated" from the armed forces, the reality was far different, and African Americans would encounter racism and discrimination in virtually every facet of their military careers, beginning with their induction into the military.

The use of the Selective Service system to provide the bulk of America's manpower in Vietnam after 1965 was one of the more controversial issues of the war, and one that would have tremendous impact on the black community. President Lyndon Johnson did not want to disrupt the civilian economy by calling up large numbers of reserves and National Guard units, so the draft seemed to offer the best alternative. Technically, it was a fair system, and all men between the ages of 18 and 26 were eligible. But in the 1950s the Pentagon instituted a complex system of educational and professional deferments aimed at limiting the potential manpower pool. In practice this meant that the overwhelmingly white middle and upper classes who could afford the cost of a college education were largely exempt from compulsory service, and the majority of draftees who would have to fight in Vietnam were from the white and black working classes. It was not a case of legal discrimination, since it was just as easy for a black student to get a deferment as a white, but a classic case of institutional or "systemic" racism. Institutional racism can be defined as practices and policies which contain inherent vestiges of racism, tends to favor one ethnic group or groups over another, and is often subtle, whether intentional or not. College deferments were just one example of the institutional racism which still pervaded the armed forces.

Throughout the 1950s and early 1960s this inequity in the draft was not a major problem, draft calls were low, and military service was still viewed as an opportunity, and not as an undue burden. Allen Thomas, Jr. was drafted on his eighteenth birthday in 1957, but like many of his contemporaries he later voluntarily re-enlisted and made a career out of the Army. As late as 1966, 75 percent of African Americans responding to a Gallup poll thought the Selective Service was fair to minorities. But as America escalated its war in Vietnam things began to change, and the higher draft calls now meant that blacks were being drafted in disproportionately high numbers. Draft eligible black men made up around eleven percent of the population during the war. In 1966, 382,000 men were drafted, and 47,500, or 13.4 percent of the total were African Americans. In 1967, they accounted for over sixteen percent of the total. By the end of the war, blacks made up 14.3 percent of the total drafted. It became increasingly difficult for an eligible but unwilling African American to avoid the draft. In 1967 less than a third of the acceptable whites were actually drafted into the service, compared to nearly two thirds of the acceptable blacks.

By 1969, another poll would find that nearly half the African Americans surveyed now believed the draft to be racist and unfair, and the biggest single grievance cited was the use of college deferments. But African Americans had other reasons for denouncing the draft and the war in Vietnam. Dr. Martin Luther King, Jr., like many critics white or black, felt it was wrong to force a young man to fight and possibly die for an unjust and immoral cause. Others, like John Lewis of SNCC, argued that since African Americans were not accorded the same rights and privileges of citizenship as whites, they did not have the same obligations. "We have a different reason for not going," explained black activist Leonard Henderson in 1968. "The whites are resisting as citizens. We resist on the grounds that we aren't citizens." (McClean, 1968, p. 63).

The composition of the local draft boards was another problem. There were over 4,080 local draft boards in the United States, and African Americans remained chronically under-represented on them throughout the war. In 1966, they constituted only 1.3 percent of the total, and by 1968, still only 4.4 percent. It was these local boards that usually determined whether an applicant received a deferment, or had to serve, and they often became a battleground between black draft resisters and unsympathetic whites. A major point of contention was the granting of Conscientious Objector deferments to those opposed to the war on religious or moral grounds. The most famous case involved heavyweight boxing champion and Nation of Islam member Muhammad Ali who refused induction in 1967 based on his religious beliefs. Ali was convicted and sentenced to five years in prison, but his sentence was overturned in 1971 on a technicality. Most members of the NOI were not as fortunate, nearly one hundred Black Muslims served time in federal prisons for draft evasion during the Vietnam War. Not only were black resisters less able to secure a deferment than their white counterparts, they spent, on average, a year longer in jail if convicted of draft evasion (Baskir and Strauss, 1978, p. 100).

Most militant black organizations, such as SNCC, and the Black Panther Party were active in the anti-draft and antiwar movements, and their members usually refused induction. But the vast majority of young black men did not contest military service; some, because they feared harsh prison sentences, but others because they still believed it was their duty. Clinton Hunt, for instance, had no hesitation about reporting.

Every new recruit was given the Armed Forces Qualification Test (AFQT) to determine his or her aptitude and general intelligence, and the results of this exam largely determined one's future career or "Military Occupational Specialty," (MOS) in the services. Whites generally enjoyed two advantages over blacks in this procedure. Most had the benefit of a better education before entering the armed forces. The other reason was more controversial. Many critics claimed the exam contained an inherent Eurocentric bias, and that it tested one's knowledge of white culture, and not intelligence. A "bonus for growing up white," in the words of some black servicemen (NAACP, 1971, p. 3). Blacks usually tested poorly on the AFQT keeping them out of the more lucrative technical fields and slotting the majority of them in service or infantry units, and this almost always meant a tour of duty in Vietnam. Interestingly enough, when the Pentagon did replace the AFQT in 1972 with a more racially neutral battery of exams black test scores rose significantly while white scores remained virtually the same (Bowman, 1984, p. 78).

African Americans were convinced that a "double standard" existed for whites and blacks in promotion and assignment policies as well. "A Negro has to give two hundred percent where a white man just has to keep his nose clean to make sergeant," complained Specialist Four Victor Hall. Journalist Wallace Terry found that sixty-four percent of the blacks he surveyed in Vietnam believed whites were promoted faster than blacks (Terry, 1970, p. 8). As was often the case, perception mirrored reality; African Americans were being promoted at a slower rate than were whites, but in addition to racism, other factors were involved. They tended to be concentrated in infantry and service units that, on average, required fewer non-commissioned officers than did the white dominated technical fields and staff positions. Attainment of rank is often as much a product of seniority as it was job performance, and because segregation and racial quotas had only ended in the military in 1948, few blacks had the service time to qualify for the most senior NCO positions. Even as late as 1972, seventeen percent of the Army's enlisted strength was black, but only seven percent of its most senior sergeants and warrant officers.

It was the administration of military justice, however, that generated the greatest number of complaints of discrimination among black servicemen. Justice is administered at two distinct levels in the armed forces. Serious transgressions, such as murder, rape, or desertion, are handled through courts-martial, similar in most respects to a civilian trial. The Department of Defense's Task Force on Military Justice in 1972 concluded that African Americans were twice as likely as white service personnel to be brought up for trial. They also found a difference in the types of crimes blacks and whites were charged with. More than forty-one percent of black defendants were charged with major military infractions, such as attacking an officer. Whites usually faced court-martial for lesser infractions; over seventy-five percent of the military's drug related violations involved white offenders. African Americans were also more likely to receive longer prison sentences than whites if convicted. Blacks served on average, three years, whereas whites only about two and a half years (Department of Defense, 1972, Vol. IV, p. 57–60).

Most defendants, white or black, usually did not contest the charges. Many were guilty as charged, and some were told, or believed, they would receive a lighter sentence in return for cooperation. Others were ignorant of their rights. But most African Americans simply had no faith in a military justice system dominated by whites. Blacks constituted less than two percent of the Judge Advocates Office's (JAG) defense lawyers, judges and prosecutors during the Vietnam War era. As late as 1972, there were only seventeen African Americans among over seventeen hundred military lawyers. And black defendants just did not trust white lawyers. One black NCO stationed in Germany told a National Association for the Advancement of Colored People (NAACP) investigative team that he had "been in the service for fourteen years and I have never seen a white JAG lawyer do anything that great for a black man." A Department of Defense survey found that two thirds of the white prisoners, but less than half of the African Americans incarcerated believed they had received a fair trial (Department of Defense, 1972, II, p. 60).

These factors contributed to a disproportionately high number of African Americans in military prisons during the war years. In 1971 blacks made up a quarter of all Marine confinements, one third of all Army prisoners, and over half of the Air Force's prisoners. Blacks constituted only eight percent of the Navy's manpower, but sixteen percent of the brig population in that service.

Lesser offenses in the armed forces, such as uniform code violations for example, were handled through a procedure known as Non Judicial Punishment (NJP). Usually known as an Article 15 in the Army and Air Force, and as a Captain's Mast in the Navy and Marines, Non Judicial Punishment has no real equivalent in civilian society. Any officer or NCO could write someone up for an infraction, but guilt and any punishment was determined by the enlisted person's commanding officer or ship's captain in a hearing. Punishment could be as light as a letter of reprimand, or as harsh as thirty days in the stockade, and reduction in rank. Again, African Americans received more than their fair share of Article 15s. The figures for the Army's Berlin command were typical. African Americans made up only fifteen percent of its complement, but received over a third of the Article 15s.

The wide discretion given officers in the handling of NJP accounted for part of the discrepancy, and to yet another double-standard; one in which blacks were written up and punished for many infractions when whites were not. Blacks were often written up for wearing a "slave bracelet" usually woven out of boot laces and worn as a sign of black solidarity, but whites were seldom given NJP for wearing peace symbols or fraternity rings, which were also considered to be uniform code violations.

Sometimes the problem stemmed from the white command structure's ignorance of or lack of respect for black culture. One member of the Nation of Islam was given several Article 15s for refusing to eat the mess hall food on certain religious holidays. Christian and Jewish prisoners could get bibles, but Muslims often had great difficulty in obtaining the Koran. In many cases it was a white racist abusing the system. Major Michael F. Colacicco had to relieve a platoon sergeant who would wake up white soldiers for work call formation, but not black ones, and then give the African Americans Article 15s for being late. The Department of Defense's own Task Force on Military Justice (1972, I, p. 63) concluded in 1972 that "there is enough evidence of intentional discrimination by individuals to convince the task force that selective punishment is in many cases racially motivated."

Whether it was the selective service, testing, or the administration of military justice, African Americans were now seriously questioning the racial policies and fairness of an institution they had held in high esteem just a few years earlier. In part it was attributable to the growing unpopularity of the war itself. Few Americans believed the war could still be won after the Tet offensive in 1968, and many blacks saw no reason to fight and die for something they saw as being essentially a white man's cause. Private Bruce Jessup believed that "America is just fighting this war so that the white man can put boo coo (sic) money in his pocket . . . to hell with this war." "If the cracker wants to stay here and fight, let him," challenged marine Claude E. Bowen, "if they kick his ass, too damned bad. Its about time somebody did." Part of it was due to changing conditions in civilian society. The Civil Rights and Black Power movements helped heighten expectations among black recruits, and many now entered service expecting to find racism and prepared to challenge it. CmSgt. Milton White, founder of the Malcolm X Society in the Air Force spoke glowingly of the "younger black airmen just entering the military system, fresh from the revolutionary civilian society outside" (White, 1970, p. 3). Private Allen E. Jones spoke for many of his black comrades when he told a reporter for the *Baltimore Afro-American*, "They say I'm just a marine, but how can I forget eighteen years of being black and all that being black means in this country."

It was factors within the armed forces, however, which directly contributed to a growing sense of alienation among black service personnel. Though the military banned official, institutional racism, the Pentagon did little to eliminate it, or even punish personal racism among whites. "Niggers eat shit," "coons please go back to Africa," and other highly racist graffiti commonly adorned the walls of bars and latrines on many military posts. Confederate flags, always a source of racial friction, often flew over installations and fire bases in Vietnam. As one African American put it, "Chuck's all right until he gets a beer under his belt, and then its nigger this and nigger that."

Despite the official attempts at a "color blind" military, the armed forces were dominated and controlled by whites, and more often than not the cultural needs of African Americans were ignored. Post exchanges (PX) seldom carried black hair care products, clothes or magazines, for example. Blacks stationed stateside could shop for these amenities off-base, but this was seldom the case overseas, especially in Vietnam. In a combat zone, these little things often assumed much greater meaning. One grateful private in Vietnam thanked *Ebony* magazine for its coverage of African Americans in the war and explained that "everytime a soul brother gets an *Ebony* or a *Jet* magazine, there is a waiting line of at least 30–50 soul brothers throughout our troop waiting to read it. The black people back in the U.S. don't know what it means to a black soldier to have magazines such as *Ebony* and *Jet* to call their own." More radical publications, such as the *Black Panther* newspaper, were even more difficult to find, and were often banned by base commanders and ship's captains.

African Americans found constant reminders that they served in a white military. At Camp Lejeune the base barbershops displayed examples of acceptable haircuts for whites, but none for blacks. In West Germany there was an Army barracks named in honor of Confederate general Robert E. Lee, but no similar tribute to any black military heroes. Even the recreational facilities were geared more for whites. As one black marine pointed out, "you don't see many of the brothers out on the skeet range." The Juke boxes in service clubs seldom carried "soul music" like James Brown, or Aretha Franklin. Instead, it was mostly "country and western" artists, music favored by the white career NCOs. The issue of music was an important one. Most of the recruits were young, between nineteen and twenty-two, and the music of their generation, soul for blacks, rock for younger whites, and country for older whites, had a profound influence on their lives. Journalist Wallace Terry reported that blacks in Vietnam believed they should control twenty-two percent of the music being played on military stations because they made up twenty two percent of the casualties (Terry, 1970, p. 14). It is interesting to note that many of the racially motivated fights that broke out in the armed forces began over a dispute involving music.

African Americans responded to the racism and official ambivalence in many ways. Many just endured it until their enlistment was up and they were free to leave. Others decided not to wait that long and deserted. Vietnam veteran Terry Whitmore cited racism and opposition to the war as his reasons for deserting. Many, especially those who hoped to make a career out of the military, still believed in the system and sought to change it peacefully, and through acceptable channels. Sailors stationed at the Navy's submarine base at Groton, Connecticut, successfully petitioned their commanding officer for more black products at the PX, and more black music at the NCO and EM clubs. Often the requests were quite moderate in nature. Black cadets at the Air Force Academy petitioned their commandant only for more equitable enforcement of the regulations, less abusive language from the instructors, and a minority studies room, open to all.

But many blacks found it difficult and dangerous to appeal through official channels. Allen Thomas, Jr., who served three tours of duty in Vietnam recalled that "if you were black and spoke up, you were a troublemaker, an instigator, whatever. If you were white, you were considered an innovator" (Westheider, 1997, p. 81). At Camp Lejeune, North Carolina, in 1969, black marines petitioned their commanding officer anonymously because they feared that even a "timid, mild-toned missive," could lead to reprisals.

Suspicious of the system and feeling like outsiders in a white dominated military, African Americans began seeking strength and comfort in an increased sense of racial solidarity. By 1968 a new black culture, based on racial pride, solidarity, and a sense of a common mission, began to emerge in the armed forces. It had its own terminology, some borrowed from civilian society, but much of it indigenous. Fellow blacks were "brothers," or "bloods," and whites, especially racist ones, were "beasts," "chucks," or "rabbits." Many of the symbols identified with black solidarity and militancy were originally developed in Vietnam. Black marines at Da Nang designed and flew one of the earliest known "Black Power" flags, which quickly became a model for others throughout the American defense establishment. Most had a red background for the blood of brothers shed in the war, and a black foreground representing black culture. The most common device in the center was a pair of crossed spears over a shield, and surrounded by a wreath, symbolizing, "violence if necessary, peace if possible." Many of the flags also bore a saying in Swahili with a similar meaning, "My Fear is for You."

Bloods in Vietnam also began to wear more personal symbols of pride and solidarity. It was a common practice for soldiers to write messages on their helmets, and many African Americans would chalk sayings such as "Black Power" or "Black is beautiful," on theirs. In addition to wearing slave bracelets, many also began carrying black power canes, usually made out of ebony with a clenched fist at the top. The upraised clenched fist was representative of the black power "salute" or "check" exchanged between brothers. Between black officers and enlisted personnel the check was often substituted for the standard military salute.

The "Dap" or ritualized handshake might have been the most important cultural expression to emerge from Vietnam. The term itself comes from a Vietnamese word, Dep, meaning beautiful, and probably originated among black prisoners at Long Binh Stockade. Each move in dapping had a specific meaning, clinching fingers together and then touching the back of the hand, for example, meant "My brother, I'm with you." There were many basic and common gestures, but numerous variations soon developed, some with over a hundred steps and taking five minutes to complete.

As the war progressed so did the trend among many bloods towards self separation, and the military became increasingly polarized along racial lines. Marine Corps historians Henry I. Shaw and Ralph Donnelly (1975, p. 71) found that "more and more, some young black marines tended to draw in upon themselves and develop a brotherhood of racial pride and to consider white marines as inherently prejudiced against them." Many African Americans did not trust whites, or feel particularly comfortable around them. "White people are dull," explained one black trooper, "they have no style and they don't know how to relax." Air Force Sergeant Jack Smedley explained that "a man wants to relax, really relax when he's off duty. He doesn't want to listen with half an ear to hear if some drunken whites are going to call him a nigger." Blacks often found themselves unwelcome in the company of whites. Stateside patterns of segregation followed the American military presence around the world, and Vietnam was no different. There were numerous bars, houses of prostitution, and restaurants that catered only to whites. Sergeant Donald Duncan reported cases of African Americans being "thrown out bodily" from all-white establishments, and the use of such violence was common.

African Americans reacted by patronizing "Black only" establishments where they could listen to Soul music, and enjoy Soul food away from hostile whites, and often in a different part of town. In Saigon, most of the white bars were located along Tu Do street, but blacks usually sought their entertainment in the Khanh Hoi district, for example.

This desire for separation also included one's living quarters, or "hooches" as they were commonly called in Southeast Asia. In Vietnam it was often a soldier or marine's prerogative to choose his own hooch mates, and soon all-black hooches became common on many bases. Captain (later Lt. Colonel) Vernon L. Connor found racially segregated barracks when he first took command of an artillery battery in Vietnam. Like many other officers, he soon put a stop to the practice, because it contributed to the "polarization of blacks against whites. I made them stop that, but you couldn't stop them from socializing with the people they wanted to" (Westheider, 1997, p. 91).

At no time, however, were the races completely divided. There was always some mixing, especially while on duty. Stewart H. Barnhoff, a company commander in Vietnam in 1971, recalled that "the black guys always hung out with the blacks and the white guys with the whites, but on duty everybody tended to work fairly well together." In many units non-racist whites were also considered brothers, and often included in the black social circle. "We are not antiwhite and don't bar whites who dig us," explained Vietnam veteran Dwight Rawls. This was especially true in combat formations, where the need to rely on one another in the face of a common enemy forged the camaraderie and unit cohesion often lacking in support and service companies. Most combat veterans would have agreed with black marine Sergeant Melvin Murrel Smith who claimed that "the friendships formed between whites and Negroes in Vietnam will never die because of what we went through together" (Johnson, 1969, p. 14).

But all too often whites identified black solidarity with black militancy and reacted with derision and hostility. Some developed a "white power" check. Dapping in particular was a major source of friction. The DoD's Task Force on Military Justice (1972, I, pp. 60–1) concluded that the Dap provoked "a reaction of white anger out of proportion to its own importance." Whites often grew angry and impatient waiting for blacks ahead of them in chow or PX lines to complete lengthy daps, and violence might result. In Japan in 1971 marine private Raymond Burns killed Corporal Thomas L. Bertler after the corporal had taunted him about dapping.

Commanding officers usually reacted by banning dapping and other overt symbols of black solidarity. In 1969 Marine Commandant General Leonard F. Chapman issued a directive essentially banning all "actions, signs symbols or words which are contrary to tradition," at work or during formation. In 1973 the Navy prohibited dapping altogether. In the Army and Air Force many base and company commanders also banned most outward manifestations of black pride and solidarity, and meted out Article 15s to, or even court-martialed, offenders.

But these attempts to suppress black solidarity backfired, and instead led to even greater self-segregation. Many began to pressure other blacks into abandoning white social contacts. Pinkie Hauser, one of the few African American women to serve in Vietnam remembers being admonished by more militant blacks for having "honkie" friends (Marshall, 1987, p. 45) For others it was just further proof that separate but peaceful coexistence with whites was not possible. Many now spoke of open warfare between the races. John R. White serving a tour in Vietnam in 1969 saw whites, not the Vietcong or North Vietnamese as his enemy. "No more talk . . . we just kill them off or they kill us off. That's just how bad it is here."

By 1968 all of the elements needed to trigger widespread racial violence in the armed forces were now present. The war was increasingly unpopular, and morale in general in the military was beginning to deteriorate. A black subculture had developed and provoked suspicion and hostility from whites. And there were those on both sides quite eager to engage in racial warfare.

But the catalyst might well have been the assassination of civil rights leader Dr. Martin Luther King, Jr. on April 4, 1968 in Memphis, Tennessee. Many whites deplored the murder and were sympathetic. Navy Seabee John Brackett recalled a "couple of good friends who were white and not racist, and that helped." But many whites openly celebrated. Brackett also remembers the "overt joy expressed by some . . . that this 'troublemaker' had been eliminated." Some whites at Cam Ranh Bay paraded around in makeshift Ku Klux Klan outfits and temporarily hoisted a Confederate flag over the Navy Headquarters building. Others were apathetic, like one white military policeman who remarked, "We have three hundred Americans dying here each week . . . King was one man."

For African Americans, King was not just "one man," and his death changed everything. Most felt bitter and disillusioned. Writing from Vietnam, Morocco Coleman claimed that "almost everywhere here you can see the unity which exists among the Negro soldiers. After the assassination of Dr. M. L. King you could also feel the malcontent." Allen Thomas, Jr. recalled that "some of the younger guys were angry and just wanted to hurt someone." James Hawkins also believed that "Dr. King's death changed things, it . . . made a lot of people angry – people with weapons" (Westheider, 1997, p. 98).

The result was the outbreak of widespread racial violence. The violence generally assumed two forms; the most common involved attacks on a member or few members of the opposite race by several individuals. Rarer, but far more alarming were large scale "rumbles" involving dozens or even more participants on both sides. Stateside, racially motivated gangfights erupted on military bases from Fort Bragg, North Carolina to Kaneohe Marine Corps Air Station in Hawaii. Overseas, bases in West Germany, Okinawa, Japan, and Vietnam were particularly affected.

In Vietnam, however, racial violence seldom broke out in combat units. There was more cohesion than in rear echelon formations, and everyone was too heavily armed to allow an argument or a confrontation to escalate into widespread violence. The one exception to this were fraggings. As morale collapsed in Vietnam officers often became the target of murder attempts by their own men. The weapon of choice was usually a fragmentation grenade – hence the term fragging – because it didn't leave any incriminating evidence. A congressional inquiry documented 1,016 incidents of fraggings between 1969 and 1972, and while there were many reasons given, including bad morale and drug use, race was a factor in many of them.

The Navy had numerous problems at shore installations, and several incidents at sea, including gangfights on the aircraft carriers *Constellation* and *Kitty Hawk*. On *Kitty Hawk* a potentially deadly armed confrontation between African Americans and a marine reaction team was averted only by the timely leadership of the vessel's black Executive Officer, Ben Cloud (Foner, 1974, pp. 239–41).

Some of the earliest fights occurred in military prisons. In April 1968 at Mannheim stockade in West Germany a large fight broke out between white and black prisoners after a white inmate made racist remarks about Dr. King's death. In August 1968 black prisoners rioted and fought whites at both the Navy's DaNang Brig, and the Army's sprawling Long Binh Stockade. It took Navy and Marine officials twenty hours to restore order at DaNang, and took the Army over three weeks to re-assert full control at Long Binh. As late as November 1972, black prisoners fought viciously with white guards at the Navy's Norfolk, Virginia Brig.

More often than not the fights began at recreational facilities, especially the on-base service clubs. The clubs made a good breeding ground for trouble because unlike many of the off-base recreational facilities they were patronized by both black and white. Alcohol, friction over music, or the ill advised use of racial slurs or "trigger" words also were contributing factors. Captain (later Lt. Colonel) Charles Shrader stated that the Enlisted Men's club at Long Binh was a "never ending source" of racial problems in his company. In May 1968 military officials closed down the EM club at Qui Nhon after a "racial melee." The problem with the service clubs was obviously not confined to Vietnam. One of the largest rumbles happened on July 20, 1969 at a Camp LeJeune service club when a black marine attempted to cut in on a white sailor dancing with a black WAVE. The ensuing violence left one dead, dozens injured, three critically, and forty-four arrested. Two years later, the Navy was forced to temporarily close its service club at the Navy Medical Center at Bethesda, Maryland following racial violence at that facility.

The racial violence alarmed military officials, and for a time seemed to threaten the ability of the armed forces to conduct its various missions around the world, including the war in Vietnam. But officers and officials believed that the vast majority of African Americans remained loyal, if disgruntled "good soldiers," and still displayed a certain amount of faith in the system. In a letter to Secretary of Defense Melvin R. Laird in April 1972, Roy Wilkins, Executive Director of the NAACP assured Laird that "the overwhelming majority of the Negro soldiers...have a deep desire to perform well for their country...they continue to cling to the belief that the United States has the capacity to correct injustices." (NAACP, 1971, p. 2). Most military officials agreed with Wilkins, and believed that the racial problems plaguing the services were largely a product of civilian society, and brought into the armed forces by a few radicals. A new stereotype of at least some black soldiers emerged in the latter half of the war, that of the "black militant," and most officers were convinced it was these militants who were causing the problem. Captain Richard Bevington claimed that racial violence in his company was caused by "a handful" of militants, and John Ellis blamed "black power types," for problems in his command.

Pentagon and Department of Defense officials believed that many of the militants belonged to organizations dedicated to subverting the armed forces. The Black Panther Party in particular, was singled out as the greatest threat to racial harmony in the military. Representative Richard H. Ichord of Missouri a member of the House Committee on Internal Security warned congress that the Panthers and similar groups "highly exploited" the issue of racism.

The Panthers were greatly admired by many of the Bloods in Vietnam. "The Black Panthers give the beast something to fear like we feared the Ku Klux Klan all our lives," explained Seaman Milton Banion, and another black sailor vowed to "join 'em, and I'd help them kill all those honky muther fuckers." Wallace Terry in 1970 (p. 140) found nearly a third of the black troops he surveyed in Vietnam willing to join the Panthers or other militant groups when they returned to civilian life.

Black soldiers may have respected the Panthers, but there were actually very few of them in the ranks. Panthers were generally prohibited by the party from serving in the "white racist" military, and the main goal of the Panthers was civilian class revolution, and not necessarily undermining the military from within. Most of the organized radicals in the armed forces were members of either old left Marxist organizations, like the Communist Party USA (CPUSA) and the Socialist Workers Party (SWP), or black nationalist groups operating almost exclusively within the military, but with some connections to civilian radicals, like the BPP. Most were tiny, short lived, and operated at a single installation, like the Peoples Justice Committee, at Fort Hood, Texas, for example. But three of them, The Movement for a Democratic Military (MDM), GIs United Against the War, and the American Serviceman's Union (ASU), were large and well organized. The ASU was probably the largest, claiming over ten thousand members and over 210 chapters worldwide.

These organizations were dedicated to fomenting revolution from within the armed forces, and were involved in a wide variety of activities. They organized demonstrations, operated "underground" newspapers, such as the ASU's *The Bond*, and stole weapons from the military. Authorities also suspected the MDM was responsible for a series of terrorist bombings, including the burning of two mess halls at Fort Ord, California, in August 1970. What they were not largely responsible for was the racial violence. Most had a Marxist orientation, and viewed the fight against the predominately white power structure as much a class struggle as a racial one. Far from advocating violence against white GIs, they counseled against it. The MDM, like the others, claimed that "all GIs must unite to fight the real enemy – the pig" (US Congress, House Committee on Internal Security, 1972, pp. 6568, 6751).

Military officials attacked the racial problems in the services in two ways. First they decided that the best way to eliminate radicalism was to eliminate the radicals. Some were simply transferred to places they could little harm. Joseph Miles, a leading activist at Fort Jackson, South Carolina, found himself posted to a remote radar station in Alaska. Others felt the fury of the military justice system. In February 1969, Lt. (jg) Susan Schnall of the GI Association was convicted of antiwar activity, given six months at hard labor, and dishonorably discharged from the Navy. Thomas Tuck, the ASU representative at Fort Knox, Kentucky was also court-martialed and dismissed from the service, a fate shared by many of the militant leadership.

But in addition to waging an internal war against the radicals the military also instituted much needed reforms, and finally became serious about eradicating both personal and institutional racism. Testing and promotion policies were changed, and non judicial punishment procedures were overhauled, eliminating some of the commanding officer's wide discretionary powers, and providing more rights to the accused. In 1969 both the Army and Marines instituted service wide race relations programs, and the Air Force began to assign at least one Equal Opportunity Employment Officer to each of its installations. Serious racial reform in the Navy began with the appointment of Admiral Elmo Zumwalt as Chief of Naval Operations in November 1970. Under Zumwalt the Navy began more than two hundred new race relations and equal opportunity programs and reconfirmed its commitment to existing ones. By 1972, and near the end of the Vietnam war, all four services would implement comprehensive affirmative action programs, opening many once virtually closed MOSs to African Americans.

Ultimately, the new reforms would prove successful, but many were not in place until after the war. Allen Thomas, Jr. claimed that "things got better for some of us after Vietnam . . . it was a lot better because some things were just no longer permitted." (Westheider, 1997, p. 173). Officials had been more serious this time about implementing reform, but another reason was the increasing number of African Americans in the command structure. Blacks made up only two percent of the officer corps during Vietnam, but the number would steadily rise to over six percent by the late 1980s. And many, like Colin Powell, the first black Chairman of the Joint Chiefs of Staff would hold senior command and policy making positions.

Much of the credit for racial reform in the armed forces belongs with the men and women who championed change during one of America's most bitter wars. Like their white comrades in arms they fought bravely but unsuccessfully on one battlefield, but achieved a victory on another. They forced the armed forces to live up to its credo of equality and opportunity, and left as their legacy a more racially egalitarian military, as an example for the rest of society.

REFERENCES

Baskir, Lawrence M., and Strauss, William A. 1978: *Chance and Circumstance: The Draft, the War and the Vietnam Generation.* New York: Random House.

Bowman, William, Little, Roger and Sicilia, Thomas G. 1984: *The All-Volunteer Force After a Decade: Retrospect and Prospect.* Washington: Pergamon-Brassey, International Defense Publishers.

Department of Defense 1971: *Annual Report for Fiscal Year 1968.* Washington: US Government Printing Office.

Department of Defense 1972: *Task Force on the Administration of Military Justice in the Armed Forces, Volumes I–V.* Washington: US Government Printing Office.

Foner, Jack D. 1974: *Blacks and the Military in American History.* New York: Praeger Publishers, Inc.

Grove, Gene 1966: "The Army and the Negro," *The New York Times Magazine,* 24 July, pp. 5–8.

Marshall, Kathryn 1987: *In the Combat Zone: An Oral History of American Women in Vietnam.* Boston: Little, Brown and Co.

National Association for the Advancement of Colored People, 1971: *The Search for Military Justice.* New York: NAACP.

Johnson, Thomas 1968: "Negroes In the Nam," *Ebony,* August pp. 31–40.

Johnson, Thomas 1969: "Negroes in Vietnam Uneasy about U.S.," *The New York Times,* 1 May, p. 1.

McClean, L. Deckle 1968: "The Black Man and the Draft," *Ebony,* August pp. 60–6.

Shaw, Henry I., Jr. and Donnelly, Ralph W. 1975: *Blacks IN the Marine Corps.* Washington: History and Museums Division Headquarters, US Marine Corps.

Stern, Sol 1968: "When the Black G.I. Comes Back from Vietnam," *The New York Times Magazine,* 24 March, pp. 27–39.

Terry, Wallace, 1970: "Bringing the War Home," *The Black Scholar,* Volume #2, November, pp. 6–18.

Terry, Wallace, 1984: *Bloods: An Oral History of the Vietnam War by Black Veterans.* New York: Random House.

United States Congress, House Committee on Internal Security 1972: *Investigation of Attempts to Subvert the United States Armed Forces.* Washington: US Government Printing Office.

Westheider, James E. 1997: *Fighting on Two Fronts: African Americans and the Vietnam War.* New York: New York University Press.

White, Milton 1970: "Malcolm X in the Military," *The Black Scholar*, May pp. 31–5.

CHAPTER EIGHTEEN

Mexican Americans and the Viet Nam War

GEORGE MARISCAL

There can be no doubt that since the turn of the century, Mexican Americans have served in the US armed forces in disproportionate numbers.[1] One factor that complicates the service of this community is the thorny issue of assimilation, its connection to patriotism and to the promise of full citizenship in the nation. For those groups who are already marked as not fully "American," the desire to "fit in" and to not call attention to one's self by refusing to practice conventional behavior is especially strong. Even in the first antiwar plays staged in the late 1960s by El Teatro Campesino, we sense the tension produced by the desire to assimilate. In the 1971 *acto* (one-act play) titled *Soldado Razo* (*Buck Private*), the narrator describes the departure of a young Chicano soldier: "So Johnny left for Vietnam, never to return. He didn't want to go and yet he did. It never crossed his mind to refuse. How can he refuse the gobierno de los Estados Unidos? How could he refuse his family?"[2] The suggestion that his family's wishes coincide with those of the US government, that the refusal to serve would disappoint both equally, reminds us that Latinos like other "unmeltable" ethnic groups are under immense pressure to "fit in" and submit to the demands of State authority.

The drive to assimilate through military service is exacerbated by one of the most pernicious inheritances from Mexican culture – warrior patriotism. The idea that masculine behavior of necessity must include a readiness to die for "la patria" is powerful in Mexican nationalist ideology. When transferred to the Chicano context it is especially dangerous since the Mexican male's rhetorical claim that he is willing to die anytime anywhere becomes a deadly reality once it is linked to US imperialist projects. As the voice of the son declares in famed *tejano* composer José Morante's "Corrido del padre de un soldado": "Soy purito mexicano/y no temo al morir" ("I'm one hundred percent Mexican/and I'm not afraid to die").[3] In their 1991 album *16 de septiembre*, to cite a more recent example, the *tejano* musical group "Little Joe y la familia" combined national icons from both the US and Mexico, and invoked cliches like "Voy a la guerra contento" ("I go happily off to war") and "Mi raza sabe morir dondequiera" ("My people know how to die anywhere") in the charged context of the Persian Gulf War.[4] Two generations earlier, New Mexican writer and World War I veteran Florencio Trujillo had written a poem to his nephew who was preparing to ship out during World War II: "Trujillo le contestó/ya vamos para los frentes/ahora lo que hemos de hacer/pues es mostrarnos valientes" ("Trujillo answered him/we're off to the front/so what we must do/is show that we are brave").[5]

In his 1979 short story, "Feliz Cumpleaños, E. U. A." ("Happy Birthday, U.S.A."), Rolando Hinojosa writes against the patriotic grain and asks his reader to imagine the unimaginable: "Sí, y como dije, después vino Korea y de repente, como si tal cosa, vino el Vietná...y allí va la raza de nuevo...ah, y esta vez muchos de los bolillos rehusaron ir – sí, raza – que no iban y no iban y no fueron... ¿qué tal si la raza no hubiera ido, eh? Se pueden imaginar." ("Yeah, like I said, then came Korea and then, just like that, came Vietnam...and there went Chicanos again...and this time a lot of white boys refused to go – yes, my fellow Chicanos – they weren't going to go and they didn't go... What would have happened if Chicanos hadn't gone? You can imagine").[6] The implied listener in Hinojosa's text is a traditional Mexican American community aghast at the thought that someone, anyone, had refused military service. If Chicanos were to just say no, how would the State respond? More important, how would the community react? In Luis Valdez's play, *The Dark Root of a Scream*, the death in Viet Nam of the character Indio is attributed in part to the pressure to serve he felt from the community:

Gato: He rapped against the war, but his time came and he had to go a huevo just like everybody else.
Priest: He was concerned what the barrio would think if he refused induction.
Gato: If he'd gone to the pinta instead of the army, all the barrio would have said he was chicken.
Priest: He was considering fleeing the country, but he knew he'd never be able to return as a community leader.[7]

In massive numbers, then, Chicanos faced with the prospect of going to Viet Nam reacted with the same sense of duty and/or fatalism that had inspired their fathers, cousins, and uncles in World War II and Korea.[8] The case of one community is telling with regard to the sacrifices made by Chicanos in the armed forces. In the small town of Silvis, Illinois, along the Mississippi river near the Iowa border, is a neighborhood established by Mexican railroad workers who had journeyed north to labor on the Rock Island line. During World War II, Korea, and Viet Nam, a single block in that community (renamed "Hero Street" in the 1960s) sent eighty-seven young men to war. Among those who died were men like Tony Pompa, a Mexican citizen who enlisted under an assumed name. As of 1994, over one hundred residents of Hero St. had served in the US military. In the area of creative writing, texts such as Américo Paredes's short stories in *The Hammon and the Beans*, Tomás Rivera's *...y no se lo tragó la tierra*, and Hinojosa's *Klail City* series and *Korean Love Songs* recount Chicano/a experiences of World War II and Korea as well as the discrimination faced by returning veterans.

I stress the Mexican American participation in US wars neither to praise or condemn those who served but to focus critical attention on the social networks that allowed some groups to resist the war while others were literally unable to do so. The conflation of duty to family and duty to country is strikingly present in one Chicano veteran's explanation of why he served: "I didn't have much of a choice. If I had refused to get drafted, what was I going to do? It would have been just as hard to refuse the draft as it was to go into the army. Where was I going to go? I had nowhere to go. That would have been real hard on my *jefitos* [parents]."[9] The easy solution of "You don't have to go!" offered to minority draftees by the relatively privileged college student-led segment of the antiwar movement simply could not account for the intense pressures and contradictions that permeated working-class communities of color.

The material conditions of poverty, job discrimination, and educational tracking together with what was felt to be the overwhelming obligation to serve and "prove" one's loyalty according to traditional notions of nation and masculinity were responsible for the relatively low number of Chicano draft resisters during the Viet Nam era. Nevertheless, Chicano men slowly joined the ranks of those who refused to participate in the killing. Denver native, Ernesto Vigil, was the first to refuse induction, and stated that he would not fight against his "brown brothers in Vietnam."[10] This sentiment and language would be picked up by other resisters like Rosalío Muñoz, David Corona (son of long-time Chicano activist, Bert Corona), Fred Aviles, and Manuel Gómez. Gómez's letter to his draft board written in 1969 stands as an early example of the structure of recognition that would emerge in later fictional representations of the war. Gómez wrote: "The Vietnamese people are not my enemy, but brothers involved in the same struggle for justice against a common enemy. We are all under the same sky. East and West are one."[11] A combination of the language of Chicano nationalism and mythic images of a post-lapsian nature, Gómez's letter is striking insofar as it previews the major tropes of Chicano antiwar literature in the early 1970s.

By the late 1960s, the fact that US involvement in Viet Nam had nothing to do with the issues in World War II was as evident to many in the Mexican American community as it was to the rest of the country. The shift from an earlier generation's unqualified patriotism to the Chicano generation's ambivalent attitudes towards the war are perhaps best exemplified in a letter written by a World War II veteran and LULAC activist father to his son who was in the military but had refused to comply with orders to Viet Nam:

> Dear Son: Your Mom and I were very shocked to read your letter and you know we have never had a Herrera yet who has refused to serve his country. Your family will never live it down and your life will be ruined. You should not question your country's motives and its foreign policy, and in the overall picture someone must suffer. . . . Your objections will be widely publicized here in Texas and your family will probably have to move out of Texas to get over the embarrassment and humiliation of what you are doing. Knowing your feelings your entire family will be more proud of you now if you go back and finish the few short months that you have to go. Think of your AGGIE BUDDIES! Your school has a glorious tradition almost as long as the Herrera family of serving our country always

without question. There has not been a single Aggie Buddy that has refused to serve, there has not been a single Herrera, don't be the first one son, don't make us ashamed of you. Go back and serve your country. Don't break our hearts. Please call us and tell us that you are going to do the right thing to your country and to your family.[12]

From the father's point of view, the profound shame the son has brought upon his family will cause them to be driven out of their home. By disrupting the long line of Mexican American service in US wars, the younger Herrera threatens to destroy one of the most important roads to assimilation.

Nowhere are the contradictions inherent in the Chicano soldier's position more evident than in the story of Everett Alvarez, Jr. Held as a POW for eight and a half years in North Viet Nam, Alvarez's participation in the US war in Southeast Asia spans the early 1960s when he became a Navy aviator to the Gulf of Tonkin incident to the release of the POWs in 1973 to the dedication of the Viet Nam Memorial in 1982. What becomes Alvarez's written account of this twenty year period, the autobiographical *Chained Eagle* is at once a conventional tale of heroism, an apology for the war, and a compendium of mutually exclusive positions regarding its meaning.[13]

Alvarez's prologue is a stunning example of patriotic discourse as it was reformulated in the 1980s by Reaganite ideologues and a large sector of Viet Nam veterans. In their view, the problem with the war was that the men who fought it were not allowed to win. The fact that such an interpretation as well as the following analysis were written by a member of a relatively disempowered minority group, the grandson of Mexican immigrants, makes it both predictable and paradoxical:

> If wars bring the ultimate destruction, they also present the noblest challenges. Prolonged captivity under brutal conditions in a hostile land pits a man against overwhelming odds. My survival depended on much more than trying to satisfy a craving for food, and overcoming the emptiness of isolation and the pain of torture. My strength came from holding fast to my faith in God and belief in the values enshrined in our Constitution: duty, loyalty, unity, integrity, honor, allegiance, courage and hope. Without my absolute belief in these core virtues of our heritage I don't believe I would have pulled through alive and sane.[14]

The confusion of military values with those implicitly stated in the US Constitution marks Alvarez's text as the product of a career Navy officer. But it also suggests the easy passage made in the minds of many Americans between the more recently elaborated responsibilities of citizens and ancient patriarchal and religious codes of conduct. As he stepped off the plane upon his return, Alvarez told the assembled crowd: "God bless the president and God bless you Mr. and Mrs. America."[15]

The material from *Chained Eagle* reproduced here represents the divisions that divided US society in general and the Alvarez family in particular. Despite the fact that their son and brother was being held by the North Vietnamese, both Alvarez's mother (Soledad) and sister (Delia) came to publically oppose the war. Delia Alvarez was an especially visible protester. She attended a World Peace Conference in Paris, and appeared on a number of national television programs in the US. What emerges from Everett's text is a portrait of a Chicano family torn apart by its loyalty to its eldest son, its belief in the promises of US culture, and (for some members) the painful realization that the morality of the war was questionable at best. As Delia Alvarez put it: "Everett will return when Vietnamese children will be able to look at the sky and clouds and not fear that a bomb will drop that will burn and tear their bodies."[16]

Much has been made about the fact that the Viet Nam War has not and perhaps cannot be absorbed by official US history. Despite attempts to "get beyond Viet Nam" by conducting "more successful" wars against developing nations, it is clear that something called Viet Nam continues to inhabit the national psyche. Myra MacPherson's *Long Time Passing: Vietnam and the Haunted Generation* (1984; rpt. 1993) plays upon the notion of lingering trauma and tragedy. Her book presented itself as an attempt to "heal wounds" and "erase our collective amnesia," yet a decade after it was published the wounds and amnesia remain open and deep. I would argue that the American war in Viet Nam can be neither "figured out" nor "factored in" at least in part because the war marked the end of uncontested "white" hegemony and radically destabilized the meaning of what it was to be an American. The racial, ethnic, and class composition of US combat units and the final Vietnamese victory together revealed the hypocrisy and inefficacy of the white male ruling class and their particular brand of liberalism. That a disproportionate number of combat troops were poor, brown, and black should have forced (but did not) a total rethinking of American identity and the rights and responsibilities of citizenship. The ramifications of this break in the liberal tradition continue to be felt in the late 1990s through neo-conservative charges of "reverse discrimination," the "oppression of the white male," and other self-serving fantasies that drive moves to roll-back the minimal gains of the Civil Rights era.

In early 1967, in a brilliant moral and political analysis of the war's disastrous effects, Martin Luther King, Jr. spoke in Manhattan's Riverside Church:

> As I ponder the madness of Vietnam and search within myself for ways to understand and respond in compassion my mind goes constantly to the people of that peninsula. I speak now not of the soldiers of each side, not of the junta in Saigon, but simply of the people who have been living under the curse of war for almost three continuous decades now. I think of them too because it is clear to me that there will be no meaningful solution there until some attempt is made to know them and hear their broken cries ... In order to atone for our sins and errors in Vietnam, we should take the initiative in bringing a halt to this tragic war ... We must continue to raise our voices if our nation persists in its perverse ways in Vietnam. We must be prepared to match actions with words by seeking out every creative means of protest possible.[17]

Dr. King's plea for an end to American ethnocentrism, his repudiation of Johnson's war policy, and his call for renewed efforts by the antiwar movement would be silenced by the assassinations of 1968 and the election of Richard Nixon. But his claim in the same speech that the war in Viet Nam had been the primary cause for the derailment of the domestic war on poverty would be picked up by Johnson himself and become a generally accepted axiom in later histories of the period.

The bankruptcy of traditional liberalism exposed in Dr. King's speech deserves our further attention. For if poor whites and poor people of color were being victimized at home because of misguided national priorities, poor whites and poor people of color were also the ones thrust into the prosecution of the war. It is the point at which Johnson's War on Poverty entered into an unholy alliance with the Pentagon that produced a conduit leading directly from the barrios and ghettos to the killing fields of Viet Nam. The primary architects of that conduit were Secretary of Defense Robert McNamara and Daniel Patrick Moynihan, the latter following up on his 1965 analysis of what he considered to be the "disorganized and matrifocal" structure of "the Negro family." In a classic piece of bureaucratic double-talk Moynihan stated: "Very possibly our best hope is seriously to use the armed forces as a socializing experience for the poor – particularly the Southern poor – until somehow their environment begins turning out equal citizens."[18] No attempt was made to figure out how the "environment" of the "southern poor" (i.e., poor African Americans) was to "somehow" become a more just and equal set of circumstances. It is the meaning of Moynihan's "somehow" that to this day has yet to be adequately defined.

The plan to socialize poor people through military service had its origins in the Task Force on Manpower Conservation report submitted to President Johnson in January of 1964. Established by President Kennedy two months before his death, the task force had been charged to investigate the fact that one out of two men tested by the Selective Service System were found unqualified for the armed forces. In Kennedy's opinion: "A young man who does not have what it takes to perform military service is not likely to have what it takes to make a living. Today's military rejects are tomorrow's hard-core unemployed."[19] As a member of the original task force, McNamara was well-positioned to make the deadly connection between "curing poverty" and supplying additional men for the military. Those men who had been previously rejected for either mental or medical reasons would be "re-tested" in order to prepare them for what Selective Service director General Lewis Hershey called "a program for the guidance, testing, counseling, training and rehabilitation of youths found disqualified for military service."[20] Although it would take more than two years for McNamara and Moynihan to concoct the final solution, the basic elements of a project that would lead hundreds of poor men to Viet Nam were in place.

Because of the situation in Southeast Asia in the mid-1960s, it had become clear that the draft pool would have to be expanded, either in an upwards (to include middle-class college students) or downwards direction. In August of 1966, at a time of escalating manpower needs, Secretary of Defense McNamara announced the creation of Project 100,000. By presenting Project 100,000 as another jobs and training program linked to the "Great Society" doctrine, McNamara could claim that disadvantaged youth would learn skills in the military that would serve them well in civilian life, thereby echoing Kennedy's original concern expressed three years earlier. In his speech before the VFW convention, McNamara's rhetoric linked the poor to the specter of the diseased: "The poor of America have not had the opportunity to earn their fair share of this Nation's abundance, but they can be given an opportunity to serve in their country's defense and they can be given an opportunity to return to civilian life with skills and aptitudes which, for them and their families, will reverse the downward spiral of human decay."[21] The goal of inducting 100,000 previously unqualified men per year was to be met by drastically lowering standards and accepting those with inferior Armed Forces Qualification Test scores. Standards for advanced training programs, however, would not be adjusted. The result was that massive numbers of poor and poorly educated minority soldiers were recruited, channeled into infantry units, and dispatched to Southeast Asia.

Over fifty percent of the so-called New Standards Men fought in Viet Nam; over fifty percent of those were African American.[22] The exact impact on Latino communities is difficult to research. Both the task force and Selective Service grouped young men into only two categories – caucasian and non-caucasian. The armed services themselves had abandoned the use of the category of "Mexican" in 1949 in response to objections to the term from Mexican American advocacy groups. In a 1967 review of Selective Service policies, however, a presidential commission found that a disproportionate number of "Negro" soldiers had died in combat (22.4 percent of all KIAs during the first eleven months of 1966) and concluded: "There is reason to believe that many of the statistics relating to the Negro would be comparable for some other minority groups, although specific information to establish this is not available."[23] Data on those groups who previously had been rejected by the services on "mental" as opposed to physical grounds (over 90 percent of all Project 100,000 inductees) clearly show the largest percentage coming from Puerto Rico and a disproportionate number of men from south Texas and other southern states. The probability that many primary Spanish-speakers did not fare well on the AFQT is high, a fact that would have placed hundreds of Chicanos and Latinos in the ranks of the new standards men.

The extent to which cultural and linguistic difference was confused with "mental inferiority" is virtually impossible to reconstruct. In a report prepared in late 1964 and published by the Department of the Army in 1965, approximately eight months before the announcement of Project 100,000, an attempt was made to define what the authors labeled "marginal men" in terms of physical, mental, and moral categories. Following up on studies conducted by the Army in 1953 ("Fort Leonard Wood study") and Air Force in 1952 ("Project 1000"), the report summarized research on whether or not men who would otherwise be rejected from military service might be given special training in order to increase their "usefulness." An entire chapter was devoted to "Army-wide Utilization of Puerto Rican Enlisted Men."[24]

The case of Puerto Rico is suggestive. Since the 1950s, the Department of the Army had operated special English-language programs in Puerto Rico. Once given a minimal proficiency, troops were transferred to the mainland for regular basic training. By the Army's own admission, these programs were less than successful; through 1964, they had suffered a 56 percent drop-out rate. Viet Nam era manpower needs and Project 100,000 combined to remove the government's continuing support of such programs. The Army's logic was that lowered standards eliminated the need for pre-induction remedial programs. Although the population of Puerto Rico ranked approximately twenty-sixth among the fifty states during the Viet Nam era, it ranked fourteenth in casualties and fourth in combat deaths. It was not until 1970 that a federal judge ruled against the Army in the case of *portorriqueño* Carlos

J. Rivera-Toledo, arguing that the Army had not complied with its own regulations regarding the testing of non-English speaking inductees. Rivera-Toledo was subsequently released from military service.

One of the first and only novels to incorporate the issue of Project 100,000 is Charles Durden's *No Bugles, No Drums* (1976). A traditional combat narrative set during one soldier's tour of duty, Durden's novel is at the same time a curious blend of antiwar sentiments and stereotypical caricatures of minority GIs. Narrator Jamie Hawkins arrives in Viet Nam and joins other new guys in a platoon which includes four "new standards men" – three African Americans and a Chicano:

> Garcia 'n' the Drill Team, like Jinx, were dubious benefactors of McNamara's brainchild. McNamara's 100,000. It has a ring, like Fortune 500, or 10 Downing Street (which, when I saw it on TV, really wasn't very impressive from the outside). McNamara's 100,000 – pulled from the compost heap of America's hopeless. That sounds bitter, but I don't know if I really care much, one way or the other. Maybe I blame McNamara for what happened. I might as well blame God. I don't expect to ever get a chance to talk to either one of 'em. But it was McNamara, not God, who put his name to the program – retrainin' the retards. Takin' people who couldn't read or write well enough to pass the Army's basic entrance exam (geared to a sixth-grade level) and puttin' 'em through a cram course. Teachin' 'em to read 'n write just enough to pass the test for cannon fodder. Teachin' 'em to write their name so they could sign their own death warrant.[25]

Durden's obvious anger over another liberal attempt at social engineering and its disastrous effects on poor minorities does not preclude his employing the character of Garcia primarily as comic relief. A poor Chicano from San Diego, Garcia speaks fractured English and harbors a dream of becoming a bullfighter. He dies in a gruesome yet ridiculous scene in which he challenges a water buffalo by waving his jacket and shouting "Toro, toro." Even in death, the character functions as an object of mockery when an enterprising GI disposes of Garcia's body in order to ship home a large quantity of marijuana in the coffin.

The indictment in the above passage of those responsible for Project 100,000, however, is stated powerfully. Subsequent studies suggest that Project 100,000 did not achieve the stated goal of teaching disadvantaged and "low-aptitude" men practical skills for post-military life. Statistics show civilians and nonveterans earning much more than their veteran counterparts. Towards the end of Durden's text, the narrator points his M-16 at a herd of local pigs, takes aim at one in particular that GIs had named McNamara, and blows it apart.

I have included a discussion of Project 100,000 because it stands as one of the landmarks in the failure and fundamental dishonesty of the liberal project. Although none of its principal architects would have considered himself racist, the ultimate consequences of their actions were unquestionably racist. Liberal discourse was structured upon racialized categories and racial language permeated policy-maker circles to such an extent that even relatively "progressive" doves like George Ball could write the following memo to President Johnson, apparently without the least bit of self-consciousness:

The South Vietnamese are losing the war to the Viet Cong. No one can assure you that we can beat the Viet Cong or even force them to the conference table on our terms, no matter how many hundred thousand white, foreign (U.S.), troops we deploy.

No one has demonstrated that a white ground force of whatever size can win a guerrilla war – which is at the same time a civil war between Asians – in jungle terrain in the midst of a population that refuses cooperation to the white forces (and the South Vietnamese) and thus provides a great intelligence advantage to the other side.[26]

"White" forces vs. people of color – the lines of battle could not be drawn more starkly. What such a world view might mean for US citizens of color is painfully apparent in any objective study of American history, especially the treatment of GIs of color in the military and in programs such as Project 100,000.

In her important history of the war, Marilyn Young comments upon the kind of situation that bears directly upon my analysis of Chicano/a experiences in Viet Nam:

A Japanese reporter, Katsuichi Honda, understood the distance between American soldiers and the ordinary scenes of Vietnamese rural life they witnessed daily without ever comprehending. It was hard to see a house of mud and thatch as more than a temporary dwelling; hardly a home in the American sense. Rice cultivation – labor intensive, back-breaking, closer to gardening than any farming even soldiers from farm country had ever seen – simply did not register with the troops, for whom neither the labor, nor the crop, nor the people who planted and depended on it were real.[27]

My thesis in this section is that in fact many American GIs in Viet Nam were able to bridge the cultural distance between themselves and the Vietnamese. Young is mistaken to assume that all Americans failed to register the reality of daily life in Southeast Asia. For many GIs of color, that reality was hauntingly close to what their own lives had been in the US.

Because Charley Trujillo's collection of Chicano oral histories, titled *Soldados* (*Soldiers*) and published in 1990, draws upon a limited sample of Viet Nam veterans all of whom are from the same rural community in central California (Corcoran), it represents in a strong way the connections Young and other historians have been unable to make. One distinguishing feature that links the experiences of Trujillo's veterans to those of other veterans of color is what I will call the structure of recognition.

Since most of the veterans interviewed by Trujillo come from families of first- and second-generation Mexican agricultural workers, it is not surprising that for these particular soldiers the Vietnamese peasant evokes a certain empathy or a fleeting recognition that in most cases dissipates as each Chicano GI is desensitized to his violent surroundings. Certainly it would be a mistake to argue for a heightened moral consciousness among all Chicano soldiers in Viet Nam. The Chicano was as susceptible as any to the brutality and random violence typical of a guerrilla war being waged in large part against civilians, and soldiers with other ethnic and racial backgrounds were capable of great compassion and an abhorrence of violence. The infamous My Lai massacre is an emblematic case. The most notorious atrocity of the war, My Lai was perpetrated by Lt. William Calley's platoon under the command of Captain

Ernest "Mad Dog" Medina, a Chicano from New Mexico and the son of a farm worker. Medina was court martialled for the murder of 102 Vietnamese civilians. He was acquitted but later admitted to surpressing evidence and lying under oath. One of the worst offenders at My Lai, guilty of multiple murders and rapes, was nineteen year-old *tejano* Esequiel Torres. Among the soldiers who reportedly refused to participate in the killing and actually aided Vietnamese civilians were two African Americans (Harry Stanley and Herbert Carter), two Chicanos (George Garza and Leonard Gonzalez), and an Irish-American (Michael Bernhardt).[28] The ability to participate in sexual crimes and random killing clearly knows no ethnic boundaries. Nevertheless, what one repeatedly finds in Chicano (and consistently in Asian American) narratives about the war is a moral ambiguity produced by an uneasy recognition of shared experiences with the Vietnamese.

The stories in Trujillo's important collection contain the raw emotional material that took aesthetic form in a one-act play staged by the Teatro Campesino at the height of the war. In this play, titled *Vietnam Campesino* (*Vietnam Peasant*, 1970), there is a scene in which the young Chicano soldier (called *el hijo*, the son) is ordered into battle:

> *General*:   I want you to burn the house of these farmworkers, boy.
> *Hijo*:   Yes, sir!
> The soldier moves toward the campesinos, who hold up a paper cutout of a small labor camp shack. They wave at him.
> *Campesinos*:   Hello, hijo.
> *Hijo*:   (Turns back to general) Hey, I can't burn my parents' home.
> *General*:   Not *those* farmworkers, stupid. (Points at Vietnamese) *These* farmworkers.[29]

Or as Johnny the buck private in *Soldado Razo* writes to his mother: "'Amá, I had a dream la otra noche. I dreamed I was breaking into one of the hooches, así le decimos a las casas de los Vietnameses. I went in firing my M-16 porque sabía que el village estaba controlado por los gooks. I killed three of them right away, but when I looked down it was mi 'apa, el carnalillo and you, jefita. I don't know how much more I can stand. Please tell Sapo and all the vatos how it's like over here. Don't let them . . ."'[30] Johnny's nightmare that the dead Vietnamese were in fact his father, mother, and brother concretizes the recognition of "the enemy," and is transformed into an anti-war message aimed at his friends back home.

Whereas the isolated comments in Trujillo's oral history contain only the vaguest intimations of a political analysis, the dramatic structure of the Teatro Campesino's play makes visible several underlying issues: the exploitation and murder of poor people in both Vietnam and the US, the fleeting potential for solidarity between colonized and exploited groups, the ideological manipulation of those groups by corporate and military managers. When the character "Hijo" is later killed by a Vietnamese peasant, the general urges Hijo's farmworker parents to attack the peasant for being a communist. The *acto* unmasks an identification with the oppressor premised upon Cold War mythologies that undermines the potential for solidarity among exploited communities and that even today is a crucial driving force behind participation by minorities in the military.

This complex system of experiences, I would argue, is what historians have yet to sort out. What I am calling a structure of recognition is that characteristic of Chicano representations of the war in which the Chicano community sees in the Vietnamese enemy a "reflection" of its own class and/or ethnic positions. The words spoken by the father of Hijo to his wife about the Vietnamese peasants: "Oye, vieja, esas gentes son iguales que nosotros" ("Look, wife, those people are just like us"), for example, are echoed by the character of the returned veteran, Ernesto, in a play by Nephtalí de León: "Isn't it enough that I was nearly bumped off in Viet Nam? Here I go halfway across the world to die in someone else's field. As if I couldn't die in these goddamn cotton fields."[31]

In 1984, psychiatrist Erwin R. Parson studied the effects of what I am calling a structure of recognition between GIs of color and the Vietnamese. Despite his unfortunate choice of terms for what he called "gook-identification," that is, "the conscious and unconscious emotional identification with the devalued, maligned, abused, and helpless aspects of the Vietnamese people," Parson's findings are interesting insofar as they corroborate those sentiments found in oral histories and literature by veterans of color.[32] In subsequent interviews with African Americans, Latinos, Native Americans, and Asian Americans, the sense that minority soldiers were in effect "fighting themselves" in Viet Nam is made perfectly clear. A Native American vet says: "We made the connection that in Vietnam, we were involved in the same kind of colonization process that was carried out by whites in this country."[33] I want to say a bit more about the experience of the Asian American GI because it is particularly troubled by such overwhelming contradictions.[34]

Because of the way in which the US military kept statistics during the 1960s and 70s, we do not know with any certainty how many Asian Americans fought in the Viet Nam War. The Department of Defense estimates that approximately 35,000 Asian/Pacific Islanders served, the highest percentages coming from the Filipino and Japanese American communities. As is the case with Mexican nationals who fought in Viet Nam such as Congressional Medal of Honor winner José Jimenez, Japanese Americans often found themselves caught in a circuitous route that led to the US military and the war. One of the most disturbing examples is that of Shojiro Yamashita who was born in the Heart Mountain Relocation Center in 1945 but who returned with his family to Japan immediately after the World War II. In 1968, after graduating from Fukuoka University, Yamashita returned to the US to join his brother. The following year, he was drafted. Six months later, he died during the invasion of Cambodia.[35] Asian Americans were at times placed in segregated units such as the so-called Team Hawaii, formed in 1969 and also including Native Americans, in order to conduct operations deep in enemy territory. Although very few Asian American-authored texts about the war have been published, many of the ones we do have contain the same structures of recognition typical of Chicano narratives.

Filipino-American author Melvin Escueta, for example, writes: "Everything about the country was very Filipino. I knew these rice paddies, my uncles had rice paddies just like them; I knew the water buffalo, my family had them; I knew those huts, I had lived in them. Everything about Vietnam struck my soul, but I locked it away."[36] The protagonist of Escueta's play, *Honey Bucket* (1976), develops the idea of shared experiences and dramatizes the racism directed at Asian Americans from within their own ranks. Chinese American veteran David Chung remembers: "The first day I arrived [in Viet Nam], an American soldier called me a 'gook...' It was very strange to land in Vietnam, look around and realize that you looked like the enemy. I was going to be shooting people who looked like my parents, my relatives, and me."[37] Upon his return to the States, Chung was told that his membership in the local VFW had been denied because his presence would upset World War II and Korean War veterans.

Telling the story of having been the butt of repeated racist attacks by a caucasian sergeant, Sam Choy recalls:

> I couldn't take it anymore. One day I got so mad I threw a knife on the floor after he called me a chink. He ordered me to pick it up. I refused. He started yelling at me. I still refused. He kept yelling all kinds of remarks like – slant-eyed Chinaman, gook, chink, and he went on and on. I just got madder. So he went to get the staff sergeant. I went to get my rifle. I waited for them to come back and when they did they started to sweet talk me to give my rifle up. I said if you come closer, I'll shoot, fired a warning shot and they froze. Then I left the tent and the corporal came after me. He tried to grab my rifle. I fired once and he froze, he was scared as hell. Then the M. P.'s came and I shot at them too. I had bad eyes, so I missed. By this time I was near the perimeter of the base and, was thinking of joining the Viet Cong; at least they would trust me."[38]

In its most dramatic form, then, the tenuous solidarity between the US soldier of color and the Vietnamese could produce a "crossing over" in which GIs considered abandoning or actually abandoned US military installations in order to live with the enemy. While it is true that many such stories may be apocryphal, the mere suggestion of individual soldiers carrying the preliminary act of recognition to its ultimate conclusion would be enough to undermine traditional practices of nationalism, patriotism, and anti-communism. In his short story "Somewhere Outside Duc Pho" (Reading 8), Daniel Cano tells the story of Chicano GI Jesse Peña who has disappeared in-country and who had been sighted leading Viet Cong patrols. But according to local legend, Peña's radical critique of the US war effort was not unique: "The story of an American leading a Vietcong squad was not uncommon. Everyone had heard it one time or another during his tour. Usually, the American was blond, tall, and thin. No one who told the story had ever seen the guy. The story was always distanced by two or three narrators, and it was more of a fable or myth, our own type of antiwar protest, I guess." In a concluding scene, a group of Chicano soldiers remark upon the irony of "fighting for democracy" in Southeast Asia when their own families in the US continued to endure discrimination and economic injustice.

The empirical evidence of GIs crossing over to fight along side the enemy is slight, although such reports are common currency in US military history and include infamous cases like the defection of Irish Catholic soldiers ("los San Patricios) to the opposite side in the Mexican War or the switching of allegiance by minority soldiers in the Spanish–American War.[39] The pressures of combat and the constraints of ideological conditioning surely make difficult any easy identification with the enemy. But the figure of the phantom GI fighting for the other side reappears in literature and testimonials about the war. Richard Holguín recalls: "Salt and Pepper were these two American Marines, one black and the other white, who had turned traitor and went to the Viet Cong side. I had seen both of them with my own eyes."[40] In Cano's *Shifting Loyalties*, the story of Jesse Peña is retold from various points of view: "You believe that shit, man. The Tiger Force," Langley had said, smirking, "was on a listening post, keepin' an eye on a squad of dinks movin' along the trail, and there, right in the middle of the VC column, they see Jesse – or a chubby Mexican-looking-type guy in fatigues, black headband, rucksack, an M-16. Dig this, Almas. The dude ain't a prisoner. He's like a...a commie, man, walking right along with them gooks. A fuckin' stroll in the park, man."[41] In a novel written some twenty years earlier, Charles Durden's *No Bugles, No Drums* (1976), we hear the story of an African American soldier, Jinx, who is known to be living with the Viet Cong. Jinx is a "new standards man" with a difference, for he has carried the kind of recognition I have been discussing to its most lethal conclusion. In a conversation immediately before he deserts, he explains to Hawkins, the narrator:

> "So much for McNamara's Hundred Thousand, huh?"
>
> "Get a nigger behind the trigger...then give 'im a ticket to Nam. Dig it? But some of us gonna survive. Sooner or later some of us niggers goin' home."
>
> "They got some poor-ass white people with that program, too."
>
> "Yeah, but it was us they wanted. Get the young blacks off America's city streets and into Nam's backwoods. They finally figured a way to kill spades 'n' slopes at the same time." He emptied the last of his beer down his throat. "If we was smart we'd get together. Niggers of the world, unite!" He banged the bottle down on the bar top. And laughed.[42]

Later in the novel, when Hawkins realizes that Jinx in fact is fighting with the Viet Cong and calling in artillery on his former platoon, he searches him out and kills him but not until many GIs have died. In the world of growing antiwar sentiment within the US military, Jinx makes a tenuous connection to other poor people of color and acts upon it. In the literary universe of crossovers, Jinx follows the trail of the "Phantom Blooker," a Caucasian fighting with the Viet Cong in Robert Roth's *Sand in the Wind* (1973), and clears a path for the deserter Cacciato who occasionally surfaces with units of the NLF in Tim O'Brien's *Going After Cacciato* (1978), for Cano's Jesse Peña, and for other characters who violate the ultimate boundary by going over to the enemy.

I do not believe it is necessary to have empirical data that shows, in deceptively neat statistical order, the number of GIs that refused orders in combat, deserted, or came to view the war as immoral. It is certainly possible that the overwhelming majority of accounts of desertions to the NLF, for example, are little more than folk tales, yet we now know that one facet of the CIA's Phoenix Program was to track down and "terminate" American soldiers living with the Vietnamese.[43] Even if only one GI acted upon a sense of recognition with the enemy, the guardians of the State would have to eliminate him. With regard to the cultural representations of GIs who "crossed over," I would argue that they are extremely important for interrogating traditional US ethnocentrism and discourses of white supremacy. When the African American protagonist of Walter Dean Myers's 1988 novel, *Fallen Angels*, remarks that a Vietnamese girl "looked like a little doll with dark black eyes that dominated a round, brown face. She could have been black, maybe Puerto Rican" or that a wounded Viet Cong had "thin arms not much different in color than mine," the traditional war narrative and its attendant tropes of nationalism and violent masculinity are momentarily subverted.[44] The transference of such fleeting textual subversions into everyday life could be subtle but meaningful. As one Chicano veteran put it upon his return to the US: "I think because we experience racism ourselves and even though we're saying those goddamn dinks, those slopes, it's making something inside here, there's this kind of understanding that we're taco benders, greasers and wetbacks."[45] It is in moments such as this that patriotism's ability to bracket differences of class and ethnicity falls apart. Exactly what "we" as an idealized American family are all willing to die for suddenly becomes a question the answer to which may have grave consequences for the nation.

I want to conclude with a short passage from Michael Herr's *Dispatches*: "Mendoza was here. 12 Sept 68. Texas."[46] Like the Mexican American soldier who appears in Norman Mailer's World War II novel, *The Naked and the Dead* or even the GIs Padilla and Chavez in Pierre Schoendorffer's award-winning documentary, *The Anderson Platoon* (1966), the presence of the Chicano "Mendoza," invoked through his graffiti at Tan Son Nhut airport in the final section of *Dispatches*, is fleeting at best. The reader can only imagine what Mendoza's story might have been, for Herr is not interested in recounting it. In what is perhaps the most famous of all Viet Nam War narratives, the Latino soldier has been granted only a ghostly presence despite Herr's appropriation of the Chicano/a term "la vida loca" to describe the insanity of the war. Perhaps we should be thankful for small favors. In the vast majority of accounts of the US war in Southeast Asia, Mendoza has been completely erased.

For those of us interested in tracking the elusive experience of the minority soldier, one other scene in *Dispatches* strikes us with special force. Attempting to determine the identity of a two-month old corpse in a US uniform, two GIs argue: "Shit, this is a gook! What'd they bring him here for?" "Look, Jesus, he's got on our uniform." "I don't give a fuck, that ain't no fucking American, that's a fucking gook!" Wait a minute," the other one said. "Maybe it's a spade . . ."[47] Whatever the ethnicity of the dead man, it is clear that skin pigmentation is the primary sign to be deciphered. Or as one character in Joe Rodríguez's *Oddsplayer* remarks: "The color of the skin fixed the enemy."[48] The dead "gook" may well have been a US Latino or Asian American and was most assuredly an American soldier of color. It is almost too horrible to consider in depth the racist connotations of this scene and its consequences for the historical record. Whoever the dead man was in reality, his life and death are forever lost in the four-letter epithet "gook."

This startling scene from *Dispatches* is reproduced in Chicano veteran Roy Benavidez's autobiography, only now as historical fact. Gravely wounded and lying among both American and North Vietnamese dead, Benavidez is unable to speak as he is loaded on to a helicopter for evacuation:

I retreated to the darkness behind my eyelids. Soon, I felt arms lifting me and sensed the sunlight fall across my face as they handed me through the doorway.

"Just put him over here with the other three on the ground," said the voice belonging to the arms holding my legs.

The other three? "Oh, Christ, No!" my mind cried as realization dawned. Half of the blood I had just dumped over Southeast Asia belonged to the Yagui Indian nation. More than once my native American features had been mistaken for Oriental. Now, by God, they were going to get me dumped with the enemy dead.[49]

Benavidez is recognized finally by a fellow sergeant and so narrowly escapes being left to die with enemy soldiers. The veracity of such stories would be difficult to prove, yet for the purposes of the present study it is enough to read them as symptoms of the potentially dire circumstances that confronted US minority soldiers in Viet Nam. For it is in these scenes, where life and death decisions are made on the basis of skin color and facial features, that the tenuous connection between Chicano GIs and the people of Viet Nam, a link that the Chicano antiwar movement would attempt to develop in a more radical internationalist direction, takes on a macabre and chilling dimension.

NOTES

1   For an official government account of this service, see *Hispanics in America's Defense* (Washington, DC: Office of Deputy Assistant Secretary of Defense for Equal Opportunity and Safety Policy, 1984). See also, Patricia A. Robles, "Hispanics' Contributions to the US. Military: An Annotated Bibliography," *Latino Studies Journal* 5 (May, 1994): 96–103.
2   Luis Valdez, *Early Works* (Houston: Arte Público Press, 1990), 132. A film adaptation of *Soldado Razo* entitled was released in 2000. On the Teatro Campesino's Viet Nam plays, see the chapter "The Chicano in War at Home and Abroad" in Jorge A. Huerta, *Chicano Theater: Themes and Forms* (Tempe: Bilingual Press/Editorial Bilingüe, 1982); Edward G. Brown, "The Teatro Campesino's Vietnam Trilogy," *Minority Voices* 4 (Spring, 1980): 29–38; Guillermo E. Hernández, *Chicano Satire: A Study in Literary Culture* (Austin: University of Texas Press, 1991).
3   For the full text, see my *Aztlán & Viet Nam: Chicano and Chicana Experiences of the War* (University of California Press, 1999), 49–50.
4   "Soldado Razo", in *16 de septiembre* (Sony, 1991).
5   "Soldaditos del '45" in *De colores* 2 (1975): 12.
6   *La palabra* 1 (1979): 56.
7   In Luis Omar Salinas and Lillian Faderman, eds., *From the Barrio: A Chicano Anthology* (San Francisco: Canfield Press, 1973), 90.
8   See the classic account: Raul Morín, *Among the Valiant: Mexican-Americans in WW II and Korea*, 3rd ed. (Alhambra: Borden, 1966). Chicano poet and Korean War veteran, José Montoya, reminds us: "Los Chicanos en Korea/Se portaron con honor/Ganaron muchas medallas/Hasta liberty in Japon/Pero al volver al cantón/Derechito a la prisión" ("Chicanos acted with honor in Korea. They won many medals and took leaves in Japan. But when they returned home they went straight to prison"). "Chicanos en Korea" in *Information: 20 Years of Joda* (San José: Chusma House, 1992), 251. Louie Mendoza, the protagonist of Arturo Islas's last novel, is a Korean War veteran who loves to hear World

War II veterans tell stories because "they made out like they knew how come they killed other guys." *La Mollie and the King of Tears* (Albuquerque: University of New Mexico Press, 1996), 124. See also, Beatriz de la Garza, *Pillars of Gold and Silver* (Houston: Arte Público, 1997) in which the principal character's journey is precipitated by the death of her father in Korea.

9 *Soldados*, 27. In their anti-draft literature, Nina Genera and Lea Ybarra made the following point to Mexican American parents: "Parents must begin to place the love of their sons before their fear of the government." *La batalla está aquí: Chicanos and the War* (El Cerrito: Chicano Draft Help, 1972), 7.

10 Ramón Ruiz, "Another Defector from the Gringo World," *The New Republic* (July 27, 1968): 11.

11 *La Raza* 1 (1970): 7. This premier issue of *La Raza* was "offered in memory of Chicanos who have died in the horror of the Vietnam War – a war created by their very own oppressors in the U.S. to further oppress and exploit those people it deems inferior."

12 Letter to Douglas MacArthur Herrera, dated October 25, 1967. Original correspondence in the John Herrera Collection, Houston Metropolitan Research Collection, Houston Public Library. For the difficult decisions faced by Chicano conscientious objecters, see the accounts in Lea Ybarra's forthcoming book, *Too Many Heroes: Oral Histories of Chicano Vietnam Veterans* (University of Texas Press).

13 Everett Alvarez, Jr. and Anthony S. Pitch, *Chained Eagle* (New York: Dell, 1989). The sequel to *Chained Eagle* is Everett Alvarez, Jr. and Samuel A. Schreiner, Jr., *Code of Conduct* (New York: Donald I. Fine, 1991).

14 Alvarez, 2. Craig Howes has shown how Alvarez's story becomes the literary and ideological model upon which subsequent POW autobiographies would be based. See his *Voices of the Vietnam POWs: Witnesses to Their Fight* (Oxford: Oxford University Press, 1993).

15 Alvarez, 312. In *Code of Conduct*, Alvarez rejects the term "Chicano": "To me words like Chicano and La Rasa [sic] meant people who had come from Mexico. Period. I didn't like the sounds of a 'Chicano movement' or a 'Chicano manifesto'" (25).

16 Quoted in Dorinda Moreno, *La Mujer – en pie de lucha iy la hora es ya!* (Mexico City: Espina del Norte, 1973), 86.

17 "A Time to Break Silence" (speech delivered on April 4, 1967) in *The Eyes on the Prize Civil Rights Reader*, eds. Clayborne Carson, et. al. (New York: Penguin, 1991), 387–93.

18 Quoted in Lawrence M. Baskir and William A. Strauss, *Chance and Circumstance: The Draft, the War and the Vietnam Generation* (New York: Knopf, 1978), 125.

19 John F. Kennedy, "Statement establishing the Task Force on Manpower Conservation" (September 30, 1963) in *One-third of a Nation: A report on young men found unqualified for military service* (January 1, 1964), Appendix A: A–1.

20 Lewis B. Hershey, "Letter to Selective Service personnel (October 31, 1963) in *One-third of a Nation*: A–49.

21 Quoted in "Readjustment of Project 100,000 Veterans," Hearing before the Subcommittee on Oversight and Investigations of the Committee on Veterans' Affairs, House of Representatives, One hundred first Congress, first session (February 28, 1990): 1. In his 1995 "reevaluation" of the Viet Nam debacle and his role in it – *In Retrospect: The Tragedy and Lessons of Vietnam* – McNamara does not make a single reference to Project 100,000. On May 15, 1995, four Chicano Viet Nam veterans, the Bolaños brothers of El Paso, Texas, all recipients of the Purple Heart, filed suit against McNamara to prevent him from earning profits from his book. The other key architect in the formulation Project 100,000, Daniel Patrick Moynihan, neglects to mention it in his review of social programs

since the 1960s, *Miles to Go: A Personal History of Social Policy* (Cambridge, Mass.: Harvard University Press, 1996).

22   See Lisa Hsiao, "Project 100,000: The Great Society's Answer to Military Manpower Needs in Vietnam" in William M. King, ed., *Viet Nam Generation, Special edition: A White Man's War: Race Issues and Vietnam* 1 (Spring, 1989): 14–37. Major studies of the war, including those by progressive historians, have devoted little space to the scandal that was Project 100,000. Mentally "deficient" characters such as Gump and Bubba in the widely-acclaimed film *Forrest Gump* take on new and disturbing meanings in the light of Project 100,000.

23   "In Pursuit of Equity: Who Serves When Not All Serve," Report of the National Advisory Commission on Selective Service (Washington, DC: US Government Printing Office, 1967): 26.

24   *Marginal Man and Military Service*, Department of the Army (December, 1965). Ironically, the authors of this study believed that its publication during "peacetime" would allow for a clear-headed analysis of the issue. Months later the massive buildup of US forces in Southeast Asia would begin.

25   New York: Viking Press, 1976, 43.

26   Memo from George Ball to President Johnson, July 1, 1965. Quoted in Marvin E. Gettleman, et. al., eds., *Vietnam and America: A Documented History* (New York: Grove Press, 1995), 282. It is not clear the extent to which the phrase "white army" was common bureaucratic usage. In his memoir, Ball refers without further comment to the same memo. George W. Ball, *The Past Has Another Pattern: Memoirs* (New York: W. W. Norton, 1982), 398. Towards the end of his recollections, Ball seems preoccupied by the preservation of a "white America": "Apart from the question of illegal immigrants, I can foresee formidable social and economic problems resulting from the increasing political influence of Hispanic-Americans" (489). He does not specify what these "problems" might be.

27   *The Vietnam Wars: 1945–1990* (New York: Harper Collins, 1991), 175.

28   For further details, see Michael Bilton and Kevin Sim, *Four Hours in My Lai* (New York: Penguin, 1992). In his 1972 attempt to explain the Chicano Movement to the East coast intelligentsia, historian John Womack wrote: "So many young men have borne so well the uses made of them in the armed services, for 'action' in Indochina or 'intelligence' in Latin America, that by now the roster of junior commissioned officers is studded [sic] with names like Ernest L. Medina (now retired)." "A Special Supplement: The Chicanos," *New York Review of Books*, 19 (August 31, 1972): 14.

29   Valdez, 116. For further analysis of Chicano-authored texts on the war, see my "Reading Chicano/a Writing about the American War in Viet Nam," *Aztlán: A Journal of Chicano Studies* 25 (Fall 2000): 13–49.

30   Valdez, 133.

31   Valdez, 115; *The Death of Ernesto Nerios*, 25. In Ed Vega's "Casualty Report," Puerto Rican veteran Sonny Maldonado attempts to deal with the experience of "looking at himself in the mirror and not recognizing the image because it was dark and as foreign as the enemy's had been." *Casualty Report* (Houston: Arte Público, 1991), 38. The situation of the Latino GI from rural Puerto Rico was especially charged since not only did he "recognize" the skin color and *campesino* culture of the Vietnamese, but the physical surroundings of the war zone were uncannily like those of home. In Jaime Carrero's 1966 play, *Flag Inside* (Río Piedras: Ediciones Puerto, 1973), the absent son Alberto writes home: "El aire tropical de Vietnam y su vegetación es paracido al de la isla" ("The tropical air of Vietnam and its vegetation is like that of the island") [19].

32 "The Gook-Identification and Post-Traumatic Stress Disorders in Black Vietnam Veterans," *Black Psychiatrists of American Quarterly* 13 (1984). Charley Trujillo has suggested to me that the Chicano GI's recognition of his own situation in that of the Vietnamese, rather than leading to a heightened critical awareness, in fact produced exaggerated forms of violence. The possible dynamics of self-hatred inherent in this interpretation are too complex (and unpleasant) for me to investigate here.

33 Joel Osler Brende and Erwin Randolph Parson, *Vietnam Veterans: The Road to Recovery* (New York: Plenum Press, 1985), 156. Unfortunately, Brende and Parson rely too heavily on ethnic stereotypes, e.g. "Hispanic machismo," "Asian fatalism," in their analysis of minority GIs.

34 The experience in Viet Nam of Asian Americans has yet to be discussed extensively in any scholarly forum. See *Amerasia Journal* 17 (1991) for the recollections of Darrell Y. Hamamoto and Lewis Kawahara and the important essay, "About Face: Recognizing Asian and Pacific American Vietnam Veterans in Asian American Studies" by Peter Nien-Chu Kiang; the novel by Korean American Ernest Spencer, *Welcome to Vietnam, Macho Man* (New York: Bantam Books, 1989); the account of Chinese American resister, Mike Wong, in William Short, *A matter of conscience: GI resistance during the Vietnam War* (Andover, Mass.: Addison Gallery of American Art, Phillips Academy, 1992); and Maxine Hong Kingston's interesting short story "Brother in Vietnam" in *China Men* (New York: Knopf, 1980) in which a Chinese American in the US Navy dreams he is a participant in a massacre: "When he stops, he finds that he has cut up the victims too, who are his own relatives. The faces of the strung-up people are also those of his own family, Chinese faces, Chinese eyes, noses, and cheekbones" (291). In Frederick Su's unpublished novel, *An American Sin*, the character David Wong says: "I killed because I was Asian fighting in an Asian War. How else could I prove I was American?" Excerpts from this novel are available at http://www.vena.com/authors/1027bi.html

35 Shojiro Yamashita's story is among those found on the Berkeley Viet Nam Veteran's Memorial website: http://www.ci.berkeley.ca.us/vvm

36 "Wounds of Vietnam heal slowly for Asian American veterans," *Asian Week* (December 9, 1983): 20. See also, Victor Merina, "The Glory and Pain of Fighting for Your Country," *Rice* (April, 1988): 35–8. Thanks to Lily Lee Adams and Cher Nicholas for bringing these articles to my attention.

37 Anne Keegan, "Oriental GIs in Vietnam: Living with the face of the enemy," *Chicago Tribune* (November 11 1988): 1, 18. A Japanese American Viet Nam War Memorial was unveiled in Los Angeles on November 11, 1995. Names on the memorial may be accessed at http://koma.org/apa/jacce_victmem.html

38 "Interview with Sam Choy," *Getting Together* 1 (April 1970): 12.

39 One of the most celebrated cases was African American soldier David Fagen who deserted to the Filipino rebels in 1899. See Michael C. Robinson and Frank N. Schubert, "David Fagen: An Afro-American Rebel in the Philippines, 1899–1901," *Pacific Historical Review* 64 (February, 1975). Such incidents link up to later ones – such as Malcolm X's ironic [?] remark in his autobiography that in 1943 he was "frantic to join . . . the Japanese army" – and give shape to a genealogy of dissent against US wars. Thanks to George Lipsitz for bringing these two cases to my attention.

40 Trujillo, *Soldados*, 177.

41 Houston: Arte Público, 1995, 78. Later in the novel, Peña's former platoon-mates speculate on his whereabouts: "There were a few nutty stories that he was traveling with the VC. Some guys said they saw him selling fish tacos in the Mekong Delta. Others

said he was running drugs near the DMZ. You know, just a big joke, stupid stuff, like he probably started a *mariachi* in Hanoi or owned a burrito stand near Haiphong" (100–1).

42   Durden, 123. We should recall that on the home front, Huey Newton of the Black Panther Party had written a letter to the leadership of the NLF (dated August 29, 1970, coincidentally the date of the largest Chicano Moratorium demonstration) in which he offered to send Panther "troops" to Viet Nam to assist "in your fight against American imperialism." Roth's *Sand in the Wind* (Boston: Atlantic Monthly Press, 1973) is also interesting for its trio of Chicano characters (Valdez, Pablo, and Ramirez), one of whom refuses to carry out orders by the end of the novel.

43   See the chilling account by an anonymous Chicano informant in Ybarra, *Too Many Heroes* (forthcoming). GI deserters, referred to as "renegades," were hunted down and given the option of committing suicide or being assassinated. They were later reported as either killed or missing in action.

44   New York: Scholastic, 1988, 52; 124. Lea Ybarra's research suggests that real-life cases of recognition between Chicanos and the Vietnamese were few. Of the twenty-five veterans interviewed, only three alluded to such recognition. "Perceptions of Race and Class Among Chicano Vietnam Veterans" in William M. King, ed., *Vietnam Generation* 2, Special issue: A White Man's War: Race Issues and Vietnam: 68–93. I would argue that for most veterans an admission of "recognition" with the Vietnamese continues to be a difficult if not taboo step outside of acceptable behavior.

45   Quoted in Ybarra, 83. In Chicano-authored fiction about earlier wars, a similar recognition produces hybrid identities and acts of crossing over. Américo Paredes's short-story "Idhiro Kikuchi," for example, tells the story of a Mexican-Japanese soldier fighting for Japan in World War II who is captured by US forces and saved from execution by a Chicano GI. In Rolando Hinojosa's *Korean Love Songs*, a Mexican American GI, David "Sonny" Ruiz, deserts to Japan and becomes Mr. Kazuo Fusaro.

46   Michael Herr, *Dispatches* (1977) (New York: Random House, 1991), 250.

47   Herr, 161.

48   Rodríguez, 63.

49   Benavidez, 4. Parallel stories appear throughout Asian American accounts of the war. US Marine Mike Nakayama writes: "The last night I spent in the field, we were overrun by a large NLF force. Out of the twelve wounded, I was one of three emergency cases who are supposed to have priority for medical treatment. I was the last to be treated. When I asked what was taking them so long, the corpsman explained that he thought I was a 'gook'" ["Nam & U.S.M.C.," *Gidra* 3 (May 1971): 17]. Donald Lau recalls: "Every now and then I would hear of an Asian American who was killed because of mistaken identity. Upon coming home I was told of an Asian American who was wounded and taken to an evac hospital . . . He was dying and a racist surgeon who made the decisions on who got priority treatment looked at him and said, 'Let's treat the Americans first.' The Asian American soldier was conscious enough to know what was going on, so he flicked the safety switch off of his pistol and fired the entire magazine into the ceiling. He then got immediate attention" [Mark J. Jue, "Asian Viet Vets want Memorial to honor own war dead," *East/West* (February 20, 1985). It is in scenes such as these, where life and death decisions were made on the basis of skin color and facial features, that the tenuous connection between American soldiers of color and the people of Viet Nam comes full circle.

CHAPTER NINETEEN

"They'll Forgive You for Anything Except Being Weak": Gender and US Escalation in Vietnam 1961–65

ROBERT DEAN

Why Vietnam? The question why US leaders committed vast sums of blood and money in a futile and enormously destructive intervention has plagued Americans for years. Despite a very large literature on the Vietnam Wars, scholars continue to produce studies seeking to illuminate the reasons for the war, and its meaning. The magnitude of the disaster – the disproportion between any measure of US "interests" in Vietnam whether strategic or economic, and the political, social, and economic costs of the war to America – raises profound questions about reason and decision-making among the elite group of men who made policy. These questions bedevil not only historians but the men who made the decisions themselves, as demonstrated by the appearance in 1995 of Robert S. McNamara's memoirs of Vietnam decision-making.[1]

McNamara's account was not received with much sympathy from historians or the public. Many fault the former Secretary of Defense for his failure to reveal a "smoking gun" which would lay bare the logic of the otherwise seemingly irrational and egregious decisions made by policy makers of the Kennedy and Johnson administrations. However unsatisfactory it may be as a complete account of the war, McNamara does attempt to grapple with the question of reason among policy makers. Perhaps his narrative has been received with such disdain because it is a litany of failure: failure to question the basic assumptions that underlay assessments of the costs and benefits of intervention, failure to ask "hard questions" about the contradictions that permeated the US relationship with Vietnam. "We failed to analyze our assumptions critically, then or later. The foundations of our decision making were gravely flawed." McNamara's tale is one of well-meaning inadequacy – the incapacity of the anointed to manage US imperial interests according to the standards of the imperial administrators themselves: "I had spent twenty years as a manager identifying problems and forcing organizations – often against their will – to think deeply and realistically about alternative courses of action and their consequences. I doubt I will ever fully understand why I did not do so here" [in July 1965].[2]

McNamara's account is unsatisfactory, not for the absence of a "smoking gun" to explain "why Vietnam," but because he offers no analysis sufficient to explain the decision makers' departure from an idealized operational reason, supposedly wielded by the "best and the brightest." While McNamara confesses inadequacy, he never really explains why, in the face of copious evidence of ongoing failure, the US government committed itself to an open-ended escalation in service to a bankrupt policy. McNamara offers a picture of the Vietnam decision-makers as smart, brave, dedicated public servants, with the best and most honorable of intentions, leading the US into folly and disaster. McNamara assumes a correspondence between a presumed "national interest" and the actions of the elite actors who made policy – but one which went awry in the case of Vietnam. The basic explanation McNamara offers is that the Kennedy and Johnson policy makers were blinded by their own rigid anti-communist ideology. Held spellbound by their own platitudes and anxieties, they were unable to understand the strategic significance of the divisions with the Communist "bloc," the power of post-colonial nationalism, and the political developments in places like Indonesia, all of which should have led the US foreign policy bureaucracy to recommend a prudent withdrawal from a not-very-important salient in the great game of containment.[3]

McNamara is, in effect, offering a cultural explanation for what some historians have labeled the "cognitive errors" of the policy process; he suggests that the particularly constricted discourse of the foreign policy bureaucracy limited the range of possible meanings attributable to the actions of the Vietnamese, the Soviets, the Chinese, etc. While his book is woefully inadequate as an explanation of the Vietnam debacle, he does hint at the importance of situating the reasoning process of the Kennedy and Johnson warrior-bureaucrats within an analysis of the cultural codes of meaning which framed it:

> I want to put Vietnam in context. We of the Kennedy and Johnson administrations who participated in the decisions on Vietnam acted according to what we thought were the principles and traditions of this nation. We made our decisions in light of those values. Yet we were wrong, terribly wrong.[4]

McNamara can't explain the failure of cost–benefit reason, because he doesn't see that another logic was at work – one centered on the system of meaning arising from the patrician tradition of neo-imperial service to the state. McNamara, of course, was himself assimilated to, rather than born into that tradition, but he implicitly employed its premises nonetheless. Gender and class are deeply implicated in the creation of a cultural context which made the military defense of imperial boundaries both an imperative of political legitimacy, and a central part of the bureaucrats' conceptions of themselves as powerful men acting as agents of history. The fateful decisions to commit American power and prestige to a military intervention in Vietnam were made by men with deeply ingrained and relatively rigid notions of manliness. Their experience in political and bureaucratic life had repeatedly provided lessons in the dangers of appearing "weak." We can perhaps illuminate aspects of the Vietnam decisions left obscure by McNamara and others by considering the role of gender in the reasoning used by the men who made the policy.

To more fully explain the contradictions of Vietnam policy requires looking at cultural practice which created and reproduced a foreign policy "establishment"; a group of privileged men, socialized to what amounts to an "imperial manhood" in a life long sequence of elite male institutions: elite boarding schools, Ivy League universities, elite college secret societies and metropolitan men's clubs, elite volunteer military service, and finally, administrative work in the national security bureaucracy of the US. Those who were not born to the patrician class of the "establishment" assimilated to its values and were admitted the inner circles through the patronage of older men (examples of key figures include Henry Stimson, Robert Lovett, John J. McCloy, or George C. Marshall).[5]

The high-level foreign policy bureaucrats appointed by Kennedy and inherited by Johnson understood themselves as continuing the tradition of the strenuous life of heroic imperial leadership descended from Theodore Roosevelt, Henry Stimson, and Dean Acheson. The foreign policy "establishment" of the nineteen-sixties was a direct descendant of the upper-class cult of martial imperial manhood expressed in the Plattsburg preparedness movement of 1913–17. Itself an old-stock patrician, neo-stoic reaction to the loss of cultural authority, a "weightless modernity," and fears of democratic disorder in a time of massive immigration, the preparedness movement cultivated the regeneration of upper-class virility and political authority through martial ordeal. The creation of a community of Spartan warrior-heroes promised individual and collective redemption from the effeminizing temptations of materialism, and promised to bring the post-1898 American imperial project into conformity with the republican ideals of manly civic virtue, service and sacrifice, drummed into patricians at Groton, St. Paul's, Andover, and elsewhere. War and the mantle of the stoic citizen-soldier promised to buttress claims to leadership by a privileged class, legitimated by a demonstrable "manliness" – body-building, close-order drill, and empire – became the rallying points for an incipient foreign policy "establishment."[6]

The legacy of this tradition is ubiquitous in the Kennedy and Johnson bureaucracy; but its direct expression was clearly visible in July 1965, during the conclaves of the "Wise Men" debating escalation in Vietnam. John J. McCloy, Plattsburg participant, WWI volunteer artillery officer, and disciple of Henry Stimson, urged Lyndon Johnson to go in with guns blazing: "The country is looking to getting on with the war." Long connection with such grand traditions of statesmanship and manly heroism gave McCloy the confidence to call for intervention, and to publicly counsel doubting citizens to defer to the "gravitas," the weighty judgment of their betters possessed by the men who inherited the legacy of his "hero statesman," Henry Stimson.[7]

During the Second World War the foreign policy bureaucrats of the Kennedy and Johnson administration had met the test of warrior manhood demanded by the narrative of the "strenuous life." They returned from victory to take up the mantle of statesmanship, "present at the creation" of a new bi-polar global imperial order.

They came of age politically during the post-war Red Scare, as junior members of a foreign policy establishment under attack by right-wing "primitives," as Dean Acheson derisively labeled the witch-hunting Congressional counter-subversives.[8] Provincial "isolationist" conservatives challenged the privileged access to power of eastern "internationalist" establishment figures both mighty and small in a bitter contest over who was to be included, and who excluded from office. The putative "loss" of China to communism provided an issue relentlessly exploited by right-wing counter-subversives as an example of Democratic "weakness," or even treason. Largely neglected in the historiography of the Red Scare is the extent to which these battles were fought on the terrain of gender and sexuality. Congressional counter-subversives used a "counter-perversion" crusade as a central enforcement tool of the purges. The homosexuals in government issue, attacks on the "lavender lads" in the State Department did not represent a peripheral "irrationality" by unsophisticated "primitives." Instead, it represented a systematic and pervasive attack on the political legitimacy of the privileged managers of the American empire through an assault on their manhood. Gay baiting and sexual blackmail were central mechanisms in the subterranean operations of the purges. Sexual and political crimes were conflated; vulnerability to one kind of offense implied vulnerability to the other. The purges ended the careers of many. Most significantly, they left indelible boundaries on the political landscape, marking limits to what kinds of policy lay within the realm of the conceivable. The lessons learned during the counter-subversion, counter-perversion crusades shaped the way that the policy makers of the Kennedy and Johnson administration calculated the possible personal and political costs and benefits of foreign policy options they faced in problems like the potential "loss" of Vietnam.

John Kennedy's campaign rhetoric and his administration's policies exemplified both the prescriptive and proscriptive aspects of this narrative of political manliness. Kennedy's identity was premised on a vision of himself as an aristocratic warrior-intellectual. He shared and exploited then-current fears of the "decline" of American manhood. The corrosive effects of material wealth, the emergence of a new "other directed" "organization man," and indulgent "Moms" all threatened the capacity of the nation to continue the fight against its ruthless imperial adversary – "World Communism." Kennedy warned of "creeping softness" – worrisome to him because he identified the strength of male bodies with the strength of the state. He worked to reinvigorate American masculinity, and to halt a threatening decline in the power of the nation, by tirelessly promoting an image of neo-republican civic virtue. Fifty-mile hikes, physical fitness programs, the Peace Corps, and the rehabilitation of the Army Special Forces (Green Berets) symbolized the new masculine vigor and engagement in heroic struggle of the Kennedy administration. Kennedy was fascinated by stories of warrior-heroes, spies, and guerrillas, who exhibited individual masculine courage. In office, he embraced men like Edward Lansdale, or Roger Hilsman, who advertised themselves as specialists in "unconventional" warfare to help defeat communist post-colonial revolution in places such as Cuba and Vietnam.[9]

Kennedy inherited the "crisis" of Vietnam from his predecessor – a scenario already rife with contradictions that would bedevil the Americans until the end. As David Anderson has argued, "the Eisenhower administration was both the creator and the captive of an illusion in Vietnam." The illusion was the fantasy of "nation-building," one that Kennedy and his successor clung to, despite constant, overwhelming evidence of its ongoing failure – and despite a repeated articulation of that evidence by participants in the decision-making process. The contradiction that blocked a "rational" assessment of US policy toward Vietnam centered on a basic confusion about the nature of the imperial undertaking which underlay American involvement. US national security managers sought to maintain imperial influence in Vietnam, but did so without a conceptual language that acknowledged the existence of an American empire. The lack of such an explicit recognition precluded, in large measure, a systematic analysis of the economic and strategic costs and benefits at stake in Vietnam. To acknowledge the true dimensions of the imperial project would have contradicted one part of the ideology which shaped the identity-narratives of the national security bureaucrats. Empire contradicted the republican ideology of democracy, with its presumption of the inevitability of "progress" through "free markets" and "open doors" that were supposed to make America morally exceptional – a "beacon of liberty" for oppressed peoples everywhere.[10]

The American imperial managers created a counter-revolutionary proxy with Ngo Dinh Diem. The Kennedy administration then struggled with the contradictions between Diem's dynastic ambitions enforced through an oppressive police state and their desires for a liberal democracy compliant with the directives of the US government. Kennedy found himself tied to a weak client devoid of indigenous political legitimacy and continually threatened by collapse. But Kennedy was driven by the political imperatives of masculine strength and weakness. The "humiliations" of the Bay of Pigs and the Vienna Summit convinced him of the necessity to demonstrate his "guts" to the Soviets, and to his domestic constituency. The lessons of the Red Scare were fresh in his mind, too. After having baited the Republicans over the "loss" of Cuba, he feared a repetition of the right-wing reaction to the "loss" of more Asian territory to the Communists. As Robert Buzzanco has ably shown, despite the repeated counsel of a significant contingent of high military officers that Vietnam was a dangerous diversion from more significant salients in the global confrontation, abandoning the uncooperative proxy regime to its fate was apparently unthinkable to Kennedy and his advisers.[11]

Kennedy hoped to contain revolution without a full-scale war, employing "men of great courage" to implement the carrot-and-stick dialectic of liberal developmentalism and counter-insurgency warfare. With the failure of Roger Hilsman's "strategic hamlet" initiative, the repression of the Buddhists, and the unwillingness of the Diem regime to prosecute the war against the National Liberation Front according to US dictates, American disenchantment with Diem peaked. Kennedy's bureaucrats first focused on Diem's brother Nhu, and his wife Madame Nhu, as the primary obstacles to the effective realization of American goals. Nhu and his wife were treated as symbols of the devious, inscrutable "oriental mind." This masculine imperial narrative cast Madame Nhu as the sexually dangerous "Dragon Lady" holding the weak Diem in thrall to her power; "Brother Nhu" was depicted as an unstable, Machiavellian, opium addicted *eminence grise* leading Diem astray. But by the fall of 1963 a significant faction within the Kennedy administration had come to regard the Diem regime as nothing more than a "medieval, oriental despotism of the classic family type."[12] Congressional support for Kennedy's counterinsurgency war demanded a veneer of democratic legitimacy Diem seemingly could not provide. Bitter that their proxy had refused to help reshape the political economy of South Vietnam in the image of a republican small-producer democracy such as had supposedly formed the "traditional American way," Kennedy's imperial managers encouraged the coup which deposed and murdered the uncooperative Diem and Nhu. The assassination of President Kennedy three weeks later passed the problem of Vietnam on to his successor, along with the men who had managed the American involvement.

Without an explicit acknowledgment of the nature of the American imperial enterprise, the national security bureaucrats of the Kennedy and Johnson administrations were thrown back on a lexicon of "honor," "credibility," "prestige," and "toughness" animated by using a doublespeak which cast the nationalist, communist insurgency as "outside aggression." The utter disarray of the succession of military juntas that followed the 1963 coup made the concept of "outside aggression" even more urgent than before, since the US had no proxy to effectively fight the nationalist insurgency. This constant effort to maintain the fiction of a "Munich analogy" was incessantly repeated despite the recognition, as Secretary of State Dean Rusk argued in January 1964, that the southern insurgency was largely indigenous: "98% of the problem is in South Vietnam, and not in cross-border operations." In the next breath Rusk endorsed stepped up operations in a covert war against North Vietnam, in the hope that it would "put muscle behind our argument that the trouble comes from the north and that when that trouble stops, our presence in South Vietnam can become unnecessary."[13]

The ability to articulate one set of propositions about the nature of the problem, and then to recommend actions which logically contradict those propositions, evident here, is a recurrent pattern in the reams of paper expended on policy "options" by the national security managers. The imperative to do so was intimately connected to the maintenance of their identities as active, powerful men, relentlessly defending boundaries against enemies, and tied also to the maintenance of political legitimacy and power. The imperatives of political legitimacy and the ideology of republican manhood also demanded a massive effort at denial and repression of the obvious parallels between the US project, and that of the French colonial enterprise, defeated at Dien Bien Phu in 1954. Charles Bohlen, ambassador to France, dispatched to entreat de Gaulle to line up behind American policy, reported back:

> General de Gaulle said that France did not agree with the U.S. in its analysis of the situation in that it did not consider that there was any real government in Vietnam.... He said that the war in essence was the same one that the French had been fighting since the end of the World War II: that the Vietnamese had no taste for this war and that the anticommunist forces in Vietnam were not up to the task. I interrupted him to tell him ... it was quite different, one was a colonial war which came out as colonial wars always do and the other was war against aggression directed and maintained from without.[14]

The clear warnings of European allies fell on deaf ears. Domestic politics helped propel the Johnson Administration closer to full-scale intervention. A set of related incidents from the spring and summer of 1964 helps illustrate the pervasive domestic politics of masculinity surrounding issues of national security and foreign policy decision-making. Lyndon Johnson had learned well the political lessons of the "loss" of China during his tenure in the Senate. He and his high-level foreign policy advisers understood the political vulnerability of the Democratic party to charges of weakness and "treason" based on the history of the counter-subversion and counter-perversion crusades of the nineteen-fifties. His greatest political apprehensions concerning American policy toward Vietnam focused on the Right; he feared being blamed for the "loss" of Vietnam. His top advisers, inherited from Kennedy, reinforced these impulses. South Vietnam, counseled McGeorge Bundy, was "both a test of US firmness and specifically a test of U.S. capacity to deal with 'wars of national liberation.' "[15]

However, Johnson and some of his political cronies and erstwhile Congressional colleagues were deeply pessimistic about the likely outcome of U.S. escalation. At the end of May, when the President sought his opinion, Senator Richard Russell (D-GA) warned his former protégé: "It's a tragic situation. It's just one of those places where you can't win. Anything you do is wrong." Russell cautioned that US military intervention would not work: "it would be a Korea on a much bigger scale and a worse scale . . . If you go from Laos and Cambodia and Vietnam and bring North Vietnam into it too, it is the damnedest mess on earth. The French report that they lost 250,000 men and spent a couple of billion of their money and two billion of ours down there and just got the hell whipped out of them." When Johnson broached his war managers' proposal to bomb infiltration routes or "oil plants" in the North, Russell bluntly, and with considerable prescience, dismissed an air war as a feasible solution to the dilemma:

> Oh, hell! That ain't worth a hoot. That's just impossible. . . . We tried it in Korea. We even got a lot of old B-29s to increase the bomb load and sent 'em over there and just dropped millions and millions of bombs, day and night, . . . they would knock the road at night and in the morning the damn people would be back traveling over it. We never could interdict all their lines of communication although we had absolute control of the seas and the air, and we never did stop them. And you ain't gonna stop these people either.[16]

Russell regarded Vietnam as a dangerous entanglement, not worth the profound risks of military intervention. Johnson asked him directly, "How important is it to us?" "It is isn't important a damn bit," Russell replied forcefully, "with all these new missile systems." American military security was not tied to any strategic imperative to hold Vietnam. Johnson was slightly taken aback: "Well, I guess it it's important to us –." "From a psychological standpoint," interjected Russell.

Johnson confided to Russell that he too had profound doubts about the wisdom of intervention in Vietnam. "I've got a little old sergeant that works for me over at the house and he's got six children and I just put him up as the United States Army, Air Force and Navy every time I think about making this decision and think about sending that father of those six kids in there. And what the hell are we going to get out of his doing it? And it just makes the chills run up my back. . . . I just haven't got the nerve to do it, and I don't see any other way out of it." But Johnson plaintively voiced bigger worries about the domestic political consequences if he failed to enlarge the war in Southeast Asia and thus "lost" territory to communism. "Well, they'd impeach a President though that would run out, wouldn't they? . . . outside of [Senator Wayne] Morse, everybody I talk to says you got to go in, including [Senator Bourke] Hickenlooper, including all the Republicans." Russell warned the President that while intervention "with all the troops" might look "pretty good right now" as a domestic and international political gesture, "it'll be the most expensive venture this country ever went into."[17]

Within minutes of the conclusion of his phone conversation with Richard Russell, LBJ consulted McGeorge Bundy. LBJ confessed that Vietnam "worried the hell out" of him – "I don't think it's worth fighting for and I don't think we can get out. . . . What the hell is Vietnam worth to me? What is Laos worth to me? What is it worth to this country?" Although he understood Vietnam or Laos to be of little intrinsic significance compared to the potential costs of war, the potential psychological effects of "softness" worried him deeply. "Of course, if you start running from the Communists, they may just chase you into your own kitchen." "That's the dilemma," Bundy agreed, "that is what the rest of that half of the world is going to think if this thing comes apart on us." LBJ wavered between his fear of appearing weak to domestic and foreign audiences and the apparent wisdom of those who counseled against escalation, simultaneously endorsing caution and disparaging the unmanly weakness of those who urged it. "Everybody I talk to that's got any sense in there says, 'Oh my God, ple-e-ease give this thought.' Of course, I was reading [Senator Mike] Mansfield's stuff this morning and it's just milquetoast as it can be. He got no spine at all. But this is a terrible thing we're getting ready to do." Bundy prodded Johnson toward a controlled technocratic toughness, to be expressed with bombs against North Vietnam: "We really need to do some target folder work, Mr. President, that shows precisely what we do and don't mean here. The main object is to kill as few people as possible while creating an environment in which the incentive to react is as low as possible."[18]

Sensing the President's hesitation to use force, Bundy tentatively ventured a suggestion that might take the political sting out of sending conscripts to fight an unpopular Asian war. The solution to the problem of "saying to a guy, 'You go to Vietnam and you fight in the rice paddies' " was to invoke the imperial brotherhood's tradition of volunteer heroism in war. "What would happen," Bundy mused, if the President were to say in a speech " 'And from now on, nobody goes to this task who doesn't volunteer.' I think we might turn around the atmosphere of our own people out there if it were a volunteer's enterprise." Johnson was skeptical, worried that volunteers would not materialize, fearing that the prospect of war was broadly unpopular. "I don't think it's just [Senators] Morse and Russell and Gruening." Bundy agreed: "I know it isn't Mr. President. It's 90 percent of the people who don't want any part of this."

Johnson continued the circular and strangely schizophrenic behind-the-scenes discourse with his political cronies. In June LBJ again consulted Senator Richard Russell. Yet again he outlined his assessment of the political and military dilemma he faced: "I don't believe that the American people ever want me to run [from Vietnam]. . . . At the same time, I don't want to commit us to a war." Russell agreed that there were no attractive alternatives: "We're just like the damn cow over a fence out there in Vietnam." The President fished for a commitment to intervention from the Armed Services Committee Chairman, recounting the pugnacious advice to defend boundaries given him by A. W. Moursund, a political crony from Johnson City, Texas.

> "Goddamn there's not anything that'll destroy you as quick as pulling out, pulling up stakes and running. America wants, by God, prestige and power." I said, "Yeah, but I don't want to kill these folks." He said, "I don't give a damn. I didn't want to kill them in Korea, but if you don't stand up for America, there's nothing that a fellow in Johnson City" – or Georgia or any other place – "they'll forgive you for anything except being weak." Goldwater and all of 'em are raising hell about . . . hot pursuit and let's go in an bomb 'em.[19]

Without hesitation, Russell warned the President of the bloody stalemate he envisioned: "It'd take a half million men. They'd be bogged down there for ten years." But the fear of the domestic political consequences of "weakness" gripped the southern Senator too, despite his clairvoyant predictions about the contemplated escalation. The "American inclination" Russell believed, was to "shoot back" when US power was challenged. Russell offered equivocal advice to LBJ; the politics of manliness dictated continuing engagement in a losing battle, but the foreseeable damage to the national interest resulting from growing military intervention demanded withdrawal. Russell again outlined the double bind facing Johnson:

> I don't know what the hell to do. I didn't ever want to get messed up down there. I do not agree with those brain trusters who say that this thing has got tremendous strategic and economic value and that we'll lose everything in Southeast Asia if we lose Vietnam. . . . But as a practical matter, we're in there and I don't know how you can tell the American people you're coming out. . . . They'll think that you've just been whipped, you've been ruined, you're scared. It'd be disastrous.[20]

LBJ seized upon the part of the Senator's counsel that reinforced his own inclination to use force, proposing his own justification for escalation: "I think that I've got to say that I didn't get you in here, but we're in here by treaty and our national honor is at stake. And if this treaty's [SEATO] no good, none of 'em are any good. Therefore we're there. And being there, we've got to conduct ourselves like men." Johnson and Russell continued tracing circles, hoping to hit upon a politically acceptable solution to the Vietnam crisis. Johnson suggested that a "proposal . . . like Eisenhower worked out in Korea" could offer a way out. Russell then offered another assessment of the political psychology of the American electorate, at odds with his earlier estimate: "I think the people, if you get some sort of agreement all the way around, would understand it. . . . I don't think they'd be opposed to coming out. I don't think the American people want to stay in there. They've got enough sense that it's just a matter of face, that we can't just walk off and leave those people down there."[21]

Throughout 1964 Lyndon Johnson played a waiting game. He fought a presidential campaign against Barry Goldwater, a right-wing hyper-masculine militarist whose handlers posed him in the cockpit of a military jet, and advertised him as "A Fighting Man," a "Courageous Man," an "All American Man . . . THE MAN for President of the United States." Johnson worked to protect himself in the game of political manliness. He cast Goldwater as a fanatic with his finger on the nuclear trigger, in contrast to his own reasoned "firmness." The Gulf of Tonkin incidents of August 2 and 4 1964, provided Johnson with an occasion to rally Congress around the flag by asking their support for an immediate military response to "aggression." Calculations about the domestic political value of a demonstration of military power also entered the equation. Immediately after the second of the real (Aug. 2) and imagined (Aug. 4) North Vietnamese attacks on the destroyers *Maddox* and *Turner Joy*, the Democratic President summoned the Congressional leadership to confer with him.[22]

Johnson entered the meeting with his resolve bolstered by political advice from friends that he should "make it look like a very firm stand." Barry Goldwater presented a special threat to Johnson's ability to project a convincing image of political manliness, they warned. "You're gonna be running against a man who's a wild man," fellow Texan and former Treasury Secretary Robert Anderson counseled, "if he can show any lack of firmness . . . this fella's gonna play all the angles." LBJ sought approval to bomb North Vietnam from conservative Republicans Bourke Hickenlooper, Charles Halleck, and Everett Dirksen, and Democrats William Fulbright, Mike Mansfield, and Richard Russell. He posed the problem in terms designed to stir the patriotic impulse to defend boundaries. "We can tuck our tails and run, but if we do these countries will feel all they have to do to scare us is to shoot the American flag."[23]

The Congressional leaders responded as the President wished, and he unleashed the waiting bombers to strike North Vietnam. The Gulf of Tonkin resolution subsequently passed by Congress at the President's request gave the executive branch *carte blanche* for future military action. Johnson's maneuvering was designed, in part, to outflank presidential rival Goldwater and the Republican Right during an election year by actions designed to seem at once tough but moderate. The "measured" bombing of North Vietnam made Johnson seem to respond strongly to "aggression," without reawakening domestic fears of another Korean-style "ground war in Asia" involving large numbers of American troops. He offered a studied contrast in masculine leadership, an image of reasoned strength, compared to the "impetuousness and impulsiveness" of Goldwater's militant and apocalyptic pronouncements.[24]

In October, Johnson was narrowly spared a dangerous reprise of the Red Scare politics of counter-perversion when his close aide Walter Jenkins was arrested in the basement men's room of the YMCA near the White House. Johnson managed to contain the political damage of the homosexual scandal by isolating and "hospitalizing" Jenkins, by disavowing any knowledge of his "perversion," and by calling in J. Edgar Hoover to certify that the White House was free of other homosexual "security risks." But most significantly, the Johnson White House quickly discovered that Walter Jenkins served in the 999th Air Force Reserve Unit, commanded by Major General Barry Goldwater, who had written all Jenkins' recent fitness reports.

Both candidates were compromised by association with a "security risk." Although the scandal made front page headlines, and stayed in the news during the two weeks leading up to the election, the outcome confounded the expectations of both campaigns and Washington political commentators. The *Chicago Tribune* pronounced it a sex scandal as serious as the recent Profumo Affair which had brought down the British Minister of War and badly damaged the Conservative government. Goldwater's supporters condemned the "moral decay" in the White House, pronounced the Jenkins affair an unforgivable breach of "national security," and condemned the scandal as part and parcel of the "weakness" of Johnson's foreign policy – all to no avail. In contrast to the Lavender Scare of the McCarthy era, the Republicans' eagerness to exploit the scandal backfired, and LBJ's poll numbers actually rose a couple of percentage points. Nonetheless, the widely publicized scandal embarrassed the administration, and provided another chastening lesson in the politics of manliness.[25]

With the February 1965 NLF attack on the US base at Pleiku, Johnson approved the escalation long urged by his high-level advisers. Johnson did not share the patrician imperial narrative of masculine toughness and struggle that animated so many of his administration, but he carried his own imperial frontier narrative. In March, President Johnson demonstrated his resolve to a group of his high-level national security bureaucrats. He promised not to "give in" to "another Munich." If the US did not defend imperial boundaries "here" [Vietnam], Johnson argued, "then Thailand" would become the battleground. "Come Hell or high water, we're gonna [sic] stay there." He urged his cabinet and staff to "beg borrow or steal to get a government" to support the US military presence in South Vietnam. The forced inactivity of the previous year had been frustrating. "We endured this thru [sic] a campaign," Johnson griped. But he made it clear that the humiliations of passivity need no longer be tolerated. The President evoked the heroic legacy of the frontier racial war of American myth. With a slightly scrambled metaphor he exhorted his men to war: "You gotta get some Indians under your scalp." By the summer of 1965 despite profound doubts about the efficacy of "white troops" in a "land war in Asia," and an essentially clear picture of the pitfalls that awaited the US Johnson approved undertaking a full-scale ground war.[26]

July 1965 saw a brief pause during the headlong escalation as Johnson convened his high-level advisers to ponder the grave implications of sending US troops to Vietnam in lots of 100,000, as Robert McNamara recommended. Visible here, perhaps more clearly than elsewhere, is the failure of cost–benefit reason that has so puzzled McNamara after the fact. George Ball, Undersecretary of State, had been the only high-level foreign policy "insider" of the Johnson administration to unequivocally argue against escalation. Ball lacked the elite boarding-school–Ivy League–clubman credentials possessed by many of his associates. His work with Jean Monnet and his international law practice gave him an intimate acquaintance with the French debacle in Indochina. Vietnam, he believed, was a dangerous distraction from the central strategic and economic concerns of the US, which still centered on Europe. He argued in several long memos prepared between October 1964, and July 1965, that the US "cut its losses" and find a negotiated settlement "under the best possible conditions." His colleagues, Bundy, McNamara, and Rusk, reacted with alarm for fear of "leaks," and treated his arguments "as an idiosyncratic diversion from the only relevant problem: how to win the war."[27]

With the July conclave Johnson conducted a formally rational inquiry into the costs and benefits of intervention. Ball was given the opportunity to play "devil's advo-cate" and argue against escalation. Ball later referred to the reasoning process used by the assembled advisers as "turning logic on its head." More accurately stated, the process reveals the way that deeply ingrained ideologies of masculine strength and political legitimacy, buttressed by the experiences of competition for power at the individual and collective level created a context of conceivable meanings, a "logic," which made Ball's proposed withdrawal from war quite literally unthinkable.[28]

While the President cautioned that "we must make no snap judgments," the very language he used reveals an obsession with masculine "toughness" and "honor." Framing the debate in operational terms, Johnson instinctively led the discussion toward the issue of "strength" and away from the assessment of economic or directly strategic costs and benefits:

> Are we the only defenders of freedom in the world? The negotiations, the pause [in the bombing campaign], all the other approaches have all been explored. It makes us look weak – with cap in hand. We have tried.[29]

The President framed the issues to place the US, under his leadership, at the center of a heroic narrative of moral and physical strength: would the assembled men act as strong men should? Would they shoulder the painful burden that others refused and defend the central cultural values of freedom, or, would they recommend that the US go abjectly to face humiliation at the bargaining table? Unstated, but understood was the assumption that such a humiliation would not only have dire international consequences but would also undermine domestic political power and legitimacy.

Before presenting his arguments against intervention, Ball first reassured the assembled fraternity of his loyalty: "if the decision is made to go ahead, I'm commit-ted." Ball did not question the propriety or wisdom of conducting an interventionist policy abroad to serve American interests. The question was simply whether or not the costs of intervention outweighed the benefits. Ball argued that the US should cut its losses, "disagreeable" as that would be, to avoid the undeniable long-term dangers of intervention. Johnson, who had read and discussed Ball's proposals for several months, found such a suggestion outside the realm of the conceivable. While he refused to consider Ball's straightforward recommendation of a negotiated with-drawal, he continued the ritual of debate: "You have pointed out the danger, but you haven't proposed an alternative. We have no mortgage on victory. . . . I think it is desirable to hear you out." Ball's option was unthinkable to the assembled conclave of national security bureaucrats too. They complained that it amounted to appease-ment, an invitation to world war because of the "similarity to our indolence at Munich." Dean Rusk agreed with his virile colleagues in their demand for unwaver-ing defense of imperial boundaries: "If the Communist world finds out we will not pursue our commitment to the end, I don't know where they will stay their hand."[30]

Johnson, of course, decided to escalate. He had McGeorge Bundy read from a prepared memo to inoculate the assembled brotherhood against the criticism they would face upon the announcement of escalation. By ritually invoking the reasoning they had rejected, the warriors hoped to steel themselves against their own repressed doubts:

> For 10 years every step we have taken has been based on a previous failure. All we have done has failed and caused us to take another step which has failed.... we have made excessive claims we haven't been able to realize.... We are about to fight a war we can't fight and win, and the country we are trying to help is quitting.... aren't we talking about a military solution when the solution is political.[31]

Rather than "turning logic on its head," as Ball put it, the war managers used a different and incommensurable logic, a sort of scholastic deduction premised on an imperial psychology of masculine strength and threat, rather than calculation of directly measurable economic or military costs and benefits. With the July 1965 decision for full intervention with ground troops, the predictions of Russell, Ball, Mansfield, and others began to be realized. The war quickly reached a bloody stalemate that wreaked its havoc on the bodies of both the Vietnamese people and the American soldiers sent to fight.[32]

Ideals of American "manhood" shaped important aspects of the way the Johnson administration prosecuted the war. Since the only culturally and politically legitimate model of American empire was that of "regeneration through violence," Johnson employed the frontier narrative of masculine heroism and race war to bring "civilization" to a wild and savage land. Thus, the metaphors, from Johnson, and from the military, cast Vietnam as "Indian Country": the enemy was a racial other, savage, and fair game for the annihilating technology of death dealt by the "air cavalry." A contradiction which continually plagued the US was the inability of the Americans to distinguish good Indians from bad – essentially a false distinction, since the American government and military held the "good" Indians, the South Vietnamese, in contempt for their weakness, effeminacy, corruption, and cowardice.[33]

Lyndon Johnson, especially, mobilized other men's bodies to do the fighting, but metaphorically cast himself and his advisers as combatants: "It's like a prizefight. Our right is our military power, but our left must be our peace proposals." Johnson cast himself as a "prizefighter up against Jack Dempsey" or the US as a barroom brawler locked in a struggle with the North Vietnamese, hoping to find a way to "get our feet on their neck." Johnson had a predilection for sexual metaphors which identified his body with imperial struggle; a tactical setback resulting from attempts to arrange "negotiations" might be equated with homosexual penetration:

> Oh yes, a bombing halt, I'll tell you what happens when there is a bombing halt. I halt and then Ho Chi Minh shoves his trucks right up my ass. That's your bombing halt.[34]

Conversely, aggressive military action against the enemy carried connotations of sexual conquest. During the spring of 1965, he reassured Congressional critics that his bombing would not spark a Chinese intervention: "I'm going up her leg an inch at a time . . . I'll get the snatch before they know what's happening, you see." To Johnson, the Gulf of Tonkin bombing symbolized a violent, sexualized male prowess: "I didn't just screw Ho Chi Minh. I cut his pecker off."[35]

The US intervention in Vietnam was the product of a long history and many complex chains of causation. The social construction of manhood among the elites who managed America's post-colonial empire is one factor that must be accounted for in the effort to fully understand that history. The way that decision-makers understood threats, the responses they considered legitimate or even conceivable, followed in significant measure from their socialization to manhood. A lifetime of immersion in masculine competition and a culture celebrating neo-stoic warrior-manhood gave many highly educated, privileged, and powerful men the conviction that "duty" and the protection of both their own power and that of the nation demanded a military defense of imperial boundaries in Vietnam. The belief that the American electorate would "forgive" its leaders "anything but being weak" pushed Lyndon Johnson and his advisors into the tragic escalation of a war they feared; a war they predicted the US could not win.

NOTES

1 Robert S. McNamara with Brian Van DeMark, *In Retrospect: The Tragedy and Lessons of Vietnam* (New York: Times Books, 1995).

2 See, for instance, the "McNamara's memoirs" thread on the H-Net H-Diplo Internet discussion group, late spring and summer 1995, especially, electronic posting, Andrew L. Johns, "Re: McNamara's Memoirs," H-Diplo, June 8, 1995; McNamara, *In Retrospect*, 33, 203.

3 While the "Munich analogy" and the "Domino Effect" continued to function as ritual invocations justifying ongoing US military involvement in South Vietnam, the CIA's answer to the question in 1964, "Would the Loss of South Vietnam and Laos Precipitate a 'Domino Effect' in the Far East?" was a qualified "no." Sherman Kent of the CIA Board of National Estimates wrote: "We do not believe that the loss of South Vietnam and Laos would be followed by the rapid, successive communization of the other states of the Far East. . . . Furthermore a continuation of the spread of communism in the area would not be inexorable, and any spread which did occur would take time – time in which the total situation might change in any number of ways unfavorable to the communist cause." Nonetheless, in his next breath, Kent argued that the "loss" of SVN "would be profoundly damaging to the U.S. position in the Far East," not for directly strategic or economic reasons, but for its effect on "prestige" and the "credibility" of the US containment effort elsewhere. See Memorandum from the Board of National Estimates to the Director of Central Intelligence (McCone), June 9, 1964, *Foreign Relations of the U.S.: Vietnam 1964.*

4 McNamara, *In Retrospect*, xvi.

5 This argument is developed at greater length in Robert Dean, *Imperial Brotherhood: Gender and the Making of Cold War Foreign Policy* (Amherst: University of Massachusetts Press, 2001). On the post-war "establishment," see Godfrey Hodgson, "The Establishment," *Foreign Policy*, no. 10, Spring 1973, 3–40. Works that employ the concept of an "establishment" include Kai Bird, *The Chairman: John J. McCloy, the Making of the American Establishment* (New York: Simon and Schuster, 1992); Hodgson, *The Colonel: The Life*

and Wars of Henry Stimson, 1867–1950 (New York: Alfred A. Knopf, 1990). Walter Isaacson and Evan Thomas, *The Wise Men: Six Friends and the World They Made: Acheson, Bohlen, Harriman, Kennan, Lovett, McCloy* (New York: Simon and Schuster, 1986), 26; Richard Barnet, *Roots of War: The Men And Institutions Behind U.S. Foreign Policy* (New York: Random House, 1972).

6 One "genealogical" example clearly illustrates a "line of descent" from TR: William and McGeorge Bundy, respectively Assistant Sec. of State for Far Eastern Affairs and National Security Advisor for Johnson. Their father Harvey Bundy worked closely with TR's erstwhile protégé, Henry Stimson during his terms as Hoover's Sec. of State and FDR's Sec. of War. McGeorge enlisted as a propagandist for the imperial tradition, by writing Stimson's memoirs after the war, and editing Dean Acheson's speeches. William married Dean Acheson's daughter, and joined the CIA in 1951, where he stayed until 1961. On the cultural construction of martial imperial masculinity, see T. J. Jackson Lears, *No Place of Grace: Antimodernism and the Transformation of American Culture, 1880–1920* (New York: Pantheon, 1981), 30–1, 98–9; Michael Pearlman, *To Make Democracy Safe for America: Patricians and Preparedness in the Progressive Era* (Urbana: University of Ilinois Press, 1984); Amy Kaplan, "Romancing the Empire: The Embodiment of American Masculinity in the Popular Historical Novel of the 1890s," *American Literary History* 2:4 (Winter 1990), 662; E. Anthony Rotundo, *American Manhood: Transformations in Masculinity from the Revolution to the Modern Era* (New York: Basic Books, 1993), 223, 233; Mark E. Kann, *On the Man Question: Gender and Civic Virtue in America* (Philadelphia: Temple University Press, 1991), esp. 288–93.

7 Meeting Notes, Camp David, Aspen Lodge, July 25, 1965, 5:00 p.m., Meeting Notes File, Box 1, Lyndon Baines Johnson Library. See also William Bundy's "Report on Meeting with Foreign Affairs Consultants," July 22, 1965, reproduced in Larry Berman, *Planning a Tragedy: The Americanization of the War in Vietnam* (New York: W. W. Norton, 1982), 134–5; John J. McCloy, Commencement Address, Haverford College, 1965, box 72, Joseph W. Alsop Papers, Library of Congress.

8 See "The Attack of the Primitives Begins," in Dean Acheson, *Present at the Creation: My Years in the State Department* (New York: W. W. Norton, 1969).

9 Robert Dean, "Masculinity as Ideology: John F. Kennedy and the Domestic Politics of Foreign Policy," *Diplomatic History*, 22:1 (Winter 1998), 29–63.

10 David L. Anderson, *Trapped by Success: The Eisenhower Administration and Vietnam, 1953–1961* (New York: Columbia University Press, 1991), 208. Republicanism, of course, expresses a strongly "gendered" vision of social order. See Mark E. Kann, *On the Man Question: Gender and Civic Virtue in America* (Philadelphia: Temple University Press, 1991).

11 See Kennedy's argument in Walt W. Rostow, *The Diffusion of Power: An Essay in Recent History* (New York: Macmillan, 1972), 270; Robert Buzzanco, *Masters of War: Military Dissent and Politics in the Vietnam Era* (New York: Cambridge University Press, 1996).

12 For invocations of the "oriental mind" to explain the national security bureaucrats' failure to successfully implement their operational schemes for the transformation of Vietnamese politics and society, see Roswell Gilpatric, Oral History interview by Dennis J. O'Brien, May 5, 1970, John Fitzgerald Kennedy Library, 24, and Roger Hillsman, Oral History interview by Dennis J. O'Brien, August 14, 1970, JFKL, 22. Henry Cabot Lodge, Telegram from the Embassy in Vietnam to the Department of State, Sept. 5, 1963, *Foreign Relations of the United States: Vietnam, August–December 1963* (Washington: US Government Printing Office, 1991), 110.

13 Memorandum from the President's Special Assistant for National Security Affairs (Bundy) to the President, January 7, 1964, *Foreign Relations of the United States: Vietnam 1964* (Washington: US Government Printing Office, 1992).

14 Message from the Ambassador in France (Bohlen) to the President, April 2, 1964, *FRUS: Vietnam 1964.*

15 Memo, Senator Mike Mansfield to President Johnson, January 6, 1964, and, Memo, McGeorge Bundy to the President, January 9, 1964, National Security File, Memos to the President, McGeorge Bundy, Box 1, folder Vol. 1, Lyndon Baines Johnson Library; Draft Memorandum to the President, Comment on Memoranda by Senator Mansfield, 7/1/64, NSF, Memos to Pres., Folder Vol. 2, LBJL; Thomas Hughes statement in *The Johnson Years: A Vietnam Roundtable*, edited by Ted Gittinger (Austin: Lyndon B. Johnson School of Public Affairs, 1993), 12–13.

16 Transcript of telephone conversation, LBJ and Senator Richard Russell, Wednesday, May 27, 1964, 10:55 a.m., in *Taking Charge: The Johnson White House Tapes, 1963–1964*, Michael R. Beschloss, ed. (New York: Simon and Schuster, 1997), 367, 369.

17 Ibid., 369.

18 Ibid., 370–1.

19 Transcript of telephone conversation, LBJ with Richard Russell, Thursday, June 11, 1964, 12:26 p.m., reproduced in Beschloss, *Taking Charge*, 401–3.

20 Ibid.

21 Ibid.

22 Advertisements, California Goldwater for President Committee, Santa Clara County [1964], in author's possession. The destroyer attacked on August 2, 1964, was in proximity to a US supported commando assault on North Vietnamese coastal installations, part of the secret OPLAN 34–A, not revealed to Congress or the public. See George McT. Kahin, *Intervention: How America Became Involved in Vietnam* (New York: Alfred E. Knopf, 1986), 219–25; or, for a discussion of Tonkin Gulf by some of the principals involved, see *Johnson Years*, Gittinger ed., 17–38. For a thorough treatment of OPLAN 34-A operations, the Tonkin Gulf incidents, and the reprisal air attacks, see Edwin E. Moise, *Tonkin Gulf and the Escalation of the Vietnam War* (Chapel Hill: University of North Carolina Press, 1996).

23 LBJ phone call with Robert Anderson, 9:46 a.m., Aug. 3, 1964, Cit. 4631–2, Audiotape WH6408.03, LBJL; Notes Taken At Leadership Meeting on August 4, 1964 (McNamara's and Rusk's statements not included), Meeting Notes File, Box 1, LBJL.

24 Hughes statement, *Johnson Years*, 45. LBJ, conversation with Robert Kennedy, 8:00 p.m. Tuesday July 21, 1964, Beschloss, *Taking Charge*, 465.

25 For coverage of the White House homosexual scandal see *The New York Times, The Washington Post*, and the *Chicago Tribune*, October 15 through 29, 1964, including: "Lyndon Aid[e] Quits in Morals Case," *CT*, Oct. 15, 1964; Morton Mintz, "Jenkins, Aide to LBJ, Resigns After Arrest," *WP*, Oct. 15, 1964; Max Frankel, "President's Aide Quits on Report of Morals Case," *NYT*, Oct. 15, 1964; James Reston, "Setback for Johnson," *NYT*, Oct. 15, 1964; "The Jenkins Case," *NYT*, Oct. 16, 1964; "White House Morality," *CT*, Oct. 16, 1964; editorial "The Security Sieve," *NYT*, Oct. 18, 1964; Arthur Krock, "The Jenkins Case: The Issue of National Security Is Raising Some Vital Questions," *NYT*, Oct. 18, 1964. Thomas Hughes statement, *The Johnson Years: A Vietnam Roundtable*, edited by Ted Gittinger (Austin: LBJ Library, University of Texas, 1993), 45.

26 Meeting Notes, March 10, 1965, Papers of McGeorge Bundy, Box 1, LBJL.

27 Extensive accounts of the July 1965 meetings and decisions can be found in George Ball, *The Past Has Another Pattern: Memoirs* (New York: W.W. Norton, 1986; Larry Berman, *Planning a Tragedy: The Americanization of the War in Vietnam* (New York: W.W. Norton, 1982); Kahin, *Intervention*; Brian VanDeMark, *Into the Quagmire: Lyndon Johnson and the Escalation of the Vietnam War* (New York: Oxford University Press, 1991); David M. Barrett, *Uncertain Warriors: Lyndon Johnson and His Vietnam Advisers* (Lawrence: University Press of Kansas, 1993). Ball, *Past*, 380–4.

28 Ibid., 383–9.

29 Notes, Cabinet Room, Wednesday, July 21, 1965, 10:40 a.m., Subject Vietnam, Meeting Notes File, Box 1, LBJL.

30 Meeting Notes, July 21, 1965,10:40 a.m.; Notes of Meeting, Cabinet Room, July 22, 1965, MNF, Box 1, LBJL.

31 Meeting Notes, July 22, 1965, 12:00 noon, MNF, Box 1, LBJL.

32 Even after the escalation had settled into stalemate, some of the war managers displayed a remarkable imperviousness to evidence which contradicted their chains of geo-strategic domino theory deduction. Walt Whitman Rostow believed that massive US intervention in Vietnam had prevented the fall of other Southeast Asian nations to Communism. He attributed the coup of the Muslim generals against Indonesia's Sukarno (in his view saving Indonesia from the communists) to the inspiration provided by the American "defense" of South Vietnam. When he sought confirmation of his theory from Richard Helms of the CIA, Helms replied that he had "searched in vain for evidence that the US display of determination in Vietnam directly influenced the outcome of the Indonesian crisis in any significant way." Instead, Helms argued, the course of Indonesian politics "evolved purely from a complex and long-standing domestic political situation." Rostow nonetheless continued to credit the US intervention with successful containment throughout Asia. See Helms to Rostow, May 13, 1966, NSC Files, Country Files, Box 248, LBJL.

33 On the cultural narratives of the period that embodied the myth of "regeneration through violence" see Richard Slotkin, *Gunfighter Nation: The Myth of the Frontier in Twentieth-Century America* (New York: HarperCollins, 1993).

34 Meeting notes, July 22, 1965, 3:00 p.m., MNF, LBJL; Meeting notes, July 28, 1965, and Meeting notes, April 1, 1965, Papers of McGeorge Bundy, box 1, LBJL; Johnson quoted in David L. DiLeo, *George Ball, Vietnam, and the Rethinking of Containment* (Chapel Hill: University of North Carolina Press, 1991), 132.

35 Johnson quoted in Gloria Emerson, *Winners and Losers: Battles, Retreats, Gains, and Ruins from a Long War* (New York: Random House, 1976), 377; and in David Halberstam, *The Best and the Brightest* (New York: Random House, 1972), 414.

CHAPTER TWENTY

The Antiwar Movement

BARBARA TISCHLER

The loosely-organized coalition that came together to stop the war in Vietnam in the late 1960s and early 1970s presents a study in contrast. It was an antiwar movement whose target was not a war at all, but a "conflict," among forces within the former French colony of Vietnam that nevertheless resulted in the loss of more than 58,000 American lives, in addition to monumental civilian and military losses within Vietnam. The movement brought together men and women whose religious and/or pacifist principles asserted the immorality of taking human life, along with cultural and political radicals of a young generation whose ideas ranged from personal liberation to revolutionary discipline and even violence. The antiwar coalition included individuals and organizations with disparate political views united in a common cause. A movement that identified itself as "Left," it experienced tension between Old and New. A peace movement, it included soldiers and recent veterans, many of whom had enlisted because they believed in the justice of the American cause in Southeast Asia. Amid cries of "Join Us!" leaders of the movement often relied on models of hierarchy and authority to legitimize their own positions, thereby failing to comprehend the contributions of dissidents within the ranks, including women, people of color, and gay people. Finally, for all the revolutionary rhetoric and analysis of the political factions of the movement, the mainstream antiwar movement was an expression of faith in participatory democracy and the venerable American idea that dissent could find a voice and play a role in affecting significant political change.

The young American men and women who joined forces to say, "No" to their government were not raised to be rebellious. As part of the Baby Boom cohort of post-war children, middle-class white young people experienced the prosperity of the post-World War II years as the norm. Their reality was far from the Depression and war that had defined their parents' youth. Relative comfort and confidence in the political and economic system seemed to validate Richard Nixon's sweeping "put-down" of Nikita Krushchev with an all-electric American kitchen. The irony was that the same affluence that brought comfort to America's young also inspired many to strive for equity and justice at home and abroad. Indeed, material comfort as an end in itself symbolized the bankruptcy of personal values and governmental policies that ignored issues of equity and justice. Young people formed the majority of activists striving for civil rights in the non-violent movement of lunch counter sit-ins and freedom rides in the early sixties. After the first sit-ins in Greensboro, North Carolina in February of 1960, the movement grew to more than 50,000, many of whom were students at local colleges. The Student Non-Violent Coordinating Committee (SNCC) represented the optimism of its youthful members that the evils of racism could be eradicated in American society.

Despite popular evocations of antiwar activism as part of a youth culture that expressed disdain for anyone over 30, future activists learned much from their elders. They heeded Dwight Eisenhower's warnings about the dangers of the military industrial complex and understood Arthur Schlesinger's optimism that the "new mood" in American politics would reject the materialism of the past in favor of a greater spiritual and philosophical richness that would restore a sense of unity to the American polity.[1] Most important, they were willing to become activists for a cause that moved them. John F. Kennedy had implored them to, "Ask not what your country can do for you, ask what you can do for your country." In 1962, the newly-founded Students for a Democratic Society, which had emerged out of the Old Left's League for Industrial Democracy but would become a prime mover in the struggle against Eisenhower, Kennedy, and Johnson's war as a representative of New Left politics, declared that

> We are people of this generation, bred in at least modest comfort, housed now in universities, looking uncomfortably to the world we inherit. When we were kids, the United States was the wealthiest and strongest country in the world; the only one with the atom bomb, the least scarred by modern war, an initiator of the United Nations that we thought would distribute Western influence throughout the world. Freedom and equality for each individual, government of, by, and for the people – these American values we found good, principles by which we could live as men. Many of us began maturing in complacency.[2]

Not content to remain complacent, many young people drawn to antiwar activism began to challenge the authority of those adult mentors who had taught them the language of optimism, liberalism, and American democracy.

In the early days of what would become a major oppositional movement, it was far from easy to challenge one's elders and one's government. For many young people, the rationale for the Gulf of Tonkin Resolution (that the destroyers Maddux and Turner Joy had been attacked in the Gulf of Tonkin) rang false. But for the American population at large that saw evening news coverage of the "incident," the need to repel any and all armed aggression against the forces of the United States seemed legitimate. A product of containment, the Resolution provided the impetus for intervention, as it passed Congress in August of 1964, with only two dissenting votes.[3] Lyndon Johnson's landslide election to the presidency over Barry Goldwater as a "peace candidate," even as he continued to order the bombing of North Vietnam, confirmed the electorate's acceptance of the Kennedy–Johnson brand of cold war liberalism and containment of communism.[4]

Johnson took his case for the deployment of ground troops in Vietnam to students at Johns Hopkins University in April of 1965. His words may sound disingenuous, even false, today, but, at the time, most Americans believed him, and it could be difficult for students or anyone else to stand up in opposition to a popular president. He told his audience that

> Viet-Nam is far away from this quiet campus. We have no territory there, nor do we seek any. The war is dirty and brutal and difficult. And some 400 young men, born into an America that is bursting with opportunity and promise, have ended their lives on Viet-Nam's steaming soil.
>
> Why must we take this painful road?
>
> Why must this Nation hazard its ease, and its interest, and its power for the sake of a people so far away?
>
> We fight because we must fight if we are to live in a world where every country can shape its own destiny. And only in such a world will our own freedom be finally secure.[5]

Early acts of protest against the war were individual rather than products of the organization and coalition-building that characterized the antiwar movement. On June 11 1963, Americans saw frightening images of Vietnamese Buddhist monk Thich Quang Duc who set himself afire on a street in Saigon to protest President Ngo Dinh Diem's repression of religious and political dissenters.[6] Neither this individual act, nor others that followed, prevented continuing attacks on Buddhists and others, but it did sear images of self-sacrifice in the name of freedom on the American consciousness. On March 16 1965, soon after the start of Operation Rolling Thunder, a massive bombing effort aimed at North Vietnam, Helga Alice Herz, a Holocaust survivor and founding member of Women Strike for Peace (WSP) in Detroit and a member of the Women's International League for Peace and Freedom, committed suicide by setting herself on fire on a Detroit street corner. In her last letter, Herz exhorted Americans to "decide if this world shall be a good place to live for all human beings or if it should blow itself up into oblivion."[7] On November 6 1965, Norman Morrison, a Quaker, set himself on fire near the Pentagon. Morrison's infant daughter was grabbed from him before she could be hurt, but he died before he reached the hospital. Three days later, Roger LaPorte, a Catholic antiwar activist, doused himself with gasoline in New York's Dag Hammarskjold Plaza. When he was rushed to the hospital, he declared, "I'm a Catholic Worker. I'm against war, all wars. I did this as a religious action." He died thirty-three hours later.[8] The drama of these acts of protest was not lost on an American public that was beginning to see the cost of the non-war in Southeast Asia. Nevertheless, public opinion remained supportive of the Johnson administration's policy of sending more bombs and more troops to protect the succession of corrupt and inept South Vietnamese governments. As a popular song of the time put it, "And though it isn't really war, we're sending fifty thousand more, to help save Vietnam from the Vietnamese."

On college campuses, many of which had been seedbeds of white civil rights activism, including participation in the Mississippi Freedom Summer of 1964 and extensive drives to register African American voters in the South, news of the widening war reached students with shock and a sense of urgency. Young people who had believed in the ideal of service and national pride espoused by John Kennedy were stunned to find those same ideals turned to the service of a war to contain communism and support undemocratic and repressive governments far from home. Further, as draft calls escalated in the mid-1960s and the number of American service personnel killed, wounded, and missing increased, the risk of having to fight and die in a war they didn't understand became very real for increasing numbers of young men. So too did the imperative to organize against the war – to struggle against American imperialism, to stop the killing of American men and women, or simply to keep one's self from the harm of war.

University and college campuses soon became the locus of the antiwar movement. Small and local at first, campus protests sponsored by the Universities Committee on Problems of War and Peace based at Wayne State University and the National Committee for a Sane Nuclear Policy (SANE) began to attract national attention. Campus chapters of SDS sponsored rallies against the war, and a variety of *ad hoc* groups emerged whose purpose was to educate students about the war and mobilize them to speak out against it. A group of faculty members at the University of Michigan sought to declare a moratorium day on which students and faculty members could study and reflect on the war. Faced with political and legislative opposition, they planned a night session that would allow for discussion and debate. On the night of March 24–5, faculty members convened the nation's first teach-in. More than 3,000 students participated in the event over the course of the night, which was twice interrupted by bomb threats and for which women students had to obtain permission to be absent from their dormitories because the University acted *in loco parentis* to protect them. One of the main speakers was Arthur Waskow of the Institute for Policy Studies in Washington, who asserted that the war was a mistake in American policy that citizens had to raise their voices in protest to correct.

Although the early teach-ins replicated the hierarchy of the classroom, with professors lecturing to rapt student audiences, students, veterans, clergymen, and others from outside the university community soon found a voice in the teach-ins, making them a valuable forum for education and debate. Within a week of the first teach-in at Michigan, similar events were held on thirty five campuses throughout the country. Although opinion on campus regarding the war was by no means unanimous (fewer than 25 percent of students polled in 1965 favored withdrawal from Vietnam or negotiations with the North Vietnamese), these events, featuring large groups of engaged and passionate students articulating their opposition to government policy, received extensive national press coverage. LBJ's Johns Hopkins speech can be seen as a response to campus critics whose voices were reaching an increasingly large public audience.[9]

Activism on campus intensified on May 21 1965, with the gathering of more than 10,000 students and faculty members on the campus of the University of California at Berkeley for Vietnam Day, a day-long gathering of marches, speeches, and forceful expressions of dissent. The Vietnam Day Committee emerged as an exemplar of civil disobedience that pushed participants in VDC actions to take a stand against the war and just as often against heavily-armed police or speeding troop trains. The Committee's actions gained publicity for the antiwar cause with a membership that reached 400 in the summer of 1965. Led by a cadre of two dozen activist/strategists, the Committee espoused the participatory democracy of SDS that often led to disagreement over tactics. Caught up in its internal debates over the "right" way to oppose the war, the VDC missed the opportunity to mobilize the kind of mass demonstrations that would later bring the antiwar movement into American homes on network news.[10]

For a coalition movement whose constituent groups pulled apart from each other philosophically as much as they pulled together, mass demonstrations that brought thousands of people together at an induction center, a military installation, or in the nation's capitol proved to be a mixed blessing. The nature of coalition politics required that groups that might have nothing else in common could come together to stop the war. For this reason, it became increasingly difficult to develop a coherent political theory or even a workable spin on events for releases to the mainstream press. Big demonstrations drew publicity, both positive and negative, but smaller-scale actions after 1966 highlighted the extent to which opposition to the war was beginning to invade life and culture in the nation as a whole. Charles DeBenedetti noted the diversity and creativity of demonstrations on the local level, which included

> a Fourth of July rally at Independence Hall of five hundred pacifists lauding draft resisters and tax refusers as "contemporary American revolutionaries"; a walk from Valley Forge to Washington by twoscore Veterans and Reservists Against the War; a two-day fast in New York by the Reverend John Neuhaus and other CALC [Clergy and Laity Concerned] leaders; the boarding of the USS Maddox in San Francisco Bay by antiwar women; large Hiroshima anniversary marches in New York, Los Angeles, and San Francisco; a two-day demonstration at the Dow Corporation plant in Midland, Michigan; a solemn vigil outside a California mortuary where the bodies of GIs killed in Vietnam were prepared for shipment home; and questions raised in meeting halls and churches throughout the country.[11]

In addition, during marches to prevent the induction of young men by the Selective Service or to protest chemical and biological research on campus,[12]

> dissidents in Tucson, Arizona, recalling that President Eisenhower had promised to fly to Korea to end the war there, raised funds by promising to buy president Johnson a one-way ticket to Vietnam. Protesters cavorted across a mock battlefield east of Toledo, Ohio, in order to disrupt war games; and Another Mother for Peace raised funds for Vietnamese civilian medical relief by selling cards that bore the words "War is Not Healthy for Children and Other Living Things." . . . The lead singer with a popular rock group, the Beach Boys, was indicted, and heavyweight boxing champion Muhammad Ali was stripped of his crown and sentenced to a maximum penalty of five years in jail and $10,000 in fines – both for refusing induction.[13]

Students and townspeople in Austin, Texas staged cultural protests against the ethos that promoted war and big-time college football on what came to be known as Gentle Thursday, and artists and writers expressed their opposition to the killing in their work with increasing frequency. On April 4 1967, Martin Luther King, Jr. spoke out against the war in New York's Riverside Church. Speaking as a preacher, he articulated a panoply of reasons that the war violated the tenets of Christianity. His powerful argument was addressed squarely at Lyndon Johnson, the president who had brought civil rights into the forefront of American politics in 1964 and 1965 but who now represented repression and death, especially to the young black men who formed a significant percentage of the troops on the ground. King told his audience that it was the task of churches and synagogues to

> urge our Government to disengage itself from a disgraceful commitment. We must continue to raise our voices if our nation persists in its perverse ways in Vietnam. We must be prepared to match actions with words by seeking out every creative means of protest possible.[14]

But as the war continued to escalate, mass action against it captured the public's imagination. The New Left in general and SDS in particular eschewed the idea that it was necessary to build a mass movement around a single issue, preferring instead to engage in coalition building to create a mass movement that would include, but not be limited to, antiwar protest. National Moratorium Day protests, large-scale marches in major cities such as New York, the protest and "levitation" of the Pentagon on October 21 1967, and the mass demonstration in Washington in November of 1969 sponsored by the National Mobilization Committee all included a variety of radical and antiwar voices. Debates over the extent to which antiwar protests should include participants from the old Communist, Trotskyist or Socialist Left contributed to efforts to forge a New Left that focused its energies on matters of war, racism, and social justice. Ideally, this New Left would be free of the sectarian politics that had divided the American Left in the past. But it was the very inclusiveness of the antiwar movement that encouraged dissension and protest from within the movement, along with the emergence of other compelling liberation movements.

The call for women's liberation within the antiwar movement was illustrated at the Jeanette Rankin Brigade protest in Washington, DC in January of 1968. New York's Radical Women, not content to accept the traditional women's role in protesting the killing, sought to transform the event into a call for women's real power. Shulamith Firestone called for women's unity, not simply as people who opposed the war but as women. She wrote in the pamphlet for the "Burial of Traditional Womanhood" march that women

> have refused to hanky-wave boys off to war with admonitions to save the American Mom and Apple Pie. You have resisted your roles of supportive girl friends and tearful widows, receivers of regretful telegrams and worthless medals of honor. And now you must resist approaching Congress playing these same roles that are synonymous with powerlessness. . . . Until we have united into a force to be reckoned with, we will be patronized and ridiculed into total political ineffectiveness. So if you are really sincere about *ending* this war, join us tonight and in the future.[15]

The "Burial" action revealed deep fissures among members of the antiwar movement: men in the movement and women activists who increasingly defined themselves as feminists could no longer be assumed to share faith in the more inclusive coalition politics that had inspired the antiwar movement just a few years earlier. At the same time, it was the antiwar movement itself that had provided women the opportunity to utilize their considerable intellectual and organizational skills that they would need to make their dissident demand for women's liberation a reality. The "burial" action in 1968 was a major step within the antiwar movement toward defining a feminist consciousness that had been foreshadowed by Casey Hayden and Mary King's "Sex and Caste" speech to members of SNCC in 1965 that had decried women's subordinate position within the Southern civil rights movement.[16]

The civilian antiwar movement is often identified with the generic spirit of activism throughout the world. While the antiwar movement is most strongly identified with white, middle-class college students, ending the war was also a major issue for African Americans, many of whom analyzed the war in international, imperialist terms as a struggle being waged by people of color. African American women saw themselves in their opposition to the war as standing in solidarity with revolutionary women of color throughout the world. Describing the importance of Vietnamese women to the struggle against the American military, a female member of the Black Panther Party noted in 1969 that

> The Vietnamese women are out there fighting with their brothers, fighting against American imperialism, with its advanced technology. They can shoot. They're out there with their babies on their backs... and they're participating in the revolution wholeheartedly just as the Vietnamese men are participating in the revolution, in the national liberation struggle. The success of their national liberation struggle is just as much dependent upon the women continuing the struggle as it is dependent on the Vietnamese men.[17]

Women whose revolutionary activity was truly a life and death matter provided inspiration for women who were beginning to identify with the liberation struggles of others but not yet ready to articulate a revolutionary ideology of their own.

It was often the case that many women's "good girl" images of themselves made it difficult to see their status within the antiwar movement at first. Margery Tabankin, an antiwar activist student at the University of Wisconsin from 1965–9, described this dynamic:

> Part of being a woman was this psychology of proving I was such a good radical, "better than the men." We felt we were motivated by something higher because we didn't have to go to war ourselves. Most guys didn't take women seriously, however. They were things to fuck.... You went through this intense experience [at demonstrations], and you went back and had sex. [However] It [sex] was much more on men's terms.[18]

For women raised to value their ability to serve men, sexually and personally (Tabankin commented that she was so taken with organizer Tom Hayden that she even did his laundry when he visited Madison to give a speech), this could be a difficult pattern to break. Creating another model for participation in the antiwar movement, a model based on comradeship and equality rather than sexual servility, involved radical changes in men's attitudes about women and women's attitudes about themselves.

Women were active participants in the group of 200–300 of Vietnam Day and Women Strike for Peace activists who walked seven and one half miles from their campus to the Oakland Army Terminal in the fall of 1965. On at least three occasions, they tried to stop the trains carrying newly inducted troops who would soon be shipped to Vietnam. Protesters held signs urging the men to turn back from their military commitment. One woman even sat on the tracks and was saved from a speeding train at the last moment by a policeman who pulled her to safety. Women also marched to the Oakland Induction Center to urge young civilian men not to allow themselves to be inducted into the military. When the tear gas canisters flew, women were not exempt from harm. They exercised their right as citizens to express their antiwar views, and they were equal opportunity recipients of police brutality. Of the Oakland troop train actions, one protester observed that "We didn't have a prayer of stopping those troop trains, but people . . . could see that we cared enough to take a chance. It made people THINK."[19] It was just such decentralized actions that eventually did encourage Americans to think, not in revolutionary terms, but in terms of the personal, human, and psychic costs of the war.

The critique of intervention, imperialism, and, by extension, American capitalism espoused by SDS and other groups rarely extended to sexism prior to 1968. The rigid hierarchical structures and "party line" of the Old Left had given way to a theory of human nature that valued multi-dimensionality and the empowerment of the individual in every area of expression from speech to sexuality. In 1962, SDS leader Tom Hayden had declared that, "the time has come for a reassertion of the personal."[20] Abbie Hoffman articulated an alternative political and cultural vision based not on theory and hierarchical organization but on fulfilling individual desires:

> I don't like the concept of a movement built on sacrifice, dedication, responsibility, anger, frustration, and guilt. All those down things. I would say, Look, you want to have more fun, you want to get laid more, you want to turn on with your friends, you want an outlet for your creativity, then get out of school, quit your job. Come on out and help build the society you want. Stop trying to organize everybody but yourself. Begin to live your vision.[21]

Hoffman's ideas represented perhaps the most radical (or most anarchistic) approach to creating a new societal paradigm. Although self-actualization and an emphasis on the personal in its most individualistic form influenced left movements throughout Europe and the United States, women activists had to work harder to be heard in the very movements that seemed to value the individual and emphasize the personal. One 1972 female Harvard graduate described her experience in the antiwar movement, which included having her skull beaten by a policeman during a demonstration at Harvard, as "weird." After all, she was a *girl* in a protest movement to prevent the slaughter of young men – "Our life was never on the line, *we* weren't going to war . . . as women, we were slightly less credible."[22]

The antiwar movement benefited from the expertise, organizational experience, and courage of women on many college campuses and in the larger world. However, the extent to which "women's issues" became contested terrain between men and women (and even among women) cannot be underestimated. Women who were radicalized by the antiwar movement found themselves marginalized by their comrades in struggle in that same movement. It is interesting not so much that the new feminism emerged out of women activists' frustration, but rather that so many women remained active in the antiwar movement into the 1970s, even as they moved toward theorizing and founding a movement of their own.

SDS faced challenges from women to consider issues of participation and leadership, but with no theoretical analysis of the role of women in radical politics, the group was ill-equipped to hear these challenges and act on them. The Port Huron Statement, the organizing statement of SDS written primarily by Al Haber in August of 1962, articulated a generational perspective on materialism, democracy, and the role of the university as an instrument of social reform, but the document said nothing at all about women. The group's dramatic increase in size and scope after the introduction of ground combat troops into Vietnam in March of 1965 fixed its sights firmly on the struggle to revolutionize American society. Efforts to raise women's issues *as* a distinct political agenda were met with the assertion that women's concerns were peripheral to the broader political agenda: ending the war, ending United States imperialism, or creating a revolution in American society. Nevertheless, as early as December of 1965, the SDS National Council included a workshop on "Women in the Movement" which produced a statement asserting that

> the problem of participation by women is a special problem – one that reflects not only inadequacies within SDS but one that also reflects greater societal problems, namely the problem of the role of women in American society.[23]

Although SDS women were not able to get the National Council to address the problem of women in the movement, their analysis was broad-ranging and cultural, refined in the same fire as that in which SDS had shaped its critique of the war, racism, imperialism, and American society itself.

The resolution passed by the SDS National Council in December of 1967 subsumed women's issues under the broader rubric of "building the anti-imperialist movement in this country." The same resolution placed the responsibility of taking the initiative to "discourage male supremacism in interpersonal relationships with both men and women."[24] The tone of this resolution, later reprinted in *New Left Notes*, was particularly offensive to women activists because it appeared to trivialize the issue of male supremacism by making it simply an issue between and among individuals. Further, it placed the burden of dealing with sexism on women rather than on SDS as a whole. In early 1969, one SDS woman wrote:

> We were still the movement secretaries and the shit-workers; we served the food, prepared the mailings and made the best posters; we were the earth mothers and the sex objects for the movement men. We were the free movement "chicks" – free to screw any man who demanded it, or if we chose not to – free to be called hung-up, middle-

class, and up-tight. We were free to keep quiet at meetings – or if we chose not to, we were free to speak up in men's terms. . . . We found ourselves unable to influence the direction and scope of projects. We were dependent on the male for direction and recognition.[25]

Women in SDS and throughout the antiwar movement began to challenge the premise that a broad ranging attack on American capitalism and imperialism would mitigate the need for ending male supremacy. They refused to accept the idea that women's issues were marginal, but this refusal came at no small price. Women who spoke out in support of women's issues were attacked with a discourse filled with sexist and near-pornographic images. Coming from comrades in the struggle to end the war and create a new society, this was painful indeed. Activist Ellen Willis reflected on this experience:

It's hard to convey to people who didn't go through that experience how radical, how unpopular and difficult it was just to get up and say, "Men oppress women. Men have oppressed *me*. Men must take responsibility for their actions instead of blaming them on capitalism. And, yes, that means *you*." We were laughed at, patronized, called frigid, emotionally disturbed man-haters and – worst insult of all on the left! – apolitical.[26]

By 1969, when SDS was on the verge of splitting over issues of how best to continue the struggle against the war while building a revolutionary movement, the ninth (and last) SDS National Convention meeting in Chicago passed a resolution declaring that sexism was a problem faced by all women and that the battle against male supremacism "doesn't stand apart from the fight against capitalism in our society, but rather is an integral part of that fight." This resolution was never passed by the SDS membership because of the battle for control that was fought out between factions within SDS, consisting of the Revolutionary Youth Movement I [Weatherman] and RYM II and forces allied with the Progressive Labor Party. This fight split SDS permanently. The rupture enabled many women to assert the importance of women's issues in various groups that would later become allied, however tenuously, in the new feminist movement.[27]

The war and the countercultural *Zeitgeist* in the United States in the late 1960s brought out an activist impulse, even an imperative to act, among Americans who might otherwise have pursued their careers and their lives with few political reference points. Popular actress Jane Fonda and singer Holly Near, along with actor Donald Sutherland, participated in the "political vaudeville" show known as FTA, which toured the country for nearly a year in 1971 and was released as a film in 1972. FTA, "Free the Army," "Free the Americans," "Fun, Travel and Adventure" (the name of a popular GI antiwar newspaper published at Fort Knox, Kentucky), or, in military parlance, "Foxtrot, Tango, Alpha," were all stand-ins for what came to be the political statement, "Fuck the Army!"

Performed on and near military bases and in coffeehouses throughout the United States and in Japan, the Philippines, and elsewhere in the Pacific Rim, the FTA show satirized military life as well as United States foreign policy. The performers crooned to the tune of "Carolina in the Morning,"

> Nothing could be finer
> Than to be in Indochina
> Making money.
> Hating is a hobby
> When you're in the China lobby
> Life is sunny

or performed a can-can on the plight of military women entitled "Tired of Bastards Fuckin' Over Me."[28]

In 1971, Jane Fonda was hardly the American woman most likely to become active in the struggle to end the Indochina War. Daughter of actor Henry Fonda, she had won an Academy Award for her role in *Klute* and had earned a reputation for her jet-setting life style rather than political activism. Inspired by the intractability of the war itself, Fonda became interested in the peace movement and sought ways to support it. In February of 1971, she helped to organize three days of war crimes testimony sponsored by Vietnam Veterans Against the War called the Winter Soldier Investigation. Later that year, she announced the formation of the FTA troupe that would perform a show written by Jules Feiffer and directed by Mike Nichols. Hoping to provide an alternative to the apolitical entertainment offered by more traditional Hollywood stars, Fonda declared that

> It has become disconcerting for many of us in Hollywood to see that Bob Hope, Martha Raye, and other companies of their political ilk have cornered the market and are the only entertainers allowed to speak to soldiers in this country and in Vietnam.

Apparently, the army brass agreed. When the FTA troupe proposed to present its debut performance at Fort Bragg, North Carolina, the commanding officer Lt. General John J. Tolson III, declared the show to be "detrimental to discipline and morale."[29] Five hundred GIs attended the show off base. Their reactions were mixed, many saying that they had hoped to see the sexy "Barbarella" character rather than the newly-politicized Fonda.

Coming to political consciousness at age 30 rather than as a young student and acquiring her analytical perspective quickly, often while flying from one protest to another, Fonda seemed eager to compress all of her political energy into support for as many radical causes as she could find in the early 1970s, telling *Life* magazine, "I never felt politics touched my life. But, as a revolutionary woman, I'm ready to support all struggles that are radical."[30] Fonda and second husband Tom Hayden helped to organize the Indochina Peace Campaign, supported the Black Panthers and United Farm Workers, and campaigned for George McGovern in his presidential run in 1972. Fonda's commentary on the progress of the Vietnamese revolution earned her the nickname "Hanoi Jane," that prompted threats against her life and the appearance of anti-Jane bumper stickers.

In spite of open hostility to Fonda and other antiwar activists, the military itself was the locus of widespread antiwar activity. Opposition to the war intensified as service personnel began to see themselves as occupying the front ranks of a multi-faceted struggle against American imperialism abroad and injustice at home.[31] Some, like the

Fort Hood Three (Dennis Mora, David Samas, and James Johnson) refused to go to Vietnam in June of 1966. They were the first active duty soldiers in the Vietnam era to do so, and they served time in federal prison for their actions. All three analyzed their disobedience in explicitly political terms. Others sought Conscientious Objector status, even while they served in the military.[32] Many men and women in the military exercised their First Amendment right as citizen soldiers to speak out against the war in the GI antiwar newspapers that appeared on and around military bases in the United States, Japan, Germany, and the Philippines.

During the Vietnam War, hundreds of underground or alternative publications produced by individuals, college groups, and organizations identified with the Left gave voice to disparate antiwar and countercultural viewpoints and aided in the organization of a broad-based and decentralized antiwar coalition. The GI antiwar press was an important part of the terrain of military rights over which antiwar soldiers and the brass frequently clashed. In the early days of the movement, the antiwar soldier or officer was an anomaly isolated by the harassment he or she faced simply for challenging prevailing military wisdom. Alternative newspapers provided assurance that there were kindred antiwar spirits, as they encouraged the growing tide of protest against the military ethos as well as the war itself.

GI newspapers were effective mechanisms for communication among antiwar soldiers. Papers printed and reprinted articles, cartoons, letters, and poetry from around the country and also printed lists of GI antiwar publications, local coffee-houses, and drop-in counseling centers in response to official military attempts to censor the papers and close down "unauthorized" GI gathering places. The disclosure of official military harassment aided the organizing efforts of the GI antiwar movement. An individual soldier punished for an unpopular, although not necessarily illegal, antiwar action could be ignored, but as the number of publicly antiwar soldiers grew, their actions, as reported in the GI press, encouraged others to express their opposition to American military policy more openly. When Lt. Henry H. Howe became the first serviceman to be prosecuted under Article 88 of the Uniform Code of Military Justice for carrying a sign that read, "End Johnson's Fascist Aggression Against Vietnam" at an antiwar march in El Paso in 1965, few groups existed to support him. Howe received a sentence of a year's hard labor and a dishonorable discharge.

By 1969, growing opposition and greater coverage of antiwar activities by military personnel improved the situation somewhat. The extensive coverage and public protests over the navy's arrest of seaman apprentice Roger L. Priest for publishing *OM, The Liberation Newsletter* (Washington, DC) helped to keep the climate of resistance alive. Faced with fourteen charges, including the encouragement of sedition and desertion, Priest declared that "the admirals and general are trying to silence dissension in the ranks by any means. This is the only way to view the heavy-handed attempts to put out of commission the antiwar, anti-military newsletter which I edit."[33] Priest received a bad conduct discharge but did not serve time in a military jail, in part because his case was publicized in the GI antiwar press. Similarly, the response to the repeated firebombing of a coffeehouse near Fort Knox, Kentucky and the attacks on the movement for a Democratic Military Center in San Diego prompted more, not less, resistance to military authority. According to *A Four-Year Bummer*,

> The organized GI Movement has grown in the last few years largely as a response of servicemen and women to the brass's attempt to repress any and all acts of dissent in the military. From individual or isolated acts of resistance, more and more GIs are moving toward more organized forms and long-range goals.[34]

Individuals and groups within the GI antiwar movement increasingly made connections with the civilian movement, and soldiers and veterans appeared as speakers at and participants in antiwar demonstrations. In the 1971 Dewey Canyon III action in Washington, DC, veterans ceremoniously threw back their military medals and decorations, often with short speeches denouncing American military policy. In 1971, GI testimony about military atrocities reached a large audience in the Winter Soldier Investigation.

The protection of the first amendment rights to free speech and a free press was a major issue in many GI antiwar papers. The military papers, along with many of their civilian counterparts, publicized the broad range of rights that soldiers began to demand as citizens. The first issue of *Fun, Travel, and Adventure* identified the papers as "Published underground – for and by the GI's at Fort Knox, Dedicated to Free Speech and the Struggle for Our Rights."[35] Military personnel understood clearly what those rights were:

- freedom from harassment for attending antiwar demonstrations off base;
- the right to produce, distribute, and possess antiwar newspapers and other anti-military documents;
- the right to wear peace signs, long hair, African unity arm bands;
- an end to institutionalized military racism;
- an end to sexism in the military;
- the right to refuse an order to fight that a soldier considered unlawful or immoral.

That this generation of soldiers spoke in terms of rights reflects the extent to which broader challenges to authority in the name of democracy fueled opposition to American policy in Southeast Asia. Soldiers found support in civilian antiwar groups and in the larger culture of protest that influenced American political life in the late 1960s and early 1970s.

Black soldiers were often driven to protest the ethos of military life by personal and collective experiences with racism in all branches of the service, and they formed their own groups and printed their own GI antiwar papers.[36] Until the Vietnam War, the military had been for many the only route out of rural poverty or the urban ghetto. Frederick Douglass had even declared that, with his uniform and musket, "there is no power on earth which can deny that he [the black soldier] has earned the right to citizenship in the United States." The career black soldier could accommodate to a military establishment that used his skills, paid him nearly a minimum wage, and gave him a pension and status in his community after twenty years of labor, and the black draftee, like his white counterpart, simply hoped to survive his hitch. But Vietnam was different, and the black men who were drafted and the black women who enlisted were sensitive to military injustice. Not surprisingly, many black soldiers analyzed the relationship of the war they were asked to fight to their own struggles for liberation.

In January of 1966, the Student Non-Violent Coordinating Committee issued a formal statement in opposition to the war, and Martin Luther King, Jr.'s break with the Johnson administration over Vietnam came the following year. James Johnson, one of the Fort Hood Three, had declared that blacks could gain nothing from participating in the war. In this context, black resistance within the military increased, along with tensions and rioting in America's cities. Reports of black soldiers being disciplined for minor infractions of dress codes and standards of military "attitude" were accompanied by coverage of serious trouble in military stockades. Riots involving black GIs in the summer of 1968 at military prisons at Da Nang and Long Binh were part of a growing pattern of resistance to the war. Many black troops protested their orders to put down rioting and disturbances. *Shakedown*, a paper published at Fort Dix, New Jersey, argued that it was important for soldiers

> to understand what riot training is really aimed at, since we all will be subjected to mandatory training and in some cases will be called to "pacify" areas here at home. Vietnam, Berkeley, Newark, and Columbia University are all recent examples of the armed power of the state in action against the people ... The most vicious use of armed power by the state has been against people of color – at first to annihilate the Indians and to take their land, later to preserve and protect the slave system, and today to control the ghettos of our country.[37]

In the GI antiwar press, expressions of solidarity with black service people included exposes of the abuses of local and military police forces. The press helped to keep military racism in the forefront of the GI antiwar movement.

Like their civilian sisters, women in the military participated in protests against the war and military life in general. Women who were dissatisfied with military life expressed some of the same ambivalence that characterized the discourse of women in the civilian antiwar movement. They were, after all, volunteers, who entered the service with the expectation that the military would value their contributions. In articles and letters in the GI antiwar press, women articulated their objection to being treated as inferior soldiers because of pervasive sexism in all branches of the service from the top down. Women complained particularly of sexual harassment and an inability to gain promotions. One medical technician, Spec. 4, wrote to *Fragging Action* about the special problems of being a military woman, citing frequent weight checks, the absence of weapons training in basic training because, "as the story goes, one very hip sister threatened to do in her C.O.," and the difficulty of attaining higher rank:

> Well, where do the promotions come in? The hard part about being a woman in the green machine is if you don't kiss the right ass or fuck the right people, forget about any more rank.[38]

Women who expressed antiwar or anti-military views were often subjected to surveillance, undesirable job assignments, or charges of drug use or homosexuality. The environment in the military was overtly hostile to gay men and women, and the military establishment effectively used accusations of homosexuality as a means of controlling outspoken GIs. Military women were haunted by this issue, as homosexuality was the cause of less-than-honorable discharges. This made it difficult to organize women around antiwar or anti-militarist politics, as gay women feared the consequences of being too outspoken. According to organizers for the United States Servicemen's Fund, gay women

> don't relate to FTA politics because the army is basically pretty good for them and our relationship to them was much more essentially political: we talked about class, the war, women. The problem . . . is that they are not in a position to move politically – they don't want to get kicked out of the army.[39]

Women who were not gay feared charges and innuendo that they could neither live with nor refute. It was not surprising that military women were wary of organizing openly. Instead, many used the existing GI antiwar press (which was a risk in itself, given the harassment of contributors to antiwar papers on many bases) to express their grievances. Women who distributed *Broken Arrow* at Selfridge Air Force Base in Michigan were questioned by the FBI as well as military authorities. WACs at Fort Bragg were intimidated by military investigators in the hope that they would "name names" to substantiate charges of drug use, homosexuality, or subversive activity by outspoken soldiers. One WAC wrote that the tactic of dragging people who were to be questioned off the job in public and threatening them with dishonorable discharges was working:

> WAC company has got us WACs so uptight and paranoid about being reported to the CID as gay, that we avoid sitting together in the dining room or on buses. It gets pretty lonely here when you can't even be close friends with other WACs for fear of being labeled gay. Don't let them scare you from relating to your WAC sisters.[40]

Women began to find a voice in the military largely, although not exclusively, as a result of the antiwar movement, just as they had in the larger culture of the political left. Nevertheless, innuendo or direct accusations of lesbianism made it difficult to organize women, both within the military and in the civilian antiwar and feminist movements as long as anti-feminists controlled the debate by equating feminism with lesbianism.

Opposition to the Vietnam war from within the military was the product of varying political perspectives. The movement espoused resistance, not only to the United States foreign policy and the war but to the military ethos itself. Antiwar soldiers, both men and women, placed themselves in the front ranks of the struggle against United States foreign policy and a broad range of injustices at home. In many cases, college campus and mainstream antiwar groups worked closely with antiwar GIs to form a coalition that crossed lines of race, class, and military service. These demands also included equality for African Americans and an end to pervasive sexism in American society in general and in the military in particular.

Why did soldiers in the 1960s assert that their right to free speech was protected by the First Amendment when their predecessors had essentially accepted the authority of the brass and the Uniform Code of Military Justice? Disillusionment with the political liberalism of her youth and loss of faith in her government is the theme noted years after her Vietnam experience by Army nurse Jeanne Rivers, who described herself as having been

> a very patriotic person. I thought that whatever we were doing, we were doing because it was right . . . I believed we were supporting the right government in Vietnam. And then, once I went there, I saw what a catastrophe the government was, and that the government was really lying to the people in the United States . . . I don't believe half, not even half, of what the government tells me now.[41]

Resistance to the war was part of a larger oppositional culture that flourished as the Vietnam War intensified after the Tet Offensive. This culture challenged traditional forms of authority and posited alternative models of government, education, family, and myriad aspects of American life. In this context, women's voices began to be heard within the civilian and GI antiwar movements. Female GIs, wives of service men, and civilian antiwar organizers marched in demonstrations, conducted consciousness-raising groups off base, and took part in symbolic acts of resistance. For example, women at Fort Bragg, North Carolina organized a group to study "workers' history, third world history, and women's history." The Fort Bragg group also offered informal courses in such essential skills as first aid, basic auto mechanics, self-defense, and carpentry.[42]

Resistance to the military ethos and demands for an end to officially-sanctioned sexism helped to broaden the base of the GI antiwar movement and to raise the consciousness of men and women in the military. The women who wrote for the GI press helped to make connections among the various demands for Constitutional rights for citizens in uniform, an end to the war, and an end to racism and sexism in the military and American society at large. Like their civilian counterparts, the men and women of the GI movement began with an understanding of their own oppression and came to realize the extent to which the personal could indeed become political.

The antiwar movement that included middle class mothers, concerned professors and clergy, soldiers, students, members of revolutionary parties, and young men who simply wanted to avoid going to war for aims and goals that they could not countenance, represented faith in American democracy and the possibility of revolutionary change, symbolic acts of non-violence, and violent acts committed to "bring the war home" in the frustrating days after 1968. Neither an expression of nihilism nor an unthinking or unconscious spirit of anarchism, the movement brought together thoughtful people across generational lines to analyze the predicament of the nation. As one Columbia University student put it in the spring of 1968:

> There is nothing more important, more precious, there is no higher end, than human life; brutality, violence, suppression are means of destroying life. A society which practices

brutality is "wrong" – I would go further, it is evil. . . . It is one thing to be functionally rational, to fit means to ends – indeed, McNamara does it quite well in the Pentagon's systems-cost analysis – but true rationality, substantial rationality, can only be men thinking and evaluating, and human thought must involve human life. Otherwise, one has the paradox and aberration of irrational violence and brutality in a functionally rational system. . . . The war in Vietnam represents, to my mind, American society's brutality run rampant. Overlooking all the political arguments against the war, all the lies told to the American people by its own government, all the sectarian political interests which are forcing the U.S. to fight this war at the expense of both the American people and the Vietnamese people, one sees in the Vietnamese war the commitment of American resources – men and money – to a policy of destruction. Could the communists do any more damage to the lives and property and freedom of the Vietnamese than the Americans have done? This is an essential moral question: it forms the basis for any political judgment which one makes. The giant of American brutality can spend 50 billion dollars a year to eliminate slums, or to provide good housing primary and secondary education for all its citizens. American society practices brutality every day in the ghettos of its air-polluted cities; read *The Autobiography of Malcolm X* – better, take a walk in Morningside Park.[43]

The antiwar movement protested the promise of American life gone terribly wrong. Arthur Schlesinger's "New Mood in American Politics" of 1960 and the cold war liberalism of the Kennedy–Johnson years reflected a society less inspired by the promise of true social reform than one mired in a war it could not figure out how to escape. In a very real sense, the antiwar movement offered the best answer to the quagmire of Vietnam in the slogan, "Out Now!"

The question remains of whether the antiwar movement actually changed American society or if it even stopped the war. Abbie Hoffman declared the movement never represented a majority of the American people, but that those who put their lives and careers on the line to end the war made it difficult for the United States to continue with "business as usual." Historian Thomas Powers agrees,

> In the end the government abandoned its policy because its domestic cost was too high, its chance of success in Vietnam too slim. There was little reason to fight on, every reason to find a way out. The opposition was not alone responsible for this shift in policy, but if there had been no opposition, the shift would not have happened when or the way it did. The American departure from Vietnam was as gradual and anticlimactic as its original intervention, but, in retrospect, just as inexorable. At the height of the war Henry Cabot Lodge used to say the other side would never surrender; it would just fade away. He was right about the process, but wrong about who would go home with empty hands in the end.[44]

NOTES

1   See Arthur M. Schlesinger, Jr., "The New Mood in American Politics," *Esquire* (January, 1960).
2   See Students for a Democratic Society, "Port Huron Statement"in Judith Clavir Albert and Stewart Edward Albert, *The Sixties Papers: Documents of a Rebellious Generation* (New York: Praeger, 1984), pp. 176–96.

3   In 1990, former Senator and presidential candidate George McGovern declared that he regretted having voted for the resolution. Keynote speech at the Charles DeBenedetti Memorial Conference, Toledo, Ohio, May 4, 1990.

4   Indeed, LBJ's famous (or infamous) "daisy" commercial that positioned Johnson as a candidate did not support the extreme step of bombing Vietnam "back to the stone age" or utilizing nuclear weapons to contain communism in Southeast Asia as candidate Goldwater and his running mate had suggested they would do.

5   Lyndon Baines Johnson speech at Johns Hopkins University, April 7, 1965, in William Appleman Williams, Thomas McCormick, Lloyd Gardner, and Walter LaFeber, *America in Vietnam: A Documentary History* (Garden City: Doubleday, 1985), pp. 242–4.

6   Charles DeBenedetti (with Charles Chatfield), *An American Ordeal: The Antiwar movement of the Vietnam Era* (Syracuse: Syracuse University Press, 1990), p. 86.

7   Amy Swerdlow, *Women Strike for Peace: Traditional Motherhood and Radical Politics in the 1960s* (Chicago: University of Chicago Press, 1993), p. 130.

8   Arthur Marwick, *The Sixties* (New York: Oxford University Press, 1998), p. 543 and Charles DeBenedetti, *An American Ordeal*, pp. 129–30.

9   See Ibid., pp. 107–8 and Thomas Powers, *Vietnam: The War at Home* (Boston: G. K. Hall, 1973), pp. 54–7.

10 Gerard J. DeGroot, "Left, Left, Left: The Vietnam Day Committee, 1965–66" in Gerard DeGroot, ed., *Student Protest: The Sixties and After* (London: Addison Wesley Longman, 1998), pp. 85–99.

11 Charles DeBenedetti, *An American Ordeal*, p. 157.

12 See Jonathan Goldstein, "Agent Orange on Campus: The Summit Spicerack Controversy at the University of Pennsylvania, 1965–1967" in Barbara L. Tischler, ed., *Sights on the Sixties* (New Brunswick: Rutgers University Press, 1992), pp. 43–61.

13 Charles DeBenedetti, *An American Ordeal*, pp. 185–6.

14 King's speech at Riverside Church is printed in Clayborne Carson, David J. Garrow, Gerald Gill, Vincent Harding, and Darlene Clark Hine, eds., *Eyes on the Prize Civil Rights Reader* (New York: Penguin, 1991), pp. 387–93.

15 Shulamith Firestone, "The Jeannette Rankin Brigade: Woman Power? *Notes 1* in Judith Hole and Ellen Levine, *The Rebirth of Feminism* (New York: Quadrangle Books, 1971), p. 117.

16 See Sara Evans, *Personal Politics: The Roots of Women's Liberation in the Civil Rights Movement & the New Left* (New York: Alfred A. Knopf, 1979), pp. 235–8.

17 See G. Louis Heath, ed., *Off the Pigs! The History and Literature of the Black Panther Party* (Metuchen, New Jersey: Scarecrow Press, 1976), p. 432.

18 Myra MacPherson, *Long Time Passing: Vietnam and the Haunted Generation* (New York: Signet, 1984), p. 552.

19 Sam Angeloff, "The Antiwar Marches and How they Happen," *Life*, (December 10, 1965): 114.

20 Tom Hayden, speech at the University of Michigan (March, 1962), cited in Sara Evans, *Personal Politics: The Roots of Women's Liberation in the Civil Rights Movement & the New Left* (New York: Vintage, 1978), p. 104.

21 Abbie Hoffman, *Revolution for the Hell of It* (New York: Dial Press, 1968), pp. 61–2.

22 Myra MacPherson, *Long Time Passing*, p. 539.

23 Kirkpatrick Sale, *SDS: The Rise and Development of Students for a Democratic Society* (New York: Vintage, 1973), p. 252.

24 Alice Echols, *Daring to Be Bad: Radical Feminism in America, 1967–1975* (Minneapolis: University of Minnesota Press, 1989), p. 122.

25 Kirkpatrick Sale, *SDS*, p. 526.

26 Ellen Willis, "Radical Feminism and Feminist Radicalism," in Sohnya Sayres, Anders Stephanson, Stanley Aronowitz, and Fredric Jameson, eds., *The '60s Without Apology* (Minneapolis: University of Minnesota Press, 1984), p. 94.

27 Echols, *Daring to be Bad*, p. 122.

28 "The Show the Pentagon Couldn't Stop," *Ramparts* (September, 1972), pp. 29–32.

29 "Left Face," *The New Republic* (March 31, 1971), p. 9.

30 "Nag, Nag, Nag: Jane Fonda Has Become a Nonstop Activist," *Life* (April 23, 1971), p. 51.

31 Military protests emerged first in the Army and the Marines, the branches of the Armed Forces that suffered the highest casualties between 1965 and 1969. After President Richard Nixon's plan for "Vietnamization"(which relied more heavily on air and sea power) was implemented, protests in the Navy and Air Force intensified. For a comprehensive account of the GI antiwar movement, see David Cortright, *Soldiers in Revolt: The American Military Today* (Garden City: Anchor/Doubleday, 1975).

32 See Gerald R. Goglio, "In the Belly of the Beast: Conscientious Objectors in the Military During the Vietnam War," in Tischler, ed., *Sights on the Sixties*, pp. 211–25.

33 "Navy Tries to Silence antiwar GI Editor," *GI Press Service*, New York; 1:3 (July 24, 1969), p. 45.

34 "GI's fight Back," *A Four-Year Bummer*, 2:7 (9 September, 1970): 2,11.

35 *Fun, Travel, and Adventure* Issue #1 (June 28, 1968): 1.

36 See *Do It Loud*, a paper published in 1969 and 1970 by the Black Brigade at Fort Bragg, N.C.; *Black Unity* from Camp Pendleton, Ca.; *Black Voice*, published in 1971–2 at Fort McClellan, Al.; *Hair*, published briefly in 1969 and revived in 1970 at Misawa Air Force Base, Japan; *About Face*, published in Heidelberg, Germany from 1970–2 by "Unsatisfied Black Soldiers" and succeeded in 1972 by *Seize the Time*; *Demand for Freedom*, published briefly in 1970–1 at Kadena Air Force Base, Okinawa; *Voice of the Lumpen*, a paper from Frankfurt, Germany that was tied to the Black Panther Party and was published in 1970–1; and *Black Tribunal for Awareness*, published briefly in Karlsruhe, Germany. See David Cortright, *Soldiers in Revolt*, pp. 287–95.

37 "Troops in the Ghetto," *Shakedown* Fort Dix, N.J. (June 6, 1969): 1.

38 "Women in the Green Machine," *Fragging Action* 2:1 (June, 1972): 5.

39 "Anniston Women's Project Report," *GI News and Discussion Bulletin* #9 (September–October, 1971): 15.

40 "CID Attacks WACs" *Bragg Briefs* 4:5 (June, 1971): 2,10.

41 Myra MacPherson, *Long Time Passing*, p. 543.

42 "Bragg Briefs" reprinted in *GI News and Discussion Bulletin* #8 (August, 1971): 15.

43 Letter from Mark Rudd to Dean David Truman, Columbia College, March 7, 1967.

44 *Vietnam: The War at Home*, p. 319.

CHAPTER TWENTY-ONE

The Veterans Antiwar Movement in Fact and Memory

JOHN PRADOS

Among the most stalwart participants in the antiwar movement were Americans who had themselves served in the armed forces, the bulk of them veterans who fought in Vietnam. Military service afforded the veterans unique credibility among antiwar activists, the media, and the American public. Military discipline enabled the veterans to craft an organization capable of coordinated actions that could be matched by few in the New Left. The military experience of the veterans endowed them with a determination to end the war and help their brothers in arms still in the military that made the veterans, in a certain sense, the shock troops of the antiwar movement. The role of the veterans antiwar movement and resources for studying it should be brought to the attention of all who are interested in American opposition to the Vietnam War.

Origins and Evolution of the Veterans Antiwar Movement

The first act of what became the veterans' play within the movement to stop the war began with a massive demonstration in New York City on April 15, 1967. Organized by the Spring Mobilization to End the War in Vietnam, a large crowd of protesters gathered in Central Park on a rainy Saturday morning, marched across 59th Street, then, after several route changes, eventually rallied at United Nations Plaza, which is located at 47th Street and First Avenue. Police estimated the crowd to number about 100,000, organizers put the figure at four times that. In San Francisco the same day another 50,000 rallied, but our interest lies in New York for there is where the march included a significant number of former military who rallied as "Veterans for Peace."

Among the vets walked Jan Barry, a former Army aviation specialist who responded to a shout for veterans to move to the front and found himself with a dozen or so people who held a banner that said "Vietnam Veterans Against the War." Barry had been in a unit at Nha Trang that supported Army Special Forces operations in Vietnam, and later held an appointment to West Point, where he had been studying to become an officer when, disgusted at the whole US stance in the war, he resigned. He had been searching for some way to openly oppose the Vietnam war and the April 1967 march would be his first rally. At the march, Barry was impressed at how crowds of onlookers who were prepared to denounce the student demonstrators hushed up when they saw veterans. The fact that a large contingent – Barry estimated it of regimental size, or up to 2,000 veterans – marched in cadence behind the banner. There lay an inkling the veterans could field a mass organization.

Attending some meetings of Veterans for Peace, along with other demonstrations in Philadelphia and Washington, Jan Barry quickly discovered there were few true veterans in the group and no real organization. Convinced there was room in the antiwar movement for activists from uniform, Barry took steps to form a new entity. He and five others held an initial meeting in New York City on June 1, 1967. They christened the group Vietnam Veterans Against the War, a phrase which had merely been a slogan on a banner in the April march. Soon the Vietnam Veterans Against the War (VVAW) became an actuality. Amorphous though it continued to be, Veterans for Peace assisted the nascent VVAW with fundraising. Like Jan Barry, many members of the new VVAW continued to work with Veterans for Peace. In places, like middle Wisconsin, whole chapters of VVAW and Veterans for Peace were virtually identical. The group also got help from others on the New Left. For example, VVAW's first office would be a desk in the corner of the headquarters of the Fifth Avenue Peace Parade Committee. Similarly, VVAW opened independent offices in 1968, but they were located in a building that belonged to a political party of the Old Left. The vets benefited from a nominal rent arrangement until the national offices moved to Chicago in 1972.

A key feature in the creation of any alliance among individuals for a political purpose is the process of what the antiwar movement termed "consciousness raising." Mobilization of any movement depends directly upon attaining a union of like-minded individuals. In much of the antiwar movement mobilization remained problematical because information available to raise consciousness varied widely from place to place; specific stimuli, such as evident manipulation or government misbehavior, also varied widely; and individuals responding to the appeals of the political alliances brought to the table many cross-cutting interests and ambitions. The veterans had significant advantages in mobilization and raising consciousness because the former military men had a common experience in their training and service, thus a precise knowledge of the institution they intended to oppose. Where America's students, parents, workers, and women had to start by finding out something about Vietnam, the veterans already knew that place intimately. Indeed, in many cases it had been the very experience of the war that turned the vets against this entire enterprise. The veterans also had a notable determination to assist their brothers in arms still in the service both in opposing the Vietnam war and improving conditions for GIs and veterans. The net result would be that veteran activists tended to have levels of commitment, knowledge, and organizational discipline difficult to match elsewhere in the antiwar movement.

In turn, in a self-reinforcing process, the ability and resolution displayed by Vietnam Veterans Against the War impressed other veterans and became a recruiting tool. When soldiers began to question the Vietnam war, once the existence of the VVAW became known, they would know where to turn. The major difficulty lay in getting out the word that VVAW was there and active. Jan Barry seized on every soapbox, radio show, television interview, or public gathering he could to speak out for veterans. Early VVAW adherents, including Carl Rogers of Ohio, and Sheldon Ramsdell, a pre-Vietnam veteran of the Navy who had had media relations training and was a photographer, were important allies in a public information campaign. One milestone passed when VVAW succeeded in gathering many signatures for an open statement opposing the war which appeared as an advertisement on a full page of *The New York Times* of November 19, 1967. The organization began to progress, starting chapters in Alabama, Oregon, Ohio, California, Texas, and New York. Some politicians also took notice, most importantly Alaska senator Ernest Gruening, an important early voice against the Vietnam war.

Another common theme in the movement opposing the Vietnam war is government repression. This too applies to VVAW from an early date. Immediately following its public declaration in the *Times*, VVAW would be probed by the Federal Bureau of Investigation (FBI) at the request of secretary of defense Robert S. McNamara, who demanded background material on signers of the VVAW manifesto. President Lyndon B. Johnson had asked for more general reporting from the Central Intelligence Agency (CIA) on foreign influences on (by which he meant evidence of communist domination of) the US antiwar movement. The CIA rendered reports on the subject a few days before publication of the VVAW manifesto and again in September 1968. The VVAW was listed as an active antiwar organization as early as the November 1967 report, but judging from the portions of this document that have so far been declassified, the CIA had been unable to find any evidence of foreign influence on the antiwar veterans. (In fact, the antiwar movement as a whole was similarly found to have foreign contacts but to be free of influence or domination.)

In the summer of 1968 VVAW mounted an action at the Democratic Party convention in Chicago to favor the nomination of Eugene McCarthy for the party's candidacy in the presidential election. The VVAW formula here was to find at least one vet from each of the fifty states who would travel to Chicago and lobby for McCarthy. The action would be mooted by the police violence and demonstrator anarchy that subsumed protest in Chicago in 1968, but the significant point is that VVAW's approach became a hallmark: the organization continually reached out for novel forms of putting across its message. This meant different kinds of protests and demonstrations, several of which will be mentioned presently.

Charles DeBenedetti, one of the foremost scholars on the antiwar movement, has found three factors that continually bedeviled the movement: all-left inclusiveness (which conveyed a political necessity to also support the more disruptive, divisive factions); weakness at the local level; and a multi-issue emphasis (to facilitate political alliance) as opposed to sole focus on the war. Vietnam Veterans Against the War managed to avoid most of these pitfalls, at least through much of its history. The vets participated in broader united fronts but resisted the temptation to support radicals of unsavory reputation. During its initial phase, from 1967 to 1969, VVAW deliberately cultivated an image of responsible dissent, clean cut vets appearing to speak in full dress uniforms, veteran "delegates" from each of the fifty states, and so on. As for weakness at the local level, *all* of VVAW's strength during the early period resided at the local level. If there were a national-cum-mass organization that would have to have been Veterans for Peace, which slowly disintegrated during this same period. Finally, VVAW, as an alliance of veterans dedicated to ending the Vietnam war, by definition avoided the pitfall of dissipating strength in pursuit of multiple issues.

While we have placed considerable attention in the argument that Vietnam Veterans Against the War possessed certain advantages, both in terms of consciousness raising and its organizational milieu, this should not be taken as a claim that VVAW merely went from strength to strength. In fact the group nearly disappeared, much as did Veterans for Peace, in 1969. Several factors help account for this development. For one, the 1968 election very much evolved as a referendum on the Vietnam war. All the candidates took positions on the war, all spoke of ending the war in one fashion or another. Even the victor, Richard M. Nixon, had promised he had a secret plan to end the war. Americans thought they had voted to end the war and many stood back expecting the Nixon administration to do just that. Only as months went by in 1969 without apparent change in the war did the quiescent antiwar movement resume its major efforts. This phenomenon affected the movement as a whole, not simply VVAW.

Second, the Vietnam Veterans Against the War lost some of its most active members, including the editor of its newspaper, who succumbed to cancer in the summer of 1969. Less active chapters plus no means of outreach were crippling the organization. In addition, more traditional associations of former military persons, such as the Veterans of Foreign Wars or the American Legion, which had looked askance at Vietnam veterans, in the late 1960s and into the 1970s began to recruit them more assiduously. With a number of its local chapters accomplishing little, VVAW had more difficulty attracting members.

A turning point came with the revival of the larger movement. In October and November of 1969 an *ad hoc* united front, the Vietnam Moratorium Committee, sponsored huge antiwar marches. On October 15 there were rallies throughout the United States, to culminate in a march on Washington for November 15. In the interval between the first moratorium and the November event, which finally drew somewhere around 600,000 protesters (by US Park Service estimate), VVAW leaders were called by march organizers to ask what the group could do for the many antiwar veterans who had come forward during the October moratorium. Indeed, a number of people who became prominent VVAW activists began openly protesting the war during the 1969 moratoriums.

With a fresh influx of members came temptations to move away from VVAW's single-minded focus on ending the war. Some possible issues were bound up in the war, including problems of GI drug use, support for war resistance by serving GIs, and Vietnam political issues like war atrocities. Others aimed more directly at veterans, including demands for honorable military discharges for all war veterans, equitable administration of Veterans Administration hospitals and GI benefits, and dealing with the psychological traumas of service in the war. With new issues came even greater impetus from the war itself. At the end of April 1970 the Nixon administration invaded Cambodia, a move which triggered an enormous upswell in the antiwar movement. Benefiting from new visibility and this event, VVAW began a steady process of growth. National membership which had stood at about 1,500 grew toward the 5,000 level.

Management of an increasingly diverse organization would be a headache for VVAW as much as other antiwar groups. A point rarely made that deserves great emphasis is that these groups were entirely voluntary. Unlike the government officials and military men who justified the war or fought it, and had pay, regular leave or vacation, and other benefits, the movement ran entirely on the strength of individuals' personal commitment. Opposition to the Vietnam war was a day-in, day-out constant, with no vacation, pay, or anything else, save for the frustration of personal hassles and of seeing much hard work, when it featured at all in the press, frequently being reduced to minor and often negative coverage buried in obscure places. With frustration a constant companion, burn-out occurred frequently. The VVAW national office went through many generations of leadership after Jan Barry's time. Al Hubbard, a former airman, emerged in 1970 as the foremost spokesman for the organization. A year later a naval officer, John Kerry, attracted the most attention. Rhetoric changed with individuals, political differences emerged, and tensions on this account were another constant theme. Barry felt uncomfortable with the more strident politics of the organization in 1970–1. Kerry discomfited many and left after a dispute within the national office.

Regardless of growth pains, changes in focus, and other obstacles, Vietnam Veterans Against the War became increasingly active and assertive. An important and innovative action occurred in early September 1970, when upwards of 150 veterans staged a four-day route march called "Operation RAW" (for "Rapid American Withdrawal") through New Jersey and Pennsylvania to Valley Forge, where they rallied with another 1,500 members and activists. Mimicing Vietnam-style military operations, specifically the variety called "search and destroy," in each of the towns the VVAW marchers passed through they conducted mock arrests and interrogations of people that demonstrated the arbitrariness of actions in Vietnam. This dramatization, soon well known as the genre "guerrilla theater," became a hallmark of VVAW actions.

A different form of dramatization featured in the vets' next major event, an inquiry into alleged war crimes by Americans in Vietnam. Called the Winter Soldier Investigation and held in Detroit in January–February 1971, the inquiry had some 125 veterans present statements on horrible incidents they had personally witnessed in Vietnam. In a painful outpouring of memories the vets recalled callous treatment of Vietnamese civilians, violations of international protocols regarding prisoners of war, torture, and violation of borders with raids into Laos.

Preparation for the inquiry had been as painful as the event itself. Vietnam Veterans Against the War initially conceived the war crimes investigation as a joint effort with another group specifically protesting atrocities but differences in planning led to a split. There had been divisions within VVAW itself over whether to hold the event in Washington, in an attempt to influence Congress, or the American heartland aimed at reaching the working class who bore the brunt of fighting in Vietnam. The faction favoring Detroit had won on that one. In Detroit there had been problems with the site, and the hotel originally contracted pulled out at a late date. Meanwhile, most of the prominent antiwar activists whom VVAW had approached to constitute a panel that would hear the testimony and support the event refused to participate, in part due to the internecine splits that had led up to the event. Most upsetting of all, an involved process by which VVAW event organizers solicited veterans willing to testify, verified their status as veterans, fleshed out the stories, and checked these in turn, had the pernicious result of bringing back the horrors of Vietnam for all those most involved in the project.

The outcome of the inquiry would be both positive and negative. On the minus side organizers were disappointed with their failure to gain major media coverage, partly due to the venue of Detroit, but also to general press downplaying of antiwar activity and to the still low profile of VVAW. With notable exceptions of the *Chicago Tribune*, Detroit newspapers, and certain columnists elsewhere, VVAW testimony would be passed over lightly. On the other hand, the veterans gained unmistakable attention of other veterans, perhaps more sensitive on this issue than society at large, and of the wider field of antiwar groups. The Detroit inquiry also solidifed VVAW in important ways, with many members in the audience convinced more than ever the message had to be carried to Washington, and more confident than ever of their fellow VVAW veterans. Some of the actions carried out during the next period would not have been possible without the degree of confidence and solidarity which developed through the Winter Soldier Investigation.

The Apogee of Vietnam Veterans Against the War

After Detroit there were VVAW regional coordinators and members of the national office convinced that the vets should go to Washington. There were also some in Congress who wanted to open up and hear the VVAW message. But visibility remained limited, even though Oregon Republican senator Mark A. Hatfield inserted the entire proceedings of the Winter Soldier Investigation into the *Congressional Record*. As with Cambodia, it was the Nixon administration which sparked the next phase of antiwar action, this time by orchestrating and supporting the February 1971 invasion of Laos by a South Vietnamese army.

For VVAW, carrying the message to Washington had to be more than one more antiwar march, and indeed the larger movement soon called a march on Washington for April 24, 1971. Seeking to distinguish their action from the large march, VVAW resolved not just to appear in the capital, but to camp there and lobby, arriving almost a week ahead of the national march and building their action to a climax the day before it. Vietnam Veterans Against the War's Washington action was called "Dewey Canyon III," following the US military's "Dewey Canyon II," codename for the operation with which US forces cleared the way for the South Vietnamese invasion of Laos.

Veterans gathered in Washington's West Potomac Park prior to moving to The Mall, where they camped out on April 19. The efforts of local coordinator Mike Oliver resulted in good relations with the Washington Police, but the Park Police had jurisdiction over The Mall, and Justice Department lawyers had gone to court for an injunction prohibiting camping on The Mall, revoking the permit VVAW had gotten for the encampment. After a stormy debate veterans voted 480 to 400 to stay in place and risk arrest rather than vacate the camp. Since the Supreme Court had overruled a federal district court in granting the injunction, this led to the fondly remembered headline: "VETS OVERRULE SUPREME COURT." As a matter of political necessity Nixon administration officials made no effort to enforce their injunction and eventually would ask a court to quash it.

For nearly a week veterans were all over the capital. Nearly 1,100 were at an initial march to Arlington Cemetery. By the end of the week 2,000 attended the final demonstration on Capitol Hill. Photographs of VVAW veterans throwing their medals over a hastily erected wooden barrier blocking access to Congress are among the icons of the Vietnam War.

Dewey Canyon brought VVAW real momentum which it proceeded to use well. A lobbying unit and Veterans Action Group were set up in Washington to work on veterans' services and benefits and lobby for draft legislation on those issues. With an infusion of donations, VVAW began publication in August 1971 of a new newspaper *The 1st Casualty.* Jan Barry, officially resigned as president of VVAW as of June 1, 1971, worked with Larry Rottman and Basil T. Paquet to compile a book of veterans' poetry that appeared the following year, as did a book collecting the testimony of the Winter Soldier Investigation. A film titled *Winter Soldier* which put the testimony into visual format, was edited and produced during 1971 to premiere at the Whitney Museum in New York City on January 27, 1972. The vets also sent delegations to Hanoi, to conferences of the World Peace Council, to the Seventeenth World Conference Against Atomic and Hydrogen Bombs in Hiroshima, and to Paris where they met with North Vietnamese negotiators in the Paris Peace talks.

Protests reached a fresh highpoint at the end of 1971 when VVAW carried out simultaneous encampments at Valley Forge, Berkeley, Killeen (Texas) and Chicago. On Christmas Eve in New York vets rallied at St. Patrick's Cathedral to read out the names of war dead. Two days later, in coordinated actions around the country, veterans occupied the Statue of Liberty; the Betsy Ross House in Philadelphia; blocked access to the Lincoln Memorial in Washington and the Air Force Recruiting station in Dorchester, Massachusetts; demonstrated outside the Chicago Stock Exchange; and in San Francisco, occupied the South Vietnamese consulate. The consulate sit-in went on for days before the VVAW protesters left voluntarily.

The most important single development within VVAW would be the decision at a national steering committee meeting in early 1972 to open the group to activists who were not military veterans. Reflecting the new approach was a name change to Vietnam Veterans Against the War/Winter Soldier Organization (VVAW/WSO). By late 1972 the antiwar group claimed to have almost 20,000 active members, of whom as many as 2,500 were in the active duty military, many in Vietnam. The group's newspaper would be changed and called *Winter Soldier* to reflect the new character.

Changes of early 1972 represented VVAW's decision to move toward becoming a mass organization. One motive flowed from the veterans' personal relationships: it was hard to sustain companionship with friends, girlfriends, and boyfriends who were, *ipso facto*, excluded from an entire realm of the person's activity. Another motive was more straightforwardly political: VVAW sought greater weight in the antiwar movement. Increasingly also, after the antiwar firestorms of Kent State and Cambodia (in 1970) and May Day (in 1971), the veterans came to recognize there were activists in the movement whose dedication and discipline matched that of the vets themselves.

Meanwhile, Vietnam Veterans Against the War had been targeted by the Nixon administration. These efforts were also reaching a high level in 1972. Immediately after the Winter Soldier Investigation one of Nixon's political operatives, Charles W. Colson, had begun trying to demonstrate that the vets were not vets. Colson's endeavors may account for Richard Nixon's comments during Dewey Canyon III that the VVAW protesters were not Vietnam veterans, a claim that backfired in the face of the veterans' numerous records of service, medals, and so forth. Colson was also behind Nixon's going out of his way, later in 1971, to meet with Vietnam veterans who supported the war. More sinister, however, were Justice Department attempts to find something to hit the veterans with, and local police, military, and Federal Bureau of Investigation (FBI) efforts to infiltrate the group. Later release of FBI records under the Freedom of Information Act, for example, shows the government had such detailed knowledge of the proceedings of meetings of the New York City VVAW chapter that that unit had to have been infiltrated. Members' apartments were also surreptitiously entered. Actions against the group's national office were not excluded. When the national office moved to Chicago in late 1972, in some ways it was like jumping from the frying pan into the fire, for the Chicago Police had a notorious "Red Squad" engaging in the same kinds of harrassment tactics.

The most notorious case of government infiltration of Vietnam Veterans Against the War bears directly on the organization's actions of 1972 and 1973. Both political parties that election year had chosen Miami for their presidential nominating conventions, and VVAW planned caravans to Miami to mount extended protests similar to Dewey Canyon. After one of the planning meetings for the protests, one of VVAW's twenty-six regional coordinators took colleagues aside to reveal that he himself was an FBI informer. This veteran, William L. Lemmer, became the basis for a government indictment prosecuting eight VVAW members for plotting to disrupt the Republican convention in Miami.

At the Democratic convention in July 1972 the veterans were lionized, afforded opportunities to make public statements, admitted to the convention floor. At the Republican convention authorities made an attempt to prevent the VVAW road convoy from ever reaching Miami. Proceeding from points around the United States on what VVAW called "The Last Patrol," the vets arrived anyway. National office staffer Barry Romo, who rose to head the organization later, had already built a relationship with Miami authorities, avoiding the difficulties that beset VVAW in Washington in 1971. With a combination of guerrilla theater, creative demonstrations, and tough confrontation when necessary, VVAW made its point.

All of this would be accomplished largely by local members (other than Romo), for the Nixon officials succeeded in getting their indictment against eight VVAW organizers. National staff and regional coordinators had to stay out of the way in order to avoid becoming caught up in the conspiracy charges administration officials were levelling at the organization. The Last Patrol action turned out to be a success for *ad hoc* efforts and personal initiative, squarely in the VVAW tradition.

When Richard Nixon was inaugurated to a second term in office in January 1973 the veterans mounted another action in Washington. Again there would be a march to Arlington. There was also a strong protest along the route of Nixon's Inauguration Day parade from the White House to the Capitol. Demonstrators successfully pelted the motorcade with tomatoes. A couple of months later in New York City the Nixon administration held a "Peace With Honor" parade. This time VVAW marched in the parade itself. When military in the review stands turned their backs on veterans in the street, VVAW protesters were able to make the point that there was no honor in America turning its back on the Vietnam it had led in the war.

The indicted veterans, called the "Gainesville Eight," went on trial in Florida in the summer of 1973. A full year of legal maneuvers had failed to turn aside this prosecution. The judge hearing the trial in federal district court would be constantly solicitous of government prosecutors, unmoved by defense motions, even after police and court officials caught two FBI agents red-handed in the act of bugging a conference between the defendants and their lawyers. In support of their members on trial the Vietnam Veterans Against the War mounted another encampment at Gainesville, where roughly 300 VVAW/WSO members stayed for days, mounting vigils, protest marches outside the courthouse, a rally at the University of Florida, and other events.

With the actual hostilities of the Vietnam war, at least for American ground troops, ended by 1973, other kinds of VVAW activity grew increasingly significant. The group became a prominent supporter of amnesty for draft resisters and GI war resisters. Limited amnesty would be granted by President Jimmy Carter in 1977. The veterans kept up their agitation for GI benefits and pressure for better quality in the Veterans Administration hospital system. These were constant VVAW themes and remained a focus of the organization right into the 1990s.

Meanwhile, most VVAW chapters had constituted what were called "rap groups," at which members could talk out issues that discomfited them, work through conflicts between chapter members, and so on. Akin to group therapy sessions, the rap groups were increasingly moderated by mediation specialists. From the rap groups emerged awareness of a particular problem of veterans, at first termed "Post-Vietnam Syndrome" or PVS. This complex of anxiety and fear set off by things that evoke previous distressing experiences eventually received formal recognition by the medical community. Now applied to all forms of traumatic experience, the complex is termed Post-Traumatic Stress Disorder (PTSD). There continues to be disagreement over whether and how PTSD differs from earlier psychiatric phenomena known as "combat fatigue" and "shell shock," but regardless of the status of VVAW's claim to discovery of PTSD, there can be little doubt the organization's role was critical in promoting awareness of and treatments for this malady.

The Vietnam War came to its final end with the fall of Saigon in April 1975. Vietnam Veterans Against the War was already in decline. The 1973 Paris Peace accord that ended the US ground combat role had defused much of the antiwar issue, and cost VVAW most of its mass following. Many VVAW members still wanted to pursue anti-imperialist issues, resisting American neocolonialism and imperialism; others wanted to draw in and focus primarily on veterans' issues. Between 1973 and 1975 the organization took both tracks, but in the latter year an effort was made by the Revolutionary Communist Party, a Marxist radical group, to infiltrate the VVAW. Espousing anti-imperialist theory, RCP ideology proved attractive to many in VVAW who saw imperialism as the major challenge. Almost simultaneously with the fall of Saigon the VVAW splintered as RCP took over some chapters. For a time the RCP conducted activities using the name VVAW, until the original organization won a lawsuit prohibiting the newer entity from using its name.

At the time of the dedication of the Vietnam Veterans Memorial in 1982 a Vietnam Veterans Against the War contingent, again not to be denied its rightful place as US servicemen, marched in the parade. Surrounded by a sea of others remembering the war, VVAW remained unique in the dedication it had brought to, and retained, in its struggle. Members of Vietnam Veterans Against the War were instrumental in the foundation of the Vietnam Veterans of America, today the largest grouping of vets from the era. With national offices still in Chicago, VVAW continues to be active with the Veterans Administration and on benefits issues. It opposed the Persian Gulf war of 1991 but proved more divided in the case of Kosovo in 1998. The organization held a twenty-fifth anniversary reunion in New York City in 1992 where probably about two hundred of its members and former members gathered. Regrettably those Vietnam Veterans Against the War who were then under Revolutionary Communist Party discipline refused to attend the VVAW commemoration. Current and former VVAW members remain prominent in PTSD treatment, veterans affairs, and American politics.

SELECT BIBLIOGRAPHY

Important sources for study of the Vietnam Veterans Against the War begin with the papers of the organization held by the State Historical Society of Wisconsin, in Madison. These are particularly strong on the preparations for the Winter Soldier Investigation. The Historical Society also houses a Social Action Collection of materials from antiwar groups across the spectrum which bears tangentially on VVAW and contains some VVAW items. Also in Madison, the Wisconsin Veterans Museum has a group of records from Portage County Veterans for Peace/Vietnam Veterans Against the War containing, among other things, copies of newsletters to VVAW regional coordinators and materials on the Gainesville conspiracy trial.

A balanced, full-length study is Andrew E. Hunt's *The Turning: A History of Vietnam Veterans Against the War* (New York: New York University Press, 1999). Hunt considers that VVAW members, more than any other individuals or groups, "succeeded in bringing the Vietnam war and its effects home to millions of Americans" (p. 199). Another full-length study is Richard Stacewicz's *Winter Soldiers: An Oral History of the Vietnam Veterans Against the War* (New York: Twayne Publishers, 1997). This is especially valuable for the detailed recollections from thirty VVAW members of how they came to oppose the Vietnam war, create or learn of the organization, and participate with it. Among the interviewees are John Lindquist and Ann Bailey, whose materials form the core of the Wisconsin Veterans Museum collection. On the other hand, Stacewicz obtained important surveillance records from the FBI under the

Freedom of Information Act, exhibited at the VVAW 25th anniversary, that he failed to make much use of in this study, making *Winter Soldiers* less useful than it would otherwise have been. The analysis views the organization as plagued by internal dissension, producing long-term achievements that were, "perhaps not all that could have been desired" (p. 433). While true enough, these comments do not hint that internal divisions were generic everywhere in the antiwar movement and followed necessarily from the fact of its voluntarism and the multiple issue and focus alliances that were necessary to build strength. The real question is whether dissension prevented effective action and here VVAW remains unchallenged in its endeavors.

Much of the veterans' antiwar movement, in motivational terms, stemmed from hopes of saving Americans still in Vietnam or in the service and destined to be sent there. In this regard an important history of both in-service and past-service Americans is Richard Moser's *The New Winter Soldiers: GI and Veteran Dissent During the Vietnam Era* (New Brunswick: Rutgers University Press, 1996). Moser sees the VVAW vets as true "citizen-soldiers," by which he means individuals politically engaged even as they served their country. Two other books are central sources that furnish background for the whole environment of Vietnam service – that is, military recruitment and the mobilization of youth for the war. One is Lawrence M. Baskir and William A. Strauss, *Chance and Circumstance: The Draft, the War and the Vietnam Generation* (New York: Knopf, 1978). Also see Christian G. Appy, *Working Class War: American Combat Soldiers and Vietnam* (Chapel Hill: University of North Carolina Press, 1993).

A number of memoirs of veterans who worked with the Vietnam Veterans Against the War testify to their personal experiences in Vietnam and how they became transformed. Most well-known among the memoirs is Ron Kovic's *Born on the Fourth of July* (New York: Simon & Schuster, 1976). Among the best memoirs is W. D. Ehrhart's *Vietnam-Perkasie: A Combat Marine Memoir* (Jefferson, NC: McFarland, 1983). An account that began questioning the war before he contributed to the foundation of VVAW is Donald Duncan's *The New Legions* (New York: Random House, 1967). Oral histories of VVAW members' Vietnam experiences are included in Al Santoli's *Everything We Had: An Oral History of the Vietnam War* (New York: Random House, 1981); and in Lynda Van Devanter's *Home Before Morning*, (New York: Beaufort Books, 1983); which collects stories of women in Vietnam. A number of novelists writing on the war are former VVAW members or associates, most notably Tim O'Brien, many of whose works directly evoke his Vietnam experience and are representative of other recollections enumerated here.

GI resistance efforts are discussed independently in detail in this collection so I shall make no effort to cover them here, other than to say VVAW constantly concerned itself with that movement so their two stories intertwine.

Another source of insight about VVAW lies in general histories of the antiwar movement. Quite valuable because of its group-centered approach (with special emphasis for religious groups) is Charles DeBenedetti and Charles Chatfield's *An American Ordeal: The Antiwar Movement of the Vietnam Era* (Syracuse NY: Syracuse University Press, 1990). Nancy Zaroulis and Gerald Sullivan take a more personalized approach, furnishing myriad details about many antiwar actions, including VVAWs, in their *Who Spoke Up? American Protest Against the War in Vietnam, 1963–1975* (Garden City NY, Doubleday, 1984). Also useful, because of his effort to create an amalgam of the antiwar movement, civil rights efforts, and other cultural trends of the era is Terry Anderson's *The Movement and the Sixties* (Oxford: Oxford University Press, 1995). The finest source to date on presidential attitudes toward the antiwar movement, including VVAW, is in Tom Wells's *The War Within: America's Battle Over Vietnam* (Berkeley: University of California Press, 1994).

Obviously important in any examination of this subject are the sources produced by and for Vietnam Veterans Against the War. The single most substantive has to be the recorded proceedings from Detroit in *The Winter Soldier Investigation: An Inquiry Into American War Crimes* (Boston: Beacon Press, 1972). That same year excerpts of the testimony were compiled into the documentary film *Winter Soldier*. Also in 1972 VVAW film people created a second documentary on the organization and its activities called *Only the Beginning*. A literary collective consisting of Larry Rottmann, Jan Barry, and Basil T. Paquet collected and edited *Winning Hearts and Minds: War Poems by Vietnam Veterans* (New York: First Casualty Press, 1972). In a slightly different configuration, Paquet and Rottmann collaborated with lead editor Wayne Karlin to compile *Free Fire Zone: Short Stories by Vietnam Veterans* (New York: McGraw Hill/First Casualty Press, 1973). Dewey Canyon III would be marked by a photo and textual collection, *The New Soldier* by John Kerry and Vietnam Veterans Against the War (edited by David Thorne and George Butler), (New York: Collier Books, 1971). For its much later anniversary the group put together a collection of poetry, commentaries, historical notes and photographs titled *Vietnam Veterans Against the War: 25 Years Fighting for Veterans, Peace, and Justice* (New York: privately printed, 1992).

On the matter of PVS and PTSD the quintessential contemporary source, which incidentally contains numerous insights into VVAW is in Robert Jay Lifton, *Home From the War: Vietnam Veterans, Neither Victims nor Executioners* (New York: Simon & Schuster, 1973). A later source which benefits from time and distance from the events of the war is Arthur Egendorf, *Healing From the War: Trauma and Transformation After Vietnam* (Boston: Houghton Mifflin, 1985).

Bits and pieces of the VVAW story appear in many places. Scott Camil's account of his travails as one of the Gainesville Eight is in "Undercover Agents' War on Vietnam Veterans," in Bud and Ruth Scultz, eds. *It Did Happen Here* (Berkeley: University of California Press, 1989). Bill Crandell's recollections of starting a VVAW chapter in Ohio, then Operation RAW and Dewey Canyon III are in "They Moved the Town," in Melvin Small and William D. Hoover, eds., *Give Peace a Chance: Exploring the Vietnam Antiwar Movement* (New York: Syracuse University Press, 1992). The feelings of a veteran who, unlike Crandell, missed the "limited incursion into the country of Congress" that was Dewey Canyon, are displayed by John Ketwig in his . . . *And a Hard Rain Fell* (New York: Macmillan, 1985). The views of other antiwar activists who worked with VVAW from the outside are in Fred Halsted, *Out Now: A Participant's Account of the American Movement Against the Vietnam War* (New York: Monad Press, 1978). Also see David Dellinger, *More Power Than We Know* (New York: Anchor Press, 1975), as well as Dellinger's memoir. *From Yale to Jail: The Life Story of a Moral Dissenter* (New York: Pantheon, 1993). For a journalist's impressions see Gloria Emerson, *Winners and Losers* (New York: Random House, 1976). Studies of what happened to returnees from the war include Murray Polner's *No Victory Parades: The Return of the Vietnam Veteran* (New York: Holt, Rinehart & Winston, 1971). Also see Bob Greene, *Homecoming: When the Soldiers Returned From Vietnam* (New York: Ballantine Books, 1990). Equally useful is John Helmer's *Bringing the War Home: The American Soldier in Vietnam and After* (New York: Free Press, 1974).

Vietnam Veterans Against the War are significant in the poetry of that conflict. Aside from the volume he collected with VVAW, Jan Barry Crumb went on to publish at least two further collections. His *Demilitarized Zones: Veterans After Vietnam* (New York: East River Anthology, 1976) includes also works by other VVAW members, including Gainesville Eight defendant Peter P. Mahoney. Many of the same poets appear in Barry's Peace is *Our Profession: Poems and Passages of War Protest* (New York: East River Anthology, 1981). Boston VVAW member David Connolly has published *Lost in America* (Woodbridge CT: Vietnam Generation, 1994). Among Barry's contributors, Bruce Weigl, John Balaban, and W. D. Ehrhart are probably the best known, and Ehrhart went on to publish possibly the best anthology, *Unaccustomed Mercy: Soldier-Poets of the Vietnam War* (Lubbock: Texas Tech University Press, 1989) which showcases, among others, the well known Horace Coleman. Ehrhart's volumes of his own poetry include several of interest. *To Those Who Have Gone Home Tired* (New York: Thunder's Mouth Press, 1984), collects his own works. *A Generation of Peace* (New York: New Voices Publishing, 1975) is the most focused on the Vietnam Experience. Next to that is probably *The Distance We Travel* (Easthampton MA: Adasta Press, 1993). Another anthology worth mention is Ehrhart's *Carrying the Darkness: The Poetry of the Vietnam War* (Lubbock: Texas Tech University Press, 1989).

On FBI informer Bill Lemmer the best source is Frank J. Donner's *The Age of Surveillance: The Aims and Methods of America's Political Intelligence System* (New York: Vintage Books, 1981). This builds on Donner's article "Confessions of an FBI Informer," *Atlantic* Magazine, December 1972. A chapter on the Gainesville Trial appears in my own book *The Hidden History of the Vietnam War* (Chicago: Ivan Dee Publishers, 1995). In the magazine *The VVA Veteran* appear my articles "Dewey Canyon III: Limited Incursion into the Country of Congress" (April/May 1997), and "The Draft and the War" (June/July 1999). On demonstration tactics used by VVAW see Henry Lesnick, ed. *Guerrilla Street Theater* (New York: Avon Books, 1973). The daily and weekly periodical press for the years of the Vietnam war naturally contains numerous articles covering specific demonstrations and protests by the Vietnam Veterans Against the War.

CHAPTER TWENTY-TWO

Sanctuary!: A Bridge Between Civilian and GI Protest Against the Vietnam War

MICHAEL S. FOLEY

On May 21, 1968, as the conspiracy trial of antiwar activist Dr. Benjamin Spock and four others began in Boston, two men – a draft resister and an Army deserter – took "symbolic sanctuary" across town at the historic Arlington Street Church. For the next ten days, young civilian antiwar activists jammed the church, engaged in a marathon teach-in, and acted as a nonviolent human barrier between the authorities and the two men. Eventually, federal authorities apprehended both men, but only after the sanctuary had attracted tremendous media attention and public interest.

Though few understood the significance of this first sanctuary at the time, it marked an important turning point for the antiwar movement. First, it set off a wave of dozens of other sanctuaries in churches across the country, most of which granted asylum to deserting American GIs. Over the next 15 months, at least 54 men (49 of whom were AWOL servicemen) took sanctuary in more than 20 cities and towns across the country, including Boston, New York, Philadelphia, Chicago, San Francisco, South Bend, Indiana, Columbus, Ohio, Providence, Rhode Island, and Honolulu, Hawaii. Second, it demonstrated for the first time (and quite clearly) that the antiwar movement and American servicemen were not necessarily antagonists. While some civilian opponents of the war no doubt regarded soldiers with suspicion, by the middle of 1968 more and more antiwar activists understood that men who enlisted or submitted to the draft did so for various reasons, most of which did not stem from strong conviction about the war, communism, or anticommunism. Finally, the sanctuary movement signaled a telling shift in the face of the antiwar movement. Increasingly, as the civilian antiwar movement began to fragment in 1968 and 1969, and as GI dissent escalated, veterans groups such as Vietnam Veterans Against the War began to assume a more prominent role in the movement. This paper argues that the tactic of sanctuary ushered in that transition.

It is puzzling that historians of the Vietnam War era and of the antiwar movement, in particular, have completely ignored or overlooked the sanctuary movement and given only cursory treatment to the alliance formed between civilian and GI antiwar activists.[1] Perhaps it has been too easy to accept the stories that portray returning soldiers as mistreated by civilian opponents of the war; images of long-haired protesters spitting on Vietnam veterans or calling them "baby killers" persist in the American consciousness despite a lack of evidence.[2] In any case, the GI and veteran antiwar movement is typically treated in isolation from the civilian movement, as if the two did not – could not – cooperate. In spite of the parallels and contrasts drawn by Andrew Hunt regarding the civilian antiwar movement and his subject, Vietnam Veterans Against the War, he and other scholars of GI and veteran dissent (David Cortright, Richard Moser and Richard Stacewicz, for example) examine their subjects largely without connecting them to the civilian antiwar movement.[3] Using Boston as a case study, this paper demonstrates, however, that these movements did not happen in a vacuum, but relied on each other at key points in their own evolution.

Moreover, a study of sanctuary is useful in examining the evolving response to the movement by police and federal agents, and the commitment made by civilian protesters to demonstrating their solidarity with GIs as they confronted the authorities. Each sanctuary in the Boston area presented the government agents with unique challenges, but over time the police and FBI learned how to best undercut the movement's momentum.

Although talk of sanctuary had been in the air for some time, it originated in Boston on that May morning somewhat haphazardly. In many ways, sanctuary was the product of a growing fragmentation within the draft resistance movement – the driving force of the antiwar movement in Boston – and the anxiety provoked by the stunning events of spring 1968. First, draft resisters – men who openly defied Selective Service laws by returning their draft cards to the Justice Department or refusing induction – began to see their movement sputter in April and May after several months of apparent success in confronting the Johnson administration at war. As I argue elsewhere, draft resistance raised the stakes for both the administration and the antiwar movement through mass civil disobedience. No longer could the administration ignore protesters and no longer could protesters simply demonstrate and go home without considering their (often privileged) place in the system. By openly defying draft laws, resisters put their own freedom on the line and forced the Justice Department and Selective Service to act. In the weeks and months following the typical draft card turn-in, resisters found themselves investigated by the FBI and saw their draft classifications changed to 1–A, and their induction process accelerated.[4]

But the administration prevented the Resistance from achieving its ultimate objective of clogging the tiny federal court system with draft cases by choosing to prosecute Dr. Spock and four other alleged movement ringleaders instead of going after the thousands of individual resisters. Without the expected steady stream of draft convictions and the attendant publicity, the movement's momentum began to slip, and so did the media's interest in more draft card turn-ins. Following the April 3, 1968 draft card turn-in on Boston Common – the largest to date – Resistance leaders started to talk about finding new ways to sustain the movement. This was a product of their escalating impatience with the war and it was set against the backdrop of Martin Luther King Jr.'s assassination, the strike at Columbia University, a potential revolution led by students in France, and the start of the Spock trial.

On the first day of the trial, Resistance leaders declared the Arlington Street Church a "liberated zone," and accepted Robert Talmanson and William Chase into the first sanctuary. Talmanson, 21, had been convicted for refusing induction; only the week before the United States Supreme Court refused to hear his case. Private Chase, 19, had served as a clerk in Cam Ranh Bay for nine months but had gone AWOL in late April; a resident of Dennis, Massachusetts, he gravitated to the Resistance because of the organization's open stand against the war. We know little about Chase except that, as he told reporters, he had to get out of Vietnam because he was "on the verge of the breaking point," and that he three times sought an army discharge. When he entered the church, he told reporters that he would not return to military duty "under any circumstances" because he was nonviolent. Both he and Talmanson, therefore, took sanctuary knowing that the church would be their final stop before seeing the inside of their prison.

Although the concept of sanctuary dated to ancient times, the first one at the Arlington Street Church appeared rooted in values that dated to the origins of European settlement in New England. Over the course of ten days, the participants treated the church more like a meetinghouse where, as in seventeenth-century New England, a community would meet to tend to all of its business, not just its religious instruction. Within hours of its start, the sanctuary began to take on a life of its own. At times, it seemed like an ongoing teach-in: participants discussed issues surrounding the war and the draft incessantly. At other times, the crowd focused on preparing for the authorities who would inevitably come. On occasion it also took on the characteristics of a big party. Several hundred people turned out on the first night for a communal dinner in the church basement. Organizers showed films of past draft card turn-ins and musicians played the blues for the crowd. A couple of nights later the rock band Earth Opera (led by future bluegrass greats Peter Rowan and David Grisman) performed on the stage in the basement of the church.[5] More than 70 people spent the first night in the church awaiting the police, and the crowds grew each night. Every day people could be found sleeping, eating, cooking, giving speeches, and having "endless conversations." Some roamed around trying to keep everyone's spirits up, trying to build solidarity. And reporters mingled throughout the building interviewing as many participants as they could. Joel Kugelmass, a Resistance leader, later called it "a very beautiful thing," because of the range of people involved. In addition to diehard activists, he said, some members of the church helped, and several women came in from the suburbs with sandwiches for everyone. In this way, sanctuary attracted new supporters to the movement.[6]

No one knew exactly when the authorities would come, who they would be, or how they would handle the crowd of supporters vowing to prevent the removal of the two men. In the first few days, Colonel Paul Feeney of the Selective Service told reporters that Bill Chase, the AWOL serviceman, was "the Army's problem," thus implying that the Army would have to apprehend Chase. US Attorney Paul Markham said that he hoped he would not have to use US Marshals to apprehend Robert Talmanson, but "if it comes to that we will have to do our duty." After a couple of days, Victor Jokel, executive assistant at the Arlington Street Church, promised that the imminent showdown between the activists in the church and the authorities would be "a moral confrontation only" and participants agreed to meet police or marshals only by blocking their way – by standing or sitting – with the intention of avoiding violence. When the authorities finally came, however, the meeting of both sides quickly escalated.[7]

The confrontation came on May 22, the third day of the sanctuary. Each day, as supporters grew more and more exhausted, they anticipated the arrival of the authorities. At approximately noon on the 22nd, about 250 supporters gathered in front of the Arlington Street Church, sensing an imminent encounter. This time, their instincts were right. At 3:15, as Resistance look-outs used walkie-talkies to communicate with those inside, a police officer began redirecting traffic off Arlington Street onto Newbury Street, thus preventing cars from passing in front of the church. At 3:30, just as films of the October 16 draft card turn-in were being shown by prosecutors across town in the Spock Trial, a Resistance activist with a bullhorn yelled "here they are" as a car bearing Paul Markham and three US Marshals arrived at the church. After entering the church through the front door the four men met Father Anthony Mullaney of St. Phillips Rectory in Roxbury who told them that they were about to "violate a moral sanctuary." Mullaney stressed to Markham, especially, that if they passed the crowd of supporters and took Robert Talmanson, the US Attorney and his marshals would be cooperating with a law that Mullaney and everyone else in the church believed to be immoral. The government men listened politely and then stepped past the priest. Robert Talmanson observed the scene from high above the sanctuary floor. He stood at the massive mahogany pulpit, over which someone had draped a large felt banner emblazoned with the large black Omega symbol of the Resistance, and read a brief statement. One could have heard a pin drop as the marshals approached Talmanson and told him that they were placing him under arrest. Talmanson replied that he would not resist and fell limp into the arms of the marshals. There had been no violence, just the promised moral confrontation, and they carried Talmanson from the pulpit.[8]

Order began to unravel, however, as the marshals attempted to leave the church. For some reason, Markham and the marshals elected not to go out the way they came in, and instead took Talmanson outside via a side door that led to an alley that runs down the right side of the church, bisecting the block from Arlington to Berkeley Streets. When the marshals emerged with Talmanson, they met the crowd of supporters who had moved from the front of the church down the alley and now stood before them with their arms interlocked. The path to their car was blocked. For approximately 45 minutes, the action stalled as Markham and the marshals plotted what to do next. Talmanson sat on the ground reading Chinese poetry with marshals standing on both sides of him. The protesters sang "the Battle Hymn of the Republic," "America," "We Shall Not Be Moved," and other civil rights songs. As a steady rain began to fall, shouts of "You're beautiful, man," and "We love you" buoyed the spirits of the arrested man.

At about 4:15, demonstrators could see that the marshals had a new plan. Fifteen Boston police officers suddenly emerged from the opposite direction of the protesters. In the late 1960s, the Ritz Carlton Hotel still operated a parking lot that guests entered from Newbury street but which also bordered the alley in which the protesters were confronting Talmanson's captors. The police arrived there and moved up the alley to offer support to their federal counterparts. They did not wear riot gear or carry tear gas guns. Eventually, some 25 police officers arrived at the Ritz parking lot aided by another six who walked down Newbury Street from Arlington to give them support. The marshals picked up Talmanson and once again tried to move him through the crowd, now numbering several hundred. When that failed, they quickly turned toward the parking lot and, with police officers forming a barrier between the marshals and the protesters, they whisked Talmanson to a waiting squad car. Along the way, several officers pushed protesters to the ground.

The police and marshals did not get Talmanson into the car fast enough, as supporters ran to sit down in front of the police car. Michael "Walrus" Colpitts laid himself out across the hood of the car while two women lay on its roof. When it became clear that there would be another delay in the action, some protesters ran into the church to get blankets and coats for the crowd to use in shielding themselves from the rain. Most were soaked to the skin. During the calm, a helicopter flew over the crowd. When one resister yelled, "Look out! Here comes the napalm!" even some of the police officers laughed.

Finally, however, the police made it clear that they meant business and were growing tired of the confrontation. A police wagon pulled up in front of the parking lot on Newbury Street. Then, all at once, the marshals pulled Talmanson from the surrounded police car and the crowd of police officers formed a phalanx that pushed through the crowd to bring the arrested man to the wagon. Officers pulled the two women from the top of the car by their hair, and as they moved through the crowd some clubbed and punched the sitting and standing demonstrators; others sprayed them in the face with mace. Some demonstrators were kicked or trampled. The police later denied using night sticks on the demonstrators, but participant and eyewitness accounts confirmed that the 20 protesters who were hurt suffered primarily from being clubbed and punched by police. One reporter for the *Boston Free Press*, an underground newspaper, evaluated tapes, still photographs and witness accounts, and concluded that the violence was "police-originated." The reporter noted that "although the police were tugged at, pushed and obstructed, at no time did any Resistance demonstrator strike or attempt to strike a police officer."[9]

Not every police officer participated in the beatings. John Phillips, no stranger to such frenzies (he, along with several others, had been beaten severely by a mob of South Boston youths for burning his draft card in 1966), later recalled that he shook hands with Deputy Superintendent Joseph Saia "in the middle of the carnage that was going on underneath us" because Saia was so obviously trying to "control things, control his officers." Likewise, Dan Tilton, who had been sitting in front of the car, recalled that after a "beefy" policeman grabbed him and threw him (practically through the air) to the ground, another cop held Tilton down on the ground, and said, "I don't want to be a part of this. Just stay where you are." Despite these examples of police restraint, many Resistance activists now feared that the Boston police had reached their limit. Historically, the New England Resistance had often been grateful that Boston police handled demonstrations and crowds better than their counterparts in other cities. Following the mêlée in the Ritz parking lot, however, activists suspected that Boston cops might start responding like Oakland or New York City police. In any case, the physical confrontation, coupled with the arrest of 16 demonstrators, added up to a stunning end to Robert Talmanson's sanctuary, and set an example that activists hoped would not be repeated when the Army came for Bill Chase.[10]

From one perspective, the skirmish with police bolstered the level of attention already being paid to draft resistance as a result of the ongoing Spock Trial. After the dust settled from the clash outside the church, Michael Ferber, a Resistance leader and one of Spock's co-defendants, arrived in the middle of a meeting called by the New England Resistance to discuss how to handle the military authorities who would undoubtedly be coming for Bill Chase; "We are all over the city," Ferber triumphantly told the crowd that after spending the day in court (where the prosecution showed films of the October 16 draft card turn-in) and walking through the Boston Common and Public Gardens, listening to the buzz. When one reporter entitled her mid-June article "The Boston Happening," it referred not just to the trial. Draft resistance and discussion of it seemed to dominate the city's discourse.[11]

Editors at the *Boston Globe*, however, offered an alternative view of the sanctuary altercation in an editorial called, "Can We Keep Our Cool?" The *Globe*, like some resisters, feared that the violence hitherto seen in other parts of the country had now spread to Boston. "Is this result inevitable?" they asked. "Isn't it possible for demonstrators to make their points and police to carry out their duties without spilling blood? Or is violence so much a part of the American heritage that real, mutual non-violence still doesn't have a chance in our society?" It appeared, then, that the apocalyptic mood that seemed to be sweeping the world wherever young people congregated, might have migrated to Boston, too.[12]

Seven days after Talmanson's arrest, Bill Chase turned himself in to authorities at the federal building in exchange for a promise of psychiatric tests; it was an anticlimactic end for those hoping to milk the sanctuary for more publicity. Resistance leaders put plans for future sanctuaries at the Arlington Street Church on hold when the church lost its insurance. (It turned out that an executive from Aetna Insurance witnessed the Talmanson arrest and ensuing commotion from his window in the Ritz Carlton Hotel and immediately called his office to have them drop the Arlington Street Church's $1.4 million in fire insurance and public liability coverage).[13]

Despite the sense of letdown among some participants, the Arlington Street Church sanctuary demonstrated two important new developments in the budding alliance between civilian and GI opponents of the war. It showed antiwar GIs that there *were* people outside the military who cared about their plight and who were willing to help; this realization came as a great comfort to those who, because of their views of the war, felt alone and isolated in the armed forces. In addition, and perhaps more important, the sanctuary established that antiwar and antidraft activists felt sufficiently strong in their support of GIs that they were willing to risk physical confrontation and injury in scuffles with police. These were not merely letter-writers, but others who were willing to put their bodies on the line for the sake of GIs.

Consequently, as Robert Talmanson and Bill Chase saw their cases work through their respective legal systems on their way to prison, enlisted men "came out of the woodwork," looking for help from the New England Resistance. Between June and December, another seven sanctuaries took place in Boston and in surrounding towns. Although each event was unique, certain patterns emerged that warrant generalization.[14]

First, each of the AWOL servicemen shared similar experiences and motives. Like Bill Chase, Allen Loehner, a 20 year-old sailor who took sanctuary in June at a Wellesley, Massachusetts church, joined the Navy to learn a trade and avoid being drafted into the Army. When stationed in Vietnam, however, he grew sick, he said, "knowing that I was killing people" with shells from his five-inch guns.[15] Likewise, Paul Olimpieri, a 21 year-old Marine who took sanctuary at the Harvard University Chapel in September, told reporters that he enlisted to avoid being drafted, but that he had then been "brainwashed" on the "use of physical torture" in boot camp. He could not wait to see action, but soon after he arrived in Vietnam he decided that the "South Vietnamese Army [was] a joke," and that most South Vietnamese did not want American forces there. After suffering wounds to his chest, arm, and ear in two separate firefights, Olimpieri found himself in a military hospital with "plenty of time to brood." The recounting of such experiences gave each sanctuary event – and the antiwar movement in Boston – a new sense of moral authority, one not carried in previous draft resistance actions. Few statements could be as effective in moving public opinion as Olimpieri's when he said, "I'm not a coward – I was awarded two Purple Hearts – but I still believe the military and the war are bad."[16]

On the other hand, sanctuary was also a natural extension of draft resistance in that it shared the same principles and goals. Indeed, by making it clear that they had given considerable thought to their options, and had decided to take these public stands against the military and the government, fully aware of the consequences, each AWOL serviceman bore moral witness to the war and openly accepted the prospect of prison as a way of generating publicity and undermining the military court system. As Mike O'Connor, a 19 year-old GI who took sanctuary at MIT in October remarked, "It has been made clear to me that by taking sanctuary, I face more time in the stockade than I would if I turned myself in." "To me it is worth it," he said. "I feel that if I can convince 100 people that the war is wrong, that it is an injustice against the basic freedoms of our country, then I will gladly serve the extra time."[17]

Second, with each sanctuary, draft resistance activists – made up mostly of middle-class, college educated civilians – came to appreciate the plight of the average working-class, high school educated GI. This represented an important shift in Resistance attitudes toward military men. The draft resistance movement (and, indeed, the antiwar movement in general) had long assumed that anyone strongly opposed to the Vietnam War would never enter the military. As Nan Stone, one of the few women leaders in the Boston draft resistance movement, later noted in a speech she gave on numerous occasions, however, it eventually became obvious to members of the Resistance that young men enlisted or submitted to the draft for many reasons, "most of which have nothing to do with agreement with U.S. foreign policy." Specifically, Stone said, the Resistance learned that servicemen usually narrowed their enlistment decision down to one of four motives. Many men feared that being drafted would leave them with no choice regarding the branch of service in which they would serve; recruiters promised "choice, not chance" if one enlisted before being drafted. Some men, especially those from poorer families, enlisted as a step toward economic advancement. And others were attracted by recruiting campaigns that promised opportunities to learn specific vocational skills and to see the world. American society, finally, indoctrinated so many men, especially working-class men, with expectations that they should join the service as a way to learn loyalty, courage, and citizenship. Organizations such as the Boy Scouts (who taught military-like discipline), and the American Legion (a veterans' organization which gave out annual citizenship awards to young men), Stone argued, fostered this sense of obligation in many young men.[18]

As a result, Resistance activists soon developed a new appreciation for GIs and their own channeling experience, and likewise began to understand the options available to working-class men in a new light. That draft resisters had suffered the antagonism of many working-class men now did not seem so unreasonable; the privileges that came with being a middle-class college student included insulation from the kind of physical harm that working-class soldiers in Vietnam faced every day. Even if a GI opposed the war, he sometimes could not tolerate college students protesting against a war about which they knew so little. Sanctuary and other outreach to GIs, therefore, fostered a new understanding – and eventually an alliance – between civilian and military dissenters.[19]

In spite of this new appreciation, the endings of sanctuary showed that although the community of supporters that developed in each event usually committed some form of civil disobedience in trying to prevent authorities from apprehending their suspect, ultimately the servicemen were the only ones who suffered significant consequences for their actions. Resistance organizers naively believed that the GIs who took sanctuary would actually be helped by it once apprehended by authorities; the attention garnered with each sanctuary, they reasoned, would prevent the military from railroading the deserters into the stockade. When the GIs did wind up in the stockade, Resistance activists could do no more than visit them regularly and try to arrange legal and financial assistance.

In the end, however, the AWOL serviceman paid the price anyway. This reality became most obvious in the case of Paul Olimpieri, the outspoken Marine who took sanctuary at Harvard. Olimpieri had read about earlier sanctuaries in Boston and Providence and contacted the New England Resistance shortly after going AWOL from Quonset Naval Air Station in Rhode Island. After first consulting with the attorney provided by the Resistance, Olimpieri persisted in choosing to make his protest publicly, and the resisters at Harvard Divinity School soon won the privilege of granting him sanctuary. By the time they took him in, Olimpieri had begun to adopt a new appearance, sporting a month's worth of new dark hair with a matching thin moustache and goatee. He wore sandals with an olive-drab Marine jacket (to which he cheerfully pinned draft resistance buttons). On the day he arrived in

Cambridge, he figured the authorities would wait a week until he became classified officially as a deserter on September 30 before arresting him.[20]

A decorated war hero like Olimpieri brought a certain moral authority to the draft resistance movement that those who had not seen combat could not provide. The seminarians publicly thanked him for seeking sanctuary with them. Harvey Cox, the venerated theologian, told reporters that the sanctuary "thrilled" him. "I'm grateful to Paul for giving us something to rejoice about," he said. Olimpieri's stories captivated his supporters. With each conversation, they learned more about the realities of fighting in Vietnam and about the realities facing working-class men faced with few alternatives to the draft. Equally important, however, Olimpieri condemned the war and the Marines. He described a Marine Corps run by "lifers who are sadistic, sick people who couldn't make it on the outside." Moreover, he criticized the American presence in Vietnam. "I don't think we have the right to decide which form of government the Vietnamese should have," he said on the first day of his sanctuary. "I feel if they don't want communism, they can win without our help like we won our revolutionary war." By claiming sanctuary, Olimpieri concluded, he sought "to tell other military personnel and civilians what is really going on" in the Marines and in Vietnam.[21]

Perhaps comments such as these led military authorities to grab Olimpieri before he attained deserter status. In the quickest end to a sanctuary to date, Military Police entered Andover Hall at 5:55 a.m. on Tuesday, September 24 (less than 48 hours after Olimpieri arrived) and, aided by Harvard police, entered the chapel. Divinity School Dean Krister Stendahl, also on hand, accepted the arrest warrant. The MPs found Olimpieri in a small second floor room behind the organ. He was chained to his wife, Lynn, and six seminarians, but the MPs came prepared. They produced a pair of bolt cutters, cut the chain, and carried him out. A piece of chain dangled from his leg as he left. Olimpieri spent the day at the Charlestown Navy Yard and anticipated a transfer back to Quonset.[22]

And then something remarkable happened: Olimpieri stunned the antiwar community by renouncing the sanctuary. Little more than twelve hours after being arrested, Paul Olimpieri stepped out onto the freshly cut lawn in front of the Marine barracks at the Charlestown Navy Yard, and held a press conference for print and television reporters. Flanked by his wife, his brother, and a new attorney, Olimpieri appeared nervous. Instead of the moustache and goatee, his face was clean shaven. One could practically see the starch in his pressed khaki uniform, and on his breast hung two Purple Heart medals. The sandals and the Resistance buttons he wore that morning were gone. "After careful consideration of my actions in the last few days, I consider them to be a mistake," he said. Olimpieri claimed that he had been "used by various groups to publicize their political goals, whatever they may be." Upon reflection, he no longer wanted to be associated with those groups. "I am just beginning to realize that things can be done through the proper channels," he concluded. "I found this out the hard way, and I hope that other servicemen will learn from my mistake."[23]

In a community which had grown used to watching resisters and supporters march off to jail defiant and unrepentant, Olimpieri's change of heart came as a shock. Few believed it conveyed his true feelings. "Paul would never say anything like this," one Resistance spokesman said. "The Marines obviously used some sort of coercion." The New England Resistance immediately issued a statement denying the charge that they had somehow used Olimpieri for their own ends. "We presented him the offer of sanctuary at the Harvard Divinity School and he readily accepted." The group also noted that they had tried to talk Olimpieri out of sanctuary and claimed that "he was well aware of the risks." But Olimpieri told reporters that he – not the Marines – called the press conference and wrote his statement. The Resistance simply could not resolve the new Paul Olimpieri with the old one. He refused to see his Resistance attorney and refused any communication with the organization. It was a terrible setback.[24]

The surprising end to the Harvard sanctuary demonstrated that, unlike draft card turn-ins in which a large number of people assumed an equal amount of risk, sanctuaries placed most of the risk on the man or men taking asylum from the military. No one expected the authorities to ignore such open defiance of the law, and although members of the Resistance community attempted nonviolently to block the inevitable arrest, the man who took sanctuary faced the punishment alone. In addition, in spite of hopes that the public nature of sanctuary would somehow protect the arrested man from unfair treatment by the military, once the police took him away, he became virtually inaccessible. Sanctuary continued to promote public confrontation with the government but the arrested servicemen usually suffered a private punishment.

This drawback notwithstanding, the sanctuary movement continued to grow over the rest of the year. Two of the largest sanctuary gatherings took place over the next month at Boston University and at MIT. The following summer, the largest number of GIs took sanctuary when three Honolulu churches granted asylum to a total of 24 men.

In Boston at least, the later sanctuaries typically saw the servicemen making very clear statements about their intentions, and noting explicitly that they were not being manipulated. At Boston University, Ray Kroll, an 18 year-old Army private, AWOL from Fort Benning, Georgia, and Thomas Pratt, a 22 year-old Marine more recently AWOL from Quonset Naval Air Station (and a friend of Paul Olimpieri), spoke to that issue. Kroll told reporters that he went looking for the New England Resistance only after he came to the decision that he "could not take part in the armed forces without going against [his] moral convictions." "I would like to make it quite clear," Kroll continued, "that the Resistance and the School of Theology are not using me in any way for anybody's gain except mine." In addition, Pratt, a clean-cut, all-American looking Marine from Norwalk, Connecticut, said, "I chose sanctuary so I could make a stand, so I could tell people how servicemen feel about the war." He knew the risks, he said. "I am ready to face the consequences."[25]

Yet at the end of the first day in Marsh Chapel, during which the number of students "protecting" Kroll and Pratt had not yet reached 100, Pratt left with his parents. He claimed to be "disenchanted with the circus setting," and said that he had only wanted to make a protest against the war. Two days later, in the custody of the Marines again, Pratt held a press conference similar to Olimpieri's. He said that he realized he had been "inexperienced and naive" in his thoughts and actions. He also accused the Resistance of exploiting him. "I feel I was used by the Resistance for their own purposes and gains," he said. "I have been on unauthorized absence status and expect to face the consequences of my action," he concluded. "I sincerely hope the Marine Corps will give me another chance."[26]

Members of the New England Resistance now began to suspect that they were being played for fools. That two Marines – indeed two *friends* – both stationed at Quonset Naval Air Station, took sanctuary separately only to attack the people who had helped them smacked of betrayal at best and intentional sabotage at worst. Ray Kroll, who remained at Marsh Chapel, lashed out at Pratt and Olimpieri. "I have little doubt in my mind that both Paul Olimpieri and Thomas Pratt were plants," he told reporters. He suggested that the military sent the two to infiltrate the Resistance as *agents provocateurs.*[27]

Fears of government penetration of the Resistance did not, however, slow the momentum of the BU sanctuary which was beginning to shape up as the largest to date. The crowd of supporters steadily grew each day from fewer than 100 to more than 1,300 as expectations of Ray Kroll's arrest heightened. Like the Arlington Street Church sanctuary, the gathering took on a life of its own. Howard Zinn later characterized it as an "ongoing free speech exercise . . . sort of like a 24 hour-a-day teach-in." At an open microphone, clergy gave sermons; resisters, academics, and anyone who wanted to, spoke to the crowd. The Resistance showed films about the war, and several bands played music at night. In the basement, approximately 20 doctors and residents, and six nurses staffed a makeshift medical center. Zinn brought one of his Government classes to the chapel and led them in a discussion of "making a public symbolic declaration of resistance to the war, and the inadequacy of normal political procedure." Although at least one disturbance broke out in the balcony of the chapel one night (several men claiming to be Vietnam veterans tore up prayer books and showered the sleeping students with debris and epithets), the sanctuary gathered momentum with each passing day. At one point, an optimistic Zinn commented to a reporter that if the sanctuary continued to be successful, and "if people continue to appear seeking sanctuary," then the BU sanctuary "may be permanent."[28]

In the end, however, the FBI had other ideas. At 5:30 in the morning on Sunday, October 6, sanctuary supporters sleeping on the floor and in the pews awoke to a voice shouting, "This is the FBI. We will give you 15 seconds to clear the aisle." The time limit expired quickly as the students turned to see 120 federal agents streaming into the chapel. As the first agent walked down the aisle, he turned to the others behind him and noted that the students were not resisting their presence; the agents would not have to move them, he suggested. A wave of agents started down the aisle, picking up students anyway. Sam Karp of the Resistance went to the microphone and told everyone to remain seated and silent. "Remember our commitment to non-violence," he said to the crowd. "Stay limp. This is their way." Slowly, the agents moved through the crowd, placing and sometimes tossing students into the pews. The sanctuary participants remained nonviolent. "No one in that place lifted a finger to resist them," Joann Ruskin, a BU junior said immediately after the raid. "It was the most beautiful thing."

If the FBI agents were not rough with the crowd in the chapel, they were not as kind to a BU television crew or Ray Kroll. After clearing a path through the sanctuary, several agents ran to the room where WBTU was filming the action, smashed open the door, and destroyed the film. Another group of agents found their way to the room where Kroll and about ten others had spent the night on cots. "Where is Ray Kroll?" they demanded. Someone asked for a warrant. "Is Ray Kroll here?" the agents asked again. Kroll identified himself and again asked for a warrant. "Don't worry about that," an agent responded. Three agents grabbed him and tried to lift him to his feet as he went limp. "Walk," one of them shouted. "Get up and walk, damn you. Walk you bastard." One witness said one agent yanked back on Kroll's hair as another pushed his head in the opposite direction. Photographs on the front page of the *Boston Globe* and *BU News* the next day show four FBI agents, all middle-aged wearing coats and ties, whisking him down the steps of Marsh chapel. The two agents on either side of him held his arms tightly; Kroll winced as one of the agents, smiling, twisted the deserter's fingers in an unnatural position. Two other agents squeezed his neck from behind and pushed the entire group through a path cleared by Boston police toward a waiting car. As Kroll attempted to go limp one last time, Ted Polunbaum, a *Newsweek* reporter, heard one agent say to Kroll, "Stand up or we'll kill you, you bastard."[29]

Although everyone involved in the sanctuary expected it to end in Ray Kroll's arrest, when it finally happened, it stunned many of them anyway. The FBI and the Boston Police Department had just given a demonstration in the use of power. The students knew that they had power, too, but Kroll's "bust" reminded them that the state had more and it knew how to use it. Although the BU confrontation with authorities did not include the violence of the Arlington Street Church sanctuary clash, in some ways, the end of this sanctuary proved more depressing.

In an article in the *BU News*, Alex Jack, a veteran civil rights and antiwar activist, and New England Resistance founder, expressed a new level of despair. The experience of this sanctuary (which he had planned) led him to openly urge revolution. "The Sanctuary at Marsh Chapel has shown, simply, that there can be no sanctuary," he wrote.

> There is no sanctuary from oppression, from racism, from militarism. The Marsh Chapel sanctuary, as previous sanctuaries, has shown that the U.S. government, the armed forces, the police, the University and the corporate interests they serve will never voluntarily stop killing people in Vietnam...They will not be deterred for conscience sake from dragging young men off to make war in protection of their illicit activities.

For the American state, the BU sanctuary showed that "no place is sacred," Jack concluded. "No rights are inviolable. No people or humanity is sacrosanct." If the government felt it had to, he wrote, "they will slaughter us all." The only solution to this condition, he argued, was the creation of a new society in which "exploitation is structurally impossible, where power is returned and exercised by the people, where there is no distinction between religion, politics or art, where in short there are no sanctuaries because no one is oppressed." Only a revolution could create the society he described, and Jack urged others to join him. "We are the children of the most monstrous and destructive society in history, a society that has no conception of or respect for human needs, a society that will annihilate the planet before sharing its wealth, a society without sanctuary for any of its victims." He concluded by calling for his generation to "rise up and utterly destroy this universe..."[30] Alex Jack's radical stance and participation in the organization of the Marsh Chapel sanctuary got him dismissed from the BU School of Theology. Only Ray Kroll, who received a sentence of three months' hard labor and who was docked two-thirds of his pay for the three months, received a harsher punishment.[31]

Unlike Alex Jack, however, most rank-and-file participants did not regard the BU sanctuary as a failure. Many believed that it had brought good publicity to the antiwar movement and bad publicity to the war and the government. Most important, Howard Zinn suggested, the sanctuary inspired close to 1,500 people to act on an issue of principle. "The most we can do if we don't liberate the world, is to liberate the spot of ground on which we stand," he said the day after the FBI bust. "We can find victory in the act of struggling for what we know is right. These five days have been days of victory. We ought to be glad they happened." Looking to the future, Louis Kampf of Resist argued that, like draft card turn-ins, sanctuaries drew people together and gave them "a sense of responsibility to each other." Too often, he noted, that sense of responsibility was fleeting. But "if resistance to the war...is to be deepened," and "if our sense of purpose is to be taken seriously," rather than worrying about elections (which few in the movement did, given the pro-war candidacies of Hubert Humphrey, Richard Nixon, and George Wallace), "resistance and peace groups might better spend their time developing strategies for building communities of resistance." No one knew how to do this, exactly, but continued outreach to GIs and providing symbolic sanctuary to those who wanted it, Kampf implied, could be key ingredients. Soon, some of Louis Kampf's own students responded to his call.[32]

To outside observers, in spite of the ignominious ends of the Harvard and Boston University sanctuaries, the sanctuary "movement" no doubt appeared to be growing as it spread from one school to another, each one larger than the last. Three weeks after Ray Kroll's arrest, students at the Massachusetts Institute of Technology organized another sanctuary, but this time it took on a secular tone. For the first time, instead of hosting the AWOL GI in a church or chapel, the MIT Resistance – an offshoot of the New England Resistance – provided asylum in the student center.

After making his statement to hundreds of supporters at MIT, 19 year-old Mike O'Connor of Goldsboro, North Carolina, twice AWOL from Fort Eustis, Virginia, and a friend of Ray Kroll's, acknowledged that, like Olimpieri, he would probably be forced to retract all of his statements upon arrest. He told the crowd, however, that his was a "statement of the heart," that they should remember it, and that with their help he would be able to withstand any coercion. In the event that he did "weaken and make any statements against this community," he urged his supporters to disregard them and "remember me for what I write and say while I am free."[33]

O'Connor's sanctuary turned out to be the one in which Boston area federal agents figured out how to best disarm the movement: they simply ignored it. Instead of swooping in to arrest the offending GI within hours or a day or two of his taking sanctuary, the FBI let the MIT sanctuary run out of steam on its own. At its peak, the crowd of people crammed into MIT's Sala de Puerto Rico numbered more than 1,000. The event included several concerts, a few short films, an almost non-stop teach-in, nonviolence training, and appearances by both Abbie Hoffman and the Living Theater. After six days, however, everyone was exhausted, especially O'Connor. The MIT Resistance declared victory and sent everyone home. O'Connor took up residence in another room in the building where, after another week, Military Police finally found and arrested him.[34]

The MIT sanctuary turned out to be the last significant sanctuary in the Boston area. Although students at Brandeis University offered sanctuary to another soldier in early December, the authorities' willingness to all but ignore it and let it sputter out on its own again undermined the protest value of the event. By January, the Resistance started to shift its focus on GIs away from sanctuary to lower profile outreach. Organizers admitted that beyond the publicity that sanctuaries garnered, and the growing numbers of students on Boston campuses who turned out for such events, these events actually played into the hands of the military. The public nature of the GI's protest had no mitigating effect on his punishment; indeed, it may have made matters worse.[35]

Consequently, the New England Resistance decided to intensify its GI outreach program. On Friday nights, Resistance members walked the few blocks from their office to the Greyhound bus terminal. There they sought out soldiers traveling for the weekend and gave them copies of *Vietnam GI*, an antiwar newspaper aimed at GIs (published in Chicago); a few people also spent their Friday nights at Logan Airport for the same reason. In addition, Resistance activists tried to make contact with disgruntled soldiers to offer counseling on how to get discharges or apply for conscientious objector status. They handed out flyers to parties and invited GIs to visit the Resistance office.[36] In one of the most ambitious strands of the outreach program, Nan Stone and Joel Kugelmass made several visits to bars and clubs in the Combat Zone (Boston's red light district), where they could usually expect to encounter plenty of alienated servicemen and frequently someone who had gone AWOL. Stone and Kugelmass then offered help in the form of lawyers and counselors. Since their antiwar experience had taught them something about the reach of the federal government, Stone and Kugelmass usually encouraged AWOLs to turn themselves in with the help of movement lawyers. In a few rare instances, however, Stone and others in the Resistance participated in a sort of underground railroad with other antiwar organizations as a way of getting deserters out of the country.[37]

Resistance members who had been part of the movement since its beginning regarded this shift to GI outreach as an indication of the organization's maturity. "As we all became a little more astute about what we were doing," Nan Stone later recalled, "we did get much more of a sense of how guys could end up in the military and even in Vietnam without believing in the war." Many servicemen, they learned, felt they had no choices. Gradually, in the second half of 1968 and into 1969, Resistance activists stopped looking at servicemen as potential enemies, and instead made them the centerpiece of their antiwar work. And so the organization continued to direct its attention toward expanding the circumference of its circle of supporters to men serving in America's armed forces.[38]

Ultimately, despite the adaptability of local and federal authorities, sanctuary foreshadowed the rise to prominence of GI issues and GI and veteran dissent as the dominant forces in the antiwar movement. By the time the last sanctuary was held in 1969, GI and especially veteran groups were gaining acceptance as the new leading edge of the antiwar movement, much as draft resistance had been two years earlier. Contrary to popular images of antiwar protesters heaping scorn upon soldiers and returning veterans, in the sanctuary phase of the movement the draft resistance community facilitated a kind of passing of the torch to the GIs and veterans who would now lead the forces of protest.

NOTES

1   Only the briefest mention of sanctuary is made in Nancy Zaroulis and Gerald Sullivan, *Who Spoke Up?: American Protest Against the War in Vietnam* (New York: Doubleday, 1984), p. 263. No other national narrative on the antiwar movement makes mention of sanctuary. See, for example, Thomas Powers, *Vietnam: The War at Home* (New York: Grossman, 1973); Lawrence S. Wittner, *Rebels Against War: The American Peace Movement, 1933–1983* (Philadelphia: Temple UP, 1984); Melvin Small, *Johnson, Nixon, and the Doves* (New Brunswick, NJ: Rutgers UP, 1988); Charles DeBenedetti, *An American Ordeal: The Antiwar Movement of the Vietnam Era* (Syracuse: Syracuse UP, 1990); Fred Halstead, *Out Now!: A Participant's Account of the American Movement Against the Vietnam War*, 2nd ed. (New York: Pathfinder, 1991); Tom Wells, *The War Within: America's Battle Over Vietnam* (Berkeley: University, of California Press, 1994).

   In addition, sanctuary has escaped coverage in other books on various subsets of the antiwar movement that might have reasonably included the subject: Mitchell K. Hall, *Because of Their Faith: CALCAV and Religious Opposition to the Vietnam War* (New York: Columbia UP, 1990); Kenneth J. Heineman, *Campus Wars: The Peace Movement at American State Universities in the Vietnam Era* (New York: New York University Press, 1993); Michael B. Friedland, *Lift Up Your Voice Like a Trumpet: White Clergy and the Civil Rights and Antiwar Movements, 1954–1973* (Chapel Hill: UNC Press, 1998); James Tracy, *Direct Action: Radical Pacifism From the Union Eight to the Chicago Seven* (Chicago: University of Chicago Press, 1996); David Farber, *Chicago '68* (Chicago: University of Chicago Press, 1988). I've tried not to be arbitrary in compiling this list: Hall, Friedland, and Tracy might have connected sanctuary to their work through religious and pacifist themes; Heineman and Farber might have connected sanctuaries at Ohio University and in Chicago during the Democratic National Convention to their narratives.

   Finally, the following more general (and, consequently, popular) accounts of the 1960s and the year 1968 also overlook sanctuary altogether: James Miller, *Democracy is in the Streets* (New York: Touchstone, 1987); Todd Gitlin, *The Sixties* (New York: Bantam, 1987); Terry Anderson, *The Movement and the Sixties* (New York: Oxford, 1995); Paul Lyons, *New Left, New Right, and the Legacy of the Sixties* (Philadelphia: Temple UP, 1996); David Burner, *Making Peace With the 60s* (Princeton, Princeton UP, 1996); David Caute, *The Year of the Barricades* (New York: Harper & Row, 1988); Ronald Fraser, ed., *1968: A Student Generation in Revolt* (New York: Pantheon, 1988); Robert V. Daniels, *Year of the Heroic Guerrilla* (New York: Basic Books, 1989).

2   The image of antiwar protesters spitting on returning veterans has recently been challenged persuasively in Jerry Lembcke, *The Spitting Image: Myth, Memory, and the Legacy of Vietnam* (New York: New York University Press, 1998). Lembcke, a Vietnam veteran and a sociologist at Holy Cross, argues that not one single instance of an antiwar protester spitting on a veteran has ever been convincingly documented.

3   Andrew E. Hunt, *The Turning: A History of Vietnam Veterans Against the War* (New York: New York University Press, 1999); Richard Moser, *The New Winter Soldiers: GI and Veteran Dissent During the Vietnam Era* (New Brunswick, NJ: Rutgers UP, 1996); Richard Stacewicz, *Winter Soldiers. An Oral History of the Vietnam Veterans Against the War* (New York: Twayne, 1997).

4   For more on draft resistance and the Spock Trial, see Michael S. Foley, "Confronting the War Machine: Draft Resistance During the Vietnam War," (Ph.D. diss., University of New Hampshire, 1999).

5   Earth Opera later recorded a song, "Sanctuary From the Law," on the album, "The Great American Eagle Tragedy" (Elektra Records, EKS-74038), the title song of which referred to the Vietnam War.

6   "Anti-War Pair Spend Second Day Sheltered in Church," *Boston Globe*, May 21 1968, p. 15; "Pair in Church 'Sanctuary' Say Next Move Up to U.S.," *Boston Globe*, May 22 1968, p. 15; Kugelmass interview, June 16 1997.

7   "Deserter, Card Burner in Church," *Boston Globe*, May 21 1968, p. 9; "Anti-War Pair Spend Second Day Sheltered in Church," *Boston Globe*, May 21 1968, p. 15; "Pair in Church 'Sanctuary' Say Next Move Up to U.S.," *Boston Globe*, May 22 1968, p. 15; "Entire 4 Hours of Melee Detailed by 2 Reporters," *Boston Globe*, May 24 1968, p. 27.

8   "Police Haul Draft Resister from Church," *Boston Globe*, May 23 1968, p. 1; "Entire 4 Hour Melee Detailed by 2 Reporters," *Boston Globe*, May 24 1968, p. 27; Keith Maillard, "Confrontation," *Boston Free Press*, Third Edition, pp. 6–7, AJP.

9   "Police Haul Draft Resister from Church," *Boston Globe*, May 23 1968, p. 1; "Globe Reporter Saw Clash From Start to Finish," *Boston Globe*, May 23 1968, p. 11; "Draft Resister Lost in Poetry," *Boston Globe*, May 23 1968, p. 2; "Entire 4 Hour Melee Detailed by 2 Reporters," *Boston Globe*, May 24 1968, p. 27; Keith Maillard, "Confrontation," *Boston Free Press*, Third Edition, pp. 6–7, AJP; Ed Harris, interview with Eugene Navias, Oct. 27 1994, ASC Oral History Project; "Participant Accounts," *Boston Free Press*, Third Edition, p. 8.

10 Phillips interview, Aug. 29 1997; Arlook interview, Aug. 12 1998; Tilton interview, June 16 1997.

11 Arlene Croce, "The Boston Happening," *National Review*, June 18 1968, p. 602.

12 "Can We Keep Our Cool?" editorial, *Boston Globe*, May 24 1968, p. 20.

13 Arlene Croce, "The Boston Happening," *National Review*, June 18 1968, p. 601; "Chase Gives Up; Promised Mental Aid," *Boston Globe*, May 30 1968, p. 17; "NER Position Paper," undated (*c.* Jan. 1969), BTP; Mendelsohn interview, Dec. 19 1997; Minutes, Special Meeting of the Prudential Committee, May 28 1968, ASC Files; George Whitehouse, interview with Joan Goodwin, May 16 1994, ASC Oral History Project, p. 17; Ralph W. Conant, Report of the Chairman of the Prudential Committee to the Annual Meeting of the Corporation," June 12 1968, ASC Files.

14 Resist Newsletters, July 29 1968 and Aug. 27 1968, Spock Papers, Series II, Box 28.

15 "Statement of Allen Loehner, SN," June 23, 1968, mimeo document, Papers of Michael Ferber (hereafter cited as MKFP).

16 "Marine Seeks Sanctuary at Harvard Divinity," *Boston Globe*, Sep. 23 1968, p. 1; Harvard Divinity School Press Release, Sep. 22 1968, MKFP.

17   "Statement of John M. O'Conner," mimeo document, MKFP.

18   Nan Stone, "GI Support Speech," undated, Nan Stone papers, copy in author's files.

19   Stone, "GI Support Speech;" For an interesting discussion of the various factors contributing to GI resentment of antiwar protesters, see Christian Appy, *Working-Class War: American Combat Soldiers in Vietnam* (Chapel Hill: University of North Carolina Press, 1993), pp. 299–306.

20   "Marine Explains Why He Dropped Out," *Boston Globe*, Sep. 24 1968, p. 7.

21   "Marine Seeks Sanctuary at Harvard Divinity," *Boston Globe*, Sep. 23 1968, p. 1; Harvard Divinity School Press Release, Sep. 22 1968, MKFP.

22   "Military Seize AWOL Marine in Harvard Divinity Chapel," *Boston Globe (Evening Edition)*, Sep. 24 1968, p. 1; "Police Arrest Olimpieri Who Condemns Students," *Harvard Crimson* Sep. 25 1968, p. 1.

23   "Sanctuary Marine Says He's All Wrong," *Boston Globe*, Sep. 25 1968, p. 1.

24   "Police Arrest Olimpieri, Who Condemns Students," *Harvard Crimson*, Sep. 25 1968, p. 1. Note: To date, I have been unable to locate Paul Olimpieri to get his side of the story.

25   "Marsh Chapel Held as Draft Sanctuary," *BU News*, Oct. 2 1968, pp. 3, 9.

26   "20 Sympathizers Protect AWOL soldier in Sanctuary at B.U.," *Boston Globe*, Oct. 2 1968, p. 5; "Marsh Chapel Held as Draft Sanctuary," *BU News*, Oct. 2 1968, pp. 3, 9; "Marine Recants Statements Made During BU Sanctuary," *Boston Globe*, Oct. 5 1968, p. 21.

27   "Marine Recants Statements Made During BU Sanctuary," *Boston Globe*, Oct. 5 1968, p. 21.

28   "Marsh Chapel Held as Draft Sanctuary," *BU News*, Oct. 2 1968, pp. 3, 9; "20 Sympathizers Protect AWOL Soldier in Sanctuary at B.U., *Boston Globe (Evening Edition)*, Oct. 2 1968, p. 5; "B.U. Sanctuary Continues for Soldier," *Boston Globe*, Oct. 3 1968, p. 3; "500 Keep B.U. Vigil Awaiting GI Arrest," *Boston Globe (Evening Edition)*, Oct. 4 1968, p. 2; Zinn interview, July 6 1998.

29   "Asked for a Warrant, They Just Stepped Over Me," *BU News*, Oct. 9 1968, pp. 3, 8; "AWOL Soldier Seized at BU," *Boston Globe*, Oct. 7 1968, p. 3.

30   Alex Jack, "The Politics of Confrontation," *BU News*, Oct. 9 1968, pp. A2–A3.

31   "Cultural Revolution at School of Theology," *Up Against the Cross*, issue # 1 (Nov. 1968), AJP; Jack interview, Mar. 21 1997; "Kroll, AWOL GI of BU Sanctuary, Gets 3 Months Hard Labor," *Old Mole*, vol. 1, #4, Nov. 5 1968, p. 3.

32   "It had Salami and Donuts, But Spirit Sustained Chapel," *BU News*, Oct. 9 1968, p. A4; "A Sense of Responsibility," Resist Newsletter, Oct. 28 1968, p. 2, Michael Zigmond Papers (hereafter cited as MZP).

33   "Statement of Jack M. O'Connor, undated (*c*. Oct. 29 1968), Robert Shapiro Papers (hereafter cited as RSP); Resist Newsletter, Dec. 20 1968, p. 8, Spock papers, Syracuse University Library, box 28.

34   "12 Days of Sanctuary at MIT," Resist Newsletter, Dec. 2 1968, p. 1, RSP; "O'Connor's Sanctuary Ends," *The Tech*, Nov. 8 1968, p. 1; "Six-Day MIT Sanctuary Ends Quietly Without Bust," *Harvard Crimson*, Nov. 4 1968, p. 1; Robert Shapiro, interview with author, Aug. 13 1997.

35   NER Newsletter, Jan. 1969, MKFP; NER Newsletter, Feb–Mar 1969, MKFP. Note: The Brandeis sanctuary for Sp/4 John Rollins, AWOL from Ft. Clayton, Panama began on December 4 and lasted two weeks. On December 19, Rollins and the sanctuary community dissolved the sanctuary and went to Ft. Devens to distribute leaflets to GIs. There Military Police arrested him.

36 NER Newsletter, Jan. 1969, MKFP; NER Newsletter, Feb–Mar 1969, MKFP; Nan Stone, interview with author, Oct. 8 1997; Joel Kugelmass, interview with author, June 16 1997; Shapiro interview, Aug. 13 1997. Note: In some ways, the Resistance began duplicating the GI Outreach Program of the Boston Draft Resistance Group, a draft counseling organization; BDRG, for example, had been distributing *Vietnam GI* at bus stations since the summer of 1968.

37 Kugelmass interview, June 16 1997; Stone interview, Oct. 8 1997; Dan and Olene Tilton, interview with author, June 16 1997; Neil Robertson, interview with author, Aug. 7 1998.

38 Stone interview, Oct. 8 1997; Kugelmass interview, June 16 1997.

CHAPTER TWENTY-THREE

Knowledge at War: American Social Science and Vietnam

MICHAEL E. LATHAM

Despite his campaign promises to "end the war and win the peace," Richard Nixon had no "secret plan" for victory in Vietnam. Samuel P. Huntington, however, endeavored to provide one. In March of 1969, the Harvard University political scientist delivered a long, detailed policy proposal to the US Agency for International Development (AID). Like many American analysts, Huntington recognized that a military success in Vietnam had become most unlikely. Thousands of air strikes, over a half-million US combat troops, and enormous amounts of aid to the Saigon regime had all failed to stop the revolution's advance. Yet Huntington still believed that it would be possible to engineer an American triumph. The key, he argued, would be to shift the struggle to another, more promising battlefield, that of national development.

As the Paris peace talks continued and the military conflict wound down, Huntington predicted, the United States would find itself with an opportunity to "persuade the enemy to compete politically and then to beat him at that competition." Where war protesters demanded an immediate withdrawal, Huntington insisted that the United States should instead plunge deeper into the conflict by dictating the terms of a settlement between the National Liberation Front (NLF) and the South Vietnamese government and then dominating the eventual results. In particular, Huntington argued that the United States should pressure South Vietnam to "trade off local authority for national power." The battle-weary NLF, he suggested, might be induced to accept formal control of specific rural provinces in exchange for tolerating the continued presence of the South Vietnamese regime at the national level. Such a result would meet the NLF's requirements for a solution that would preserve its organization and still allow it to continue political proselytizing or renew military struggle if necessary. Yet it would also throw a major advantage to Saigon by leaving the revolutionaries vulnerable to the forces of modernization unleashed by the American presence. "The underlying problem in Vietnam," Huntington emphasized, "has been to bridge the gap between the countryside and the cities," a task that the revolution had proven unable to complete. The United States, however, could accelerate its programs of "inducing substantial migration of people from the countryside to the cities," "promoting economic development in rural areas," building "marketing and transportation links," and creating more vital non-Communist political organizations. Continued American effort, Huntington confidently proclaimed, would present the revolutionaries with a "difficult choice." "If the NLF attempts to isolate the areas under its control from these developments," he argued, "it is likely to be confronted by population drainage and an increasing gap between the economic and social well-being of its areas and those areas integrated into the national economy... If, on the other hand, the NLF permits extensive contacts to develop between its areas and the cities, the social and economic grievances in large part responsible for its appeal will be undermined by economic development and the opportunities for entrepreneurship opened up...." Time, Huntington insisted, was still on America's side. Contact with the international, capitalist marketplace, exposure to modern communications, and continued urbanization would all foster a new, democratic party politics and drive Vietnam out of the phase of development in which an agrarian-based revolution had gained the upper hand. That strategy, of course, might still require high levels of violence. "Inducing" the movement of people from rural areas to cities meant creating refugees, a process thus far promoted through relentless bombing, the creation of free-fire zones, and crop destruction. Yet for Huntington these were minor matters, problems not really worth addressing in his larger scheme. American power, he cheerfully concluded, could engineer a "political take-off," a transformation of Vietnamese society so profound it would produce the victory that all other strategies had failed to deliver.[1]

Read with great interest and treated as a classified document by both AID and US Army officials, Huntington's proposal reflects a larger pattern of analysis. Like Huntington, many American social scientists produced knowledge designed to identify the specific levers American policymakers might use to manipulate Vietnam's society and the course of its history. Committed to Cold War goals, they came to see Vietnam less as an intriguing subject for study in its own right than as a field in which complex historical, social, and political problems might be reduced to technical ones, suitable for the deployment of American power. Yet they also encountered a war that forced them to make choices about their professional goals, sense of national duty, and personal values. This essay explores those issues by illustrating three of the many contexts in which social scientists went to war in Vietnam: Michigan State's nation-building mission; the practice of psychological warfare; and the RAND Corporation's analysis of the revolution. As these three cases reveal, individuals confronted common problems, but sought to resolve them in disparate ways. Employed by the US government and eager to combat the threat they identified in Communist expansion, Michigan State's experts, like Huntington, were willing to subordinate their academic roles in service to the state. Many American psychologists were also willing to discard the ideals of broad, dispassionate inquiry and the internally generated questions of their own professional discipline to work on an array of problems bounded by the specific assumptions and objectives of their government sponsors. Other social scientists, however, including some working for RAND, ultimately became convinced that

Vietnam was not readily malleable and turned against the war and its escalating brutality. In time, their questions also contributed to a long, divisive debate over the role of the university and the obligations of intellectuals. Among American social scientists, as in so many other sectors of the nation's culture, the Vietnam war shattered an established consensus and provoked a painful and productive reassessment of democratic principles, personal integrity, and moral responsibility.

Social Research and the National Security State

As historian Stuart Leslie argues, the political economy of the Cold War effectively redefined America's scientific establishment. During World War II, the US government issued an unprecedented number of research and development contracts to the nation's universities. The investment also paid off. Radar, sonar, long-range rockets, and the atomic bomb became the "wonder weapons of the war," devices that contributed powerfully to victory over the Axis. The Manhattan Project in particular, bolstered by a collection of brilliant physicists, chemists, and engineers, created relationships between government demands and academic expertise that tightened as the Cold War intensified. By the end of the Korean War, the Defense Department became the largest single patron of scientific research and its funding levels surpassed the previous World War II peak. By 1960, defense research and development soared to an annual level of $5.5 billion. Universities, moreover, were central to the entire process for only they "could both create and replicate knowledge and train the next generation of scientists and engineers." Defense spending altered curricula, changed standards for professional advancement, and provided support for institutional expansion as it helped forge "a new kind of postwar science, one that blurred traditional distinctions between theory and practice, science and engineering, civilian and military, and classified and unclassified, one that owed its character as well as its contracts to the national security state."[2]

Though its impact was most dramatic in the physical sciences, especially in the realm of weapons development, World War II and the Cold War profoundly influenced American social research as well. Economists mapped out complex military supply tasks, political scientists expanded their work in game theory and conflict simulation, and psychologists designed intelligence tests for the armed forces. The pursuit of victory also stimulated a sharp increase in interdisciplinary research as funding poured into new "area studies" programs and federal agencies collaborated with private foundations to create specialized, policy-oriented institutes at elite universities. In 1947, the Carnegie Corporation helped found Harvard's Russian Research Center, an organization that analyzed captured documents, interpreted Soviet social and economic trends for US intelligence agencies, and interviewed Russian refugees. At the Massachusetts Institute of Technology (MIT), the programmatic relationship between knowledge production and Cold War demands was equally tight. In 1950, the State Department asked the university for help in making Western radio broadcasts less vulnerable to Soviet jamming. When a group of MIT academics recommended a wider inquiry into the opportunities to be exploited by communicating with the Soviet people, the Central Intelligence Agency (CIA) agreed to fund a new, interdisciplinary Center for International Studies. With an economist and former CIA official as director, the center soon employed over seventy people, including six core faculty and a wide array of visiting social scientists, postdoctoral fellows, and foreign associates. Like the Harvard center, the MIT group conducted research into questions determined by its federal clients to the detriment of problems arising from the normal process of scholarly inquiry. It also sent the knowledge it produced directly to national security agencies, often before it appeared in published form.[3]

During the 1950s, the "loss" of China, detonation of a Soviet atomic bomb, and war in Korea all helped create an atmosphere in which a failure to contain communism anywhere might be considered a crisis everywhere. They also convinced many academics that victory over the Communists would demand a full mobilization of their knowledge about the foreign world and the way changes in its politics, economics, and populations might be guided. Those scholars that criticized the Cold War mission moreover, became vulnerable to McCarthyist attacks. In 1953, congressional committees bent on eliminating internal subversion and hostile ideology subpoenaed over 100 college and university faculty.[4] Even after Congressional witch-hunting tapered off in the mid-1950s, professors still confronted loyalty oaths, internal investigations, and sanctions by their colleagues and administrative superiors. Anticommunism, many universities concluded, was a far more pressing matter than tolerance for dissent or respect for intellectual freedom. Cold War pressures and opportunities, many social scientists decided, were more compelling than the intellectual norms of open peer review, objectivity, and the pursuit of knowledge unbounded by demands for political utility.

As the Cold War continued to expand beyond the borders of Europe, Vietnam rapidly emerged as a pivotal "test case" of American power. It was in Vietnam, officials believed, that the United States might demonstrate to ideological adversaries and worried allies that it could marshal the resources and the knowledge to determine the future of an "underdeveloped" world. After the Viet Minh victory over the French and the settlement at Geneva in 1954, the Eisenhower administration began to recruit American academics to advise and assist the South Vietnamese regime. Soviet pledges to sponsor "wars of national liberation" in decolonizing areas raised further alarms for John F. Kennedy and the experts he brought with him into the White House. For officials like national security adviser McGeorge Bundy and policy planner Walt Rostow, Vietnam became a high-stakes laboratory in which social scientific theories of modernization, nation-building, and "internal war" might be developed and deployed. Fighting a guerrilla struggle in Vietnam, they believed, required studying the economics of national growth, the psychology of the revolutionary, and the politics of nationalism. That research, moreover, was not a matter to be divorced from military exigency. Indeed, social science and violence were to go hand in hand. As a report sponsored by the Smithsonian Institution under the leadership of MIT political scientist Ithiel de Sola Pool insisted in 1963, counterinsurgency was of special concern to social scientists because that form of warfare was "intimately related to questions about the social structure, culture, and behavior patterns of the populations involved in such conflicts. Without question, social science research is in a strong position to contribute useful knowledge in designing and developing internal security forces."[5] When American intervention accelerated, the US government made Vietnam the focus of an immense scholarly industry. Artillery, helicopters, defoliants, and napalm made up only part of America's lethal arsenal. Social research on such topics as the "felt needs" of the rural population, the impact of radio and television, the role of women, and the patterns of village-level communication was also expected to help destroy a revolution few Americans knew anything about.

"Rationalizing" the South: Michigan State and the Diem Regime

John Hannah, president of Michigan State University (MSU), was particularly confident about the potential for American social science to turn the tide in Vietnam. Determined that "colleges and universities must be regarded as bastions of our defense, as essential to the preservation of our country and our way of life as supersonic bombers, nuclear-powered submarines and intercontinental ballistic missiles," Hannah authorized one of the earliest attempts to bolster the fragile South Vietnamese regime with American expertise.[6] Between May of 1955 and June of 1962, Michigan State deployed over one hundred full-time staff and channeled approximately $25 million in US funding to defend the government organized under Ngo Dinh Diem.[7] Because of its massive scale and intimate collaboration with both the American and South Vietnamese governments, the MSU experience presents a striking example of the way that academics in service to the state often risked their independence as well as their integrity.

Michigan State political scientist Wesley Fishel, an advisor and confidant to Diem since the early 1950s, had little doubt that his university could help build a new, independent South Vietnam where none had ever existed before. After conducting a survey of the country's needs in the fall of 1954, Fishel led a team to Saigon and stood by Diem as he decided not to hold the national reunification elections mandated by the Geneva Accords. Vietnamese society, Fishel explained in a curious choice of words, was the "product of political miscegenation." French colonists had unwisely built "a weighty superstructure of Western organizations, principles, laws, and techniques" on a "traditional base, influenced by Confucian, Taoist, and Buddhist ideals and values...." South Vietnam's new constitution, National Assembly, and programs of agricultural assistance, he expected, would help supply a "sense of identity between the people and their government."[8] Michigan State's purpose, as Fishel defined it, was to accelerate that process by rationalizing Vietnam's unwieldy social structure and training the public administrators, civil servants, and police needed to foster security and a modern, popular, nationalism under Diem's leadership.

Under contract to both South Vietnam and the United States, the MSU team quickly discovered that collaboration involved compromise and conflict. One of the group's first tasks was to help resettle the approximately 900 thousand refugees that poured into the South following Vietnam's partition. A Catholic from central Vietnam himself, Diem viewed the predominantly Catholic refugees as an ideal power base for his government and used the provision of land, medicine, food, public works, and government employment as a way to solidify personal control in the countryside. When MSU consultants objected to the comparatively poor treatment of the Buddhist arrivals and recommended that aid distribution be decentralized to involve the participation of the refugees themselves, Diem stubbornly refused. Very early into their tenure in Vietnam, MSU's economists, political scientists, and anthropologists found that although Diem was glad to accept the resources they delivered, he proved most unwilling to adopt the reforms they recommended.[9]

The MSU team had a similar experience when it attempted to train South Vietnam's police forces. Between 1955 and 1958, MSU consultants organized a National Police Academy, printed over three million identity cards, built a crime detection laboratory, and taught courses in such areas as homicide investigation, arrest techniques, data management, and criminal law. Yet here, too, they found Diem's regime and its representatives far more interested in equipment distribution than lectures on legal procedures or constitutional justice. As one Michigan State faculty member put it, the Sûreté "had no trouble in accepting . . . revolvers, ammo [and] communication equipment but being receptive to American democratic principles, that's something else."[10] When MSU team members pressed Diem to convert his sixty thousand-strong Civil Guard from a paramilitary force into a civil agency responsible only for local law enforcement, he again refused. In the end, the social scientists wound up distributing weapons, surveillance technology, and little else.

Michigan State also came into conflict with the United States government. Frustrated over the refugee and police experiences, the MSU team hoped that its administrative education program would generate more productive nation-building efforts. On a nine-acre site in Saigon, MSU economists, political scientists, psychologists, and financial experts built a school to train personnel from South Vietnam's national bank, health ministry, and civil service. Yet here as well the social scientists found their range of activity tightly circumscribed by the will of their sponsors. When the team sought to produce more empirical research, publish studies of Vietnamese society, and engage in less immediately policy-oriented tasks, American aid officials objected to their work as a waste of money likely to provoke a wrathful congressional investigation. Fearful that MSU economists might advocate undesirable views, US officials also demanded the right to inspect course syllabi.[11] The message for the MSU team members was clear – their tasks were to come from the direction of their government clients, not their own curiosity, educational commitments, or disciplinary practices. The knowledge desired was instrumental, not disinterested.

MSU even lost control over the personnel operating under its name when it consented to provide housing and public cover for several CIA agents. Active from 1955 until 1959, the agents reported directly to the US Embassy and made little pretense of promoting democratic nation-building. Conducting security checks on police recruits and training spies and interrogators in counterespionage, the unit also built a jail complete with bugged cells to imprison suspected revolutionaries. When *Ramparts* magazine finally exposed the connection between the CIA and Michigan State in 1966, both Hannah and Fishel were subjected to critical questioning by the nation's press, MSU students, and Michigan's legislature about the way the university had represented its role in Vietnam.[12]

Despite the clear contradictions to its stated purposes in democratic nation-building and social scientific inquiry, the MSU team remained in Vietnam for seven years. In the end, it was Ngo Dinh Diem, angered over critical articles published by MSU professors in American journals, who terminated the contract in 1962. Like the US government itself, Michigan State's social scientists were slow to question their assumptions about the war, even as they became increasingly aware of South Vietnam's brutal repression. Although a few disenchanted veterans of the project returned to the United States to express their misgivings, the MSU team directors generally tried to placate their government clients.[13] Where Wesley Fishel and his associates might have protested publicly and used their intellectual legitimacy to call American and South Vietnamese policies into question, they chose instead to collaborate with Diem and, in the process, reinforced the authority of a state that routinely abused, imprisoned, and executed its opponents. Michigan State social scientists, like many American experts, made the mistake of believing that Vietnamese society could be easily refashioned. Confident they could identify the essential social mechanisms, the scholars expected to engineer responsible, attractive democracy and derail a powerful revolution. Ignorant of the power relations, class dynamics, and nationalist forces at work around them, many on the MSU team assumed they could reduce deeply-rooted political problems to issues of technique and administration. In this regard, they also helped push Vietnam and the United States deeper into tragedy.

Psychological Warfare and Behavioral Conditioning

Certain that the failures in Vietnam had more to do with Diem than the war's underlying rationale, the Johnson administration deepened America's commitment through the mid-1960s by deploying ever larger numbers of combat troops, stepping up a destructive air war, and trying to enhance "pacification" capabilities. Social scientists played a leading role in that escalation, and because psychologists stood in the front ranks of a war for the "hearts and minds" of Vietnam's population, their work provides a stunning case of the way knowledge and violence intersected. During the Korean War, the Defense Department had become particularly interested in the techniques of mass communication and ideological indoctrination. By the early 1960s, the military sponsored about $15 million of psychological research annually, an amount that would nearly triple before the end of the decade.[14] Psychologists, committed to a behavioral model, claimed that their discipline could illuminate the universal laws governing identity, relationships, and personality formation. In Vietnam, they promised to unlock the mysterious social psychology of revolution and provide the tools to drive human aspirations in different directions. Where the military had once used psychology to select soldiers or match men to machines, it now hoped to reorder a population's sense of itself and the war around it.

Psychological studies of the "Vietnamese mind," moreover, described an ideal site for the techniques of behavioral conditioning. According to many analysts, Vietnam was a "traditional" society in the midst of a jarring transition. As the older values that once integrated family and village life were disrupted by "modern" Western technology, markets, and communications, peasants supposedly groped for a new sense of security and pursued personal interests that the United States could easily manipulate. In one secret report provided to the US Army, psychologist Titus Leidesdorf described the Vietnamese a "singularly self-centered people" and a prime "operational target." What a Vietnamese person did, he claimed, was usually driven by a "commitment to himself and his own needs, not to some grand purpose, some great ideal, or some compelling loyalty. . . . [W]hile the Westerner (and particularly the American) accepts direction from others, commits himself to external causes and obligations, and endeavors to submerge his selfish interests in some greater social purpose (usually experiencing a sense of guilt if he fails to do so), the Vietnamese *qua* Oriental is free from this sense of compulsion, and rather comfortably so." The Vietnamese character, Leidesdorf argued, revealed little philosophical depth and a high degree of vulnerability to the tools of behavioral modification. Since the Vietnamese were "intensely individualistic in outlook and purpose – often bovine, passive, and seemingly uninspired (in Western terms), but adequately motivated to pursue [their] own interests," they would respond strongly to American programs meeting concrete material needs. Communism, he continued, was attractive "not because of its intellectual or ideological appeal," but simply because "its structure, its discipline, and its determinism provide a kind of social womb."[15]

Psychologists like Leidesdorf, displaying an abysmal understanding of Vietnamese history and nationalism, completely ignored the sacrifices, commitment, and determination that animated the revolutionaries. They cast the Vietnamese as infantile, assumed cultural and intellectual superiority over them, and claimed that, since ideology really wasn't an issue, American wealth and prestige could easily destroy the revolution's momentum. The Simulmatics Corporation, a think tank that employed many Harvard and MIT experts, defined the situation in similar terms. Psychological testing revealed that the Vietnamese peasantry lived in an "anomic environment," a kind of socio-political void lacking "well-staffed communal organizations" that might make it resistant to the "bullying" of the NLF. From the "worm's eye point of view of the peasant," ideology mattered far less than the "monopoly of force."[16] Surely, the consultants suggested, American power and wealth could move into the gap to win, or buy, popular allegiance.

As the war progressed, psychological warfare became an integral part of American strategy. When analysts found that the government's Regional and Popular Forces were not fighting effectively, Simulmatics Corporation experts went into the field to find out why. After analyzing 1,300 respondents with a "thematic apperception test," a "self-anchoring scale" and "dream reports" in addition to other diagnostic tools, they learned that the South Vietnamese recruits were alienated by the corrupt regime they were ordered to defend. Such a conclusion might have led to deeper questions about a war in which the United States upheld a regime with precious little popular respect or legitimacy. The psychologists, however, settled on a more simple remedy. A program of "emotional and behavioral conditioning to national symbols," they suggested, would regenerate a fighting spirit. While the government expressed its concern for the soldiers' welfare, "officials, flags, literature" and "radio programs emanating from Saigon" would develop "functional ties," "facilitate identification with national goals," and help "stimulate hostility toward the VC and communism."[17]

When directed toward the enemy, behavioral conditioning could also take on frightening dimensions. One bizarre technique, labeled "Wandering Souls," involved setting up noise-making loudspeakers near an NLF-controlled village to prevent the guerrillas from resting during the day. Once night fell, American helicopters would then fly over enemy-held terrain broadcasting propaganda messages or "eerie sounds" intended to make guerrillas think of the dead among them that would never find peace because they were buried in unmarked graves. Though US Army officials admitted that the NLF knew the sounds came from aircraft, they believed such tactics weakened the enemy's resolve by proving that the Americans knew their deepest fears.[18] Other measures revealed behavioral conditioning at its most violent. Over the course of the war American aircraft dropped millions of leaflets across the Vietnamese countryside. While some offered revolutionaries "safe conduct" if they defected or stressed the loneliness of soldiers fighting far away from families, many took a more direct approach. One American leaflet, prepared in 1967, warned its readers that: "Each day, each week, each month, more and more of your comrades, base camps and tunnels are destroyed. You are shelled more often. You are bombed more often. You are forced to move very often. You are forced to dig deeper. You are tired. You are sick. Your leaders tell you victory is near. They are wrong. Only death is near. Do you hear the planes? Do you hear the bombs? These are the sounds of death: your death. Rally [to the government side] now to survive...."[19] In another tactic, armed propaganda teams would clear a settlement and tell peasants that, because they had collaborated with the NLF, their village was now a target. While the villagers watched from a distance, their houses and fields would be destroyed. Convinced that the approach "rub[bed] in the accuracy of modern artillery" army planners believed it was "an effective way of lowering morale and the will to resist."[20]

In the long run, such tactics probably inspired hatred for the United States and the South Vietnamese government at least as much as they deterred revolutionaries from carrying on their struggle. Searching for the instruments of social control, psychologists ignored the historical and social context in which the war was fought. Promising to manipulate a supposedly "passive" and "self-interested" population into relinquishing its commitments, their Pavlovian approaches also helped clear the way for ever more violent means of "reinforcement." Psychologists, in such cases, raised false expectations, legitimated a relentless escalation, and prolonged the war's ordeal.

Analyzing the Enemy: RAND and the Revolution

Not all social scientists were quite so confident in their predictions of American victory and, unlike the proponents of psychological warfare, many RAND Corporation analysts raised fundamental questions about the war effort. Originally created in 1946 to conduct physical and operations research for the Air Force, RAND (an acronym for "Research and Development") was a federal contract research center, an organization founded for the exclusive purpose of providing guidance to policymakers. RAND's social science division spent much of the 1950s ensconced in its Santa Monica offices poring through military data, exploring the psychology of deterrence, and crafting the doctrines of American nuclear strategy. By the early

1960s, however, the Department of Defense wanted to know more than how to use the bomb, it also sought to understand the causes of "third world" revolution. Under new orders, RAND experts arrived in Vietnam to study the war in the countryside. An investigation of RAND's work raises fascinating and troubling questions about the way evidence was obtained, the quality of classified analysis, and the way that policymakers responded to knowledge challenging their deeply held assumptions.

Though RAND generated reports on topics ranging from Montagnard tribes to propaganda techniques, much of its analytical effort focused on the enemy. Between 1964 and 1968, RAND conducted over 2,400 interviews with Vietnamese peasants, enemy defectors, and prisoners of war. The results, totaling some 62,000 transcript pages, produced some startling conclusions. In contrast to the repeated US government claims that North Vietnam was the driving force behind an unpopular war of Communist aggression, RAND studies revealed that the revolution had deep historical causes and that its Southern participants were motivated by an intense sense of nationalism. After interviewing 78 Vietminh veterans and 34 newly recruited NLF cadres, W. P. Davidson and Joseph Zasloff determined that their subjects were profoundly committed to "reunification by any means" and perceived the South Vietnamese government as an obstacle to that goal. Revolutionaries identified their current struggle with Vietnam's historic pursuit of independence against the powers of China, France, and Japan. In their minds, the United States had become yet another imperial power seeking to dictate their country's future. Davidson and Zasloff also found that their interviewees bitterly resented South Vietnam's repressive violence: "One former Vietminh, who had been elected a village official in 1954 and claimed to have been loyal to the Saigon government, told the following story. Suspected of being a Viet Cong agent, he was sentenced without trial to five years in prison. Meanwhile, his eldest sister was secretly done away with by government officials; and Saigon troops mopped up his home village, arrested his wife, and shot her. In a second sweep of his village by government forces, his house and furniture were burned and his fourteen year-old daughter died from illness and sadness, or else committed suicide; he wasn't sure which." The government, peasants also explained, perpetuated their poverty and supported a wealthy elite. Villagers described having to pay bribes to local officials, doing mandated, unpaid labor on government projects, and dealing with a militia that routinely stole their livestock or rice. Though the revolutionaries might occasionally coerce a recruit, it didn't take much for the NLF to gain the allegiance of a people "eager to join a cause that offered them greater opportunities."[21]

RAND reports demonstrated that the revolution was also extremely well-organized and resistant to American force. Political scientist Nathan Leites discovered that the NLF cultivated a relationship with the peasantry that clearly distinguished it from the established government. Interviews and captured documents revealed that the revolutionaries adhered to a code that "discourages and condemns the abuse of power by its cadres for their private gain or pleasure, concerned as it is not only about the likely popular reactions to patent injustices but also about the damage that such improper conduct might do to the spirit of righteousness from which the cadres draw much of their strength." Though the NLF could ruthlessly attack its opponents, Leites argued that it also operated with a high level of personal discipline, tried to improve peasant life, and won rural loyalty. As he concluded, "in social and geographic origins, in dress, behavior, and in standard of living the people identify themselves more readily with the VC than with representatives of the GVN [South Vietnamese Government]."[22] In their study of Dinh Tuong, a province near Saigon, David Elliott and W. A. Stewart also found the NLF working through a disciplined, resilient system. Cadres played crucial roles in conveying policy directives from district and provincial authorities down to local villages and held together a "balanced, well-coordinated, closely interrelated, political–military organization in which each element supports every other element and multiplies its effectiveness." Even in the face of intense firepower, the NLF managed to adapt its organization, preserve lines of communication, and maintain its base and safety areas through the active cooperation of peasants that provided guerrillas with rice, transported wounded, and carried ammunition. Destroying the revolution without alienating the peasantry, the two argued, would be a most difficult task.[23]

With hindsight, such research appears to have provided a perceptive, accurate picture of a movement that the architects of American policy continued to underestimate. Yet RAND researchers did not always agree with each other and, all too often, evidence that should have given pause to the advocates of further engagement was swept aside in favor of material telling policymakers what they wanted to hear. Where Elliott and his associates argued that the war's course would be long, difficult, and uncertain, Leon Gouré and Charles Thompson provided an assessment more to Lyndon Johnson's liking. "Air power, armor, and artillery," they declared, were terrifying and exhausting an enemy no longer able to protect itself. Defoliation and crop spraying had compounded the NLF's plight by "denying them areas where they can camp or organize ambushes safe from observation and by reducing their ability to obtain food." Villagers were increasingly reluctant to assist the NLF and afraid of government retaliation. According to Gouré and Thompson, the revolutionaries were on the ropes. "Combined military, political, and psychological operations," they insisted, could "capitalize on the vulnerabilities that have begun to appear in Viet Cong morale and in the attitude of villagers under their control" and "undermine the popular support which, according to Viet Cong statements, is so vital to the success of their movement."[24] According to at least one source, the work of Gouré and Thompson strongly reinforced Johnson's determination to continue heavy bombing throughout South Vietnam.[25] As a senior Defense Department research director recalled, policymakers evaluated social scientific research with a set of ideological assumptions firmly in mind. Unwilling to pore through the mass of methodological explanation and subtle analysis, they looked instead for the "one-page 'fact sheet.'" When conclusions fit their expectations, they invoked the legitimacy of social science to defend a position. When evidence challenged intuition, however, a policymaker was "more likely to dismiss the report as poorly done than to inquire searchingly into the basis for his own beliefs, or ask for a critical review of the report to see whether it might possibly be correct."[26] As the United States moved deeper into the Vietnam War, even the best social science did little to shake Washington's confidence in the eventuality of military victory.

RAND researchers also did their work in conditions that raised difficult moral questions. Gaining access to defectors and prisoners meant having to cooperate with the South Vietnamese security apparatus, and interviewers like Duong Van Mai Elliott frequently met their subjects in detention centers and jails. While intrigued to learn about the motivation of the revolutionaries, Elliott found the work increasingly disturbing. Behind barbed wire, in dark interrogation rooms, prisoners answered her questions but also, unprompted, told her that "they had been beaten or had had soapy water poured down their throats and noses; that they had been struck repeatedly on the palms of their feet; that they had been subjected to electric shocks." Other Vietnamese interviewers hired by RAND heard similar stories and they rightly judged that torture was common practice. Fearful that the South Vietnamese government would retaliate against them or their families, they told their RAND superiors what they discovered but did not publicize it. When South Vietnam's brutality continued despite growing criticism in the US media, researchers found themselves facing difficult choices. Ultimately, Duong Van Mai Elliott's experiences helped change her understanding of the war. While many of her RAND superiors continued searching for ways to win in Vietnam, she lobbied the US Congress for an American withdrawal.[27]

As the war ground on, more RAND analysts also dissented, the most famous of them a former Pentagon aide named Daniel Ellsberg. As early as June of 1968, Ellsberg started to condemn the war he had once helped plan. At a Chicago conference dedicated to exploring the "Lessons and Mislessons" of Vietnam, Ellsberg mounted a determined attack on American policy. The United States, he charged, was defending a corrupt and ineffective regime. Strategic bombing had also killed thousands of innocent civilians while failing to weaken North Vietnam's determination to support the revolution. Responding to claims that American popular opposition to the war reflected only the normal ebb and flow of public opinion, Ellsberg also described the war as a reprehensible venture. Americans had risen to protest not out of a bland isolationism but instead in reaction to "the spectacle of non-combat casualties being inflicted in Vietnam, and massive refugee movements imposed, by processes which qualified experts tell us are unnecessary, ineffective, and even counterproductive." Americans, he continued, were justifiably alienated by "*this* war: including among other things, the manner we got into it, the manner we have explained it, the manner we are conducting it, and perhaps above all, our evident lack of lasting progress or prospects of success."[28] Finally, as he reviewed secret documents for a history of the war ordered by Secretary of Defense Robert McNamara, Ellsberg's dissent turned into defiance. In 1969, he photocopied the classified material in his office safe and sent it to the Senator J. William Fulbright in hopes that the Committee on Foreign Relations would launch an inquiry. Deeply troubled by his own sense of moral responsibility, Ellsberg then took the decisive step of sending the documents to the *New York Times*. When published in June of 1971, the "Pentagon Papers" presented a damning indictment of American policy and a portrait of official deception stretching back years. In the end, most RAND social scientists found Vietnam a far more complex place than policymakers assumed and the bulk of their research raised serious questions about the war's rationale and American capabilities.

Confronted with their evidence, they found themselves unable to engineer a victory and, in some cases, resolved to hasten an exit.

As the Vietnam War churned on through the late 1960s and into the 1970s, many American social scientists joined Ellsberg in turning against it. The most articulate among them also came to argue that the war was not merely the result of bad policy but instead the sign of a sickness at the core of American society, a moral failure about which one could no longer remain detached or indifferent. Perhaps no one made that point more sharply than MIT linguistics professor Noam Chomsky in his landmark essay, "The Responsibility of Intellectuals." "We can hardly avoid asking ourselves," he wrote, "to what extent the American people bear responsibility for the savage American assault on a largely helpless rural population... As for those of us who stood by in silence and apathy as this catastrophe slowly took shape over the past dozen years, on what page of history do we find our proper place?" According to Chomsky, intellectuals bore a particularly heavy moral burden because they were "in a position to expose the lies of governments, to analyze actions according to their causes and motives and often hidden intentions." Their access to information, comparative leisure, and freedom of expression, he maintained, gave them the chance to "seek the truth lying hidden behind the veil of distortion and misrepresentation, ideology, and class interest...."[29] That so many had failed in that obligation, he and other critics claimed, revealed that the "experts" had lost all integrity. Hiding behind claims of privileged knowledge and objective rigor, they had sought to contain debate and prolonged an unnecessary, unjust war.

Faced with questions like the ones that Chomsky presented, social scientists took disparate stances. Anti-war faculty helped galvanize collective opposition by leading teach-ins, expressing their dissent in writing, and supporting students that carried protest into the streets. Scholars like Samuel Huntington and Ithiel de Sola Pool, however, claimed that even their defense-supported scholarship allowed them to create new, intrinsically valuable knowledge. They also continued to enjoy high levels of professional prestige and government backing. Yet, in many ways, the Vietnam War marked a turning point and the debate over social research helped foster a growing sense that "the political and the intellectual were inseparable."[30] Coupled with the news of My Lai, the invasions of Cambodia and Laos, and the killings at Kent State and Jackson State, the war efforts of social scientists stimulated growing resistance. At universities like Berkeley, Columbia, MIT, Stanford, and Southern Illinois, administrators faced massive opposition to war research and, in some cases, moved to divest themselves of Defense Department contracts. At a conference dedicated to "Scholarly Integrity and University Complicity" in 1970, historian Gabriel Kolko argued that when a university conducted war-related research it "compromised its deepest obligations to the majority of its students and faculty, as well as the traditional aims of the university in Western history...."[31] By that point, many scholars agreed that the war researchers had ceded the direction of their work, allowed classification to conceal their responsibility, and abused their authority.

Among many social scientists, the tensions between national security claims and intellectual freedom helped shatter a Cold War consensus. Where many experts were eager to help the United States "pay any price" and "bear any burden" in 1961, the

Vietnam War's close found them far more concerned with their independence and more cautious in evaluating government demands. Where anti-communism once preserved a solid front and dissent once provoked McCarthyist repression, many social scientists came to take on more critical roles, paying close attention not only to the content of research but also the power relations that shaped its production and the purposes to which it might be lent. As the United States seeks to mobilize its reservoir of expertise in a post-Cold War world, those issues remain pressing ones.

NOTES

1   Samuel P. Huntington, "Getting Ready for Political Competition in Vietnam," unpublished document, 1969, Records Group 472, National Archives, College Park, MD.
2   Stuart W. Leslie, *The Cold War and American Science: The Military–Industrial Academic Complex at MIT and Stanford* (New York: Columbia University Press, 1993), 1–2, 8.
3   Roger L. Geiger, *Research and Relevant Knowledge: American Research Universities Since World War II* (New York: Oxford University Press, 1993), 50–69.
4   Ibid., 39.
5   Seymour J. Deitchman, *The Best-Laid Schemes: A Tale of Social Research and Bureaucracy* (Cambridge: MIT Press, 1976), 34.
6   John Ernst, *Forging a Fateful Alliance: Michigan State University and the Vietnam War* (East Lansing: Michigan State University Press, 1998), 6.
7   Robert Scigliano and Guy H. Fox, *Technical Assistance in Vietnam: The Michigan State Experience* (New York: Praeger, 1965), 4, 40.
8   Wesley R. Fishel, "Problems of Democratic Growth in Free Vietnam," in *Problems of Freedom: South Vietnam Since Independence* (New York: Free Press, 1961), 9, 19.
9   Ernst, 21–39.
10 Ibid., 65.
11 Scigliano and Fox, 47–8.
12 Ernst, 67, 128–9.
13 Ibid., 120–1.
14 Ellen Herman, *The Romance of American Psychology: Political Culture in the Age of Experts* (Berkeley: University of California Press, 1995), 129.
15 Titus Leidesdorf, "The Vietnamese as Operational Target," unpublished document, not dated, Records Group 472, National Archives, College Park, MD.
16 Simulmatics Corporation, "Studies of Entrepreneurship and National Integration in South Vietnam," unpublished document, 1968, Records Group 472, National Archives, College Park, MD.
17 Simulmatics Corporation, "Final Report: A Socio-Psychological Study of Regional/ Popular Forces in Vietnam," unpublished document, 1967, Records Group 472, National Archives, College Park, MD.
18 Peter Watson, *War on the Mind: The Military Uses and Abuses of Psychology* (New York: Basic Books, 1978), 410.
19 Jonathan Schell, *The Village of Ben Suc* (New York: Knopf, 1967), 15–16.
20 Watson, 412.
21 W. P. Davidson and J. J. Zasloff, *A Profile of the Viet Cong Cadres* (Santa Monica: RAND Corporation, 1966), vi, 10–12.

22 Nathan Leites, *The Viet Cong Style of Politics* (Santa Monica: RAND Corporation, 1968), xvi, xxii. Ironically, that conclusion did not move Leites to question the possibility of American victory. Instead, he and fellow RAND analyst Charles Wolf, Jr. soon recommended that the United States simply abandon the "hearts and minds" approach in favor of more carefully targeted coercive violence intended to raise and reinforce the cost of rebellion. Where a revolution had already gained popular support, they advocated instrumental force, not withdrawal or even a reassessment of war goals. See Leites and Wolf, *Rebellion and Authority: An Analytic Essay on Insurgent Conflicts* (Chicago: Markham, 1971).

23 David W. P. Elliott and W. A. Stewart, *Pacification and the Viet Cong System in Dinh Tuong: 1966–1967* (Santa Monica: RAND Corporation, 1969), 1, 41.

24 Leon Gouré and C. A. H. Thompson, *Some Impressions of Viet Cong Vulnerabilities: An Interim Report* (Santa Monica: RAND Corporation, 1965), v–vii.

25 Watson, 28.

26 Deitchman, 390–91.

27 Duong Van Mai Elliott, *The Sacred Willow: Four Generations in the Life of a Vietnamese Family* (New York: Oxford University Press, 1999), 321–23, 335–36.

28 Daniel Ellsberg, *Some Lessons From Failure in Vietnam* (Santa Monica: RAND Corporation, 1968), 2–3, 6–8.

29 Noam Chomsky, "The Responsibility of Intellectuals," in *American Power and the New Mandarins* (New York: Pantheon, 1969), 324.

30 Robert R. Tomes, *Apocalypse Then: American Intellectuals and the Vietnam War, 1954–1975* (New York: New York University Press, 1998), 31.

31 Gabriel Kolko, "The Political Significance of the Center for Vietnamese Studies and Programs," *Bulletin of Concerned Asian Scholars* 2 (1971): 39–49.

REFERENCES

Chomsky, Noam 1969: "The Responsibility of Intellectuals", *American Power and the New Mandarins.* New York: Pantheon, pp. 323–66.

Davidson, W. P., and Zasloff, J. J. 1966: *A Profile of the Viet Cong Cadres.* Santa Monica: RAND Corporation.

Deitchman, Seymour J. 1976: *The Best-Laid Schemes: A Tale of Social Research and Bureaucracy.* Cambridge: MIT Press.

Elliott, David W. P., and Stewart, W. A. 1969: *Pacification and the Viet Cong System in Dinh Tuong: 1966–1967.* Santa Monica: RAND Corporation.

Elliott, Duong Van Mai 1999: *The Sacred Willow: Four Generations in the Life of a Vietnamese Family.* New York: Oxford University Press.

Ellsberg, Daniel 1968: *Some Lessons From Failure in Vietnam.* Santa Monica: RAND Corporation.

Ernst, John 1998: *Forging a Fateful Alliance: Michigan State University and the Vietnam War.* East Lansing: Michigan State University Press.

Fishel, Wesley R. 1961: "Problems of Democratic Growth in Free Vietnam", *Problems of Freedom: South Vietnam Since Independence.* New York: Free Press, pp. 9–28.

Geiger, Roger L. 1993: *Research and Relevant Knowledge: American Research Universities Since World War II.* New York: Oxford University Press.

Gouré, Leon and Thompson, C. A. H. 1965: *Some Impressions of Viet Cong Vulnerabilities: An Interim Report.* Santa Monica: RAND Corporation.

Herman, Ellen 1995: *The Romance of American Psychology: Political Culture in the Age of Experts*. Berkeley: University of California Press.

Huntington, Samuel P. 1969: "Getting Ready for Political Competition in Vietnam," unpublished document. Records Group 472, National Archives, College Park, MD.

Kolko, Gabriel 1971: "The Political Significance of the Center for Vietnamese Studies and Programs", *Bulletin of Concerned Asian Scholars*, 2, 39–49.

Leidesdorf, Titus n.d.: "The Vietnamese as Operational Target," unpublished document. Records Group 472, National Archives, College Park, MD.

Leites, Nathan 1968: *The Viet Cong Style of Politics*. Santa Monica: RAND Corporation.

Leites, Nathan and Wolf, Charles Jr. 1971: *Rebellion and Authority: An Analytic Essay on Insurgent Conflicts*. Chicago: Markham.

Leslie, Stuart W. 1993: *The Cold War and American Science: The Military–Industrial–Academic Complex at MIT and Stanford*. New York: Columbia University Press.

Schell, Jonathan 1967: *The Village of Ben Suc*. New York: Knopf.

Scigliano, Robert and Fox, Guy H. 1965: *Technical Assistance in Vietnam: The Michigan State University Experience*. New York: Praeger.

Simulmatics Corporation 1967: "Final Report: A Socio-Psychological Study of Regional/Popular Forces in Vietnam," unpublished document. Records Group 472, National Archives, College Park, MD.

Simulmatics Corporation 1968: "Studies of Entrepreneurship and National Integration in South Vietnam," unpublished document. Records Group 472, National Archives, College Park, MD.

Tomes, Robert R. 1998: *Apocalypse Then: American Intellectuals and the Vietnam War, 1954–1975*. New York: New York University Press.

Watson, Peter 1978: *War on the Mind: The Military Uses and Abuses of Psychology*. New York: Basic Books, 1978.

CHAPTER TWENTY-FOUR

The War on Television: TV News, the Johnson Administration, and Vietnam

CHESTER J. PACH, JR.

President Lyndon B. Johnson's discontent with television coverage of the Vietnam War exploded on September 20 1967, when he welcomed a group of Australian broadcasters to the White House. Several thousand Australian troops were fighting in Vietnam, and Australian television crews were covering the war. "This is our first television war," one of the visitors remarked, and the lack of formal censorship meant that some reports, like a story that CBS had carried the previous evening on a US marine sweep through a South Vietnamese village, contained "hard-hitting comment." Just the mention of TV news coverage of the war provoked a presidential outburst. The real story in the villages, Johnson replied, was marines opening their hearts to the peasants and undertaking civic action projects, such as building schools. "But television doesn't want that story," Johnson insisted. "I can prove that Ho [Chi Minh] is a son-of-a-bitch if you let me put it on the screen – but they want me to be the son-of-a-bitch." The worst media offenders were NBC and the *New York Times*, both of which, he alleged, were "committed to an editorial policy of making us surrender." NBC correspondents Wilson Hall and Dean Brelis, Johnson concluded, only reported "American losses" and enemy "successes."[1]

The president, of course, was wrong about Hall and Brelis, whose reports from Vietnam were more balanced than LBJ's one-sided caricature. And his comments, as press secretary George Christian later explained, surely reflected the frustration he felt at a time when the war had grown so unpopular that one White House aide seriously proposed a thirty-day moratorium on criticism of the president's war policies, perhaps with a catchy title like "Stop Bombing LBJ," "Halt the Howling," or "Desist from Dissent."[2] But the president's remarks also indicated that Johnson considered the

The author would like to thank Mike Parrish for assistance at the Lyndon B. Johnson Library; Steve Roca, for help at the National Archives; and Richard Dodgson for research assistance.

news media in general – and TV news in particular – a major adversary in his efforts to show that the United States was making progress in meeting aggression and sustaining self-determination in South Vietnam. In a war whose "main front" was "here in the United States," as Johnson believed, the television screen became an important battlefield, one that president mistakenly considered decisive.[3]

Vietnam was the first war covered extensively on US television, and by the time of the commitment of American combat troops in 1965 more than half of the American people relied on TV as their principal source of news. US military authorities did not censor the news from Vietnam, as they had in previous twentieth-century conflicts. Why? "Because we are fools," the president told one group of journalists in the fall of 1967.[4] But administration officials had rejected censorship in 1965 and again in 1967 because they doubted it would work and even feared that it would provoke a backlash of hostile commentary. Instead, their goal was "maximum candor consistent with security considerations." Such openness aimed at producing cooperative relations between US information officers and reporters as well as "accurate and constructive news coverage" of the war.[5]

Realities in Vietnam fell far short of this ideal. Reporters sometimes questioned the credibility of information they received in the daily briefings in Saigon that had become known as the Five O'clock Follies. Political and military officials in Washington and Saigon had differing views about how much candor US security would allow, as a nasty incident involving Arthur Sylvester, the assistant secretary of defense for public affairs, clearly revealed. Sylvester had a reputation for considering candor a matter of convenience. Shortly after the Cuban Missile Crisis in 1962, he declared that the government had a "right, if necessary, to lie to save itself." While holding a press conference in Saigon, he denied that the United States was providing South Vietnam with certain kinds of combat equipment. As he spoke, a US warship sailing into port behind him belied his assertion. In July 1965, he made another trip to Vietnam and held a stormy meeting with US correspondents in Saigon. After disparaging their reporting, he tried to intimidate them. "We'll go around you to your editors," he threatened. "And that's the way we'll get you fellows straightened out." Then, according to CBS correspondent Morley Safer, Sylvester "put his thumbs in his ears, bulged his eyes, stuck out his tongue and wiggled his fingers." For good measure, he blurted out, "Look, if you think that any American official is going to tell you the truth, you're stupid." Barry Zorthian, the chief of US information activities in Vietnam and the leading proponent of maximum candor, bemoaned the damage that Sylvester had done. But as the United States went to war in Vietnam, relations between the news media and public affairs officials were strained.[6]

They only got worse after a sensational report by Safer on the "CBS Evening News." "This is what the war in Vietnam is all about," Safer declared as he accompanied US marines into the village of Cam Ne on August 3 1965. The marines encountered hostile fire, but their search of the village yielded just one elderly prisoner. The only known fatality was a child, the victim of a marine bullet. Safer reported that a marine had confided that his unit had orders to destroy Cam Ne. The film showed one marine using a cigarette lighter and another a flame thrower to set fire to thatched huts. "One hundred fifty homes were leveled in retaliation for a burst of gunfire," hardly the way, Safer concluded, to convince a peasant that "we are on his side."[7]

The report infuriated Johnson. CBS, he insisted, was "out to get us." He telephoned his friend Frank Stanton, the president of CBS, early one morning and began a diatribe by sneering that CBS had provided him with a breakfast of "shit on a shingle." The president believed that Safer had "Communist ties," but investigations showed only that he was a Canadian. Yet lack of US citizenship, in the eyes of the president and some of his aides, was itself damning. "We will never eliminate the irresponsible and prejudiced coverage of men like Peter Arnett [a New Zealander working for the Associated Press] and Morris Safer [sic], men who do not have the basic American interest at heart," wrote White House aide Bill Moyers to the president. "But we will try to tighten things up." Sylvester urged the replacement of Safer with an American correspondent who could provide a "balanced account of controversial situations," but CBS News President Fred Friendly refused to yield to the pressure.[8]

Administration officials recognized, however, that their problems were greater than one reporter or one story. Sylvester recommended alerting US troops to "the press problem," so that there would be fewer opportunities for reporters to film dramatic scenes like those at Cam Ne. Others, though, said that US forces had "to get used to fighting in the open." Chester Cooper, a member of the National Security Council staff, maintained that the most important issue was not public relations but how to fight the war so that military operations did not alienate the Vietnamese people. The upshot of these discussions, though, was not a reconsideration of the effectiveness of search and destroy operations. Instead, the Johnson administration counted on finding ways "to build the necessary understanding" of US involvement in this "new kind of 'twilight' war." Doing so included meetings with network executives and editors to explain US policy and to press for sympathetic reporting; leaking information to friendly reporters; and renewed efforts to improve the briefings for correspondents in Saigon.[9]

Despite the administration's concern about "poisonous reporting" by "immature correspondents," several prominent TV journalists expressed support for the president's Vietnam policies. Television reporters often referred to "our" soldiers or ships, even though Robert Northshield, the executive producer of the "Huntley–Brinkley Report," stated that such language turned the networks into "a government propaganda arm." TV journalists did not wish to compromise their integrity; they tried to report fully and effectively within the limits of daily programs that provided, after commercials and credits, only twenty-two minutes for news. But like the majority of Americans, many backed the US war effort. Walter Cronkite, the anchor of the "CBS Evening News," visited Vietnam in July/August 1965 and was "impressed with our effort," so much so that he was embarrassed by the "rude challenges" of "younger reporters" to the briefers at the Five O'clock Follies. ABC commentator and, later, coanchor, Howard K. Smith, defended administration Vietnam policies in speeches on college campuses and in an evening broadcast in July 1966 in which he concluded, "It is entirely good what we're doing." Chet Huntley, the coanchor of NBC's "Huntley–Brinkley Report," protested that his reputation as a hawk was undeserved. Still, he insisted in February 1966 that "there is no alternative in Vietnam to fighting it out," while stepping up US efforts to strengthen the effectiveness of the Saigon government. David Brinkley, the other half of the NBC team, recalled that he "despised" the Vietnam War and "said so night after night after night." Yet despite his opposition, Brinkley did not express his reservations frequently or consistently in 1965/66.[10] Indeed, only on rare occasions as US troops poured into Vietnam did network TV journalists question Johnson's decision to fight.[11]

Much of the coverage of the US war effort on the network evening newscasts during 1965/66 was actually quite favorable. Many stories emphasized the scale of the US war effort, the sophistication of American technology, and the power and mobility of troops. Typical was NBC correspondent Jack Perkins's story about the First Air Cavalry Division, which arrived in South Vietnam in September 1965. Jack Perkins described the unit as "completely portable" so that it could easily move around the country in helicopters and "fight the war it was designed for." Five months later, Perkins filed another story in which he stated that the division had indeed compiled a "remarkable record of success" at killing the soldiers of the National Liberation Front (NLF). Even more notable was the record "kill ratio" of forty-three to one that the 173d Airborne Brigade established in March 1966 during Operation Silver City. "It was like one of these old John Wayne Indian movies," a battalion commander told viewers of the "CBS Evening News" in terms they could find both familiar and reassuring. "We were in a circle; they just kept charging; they just kept getting killed." Sometimes the evening newscasts showed that Americans were not just doing well but also doing good. After a film report in January 1966 about US troops evacuating the residents of a Catholic orphanage in NLF territory, Huntley explained that the purpose of the story was not "to show what swell guys Americans are but to try remember what men are and what children are and what war is." Whether or not they were "swell guys," administration officials usually enjoyed deferential treatment on the evening newscasts as they explained US policies. Long before the seven-second sound bite became a staple of TV news, Johnson, Secretary of State Dean Rusk, and Secretary of Defense Robert S. McNamara could count on the evening newscasts showing uninterrupted excerpts as long as one to two minutes from press conferences, speeches, or major statements.[12]

Critics of the war hardly fared as well. In books about media coverage of the antiwar movement, Todd Gitlin and Melvin Small have shown that reporters concentrated on the number of demonstrators or their appearance, rather than the arguments they made against US involvement in Vietnam.[13] But the coverage could vary, with establishment figures, such as antiwar senators, often getting significant opportunities to express their dissent. Radical critics got treatment that was far more brusque, as in NBC's report in March 1966 about the National Coordinating Committee to End the War in Vietnam. After meeting with NLF representatives in Budapest, committee chair Frank Emspach insisted that the United States had intervened in a civil war with poison gas and "biological" weapons. Huntley scornfully dismissed Emspach's allegations. If the charges about US methods of warfare were true, Huntley sneered, then all western reporters and diplomats in Vietnam "must be stupid, blind, naive, or downright liars." Rarely did an anchor express personal conclusions with such vehemence.[14]

For Huntley and for others, legitimate controversy over the war could occur only within narrow limits. The president agreed. Repeatedly Johnson alleged that critics of the war were Communists or that their dissent played into Hanoi's hands. As opposition to the war increased, so did the president's suspicions. "Most of the protests are Communist-led," he told *Time* correspondent Hugh Sidey. When CBS White House correspondent Robert Pierpoint suggested a halt in the bombing of North Vietnam as a step toward peace talks, Johnson replied, "You're a member of that Communist conspiracy." After a demonstration at the Pentagon in October 1967, Johnson said that the FBI had discovered that "a substantial number" of the protesters who burned their draft cards "were crazy people" who had been "in mental institutions." Johnson said he "did not want to be like a McCarthyite," referring to the extreme Red-baiting of Wisconsin Senator Joseph R. McCarthy in the early 1950s. "But this country is in a little more danger than we think."[15]

While much of the TV coverage showed a tide of US successes in Vietnam during 1965/6, there were troubling undercurrents. Large-scale operations sometimes failed to produce commensurate results. A succession of reports concluded that US traps "snapped close on thin air," that the enemy fled before GIs could engage them, and that firepower was displacing or – worse – killing civilians. ABC's Lou Cioffi summarized a major, continuing problem when he explained in October 1965 that "the United States has brought in a fantastic amount of military power here in Vietnam. But so far we've not been able to figure just exactly how to use it effectively in order to destroy the Vietcong."[16] Persistent difficulties also bedeviled programs to pacify villages and hamlets, and there was a "gap between promise and performance." Cronkite informed viewers in February 1966 that US officials had set a modest goal – just 14 percent of the South Vietnamese people living in secure locations by the end of the year. But there was no pacification plan for the displaced villagers of Kim Son, uprooted in early 1966 by Operation Eagle's Claw. "Their misery, their sickness, their fear all are shared by other villagers all over Vietnam," declared CBS's Laurence. "And until pacification really begins, these children and their children will suffer the same wartime fate as their fathers and grandfathers."[17]

Taken together these reports did not suggest that US forces were losing the war or that victory was beyond their grasp. But these stories made clear that the war would be long, difficult, and costly. At the end of 1965, ABC's Malcolm Browne even predicted that it might take twenty-five years to prevail over the North Vietnamese and the NLF.[18]

Also disturbing were TV's occasional glimpses of the horrors of the conflict in Vietnam. In a war against an elusive enemy, camera operators only infrequently filmed heavy fighting. But graphic scenes often did not make the final cut because editors in New York were keenly aware that their programs aired at the dinner hour. When CBS obtained film of GIs cutting off the ears of a dead NLF soldier, there was an intense debate about how much to show. The report that viewers saw in October 1967 did not contain footage of the actual mutilation, although correspondent Don Webster still described it as "appalling." Even though editors made decisions on the basis of their "queasy quotient," as *CBS Evening News* senior producer Sanford Socolow called it, some film could still be quite unsettling. In December 1965, for example,

NBC showed a story about Michael R. Yunck, a marine colonel with a severe leg wound. Speaking of his shattered limb as doctors prepared to operate, Yunck said, "I know, I know there's not much left because I was carrying that damn thing in my hands all the way back. I was afraid the whole damn thing was going to come off." Doctors had to amputate Yunck's leg, and NBC carefully trimmed the film so that viewers could not see his wound or the surgery. "The only decision was how much we could stand," explained NBC's Northshield. Surely, the film approached the limit. Other reports showed the brutality of war without being ghastly, as when CBS carried a story in September 1965 about Vietnamese civilians scavenging for food in a US marine garbage dump that contained live ammunition and another two months later about a widow at Fort Benning, Georgia, holding her baby and tearfully reading one of the last letters from her fallen husband. Such stories aired only occasionally. Yet just counting their frequency fails to consider the emotional power of these harrowing stories.[19]

Johnson recognized the power of television – the news medium that the public considered most reliable – and he took the lead in administration efforts to secure favorable coverage of the US war effort. LBJ watched the news on banks of three monitors in the Oval Office, his White House living quarters, and his Texas ranch. He was so obsessed with the news that he even had three sets installed in his hospital room when he had surgery. The president believed that reporters were "puppets" that responded "to the pull of the most powerful strings." Johnson sometimes tried to manipulate those supposed strings by calling reporters to complain about critical stories, although the frequency of those calls has been exaggerated. Dan Rather estimated that he got between twelve and fifteen such calls during the four years that he covered the Johnson White House. NBC's Brinkley recollected that the president would call about two or three times per month – but never to discuss news stories, only to talk about himself. Johnson was also famous for his "treatment," the unique combination of cajolery and bullying in face-to-face meetings that had made him such an effective Senate majority leader. But the treatment often failed to produce the same results with reporters and editors that it did with wavering legislators. CBS's Pierpoint, for example, got "really angry" when Johnson mentioned his friendship with Frank Stanton in a transparent effort to intimidate. Johnson would sometimes talk to journalists in his bedroom or bathroom. Some reporters found these conversations bizarre. Rather remembered leaving the president's bedroom not thinking about "the substance" of LBJ's comments, but instead wondering about such things as the "eleven bottles of Lavoris . . . , all in various stages of use." Other journalists found that such meetings helped "humanize" a figure who might otherwise seem remote. Brinkley simply reached the conclusion that Johnson was "crude and coarse."[20]

Johnson tried to use appearances on television to win public support for the war, but these efforts also produced disappointing results. "I think television is the medium which will basically establish your reputation, just as radio basically established that of President [Franklin D.] Roosevelt," gushed Robert E. Kintner soon after leaving his position as president of NBC to become a White House advisor. Television, Kintner explained, provided the best way to reach the American people "directly with your own words rather than through editorial interpretation." But rarely was Johnson able to come across as effectively in American living rooms as he did in the Oval Office or on the telephone. Problems with eyeglasses and teleprompters; self-consciousness about a "Texas twang" in his voice; and resentment over invidious comparisons to the cool charm of John F. Kennedy only added to Johnson's uneasiness before the camera. What rankled as well were charges of a credibility gap – the president's use of the media to disseminate optimism, evasions, and half-truths about Vietnam. The American people longed for "statements that we can win in South Vietnam, and not ten years from now," Kintner informed Johnson in mid-1966. But the president could not provide such assurances, even though US troop strength approached 400,000 at the end of the year. By early 1967, polls showed that critics for the first time outnumbered supporters of the president's policies in Vietnam.[21]

Johnson blamed his difficulties on slanted and hostile media coverage. "On NBC today it was all about what we are doing wrong," he told his national security advisors in December 1965. According to LBJ, "nothing was being published to make you hate the Viet Cong; all that is being written is to hate us." Sometimes Johnson accounted for such allegedly unbalanced coverage by insisting that North Vietnam was doing "a far better propaganda job than we do." On other occasions he returned to the theme of Communist subversion. The networks, he told the president of NBC in February 1967, were "infiltrated" and he was "ready to move on them if they move on us." Such outlandish statements indicate that Johnson probably would not have been happy with anything less than what Arthur Sylvester had suggested in that tempestuous meeting of July 1965 – that the media act as the "handmaiden" of administration policy.[22]

By mid-1967, White House officials expressed their discontent about television coverage of the war with new urgency. Once more several of Johnson's top advisors blamed reporters, rather than the harsh realities of the war, for bleak news from Vietnam. The correspondents in Vietnam, the president's aides asserted, were hostile or cynical and their stories distorted. Leonard Marks, the director of the US Information Agency, who had visited Vietnam in July, for example, charged that journalists "are out there to win Pulitzer prizes for sensational articles rather than objective reporting." Secretary of Defense McNamara, also just back from Vietnam, believed that reporters there were in "a very bad mood," that they were skeptical and antagonistic, judgments that McNamara's traveling companions – General Earle G. Wheeler, the chair of the Joint Chiefs of Staff, and Nicholas deB. Katzenbach, the under secretary of state – also shared. Katzenbach maintained that too many correspondents had "been out there too long," while Marks insisted that the reporters were too young and lacked "in-depth background about what has taken place in Vietnam."[23]

The theme in the reporting that most troubled Johnson and his principal aides during the summer of 1967 was that the war was a stalemate. The most influential expression of this view came in a front-page article in the *New York Times* on August 7, by R. W. Apple, Jr., the newspaper's Saigon bureau chief. "The war [was] not going well," according to "most disinterested observers" to whom Apple spoke.

Enemy military forces were now larger than ever; only a small portion of South Vietnam was secure; without US troops, the South Vietnamese government "would almost certainly crumble within months." "Victory is not close at hand," Apple concluded. "It may be beyond reach."[24]

Only a day after the publication of Apple's article, Walter Cronkite declared on the "CBS Evening News" that there was "no evidence of any dramatic progress in the war." A film report then followed in which correspondent Bert Quint found many of the same problems as had Apple–that US officers spoke far more pessimistically in private than in public, that in this war of attrition it was difficult to know which side would wear out first.[25] Quint said that high-level denials of stalemate rang hollow, denials that all three major network newscasts had carried during the past month and that McNamara, Wheeler, and General William C. Westmoreland, the US commander, had repeated emphatically in high-level meetings.[26] Yet the sources on which Apple, Quint, and other reporters relied included generals who did not share the official optimism. These reporters also may have been picking up on some of the president's own rhetoric, as Johnson had called the Vietnam War "a bloody impasse" in his Memorial Day proclamation.[27]

The news reports about stalemate in Vietnam came at a time when Johnson could no longer afford such criticism. Polls revealed in August that only one-third of the US public supported Johnson's handling of the war and only 39 percent approved of his overall performance as president.[28] Ordinary Americans paid a price for the war, as casualties mounted, draft calls increased, the budget deficit deepened, inflation crept upward, spending on Great Society programs diminished, and the administration and Congress discussed a tax increase. Prominent critics – both hawks and doves – assailed Johnson's war policies on Capitol Hill. Senator Ernest Hollings (Dem.–SC) told Walt W. Rostow, the president's assistant for national security affairs, that he was worried about continuing Senate support for Johnson's war policies. Hollings said the mood in the Senate was "affected by stories of the Marines getting ambushed in the DMZ . . . and a general feeling that we are on a treadmill in Viet Nam." Senate Democrats facing reelection confronted increasing pressure to break with Johnson because of popular discontent with the war. "Every political advisor I have says the only way I can save myself is by attacking the President," confided Joseph Tydings of Maryland. "I won't do that, but it's going to be tough."[29]

Johnson was keenly aware of the magnitude of his problems. In a talk to a group of educators, he admitted, "I am in deep trouble." The prospects for 1968 were unsettling, as some polls showed Johnson running behind possible Republican nominees, such as Governor George Romney of Michigan. Johnson even privately expressed doubts about seeking reelection. But whoever the Democratic nominee might be, he would face real difficulty without a change in public attitudes toward the war.[30]

Johnson refused to make major alterations in his Vietnam policies in hope of resolving these problems. During the summer and early fall, he made only incremental changes   an additional 45,000 troops, which was far short of the 200,000 increase that Westmoreland had requested, and the removal of some restrictions on bombing targets in North Vietnam, especially in the vicinity of Hanoi and Haiphong.

But, in the president's view, both massive escalation and a dramatic, unilateral peace initiative, such as a bombing pause, carried unacceptable risks.[31]

Instead, the Johnson administration launched a new public relations offensive aimed at showing that there was no stalemate in the war – that the United States was achieving its goals in Vietnam. "The Administration's greatest weakness was its inability to get over the complete story" on Vietnam, Johnson told ABC reporter Howard K. Smith. The result, he believed, was that the American people were "skeptical, cynical, and – more often than not – uninformed." In mid-August, Johnson approved the creation of a Vietnam Information Group, a task force working closely with the National Security Council that could prepare briefing papers, write speeches, and distribute upbeat reports that administration officials could leak to friendly journalists.[32] The White House also asked Westmoreland, and Ellsworth Bunker, the US ambassador in Saigon, to "search urgently for occasions to present sound evidence of progress in Vietnam . . . [The] President's judgment is that this is at [the] present stage a critically important dimension of fighting the war."[33]

Johnson took the lead in this Progress Campaign. He met with journalists, members of Congress, and various interest groups such as union officials, educators, and business leaders. Repeatedly he said that the war was not stalemated; that official studies demonstrated genuine, measurable progress; that domestic divisions only bolstered Hanoi's hopes that US resolve would wither. Johnson also occasionally read snippets from an historical memorandum to remind visitors that in previous wars "discouragement over prospects for victory" had cut "deep into hope and determination." He admonished his top advisors "to sell our product" and "to get a better story to the American people."[34]

These sales pitches produced varying reactions, as when Johnson spoke to a group of CBS reporters and executives. Harold Kaplan, the head of the Vietnam Information Group, compared meeting this group to venturing into a contested hamlet in South Vietnam – "it was all right for lunch" but "I'm not sure I'd spend the night there." Kaplan suggested that any presentation begin by "telling them why TV coverage of Vietnam is a travesty and a scandal, but then the dialogue gets mellower. . . . With a bit of luck, you can make a few points."[35] The president apparently got lucky. Various members of the CBS delegation considered Johnson's presentation "a monologue – but a fascinating one," "a great experience," and "a wholly new view of the President." "Why can't he do that on television?" one listener asked. But some presidential aides were less enthusiastic. Christian rated the meeting a "B" because Johnson "was too belligerent at first, and the long monologue . . . was a little overpowering."[36] White House counsel Harry McPherson was even more critical. He thought the president had "bullied" a questioner and turned "a pretty receptive occasion into a somber affair." McPherson bluntly faulted Johnson for "the long monologue" which became "a long hard sell." "It just got boring, Mr. President."[37]

More successful were administration efforts to generate favorable television coverage, especially when the Progress Campaign reached its high point in mid-November. Westmoreland and Bunker came to Washington to assure the news media and the public that the war was going well. ABC showed film of the general and the president strolling in the Rose Garden followed by McNamara's statement that Westmoreland was one of the century's greatest military commanders. The administration arranged for a joint appearance of the general and the ambassador on NBC's "Meet the Press" and for Westmoreland to speak at the National Press Club. "We have reached the point when the end begins to come into view," the general declared hopefully. All three networks emphasized the good news that he expected the South Vietnamese to take over a larger share of the fighting, which would allow a reduction of US combat forces within the next two years.[38] Johnson reinforced the message of progress during a press conference that was one of his most effective performances on television. Using a lapel microphone that allowed him to move around easily, Johnson vigorously denounced the "storm trooper" tactics of irresponsible protesters, while expressing confidence that US forces would bring home "an honorable peace." "That was the real Lyndon Johnson," exclaimed *Time*'s Sidey, "who only a few of us have seen too rarely."[39]

In their meetings, Westmoreland and Johnson concentrated on how to continue the Progress Campaign. After all, as Rostow reminded the president, the "main front" of the war was "here in the U.S." and was "primarily affected by what the Saigon press corps and TV crews file." Westmoreland – the military commander – returned to Saigon with an extensive agenda of public relations initiatives. Absolutely essential was "an improved image" for the Saigon government through "appropriate publicity" for an "anticorruption campaign" and through vigorous and effective South Vietnamese military operations that could take "center stage." Also important was reducing anxiety about heavy US casualties, since many of the wounded were "only scratched," and "improving the credibility of [enemy] body count reports." An increase in US visitors to Saigon, Johnson and his top advisors hoped, would create new emissaries of progress on the home front. Westmoreland and Bunker also planned a regular "TV report to the nation," but the White House dropped the idea when the networks balked at providing air time for news programming they did not produce and could not control.[40] Together these measures placed the emphasis on visible progress – improvement that the visual medium of television could cover and that the American people could easily understand.

Yet fighting in Vietnam – a "savage" battle at Dak To as NBC anchor Chet Huntley described it – undercut the administration's emphasis on progress. Three weeks of intense combat against North Vietnamese troops dug into jungle slopes and mountains reached a climax while Westmoreland was in Washington. US soldiers paid a fearful price, as Dean Brelis reported from Hill 882. "Look at my leg," screamed one horribly wounded GI. "There's nothing left." Far from the battlefield, Westmoreland asserted that US mobility was helping to grind down enemy strength and achieve victory. CBS juxtaposed Westmoreland's confidence with correspondent Murray Fromson's "on-the-scene" skepticism about whether the North Vietnamese, "who had put themselves back in the headlines and on the minds of many Americans who are weary of the war," were really losers. ABC correspondent Ed Needham's wrap-up report after the North Vietnamese had abandoned Hill 875 was filled with "unhappy scenes," since Dak To had claimed more US lives than any previous battle in the war. "It was a hard fight," Needham concluded as the film showed a helmet on the ground with a hole ripped through it. "It hardly seems worth it."[41]

Despite the carnage at Dak To, the Progress Campaign paid some dividends by mid-December. Polls showed that half the American people believed that the United States was making progress in Vietnam, while only a third thought it was "standing still" – a reversal of public sentiment since the end of July. Support for Johnson's handling of the war rebounded to 38 percent, although 49 percent still disapproved. Doubts about the wisdom of US involvement deepened, however, as public opinion was almost evenly divided – 45 to 46 percent – about whether it had been a mistake to send US combat forces to Vietnam. Those who approved of Johnson's overall performance in office outnumbered those who were dissatisfied, 46–41 percent. Yet the measures of the president's popularity did not rise until after Westmoreland came home and pointed to light at the end of the tunnel.[42] What most people wanted – what the Johnson administration led them to expect – was good news from Vietnam, steady progress that would soon make possible disengagement from the war.[43]

Yet as 1967 came to a close, TV news programs carried stories that suggested that such progress would come neither easily nor steadily. Correspondent John Laurence visited a refugee camp to check on the villagers from Dai Lac, whose relocation from an area controlled by the NLF the CBS Evening News had covered a month earlier. The South Vietnamese government had promised an improved life away from the NLF, but the refugees were struggling to survive. They had been living in tents for a month, and they had not gotten any rations for ten days. Corruption, bureaucratic rigidity, and indifference prevented the refugees from obtaining the government identification cards necessary to secure emergency assistance. Ambassador Bunker toured the camp and said help would arrive shortly, but none had. The US refugee advisor could not cut through the red tape to provide food. Laurence then interviewed Vice President Nguyen Cao Ky, who maintained that such problems did not occur. The problem was slowly solving itself, Laurence concluded, as all but a small portion of the 6,500 refugees had left the camp either for cities or for what remained of their village. Surely, this was no way to win hearts and minds.[44]

While most reports emphasized the high quality of US fighting forces, there were some indications in late 1967 that drugs were threatening combat effectiveness. Laurence declared that American soldiers were "tuning in to the pleasures of smoking pot," which was readily available, as film of him making a purchase in Saigon demonstrated. One soldier, who obviously inhaled, explained that "you can actually see hallucinations out there" or "go against your own men, if you're out in the field." A few weeks later, Vietnam veteran John Steinbeck IV estimated that 75 percent of GIs smoked marijuana. NBC correspondent John Chancellor, who covered Steinbeck's press conference, noted that the Pentagon insisted that less than one percent of uniformed forces got high. Laurence explained the increasing use of marijuana not as a response to the strains of the war or a symptom of deteriorating discipline, but an indication of the wiliness of the enemy. "The Communists are battling American troops not only with fire power, but with drugs," Cronkite declared in his introduction to Laurence's report. US intelligence, Laurence explained, had determined that the NLF largely controlled marijuana sales to GIs.[45]

The most comprehensive assessment of the war by a TV correspondent came from ABC's Roger Peterson, who filed a highly skeptical report at the end of his assignment in Vietnam in November 1967. "I leave Vietnam with the feeling there will never be enough time" to achieve sufficient progress, Peterson declared, if events kept moving "at the [current] snail-like pace." Pacification, he asserted, "continues to stumble along," and "it might take a decade or two" for the South Vietnamese Army "to become an effective fighting force." The "stumbling, infantile democracy" in South Vietnam might "look good from 10,000 miles away. But close up . . . it's as corrupt and inefficient as its predecessors." The solution, Peterson insisted, was for the US officials to "stop saying please" and "demand a return for the money and blood spent over here." So while there was "more light in the tunnel," Peterson concluded, "the end still seems several years away."[46]

As Peterson's report suggested, the Johnson administration, despite its ambitious Progress Campaign, could control neither the news from Vietnam nor the war itself. The Progress Campaign brought some modest, short-term gains. But the appearance – and illusions – of progress vanished quickly, dramatically, and painfully when the Tet Offensive began at the end of January 1968.

"What the hell is going on," asked a bewildered Walter Cronkite after learning of a powerful wave of North Vietnamese and NLF assaults throughout South Vietnam that coincided with the lunar new year holiday of Tet. "I thought we were winning the war." Many viewers must have felt similar consternation as they watched television news reports of military police fighting off an attack on the grounds of the US embassy in Saigon. During the next few days, the networks carried a flurry of stories that showed South Vietnam under "hard, desperate, communist attack." Damaged US aircraft littered the air base at Danang, where the NLF took the war into the city for the first time. South Vietnamese troops were so busy trying to expel a North Vietnamese regiment from Ban Me Thuot, NBC's Wilson Hall said, that they had not even counted the dead. At Nam O, terrified civilians rushed from their homes to escape the deadly crossfire. Saigon was "a city besieged," where fires and air strikes sent columns of smoke into the air. Correspondents emphasized the unprecedented, astonishing, and frightening sights of Saigon – tanks in the streets, fighter aircraft hitting targets in residential neighborhoods, refugees who had come to the city to escape the war fleeing once again. The normal routines of the city had come to a halt; only the coffin makers were open for business, ABC reported.[47]

The nasty street fighting in Saigon produced the most spectacular image of violence during Tet. A startling photograph of the incident appeared on the front page of many US newspapers, and on the evening of February 2 1968, millions of television viewers saw stunning film of the same event. "Government troops were ordered to get as much revenge as they could," declared Howard Tuckner, NBC's reporter in Saigon. After scenes of skirmishing around the An Quang Pagoda, the film showed a prisoner, wearing a plaid shirt and shorts, walking in the custody of South Vietnamese marines. "The chief of South Vietnam's National Police Force, Brigadier General Nguyen Ngoc Loan, was waiting for him." Tuckner said no more. Loan waved his pistol, pointed it at the prisoner's head, and fired. The photograph in the newspapers captured the moment of death; the film provided additional, excruciating glimpses of the corpse with blood draining from the skull. "Rough justice on a Saigon street" is how NBC's John Chancellor described the execution. But reactions varied with the viewer. "Although his public relations leave a lot to be desired," Rostow wrote to the president, "I'm not sure that Loan isn't one of the heroes of the battle thus far."[48]

Television reporters also found harrowing violence and high drama at Hue, where a savage battle persisted long after the first wave of the Tet attacks had receded. US marines advanced from "house to house" and "room to room," enduring "one nasty little firefight after another." "Death is literally just around the corner," observed ABC's Sam Jaffe. At the end of February, the marines finally seized the Citadel, a walled fortress where Vietnamese emperors had once lived. They prevailed, according to CBS's Don Webster, "on the basis of sheer courage."[49]

The network newscasts devoted more attention to Khe Sanh than any other battle during the Tet Offensive. At this remote northern outpost, 6,000 US marines confronted growing isolation, as 20,000 North Vietnamese troops laid siege from the nearby hills. Many film reports concentrated on the uncertainties of daily life for the embattled garrison. What made this drama compelling was the enormous significance that high US officials attached to Khe Sanh. Westmoreland expected the North Vietnamese to seek a decisive battle – one that might equal the victory over the French at Dienbienphu in 1954. Johnson was determined that history not repeat itself. So great was his concern that he got special daily reports from Westmoreland about the situation at Khe Sanh. "It may be the biggest battle of the war, or it may be the biggest bust," CBS correspondent Fromson asserted in mid-February as he questioned whether US officials had sufficient information about enemy intentions. The waiting finally ended in late March. The climactic assault never came, and the North Vietnamese withdrew.[50]

As the Tet Offensive ebbed, television journalists tried to evaluate its significance. The most famous assessment came from Walter Cronkite, who spent a week in Vietnam and offered his conclusions in a remarkable half-hour special on February 27. Once a supporter of the US war effort, Cronkite returned from Vietnam doubtful that victory was possible. Even though they suffered staggering casualties and had relinquished practically all the territory they had seized, the North Vietnamese and NLF, Cronkite found, had succeeded in destroying the illusion of security that existed in the cities and in setting back pacification in the countryside. Cronkite no longer accepted the hopeful predictions of US officials, who found "silver linings" in "the darkest clouds." "To say that we are closer to victory today is to believe, in the face of the evidence, the optimists who have been wrong in the past. To suggest that we are on the edge of defeat is to yield to unreasonable pessimism. To say that we are mired in stalemate seems the only realistic, yet unsatisfactory conclusion." The only solution was disengagement and negotiation, "not as victors but as honorable people who lived up to their pledge to defend democracy and did the best they could."[51]

"If I've lost Cronkite, I've lost the country," the president despaired. Cronkite's advocacy of disengagement did have a significant effect on Johnson, but only because it confirmed the widespread dissatisfaction with the administration's policies. By late February, surveys showed that only 32 percent of the American people endorsed Johnson's handling of the war. Those who thought the United States was making progress had plunged from 51 percent in November 1967 to 32 percent. And for the first time, half – exactly 50 percent – thought it had been a mistake to send US troops to Vietnam. Johnson also lost the backing of the Wise Men – an informal advisory panel of establishment figures – who informed him in late March that "we can no longer do the job we set out to do in the time we have left and we must begin to take steps to disengage." "We have no support for the war," the beleaguered president complained. When he finally spoke to the nation on television on March 31 – his first address on the war since the beginning of the Tet Offensive – he announced a partial bombing halt of North Vietnam, called for negotiations, and declared that he would not seek another term as president. His presidency had become the latest casualty of the Vietnam War.[52]

Johnson once more complained bitterly about television coverage of the war. He only hinted at his dissatisfaction when he spoke to the National Association of Broadcasters on the morning after his withdrawal from the presidential campaign. "As I sat in my office last evening, waiting to speak, I thought of the many times each week when television brings the war into the American home." No one, Johnson asserted, could know "exactly what effect those vivid scenes have on American opinion," and historians could "only guess" at the influence television might have had during crises in earlier wars. Still, the president's implied but unmistakable conclusion was that television was somehow responsible for the collapse of popular support for his administration's war policies. Johnson took the criticism of his policies and his leadership quite personally. In what CBS correspondent Pierpoint described as "a bitter and moody" monologue aboard Air Force One in early May 1968, Johnson made this astounding assertion: "The only difference between Kennedy's assassination and mine is that mine's a live one – a little more torturous."[53]

The Nixon administration went even further than its predecessor in blaming the television networks for US problems in Vietnam. President Richard M. Nixon believed that he faced unprecedented antipathy from news reporters, editors, and executives. He directed White House aides to monitor the daily news telecasts; prepare summaries that would alert him to unfair coverage; and maintain lists of journalists ranked according to their friendliness toward the administration that could be used in allocating favors, such as invitations to White House social events, or for inflicting retaliation, such as exclusion from all sources of White House information other than routine press handouts. Believing that he was a master of electronic communication, Nixon relied heavily on televised speeches to appeal directly to what he called the "silent majority," patriotic citizens who supported his Vietnam policies. At the same time, Vice President Spiro T. Agnew tried to mobilize public opposition to the networks by charging that they were under the control of Eastern, liberal elites, who deliberately gave the news an anti-Nixon slant. Nixon thought that he had shrewdly shifted credibility problems from the White House to the networks. Public relations, in which television had a central role, became a critical accompaniment to war-related political, military, and diplomatic strategies, as the Nixon White House emphasized the image of a resolute president surmounting antiwar critics and hostile news media in his quest for "peace with honor" in Vietnam.[54]

The Johnson–Nixon argument that television coverage played a critical, even decisive, role in undermining US public support for the war has not persuaded many authorities on the news media. There is no detailed, systematic information, such as public opinion polls, that might indicate how viewers reacted to coverage of the war on the evening news. Without such data, one media critic, Michael Arlen, has suggested that TV reporting actually made the violence of the war less shocking, as viewers became accustomed, night after night, to the brutality of Vietnam. Other scholars, such as Daniel Hallin, have shown that criticism of the war increased on TV newscasts as opposition to war expanded among mainstream figures, such as members of Congress. Hallin and others have also pointed out that public opinion turned against Johnson's handling of the war during 1965–7, when television reporting was most favorable to administration policies. Their conclusion is that Johnson and Nixon have exaggerated or misunderstood the effects of TV news in shaping public attitudes toward the Vietnam War.[55]

Yet it is equally a mistake to discount or dismiss TV news. Johnson and his aides were clearly worried about television coverage of the war. They shaped policies to counteract what they considered to be critical, unfair, and sensational reporting. TV coverage of Tet was spectacular and unsettling, both for viewers who had become accustomed to the misleading optimism of the Progress Campaign and for top government officials, who recognized the damage to their credibility. White House counsel Harry McPherson recalled that during the Tet Offensive he was "more persuaded by what . . . [he] saw on the tube" than the confidential information that came from official sources. On the eve of his speech withdrawing from the presidential race, Johnson insisted that no president could govern effectively in the face of opposition from the major news media.[56] Public relations had been a critical part of Johnson's management of the war effort since the commitment of US combat forces in 1965. But as popular support for the administration's Vietnam policies crumbled and then collapsed, the president thought that his problem was that he had failed to win the war on television. McPherson, however, understood that the real problem was with the war that television showed.

NOTES

1 Notes, president's meeting with Australian broadcast group, September 20 1967, Folder "Sept. 1967 – Meetings with Correspondents," Box 3, Meeting Notes File, Lyndon B. Johnson Library, Austin, Texas (hereafter LBJL); report by Schoumacher, CBS, September 19 1967, A113, Assistant Secretary of Defense for Public Affairs, Record Group 330, National Archives, College Park, Maryland (hereafter DOD Weekly News Summary).

2 Author interview with George Christian, August 25 1999; memo, Panzer to President, October 21 1967, Folder October 1967, Box 398, Office Files of Fred Panzer, LBJL.

3 Notes, meeting with Saigon advisers, November 21 1967, Tom Johnson's Notes of Meetings (hereafter TJ Notes), Box 1, LBJL.

4 Notes, president's meeting with 16 foreign editors, October 11 1967, Box 1, TJ Notes.

5 Barry Zorthian Oral History Interview, I: 7, LBJL; Hammond (1988), 145; Pach (1994), 92.

6 Zorthian Oral History Interview, II: 3–8; Martin Gershen, "The 'right to lie,'" *Columbia Journalism Review* 5 (Winter 1966/67): 14–16; Morley Safer, "Television Covers the

War," reprinted in US Congress, Senate, Committee on Foreign Relations, *News Policies in Vietnam*, Hearings, August 17 and 31 1966, 89th cong, 2d. sess., 92; author interviews with John Rich, February 23 2000, and with Jack Perkins, February 24 2000.

7   Report by Safer, CBS, TV-6412.2, Museum of Broadcast Communications, Chicago, Illinois (hereafter MBC).

8   Zorthian Oral History Interview, II: 8; memo, Rather to Reedy, n.d.; and memo, Moyers to president, n.d., both in Folder Aug. 1–15, 1965, Box 9, Handwriting File, LBJL; Hammond (1988), 188–91; Morley Safer, *Flashbacks: On Returning to Vietnam* (New York: Random House, 1990), 88–97; Pach (1994), 103.

9   Memo of conversation, August 10 1965, *Foreign Relations of the United States, 1964–1968*, vol. 3: *Vietnam: June–December 1965* (Washington, DC: Government Printing Office, 1996), 322–5; Dallek (1998), 286–8.

10   Alfred E. Kroeger, "Vietnam: Television's Cruelest Test," *Television* 23 (May 1966): 26; Walter Cronkite, *A Reporter's Life* (New York: Alfred A. Knopf, 1997), 249–52; Howard K. Smith, *Events Leading Up to My Death: The Life of a Twentieth-Century Reporter* (New York: St. Martin's, 1996), 325–9; memo, Cater to President, May 14 1965, Folder Douglas Cater Memos [1 of 2], Reference File – Vietnam, Box 1, LBJL; "ABC Scope: The Vietnam War," Part 34, "Howard K. Smith, One Man's Opinion," July 16 1966, TV 1505.1, MBC; Chet Huntley Oral History, 10, LBJL; Huntley, "Emphasis" script, February 3 1966, Folder 11, Box 11, Papers of Chet Huntley, State Historical Society of Wisconsin, Madison, Wisconsin (hereafter SHSW); author interview with David Brinkley, February 22 2000.

11   "Vietnam: December 1965," NBC, December 20 1965.

12   Reports by Perkins, NBC, September 13 1965, A6, and February 24 1966, A29; comments by Huntley, NBC, January 24 1966, A25; report by Laurence, CBS, March 22 1966, A33, all in DOD Weekly News Summary.

13   Gitlin (1980); Small (1994).

14   Report by Matney and comments by Huntley, NBC, March 25 1966, A34, DOD Weekly News Summary.

15   Hallin (1986), 116–18; Dallek (1998), 286–8, 467; author interview with Robert Pierpoint, October 1 1999; notes, meeting with Democratic leadership, October 31 1967, Folder October 31 1987, Box 81, Diary Backup, LBJL.

16   Report by Cioffi, ABC, October 14 1965, A10; report by Browne, ABC, October 8 1965, A10; report by Perkins, NBC, January 20 1966, A24; report by Nessen, NBC, March 8 1966, A31, all in DOD Weekly News Summary.

17   Report by Cioffi, ABC, February 11 1966, A28; comments by Cronkite, CBS, February 14 1966, A28; report by Collingwood, CBS, February 21 1966, A29; report by Laurence, CBS, February 23 1966, A29; report by Brelis, NBC, June 30 1966, A47; and comments by Cronkite, CBS, October 14 1966, A63, all in ibid.

18   Report by Browne, ABC, November 23 1965, A16, ibid.

19   Pach (1994), 94–5; David Farber, *The Age of Great Dreams: America in the 1960s* (New York: Hill and Wang, 1994), 154–5; Kroeger, "Vietnam: Television's Cruelest War," 24–6; report by Laurence, CBS, September 14 1965, A6; report by Cronkite, CBS, November 24 1965, A16; and report by Webster, CBS, October 9 1967, A116, all in DOD Weekly News Summary.

20   Burns W. Roper, "Emerging Profiles of Television and Other Mass Media: Public Attitudes, 1959–1967," copy in Folder Television, Box 421, Panzer Files; Kearns (1976), 7, 245–6; Culbert (1981), 214, 219, 222; Dan Rather Oral History, 25–6, 40–1, LBJL; author interview with Pierpoint; author interview with Brinkley.

21 Memo, Kintner to President, April 27 1966, Folder Chronological, Apr. 1966 A–Z, Box 1; memo, Kintner to President, May 30 1966, Folder Memos 5/20/66–5/31/66, Box 7, both in Office Files of Robert E. Kintner, LBJL; Huntley Oral History, 17; Turner (1985), 176; Braestrup (1977), 1: 700.

22 Notes of meeting in Cabinet Room, December 17 1965, Box 1, Meeting Notes File; LBJL; Safer, "Television Covers the War," 91.

23 Notes, meeting of the president with Rusk, McNamara, Rostow, and Christian, July 12 1967; and notes, meeting of the president with McNamara, July 12 1967, both in Box 1, TJ Notes.

24 *New York Times*, August 7 1967.

25 Remarks by Cronkite and report by Quint, CBS, August 8 1967, A107, DOD Weekly News Summary.

26 See, for example, Morton interview with McNamara, CBS, July 6 1967, A102; remarks by Jennings, ABC, and by Brinkley, NBC, both July 7 1967; remarks by Brinkley and report by Burrington, NBC, July 10 1967; remarks by Reasoner, CBS, and Reynolds, ABC, both July 12 1967, all in A103, ibid. For denials of stalemate in high-level meetings, see, for example, notes, meeting of the president with Rusk, McNamara, Rostow, Christian, and Johnson, July 12 1967; notes, president's meeting with McNamara, Wheeler, Westmoreland, and Christian, July 13 1967; and notes, president's meeting with the Cabinet, July 19 1967, all in Box 1, TJ Notes.

27 *Public Papers of the Presidents of the United States: Lyndon B. Johnson, 1967*, 2 vols. (Washington, DC: GPO, 1968), 1: 554–5.

28 Table, "Public Approval of LBJ's Handling of the War...," October 5 1967, Folder October 1967, Box 398, Panzer Files; Braestrup (1977), 1: 700.

29 Memo, McPherson to President, August 25 1967, Folder Memoranda for the President 1967 (2), Box 53, Office Files of Harry McPherson, LBJL; memo, Rostow to president, August 1 1967, Folder vol. 37 [2 of 2], Box 20, Memos to the President, National Security File (hereafter NSF), LBJL.

30 Notes, president's meeting with educators from Cambridge, Massachusetts, colleges and universities, September 26 1967; and notes, president's meeting with Rusk, McNamara, Rostow, Helms, and Christian, October 3 1967, both in Box 1, TJ Notes; George H. Gallup, *The Gallup Poll: Public Opinion, 1935–1971*, 3 vols. (New York: Random House, 1972), 3: 2076.

31 Buzzanco (1996), 294–9; Dallek (1998), 470–9.

32 Notes, meeting between president and Smith, March 31 1967, Folder Notes on Meetings – President, 1967, Box 1, Papers of George Christian, LBJL; memo, Tom Johnson to Christian, August 15 1967, PR 18, Confidential File, Box 83, White House Central Files, LBJL; memo, Christian to President, August 22 1967, Folder August 1967 [4 of 5], Box 24, Handwriting File.

33 Berman (1989), 84–5.

34 Notes, president's meeting with McNamara, Rusk, Rostow, and Christian, October 4 1967; notes, president's meeting with Bunker, Rusk, McNamara, Wheeler, Helms, Rostow, and Christian, November 15 1967; notes, meeting with Saigon advisers, November 21 1967, all in Box 1, TJ Notes.

35 Memo, Kaplan to Rostow et al., October 31 1967, Folder Classified (1 of 2), Box 12, Christian Papers.

36 Memos, Maguire to president, November 3 1967; Rostow to Markham, November 4 1967; and Christian to president, November 4 1967, all in Folder November 2 1967, Box 81, Diary Backup.

37 Memo, McPherson to president, November 4 1967, Folder Memoranda for the President 1967 (1), Box 53, McPherson Files.

38 Remarks by Cronkite, CBS; and report by Gill, ABC, both November 16 1967, A121; remarks by Brinkley, NBC, and by Cronkite, CBS, both, November 21 1967, A122; DOD Weekly News Summary; "Radio–TV Defense Dialog," November 18–19 1967, Folder 3 – Radio–TV Defense Dialog, Jul.–Dec. 1967, Papers of Robert Goralski, WSHS.

39 Letter, Sidey to President, November 17 1967, Folder November 1967 [4 of 4], Box 26, Handwriting File; memo, Fleming to President, November 17 1967, Folder Network Pool II, Box 4, Christian Papers; *Public Papers, 1967*, 2: 1058–49; Turner (1985), 204–5.

40 Memo for record, November 22 1967, Folder 25 (History File) II, Box 14, Papers of William C. Westmoreland, LBJL.

41 Remarks by Huntley, NBC, November 20 1967; report by Brelis, NBC, November 21 1967; interview with Westmoreland and report by Fromson, CBS, November 21 1967, all in A122; and report by Needham, ABC, November 24 1967, A123, all in DOD Weekly News Summary.

42 Indeed, Johnson's polls ratings on Vietnam and his overall handling of his job reached new lows in late October, according to public opinion surveys by Louis Harris. Memorandum, Panzer to President, November 11 1967, Folder November 1967, Box 398, Panzer Files.

43 Braestrup (1977) 1: 695, 700; Gallup, *The Gallup Poll*, 3: 2074, 2075, 2078, 2091, 2096; Dallek (1998), 499; Pach (1998), 61–2.

44 Reports by Laurence, CBS, December 23 1967 and December 26 1967, A127, DOD Weekly News Summary.

45 Remarks by Cronkite and report by Laurence, CBS, November 29 1967, A123; and report by Chancellor, NBC, December 27 1967, A127, ibid.

46 Report by Peterson, ABC, November 27 1967, A123, ibid.

47 Report by Syvertsen, January 30, CBS; comment by Brinkley, February 1 1968, NBC; report by Nessen, February 1 1968, NBC; report by Syvertsen, February 1 1968, CBS; report by Tuckner, February 1 1968, NBC; report by Webster, February 1 1968, all in A132, ibid; report by Webster, February 2 1968, CBS; report by Hall, February 2 1968, NBC; report by Peterson, February 2 1968, ABC, anchor comments, February 2 1968, ABC, all in A133, ibid; Oberdorfer (1971), 158; Pach (1994), 107–8. For a thorough study of television reporting on the Tet Offensive, see Pach (1998), and for an abridged version, see Pach (1999). The author wishes to thank the German Historical Institute and *South Central Review* for permission to reproduce material from those articles.

48 Remarks by Chancellor, February 1 1968, NBC, A132; comments by Huntley and report by Tuckner, February 2 1968, NBC; and report by Peterson, February 2 1968, ABC, all in A133, DOD Weekly News Summary; George A. Bailey and Lawrence W. Lichty, "Rough Justice on a Saigon Street: A Gatekeeper Study of NBC's Tet Execution Film," *Journalism Quarterly* 49 (Summer 1972): 221–9, 238; memo, Rostow to president, February 8 1968, Folder vol. 60 [2 of 2], Box 28, Memos to the President, NSF.

49 Report by Laurence, CBS, February 5 1968; A133; report by Webster, CBS, February 7 1968, A133; report by Gralnick, CBS, February 19 1968, A135; and report by Jaffe, ABC, February 21 1968, A135, all in DOD Weekly News Summary.

50 Peter Brush, "The Battle of Khe Sanh, 1968," in *The Tet Offensive*, ed. Marc Jason Gilbert and William Head (Westport, CT: Greenwood, 1996), 192–5; report by Fromson, CBS, February 16 1968, A135, DOD Weekly News Summary.

51 "Who, What, When, Where, Why: Report from Vietnam by Walter Cronkite, CBS, February 27 1968, A596, Museum of Television and Radio, New York, NY.

52   Braestrup (1977), 1: 693, 695, 698–9; Richard Immerman, "'A Time in the Tide of Men's Affairs': Lyndon Johnson and Vietnam," in *Lyndon Johnson Confronts the World: American Foreign Policy, 1963–1968*, ed. Warren I. Cohen and Nancy Bernkopf Tucker (New York: Cambridge University Press, 1994), 78–9; *Public Papers of the Presidents of the United States: Lyndon B. Johnson, 1968–69*, 2 vols. (Washington, DC: Government Printing Office, 1970), 1: 469–76.
53   *Public Papers, 1968–69*, 1: 482–6; notes, Air Force One to Independence, May 5 1968, Folder 12, Box 6, Papers of Robert Pierpoint, WSHS.
54   Small (1999), 59–95; Kimball (1998), 1–15.
55   Arlen (1982); Hallin (1986), 211–15; Wyatt (1993).
56   Culbert (1981) 239–40; Randall Bennett Woods, LBJ, Politics, and 1968," *South Central Review* 16–17 (1999–2000): 21–2.

FURTHER READING

Arlen, Michael 1982: *Living-Room War*. New York: Penguin Books.

Berman, Larry 1989: *Lyndon Johnson's War: The Road to Stalemate in Vietnam*. New York: Oxford University Press.

Braestrup, Peter 1977: *Big Story: How the American Press and Television Reported and Interpreted the Crisis of Tet 1968 in Vietnam and Washington*. 2 vols. Boulder, CO: Westview Press.

Buzzanco, Robert 1996: *Masters of War: Military Dissent and Politics in the Vietnam Era*. New York: Cambridge University Press.

Culbert, David 1981: "Johnson and the Media," *Exploring the Johnson Years*, ed. Robert A. Divine. Austin: University of Texas Press, 214–48.

Dallek, Robert 1998: *Flawed Giant: Lyndon Johnson and His Times, 1961–1973*. New York: Oxford University Press.

Gitlin, Todd 1980: *The Whole World Is Watching: Mass Media in the Making and Unmaking of the New Left*. Berkeley: University of California Press.

Hallin, Daniel C. 1986: *The "Uncensored War": The Media and Vietnam*. New York: Oxford University Press.

Hammond, William M. 1988: *Public Affairs: The Military and the Media, 1962–1968*. Washington, DC: Center of Military History, United States Army.

Hammond, William M. 1996: *Public Affairs: The Military and the Media, 1968–1973*. Washington, DC: Center of Military History, United States Army.

Kearns, Doris 1976: *Lyndon Johnson and the American Dream*. New York: Harper and Row.

Kimball, Jeffrey 1998: *Nixon's Vietnam War*. Lawrence: University Press of Kansas.

Oberdorfer, Don 1984: *Tet!* New York: Da Capo.

Pach, Chester J. Jr. 1994: "And that's the way it was: The Vietnam War on the network nightly news," *The Sixties: From Memory to History*, ed. David Farber. Chapel Hill: University of North Carolina Press, 90–118.

Pach, Chester J. Jr. 1998: "Tet on TV: U.S. nightly news reporting and presidential policy making," *1968: The World Transformed*, ed. Carole Fink, Philipp Gassert, Detlef Junker. New York: Cambridge University Press, 55–81.

Pach, Chester J. Jr. 1999–2000: "TV's 1968: war, politics, and violence on the network evening news, *South Central Review*, 16–17: 29–42.

Small, Melvin 1999: *The Presidency of Richard Nixon*. Lawrence: University Press of Kansas.

Turner, Kathleen J. 1985: *Lyndon Johnson's Dual War: Vietnam and the Press.* Chicago: University of Chicago Press.

Wyatt, Clarence 1993: *Paper Soldiers: The American Press and the Vietnam War.* New York: W. W. Norton and Company.

Select Bibliography

AMY E. BLACKWELL

Acheson, Dean. *Present at the Creation: My Years at the State Department.* New York: W. W. Norton, 1969.

Adams, Sam. *War of Numbers: An Intelligence Memoir.* South Royalton, Vt.: Steerforth Press, 1994.

Addington, Larry. *America's War in Vietnam: A Short Narrative History.* Bloomington: Indiana University Press, 2000.

Aitken, Jonathan. *Nixon: A Life.* Washington, DC: Regnery, 1993.

Aliano, Richard. *American Defense Policy from Eisenhower to Kennedy: The Politics of Changing Military Requirements, 1957–1961.* Athens: Ohio University Press, 1975.

Allen, Douglas, and Ngo Vinh Long, eds. *Coming to Terms: Indochina, the United States, and the War.* Boulder, Colo.: Westview Press, 1991.

Allison, Graham. *Essence of Decision.* Boston: Little, Brown, 1971.

Ambrose, Stephen. *Eisenhower: The President.* New York: Simon & Schuster, 1984.

——. *Nixon.* 3 vols. New York: Simon & Schuster, 1987–1991.

Ambrose, Stephen, and James Alden Barber, eds. *The Military and American Society.* New York: Free Press, 1972.

Anderson, David. *Trapped by Success: The Eisenhower Administration and Vietnam, 1953–1961.* New York: Columbia University Press, 1991.

——. *Roots of War: The Men and Institutions Behind U.S. Foreign Policy.* New York: Atheneum, 1972.

Anderson, David L., ed. *Facing My Lai: Moving Beyond the Massacre.* Lawrence: University Press of Kansas, 1998.

——. ed. *Shadow on the White House: Presidents and the Vietnam War, 1945–1975.* Lawrence: University Press of Kansas, 1993.

Andradé, Dale. *Trial by Fire.* New York: Hippocrene, 1995.

Andrews, William R. *The Village War: Vietnamese Communist Revolutionary Activities in Dinh Tuong Province, 1960–1964.* Columbia: University of Missouri Press, 1973.

Angers, Trent. *The Forgotten Hero of My Lai: The Hugh Thompson Story.* Lafayette, La.: Acadian House, 1999.

Appy, Christian. *Working-Class War.* Chapel Hill: University of North Carolina Press, 1993.

Arnold, James R. *The First Domino: Eisenhower, the Military, and America's Intervention in Vietnam.* New York: Morrow, 1991.

Asprey, Robert. *War in the Shadows: The Guerrilla in History.* 2 vols. Garden City, NY: Doubleday, 1975.

Bacevich, A. J. *The Pentomic Era: The U. S. Army Between Korea and Vietnam.* Washington, DC: National Defense University, 1986.

Baker, Mark. *Nam: The Vietnam War in the Words of the Men and Women Who Fought There.* New York: Morrow, 1981.

Ball, George. *The Past Has Another Pattern.* New York: W. W. Norton, 1982.

Ballard, Jack S. *Development and Employment of Fixed-Wing Gunships, 1962–1972.* Washington, DC: US Office of Air Force History, 1982.

Baritz, Loren. *Backfire: A History of How American Culture Led Us into Vietnam and Made Us Fight the Way We Did.* New York: Morrow, 1985.

Barnet, Richard. *The Economy of Death.* New York: Atheneum, 1970.

Barrett, David M. *Uncertain Warriors: Lyndon Johnson and His Vietnam Advisers.* Lawrence: University Press of Kansas, 1993.

Bates, Milton J. *The Wars We Took to Vietnam: Cultural Conflict and Storytelling.* Berkeley: University of California Press, 1996.

Bator, Victor. *Vietnam: A Diplomatic Tragedy.* Dobbs Ferry, NY: Oceana Publications, 1965.

BDM Corporation. *A Study of Strategic Lessons Learned in Vietnam.* McLean, Va.: BDM Corporation, 1980.

Beattie, Keith. *The Scar That Binds: American Culture and the Vietnam War.* New York: New York University Press, 1998.

Becker, Elizabeth. *America's Vietnam War: A Narrative History.* New York: Clarion, 1992.

Bergerud, Eric. *The Dynamics of Defeat: The Vietnam War in Hau Nghia Province.* Boulder, Colo.: Westview Press, 1991.

Berman, Larry. *Planning a Tragedy: The Americanization of the War in Vietnam.* New York: W. W. Norton, 1982.

——. *Lyndon Johnson's War: The Road to Stalemate in Vietnam.* New York: W. W. Norton, 1989.

Berman, William C. *William Fulbright and the Vietnam War.* Kent, Ohio: Kent State University Press, 1988.

Bernstein, Irving. *Guns or Butter? The Presidency of Lyndon Johnson.* New York: Oxford University Press, 1995.

Beschloss, Michael R., ed. *Taking Charge: The Johnson White House Tapes, 1963–1964.* New York: Simon & Schuster, 1997.

Betts, Richard K. *Soldiers, Statesmen, and Cold War Crises.* Cambridge, Mass.: Harvard University Press, 1971.

Bibby, Michael, ed. *The Vietnam War and Postmodernity.* Amherst: University of Massachusetts Press, 2000.

Biggs, Bradley. *Gavin.* Hamden, Conn.: Archon Books, 1980.

Billings-Yun, Melanie. *Decision Against War.* New York: Columbia University Press, 1988.

Bilton, Michael, and Kevin Sim. *Four Hours in My Lai.* New York: Viking, 1992.

Blaufarb, Douglas. *The Counterinsurgency Era: U.S. Doctrine and Performance.* New York: Free Press, 1977.

Bloodworth, Denis. *An Eye for the Dragon: Southeast Asia Observed 1954–1970.* New York: Farrar, Straus, and Giroux, 1970.

Blum, Robert. *Drawing the Line: The Origin of the American Containment Policy in East Asia.* New York: W. W. Norton, 1982.

Bodard, Lucien. *The Quicksand War: Prelude to Vietnam.* London: Faber & Faber, 1967.

Boettcher, Thomas. *Vietnam: The Valor and the Sorrow.* Boston: Little, Brown, 1985.

Borer, Douglas. *A Superpower Defeated: Vietnam and Afghanistan Compared.* London: Frank Cass, 1999.

Bornet, Vaughan. *The Presidency of Lyndon B. Johnson.* Lawrence: University Press of Kansas, 1983.

Bouscaren, Anthony. *The Last of the Mandarins: Diem of Vietnam.* Pittsburgh, Pa.: Duquesne University Press, 1965.

Bows, Ray. *Vietnam Military Lore: Legends, Shadows and Heroes.* Hanover, Mass.: Bows & Sons, 1998.

Boyle, Richard. *Flower of the Dragon: The Breakdown of the U.S. Army in Vietnam.* San Francisco: Ramparts Press, 1972.

Bradford, Zeb B., and Frederic J. Brown. *The United States Army in Transition.* Beverly Hills, Calif.: Sage Publications, 1973.

Bradley, Mark Philip. *Imagining Vietnam and America: The Making of Postcolonial Vietnam, 1919–1950.* Chapel Hill: University of North Carolina Press, 2000.

Braestrup, Peter. *Big Story: How the American Press and Television Reported and Interpreted the Crisis of Tet 1968 in Vietnam and Washington.* 2 vols. Boulder, Colo.: Westview Press, 1977.

——. ed. *Vietnam as History: Ten Years After the Paris Peace Accords.* Washington, DC: University Press of America, 1983.

Brandon, Henry. *The Retreat of American Power.* New York: Doubleday, 1974.

Brigham, Robert K. *Guerrilla Diplomacy: The NLF's Foreign Relations and the Viet Nam War.* Ithaca, NY: Cornell University Press, 1998.

Brodie, Bernard. *War and Politics.* New York: Macmillan, 1974.

Brown, T. Louise. *War and Aftermath in Vietnam.* New York: Routledge, 1991.

Brown, Weldon A. *Prelude to Disaster: The American Role in Vietnam, 1940–1963.* Port Washington, NY: Kennikat Press, 1975.

——. *The Last Chopper: The Denouement of the American Role in Vietnam, 1963–1975.* Port Washington, NY: Kennikat Press, 1976.

Browne, Malcolm. *The New Face of War.* Indianapolis: Bobbs-Merrill, 1965.

Buckingham, William A., Jr. *Operation Ranch Hand: The Air Force and Herbicides in Southeast Asia, 1961–1971.* Washington, DC: US Office of Air Force History, 1982.

Burchett, Wilfred. *Grasshoppers and Elephants: Why Vietnam Fell.* New York: Urizen Books, 1977.

Burke, John P., and Fred I. Greenstein. *How Presidents Test Reality: Decisions on Vietnam 1954 and 1965.* New York: Russell Sage Foundation, 1989.

Burkett, B. G., and Glenna Whitley. *Stolen Valor: How the Vietnam Generation Was Robbed of Its Heroes and Its History.* Dallas, Tex.: Verity Press, 1998.

Butler, David. *The Fall of Saigon.* New York: Dell, 1985.

Buttinger, Joseph. *The Smaller Dragon: A Political History of Vietnam.* New York: Praeger, 1958.

——. *Vietnam: A Dragon Embattled.* 2 vols. New York: Praeger, 1967.

——. *A Dragon Defiant: A Short History of Vietnam.* New York: Praeger, 1972.

——. *Vietnam: The Unforgettable Tragedy.* New York: Horizon Books, 1977.

Buzzanco, Robert. *Masters of War: Military Dissent and Politics in the Vietnam Era.* New York: Cambridge University Press, 1996.

——. *Vietnam and the Transformation of American Life.* Malden, Mass.: Blackwell Publishers, 1999.

Cable, James. *The Geneva Conference of 1954 on Indochina.* New York: St. Martin's, 1986.

Cable, Larry E. *Conflict of Myths: The Development of American Counterinsurgency Doctrine and the Vietnam War*. New York: New York University Press, 1988.

——. *Unholy Grail: The US and the Wars in Vietnam, 1965–8*. New York: Routledge, 1991.

Caldwell, Malcolm, and Lek Tan. *Cambodia in the Southeast Asian War*. New York: Monthly Review Press, 1973.

Califano, Joseph A., Jr. *The Triumph and Tragedy of Lyndon Johnson: The White House Years*. New York: Simon & Schuster, 1991.

Campagna, Anthony S. *The Economic Consequences of the Vietnam War*. Westport, Conn.: Praeger, 1991.

Cao Van Vien. *The Final Collapse*. Washington, DC: Government Printing Office, 1983.

Capps, Walter H. *The Unfinished War: Vietnam and the American Conscience*. Boston: Beacon Press, 1982.

Castle, Timothy N. *At War in the Shadow of Vietnam: U.S. Military Aid to the Royal Lao Government, 1955–1975*. New York: Columbia University Press, 1993.

——. *One Day Too Long: Top Secret Site 85 and the Bombing of North Vietnam*. New York: Columbia University Press, 1999.

Chaffard, Georges. *Les deux guerres du Vietnam: de Valluy à Westmoreland*. Paris: La Table Ronde, 1969.

Chandler, Robert W. *War of Ideas: The U.S. Propaganda Campaign in Vietnam*. Boulder, Colo.: Westview Press, 1981.

Charlton, Michael, and Anthony Moncrief. *Many Reasons Why: The American Involvement in Vietnam*. New York: Hill and Wang, 1978.

Chester, Lewis, Godfrey Hodgson, and Bruce Page. *An American Melodrama*. New York: Viking, 1969.

Chomsky, Noam. *American Power and the New Mandarins: Historical and Political Essays*. New York: Vintage, 1969.

——. *At War With Asia: Essays on Indochina*. New York: Random House, 1970.

——. *Towards a New Cold War: Essays on the Current Crisis and How We Got There*. New York: Pantheon, 1982.

——. *Year 501: The Conquest Continues*. Boston: South End Press, 1992.

——. *Rethinking Camelot: JFK, the Vietnam War, and U. S. Political Culture*. Boston: South End Press, 1993.

Chong, Denise. *The Girl in the Picture: The Story of Kim Phuc, the Photograph, and the Vietnam War*. New York: Viking, 2000.

Clarke, Jeffrey. *Advice and Support: The Final Years of the U. S. Army in Vietnam*. Washington, DC: United States Army Center of Military History, 1988.

Clifford, Clark, with Richard Holbrooke. *Counsel to the President: A Memoir*. New York: Random House, 1991.

Clodfelter, Mark. *The Limits of Air Power: The American Bombing of North Vietnam*. New York: Free Press, 1989.

Cobb, William W., Jr. *The American Foundation Myth in Vietnam: Reigning Paradigms and Raining Bombs*. Lanham, Md.: University Press of America, 1998.

Cohen, Warren I. *Dean Rusk*. Totawa, NJ: Cooper Square Publishers, 1980.

Cohen, Warren I., and Nancy B. Tucker. *Lyndon B. Johnson Confronts the World: American Foreign Policy, 1963–1968*. New York: Cambridge University Press, 1994.

Colbert, Evelyn. *International Politics in Southeast Asia, 1941–1954*. Ithaca, NY: Cornell University Press, 1977.

Colby, William, and Peter Forbath. *Honorable Men*. New York: Simon & Schuster, 1978.

Colby, William, with James McCargar. *Lost Victory*. New York: Contemporary Books, 1989.

Collins, J. Lawton. *Lightning Joe: An Autobiography.* Baton Rouge: Louisiana State University Press, 1979.

Collins, James Lawton, Jr. *The Development and Training of the South Vietnamese Army, 1950–1972.* Washington, DC: Department of the Army, 1975.

Colodny, Len, and Robert Gettlin. *Silent Coup: The Removal of a President.* New York: St. Martin's Press, 1991.

Committee of Concerned Asian Scholars. *The Indochina Story.* New York: Pantheon, 1970.

Conference on the History of Vietnam. *Some Lessons and Non-Lessons of Vietnam: Ten Years After the Paris Peace Accords.* Washington, DC: Woodrow Wilson International Center for Scholars, 1973.

Congressional Research Service. *The U.S. Government and the Vietnam War: Executive and Legislative Roles and Relationships, Part I: 1945–1961.* Prepared for the Committee on Foreign Relations, United States Senate. Washington, DC: Government Printing Office, 1984.

——. *The U.S. Government and the Vietnam War: Executive and Legislative Roles and Relationships, Part II: 1961–1964.* Prepared for the Committee on Foreign Relations, United States Senate. Washington, DC: Government Printing Office, 1984.

Cooper, Chester. *The Lost Crusade: America in Vietnam.* New York: Dodd, Mead, 1970.

Corson, William. *The Betrayal.* New York: Ace Books, 1968.

Cortright, David. *Soldiers in Revolt: The American Military Today.* Garden City, NY: Doubleday, 1975.

Currey, Cecil B. *Self-Destruction: The Disintegration and Decay of the United States Army during the Vietnam Era.* New York: W. W. Norton, 1981.

——. *Edward Lansdale: The Unquiet American.* Boston: Houghton Mifflin, 1988.

——. *Long Binh Jail: An Oral History of Vietnam's Notorious U.S. Military Prison.* Washington, DC: Brassey's, 1999.

Dallek, Robert. *Flawed Giant: Lyndon Johnson and His Times 1961–1973.* New York: Oxford University Press, 1998.

Davidson, Phillip B. *Secrets of the Vietnam War.* Novato, Calif.: Presidio Press, 1990.

——. *Vietnam at War: The History, 1946–1975.* Novato, Calif.: Presidio Press, 1988.

Dawson, Alan. *55 Days: The Fall of South Vietnam.* Englewood Cliffs, NJ: Prentice-Hall, 1977.

DeBennedetti, Charles. *The Peace Reform in American History.* Bloomington: Indiana University Press, 1980.

DeBennedetti, Charles, and Charles Chatfield. *An American Ordeal: The Antiwar Movement of the Vietnam Era.* Syracuse, NY: Syracuse University Press, 1990.

DeForest, Orrin, and David Chanoff. *Slow Burn: The Rise and Bitter Fall of American Intelligence in Vietnam.* New York: Simon & Schuster, 1990.

DeGroot, Gerald J. *A Noble Cause?* London: Longman, 1999.

Deitchman, Seymour J. *The Best-Laid Schemes: A Tale of Social Research and Bureaucracy.* Cambridge, Mass.: MIT Press, 1976.

Dellinger, David. *Vietnam Reconsidered: Covert Action to Invasion to Reconstruction.* Boston: South End Press, 1986.

DiLeo, David L. *George Ball, Vietnam, and the Rethinking of Containment.* Chapel Hill: University of North Carolina Press, 1991.

Divine, Robert A. *Eisenhower and the Cold War.* New York: Oxford University Press, 1981.

——. ed. *Exploring the Johnson Years.* Austin: University of Texas Press, 1981.

Donovan, James. *Militarism U.S.A.* New York: Scribner's, 1970.

Downs, Frederick. *The Killing Zone: My Life in the Vietnam War.* New York: Norton, 1978.

Drachman, Edward R. *United States Policy Toward Vietnam, 1940–1945.* Rutherford, NJ: Farleigh Dickinson, 1970.

Duffy, Dan. ed. *Informed Dissent: Three Generals and the Vietnam War, Essays by Robert Buzzanco and Asad Ismi.* Chevy Chase, Md.: Vietnam Generation/Burning Cities Press, 1992.

Duiker, William J. *The Communist Road to Power in Vietnam.* Boulder, Colo.: Westview, 1981.

——. *Vietnam: Nation in Revolution.* Boulder, Colo.: Westview, 1983.

——. *Sacred War: Nationalism and Revolution in a Divided Vietnam.* New York: McGraw-Hill, 1995.

——. *Ho Chi Minh.* New York: Hyperion, 2000.

Dunn, Peter M. *The First Vietnam War.* London: C. Hurst & Co., 1985.

Eckhardt, George. *Command and Control, 1950–1969.* Washington, DC: Department of the Army, 1974.

Edelman, Bernard, ed. *Dear America: Letters Home from Vietnam.* New York: Norton, 1985.

Edmonds, Anthony O. *The War in Vietnam.* Westport, Conn.: Greenwood, 1998.

Eisenhower, Dwight. *The White House Years: Mandate for Change, 1953–1956.* Garden City, NY: Doubleday, 1963.

——. *The White House Years: Waging Peace, 1956–1961.* Garden City, NY: Doubleday, 1965.

Elliott, David. *The Vietnamese War: Revolution and Social Change in the Mekong Delta.* Armonk, NY: M. E. Sharpe, 2000.

Ellsberg, Daniel. *Papers on the War.* New York: Simon & Schuster, 1972.

Ely, John Hart. *War and Responsibility: Constitutional Lessons of Vietnam and its Aftermath.* Princeton: Princeton University Press, 1993.

Emerson, Gloria. *Winners and Losers: Battles, Retreats, Gains, Losses, and Ruins from a Long War.* New York: Random House, 1976.

Enthoven, Alain, and K. Wayne Smith. *How Much Is Enough? Shaping the Defense Program, 1961–1969.* New York: Harper & Row, 1971.

Ernst, John P. *Forging a Fateful Alliance: Michigan State University and the Vietnam War.* East Lansing: Michigan State University Press, 1998.

Errington, Elizabeth Jane, and B. J. C. McKercher, eds. *The Vietnam War as History.* New York: Praeger, 1990.

Esper, George, and The Associated Press. *The Eyewitness History of the Vietnam War, 1961–1975.* New York: Ballantine, 1983.

Evans, Rowland, Jr. and Robert D. Novak. *Nixon in the White House.* New York: Random House, 1971.

Falk, Richard A, ed. *The Vietnam War and International Law.* 4 vols. Princeton: Princeton University Press, 1967–76.

Fall, Bernard B. *Viet-Nam Witness, 1953–66.* New York: Praeger, 1966.

——. *Hell in a Very Small Place: The Siege of Dien Bien Phu.* Philadelphia: Lippincott, 1967.

——. *Last Reflections on a War.* New York: Doubleday, 1967.

——. *The Two Vietnams: A Political and Military Analysis.* New York: Praeger, 1967.

——. *Street Without Joy.* Harrisburg, Pa.: Stackpole Co., 1963. Reprint, Mechanicsburg, Pa.: Stackpole Books, 1994.

Fifield, Russell H. *Southeast Asia in United States Policy.* New York: Praeger, 1963.

——. *Americans in Southeast Asia: The Roots of Commitment.* New York: Crowell, 1973.

FitzGerald, Frances. *Fire in the Lake: The Vietnamese and the Americans in Vietnam.* New York: Random House, 1972.

Flood, Charles Bracelen. *The War of the Innocents.* New York: McGraw Hill, 1970.

Foner, Philip S. *U. S. Labor and the Vietnam War.* New York: International Publishers Co., 1989.

Ford, Ronnie E. *Tet 1968: Understanding the Surprise.* London: Frank Cass, 1995.

Fox, Roger. *Air Base Defense in the Republic of Vietnam, 1961–1973.* Washington, DC: Office of Air Force History, 1979.

Franklin, H. Bruce. *M. I. A., or Mythmaking in America.* New Brunswick, NJ: Rutgers University Press, 1993.

——, ed. *The Vietnam War: In American Stories, Songs, and Poems.* Boston: Bedford/St.Martin's, 1996.

——. *Vietnam and Other American Fantasies.* Amherst: University of Massachusetts Press, 2000.

Freedman, Lawrence. *Kennedy's Wars: Berlin, Cuba, Laos, and Vietnam.* New York: Oxford University Press, 2000.

Fulbright, J. William. *The Arrogance of Power.* New York: Random House, 1966.

——. *The Price of Empire.* New York: Pantheon Books, 1989.

Futrell, Robert. *The United States Air Force in Southeast Asia: The Advisory Years to 1965.* Washington, DC: Office of Air Force History, 1981.

Gaddis, John. *Strategies of Containment: A Critical Appraisal of Postwar National Security Policy.* New York: Oxford University Press, 1982.

Galbraith, John Kenneth. *Ambassador's Journal: A Personal Account of the Kennedy Years.* Boston: Houghton Mifflin, 1969.

——. *How To Control the Military.* New York: Signet, 1969.

Galloway, John. *The Gulf of Tonkin Resolution.* Rutherford, NJ: Farleigh Dickinson University Press, 1970.

Gallucci, Robert L. *Neither Peace Nor Honor: The Politics of American Military Policy in Vietnam.* Baltimore, Md.: Johns Hopkins University Press, 1975.

Gardner, Lloyd. *Approaching Vietnam: From World War II through Dienbienphu, 1941–1954.* New York: W. W. Norton, 1988.

——. *Pay Any Price: Lyndon Johnson and the Wars for Vietnam.* Chicago: I. R. Dee, 1995.

Garthhoff, Raymond. *Détente and Confrontation: American–Soviet Relations from Nixon to Reagan.* Washington, DC: Brookings Institution, 1985.

Gavin, James. *War and Peace in the Space Age.* New York: Harper and Row, 1958.

——. *Crisis Now.* New York: Random House, 1968.

Gelb, Leslie, and Richard Betts. *The Irony of Vietnam: The System Worked.* Washington, DC: Brookings Institution, 1979.

Gettleman, Marvin. et al., eds. *Vietnam and America: A Documented History.* New York: Grove Press, 1985.

Geyelin, Philip. *Lyndon B. Johnson and the World.* New York: F. A. Praeger, 1966.

Gibbons, William Conrad. *The U. S. Government and the Vietnam War: Executive and Legislative Roles and Relationships.* Princeton: Princeton University Press, 1986.

Gibson, James. *The Perfect War: The War We Couldn't Lose and How We Did.* New York: Vintage, 1988.

Giglio, James N. *The Presidency of John F. Kennedy.* Lawrence: University Press of Kansas, 1991.

Gilbert, Marc Jason, and William Head, eds. *The Tet Offensive.* Westport, Conn.: Praeger, 1996.

Gilbert, Marc Jason, ed. *The Vietnam War: Teaching Approaches and Resources.* Westport, Conn.: Greenwood, 1991.

Goff, Stanley, and Robert Sanders. *Brothers: Black Soldiers in the Nam.* Ed. by Clark Smith. Novato, Calif.: Presidio Press, 1982.

Goldman, Peter, and Tony Fuller, with Richard Manning, et al. *Charlie Company: What Vietnam Did to Us*. New York: Morrow, 1983.

Goodman, Allan. *Politics in War: The Bases of Political Community in South Vietnam*. Cambridge, Mass.: Harvard University Press, 1973.

———. *The Lost Peace*. Stanford, Calif.: Hoover Institute Press, 1978.

Goscha, Christopher E. *Thailand and the Southeast Asian Networks of the Vietnamese Revolution, 1885–1954*. London: Curzon Press, 1999.

Goulden, Joseph C. *Truth Is the First Casualty: The Gulf of Tonkin Affair Illusion and Reality*. Chicago: Rand McNally, 1969.

Graff, Henry F. *The Tuesday Cabinet: Deliberation and Decision on Peace and War Under Lyndon B. Johnson*. Englewood Cliffs, NJ: Prentice-Hall, 1970.

Greene, Bob. *Homecoming: When the Soldiers Returned from Vietnam*. New York: Putnam, 1989.

Gregory, Barry. *The Vietnam War*. 12 vols. Freeport, NY: Marshall Cavendish, 1988.

Griffen, William L., and John Marciano. *Lessons of the Vietnam War: A Critical Examination of School Texts and an Interpretive Comparative History Utilizing the Pentagon Papers and Other Documents*. Lanham, Md.: Rowman & Littlefield, 1979.

Gurtov, Melvin. *The First Vietnam Crisis: Chinese Communist Strategy and United States Involvement, 1953–1954*. New York: Columbia University Press, 1967. Reprint, Westport, Conn.: Greenwood Press, 1985.

Haines, Harry, ed. *GI Resistance: Soldiers and Veterans against the War*. Special issue of *Viet Nam Generation* 2, no. 1 (1990).

Halberstam, David. *The Making of a Quagmire*. New York: Random House, 1965.

———. *The Best and the Brightest*. New York: Fawcett Crest, 1972.

Haldeman, H. R., and Joseph DiMona. *The Ends of Power*. New York: Times Books, 1978.

Haley, P. Edward. *Congress and the Fall of South Vietnam and Cambodia*. Rutherford, NJ: Fairleigh Dickinson University Press, 1982.

Hall, Mitchell K. *Because of Their Faith: CALCAV and Religious Opposition to the Vietnam War*. New York: Columbia University Press, 1990.

Hallin, Daniel C. *The Uncensored War: The Media and Vietnam*. New York: Oxford University Press, 1986.

Halperin, Morton. *Bureaucratic Politics and Foreign Policy*. Washington, DC: Brookings Institution, 1974.

Hamilton-Paterson, James. *The Greedy War*. New York: McKay, 1972.

Hammel, Eric. *Khe Sanh, Siege in the Clouds: An Oral History*. New York: Crown, 1989.

———. *Fire in the Streets: The Battle for Hue, Tet 1968*. Chicago: Contemporary Books, 1991.

Hammer, Ellen. *The Struggle for Indochina*. Expanded ed. Stanford, Calif.: Stanford University Press, 1966.

———. *A Death in November: America in Vietnam, 1963*. New York: E. P. Dutton, 1987.

Hammond, William M. *Public Affairs: The Military and the Media, 1962–1968*. Washington, DC: United States Army Center of Military History, 1988.

Harrison, James. *The Endless War: Vietnam's Struggle for Independence*. New York: McGraw-Hill, 1983.

Hasford, Gustav. *The Short-Timers*. New York: Harper & Row, 1979.

Hassler, Alfred. *Saigon, USA*. New York: Richard W. Baron, 1970.

Hatcher, Patrick Lloyd. *The Suicide of an Elite: American Internationalists and Vietnam*. Stanford, Calif.: Stanford University Press, 1990.

Hayes, Samuel P., ed. *The Beginning of American Aid to Southeast Asia: The Griffin Mission of 1950*. Lexington, Mass.: D. C. Heath & Co., 1971.

Hearden, Patrick J. ed. *Vietnam: Four American Perspectives: Lectures.* West Lafayette, Ind.: Purdue University Press, 1990.

——. *The Tragedy of Vietnam.* New York: Harper Collins, 1991.

Heath, Jim F. *Decade of Disillusionment: The Kennedy–Johnson Years.* Bloomington: Indiana University Press, 1975.

Heineman, Kenneth H. *Campus Wars: The Peace Movement at American State Universities in the Vietnam Era.* New York: New York University Press, 1994.

Hellman, John. *American Myth and the Legacy of Vietnam.* New York: Columbia University Press, 1986.

Henden, Herbert, and Ann P. Haas. *Wounds of War: The Psychological Aftermath of Combat in Vietnam.* New York: Basic Books, 1985.

Hennessy, Michael A. *Strategy in Vietnam: The Marines and Revolutionary Warfare in I Corps, 1965–1972.* New York: Praeger, 1997.

Herman, Edward, and Noam Chomsky. *Manufacturing Consent: The Political Economy of the Mass Media.* New York: Pantheon, 1988.

Herring, George C. *America's Longest War: The United States and Vietnam, 1950–1975.* 2d ed. New York: McGraw-Hill, 1986.

——. *LBJ and Vietnam: A Different Kind of War.* Austin: University of Texas Press, 1994.

——. ed. *The Secret Diplomacy of the Vietnam War: The Negotiating Volumes of the Pentagon Papers.* Austin: University of Texas Press, 1983.

Herrington, Stuart A. *Peace with Honor? An American Reports on Vietnam, 1973–1975.* Novato, Calif.: Presidio Press, 1983.

Hersh, Seymour M. *My Lai 4: A Report on the Massacre and its Aftermath.* New York: Random House, 1970.

——. *Cover-Up.* New York: Random House, 1972.

——. *The Price of Power: Kissinger in the Nixon White House.* New York: Summit Books, 1983.

Herz, Martin F. *The Prestige Press and the Christmas Bombing.* Washington DC: Ethics and Public Policy Center, 1980.

——. *The Vietnam War in Retrospect.* Lanham, Md.: University Press of America, 1984.

Hess, Gary R. *The United States' Emergence as a Southeast Asian Power, 1940–1950.* New York: Columbia University Press, 1987.

——. *Vietnam and the United States: Origins and Legacy of War.* Boston: Twayne, 1990.

Hewes, James E., Jr. *From Root to McNamara: Army Organization and Administration, 1900–1963.* Washington, DC: Department of the Army, 1975.

Hickey, Gerald C. *Village in Vietnam.* New Haven, Conn.: Yale University Press, 1964.

Higgins, Hugh. *Vietnam.* 2nd ed. Exeter, NH: Heinemann Educational Books, 1982.

Hilsman, Roger. *To Move a Nation: The Politics of Foreign Policy in the Administration of John F. Kennedy.* Garden City, NY: Doubleday, 1967.

Hodgkin, Thomas L. *Vietnam: The Revolutionary Path.* New York: St. Martin's Press, 1981.

Holm, Tom. *Strong Hearts, Wounded Souls: Native American Veterans of the Vietnam War.* Austin: University of Texas Press, 1996.

Holsti, Ole, and James N. Rosenau. *American Leadership in World Affairs: Vietnam and the Breakdown of Consensus.* Boston: Allen & Unwin, 1984.

Hooper, Edwin, et al. *The United States Navy and the Vietnam Conflict: The Setting of the Stage to 1959.* Washington, DC: Naval History Division, Dept. of the Navy, 1976.

Hoopes, Townsend. *The Devil and John Foster Dulles.* Boston: Little, Brown, 1973.

——. *The Limits of Intervention.* New York: David McKay, 1973.

Hosmer, Stephen T., et al. *The Fall of South Vietnam.* Boston: Allen & Unwin, 1984.

Hull, Roger H., and John C. Novogrod. *Law and Vietnam*. Dobbs Ferry, NY: Oceana, 1968.

Hunt, Richard A. *Pacification: The American Struggle for Vietnam's Hearts and Minds*. Boulder, Colo.: Westview Press, 1995.

Hunt, Richard A., and Richard H. Shultz, Jr. *Lessons from an Unconventional War: Reassessing U. S. Strategies for Future Conflicts*. New York: Pergamon Press, 1981.

Iriye, Akira, and Yonosuke Nagai. eds. *The Origins of the Cold War in Asia*. New York: Columbia University Press, 1977.

Irving, Ronald E. M. *The First Indochina War: French and American Policy, 1945–54*. London: Croom Helm Ltd., 1975.

Isaacs, Arnold R. *Without Honor: Defeat in Vietnam and Cambodia*. Baltimore, Md.: Johns Hopkins University Press, 1983.

———. *Vietnam Shadows: The War, Its Ghosts, and Its Legacy*. Baltimore, Md.: Johns Hopkins University Press, 1997.

Isaacson, Walter. *Kissinger: A Biography*. New York: Simon & Schuster, 1992.

Isserman, Maurice, and Michael Kazin. *America Divided: The Civil War of the 1960s*. New York: Oxford University Press, 1999.

Jamieson, Neil L. *Understanding Vietnam*. Berkeley: University of California Press, 1993.

Jeffords, Susan. *The Remasculinization of America: Gender and the Vietnam War*. Bloomington: Indiana University Press, 1989.

Joes, Anthony James. *The War for South Viet Nam, 1954–1975*. Revised ed. Westport, Conn.: Praeger, 2001.

Johnson, Chalmers. *Autopsy on People's War*. Berkeley: University of California Press, 1973.

Johnson, Harold K. *Challenge: Compendium of Army Accomplishments: A Report by the Chief of Staff, July 1964–April 1968*. Washington, DC: Department of the Army, 1968.

Johnson, Lyndon. *The Vantage Points: Perspectives of the Presidency, 1963–1969*. New York: Holt, Rinehart & Winston, 1971.

Joseph, Paul. *Cracks in the Empire: State Politics in the Vietnam War*. Boston: South End Press, 1981.

Jurika, Stephen, Jr. ed. *From Pearl Harbor to Vietnam: The Memoirs of Admiral Arthur W. Radford*. Stanford, Calif.: Hoover Institution Press, 1980.

Kahin, George McT. *Intervention: How America Became Involved in Vietnam*. Garden City, NY: Doubleday, 1987.

Kahin, George McT., and John Lewis. *The United States in Vietnam*. New York: Delta, 1969.

Kaiser, David. *American Tragedy: Kennedy, Johnson, and the Origins of the Vietnam War*. Cambridge, Mass.: Belknap Press of Harvard University Press, 2000.

Kalb, Marvin, and Bernard Kalb. *Kissinger*. Boston: Little, Brown, 1974.

Kaplan, Lawrence S., Denise Artaud, and Mark R. Rubin. eds. *Dien Bien Phu and the Crisis of Franco-American Relations, 1954–1955*. Wilmington, DE: SR Books, 1990.

Karnow, Stanley. *Vietnam: A History*. New York: Viking Press, 1983.

Kattenburg, Paul. *The Vietnam Trauma in American Foreign Policy, 1945–1975*. New Brunswick, NJ: Rutgers University Press, 1980.

Kearns, Doris. *Lyndon Johnson and the American Dream*. New York: Harper and Row, 1976.

Keiser, Gordon. *The US Marine Corps and Defense Unification, 1944–1947: The Politics of Survival*. Washington, DC: National Defense University, 1982.

Kendrick, Alexander. *The Wound Within: America in the Vietnam Years, 1945–1974*. Boston: Little, Brown, 1974.

Kern, Montague, Patricia W. Levering, and Ralph B. Levering. *The Kennedy Crises: The Press, the Presidency, and Foreign Policy*. Chapel Hill: University of North Carolina Press, 1983.

Kiernan, Ben., ed. *How Pol Pot Came to Power: A History of Communism in Kampuchea, 1930–1975.* London: Verso, 1985.

——. *Genocide and Democracy in Cambodia: The Khmer Rouge, the United Nations, and the International Community.* New Haven, Conn.: Yale University Press, 1993.

King, Edward. *The Death of the Army: A Pre-Mortem.* New York: Saturday Review Press, 1972.

Kinnard, Douglas. *President Eisenhower and Strategy Management: A Study in Defense Politics.* Lexington: University Press of Kentucky, 1977.

——. *The War Managers.* Hanover, NH: University Press of New England, 1977.

——. *The Secretary of Defense.* Lexington: University Press of Kentucky, 1980.

——. *The Certain Trumpet: Maxwell Taylor and the American Experience in Vietnam.* New York: Brassey's, 1991.

Kinney, Katherine. *Friendly Fire: American Images of the Vietnam War.* New York: Oxford University Press, 2000.

Kissinger, Henry. *White House Years.* Boston: Little, Brown, 1979.

——. *Years of Upheaval.* Boston: Little, Brown, 1982.

——. *Diplomacy.* New York: Simon & Schuster, 1994.

Klatch, Rebecca E. *Generation Divided: The New Left, the New Right, and the 1960s.* Berkeley: University of California Press, 1999.

Knoll, Erwin, and Judith Nies McFadden, eds. *American Militarism 1970.* New York: Viking, 1969.

Knoll, Edwin, and Judith Nies McFadden. *War Crimes and the American Conscience.* New York: Holt, Rinehart & Winston, 1970.

Kolko, Gabriel. *The Roots of American Foreign Policy: An Analysis of Power and Purpose.* Boston: Beacon Press, 1969.

——. *Confronting the Third World: United States Foreign Policy, 1945–1980.* New York: Harper and Row, 1972.

——. *Anatomy of a War: Vietnam, The United States, and the Modern Historical Experience.* New York: Pantheon, 1985.

——. *Vietnam: Anatomy of a Peace.* New York: Routledge, 1997.

Kolko, Gabriel, and Joyce Kolko. *The Limits of Power: The World and United States Foreign Policy, 1945–1954.* New York: Harper & Row, 1972.

Komer, Robert W. *Bureaucracy Does Its Thing: Institutional Constraints on U.S.–GVN Performance in Vietnam.* Santa Monica, Calif.: Rand Corporation, 1972.

Korb, Lawrence. *The Joint Chiefs of Staff: The First Twenty- Five Years.* Bloomington: Indiana University Press, 1976.

——. *The Fall and Rise of the Pentagon: American Defense Policies in the 1970s.* Westport, Conn.: Greenwood Press, 1979.

Kovic, Ron. *Born on the Fourth of July.* New York: McGraw- Hill, 1976.

Krepinevich, Andrew F, Jr. *The Army and Vietnam.* Baltimore: Johns Hopkins University Press, 1986.

Krock, Arthur. *Memoirs: Sixty Years on the Firing Line.* New York: Funk & Wagnalls, 1968.

Krohn, Charles A. *The Lost Battalion: Controversy and Casualties in the Battle of Hue.* Westport, Conn.: Praeger, 1993.

Krulak, Victor. *First to Fight: An Inside View of the U. S. Marine Corps.* Annapolis, Md.: Naval Institute Press, 1984.

Kunz, Diane B., ed. *The Diplomacy of the Crucial Decade: American Foreign Relations During the 1960s.* New York: Columbia University Press, 1994.

Kurland, Gerald. *The Gulf of Tonkin Incidents.* Charlotteville, NY: Sam Har Press, 1975.

Lacouture, Jean. *Vietnam Between Two Truces*. New York: Random House, 1966.

———. *Ho Chi Minh: A Political Biography*. New York: Random House, 1968.

Lake, Anthony, ed. *The Vietnam Legacy: The War, American Society, and the Future of American Foreign Policy*. New York: New York University Press, 1976.

Lancaster, Donald. *The Emancipation of French Indochina*. New York: New York University Press, 1961.

Lang, Daniel. *Casualties of War*. New York: McGraw-Hill, 1969.

Langguth, A. J. *Our Vietnam/Nuoc Viet Ta: The War 1954–1975*. New York: Simon & Schuster, 2000.

Lansdale, Edward G. *In the Midst of Wars: An American's Mission to Southeast Asia*. New York: Fordham University Press, 1991.

Latham, Michael. *Modernization as Ideology: American Social Science and "Nation Building" in the Kennedy Era*. Chapel Hill: University of North Carolina Press, 2000.

Lee, Steven Hugh. *Outposts of Empire: Korea, Vietnam, and the Origins of the Cold War in Asia, 1948–1954*. Buffalo, NY: McGill-Queen's University Press, 1995.

LeGro, William E. *Vietnam from Cease-Fire to Capitulation*. Washington, DC: US Army Center of Military History, 1981.

Lembcke, Jerry. *The Spitting Image: Myth, Memory, and the Legacy of Vietnam*. New York: New York University Press, 1998.

Levine, Alan J. *The United States and the Struggle for Southeast Asia, 1945–1975*. Westport, Conn.: Praeger, 1995.

Levy, David W. *The Debate over Vietnam*. Baltimore: Johns Hopkins University Press, 1991.

Lewis, Lloyd B. *The Tainted War: Culture and Identity in Vietnam War Narratives*. Westport, Conn.: Greenwood, 1985.

Lewy, Guenter. *America in Vietnam*. New York: Oxford University Press, 1978.

Lifton, Robert Jay. *Home from the War: Vietnam Veterans: Neither Victims Nor Executioners*. New York: Simon & Schuster, 1973.

Lind, Michael. *Vietnam the Necessary War: A Reinterpretation of America's Most Disastrous Military Conflict*. New York: Free Press, 1999.

Littauer, Ralph, and Norman Uphoff, eds. *The Air War in Indochina*. Boston: Beacon Press, 1972.

Litwak, Robert S. *Détente and the Nixon Doctrine: American Foreign Policy and the Pursuit of Stability, 1969–1976*. New York: Cambridge University Press, 1984.

Lockhart, Greg. *Nation in Arms: The Origins of the People's Army of Vietnam*. Sydney, Australia: Allen & Unwin, 1989.

Lodge, Henry Cabot. *The Storm Has Many Eyes: A Personal Narrative*. New York: Norton, 1973.

Logevall, Frederik. *Choosing War: The Lost Chance for Peace and the Escalation of War in Vietnam*. Berkeley: University of California Press, 1999.

Lomperis, Timothy J. *The War Everyone Lost – and Won: America's Intervention in Viet Nam's Twin Struggles*. Revised ed. Washington, DC: Congressional Quarterly Press, 1993.

———. *From People's War to People's Rule: Insurgency, Intervention, and the Lessons of Vietnam*. Chapel Hill: University of North Carolina Press, 1996.

Louvre, Alf, and Jeffrey Walsh. eds. *Tell Me Lies about Vietnam: Cultural Battles for the Meaning of the War*. Philadelphia: Open University Press, 1988.

Lowe, Peter., ed. *The Vietnam War*. New York: St. Martin's, 1999.

Lukas, J. Anthony. *Nightmare: The Underside of the Nixon Years*. New York: Viking, 1976.

Lyon, Peter. *Eisenhower: Portrait of the Hero*. Boston: Little, Brown, 1974.

Maclear, Michael. *The Ten Thousand Day War: Vietnam: 1945–1975*. New York: St. Martin's Press, 1981.

MacPherson, Myra. *Long Time Passing: Vietnam and the Haunted Generation*. Garden City, NY: Doubleday, 1984.

Mallin, Jay. *Terror in Vietnam*. Princeton, NJ: Van Nostrand, 1966.

Mangold, Tom, and John Penycate. *The Tunnels of Cu Chi: The Untold Story of Vietnam*. New York: Random House, 1985.

Mann, Robert. *A Grand Delusion: America's Descent into Vietnam*. New York: Basic Books, 2001.

Mantell, David. *True Americanism: Green Berets and War Resisters, a Study of Commitment*. New York: Teachers College Press, 1974.

Mariscal, George, ed. *Aztlán and Viet Nam: Chicano and Chicaca Experiences of the War*. Berkeley: University of California Press, 1999.

Marolda, Edward, and Oscar Fitzgerald. *The United States Navy and the Vietnam Conflict, Vol. II: From Military Assistance to Combat, 1959–1965*. Washington, DC: Naval Historical Center, 1986.

Marr, David G. *Vietnamese Anticolonialism, 1885–1925*. Berkeley: University of California Press, 1971.

——. *Vietnamese Tradition on Trial, 1920–1945*. Berkeley: University of California Press, 1981.

——. *Vietnam 1945: The Quest for Power*. Berkeley: University of California Press, 1995.

Marrin, Albert. *America and Vietnam: The Elephant and the Tiger*. New York: Viking, 1992.

Mason, Robert. *Chickenhawk*. New York: Viking Press, 1983.

Matusow, Allen J. *The Unraveling of America: A History of Liberalism in the 1960s*. New York: Harper & Row, 1984.

McCarthy, Joseph E. *Illusion of Power: American Policy Toward Vietnam, 1954–1966*. New York: Carlton, 1967.

McCarthy, Mary. *The Seventeenth Degree*. New York: Harcourt Brace Jovanovich, 1974.

McChristian, Joseph A. *The Role of Military Intelligence, 1965–1967*. Washington, DC: Department of the Army, 1974.

McCoy, Alfred W., with Cathleen B. Read and Leonard P. Adams II. *The Politics of Heroin in Southeast Asia*. New York: Harper & Row, 1972.

McGarvey, Patrick J., ed. *Visions of Victory, Selected Vietnamese Communist Military Writings, 1964–1968*. Stanford, Calif.: Hoover Institute Press, 1969.

McGehee, Ralph W. *Deadly Deceits: My 25 Years in the CIA*. New York: Sheridan Square Publications, 1983.

McLellan, David S. *Dean Acheson: The State Department Years*. New York: Dodd, Mead, & Co., 1976.

McMahon, Robert J., ed. *Major Problems in the History of the Vietnam War: Documents and Essays*. 2nd ed. Lexington, Mass.: D. C. Heath, 1995.

McMaster, H. R. *Dereliction of Duty : Lyndon Johnson, Robert McNamara, the Joint Chiefs of Staff, and the Lies That Led to Vietnam*. New York: Harper Collins, 1997.

McNamara, Robert S., with Brian VanDeMark. *In Retrospect: The Tragedy and Lessons of Vietnam*. New York: Times Books, 1995.

McNamara, Robert S. et al. *Argument without End: In Search of Answers to the Vietnam Tragedy*. New York: Public Affairs, 1999.

McPherson, Harry. *A Political Education: A Washington Memoir*. Austin: University of Texas Press, 1995.

McQuaid, Kim. *The Anxious Years: America in the Vietnam-Watergate Era*. New York: Basic Books, 1990.

Mecklin, John. *Mission in Torment: An Intimate Account of the U. S. Role in Vietnam*. New York: Doubleday, 1965.

Melanson, Richard A. *Writing History and Making Policy: The Cold War, Vietnam, and Revisionism*. Lanham, Md.: University Press of America, 1983.

Melanson, Richard A., and David Meyers. eds. *Reevaluating Eisenhower: American Foreign Policy in the 1950s*. Urbana: University of Illinois Press, 1987.

Middleton, Drew. *Air War-Vietnam*. New York: Arno Press, 1978.

Miller, Merle. *Lyndon: An Oral History*. New York: Ballantine Books, 1980.

Millett, Allan. *Semper Fidelis: The History of the United States Marine Corps*. New York: Free Press, 1982.

Milstein, Jeffrey S. *Dynamics of the Vietnam War: A Quantitative Analysis and Predictive Computer Simulation*. Columbus: Ohio State University Press, 1974.

Moise, Edwin E. *Land Reform in China and North Vietnam: Consolidating the Revolution at the Village Level*. Chapel Hill: University of North Carolina Press, 1983.

——. *Tonkin Gulf and the Escalation of the Vietnam War*. Chapel Hill: University of North Carolina Press, 1996.

Moore, Harold G., and Joseph L. Galloway. *We Were Soldiers Once...and Young: Ia Drang, The Battle That Changed the War in Vietnam*. New York: Random House, 1992.

Morris, Roger. *Uncertain Greatness: Henry Kissinger and American Foreign Policy*. New York: Harper & Row, 1977.

Morrison, Wilbur H. *The Elephant and the Tiger: The Full Story of the Vietnam War*. New York: Hippocrene, 1990.

Moser, Richard. *The New Winter Soldiers*. New Brunswick, NJ: Rutgers University Press, 1996.

Moss, George D. *Vietnam: An American Ordeal*. 2nd ed. Englewood Cliffs, NJ: Prentice Hall, 1994.

Mrozek, Donald. *Air Power and the Ground War in Vietnam: Ideas and Action*. Maxwell Air Force Base, Ala.: Air University Press, 1988.

Nalty, Bernard C. *The Vietnam War*. New York: Barnes & Noble, 2000.

Neese, Harvey, and John O'Donnell. eds. *Prelude to Tragedy: Vietnam, 1960–1965*. Annapolis, Md.: Naval Institute Press, 2001.

Newman, John M. *JFK and Vietnam: Deception, Intrigue, and the Struggle for Power*. New York: Warner, 1992.

Ngo Vinh Long. *Before the Revolution: The Vietnamese Peasants Under the French*. Cambridge, Mass.: MIT Press, 1973. Reprint, New York: Columbia University Press, 1991.

Nguyen Cao Ky. *Twenty Years and Twenty Days*. New York: Stein & Day, 1976.

Nguyen Tien Hung, with Jerrold Schecter. *The Palace File*. New York: Harper & Row, 1986.

Nguyen Thi Dieu. *The Mekong River and the Struggle for Indochina: Water, War, and Peace*. Westport, Conn.: Praeger, 1999.

Nicosia, Gerald. *Home to War: A History of the Vietnam Veterans' Movement*. New York: Crown Publishers, 2001.

Nixon, Richard. *RN: The Memoirs of Richard Nixon*. New York: Grosset & Dunlap, 1978.

——. *No More Vietnams*. New York: Arbor House, 1985.

Nolan, Keith W. *The Battle for Hue: Tet 1968*. New York: Dell, 1985.

——. *The Battle for Saigon: Tet 1968*. New York: Pocket Books, 1996.

Nolting, Frederick. *From Trust to Tragedy*. New York: Praeger, 1989.

Nordell, John R., Jr. *The Undetected Enemy: French and American Miscalculations at Dien Bien Phu*. College Station: Texas A&M University Press, 1995.

O'Ballance, Edgar. *The Wars in Vietnam: 1954–1973*. New York: Hippocrene, 1975.

——. *The Wars in Vietnam: 1954–1980*. New York: Hippocrene, 1981.

Oberdorfer, Don. *TET!* Garden City, NY: Doubleday, 1984.

O'Brien, Tim. *Going After Cacciato: A Novel*. New York: Delacorte Press/S. Lawrence, 1978.

——. *The Things They Carried*. New York: Houghton Mifflin, 1990.

O'Connor, John J. *A Chaplain Looks at Vietnam*. New York: World, 1968.

Olson, James S., and Randy Roberts. *Where the Domino Fell: America and Vietnam, 1945–1990*. 2nd ed. New York: St. Martin's, 1996.

——. *My Lai: A Brief History with Documents*. Boston: Bedford Books, 1998.

Osborn, George K., et al., eds. *Democracy, Strategy, and Vietnam: Implications for American Policymaking*. Lexington, Mass.: Lexington Books, 1987.

Osborne, Milton. *The Mekong: Turbulent Past, Uncertain Future*. New York: Atlantic Monthly Press, 2000.

Osgood, Robert E. *Limited War Revisited*. Boulder, Colo.: Westview Press, 1979.

——, and Robert W. Tucker, et al. *Retreat from Empire? The First Nixon Administration*. Baltimore: Johns Hopkins University Press , 1973.

Palmer, Bruce. *The 25-Year War: America's Military Role in Vietnam*. New York: Simon & Schuster, 1985.

Palmer, Dave Richard. *Summons of the Trumpet: U. S.–Vietnam in Perspective*. New York: Ballantine Books, 1984.

Palmer, Gregory. *The McNamara Strategy and the Vietnam War: Program Budgeting in the Pentagon, 1960–1968*. Westport, Conn.: Greenwood Press, 1978.

Pan, Stephen, and Daniel Lyons. *Vietnam Crisis*. New York: Twin Circle, 1966.

Papp, Daniel S. *Vietnam: The View from Moscow, Peking, Washington*. Jefferson, NC: McFarland & Co., 1981.

Parker, William D. *U. S. Marine Corps Civil Affairs in I Corps, Republic of South Vietnam: April 1966 to April 1967*. Washington, DC: Historical Division, Headquarters, U. S. Marine Corps, 1970.

Parmet, Herbert. *JFK: The Presidency of John F. Kennedy*. New York: Penguin Books, 1984.

Paterson, Thomas, ed. *Kennedy's Quest for Victory: American Foreign Policy, 1961–1963*. New York: Oxford University Press, 1989.

Patti, Archimedes L. *Why Vietnam? Prelude to America's Albatross*. Berkeley: University of California Press, 1981.

Peers, Gen. William R. *The My Lai Inquiry*. New York: Norton, 1979.

Perry, Mark. *Four Stars*. Boston: Houghton Mifflin, 1989.

Pettit, Clyde E. *The Experts: 100 Years of Blunder in Indo-china*. Secaucus, NJ: Lyle Stuart, 1975.

Pike, Douglas. *Viet Cong: The Organization and Techniques of the National Liberation Front of South Vietnam*. Cambridge, Mass.: MIT Press, 1966.

Pisor, Robert. *The End of the Line: The Siege of Khe Sanh*. New York: Ballantine, 1983.

Podhoretz, Norman. *Why We Were in Vietnam*. New York: Simon & Schuster, 1982.

Porter, Gareth. *The Myth of the Bloodbath: North Vietnam's Land Reform Reconsidered*. Ithaca, NY: Cornell University Press, 1972.

——. *A Peace Denied*. Bloomington: Indiana University Press, 1975.

——. *Vietnam: The Definitive Documentation of Human Decisions*. Stanfordville, NY: E. M. Coleman Enterprises, 1979.

——. ed. *Vietnam: A History in Documents*. New York: New American Library, 1981.

Post, Ken. *Revolution, Socialism and Nationalism in Viet Nam*. 5 vols. Brookfield, Vt.: Dartmouth Publishing Co., 1989–94.

Powell, Lee Riley. *J. William Fulbright and America's Lost Crusade: Fulbright's Opposition to the Vietnam War*. Little Rock, Ark.: Rose Pub. Co., 1984.

Powers, Thomas. *The War at Home: Vietnam and the American People, 1964–1968*. New York: Grossman Publishers, 1973. Reprint, Boston: G. K. Hall, 1984.

Prados, John. *The Sky Would Fall*. New York: Dial, 1983.

——. *The Hidden History of the Vietnam War*. Chicago: Ivan R. Dee, 1995.

——. *The Blood Road: The Ho Chi Minh Trail and the Vietnam War*. New York: Wiley, 1999.

Prados, John, and Ray Stubbe. *Valley of Decision: The Siege of Khe Sanh*. Boston: Houghton Mifflin, 1991.

Pratt, John Clark, comp. *Vietnam Voices: Perspectives on the War Years, 1941–1982*. New York: Penguin, 1984.

Previdi, Robert. *Civilian Control Versus Military Rule*. New York: Hippocrene Books, 1988.

Prouty, Fletcher. *JFK: The CIA, Vietnam and the Plot To Assassinate John F. Kennedy*. New York: Birch Lane, 1992.

Race, Jeffrey. *War Comes to Long An: Revolutionary Conflict in a Vietnamese Province*. Berkeley: University of California Press, 1972.

Randle, Robert F. *Geneva 1954: The Settlement of the Indochinese War*. Princeton: Princeton University Press, 1969.

Ravenal, Earl C. *Never Again: Learning from America's Foreign Policy Failures*. Philadelphia: Temple University Press, 1978.

Raymond, Jack. *Power at the Pentagon*. New York: Harper & Row, 1964.

Record, Jeffrey. *The Wrong War: Why We Lost in Vietnam*. Annapolis, Md.: Naval Institute Press, 1998.

Reston, James, Jr. *Sherman's March and Vietnam*. New York: Macmillan, 1984.

Rogers, Bernard William. *Cedar Falls–Junction City: A Turning Point*. Washington, DC: Department of the Army, 1974.

Rose, Lisle A. *Roots of Tragedy*. Westport, Conn.: Greenwood Publishing Group, 1976.

Rosenberg, Milton, Sidney Verba, and Phillip Converse. *Vietnam and the Silent Majority: The Dove's Guide*. New York: Harper & Row, 1970.

Rostow, Walt W. *The Diffusion of Power: An Essay in Recent History*. New York: Macmillan, 1972.

Rotter, Andrew. *The Path to Vietnam: Origins of the American Commitment to Southeast Asia*. Ithaca, NY: Cornell University Press, 1987.

Rowe, John Carlos, and Rick Berg, eds. *The Vietnam War and American Culture*. New York: Columbia University Press, 1991.

Roy, Jules. *The Battle of Dienbienphu*. New York: Harper & Row, 1965.

Rudenstine, David. *The Day the Presses Stopped: A History of the Pentagon Papers Case*. Berkeley: University of California Press, 1996.

Rusk, Dean, with Richard Rusk. *As I Saw It*. ed. by Daniel S. Papp. New York: W. W. Norton, 1990.

Russell, Bertrand. *War Crimes in Vietnam*. New York: Monthly Review Press, 1967.

Rust, William J. *Kennedy in Vietnam*. New York: Scribners, 1985.

Salisbury, Harrison. ed. *Vietnam Reconsidered: Lessons from a War*. New York: Harper & Row, 1984.

Sansom, Robert L. *The Economics of Insurgency in the Mekong Delta*. Cambridge, Mass.: MIT Press, 1970.

Sardesai, D. R. *Vietnam: The Struggle for National Identity*. Boulder, Colo.: Westview Press, 1992.

Sarkesian, Sam. *Unconventional Conflicts in a New Security Era: Lessons from Malaya and Vietnam*. Westport, Conn.: Greenwood, 1993.

Schalk, David L. *War and the Ivory Tower: Algeria and Vietnam*. New York: Oxford University Press, 1991.

Schandler, Herbert. *Lyndon Johnson and Vietnam: The Unmaking of a President*. Princeton: Princeton University Press, 1977.

Schell, Jonathan. *The Military Half: An Account of Destruction in Quang Ngai and Quang Tin*. New York: Knopf, 1968.

Schlesinger, Arthur, Jr. *A Thousand Days: John F. Kennedy in the White House*. Boston: Houghton Mifflin, 1965.

——. *The Bitter Heritage: Vietnam and American Democracy, 1941–1966*. Boston: Houghton Mifflin, 1967.

——. *Robert Kennedy and His Times*. Boston: Houghton Mifflin, 1978.

Schlight, John. *The United States Air Force in South Vietnam*. Washington, DC: Office of Air Force History, 1988.

Schoenbaum, Thomas J. *Waging Peace and War: Dean Acheson in the Truman, Kennedy, and Johnson Years*. New York: Simon & Schuster, 1988.

Scholl-Latour, Peter. *Death in the Rice Fields*. New York: Penguin, 1986.

Schulzinger, Robert D. *Henry Kissinger: The Doctor of Diplomacy*. New York: Columbia University Press, 1989.

——. *A Time for War: The United States and Vietnam, 1941–1975*. New York: Oxford University Press, 1997.

Scigliano, Robert. *South Vietnam: Nation Under Stress*. Boston: Houghton Mifflin, 1963.

Scigliano, Robert, and Guy H. Fox. *Technical Assistance in Vietnam: The Michigan State Experience*. New York: Praeger, 1965.

Scott, Peter Dale. *The War Conspiracy*. Indianapolis: Bobbs Merrill, 1972.

Serong, Brigadier F. P. *The 1972 Easter Offensive (Southeast Asian Perspectives*, no. 10). New York: American Friends of Vietnam, 1974.

Shaplen, Robert. *The Lost Revolution: The U.S. in Vietnam, 1946–1966*. Revised ed. New York: Harper Colophon, 1966.

——. *Time Out of Hand: Revolution and Reaction in Southeast Asia*. New York: Harper Colophon, 1970.

——. *The Road from War: Vietnam 1965–1971*. New York: Harper Colophon, 1971.

——. *Bitter Victory*. New York: Harper & Row, 1986.

Shapley, Deborah. *Promise and Power: The Life and Times of Robert McNamara*. Boston: Little, Brown, 1993.

Sharp, U. S. G. *Strategy for Defeat: Vietnam in Retrospect*. San Rafael, Calif.: Presidio, 1978.

Sharp, U. S. G., and William C. Westmoreland. *Report on the War in Vietnam (as of 30 June 1968)*. Washington, DC: Government Printing Office, 1968.

Shawcross, William. *Sideshow: Kissinger, Nixon and the Destruction of Cambodia*. New York: Simon & Schuster, 1981.

Shay, Jonathan. *Achilles in Vietnam: Combat Trauma and the Undoing of Character*. New York: Simon & Schuster Trade Paperbacks, 1995.

Sheehan, Neil. *A Bright Shining Lie: John Paul Vann and America in Vietnam*. New York: Random House, 1988.

——. *After the War was Over: Hanoi and Saigon*. New York: Random House 1992.

Short, Anthony. *The Origins of the Vietnam War*. New York: Longman, 1989.

Shulimson, Jack. *U. S. Marines in Vietnam: An Expanding War, 1966*. Washington, DC: History and Museums Division, US Marine Corps, 1982.

Shulimson, Jack, and Charles Johnson. *U. S. Marines in Vietnam: The Landing and the Buildup, 1965.* Washington, DC: History and Museums Division, US Marine Corps, 1978.

Siff, Ezra Y. *Why the Senate Slept: The Gulf of Tonkin Resolution and the Beginning of America's Vietnam War.* Westport, Conn.: Greenwood, 1999.

Sigler, David B. *Vietnam Battle Chronology: U. S. Army and Marine Corps Combat Operations, 1965–1973.* Jefferson, NC: McFarland, 1992.

Simpson, Howard R. *Dien Bien Phu: The Epic Battle America Forgot.* McLean, Va.: Brassey's, 1994.

Small, Melvin. *Johnson, Nixon, and the Doves.* New Brunswick, NJ: Rutgers University Press, 1989.

——. *Covering Dissent: The Media and the Anti-Vietnam War Movement.* New Brunswick, NJ: Rutgers University Press, 1994.

——. *The Presidency of Richard Nixon.* Lawrence: University Press of Kansas, 2000.

Small, Melvin, and William D. Hoover. eds. *Give Peace a Chance: Exploring the Vietnam Antiwar Movement.* Syracuse, NY: Syracuse University Press, 1992.

Smith, Gaddis. *Dean Acheson.* New York: Cooper Square, 1970.

Smith, R. B. *An International History of the Vietnam War.* 3 vols. New York: St. Martin's Press, 1983–91.

Smyser, William R. *The Independent Vietnamese.* Athens: Ohio University Center for International Studies, 1980.

Snepp, Frank. *Decent Interval: An Insider's Account of Saigon's Indecent End.* New York: Random House, 1977.

Snyder, J. Richard, ed. *John F. Kennedy: Person, Policy, Presidency.* Wilmington, Del.: SR Books, 1988.

Sobel, Lester A. ed. *South Vietnam: U.S.–Communist Confrontation in Southeast Asia.* 7 vols. New York: Facts on File, 1966–73.

Solis, Gary D. *Son Thang: An American War Crime.* Annapolis, Md.: Naval Institute Press, 1997.

Sorensen, Theodore. *Kennedy.* New York: Harper & Row, 1965.

Sorley, Lewis. *Thunderbolt: General Creighton Abrams and the Army of His Times.* New York: Simon & Schuster, 1992.

——. *Honorable Warrior: General Harold K. Johnson and the Ethics of Command.* Lawrence: University Press of Kansas, 1998.

——. *A Better War: The Unexamined Victories and the Final Tragedy of America's Last Years in Vietnam.* New York: Harcourt, Brace, & Co., 1999.

Spanos, William V. *America's Shadow: An Anatomy of Empire.* Minneapolis: University of Minnesota Press, 1999.

Spector, Ronald. *Advice and Support: The Early Years of the U.S. Army in Vietnam, 1941–1960.* New York: Free Press, 1985.

——. *After Tet: The Bloodiest Year in Vietnam.* New York: Free Press, 1993.

Stanton, Shelby L. *The Rise and Fall of an American Army: U. S. Ground Forces in Vietnam, 1965–1973.* Novato, Calif.: Presidio, 1985.

Stevens, Robert W. *Vain Hopes, Grim Realities: The Economic Consequences of the Vietnam War.* New York: New Viewpoints, 1976.

Stoessinger, John G. *Henry Kissinger: The Anguish of Power.* New York: Norton, 1976.

Stone, I. F. *The Killings at Kent State: How Murder Went Unpunished.* New York: Vintage Books, 1971.

Sturken, Marita. *Tangled Memories: The Vietnam War, the AIDS Epidemic, and the Politics of Remembering.* Berkeley: University of California Press, 1997.

Summers, Harry. *On Strategy: A Critical Analysis of the Vietnam War.* Novato, Calif.: Presidio Press, 1982.

Szulc, Tad. *The Illusion of Peace: Foreign Policy in the Nixon Years.* New York: Viking Press, 1978.

Taylor, John. *General Maxwell Taylor: The Sword and the Pen.* New York: Doubleday, 1989.

Taylor, Leonard B. *Financial Management of the Vietnam Conflict.* Washington, DC: Department of the Army, 1974.

Taylor, Maxwell D. *The Uncertain Trumpet.* New York: Harper & Row, 1959.

——. *Responsibility and Response.* New York: Harper & Row, 1967.

——. *Swords and Plowshares.* New York: W. W. Norton, 1972.

Taylor, Sandra C. *Vietnamese Women at War: Fighting for Ho Chi Minh and the Revolution.* Lawrence: University Press of Kansas, 1999.

Terry, Wallace, ed. *Bloods: An Oral History of the War by Black Veterans.* New York: Random House, 1984.

Terzani, Tiziano. *Giai Phong: The Fall and Liberation of Saigon.* New York: St. Martin's, 1976.

Thayer, Carlyle. *War by Other Means: National Liberation and Revolution in Viet-Nam, 1954–60.* Cambridge, Mass.: Unwin Hyman, 1989.

Thayer, Thomas C. *War Without Fronts: The American Experience in Vietnam.* Boulder, Colo.: Westview Press, 1985

Thies, Wallace. *When Governments Collide: Coercion and Diplomacy in the Vietnam Conflict, 1964–1968.* Berkeley: University of California Press, 1980.

Thompson, James Clay. *Rolling Thunder: Understanding Policy and Program Failure.* Chapel Hill: University of North Carolina Press, 1980.

Thompson, W. Scott, and Donaldson Frizzell, eds. *The Lessons of Vietnam.* New York: Crane, Russak, 1977.

Tilford, Earl H., Jr. *Crosswinds: The Air Force's Setup in Vietnam.* College Station: Texas A&M University Press, 1993.

Tischler, Barbara L., ed. *Sights on the Sixties.* New Brunswick, NJ: Rutgers University Press, 1992.

Tolson, John J. *Airmobility, 1961–1971.* Washington, DC: Government Printing Office, 1973.

Tønneson, Stein. *The Vietnamese Revolution of 1945: Roosevelt, Ho Chi Minh, and De Gaulle in a World at War.* Newbury Park, Calif.: Sage Publications, 1991.

Tran Van Don. *Our Endless War.* San Rafael, Calif.: Presidio, 1978.

Tregaskis, Richard. *Vietnam Diary.* New York: Popular Library, 1963.

Trewhitt, Henry L. *McNamara: His Ordeal in the Pentagon.* New York: Harper & Row, 1971.

Trullinger, James Walker Jr. *Village at War: An Account of Revolution in Vietnam.* New York: Longman, 1980.

Truong Nhu Tang. *A Vietcong Memoir: An Inside Account of the War and Its Aftermath.* San Diego: Harcourt Brace Jovanovich, 1985.

Tucker, Spencer. *Vietnam.* Lexington: University Press of Kentucky, 1999.

Turley, Col. Gerald H. *The Easter Offensive.* Novato, Calif.: Presidio, 1985.

Turley, William S. *The Second Indochina War: A Short Political and Military History, 1954–1975.* New York: Mentor, 1986.

Turner-Gottschang, Karen, with Phan Thanh Hao. *Even the Women Must Fight: Memories of War from North Vietnam.* New York: Wiley, 1998.

Turner, Kathleen. *Lyndon Johnson's Dual War: Vietnam and the Press.* Chicago: University of Chicago Press, 1985.

VanDeMark, Brian. *Into the Quagmire: Lyndon Johnson and the Escalation of the Vietnam War.* New York: Oxford University Press, 1991.

Van Tien Dung. *Our Great Spring Victory.* New York: Monthly Review Press, 1977.

Vietnam Veterans Against the War. *The Winter Soldier Investigation: An Inquiry into American War Crimes.* Boston: Beacon Press, 1972.

Vogelgesang, Sandy. *The Long Dark Night of the Soul: The American Intellectual Left and the Vietnam War.* New York: Harper & Row, 1974.

Vo Nguyen Giap, *People's War, People's Army.* New York: Praeger, 1962.

Walt, Lewis. *Strange War, Strange Strategy: A General's Report on Vietnam.* New York: Funk & Wagnalls, 1970.

Walton, Richard J. *Cold War and Counterrevolution: The Foreign Policy of John F. Kennedy.* New York: Viking Press, 1972.

Warner, Denis. *The Last Confucian.* New York: Macmillan, 1963.

Warner, Roger. *Back Fire: The CIA's Secret War with Laos and Its Link to the War in Vietnam.* New York: Simon & Schuster, 1995.

——. *Shooting at the Moon: The Story of America's Clandestine War in Laos.* South Royalton, Vt.: Steerforth Press, 1996.

Weiner, Milton Gershwin, and Marvin B. Schaffer. *Border Security in South Vietnam.* Santa Monica, Calif.: Rand, 1971.

Weller, Jac. *Fire and Movement: Bargain-Basement Warfare in the Far East.* New York: Thomas Y. Crowell, 1967.

Wells, Tom. *The War Within: America's Battle over Vietnam.* Berkeley: University of California Press, 1994.

Werner, Jayne, and David Hunt, eds. *The American War in Vietnam.* Ithaca, NY: Southeast Asia Program, Cornell University, 1993.

Werner, Jayne S., and Luu Doan Huynh. *The Vietnam War: Vietnamese and American Perspectives.* Armonk, NY: M. E. Sharpe, 1993.

Wesseling, Louis. *Fuelling the War: Revealing an Oil Company's Role in Vietnam.* New York: I. B. Tauris, 2000.

West, Francis J. *The Village.* New York: Harper & Row, 1972.

West, Richard. *War and Peace in Vietnam.* London: Sinclair-Stevenson, 1995.

Westheider, James E. *Fighting on Two Fronts: African Americans and the Vietnam War.* New York: New York University Press, 1997.

Westmoreland, William C. *A Soldier Reports.* Garden City, NY: Doubleday, 1976.

Wexler, Sanford. *The Vietnam War: An Eyewitness History.* New York: Facts on File, 1992.

Wheeler, John. *Touched with Fire: The Future of the Vietnam Generation.* New York: F. Watts, 1984.

Whitlow, Robert. *U. S. Marines in Vietnam: The Advisory and Combat Assistance Era, 1954–1964.* Washington, DC: History and Museums Division, US Marine Corps, 1977.

Wicker, Tom. *JFK and LBJ: The Influence of Personality upon Politics.* Baltimore: Penguin Books, 1973.

Windchy, Eugene G. *Tonkin Gulf.* New York: Doubleday, 1971.

Winters, Francis X. *The Year of the Hare: America in Vietnam, January 25, 1963 – February 15, 1964.* Athens: University of Georgia Press, 1997.

Wintle, Justin. *The Viet Nam Wars.* New York: St. Martin's, 1991.

Wirtz, James. *The Tet Offensive: Intelligence Failure in War.* Ithaca, NY: Cornell University Press, 1991.

Wolff, Tobias. *In Pharaoh's Army: Memories of the Lost War.* New York: Knopf, 1994.

Woodruff, Mark R. *Unheralded Victory: The Defeat of the Viet Cong and the North Vietnamese Army, 1961–1973.* Arlington, VA: Vandamere Press, 1999.

Wright, James D. *The Dissent of the Governed: Alienation and Democracy in America*. New York: Academic Press, 1976.

Yarmolinsky, Adam. *The Military Establishment: Its Impact on American Society.* New York: Harper & Row, 1971.

Yergin, Daniel. *Shattered Peace: The Origins of the Cold War and the National Security State*. Boston: Houghton Mifflin, 1977.

Young, Marilyn. *The Vietnam Wars: 1945–1990*. New York: Harper Collins, 1991.

Yuen Foong Khong. *Analogies at War: Korea, Munich, Dien Bien Phu and the Vietnam Decisions of 1965*. Princeton: Princeton University Press, 1992.

Zaffiri, Samuel. *Hamburger Hill: May 11–20, 1969*. Novato, Calif.: Presidio Press, 1988.

Zagoria, Donald. *Vietnam Triangle: Moscow/Peking/Hanoi*. New York: Pegasus, 1972.

Zasloff, Joseph J., and MacAlister Brown. eds. *Communism in Indochina: New Perspectives*. Lexington, Mass.: Lexington Books, 1975.

Zasloff, Joseph J., and Allan A. Goodman. eds., *Indochina in Conflict: A Political Assessment*. Lexington, Mass.: Lexington Books, 1972.

Zumwalt, Elmo R. *On Watch: A Memoir*. New York: Quadrangle, 1976.

Index